SERMONS ON THE ACTS OF THE APOSTLES

CHAPTERS 1–7

John Calvin

Forty-four sermons delivered in Geneva
between 25 August 1549 and 11 January 1551

Translated into English by
ROB ROY McGREGOR

THE BANNER OF TRUTH TRUST

THE BANNER OF TRUTH TRUST

3 Murrayfield Road, Edinburgh EH12 6EL, UK
P.O. Box 621, Carlisle, PA 17013, USA

*

Translated from
Sermons on the Acts of the Apostles,
edited by Willem Balke and Wilhelmus H. Th. Moehn,
Supplementa Calviniana, volume 8
(Neukirchen-Vluyn:
Neukirchener Verlag des Erziehungsvereins, 1994).

First Banner of Truth edition, 2008

ISBN–13: 978 0 85151 968 5

*

Typeset in 11/15 pt Adobe Caslon Pro at
The Banner of Truth Trust, Edinburgh
Printed in the USA by
Versa Press, Inc.,
Peoria, IL

CONTENTS

v

Contents

Contents

Translator's Preface

John Calvin's comprehensive view of Scripture was fixed early on. His preaching reflects the consistency of his theology based on a comprehensive understanding of both the Old and New Testaments. He believed that God spoke to the ancient fathers of Israel and revealed through word and deed his intention for the people, his people, to be his witnesses and the means by which he would reveal his character and power in their day in anticipation of the fulfilment of his universal design in and through Jesus Christ. The implementation of God's design, as Calvin understood and insisted upon, depended on the people's faithful adherence to God's revealed will. Their adherence to the revelation demanded obedience founded on God's integrity, not only in the days of the ancient fathers, but also in the days on which the Light of the World has shone and is still shining.

Calvin's preaching is replete with high moral standards that are Christlike in scope. The believer's moral character and behaviour stem from the indwelling presence of the Holy Spirit and from the knowledge of God's self-revelation in Jesus Christ. In other words, Calvin teaches consistently that the purpose of revelation, which is understood and expressed in one's theology, however correct, is to mould the life of believers into the image of God's Son Jesus Christ. That failing, theology fails. God's kingdom, although described in theological terms, consists in viable Christlikeness in the form of the fruit of the Spirit, both in this life and in the life to come. That, I believe, is a concise expression of Calvin's understanding of 'spirituality' as revealed in Holy Scripture.

Calvin's extant sermons on the Acts of the Apostles[1] rest on that understanding. His treatment of the sacraments emphasizes the church's need of them as signs of God's gracious washing away of sin and resurrection to new life and the church's need for assurance of incorporation into the body of Christ. But are all those who receive baptism and partake of the Lord's Supper true members of the body? Calvin is adamant! No more so than Jews ingrained with Judaism constituted the true Israel. As the Jews of old were obstreperous and rebellious, despite God's revelations and unremitting oversight, guidance, and provision, so were contemporary Christians fractious and self-willed, all of which underlines the innate, evil impulse to idolatry. Nothing short of the willing and sometimes determined intellectual submission to God's will in Christ will suffice. In face of what appears to be a deliberate delay on God's part in fulfilling his promises, the faithful in both Old and New Testament dispensations are expected to be patient and await their fulfilment in the time of God's choosing, no matter how remote, no matter the hardships, no matter the persecutions. Persistence and perseverance are the perennial watchwords of faith.

---

[1] In their Introduction, the editors make this comment: 'The text of the 44 sermons on Acts 1 to 7 have survived in a manuscript of the Bibliothèque Publique et Universitaire in Geneva, shelf mark Ms. fr. 25. According to the Catalogue of Denis Raguenier, this is the first volume in a series of two volumes on Acts 1 to 16. The second volume with sermons on Acts 8 to 16 and two other volumes with sermons on Acts 17 to 28 have been lost' (xi).

Jesus never promised his followers an indulgent life in this world, nor does John Calvin, a position antithetical to that of the Roman Catholic Church of his time, where all kinds of human depravity were absolved, not by the broken body and shed blood of Jesus Christ, but by ritual, incantation, and empty gestures – all of which were foolish inventions of superstitious and idolatrous minds. Calvin's preaching condemns that and all teaching which concedes to human weakness and exploits man's arrogant penchant for self-deception. His sermons on Acts regularly reveal the depths and extent of sin in the human heart, ranging from covert and unacknowledged idolatry, theft, false witness, adultery, larceny, and robbery, to unobtrusive hypocrisy, to subtle greed, the latter being vices so imperceptible and pervasive that they go unrecognized even when repeatedly illuminated by faithful preaching.

The recurrence of those themes is such that one would think Calvin might despair of ever leading his flock to the right and pure path. But his faith and trust in God's unalterable purpose and the Holy Spirit's sure guidance are such that he knows God's pure kingdom will prevail – by the hardest – against all the cunning deceit and devious devices of Satan, the Liar and the Father of Lies. For that reason, Calvin exhorts the people to be wary of the soft and self-indulgent life which blinds Christians to the rigorous moral demands of the Christian faith.

The rigour reflected in Calvin's sermons on Acts is no less than that expressed by Jesus in the Gospels, by Paul in his Epistles, and by all the other writers of the New Testament. Like them, Calvin emphasizes that that very rigour is proof that God's love and grace provide an escape from the horrors of the separation from God occasioned by sin and man's intransigence therein. That love and grace, gentle and compassionate toward the repentant sinner, nonetheless demand a holiness, a righteousness of life that transcends intellectual concurrence and consensus in theological doctrine. God's kingdom is holy. It is where he—Father, Son, and Holy Spirit—lives, the promised and anticipated habitation of those who, by dint of will and unrelenting effort, with the help of the Holy Spirit, develop within themselves the character, the living image of the Lord Jesus Christ. Like character seeks like character and will find its home only where righteousness is at home. Such, we may surmise from Calvin's preaching, is the character of God's kingdom of peace.

True to form, Calvin never misses an opportunity to inveigh against 'the pope and his ilk'. He challenges the legitimacy of the papal priesthood on the grounds that it was established by the will of men and not, as was the Jewish priesthood, by the law given to Moses. Theirs is a hodgepodge of human fabrications, superstitions, and idols which supplants the pre-eminence of Jesus Christ, who, Calvin affirms, 'must always occupy the highest rank, and his gospel must be received with all fear and reverence without the addition or deletion of anything under any pretext', for by deleting and adding, 'we renounce what the Son of God has done.' That practice in the Papacy leads Calvin to say, 'That is why the pope and Muhammad are companions and have spoken with the same voice.' Like Muhammad, who 'after dispensing his devil-inspired teachings, which bewitched the poor world [by] declar[ing] that everything he had taught was revealed by the Holy Spirit', the pope also declares that everything he teaches has been revealed by the Holy Spirit (Sermon 35).

Readability and accuracy, especially conceptual accuracy, have been my goal in translating these forty-four sermons on chapters 1 to 7 of the Acts of the Apostles. To that end, I have on occasion restructured Calvin's long sentences so that the development of the thought is more comprehensible for the reader. Calvin's use of the passive voice, a commonplace of the 16th century, has been replaced by the active voice when feasible, but has been retained in most cases because of the sequential development of Calvin's thought within the paragraph. Not uncommonly, Calvin speaks rapidly as he expresses 'reformed' concepts fully, as if in a single breath. To accommodate that style, I have used a 'looser' punctuation than I would have preferred, but always with the view to avoiding misreading or misunderstanding.

Scripture references have been placed in parentheses instead of in footnotes, where the editors of the French text placed them, occasionally with a notation that the reference is in the margin. References found within the lection of the day are not noted.

The text used for this translation was *Sermons on the Acts of the Apostles*, edited by Willem Balke and Wilhelmus H. Th. Moehn, and may be found in the *Supplementa Calviniana*, volume 8 (Neukirchen-Vluyn: Neukirchener Verlag des Erziehungsvereins, 1994). Those who read French and Latin will find in the notes a compilation of references and sources that deserves more than passing thanks. The editors' comments included with this translation are given in the footnotes.

I undertook the translation of Calvin's sermons on the book of Acts in early 2002, eight years after my retirement from Clemson University, Clemson, South Carolina, as Professor Emeritus of French and Latin, because I could find no English version of the sermons. To my knowledge, these sermons have not been translated into English until now. Consequently, I undertook the project because of my appreciation of the theological acumen of their preacher and because of my predilection for sedentary activities, wherein sun shall not smite me by day, nor moon by night!

I am ever grateful to my wife for efficiently running the family household, for doing the annual state and federal taxes, and for making it possible for me to be a drone. On the other hand, in this venture with Calvin, I have no reason to thank her or my son for their patience and indulgence, inasmuch as I have deprived them of no husbandly or paternal obligations, time, or affection, having worked unobtrusively and late at night after lights out, so to speak, 'getting my Calvin fix'. They were happy to see me contentedly occupied and in good health. I do, however, thank them for graciously indulging me routinely for decades, a mark of patience my acquaintances will understand and appreciate.

I owe special thanks to Dr William B. Evans for reading the manuscript and writing the Introduction. Dr Evans is Eunice Witherspoon Bell Younts and Willie Camp Younts Professor of Bible and Religion and Chairman of the Department of Bible, Religion, and Philosophy at Erskine College, Due West, South Carolina, where, at Erskine Theological Seminary, I am Adjunct Professor of Ancient Languages.

One wonders, after perusing any sequence of Calvin's sermons, whether the sixteenth-century Reformer would be welcomed in many Protestant, even Presbyterian pulpits, today. Calvin is hailed for his biblical theology, but largely ignored with respect to his insistence upon the transformed-life, life-long self-abnegation demanded of genuine Christian discipleship. The motive behind his insistence arises from his acute awareness that God, after expressing his fatherly love and gracious acceptance of the wayward, remains the uncompromising judge of all humankind, Christian or not. That awareness of judgment should, Calvin says, 'make our hair stand on end' and drive us to repentance, without which there is no forgiveness.

It is hoped that the reader of these sermons will seek not just to confirm the sermons' agreement with 'Calvinistic' theology, but particularly to experience Calvin's sincere and profound personal response to the loving and merciful God whose Son is on the threshold of judging with finality the whole world with mercy and justice.

ROB ROY MCGREGOR
Anderson, South Carolina
USA
March 2006

INTRODUCTION

The contributions of John Calvin as a Reformer, theologian, and student of Scripture are, of course, well known. His *Institutes of the Christian Religion*, first published in 1536 and achieving definitive form in the Latin edition of 1559, have influenced many generations of Presbyterian and Reformed readers. Likewise, the commentaries he wrote on most of the books of the Bible are rightly regarded as monuments of careful biblical scholarship which repay careful study even today. Less well known is Calvin's preaching, despite the fact that he devoted a great deal of his time to pulpit ministry in Strasbourg and Geneva.

It is only during the twentieth century, and especially the post-World War II period, that Calvin's sermons have begun to receive the scholarly attention they so richly deserve. Due to the work of scholars such as Émil Doumergue, Erwin Mülhaupt, T. H. L. Parker, Richard Stauffer, and Hughes Oliphant Old,[1] we

---

[1] See, e.g., Émil Doumergue, *Calvin, le prédicateur de Genève* (Édition Atar: Genève, 1909); Erwin Mülhaupt, *Die Predigt Calvins. Ihre Geschichte, ihre Form, und ihr religiösen Grundgedanken* (Berlin, 1931); Leroy Nixon, *John Calvin: Expository Preacher* (Grand Rapids: Eerdmans, 1950); T. H. L. Parker, *The Oracles of God: An Introduction to the Preaching of John Calvin* (London: Lutterworth, 1947); *Calvin's Preaching* (Edinburgh: T & T Clark, 1992); Richard Stauffer, *Dieu, la création et la providence dans la prédication de Calvin* (Bern: Peter Lang, 1978).

now have a much greater knowledge of Calvin's preaching activity, and ongoing efforts are underway to provide critical texts of all extant Calvin sermons in the series *Supplementa Calviniana*. This excellent English translation of Calvin's sermons on The Acts of the Apostles represents the fruit of this careful labour in that it is translated from this more recent critical edition.

Calvin's Preaching Activity

Though the details are unclear, Calvin apparently did some preaching prior to his arrival in Geneva in 1536, and he preached regularly there until his expulsion from the city in 1538. Called to pastor the congregation of French exiles in Strasbourg, Calvin continued his homiletical endeavours there until he was recalled to Geneva in 1541.

The excellence of Calvin's preaching was widely recognized, and in 1549 an organized and subsidized effort was begun to transcribe his sermons. Such recording of the sermons was the only way to preserve them for posterity because Calvin preached without notes or a manuscript! A French refugee named Denis Raguenier, who had developed an efficient system of shorthand, was engaged to transcribe Calvin's sermons, and he proved to be well equipped for this demanding task. Raguenier continued his work until 1560, at which time other secretaries took over the task.

As Calvin's biographers, from Theodore Beza onward, have underscored, Calvin was an indefatigable preacher. Because of the Raguenier transcriptions, we have much greater knowledge of Calvin's preaching from the period 1549 until his death in 1564. During this period the Reformer's regular practice was to preach twice every Sunday and then once during the remaining days of every other week. (During the week that he did not preach Monday through to Saturday, he typically presented three theological lectures). On Sunday mornings Calvin preached from the New Testament. The Sunday afternoon sermons typically came from texts in the Psalter, while the weekday sermons were generally based upon Old Testament texts.[1] The length of the sermons translated in this volume suggests that Calvin typically preached for an hour or more. Certainly few if any other preachers in all of Christian history can claim to have sustained such a workload, and this demanding schedule enabled Calvin to preach through much of the Scriptures during his career at Geneva.

Characteristics of Calvin's Preaching

John Calvin is rightly regarded as the greatest theologian of the magisterial Reformation. We would expect that his preaching was informed and buttressed by his theological commitments, and we are not disappointed. T. H. L. Parker rightly observes, 'The impulsion, or compulsion, to preach was theological. Calvin preached because he believed. He preached in the way he did because he believed what he did.'[2] His approach to preaching was driven and shaped, first of all, by his extraordinarily high regard for the authority and power of God's written word. For Calvin, the Scriptures are indeed God's word to his people—the human authors of the biblical books were so moved by the Holy Spirit that the final product is God's word. And because the Scriptures are God's word they are without error as originally given. The authority of Scripture is the authority of God himself. In order to emphasize the complete trustworthiness of the Bible, Calvin even

---

[1] On Calvin's preaching schedule, see Parker, *Calvin's Preaching*, pp. 59-64.

[2] Parker, *Calvin's Preaching*, p. 1.

sometimes speaks of the Holy Spirit as 'dictating' the words of Scripture to the human authors.[1]

At the same time, Calvin was also quite aware of the human dimension of Scripture. As a scholar trained in the humanist tradition of the Renaissance, he had a keen eye for the stylistic differences between writers, and he was also aware that problems had crept into the biblical text at certain points because of imperfect transmission by copyists. Calvin also emphasizes the way that God 'accommodates' divine truth to the limitations of human capacity, placing the revealed mysteries down on a level, as it were, where finite and sinful human beings can begin to apprehend them.[2] All this drove Calvin not only to take the Scriptures with great seriousness but also to devote enormous attention and energy to the proper interpretation of Scripture, and to the presentation of their teachings in a compelling way to God's people.

Calvin was also convinced that God's word is powerful, that there is an inextricable bond between the written word and the Holy Spirit, who works in human hearts to accomplish God's purposes. In dependence upon passages such as Hebrews 4:12, Calvin recognized that where God's word is read and preached God himself is present and active. Sometimes this is a gracious and saving presence, while at other times God may use his word to harden and to judge.[3] Of particular interest here is Calvin's conviction that the

---

[1] See Calvin, Commentary on *2 Tim.* 3:16. On Calvin's view of inspiration, see B. B. Warfield, 'Calvin's Doctrine of the Knowledge of God', in *Calvin and Augustine* (Philadelphia: Presbyterian and Reformed, 1956), pp. 48-70; Edward A. Dowey, Jr., *The Knowledge of God in Calvin's Theology*, third ed. (Grand Rapids: Eerdmans, 1994), pp. 90-105.

[2] See Calvin, *Institutes*, II.11.13; and Commentary on *1 Cor.* 2:7.

[3] See Calvin, *Institutes*, I.9.3; Commentary on *Heb.* 4:12. See also Ronald S. Wallace, *Calvin's Doctrine of Word and Sacrament* (Grand Rapids: Eerdmans, 1957), pp. 91-95.

Scriptures rightly preached are God's word to his people. Insofar as the preacher proclaims the message of Scripture, that message is more than simply the word of a human being. It is the very word of God. Thus emerges what John Gerstner aptly termed Calvin's 'two-voice theory of preaching'.[1]

We may infer from this view of the authority and power of God's word that Calvin took the task of preaching with great seriousness. He had no use for ministers who went into the pulpit unprepared. His preaching was informed by careful study of the biblical text in the original languages. He had studied both Greek and Hebrew at the University of Paris, and was intimately familiar with the methods of textual analysis emerging out of Renaissance humanism.[2] Moreover, his preaching was enriched by the detailed exegetical study that produced his commentaries on many of the books of the Bible. Interestingly, however, with all his other duties in Geneva Calvin had little time to prepare sermons in detail. Rather, the evidence suggests that he preached extemporaneously with only the Hebrew Bible or the Greek New Testament in front of him in the pulpit.[3] While he doubtless gave considerable thought to what he would say beforehand, a good deal of the sermon content emerged spontaneously out of Calvin's deep and detailed knowledge of Scripture, the Christian tradition, and the needs of the congregation.

[1] See John Gerstner, 'Calvin's Two-Voice Theory of Preaching', *Reformed Review* 13 (1959):15-26. See also Wallace, *Word and Sacrament*, pp. 90-91; Calvin's sermon on *Acts* 7:37-38 in this volume.

[2] On Calvin's background and training as a scholar, see E. Harris Harbison, *The Christian Scholar in the Age of the Reformation* (New York: Charles Scribner's Sons, 1956), pp. 137-164.

[3] See Parker, *Calvin's Preaching*, pp. 80-81, 172-178.

Calvin's method of preaching was expository. That is, his sermons were exercises in the explanation and application of Scripture. Abandoning the medieval practice of preaching on isolated texts specified by a lectionary, Calvin returned to the patristic practice of *lectio continua*, that is, preaching through entire books of the Bible, a practice that had been pioneered by great preachers of a much earlier age such as Origen and Augustine.[1] As the sermons in this volume demonstrate, Calvin would typically focus on a few verses, picking up where he had left off in the previous sermon in the series. He would then explain the meaning of the text in clear, simple, and straightforward terms.

But the Reformer was not content with mere explanation. He was also deeply concerned to apply the meaning of Scripture to the challenges of his day and the needs of his congregation. For Calvin, Scripture always contains an imperative challenging the listener to greater faith, obedience, and piety. And so Calvin emphasizes not only the responsibilities of the minister to preach the word faithfully, but also the responsibility of the congregation to heed the word of God as it is preached, and to seek out the pure preaching of the word.

> When acknowledging our faults, we have to ask God for forgiveness. Having done that, let this passage admonish us so that we may better receive God's word and pay attention to the teaching of the gospel more willingly than we have up till now. Why has the gospel borne so little fruit in us? Because most of us do not take a liking to it and have very little concern for it. It is true that the gospel is indeed preached and people come to the sermon, but as a duty. After much has been said at those times, what do we carry away with us? We should engage in this kind of self-examination every

---

[1] On Calvin's place in the history of preaching, see Hughes Oliphant Old, *Worship: Reformed According to Scripture*, rev. ed. (Philadelphia: Westminster/John Knox, 2002), pp. 74-77.

time we hear a sermon so that we can think about what we ought to get out of it and how we ought to apply it for our advantage. The sermon is not a lot of hot air. One day we will have to give an account of all that we have heard during preaching although we have let it go in one ear and out the other.[1]

Calvin knew full well that sinful human beings do not naturally submit to God, but he exhorted his congregation in the confidence that the Holy Spirit is present and active in the preaching of the Word.

As is often noted, Calvin's preaching is distinctive for its lack of pretence and artifice. His sermons do not contain showy displays of learning. He leaves his scholarly apparatus, though not the fruits of his scholarship, in the study—for example, in these sermons one finds few references to the original languages. This stands in marked contrast to some preachers today who seek to demonstrate their scholarly credentials with pretentious references to 'the original Greek' or to 'the Hebrew text'. Likewise, Calvin eschews rhetorical flourishes and contrivances for their own sake. Though well schooled in the rhetorical techniques of classical antiquity and adept in their use, Calvin was careful to use them only as servants to the meaning of the text. In fact, he seems to have been apprehensive that the wrongful use of rhetoric might drown out the voice of the Holy Spirit. In a letter to the Duke of Somerset in England, Calvin wrote:

> You are also aware, Monseigneur, how he [i.e., St Paul] speaks of the lively power and energy with which they ought to speak, who would approve themselves as good and faithful ministers of God, who must not make a parade of rhetoric, only to gain esteem for

---

[1] Calvin's sermon on *Acts* 4:32-37. See also sermons on *Acts* 5:1-6 and *Acts* 5:17-21.

themselves, but that the Spirit of God ought to sound forth by their voice, so as to work with mighty energy.[1]

Calvin also had a striking sense of the peculiar role of the minister as mediating the word of God to the congregation. On the one hand, Calvin as a preacher stood in solidarity with his congregation. He typically used the first person plural forms 'we' and 'us' instead of the second person 'you'. That is to say, he stood together with the congregation under the authority of God's word. At the same time, he also recognized the unique role of the minister as one who is commissioned to proclaim the oracles of God. For example, he exhorted his Genevan congregation in the following terms:

> If we desire to be instructed appropriately, let us hold fast to what is contained in the law, in the prophets, and in the gospel as the source of everything we need. And then let us, as we hold to that knowledge, honour it as it deserves to be honoured, and let us be assured that this is the way God ordained to speak to us and that we must not turn a deaf ear to men when they faithfully proclaim the message entrusted to them. Let us hear them as if they were angels descended from heaven.

> And then we must note that this is an inviolable procedure: God has always spoken to us by means of his servants. And when he sends us men to proclaim his will, we must not receive it as coming from them. Otherwise, it would not be the will of God. But when we acknowledge that what they proclaim is drawn from the true source, which is the teaching of the prophets and the gospel, we

[1] Calvin, Letter to the Duke of Somerset, 22 October, 1548, quoted in John H. Leith, 'Calvin's Doctrine of the Proclamation of the Word and Its Significance for Today', in *John Calvin and the Church: A Prism of Reform*, ed. Timothy George (Louisville, KY: Westminster/John Knox, 1990), p. 210.

must receive it without any resistance, for if we reject it, the devil will surely be our teacher.[1]

With this glorious privilege came the awesome responsibility to preach with courage despite the dangers and threats that may be faced. And so Calvin in his preaching steadfastly refused to trim his sails or pander to the audience. He did not shy away from naming the spiritual and moral failings of the Genevan populace. Of course, he also rarely missed an opportunity to skewer the pope of Rome and his minions for what Calvin regarded as their idolatry, abuse of power, and disobedience to Scripture. Of particular interest, in today's context of a resurgent Islam, are the parallels that Calvin draws between the pope and the prophet Muhammad, whom the Reformer regarded as 'the two horns of the devil set on killing the poor world and imprisoning it.'[2] In both these instances, we must recall that sixteenth-century Europe sensed a very real political and military threat from Islam, and that Calvin's congregations in Geneva included many who had fled for their lives from Roman persecution in France, and for whom reports of Protestant martyrdom were a daily occurrence.

The Preservation and Influence of Calvin's Sermons

As noted above, between 1549 and 1560 Calvin's sermons were transcribed in shorthand by Denis Raguenier, with other secretaries taking over the task until the close of Calvin's ministry in 1564. These shorthand transcriptions were subsequently written out in longhand and then bound into volumes.

---

[1] Calvin's sermon on *Acts* 7:37-38.

[2] Ibid. See also sermon on *Acts* 7:35-37.

Eventually over forty of these volumes were produced, and they were stored under the care of the deacons of the Reformed Church in Geneva. From these texts a significant number of Calvin's sermons were published and translated into other languages, especially English. In 1613 the volumes of Calvin's sermons were moved to the University Library in Geneva. Regrettably, as time went on these treasures were not properly valued by the University, and most of the volumes were sold for a pittance in 1805 in order to clear shelf space in the library. Eventually some of these original-transcription volumes were recovered, but the majority remain outstanding. It is now estimated that only 680 of Calvin's sermons are preserved in transcribed manuscript form, with certain others being preserved in their early published form.[1]

Calvin's sermons were especially popular in the British Isles, and a surprising number of them were translated into English and published. Their popularity is due in part to the fact that many of the Marian exiles found refuge in Geneva, where they sat under Calvin's expository ministry with rapt attention. Upon the accession of Elizabeth I in 1558, following the death of Mary Tudor, these exiles returned to England and Scotland and assumed leadership of the Reformation in their native lands.[2] While Calvin's influence in England was soon to fade, his theological and homiletical legacy lived on with much greater vigour in Scotland, where, as Hughes Oliphant Old notes, the 'expository preaching of books of the Bible in course became a continuing feature of the Scottish pulpit.'[3]

---

[1] On the preservation and transmission of Calvin's sermons, see Parker, *Calvin's Preaching*, pp. 65-75, 153-162.

[2] On Calvin's influence upon English preaching, see T. H. L. Parker, *The Oracles of God: An Introduction to the Preaching of John Calvin* (London: Lutterworth, 1947), pp. 108-127.

[3] Old, *Worship*, p. 77.

The Translator

In addition to being one whom I am privileged to call a good personal friend, Dr Rob Roy McGregor is a distinguished scholar of Romance languages, whose enviable facility with Latin and French gives him full entrance into the fullness of Calvin's *oeuvre*. This particular translation, in addition to being based on the best available critical text, captures the liveliness, urgency, clarity, and verve of Calvin's sermons in a way that enables the reader to leap over many centuries and to experience Calvin's vitality and power as a preacher. As the Translator's Preface suggests, this translation effort has clearly been a labour of love that is now bequeathed to the larger English-speaking world for its benefit and edification.

WILLIAM B. EVANS
Erskine College
August 2006

I

JESUS' WORK AND TEACHING UNTIL HIS ASCENSION

SUNDAY, 25 AUGUST 1549

The former treatise have I made, O Theophilus, of all that Jesus began both to do and teach, ² Until the day in which he was taken up, after that he through the Holy Ghost had given commandments unto the apostles whom he had chosen (Acts 1:1–2).

Since everything God has given us by way of doctrine is intended for our benefit, we do well to consider the advantage we receive from all we read and find in holy Scripture. Similarly, this consideration must make us more diligent in our desire to understand how we profit from what a prophet or apostle tells us. It must motivate us even more to seize the advantage we are to gain from it. Therefore, since we are going to comment on what Luke says about how the apostles began to fulfil the commission given by their master, Jesus Christ, we must be very attentive to what he tells us.

At the outset, we see it was not without purpose that Jesus Christ promised to send the Holy Spirit to his apostles, first, to instruct them in the doctrine they were to proclaim to the people and, second, to strengthen them so they might withstand the conflicts which would befall them. Therein we see he in no way deprived his apostles of what he had promised.

Later, we see how Jesus Christ's shed blood has borne fruit, for if there were no church on earth, what fruit would his death and suffering produce? But when we understand that God built his church using faith, we also understand that Jesus Christ did not shed his blood in vain.

Moreover, we see here the power of Jesus Christ in establishing his church, even in spite of the world's resistance, because those who were powerful and in control at that time, or seemed to be, resisted the church and raised every possible barrier to keep it from being established and thus impede the gospel's progress. Yet he overcame enormous obstacles with towering success. The way he did it shows clearly that all the glory must be attributed to him alone. For if he had chosen great, knowledgeable, or powerful personages, it could be said they had much to do with it and shared his glory. But what do we see here? Poor people of no account, undesirables. For all Christians at that time were thought of as dogs. Everyone held them in contempt. Everyone also thought the apostles were the refuse of the world, as Paul notes (*1 Cor.* 4:13). But knowing that is the kind of people God has chosen to preach the gospel in his name, what could we say but 'What an odd lot of unsuitable overseers for that job'? That would be our immediate reaction from our perspective. Nonetheless, God used them to preach the gospel everywhere despite the fact that princes and their officers resisted it with all their might.

In addition, they did not have weapons to establish the gospel violently; they had only the word of God, and the common folk sided with them. Therein we see the fulfilment of what was said in the Psalm: that the nations and the kings agreed together and said, 'We want to be your people' (*Psa.* 138:4). Yes, that was said of David, but it signified Jesus Christ as well.

When reading such things, can we not recognize the authority of the Gospels? Yet we see how Satan kept trying to collect all possible devices in his effort to overthrow every teaching of salvation, for he is first the enemy of the glory of God and then the enemy of man's salvation. Now, we know that the gospel is the glory of God and the salvation of our souls. So there is a reason Scripture says Satan kept trying to get people to reject the gospel. We see, however, that the gospel has been established and that in this story Satan has long waged war on it and is never without henchmen. Even if we compare followers of the gospel with followers of Satan, we will find not a hair's difference between them. We will even find that most of those who have received the gospel will be dedicated to evil. We saw it in the Psalm just mentioned: the majority are hypocrites (*Psa.* 138:4). The number of the faithful, then, is very small. It seems everyone has conspired to serve Satan. Therefore, since such has been the case from the beginning of the gospel, we must conclude that such will be the case until the end.

We must also note the apostles' steadfastness. Although men of no authority, they were not intimidated. Although weak and inexperienced, they travelled throughout the world preaching the gospel and persevered until the end. From that, we know they were able to accomplish their task in spite of every difficulty and every hindrance because they entrusted themselves to God.

In addition, we have to consider their long-suffering. However greatly persecuted, they never lost courage. Why not? Because they knew their calling was not to triumph in this world. And we too, following their example, must prepare ourselves if we see rebuke coming because of the gospel, and we must not weary of persevering. Why not? Because we have our triumph waiting for us high in heaven. In this world, on the other hand, we must suffer after the example of our Lord Jesus Christ and the apostles. That is what we have to take note of in the present passage.

Therein we must also see God's providence in maintaining his church; therein we must take comfort, for we know that God's church is, in this world, like a tiny ship tossed about by a tempest-uous sea. But how does God maintain the church? Jesus Christ sustains it by his might! If Jesus Christ were not watching over the faithful, what would become of us, considering our condition? But we have reason to be confident, for God has shown great solicitude for his church and has, by the preaching of the apostles, established his church, where his name is invoked and his gospel expounded. That is but one more useful point in the present passage.

Now if God had not left us this scripture, we would not see the truth of Jesus Christ fulfilled regarding his promise to send his Holy Spirit from on high, and we would not know which road or course to follow. Satan has so completely filled the world with lies that there would be no memory of God's promises or his gospel, and we would be uncertain about the things we need to know, things we could not have learned about had God not left us this passage as a reminder that it is he who speaks and not a mortal man.

What an invaluable treasure God has left us in this account! Here we see how God established his church, and we learn that he maintains it by his power. We see in it the excellence of the gospel, whose success Satan's ever so great violence did not thwart. What an inestimable treasure God left us when showing us that the gospel of Jesus Christ will reign forever, truly at the foot of the cross, just as this merciful God will be pleased to train our endurance. For we must always be poised to engage every battle, ever steadfast, even when it seems we are going to be abandoned and swallowed up by everything. Such are the things which are revealed here and which we must learn here, provided we receive the gifts of God's grace by faith.

Now, aware of how useful this book is for us, let us consider Luke's starting point. He recalls the intent of his Gospel. 'We have', he says, 'upheld the primary intent of all the things which

Jesus began to do and to teach, right up to the day he was lifted on high, after instructing his apostles by his Holy Spirit and informing them of the duty he wanted them to discharge.' That, he says, is what we have deduced thus far. Now, he recites these things to show that he will continue his account and that Jesus Christ not only descended into this world to save us, but that he now ever extends his hand to help us.

That is why Luke speaks of the events he wrote concerning Jesus Christ's deeds. It is as if he were saying, 'The manifestation of Jesus Christ was not a fleeting, temporal phenomenon, but evidence that he will always be with us and that he was raised from the dead to govern his church as it suffers in the midst of its many enemies, for he always persists in showing he is our 'Saviour, Head, and Guide'. That, in short, is what Luke means in this passage.

Now when he talks about what he related in his Gospel, he uses two verbs, namely that Jesus Christ began both to do and to say, that is, to teach. This passage has been abused by those who want to expound it by saying Jesus Christ demonstrated a good way to live before teaching. It is true a worthy preacher's duty is to live an exemplary life before speaking in order to show he brings the word of God in earnest. That is quite true, but such is not the message of this passage. Luke is speaking here of Jesus Christ in the same way he did at the end of his Gospel (*Luke* 24:19), namely that Jesus Christ had a divine power not just in doing miracles but also in his speaking. It is true the expression 'what he did' shows that the works he performed while in this world demonstrate he is the Son of God. In this passage, Luke wishes to show he understood Jesus Christ's works as well as his words.

Now in that statement we see that the value of Luke's Gospel is in its declaration that Jesus Christ came to fulfil what the prophets had proclaimed beforehand. Indeed, Jesus Christ's charge was to snatch us from eternal death. To the extent his charge did not have the power it should have had over us, he wanted his miracles to confirm it. That, then, is what we should learn from this passage, for what is our wisdom if not the teaching of the gospel?

Indeed, if we ask a number of people what the meaning of Luke's Gospel is, they will say they have no idea. All the more, then, should we be attentive to Luke's teaching concerning the words and deeds of Jesus Christ, namely that the remission of our sins must be made in his name and that repentance must then follow. True, it is premature for Luke to say, 'Jesus Christ has done and taught', but the fact remains that his full meaning is comprised in those two words.

The purpose of everything the apostles said was to make known what Jesus Christ had said and done on earth. So then, when they tell us that the remission of sins is in Jesus Christ, it is so we can know not just that we are lost – if we have not been brought to God the Creator to receive grace through him – but that we have to be accounted righteous through his obedience. Thus we enter into grace because Jesus Christ is our Guarantor and because he, being perfectly righteous, makes us participants in his righteousness so that we will, through him, be made pleasing to God his Father. From his grace, then, comes both the forgiveness of our sins and our boldness to call God 'our Father' and request of him everything we need. Since we pray to God in the name of Jesus Christ, he cannot refuse him.

Repentance follows. In other words, people must condemn themselves and then renounce and despise themselves so they can beseech God to refashion them in his image, which they have erased. That is our starting point, if we wish to repent properly, not as the papists, who have abused true repentance by turning it into fasting on a Wednesday and muttering or performing some affectation or other. We must begin at a higher level by yielding ourselves to God, acknowledging our total spiritual poverty and grieving over our faults. Likewise, what belongs to our human nature must be put to death so God can reign in us. That is what repentance is. Walking in newness of life. Now, the ability to do that does not come from man. Consequently, everything must be renewed. Otherwise, we do not know what it means to be a Christian, and if we say we are Christians – and there are those who make the claim unashamedly – our Lord condemns us. Yet, we must pay attention to this teaching so that each of us will be instructed according to our capacity. Even though we do not all have the same capacity, we must all experience repentance.

It is also true Jesus Christ did not come into the world just to teach us what we should do, but to teach us what we should say and to draw sinners away from sin. We are indeed all sinners. Our sins must be blotted out by Jesus Christ, which was accomplished by his death, for the effect of his death was to cancel the debt Satan held against our sins. Jesus Christ had to attach it to his cross. We see, then, that the Son of God not only spoke, but he also did what he had declared. In other words, he showed himself to be our Redeemer when he yielded that perfect obedience to remove our sins, and then rose from the dead to loose us from the bonds of Satan and death. In this way, he forever removed death's power to inflict its cruelty upon us, as it had done previously.

In addition to preaching repentance, Jesus, by his death, even crucified our old Adam (cf. *Rom.* 6:6). So now we can put our affections to death, which is beyond our power to do, except that such power has been given to us through his sacrifice. Consequently, by putting our old Adam to death and making us members of his body, he grants us that power and gives us the grace to conquer ourselves. Then, by his resurrection he has acquired for us this power by which we can, as Paul says, bear fruit in him. Such are Jesus Christ's deeds. But it remains for us to know what those deeds are. Without that knowledge, we cannot put our confidence in him, which we must do, for 'Cursed is the man who trusts in man and who makes the flesh his arm' (*Jer.* 17:5). Shall we then find our glory in men when not even the angels are glorious or immortal, except insofar as God sustains them? For they are immortal only to the extent that God has willed it and granted them that grace. And yet if Jesus Christ had declared himself to be just a mortal man, could we put our confidence in him? Certainly not! He must be the Son of God, which his deeds and his sayings have demonstrated. It is now clear that with the death and resurrection of Jesus Christ we have his miracles to serve as a seal and assure us that it is to him we must go for our complete salvation. For John says that by this Word, who is the Son of God, all things were created and are maintained (*John* 1:3). That, too, is what Luke says.

Now let us return to the remarks we have just made, namely that we are well taught in the gospel when we learn first that Jesus Christ came into the world to bring us the ambassadorship of God his Father. Now this ambassadorship consists of two points: that we learn to renounce ourselves and then put that learning into action. We see that Jesus Christ has not only spoken but has also fulfilled what he taught, thereby truly showing himself to be our Redeemer. But so that we may know that he is not simply a mortal man, but that he is the Son of God, he demonstrated the certainty of his majesty so that we may have a firm foundation for our confidence in him. When we grasp all that, we will be able to assert that we are Christians. Otherwise, our faith will be false if we take the name Christian without knowing what the gospel contains.

Luke adds that he spoke of what Jesus Christ had done and said 'until the day in which he was taken up, after instructing his apostles by the Holy Spirit'. In that verse, he shows that Jesus Christ did not appear on earth briefly only to disappear suddenly, but that he provided for his teaching to last forever and, to that end, appointed his apostles, who are likewise to perform miracles. Our conclusion must be, then, that Jesus Christ is the Redeemer until the end because he left us with his teaching as well as the responsibility and authority to do all the things he had done. By pointing that out, Luke wishes to show the apostles carried out their commission and fulfilled their duty.

Because the words he uses are weighty, we must consider them seriously. He says that Jesus Christ gave his apostles a charge and that that charge was then given to them by the Holy Spirit. With that statement he indicates the office entrusted to them: just as he chose his apostles to bear his word, so must they be busy about the task. So it is not theirs to preach their imaginations and fantasies, but to declare what they have received from God. Now if a man is sent with a message, will he be received as a messenger if he does not faithfully relate what he was given to say? Or will an ambassador be approved if he has not implemented his mandate? By no means! That is a crime of lese-majesty. Therefore, because the apostles' office exceeds every other ambassadorship and they bear a reconciliation which God makes with us and declare that we are companions of angels, human beings will surely be permitted to forgo their dreams. We must note, then, that Jesus Christ bestowed upon them their Bible and the message they were to deliver. In summary, what Luke calls the charge Jesus Christ entrusted to his apostles is the preaching of the message they received from him.

So we see the apostles did not receive the office of teacher until they had first been disciples. For if the apostles were constrained not to go beyond the limits of the teaching they received from Jesus Christ, will other men have greater authority to do so? The pope can assume no greater title than to say he stands in the place of the apostles. Having only apostolic rank and authority, where does he get the authority to bind people's consciences? If he claims such authority, let him name the source of that authority. Not even Peter would have dared make such a claim, for he too would have exceeded his charge. However, let us note first that Jesus Christ did not turn the reins over to the apostles to teach what they wished; he entrusted to them a particular lesson. Do not let those responsible for bearing the word of God presume to add to it something of their own or to remove from it any teaching contained in the law, the prophets, and the gospel. Rather let them faithfully distribute what they have received from God, as Paul says when speaking of the Lord's Supper (*1 Cor.* 11:23). We must apply what he says about the Lord's Supper to everything else Jesus Christ said. That is why it is written: 'This is my beloved Son. Hear him.' For it is not written: 'Listen to him as to an ordinary man.' He has a precedence that is his alone.

In addition, we are confirmed in the apostles' teaching when we understand they received it from God. It is said here that Jesus Christ instructed them and that they fulfilled their charge faithfully. It is therefore Jesus Christ who speaks through them and forthwith, Luke says, instructs them by the Holy Spirit. Even if Luke had not added that statement, the name of Jesus Christ would have sufficed, for we understand that he is the Saviour of the world and has clearly shown by his miracles that he is the Son of God. But so that the teaching might be even more emphatically authorized, he says 'by the Holy Spirit', as if to say Jesus Christ did not instruct his apostles by that human nature shared with us, but by the same Spirit of God that was upon him, as it is written in Isaiah (*Isa.* 42:1).

Thus we see how Luke wanted to emphasize that Jesus Christ did not entrust the gospel to the apostles as long as he was our brother here on earth, but that he entrusted it to them as Son of God. In that, we also see how God recommends his word to us, and for good reason. We are filled with ingratitude, which means we

hold his word in contempt in spite of the fact he wants everything
to tremble the instant he utters his voice. And yet who is moved
when his word is proclaimed? Some are put to sleep by it; others
neither honour nor reverence it. So it is for good reason that God
is so insistent to instruct us in his teaching. He wants us to learn to
receive it better than we normally do. And yet it is certain we will
be without excuse if we do not receive it, seeing that Jesus Christ
says he is the author of it and adds he bestowed it by the power of
the Holy Spirit. That is what we must pay strict attention to.

Now subsequent to that is the election of the apostles,
which we cannot deal with now. But since we have received the
teaching in the way I have described, we need to remember what Jesus
Christ has done. He has ratified that teaching by dying and sealed
it with his miracles. Since that is true, what can we do but receive
it? Let us then learn to strengthen our faith in all that Jesus Christ
has done for our salvation. And let us not permit his death to be
nullified by our ingratitude. Let us receive his miracles and not
let them fly off with the wind. Now, when asked whether we are
Christians, let us always say 'yes'!

Furthermore, because we are going to celebrate the holy Supper of our Lord next Sunday,[1] we are not to come unadvisedly, for
Jesus Christ shows us the great worth of the blessings we receive in
it. So since on Sunday we are to receive this pledge which God has
granted us and since we belong to Jesus Christ as members of his
body, let us earnestly and circumspectly affirm our duty to follow
his command so that this affirmation will not be made in vain, lest
we be called treacherous violators of the faith.

Since in this way we have Jesus Christ in his fullness with the
Holy Spirit, we must have proper respect for his gospel and yield
ourselves to it in such a manner that when we say we belong to
him, our lives bear witness thereto. Such must be our behaviour if

[1] i.e., 1 September 1549.

we wish to come to this table, not as guilty people, but to put off our old flesh, that corruption which belongs to our nature. And yet we must be all the more attentive to his gospel so that we will not receive the holy Supper in vain and so that what he has done will avail for us and by his Holy Spirit bear fruit in us.

Following that sacred teaching, let us bow before the face of our gracious God, praying that if we have been till now so unfortunate as not to taste the power of his word, he will henceforth favour us with hearing it and nourish us with it, not as little children on milk, but as those who, with strong meat, are sustained by his grace until we arrive at the perfection to which he calls us. Now let us all say, Heavenly Father . . .

2

How Peter's Sermon Bore Fruit

Sunday, 22 December 1549

Therefore let all the house of Israel know assuredly, that God hath made that same Jesus, whom ye have crucified, both Lord and Christ. [37] Now when they heard this, they were pricked in their heart, and said unto Peter and to the rest of the apostles, Men and brethren, what shall we do? [38] Then Peter said unto them, Repent, and be baptized every one of you in the name of Jesus Christ for the remission of sins (Acts 2:36–38).

Because many people have no regard for God and are in this world like wild animals, without hope of salvation and without godliness, Peter in particular, wishing to bring the Jews to our Lord Jesus Christ, capitalizes on the fact that they belong to a house God chose and elected from among all others because they were descended from the lineage of Jacob. And since our Lord called himself the God of Abraham, of Isaac and Jacob, he also called the Jews into his fellowship and tried to establish them among the number of his children and heirs. That is why Peter reminded them of their lineage, so they might know that the Messiah's salvation, promised in the law, was for them. Yet he tells them that in vain do they boast of belonging to that lineage if they do not receive the benefit offered to them. And why does God so magnify the house of Abraham? Precisely so that he will have a people to serve him and call upon him and recognize him as their God and Lord. And those who refuse, them he considers unworthy of the house, cuts them off and casts them away.

It is true that was said to the Jews when they had an opportunity to receive the gospel when the apostles preached it. But now we are all members of one church. And since our Lord has torn down the wall between them and us, we now bear the name Christian, which is greater and more excellent than that of the house of Jacob. For Jesus Christ wanted to make us participants in that name which was conferred upon him by God his Father. Let us consider not only that what was promised to the Jews belongs to us but also that, since Jesus Christ is offered to us, he has been anointed by the Holy Spirit and given all power by God his Father. Let us be assured of our salvation, for he has taken us under his protection. Now, Peter not only says that is what people think and believe, but he also wants us to know for certain that Jesus Christ is our redemption and that through him alone we have salvation. He also wants the confidence we draw from that truth to be so firmly grounded that we will never doubt, no matter what trial befalls us.

Indeed, we see that the devil spares no effort to ruin us and, primarily, to turn us from that confidence. If, then, our certainty is not such that we can repulse all the devil's assaults, what would happen? Will we think about what our salvation might have been? Yet Peter had a reason for using the expression 'Let all the house of Israel know assuredly'. He uses it like a statement customarily attached to letters to certify their authenticity. And in that usage we see he wanted to make a distinction between our faith and a wavering opinion. For many will be found who will say they have faith, but if they look into their hearts, they will find they foolishly believe they have that faith which they truly believe they have simply because they think they do. Just let some slight hint of testing arise, and they are overwhelmed!

Now that is not the way God wants us to believe in him. He wants our confidence in him to remain as unchanging as he is, as Paul says in his second letter to the Corinthians, 'that the Son of God, Jesus Christ, was not Yes and No, but in him was Yes. For all the promises of God in him are Yes, and in him Amen, to the glory of God' (*2 Cor.* 1:19–20). In the same way, just as Jesus Christ is unchangeable, so let our faith hold firmly to the steadfastness of the gospel during every trial.

In addition, it was not without reason that Peter says Jesus Christ was devoted to God, for if we know only the Son of God in his essence, we will have small consolation. But knowing that he offered himself to God his Father for our reconciliation and that he gave himself for us, we can have confident faith in him. Now, it is not enough for confident faith to say, 'I believe that Jesus Christ came into this world and endured death and suffering'; we must face the main issue: Why did he come? When we realize that God consecrated him and conferred on him the office of priest, which he accepted for our redemption, we will understand that we now have a place in heaven because we have a priest who leads us to it, and we will also understand that he was solemnly consecrated for this purpose by God his Father. When he has taken us under his protection, he will teach us that God's will is for us to believe in him. That is how we will be able to put our trust in him. For we are well justified in finding consolation and seeking no further when we find the remission of our sins in the death of Jesus Christ. Now, this is not a private death, one which belongs particularly to a single individual, but through it our sins are forgiven and God receives us as if we were righteous and innocent. Through his death we can also call upon God in the strong confidence that Jesus Christ was anointed advocate and established in that office to intercede for us.

We see that he is by nature the Son of God. Therefore, through him we are his children by adoption. Thus we learn how important it is to believe in Jesus Christ. It is not enough to consider his essence and to be able to say he took on human flesh by the Virgin Mary, died and was raised alive and ascended into heaven, but we must know that the role of him who came was to cleanse us of all our iniquities so that God can accept us as his children and preserve us in his household. Thereafter he directs and governs us by his Holy Spirit so that sin will not rule in us and so that we will be sustained by him when we face all temptations.

Look, the devil is intent on ruining us and does not stop deluging us with his wiles. As for assaults against us, nothing excels the world's onslaught, and yet if we consider Jesus Christ just as he came into this world and just as we go to him in our human condition, he will protect us from all assaults as long as he is the agent of God his Father, not to reign in his stead, but to make us kings under him and conquerors of our enemies, as was explained last Sunday[1] in the Psalm that says he will reign in the midst of his enemies (*Psa.* 110:2).

Now we have many enemies assailing us from all sides: the devil, the world, and our own flesh, but that does not keep Jesus Christ from reigning in us, provided we are led by him. So we see that Jesus Christ is not king for himself or for his own advantage, but for us, and all the victories he won are for our advantage.

Yet Peter accuses the Jews of ingratitude and cruelty when he says they crucified Jesus Christ, which is like saying, 'Know that you had a redeemer who had been promised in the law, and yet you murdered him.' That is the second time he accuses them of crucifying Jesus Christ, and the second accusation is sharper than the first. For he was charging them only with killing an innocent

---

[1] Calvin is referring to the sermon of 15 December 1549, which has been lost. Psalm 110:2 is quoted in Acts 2:34–35. [Editors' note]

man when he said: 'You men of Israel, hear these words; Jesus of Nazareth, a man approved of God by mighty works and wonders and signs, you have taken, and by wicked hands have crucified and slain' (*Acts* 22:22–23). And now he tells them they undertook open war against God when they killed the one who had been given to them as their Saviour. Now that was a sacrilege abhorrent enough to confound them!

Even if the Jews to whom Peter was speaking did not put Jesus Christ to death with their own hands, but sued for his death and consented to it, he accuses them as if they were in fact guilty of it. For God does not look upon the hand alone, but upon the heart's intention. They were murderers with their tongues when crying out to Pilate, 'Crucify him, crucify him' (*Luke* 23:21). Let us not think, therefore, that we are excusable when we have not committed a transgression in such a way that people can blame us for it. But when our conscience convicts us, that is sufficient to incur condemnation.

Still we must note that Peter did not wish to embark on this reproach of the Jews to defame them but to help them. For, as has been mentioned in recent days, if people are not of contrite heart and do not bemoan their sins, they will never be disposed to receive the promise of salvation. As long as they are at ease, they find no pleasure in God's goodness and turn their backs on him. But when we are shown our vices and are displeased with them and so greatly ashamed of them that we do not know what to do, then we receive our Lord and let him enter us. Until then we had closed the door to him. And that is why Peter accuses the Jews once again of crucifying Jesus Christ.

We see that Paul affirms to the Corinthians: 'It is not to shame you' (*1 Cor.* 4:14). And again he repeats: 'I do not want to shame you', and that is the true meaning of what Peter says here. For when the Holy Spirit judges men, it is not because he wants to confound them, as if wanting to stomp on them and spit in their face. That is not his intention. What is, then? By condemning us, he wants to pardon us completely. But until we are cut to the quick by the knowledge of our sins, it is impossible for us to grasp the good which God wants to do for us. For as long as man delights in his vices, he rejects God's favour. That fact will be very easy to recognize once we consider our own natural disposition, which is to make of vice a virtue: we discern other people's imperfections without difficulty and find ways to condemn them. But if we are obliged to recognize the same faults in ourselves, we cannot possibly be persuaded that we have any. Such is our experience every day, more often than need be. Consequently, God has to bring us to this point forcibly, as it were, so we will feel shame for our sins and receive his grace, as we have already said. Yet, let us consider ourselves and recognize that although we find such an undertaking galling, we must nonetheless endure it like drinking a bitter medicine that will do us good.

There are many who find this teaching very irksome and say, 'Why all this wrangling? Would it not be enough to tell us what we should do without constantly goading us?' Well, let us note briefly how Peter proceeds here. He does not say to the Jews, 'You must do thus and so', but, 'You are murderers; you have killed the one sent to be your saviour.' That is what he rebukes them for, in the tradition of all the prophets. The apostles of Jesus Christ do no less. For that is the purpose of Paul's admonition to the Corinthians. He needs to throw them into confusion and make them experience shame for their sins. So he says to them, 'I must declare your baseness. You are vainglorious and foster in-cest, lechery among yourselves, then you go mingle with idolaters and engage in frivolous disputes and speculations, even going so far as to doubting the resurrection, and yet you wish to be called Christians. No and no! Go hide yourselves with all the glory you get from that.' And why does he speak this way? It is not because he does not love them or desire their conversion, but since they are satisfied in their evil and he cannot otherwise bring them to acknowledge their sins, he uses those kinds of severe words. So since that is the way of the Holy Spirit, let us learn to endure stings to the quick and bow our heads when our vices are thrown up before us so that God, who is our Judge, may be our Father and receive us as his children, according to his infinite mercy.

And besides, when we see that Peter calls 'murderers' those who did not lend a hand in crucifying Jesus Christ, let us remember what I have already said, that although we did not crucify Jesus Christ bodily but consented to his death, we are as guilty as the wicked men who murdered him. The apostle says that is the way we crucify Jesus Christ anew. If, after knowing the truth of the gospel, we turn from it, we ourselves crucify him and place him there as a spectacle on a scaffold. For since Jesus Christ grants us the grace of calling us to himself by his word and of receiving such a blessing from him, do we not put him mockingly on the scaffold when we balk at that holy calling to which he has called us? Paul also says that Jesus Christ is crucified afresh by our offences (*Heb.* 6:6).[1] However, if we are so wicked as to turn away from God's truth, we are more the murderers of Jesus Christ than those who crucified him with their own hands. Why so? Because when he was crucified, it was as a servant, as Paul says (*Phil.* 2:7). But now that he is exalted and the Father has given him a name that is above every name, and now that he is raised on high and the devils of hell tremble at the sound of his name, will we come and mock him? Will we come again and crucify him? We must not doubt that we are guiltier than those who crucified him when he was in that servile and lowly condition. Then we must look at this more closely than is our custom so that we will not fall under

---

[1] Calvin, like many others of his time and since, believed Paul to be the author of the Letter to the Hebrews.

this condemnation Paul pronounces against those who crucify Jesus Christ afresh by their offences and disordered lives.

Just as Luke declared that Peter admonished the Jews very harshly in his effort to bring them to the knowledge of their sins, so he shows that this teaching was not useless, for God gave such authority to Peter's sermon that those who heard it were pricked and grieved in their hearts for committing such an egregious and villainous act. According to Luke's account, that is the first fruit produced by that sermon.

Then he adds that they asked Peter and the other apostles what they should do. For it is not enough to be pained by the knowledge of one's sin. One must seek the remedy. And yet Luke says the answer they received was that they should repent, that through Jesus Christ they would receive remission of their sins, and that, as a sign thereof, they should be baptized in his name.

Now that is how the teaching first bore fruit. To the extent that the Jews who had previously despised the Son of God and were hardened in that very damnable act they had committed, to that extent they are so humiliated and dejected that they ask only to yield themselves to the will of God in all reverence and humility. That is the meaning of the expression 'pricked in their heart', which Luke uses here. We must use that teaching so that we may know that the word of God is not fruitless in us. May we experience such grief from the knowledge of our sins that we do not fail to repent, as Paul also says when speaking of it: 'I know I grieved you, but I shall not repent of making you feel sad, because I know that that sadness will be changed into joy' (*2 Cor.* 7:8–9). Therefore, we must not repent of being sad for feeling our sins, provided that, humble before God, we seek all our consolation where he promised we would find it, in Jesus Christ, so that he might ease the anguish we felt in our hearts. That is what Luke intends in this passage. For if we are so hardened that we react by throwing up our chin when someone rebukes us for our vices, we give evidence of our reprobation. It is even said that the word of God is an iron hammer that breaks rocks to pieces (*Jer.* 23:29). So if an admonition directed against us does not humble us, are we not well justified in saying we have a perverse and accursed nature?

Yet, let us note what was said earlier, namely that since we are enemies of God by doing evil, the way to come to him is to find displeasure in our vices. For until we know the depth of the sins which are in us, we will in no way profit from the reproofs we receive, but will turn everything into a profane teaching, for there will be many who know how to mock superstitions and idolatrous ceremonies but, because of their sins, fail to recognize their ruin and God's judgment on them. Therefore, we must study this lesson all the more because we know we need it.

Moreover, we must note that since the word of God is called a 'sharp sword' (*Heb.* 4:12), it must, when preached to us, pierce us to the heart and examine what lies deep in its shadows. If we have not felt that power, we do not yet know what it is to be taught by God. Paul, when glorying in his preaching, says he was a priest to offer a solemn sacrifice to God (*Rom.* 15:16; *Phil.* 2:17). He makes a comparison with the priest who has the sword in his hand to kill the sacrificial animal, because the sacrifice could not be offered unless the animal was killed. So he says he mortified men so that they might be a sacrifice pleasing to God. If, therefore, Paul's preaching bore fruit in this way by mortifying men and leading them to knowledge of their sins, we must conclude that, until we are pricked in the heart and experience grief for offending, we will not profit from the teaching.

Now we must join these two things together, namely, the goading of the heart and the counsel which the Jews asked for when wanting to know what they were to do. There are many who will keenly feel a goading and anguish in their heart but all the same will not allow themselves to wander and caper heedlessly to such a degree that they bring themselves to ruin. We see what happened to Cain and Judas. It is true that Cain does say he offended, knows his sin, and has great anguish in his heart (*Gen.* 4:13). Judas admits he sinned by selling innocent blood and makes a proper confession (*Matt.* 27:4). We must not, then, think he admits it hypocritically. He readily condemns himself before both God and men. Cain, on the other hand, goes away trembling and with deep anguish in his heart. And yet, what end do both men come to? They die desperate and lost because, while having that goading in their hearts and knowing their sin, they still refused to ask for advice about what to do.

Unbelievers have the same experience. I include even those who do not have preaching. Although God does not speak to the wicked by the voice of men, still they must have some goad to prick them and incite them to consider that there is a God who will be their judge. Then, afterwards, they will feel that heaviness and anguish in their hearts. All their feeling will be like a rage, such that they will not be able to avoid that diabolical fury, and will enter a state of despair from which they will never be able to escape. It is like a wild boar backed into a corner. He will froth at the mouth. The more he is watched, the more he will lash out with his tusks to kill everything around him if he could. The same is true for these good-time boys. They will just mock whatever they hear from the pulpit, as a number of them have done. But if someone rebukes them for their faults, they will indeed be pricked, not to repent, but to froth in their fury and lash out against God and his word with their teeth. And when they are observed doing so, it is a good sign they are pricked, but to their condemnation.

There are others who profit no more than the above. They gladly lull themselves to sleep and remain so dull of mind that the teaching cannot penetrate them. They are like the sick people around us. Some are so numb they feel nothing when touched. That is a sickness unto death. Others have a hot fever which makes them delirious, so delirious they cannot be restrained. So is it with these spiritually sick people. Some are so hardened they refuse to feel any judgment of God, so hardened they come to this evil which Paul calls hardness of heart (*Eph.* 4:18–19), and that sickness is incurable. There are others who become angry when confronted with rebukes. They are pricked and feel regret in their heart. But will this lead them to seek counsel? No, it incites them even more and makes them intensely spiteful.

Now, let us note what Luke says. After sorrow entered the Jews, they asked for counsel. In that statement, he shows two things. The first is that men receive a rebuke which bears them no fruit because they do not amend their lives. Second, he wanted to draw attention to an obedience which came upon those Jews who submitted themselves completely to God and sought only to do what they were told. When Peter told them they were murderers and spoke to them sharply, they did not reply, but humbled themselves, saying, 'We are ready to do all that you tell us.' That is very far from rising up against him and disparaging him and his teaching. No, they recognized their fault and confessed it, saying, 'You have brought us such a good medicine that we will live henceforth unto God, whereas we used to live unto the devil.'

Therefore, we see what we must do if we want to profit from the teaching. We must sense our evil in order to be grieved by it and seek ways to shake it off. Are we so disposed? Let us understand that God is ready to receive us and that, when he condemns us, it is to cleanse us; when he pricks us, it is to heal us; and when he threatens us, it is to call us unto himself.

Thereafter, let us be gentle and gracious so that when we feel the harshness of those who preach the gospel, we will realize they intend to strike like lightning so that we will conform to the word with all obedience and so avoid kicking against the goad (cf. *Acts* 26:14). For God is able to rein us in when we try to act like wild horses. Otherwise, we will call ourselves Christians to no avail. And if we do not take advantage of the examples proposed for us here, we heap double condemnation upon ourselves (cf. *Luke* 12:47).

We must be all the more mindful of these things since we are to come to the table of Jesus Christ next Wednesday[1] to make an open declaration that we wish to obey God and submit ourselves unreservedly to him and his word. Let us now look briefly at how we will recognize the falseness within us. We come to this place to declare publicly that we want to live in Jesus Christ, praying that he will be pleased to live in us – but that is not what happens! We gather here and go through the motions in the presence of both God and his angels. Now do we think that he will gladly endure such pretence? When coming to the Lord's table, we come seeking Jesus Christ, and when the gospel is preached to us, he is there in our midst, calling us to his table to participate in his body and blood, indeed in his whole self. Therefore, when we see that the blood of Jesus Christ is our spiritual substance, our open avowal must be such that we ask only to be joined to him, for as soon as we are separated from him, we join ourselves to the devil. Do we think God can tolerate such cowardliness when we are unwilling to allow Jesus Christ to reign in us and thus reject him? Therefore, let us make up our minds that when coming to commune at the table of Jesus Christ, we do what is demonstrated here, namely that we confess our sins in such a way that, instead of delighting in them, we have that pricking of the heart spoken of here so that we can come and seek in the Lord's Supper what we are supposed to find in it. It is true that we will not

[1] Calvin is referring to the Lord's Supper held on Christmas Day, Wednesday, 25 December 1549. [Editors' note]

be appropriately prepared for approaching this holy table, but knowing our infirmity, we must very reverently seek in it what is lacking in us. That is also why the Lord's table is offered to us many times. We are so weak that we are no sooner lifted up than we fall again straightway.

We must, therefore, be appropriately prepared not just when the time for the Lord's Supper approaches; God must always strengthen us, and we must ever and increasingly profit from his teaching in such a way that this will be a perpetual practice throughout our lives. And yet, as we seek in God the remedy for our sins, let us not doubt his readiness to receive us mercifully and extend his hand to draw us unto himself. That, then, is how, in our search for God, we find what Peter proposes here, namely that God will come to meet us and heal our ills, provided we can allow him to be our physician. But we will hold that for next Sunday.

Following this holy teaching, let us bow before the face of our gracious God in acknowledgment of our faults, beseeching him to be pleased to grant that we, being displeased with our vices, may seek all our pleasure and consolation in him and his teaching and, in this way, come to Jesus Christ humbly so that he will lead us to the heavenly kingdom after communicating to us in this world his body and blood for the nourishment and sustenance of our souls as long as they remain in these mortal bodies. Now let us all say, Almighty God, heavenly Father . . .

3

On Coming to Christ

Then Peter said unto them, Repent, and be baptized every one of you in the name of Jesus Christ for the remission of sins, and ye shall receive the gift of the Holy Ghost (Acts 2:38).

We saw previously how we come to God. We must be touched in heart and acknowledge our faults in order to humble ourselves before him. Furthermore, we have shown it is not enough to acknowledge our sins unless we put ourselves in God's hands and are prepared to receive the counsel he gives us. Judas, Cain, and their ilk did indeed acknowledge their sin but consequently fell into despair because they did not seek counsel concerning what they should do. Therefore, when God reproves us for our faults, we must take care not to lose courage, as the Jews did, who, upon learning of their offence and being aggrieved in themselves for committing it, said, 'Brethren, what shall we do?' (*Acts* 2:37)

We now need to show that a sinner who responds the same way will not be disappointed. As we see, after the Jews acknowledged their fault and declared openly they would do whatever the apostles told them, Peter adds God's counsel: 'Repent'. In Psalm 51 we read that a contrite heart and a broken spirit are a sacrifice pleasing to God and that he never rejects the one who comes to him in such humility (*Psa.* 51:19). God greatly consoles us by assuring us that if we come to him in sorrow for offending him, he will accept that contrition as a sweet-smelling sacrifice; he will receive us and sanctify us by his grace. And that very consolation should stir us to repentance, but there are very few who think about that because sins reign too much in us, and the devil intoxicates us or, rather, charms us so much that we do not think about the perdition which is on our doorstep. Nevertheless, the fact remains that we do well to be affected by our Lord's readiness to receive us if we go to him in repentance.

Let us consider now that when God disposes us to come to him, we must do so immediately, just as Peter tells the Jews, 'Repent, and be baptized every one of you in the name of Jesus Christ for the remission of sins, and you shall receive the gift of the Holy Spirit.' So we have here Peter's first point, which is like an exhortation to the Jews to repent; the second is a promise of the remission of sins. The third is to show the remission of our sins must be founded on the name of Jesus Christ; and the fourth is the witness of the remission of our sins, namely, baptism. That is what we must declare.

To understand each point more easily, we need to know what repentance is. We now know the term has been misused for a long time, for when they speak of repentance in the Papacy, only a few external practices will come to mind, such as eating no meat on Fridays or Saturdays, fasting occasionally, gadding about on pilgrimages, mumbling in front of some statue, having a mass sung, and the like. That is what repentance means to the ignorant. Now when Scripture speaks of it, it means something very different. It is, in a word, the turning of a man to God. For by nature we are alienated from God and can do nothing but the things he condemns. That, therefore, is the condition of man in himself, that is, a condition totally repugnant to the righteousness of God. Now here is God calling us to himself by repentance. Take the case of a man whose back was turned on God. When God in his grace gives him knowledge of his sin through the preaching of his word and so brings him to repentance, he then turns around and contemplates God face to face. In that, we see repentance does not lie in outward nonsensical actions, such as abstaining from eating meats on one day rather than on another and engaging in a thousand other monkey tricks like those performed by the Papacy. But repentance has its seat in the spirit and in the heart. That is why we must pay close attention to what we have touched on. For when we come to God, will we come with feet or hands or tongue? Not at all! The heart must work at it. And in fact, this word, as used in Scripture, tells us mainly that we have become new creatures (*2 Cor.* 5:17).

So we see now both how repentance encompasses man's turning to God and how its principal seat lies in the heart and in the spirit. And that is why Scripture, when speaking of our conversion, also confronts us with the weakness of our flesh: the old man must be put to death (*Eph.* 4:22–24), that is, the nature with which we are born as human beings must be removed, for there is only wickedness in us. Therefore, we must begin by blaming ourselves and by conquering what constitutes our own condition. Then, God must rule in us and cover us with his grace, for it would not be enough for us to be put to death if God did not give us a new life so that he might use us entirely in his service. And this is how we can experience repentance: it is when God gives us the grace to bring all our desires into captivity, when all that makes up our human nature is conquered and we are so governed by his Holy Spirit that our lives are completely ruled by his word, whereas formerly we were devoted to evil.

So then, when Peter says to the Jews, 'Repent', it is as if he were saying to them, 'Until now you were lost people because your backs were turned on God. Now it is a matter of changing your lives, which cannot be done until you recognize the danger you are in. So that is where you must begin if you wish to escape. And still it is not enough that you recognize your evil; you must seek the means to be delivered from it, as we have said, which will be when you completely renounce what comes out of your nature so that you can give yourselves in obedience to God.' That is how Peter calls the Jews to repentance. It is true that all we have here is this word 'repent', but we need to note that Luke did not want to relate Peter's sermon in its entirety. He gives only a summary of what was said, as one who would like to summarize what this sermon deals with! Here is what has been touched on so far concerning repentance. First, the Christian must experience personal grief for offending God; second, he must recognize that his salvation depends on the remission of his sins; third, he must realize both that he obtains this good through Jesus Christ; and that, finally, with baptism, God wishes to seal with a visible sign the remission of his sins and provide him with a witness to God's grace. That, then, is an abbreviated account of the meaning of repentance, which could be treated in longer discourses.

That is how Luke handles the subject and will again later. For if he had wanted to record the apostles' sermons and exhortations in detail, he would have had to make long entries because Paul even exhorted the people until long after midnight (*Acts* 20:7), as we shall see. Now there would be a great deal to record if he wanted to set all that down in writing. But, as I said, it is enough that he mentions the principal point, as, when speaking of repentance, he uses only the word 'repent'. He does not describe all we have just stated, nor does he say that we must be freed of all earthly concerns if we are to be conformed to Jesus Christ. Similarly he does not say that the man who wishes to repent is not to die to himself once for all, but that he is like a man engulfed in his human desires and yet lives not for himself, but is living his new life, which comes from Jesus Christ. That is how Scripture speaks of repentance, and let us not doubt that Peter elaborated to the Jews the meaning of repentance and the way men can repent in such a way that their repentance is effective.

Now when we are thus refashioned, life thereafter is like the fruit of a tree. We shall not say that the goodness of a tree is in the branches, but that one knows it by its fruit. The same is true of repentance. It must produce its fruit; otherwise, you will not recognize that a man is converted. And for that reason it is said, 'Bring forth fruits meet for repentance' (*Matt.* 3:8; *Luke* 3:8). We must therefore show by results that we are truly repentant, for it will only be boasting filled with lies if we say we are repentant but our lives do not reflect our words. It is true we will not by our effort enter upon this renewal of life unless God gives us the grace to do so, but the fact remains that the path is completely laid out and we have only to beseech him to direct us when we are alienated from him.

To be noted also is that although our Lord does not lead us to repentance upon our first request, we must not give up, but entreat him many times inasmuch as we must not think it a small thing for man to be brought into conformity with the image of God. Let us not think then, when we have arrived at repentance, that we have attained a perfection like his. Far from it! But we must draw ever nearer to him and make daily progress. It is not enough to begin. We must carry through.

When seeing that Peter exhorts the Jews to repent, we must note that it is not enough to repent once, as I have already pointed out, but we must persist. And contrarily, beyond the fact that repentance cannot be achieved with the first effort, let us daily take care that vices not flourish in us. We are like fertile ground, good for producing weeds rather than useful plants. And when God has

removed the evil affections which are in us, our nature is still so perverse that they will spread their roots and increase and grow larger
than before. That is why Jesus Christ, saying we must be grafted into
him, declares that the function of God his Father is to graft us into
him, but he must prune us and cut out what is of no use to us, so that
we can bear good fruit (*John* 15:1). In the same manner, vines must
be pruned each year. Otherwise they would become weak and not
bear fruit. Therefore, after grafting us, God must prune us and cause
us to produce fruit which is pleasant in his sight. Those then are the
reasons we know it is not enough to experience this repentance just
once; we must continue to repent, for repentance is never finished
until the old man is completely discarded.

Moreover, our nature is so fertile for evil that it always
produces a new vice, and our Lord has no sooner removed one
vice from us than the process must be repeated. For vices well
up within us one after another like water from a fountain. So
then we need to try hard every day to repent so as to return more
effectively to the will of God. And that is a thing badly practised,
although it is very necessary, for we do not think about our sins to
abandon them or remember the will of God to follow it. And yet
each one of us, man or woman, must try daily to consider: 'Well
now, how have I conducted my life up till now? How have I used
the fear of God to advantage? I find that each day requires a new
beginning, for I do not chastise myself for some admonition or
other I may receive.' That is how we must examine ourselves. When
we experience this sorrow for offending God, we must not doubt
that our Lord supplies what lacks and thereby brings us to the true
repentance mentioned here. That is the way we must approach him.
Otherwise, if we ever think we take one step closer to him, we take
two steps back.

Now we must not be surprised if we are unable to prick our
own conscience, because we do the very opposite. We are grieved

if someone speaks of our vices in public. We do not want anyone to reproach us for them. We do not want to think about them in private either. And yet Solomon says – and not without cause – that the man who is often afraid is blessed (*Prov.* 28:14), not that we should be afraid of putting ourselves in such defiance that we cannot return to God, but that we should be quick to confront our vice head on and take heed to correct it while God gives us the grace to put our mind to it. Now since very few of us do that and are blessed, many more of us do not do that and are not blessed. And no matter how much we boast of being Christian, we indicate clearly, unless we change our ways, that ours is but empty boasting. For we should know that Christian teaching consists of these two points, namely, repentance and the remission of sins. We have no other instruction from God. After Jesus Christ instructed his apostles, he said, 'Preach repentance and the remission of sins' (*Luke* 24:47). We must be refashioned through repentance if we wish to receive remission of our sins. For up to that point, we shall not be able to lean upon God's goodness and entrust ourselves to him as we should. And that is why we see many people who are far from being Christians. For, as I said earlier concerning repentance, they never want to acquire knowledge of their sins and do not want to be badgered about them, and yet it is in repentance that all our well-being lies. May we, through the reproofs directed against us, be able to seize this repentance which will let us taste the goodness of God so that we may entrust ourselves entirely to him.

In addition, we must note that just as Peter, wanting to bring the Jews to repentance, reprimanded them severely for their faults, so must the one who preaches to us reprove us daily for our sins. Otherwise, we would have a gospel made to our order. It would not be the one God has given us. That fact greatly annoys us, whatever the situation. Some are vexed and others gnash their teeth, but we must nonetheless uphold the teaching of God in the midst of his church. If we think we are doing them a favour by being lenient, we shall be contributing to their ruin. It is a great pity that we cannot be persuaded that that is true. As I have already said, when God calls us, a change must take place in us, as if we had become new men. That is how Scripture speaks of it and how we must use repentance to advantage.

Now let us look briefly at what one will find in our lives. It is true we have the gospel, but if someone examines our deeds and evaluates what kind of people we are, will he find that there is some change in us? Not at all! For we are not adhering to the path set before us. When the subject of repentance comes up, we should look circumspectly within ourselves. Well, we are very far from our goal. If we have taken three or four steps, we must take hundreds more and continue on our path until we reach the destination to which God calls us. That is how we must exhort ourselves to pursue this repentance; but till now we have only learned that it remakes our life. We have wanted Jesus Christ to come to us, but it has not occurred to us to approach him.

From that perspective then, let us, as we hear this passage, imagine something shameful that would cause us deep sorrow, for if we were the kind of people we should be, no one would have to speak to us the way Peter spoke to the Jews. The gospel has long been preached to us and we have long been exhorted to repent. Yet we have not done so. Does it not dishearten us that instruction profits us so little? If we wish to draw our conclusions from the facts, consider what people will be able to say about us based on the vices which reign among us. It is true that we would be well advised to renounce the vanities and vainglories of this world and remove from our midst all those things which can move us to evil. Nevertheless there has never been a greater excess of clothing than there is among us now. Still, this clothing is only like leaves covering branches, just small things, although rather significant. But as with other abominable things, it too is but a vapour. The blasphemies, the broken vows, the renunciations of God – have they ever been greater than now? Then there are ordinances against gambling for money. We see the situation going from bad to worse. There are wicked wretches who will one day gamble away their money, and their wives and poor families will have to languish in hunger because of such despicable people's bad management. Sensuous dances will be forbidden, followed by indecent and profane songs and dissolute habits. The ordinances will be proclaimed publicly, but where is the fear that we owe first and foremost to God, then to those over us? What obligation do we have to abstain from all those things?

Let us now come to the greatest sins. Let us determine whether we can indeed glorify ourselves in our pride. Where is our glory? Let us consider how Paul speaks to the Corinthians: 'And you, merchants (for we know that Corinth was a rich and opulent city, much larger than and different from this one), you think so highly of your wealth and power, go hide yourselves with it and your pride. You are lechers, you associate with idolaters, you occasion a thousand offences, then, in the guise of being rich and powerful, you want people to think you are good Christians. No, no! That is not how Christianity works.' About that much more can be said. For all that is a matter of minor concern, as I said, when compared with the blasphemies, usuries, robberies, lecheries, excesses, controversies, injustices, and strife which dominate our behaviour. As for the wrongs and injustices we do to one another, have there ever been more lawsuits and controversies than we have now? What good does it do to have this teaching of peace by which God exhorts us to learn how to endure even the wrongs others do to us? When there are differences between us, may he teach us to be reconciled rather than go to court. Then, how many refrain from blasphemies? But to the contrary, many take pleasure in tearing God's name to pieces. Body, belly, head! Everything sails out of the mouths of those despicable monsters. Then if they are rebuked, they want to lay the blame on their anger. Indeed! And wretched people! Must God be subjected to fits of anger? After you mangle his name this way, will he be content to say that you are angry and that he will just have to endure that kind of behaviour? Oh, you will not last long that way! Afterwards, deceitful and false dealings will ensue; usurers will reign to suck the blood of their neighbour. And those vile thieves will exert a greater cruelty on the poor and be worse than wolves. They will connive together and gnaw a poor man down to the bones. Lecheries will multiply in abundance. And when seeing those kinds of things, will people think they are better off with the teaching than before? In no way! But in that, they know quite well that we have no idea what repentance is all about. So let us think about ourselves and remember that it is not a bad thing to be pricked in our consciences. Gentle medicines will do us no good. We need serious surgery and cauterization of our wounds, because evil is so deeply rooted in us that even harsher measures will have to be taken, for mild measures would only sustain the evil and cover the filth in us. Then, after the example of those Luke talks about here, let us allow ourselves to be rebuked severely for our vices so that after we are empty of them, God may be pleased to fill us with his grace. So that is what we must note concerning this matter of repentance.

There remains the matter of the remission of sins for us to consider. If we preached only repentance and omitted the remission of sins, what would we be able to say? It is certain we would be able to conceive only fear if God did not come later and say to us, 'Now no matter what bitterness and hardness you may experience, it is still true that I wish to soften that anguish of heart which is in you. It is true that you well deserve my condemnation, but I still want to pour out my mercy upon you and receive you as if you were righteous, just as I receive my Son Jesus Christ. You will be my well-beloved children and I shall show you that I am your Father.' So when our Lord adds that consolation to the teaching of repentance, he shows that after a man is thus humbled by the knowledge of his sin, he is unwilling to leave him desolate, but draws him to himself through Jesus Christ, in whom the penitent finds all his joy and all his comfort and so is strengthened.

So that is how we must unite these two matters. That is, we are to become troubled within ourselves; then we are to recognize that God does not wish to impute our sins to us, for he receives us in the name and merit of our Lord Jesus Christ, whose obedience supplies all that is lacking in us. If we are wicked and wretched, Jesus Christ abolishes all that, for he is the fountain of every virtue. If we are but sin, he is righteousness. If we are defiled, he is the fountain of living water to cleanse us. If we are weak, he is the goodness of God to strengthen us. If we are poor, he is so abundantly rich that we must not fear, when we come to him, that we will lack anything. That is why repentance and remission of sins must not be separated. That is why Peter, after rebuking those who offended God, adds: 'Your sins will be forgiven.'

Besides, as we have said, we must continue repenting through-out our lives because the promise which is added is eternal. For when God has pardoned us, when we, being inclined to evil, fall again, he must exercise that kindness toward us and forgive us not once, not twice, but every time and as many times as we return to him in repentance and ask his forgiveness, praying that he will be pleased to make the blood of Jesus Christ avail for us.

Now the papists have failed miserably in the matters of forgiveness and repentance, as we shall see later. As for this word 'repentance', it is the principal way we are refashioned in the image of God. Now we have shown that the papists have not an inkling about the subject. They will not say that repentance is conversion to God, but they speak of repentance to I-know-not-what extent in their diabolical ceremonies. Then they add oral confession and satisfaction by works. Now the same is true when it comes to the remission of sins. They will indeed say that in baptism we have the forgiveness of our sins freely bestowed, but then they say we must bring to God satisfaction for our sins to compensate him. They say that sins are debts, for which we are liable according to his judgment, and yet we must bring him works to recompense him. That is what they mean when they say that forgiveness of sins is given to us only once and that, when a child is baptized, he is truly cleansed of all his sins, but afterwards he must offer satisfaction for those he commits.

They add yet another even more damnable blasphemy, namely, when we Christians do what God has commanded, we do nothing, and we must do more than is required of us if we are to please him. It is as if a man owed his creditor, pays his debt, and does nothing more for him: 'Well, here is what I owe; like it or lump it.' That is how the papists want to treat the matter. Let us now consider for a moment whether God approves or condemns such an approach. When he wishes to condemn such hypocrisies, he says this, 'Who gave you those tasks to perform? Or who has been your employer if I pay you? As for me, I disavow all that and, whereas you think I take pleasure in those things, I hold them in abomination.'

When they speak of the remission of sins, they will say that Jesus Christ helps us with it, but that we win it by our works and that that is the way our sins are pardoned. Now Scripture teaches the opposite. As for our works, provided we could do good works, they are all useless and do not please him, except insofar as they are offered to him in the name of and through Jesus Christ, because we are servants, indeed useless servants, and can do nothing for him except what we owe a hundred times over. It is like a servant who labours all day in his master's vineyard and does double duty. When he comes home in the evening after working very hard all day, will his master arise from table to serve him to repay him for the hard work he has done? Did he do anything for his master which was not his duty (*Luke* 17:7–10)? So then, our works, even our best ones, are so incapable of compensating for our sins that everything which proceeds from us is only sin, and God condemns it. In this way let us realize that we have the forgiveness of our sins through Jesus Christ, just as we have the witness of forgiveness in baptism. That is what we must learn about this point, and, as for repentance, we must learn to come to him and beseech him to be pleased to remake us by his Holy Spirit so that we may know these things as he wishes us to understand them.

> And because we are not capable of understanding them as we should, except as he illuminates us by his grace, let us beseech him to be pleased to touch us to the quick with the kind of repentance just discussed, so that we, being aggrieved in ourselves, will seek in him all our help and comfort, as he is our only happiness. Thus let us all say, Almighty God, heavenly Father . . .

4

To Whom the Promise Belongs

Sunday, 19 January 1550

For the promise is unto you, and to your children, and to them that are afar off, even as many as the Lord our God shall call. [40] *And with many other words did he testify and exhort, saying, Save yourselves from this untoward generation* (Acts 2:39–40).

Last Sunday,[1] we dealt with baptism, how it is never without its effect and its power, provided there is no obstacle on our part, for God is faithful to his promises and wishes to show us it is not in vain that he demonstrates through baptism both that we are washed and cleansed of all our stains by the blood of Jesus Christ and that we are renewed in it by the Holy Spirit. It is not, then, without cause that baptism symbolizes the same for us.

Let us receive what our Lord presents to us in it. And it is certain we will feel what Peter declares, namely that the Holy Spirit will be given to us (*Acts* 2:38), and that God will, by his power, fulfil all he promises and signifies by the gift of the Holy Spirit.

The reason for that is now added. Inasmuch as the promise belongs to the Jews, Peter said to them in effect: 'It is to you that God is speaking. You have his promises through his word. Your

---

[1] Calvin is referring to the sermon of 12 January 1550, which has been lost. [Editors' note]

role must necessarily be to trust what he declares.' From that we have to derive the good and very useful teaching that we must trust God's grace and consider his promises as completely fulfilled the moment he utters them. For questioning whether he will or will not do what he has said to us once and once only is one of the greatest blasphemies we can ever commit against God. For there is nothing he reserves for himself more than that respect we are to have for his word, that as soon as he speaks, the thing is accomplished. That is why he shows us that the world was made and created by his word alone (*John* 1:3). That then is an especially excellent testimony of the dependability of the word of God. Moreover, when he calls us to the hope of eternal life, we are to consider his desire to save us as completely assured. Why? Because God has spoken. That then is what Peter wanted to signify when he said, 'For the promise is unto you, and to your children.'

For that reason, if you wish to honour God as is fitting, you must realize that he does not want to deprive you of what he has said, provided you do not profane him by your unbelief. He wishes to tell you how faithful he is to all his promises. In addition, he wants us to know he is not fickle like mortals, who promise one thing and do another. So let us be aware that God opens his heart to us when he opens his mouth to speak and that we must not question, saying, 'Is it so or not?'

Now there is in this passage yet another teaching. In the sacraments we must always have our eyes fixed on the word of God. The sacraments, as discussed previously, are nothing and have no power except insofar as they are authorized by the word and stamped by it. It is like money which cannot be circulated without the sign and mark of the prince. Likewise, the water in baptism serves no purpose apart from the word of God, where the water is for us a mark and sign that we are washed by the blood of Jesus Christ.

42

So, do we want the sacraments to bear fruit in us? The promise must come first. For it is not without reason that Peter adds, 'It is to you that this promise belongs.' By that he means that if there were no promise, baptism would be null and void. And still we must note not only that the sacraments serve no purpose without the promise, but also that we are informed that when we introduce a sacrament, that is, a sign, unsupported by the word of God, we have only a sham and deception. Like the papists, they will say they have seven sacraments, but when asked what these sacraments – as they call them – are based on and whether they are supported by the word of God, we find that the papists forged them in their head. And the papists have their confirmation, that foul anointing which nullifies the baptism of Jesus Christ. They will make a good case for its being a sacrament. The designation is very honourable, but one will discover that God did not ordain it.

Let us then weigh this verse carefully: 'For the promise is unto you, and to your children.' Let us also consider the true usage of the sacraments God has given us. It will be seen that we always confine them to his word. And because the promises always bring us back to Jesus Christ, it is with them that we must offer and receive the sacraments which God ordains, for we see they were founded on his word, and we must reject all those which men forge in their head. What is more, we understand, generally speaking, that we must stand fast on God's word in order to have a well-founded faith; otherwise, our faith will be only an opinion and a foolish belief which will easily be overcome whenever the devil wishes to attack. So if we want to have a strong, unchangeable faith, we must build it on the truth of God and cling to that truth. For there is a mutual concordance, as they say, between faith and God's promises.

Thus we see there are very few believers, even though they all say they are. If you ask many people what indication they have for calling themselves 'believers' and 'Christians', they will say, 'I believe what is preached', but no mention is made of depending on God and what he has spoken once and for all. Since that is the case, to be true believers, we must learn that when we hear the promises, it is God who makes them and will unquestionably keep them.

We must now note that Peter does not attribute to himself what he states here about our salvation, namely, the remission of sins and the gift of the Holy Spirit. On the contrary, he wishes to show that although God uses men to draw others to the knowledge of these things, all the glory of it belongs to God. It is as if he were saying, 'It is true that I proclaim to you the forgiveness of sins and that I declare to you that you have salvation through Jesus Christ, as you see that the promise is made to you concerning it. Nevertheless, do not look to me; learn about the one I serve and whose words I bring to you.' That is how we must view the matter, for we now have the gospel and men to proclaim it to us, but it did not grow in their garden, as the saying goes. It is God who set forth its law and ordained its government, and men are only its servants. For that reason we must be totally convinced it is God who established the gospel, even though it is administered by the hand of men.

Let us now come to what Peter says: 'Unto you, and to your children'. In the first place, he addresses those who are of age. That is why he says to them, 'Repent.' From the outset he confronts them with repentance with the view to speaking about baptism. Those who are at the age of discretion cannot be baptized (I mean those who are not the people of God), unless they have repented of their sins and confessed to being Christian. But Peter repeatedly adds that the promise is to the children of the Jews, as indeed we see that it is our Lord's promise to Abraham, when he says to him, 'I shall be your God and the God of your seed for a thousand generations' (cf. *Gen.* 17:7). That is how our Lord wishes to declare himself the Saviour of those who are in his church at the present time as well as the Saviour of those who come afterward and their children, because he recognizes and accepts them as his own. And that is what Peter is saying here: 'The promise is unto you, and to your children.'

In that statement we have a singular consolation inasmuch as we understand God is not content to be our Saviour at the time we can call upon him and he answers our prayer, but he extends his mercy to our children and wishes them to be participants in the same grace which he bestows upon us liberally. That means the children are in their mother's womb like animals in respect of awareness. Yet God acknowledges them as his own and promises them eternal life. That is to show his great goodness toward us, that great goodness which he wishes so much to impress upon us and extend to our posterity and lineage.

And yet, let us look more closely at this passage: 'The promise is unto you, and to your children.' Now when baptism is added later, it is to ratify that promise. That is why we baptize our small children today. Baptism is not a creation of men, but of God. For just as he spoke to Abraham in the time of the law and commanded circumcision, so he now does for us with the institution of baptism. So then, when our Lord receives our children as his own, they must be marked with his sign, and that promise must be confirmed by baptism.

When speaking to the Jews, Peter adds: 'And to them that are afar off'. For at that time, only the Jews were of God's church and had a special privilege over all other peoples. But when Jesus Christ appeared, he broke down the wall of partition separating the Jews from other nations (*Eph.* 2:14). There was a great difference between the Gentiles and the Jews, and the majority of the world was excluded from the kingdom of heaven. Therefore, Peter informs the Jews that since our Lord showed the way by which they must come to him and that they were the first to whom he revealed himself, their condemnation will be double unless they take advantage of the many acts of grace and kindness bestowed upon them. Then he shows it is no longer to a single nation that our Lord promises salvation, but that his grace extends to all in general, although they are far from his kingdom. Paul also spoke of it to the Ephesians: 'Consider what sort you were before God called you to the knowledge of him; you were poor, ignorant people, lost, and without God and without religion, excluded from the kingdom of God' (*Eph.* 2:11–12). Although the Gentiles worshipped idols and had some appearance of religion, the fact remains that the more they moved away from their salvation the more they thought they were drawing nearer. They did not have the knowledge of God; but when Jesus Christ came, he not only brought us to a knowledge of God but also reconciled us to him, becoming our peace and mediator to reconcile us with God, as indeed we now see that the gospel proclaims that peace which Jesus Christ himself proclaims to us. And when men declare it, we must receive it as proceeding from his mouth.

And also, let us be aware that the gospel is proclaimed to everybody, both to Gentiles and to Jews. For Peter shows that our Lord wants not only to show grace to the race of people he had chosen but also to be merciful to everybody, demonstrating that there was no difference between Jew and Gentile, that God will save those who were far from him, and that he is not so bound to the Jews that he will not also call the Gentiles into the knowledge of his truth so they may obtain grace and salvation.

Here we have an exhortation which bears careful examination – in particular, since God calls us, we must be more diligent in coming to him. Moreover, if we compare ourselves to the many poor ignorant people who are in the world today, we will find that

God is granting us extraordinary acts of kindness and wonderful privileges. If we begin, for example, with the Turks and the Gentiles, we find poor blind peoples who have no knowledge of God or of his word and are mired in their ignorance. As for the Jews, they will indeed say they know God, but their eyes are veiled and they cannot see because they do not have Jesus Christ, who is the light and the splendour of God's glory. As for the papists, we will find that everything they do is in error. Even though they think they have the true knowledge of God, they corrupt everything so badly that they are far from knowing God to honour him as they should, and they even dishonour and blaspheme him in all their actions.

And yet here God comes to call us. He extends his hand to us. Should we not then be moved to come to him? If we fail to respond, will we not deserve a more grievous judgment than others? This much is certain. When God comes to judge the world, the Turks, Gentiles, papists, and other unbelievers will be treated much more gently than we, unless we take better advantage than we usually do of the kindnesses and benefits God provides for us daily. Such must be uppermost in our minds.

On the other hand, we see here that the gospel has been preached everywhere, not because men have hungered for it, but because God commanded it to be done. For it is clearly not by the work of mortal man that those far removed from God for a time have come to him and been received into his dwelling. So let us know that, despite our being descended from Gentiles, God's grace is so effective that we have no reason to argue whether the gospel belongs to us and whether Jesus Christ has gained our salvation. It is especially pointed out that those who were far from him and without knowledge of him are now ranked among his children. Now that is the way God has called us through the gospel, like a trumpet calling us to assemble with his people. We must not, then, doubt that Jesus Christ is ours. Let us come to him if we do not wish to be completely without excuse, because he calls us in many ways.

Now after expounding that, Luke adds that Peter exhorted his hearers with these words, saying, 'Steer clear of this perverse generation', or 'Save yourselves' (*Acts* 2:40). By that he means that Peter both declared the pure truth of God and tried to remedy the evil which was probably among the faithful at that time. Inasmuch as the Jews had been steeped in false teachings because the priests and teachers of the time were wicked and not concerned to bring the people to God, but concerned only for their own well-being and personal profit, they were disseminating false teachings. And for that reason Peter says, 'Save yourselves from this untoward generation', as if he were saying, 'My friends, I have shown you what your salvation consists in. That is the path you most hold to. But because you are given to turning aside and to wandering hither and yon, I am teaching you the right path. Steer clear of this perverse generation!'

Here we must note that it is not enough to be shown what we must believe and adhere to, but when the devil sows errors to turn us from the path of salvation, that fact must be pointed out clearly, as with a finger, so that we may protect ourselves from them, as is our great need right now, especially as they exist in the Papacy. If you say that only Jesus Christ, in whom we can hope for salvation, has reconciled us to God his Father by his death and passion, the poor ignorant people will believe none of it. And why not? Because they are taught the very opposite, for there is as much difference between the teaching of Jesus Christ and the teaching of the pope as there is between day and night. It is true the papists will certainly say Jesus Christ is their Saviour; yet they will not abandon their confidence in their merits. They will indeed come and call upon God and bring in intercessors to pray to God for them whenever they wish. They will not be satisfied to have the one who was made the eternal mediator and intercessor between God and men, namely, Jesus Christ. But they will want to have the Virgin Mary and the Saints, male and female, and when they have assembled all these superstitions, they will call that 'the worship of God'. If they are told they must worship God and follow his commandments, they will agree, but that will mean having masses sung, abstaining from meat a few days, making pilgrimages and doing other insignificant trifles. They will prefer the fabrications of men to the teachings of the gospel; they will always have their works of satisfaction, their meritorious works. In short, they are so mired in that idolatry they cannot be pulled free. And we must not be astonished by that, for since they have abandoned God, he has of necessity abandoned them, and they give themselves to every kind of ungodliness and filthiness. We will see these dissemblers, these ministers of Satan, who will be there to protest so that it seems they have the greatest zeal in the world. Yes, truly, but it is to lead the pitiable people to damnation and to harden them more and more in their abomination and nullify God's power.

It is true there are some who seem to preach the word, but if they have declared a single word of it, they will think they are gravely offended if someone asks them more about the subject. All they will do is dissemble so as to please some and ridicule the others. Now that is not the way to go about it. We must cut deep to uproot what Satan has planted (cf. *Matt* 13:24–30, 36–43). For even if we try hard to pull up the weeds he has sown, his helpers are still there to sow others so he can destroy and suffocate the good seed which the Lord has sown. Yet Paul says that ministers must not only be learned and instructed in doctrine but also powerful both to resist the attacks of the enemies of God and his word and to uproot the seeds the devil has sown for a time (cf. *1 Tim.* 3:2, 6–7; *Titus* 1:9).

Hence all the doctrine preached by the Papacy is only abomination, although there are some individuals, as I have said, who wish to be seen as good evangelists. If we wish to share in the blessings which Jesus Christ has brought us, we must not keep company with unbelievers, for we cannot serve God and the devil. By adhering to the teaching of the papists, we nullify the true worship of God. So then let us acknowledge the benefits which God has provided inasmuch as he has both declared his will for us and removed us from all those abominations of the Antichrist which currently dominate the Papacy. There was no other way for God to save us than to remove us from it. Otherwise, we would be lost along with those unfortunate people who have no knowledge of God and his teaching.

It is true there will be many individuals, as I have said, who will claim to preach the gospel and not want to be thorough hypocrites. But if you then exhort them to declare publicly against the errors they think the people engage in, they will say they do not wish to place themselves in danger and must avoid an occasion for sin. Really? And when the poor ignorant people fall into a ditch, will they be made to sin when someone pulls them out? Must we not cry out, 'Keep yourselves from this perverse generation', when we realize that everyone is going to hell? Let us not think our Lord can tolerate seeing himself and his word mocked this way any more than he can tolerate seeing those who are responsible for his flock watch it perish this way without concern.

Further, we see their impudence when they accuse us of excessive severity and say, 'You do not need to lash out this way against the pope and his people and call him Antichrist. You can preach the gospel well enough without such accusations. What good does it do to say that priests are ravenous wolves who will devour the flock of Jesus Christ and poison everyone with their false doctrine?' Those men are really dreadful teachers. They should have been born sooner so they could have taught Peter how to preach and instruct him what to say. That is the way those scoundrels imitate evangelists for a sop as much in France as in Italy, being urged on by their wits to deceive and please men by all they proclaim. But we do not have to do that. We must be confident that what we understand is from God and his Holy Spirit, for in truth we are taught by God in this passage that if we wish to come to him through our Lord Jesus Christ, we must rid ourselves of this perverse generation. For we cannot do that unless we separate ourselves from their lies and deceits. It is generally believed that since God's promises are ours, we are no longer encompassed by the defilements of this world – and there are no worse defilements than those in the world, for we see that the devil is always sowing it with error upon error, lie upon lie, so that, by turning to Jesus Christ and beseeching him to favour us with deliverance, we may live more and more in him and be changed more and more by him.

Now just as Peter spoke of the perverse generation of his time, so must we understand we must do the same today, not only among the papists, but also among those who have made profession of receiving God's teaching. And we must remember that the word of God must be proclaimed and preached fervently and that unacknowledged sins must be rooted out, for the devil works hard to undermine everything we build up. Let us see to the matter early on because if we leave the poison there too long without counteracting it, it will infect the whole body and bring death. We must cry out against this infection: 'Save yourselves from this untoward generation.' And if anyone says we can preach without such vehemence, we must consider that Peter speaks just as Jesus Christ spoke before. For even though the scribes and Pharisees had God's teaching and were mingling their false teachings with it, Jesus Christ nevertheless cries out in opposition, as if wanting to destroy everything. Now we see which of them is much worse than the other, the scribes or the Pharisees. It is true that Jesus Christ reproaches them for closing the door on the teaching. They do not wish to enter, and yet they prevent those who come to the door from entering (*Matt.* 23:13; *Luke* 11:52). But the Pharisees are more dangerous, for they turn aside those who are already on the narrow way and lead them away from holy enterprises.

Are we servants of God if we turn a blind eye to that? Are we to keep silent when we see some people indulging every evil practice and others filled with greed, usury, and strong-arm tactics? If we do, villainous and dissolute acts and inconstancies will have a stronger upper hand than ever. Others will come to vent their damnable blasphemies against God and his word, saying, 'And since Jesus Christ has died for us, is it not enough that we know it without citing that Old Testament, as if Jesus Christ had not come into the world?' Oh, let us flee from such blasphemers! When we hear such blasphemies, we must fear that our Lord will immediately give Satan permission to throw us all into consternation and that in our bewilderment we will be at a loss to know what to do – as is in fact already the case. Many more will yet be found that God has completely abandoned. They are no longer aware that salvation is by Jesus Christ, through his word and by his acts of grace toward us. Those blasphemers will shred him into small pieces and have no more reverence for his holy name than dogs have. That is good reason enough to say, 'Save yourselves from this untoward generation.'

Suppose I see a man so near a precipice that if he takes but one or two more steps he will fall into it and be killed. Will it be enough if I but say to him, 'Watch where you are going'? Not at all! But I must shout: 'Hey! Don't take another step! Stop where you are or you'll break your neck!' That is exactly what we must do, for we see many on the verge of stumbling fatally. If we leave them alone without a word of caution, we betray God and you as well. When we see that some are given to adulteries and excesses, and others to usuries, strong-arm tactics, and so many other wicked deeds, we have to shout, 'Hey! Not another step! You are nearing the pit of hell! If you fall in, you will never get out and, count on it, you will be in unending torment!' Such is the responsibility we receive from our Lord Jesus Christ and learn from his word. So must we fulfil it.

Time now prevents us from saying more. We shall keep the rest for another time. But we need to remember that if we do not ask God to help us and fill us with the desire for his name's honour and glory and for the advancement of his kingdom and the welfare and advantage of our neighbours, we will not be able to draw near to him and abandon that perverse generation which entices us into its condemnation. To do that, we must receive the word of God with all reverence, and his word must be our bread and healing balm – bread, because it is that spiritual food which eternally nourishes our souls; healing balm, because it cleanses all stains which so defile and deform our souls that they dare not present themselves before God. That is why we must cry out against the dissolute acts and inconstancies so prevalent now, for after we have warned them that they are going to hell, they still pay no attention, but rather abound increasingly in their wickedness. We must confront them, and if we see that those who are to correct others are themselves encouraging them, then we have to cry out, 'You poor people are destroying yourselves; you are hard on the heels of your ruin. Watch out!' For those who encourage the wicked in their iniquity strangle them more than the hangman who would put a rope around their neck. Do not be surprised then that we who wish to please God must be humble enough to prostrate ourselves, for we shall never come to Jesus Christ unless we abase ourselves so he can lift us up and so nothing can keep us from following the pure teaching of God, such as he reveals it to us.

Following that holy teaching, let us fall before the face of our gracious God in recognition of our faults, praying that he will be pleased to lead us in such a way by his Spirit that our lives will be dedicated to the glory of his name, and that in that way we will show we are truly his people and want to follow the good calling to which he has called us. Thus let us all say, God Almighty, heavenly Father . . .

5

The Three Marks of the Church

Sunday, 26 January 1550

Then they that gladly received his word were baptized: and the same day there were added unto them about three thousand souls. [42] *And they continued stedfastly in the apostles' doctrine and fellowship, and in breaking of bread, and in prayers* (Acts 2:41–42).

As we have seen, Peter's sermon began to bear fruit when those who were unacquainted with that teaching were admonished and ask what they must do (*Acts* 2:37). That is good fruit indeed and an indication that the word of God has not lost its effectiveness.

Now Luke explains more fully what happened: 'Those who gladly received his word were baptized: and the same day there were added unto them about three thousand souls.' Here we see an imposing and remarkable power. With a single sermon Peter leads three thousand individuals to Jesus Christ! In that, we are to see how God works powerfully and are not to be so dazzled that we find it strange. True, we are to admire the works of God in order to glorify him in them, but we must not find them strange, as I said, since heaven and earth were created by his word alone (*John* 1:3). So, since we are dealing with the same word, even though proclaimed by human beings, we must not doubt that it is powerful and that our Lord empowers it for the glorification of his name and the building up of his church, just as he has done from the beginning.

This is a noteworthy passage, for it concerns us inasmuch as we are so corrupt and wretched by nature that we are barred from the kingdom of God unless – as John 3 says – we become new creatures (*John* 3:3). So we must be born a second time. Since we are born into and belong to this world, our Lord denies that we belong to him in any way. How then can we be born again to become children of God? It is by his word, which must work deeply within us and be imprinted on our hearts before we can be regenerated and become children of God. We must also note that Luke adds that those who turn to God do so resolutely and willingly, an observation which teaches us that when God presents himself to us and wishes to draw near to us, we must draw near to him. It is true we cannot do so on our own; we have to ask him to produce in us by his Holy Spirit the burning desire to receive his word, as the Jews do in this passage.

From the moment we see that the word of God is effective, we must endeavour to listen attentively to what it teaches so that we may profit from it and humble ourselves because the testimony of the word will condemn us severely in the day of the Lord if we fail to apply it more advantageously than has been our custom. If a single sermon by Peter so effectively won three thousand individuals to Jesus Christ, what will three thousand sermons do? Therein do we recognize our perversity. What good will three thousand days of preaching do us? Very little, for with great difficulty will we find that one person has been brought to Jesus Christ. Yet, we can see from experience how ineffective the word of God is for us, since despite its many admonitions we cannot turn to God. It is true we will protest mightily, saying we desire the teaching, but what effort do we make to follow it and obey it? At the same time we would have to be teachable and allow the word to lead us, since it tells us that God calls us to the hope of salvation.

To that Luke adds, 'They continued steadfastly in the apostles' doctrine and fellowship, and in the breaking of bread.' Now it is not enough to show we are quick to receive what our Lord tells us. But we must be faithful and persevering. We shall see many who are rather easy to instruct but fall away immediately. Others will put on a good appearance at the outset and seem to be zealous for the word but in the end will grow cold or become so hardened in their first error that they fancy God's word is useful to them only as a fiction, and so hardened that they have less common sense and intelligence than poor dumb animals. Yet, Luke adds these two items: first, as soon as God speaks to us, let us be ready to hear him and obey what he commands; then, as soon as we are firm in our faith, let us not display our arrogance by showing our courage at the outset only to end up abandoning everything, but let us be founded on and rooted in his teaching so that it will be evident we are so steadfast that we will not fall away for any reason. We see how Paul makes that point in 2 Corinthians[1] and Ephesians: 'I thank God that as soon as the gospel was preached to you, you received it gladly; and not only did you receive it, but you have also persevered in it until now.' In that statement he declares what our responsibility is and what indicates that we are Christian. To the Ephesians he says the gospel was sealed in their hearts (*Eph.* 1:13), such that they are thereby established and secure and have in reality received the teaching. From the outset, then, we are to be aware that we need not pressure ourselves to come to God, as if forced, but to come gladly and freely, zealously and fervently desiring to persevere.

Now it is true that receiving the word and persevering in it are very difficult, but our Lord will truly bless us as he did them, provided we do not place obstacles in his way and provided we, when not feeling disposed to come to him, beseech him to humble

[1] In reality, this concerns the first letter. Cf. 1 Corinthian 1:4-7; Ephesians 1:15-17; 3:13-17. [Editors' note]

us to the point that we will wholly return to obedience so as to hear what he says to us and to persevere in it until the end. And when we recognize we are separated from him, we must desire to draw near to him, and pray he will not allow us – at the very moment he has granted us the grace of revealing himself to us through his word – to be drawn away from the teaching about salvation. That is how we must commit ourselves to him so he will give us the steadfastness to persevere in his teaching. Every day we see many people who wander from it. As a result, they initially appear to be followers of the gospel and great advocates of the word but fall away in the end, becoming despisers of God, worse than rabid dogs. And how is it that the devil can thus turn us from the narrow path and from the moral strength which we have experienced? It is because of our indifference that we have grown too cold to pray to God. So if we want to be well fortified against all the devil's tricks, which he spreads around us to lead us astray, we must pay closer attention than before to the exhortations and admonitions which confront us, and we must persevere in the doctrine which we are taught daily in his name.

Let us now look at what the faithful have persevered in. There is no doubt that Luke did not intend to include everything available to us in the Christian faith. Yet, by what he tells us we know the three marks which constitute God's church, namely, the proclamation of the word of God among us, the Lord's Supper, and our communion together in true love. Without those marks, Luke says, we cannot truly follow the teaching of the apostles. It is true some consider that communion to be the Lord's Supper, the breaking of bread, for Scripture considers the breaking of bread to be the Lord's Supper. The true explanation for this is that all of us, being united with the body of Jesus Christ, share in this breaking of bread, which is his holy Supper, to show that we must live in peace and harmony with our neighbours, just as the members of a body are joined together in harmony. That is what we confess in the creed after confessing our belief in the church of God when we say we believe in the communion of the saints. In that communion, the saints truly have fellowship when they are all instructed in the word of God and in the same doctrine, when they use the sacraments as ordered by God and when they assemble to pray together publicly. So if we want to ascertain whether a true mark of the church is from God, we must determine whether it meets the criteria mentioned in this passage.

The pope will boast openly that he has the church on his side. We know that is a complete abomination. What he calls the 'church of God' is just a synagogue of Satan. It is the great brothel where he leads all idolaters in debauchery. In short, it is the place of every foul and vile act, where poor souls are polluted and infected with damnation. How is it then that he can say he has the church of God on his side? Whenever he wants to boast about that, we will very gladly define 'the church of God' for him. To do so, we must consider whether he has a church like the one our Lord requires and has been building from the beginning. We can do no better than define it by what our Lord declares through Luke's words when he says that the church exists wherever there is true perseverance in the teaching of the apostles, wherever there is loving fellowship among the faithful, and wherever the sacraments are administered as stipulated and the word is preached in its truth.

Now let us point out what the teaching is in the pope's synagogue, which he wants us to call the church. First, we know that everything practised there is only an invention of Satan, for they have perverted the truth of the gospel. Every article of their teaching is corrupt. They have forged articles of faith, each one contrary to those we receive from the apostles' teaching. Do they and their teaching lead the people to God? To the contrary. By their human traditions they lead them far astray. Moreover, they forcibly constrain people to adhere to what they have prescribed for them.

Thus, having meticulously examined whether the apostles' teaching exists in the Papacy, we discover that there is not the remotest resemblance. Even if we compare the true worship of God with what they have invented, we shall see there is as much difference between the former and the latter as there is between God and the devil. For what they call 'worship of God' is but a damnable blasphemy against his divine majesty and an abomination before him.

Then we remember that the absolute assurance of our salvation must be in Jesus Christ, that we cannot have a single worthy thought unless it comes from God, that our works, such as they are, however fine they may appear to men, are but a stench to God, and that until God regenerates us we are imperfect. What is more, all our works, even though performed with the aid of the Holy Spirit, are so blotched by our perverse nature that we never have a perfect zeal for serving God. Also, we realize we are never inclined to come to God unless we have been invested with our Lord Jesus Christ's righteousness, which is inaccessible to us unless he alone makes us sharers in it.

Now that we acknowledge all these imperfections in ourselves and rely only on God's goodness to make up for our deficiency, let us look at the Papacy's procedure. To be sure, they will say, 'It is true we are weak by nature, but when we do good works and God works in us, we act together. He does a part of the work and we do the rest, and we motivate him by our merits to help us, so that if we fall a bit short, we make up for it with our meritorious works.' So that is how people are drawn in to putting their confidence in their own merits rather than coming to Jesus Christ. In that, we see the vast difference between God's teaching and the pope's. If we say to them that when God calls us to himself and we need an advocate because we are unworthy to present ourselves before him and have only the one mediator Jesus Christ between him and ourselves (*1 Tim.* 2:5), the papists, to the contrary, will invoke Peter and Paul and the Saints for help and waste their time with meaningless prattle and prostrate themselves before wooden and stone images, and will even say the Lord's Prayer to powerless idols or to some image placed there by Saint Gertrude or some other whose soul is in the pope's paradise, that is, hell. They will brazenly offer their prayers to them as if they understood their petitions and answered them. Still, if you ask them whether they have the apostles' teaching, they will certainly answer yes. But clearly they do not. They have so corrupted every good doctrine and exchanged the right use of the sacraments for insignificant drivel and diabolical ceremonies that the mark and sign for which they were instituted can no longer be recognized. We have baptism and the Lord's Supper to confirm us in God's word and in his promises so that we will not doubt them. The pope has added sacraments to suit himself and urges that they be more closely observed and maintained than Jesus Christ's. Moreover, he is not content to sully the true sacraments with his mindless comments, which he has so heaped upon baptism that we are horrified at the thought of it. In addition, he has favoured adding five others with his own hand, showing that he is not satisfied with being as great as Jesus Christ but wants to be twice as great and more!

As for the Lord's Supper, we can see how many blasphemies he has polluted it with. His mass is an invention of Satan, for nothing in it resembles a sacrament. Even so, he will declare that it is a sacrifice pleasing to God the Father and will appease him on our behalf and win the remission of the sins of the living and the dead – all of which is an odious blasphemy against Jesus Christ, who alone has that office which the pope and his ilk take upon themselves in their mass, which is clearly an idol raised against the honour of God and the glory of his holy name and leads people to hell. In that, we see a gross stupidity in those poor wretches and conclude that the church is as much among them as it is in hell.

Now to define the church in a few words: just as a body without a soul is but a rotting carcass, so the church deprived of the word of God is but a chaos.

Now that we have determined that the church does not exist in the Papacy, let us look straightway at ourselves and see how and when we have a church. Since our Lord has chosen us as his flock, we must take care to have what is shown to us in this passage, namely that we are persevering in the apostles' teaching, that we are united with one another in love and brotherly affection, and that we employ the sacraments rightly, and invoke God with one heart and one mind. When those features are present, we can confidently say we have a church such as God requires. So then, let people think what they will of us. Let them call us 'heretics'. Let the pope anathematize us to his heart's content as being separated from the church. We must nonetheless truly acknowledge that the church of God is none other than the one I have described, and that God is pleased with it and approves of it. Let them say what they will about us. It is enough that we have what God commands and that we know the church consists of those things. The more we are obliged to be deeply engaged in finding strength in the teaching of God and profiting from it day by day, in continuing in fellowship with one another in genuine love, in invoking the name of the Lord, and celebrating the sacraments truly and rightly, the more we realize that this is God's church. It is true the pope's church looks like the church, but if you take a good look at it, you will find nothing founded on the word of God.

We must be aware of that if we wish to be certain of our Christian faith, as Paul points out when declaring the whole church is founded on the teaching of the prophets and apostles

(*Eph.* 2:20). It is true Luke mentions only the apostles' teaching, but it is joined with that of the prophets. In fact we find passages from David and the other prophets[1] in Peter's sermon. Just as the burden of the gospel is to show what the office of Jesus Christ is, so is its burden to show that he is the end of the law (*Rom.* 10:4). It is not an unknown teaching, but the apostles' teaching that we need for giving form to the church, which was left to them by Jesus Christ, in whom we have all the fullness of wisdom (*Col.* 2:2–3).

But there are very few who think about what I am saying. Currently, everyone admits to being a Christian and to belonging to the church, but if you ask them what they believe, they cannot tell you. If they utter the words with their mouth, their hearts have an opposite opinion. Consequently, you will not find a smidgen of Christian faith in them. Yet the fact remains that our Lord declared that his teaching is destined for our salvation or our condemnation (cf. *Mark* 16:16; *John* 3:18). He speaks about our salvation when he says we are persevering in his teaching, and about our condemnation when he says that if we reject it, we are already banished from his kingdom. Now it is true that each individual cannot be so learned that he is able to determine whether the teaching he holds is the same as the apostles' or not. The fact is that each of us, from the least to the greatest, must possess the fundamental teaching that the forgiveness of our sins and our salvation come from Jesus Christ, and that the Holy Spirit confirms us in God's word and promises. That, I say, is the teaching which we must adhere to. It is also what we must learn from the word while remembering it is not enough to adhere to the apostles' teaching. We must also profit from it.

So far, I have spoken very few words, but they contain much substance. We see that the whole of Scripture leads us to one point:

---

[1] *Acts* 2:17-21 = *Joel* 3:1-5; *Acts* 2:25-28 = *Psa.* 16:8-11; *Acts* 2:30 = *Psa.* 132:11; *Acts* 2:31 = *Psa.* 16:10; *Acts* 2:34-35 = *Psa.* 110:1.

knowing Jesus Christ as our only Saviour and the only Mediator between God and us (*1 Tim.* 2:5). Moreover, we must maintain this confidence in him so that in the end we will know we have not believed in vain, because we will have persevered in that teaching. It is not enough that we have received the word. We must persevere in it and demonstrate that it does in fact have its root in God, and we will demonstrate that fact by diligently attending preaching services and having fellowship in the sacraments and in prayers. It is true the text speaks here of public prayers, but that does not prevent each of us from praying in private. Since we are unduly dilatory in prayer unless prodded often, we do well to join together in prayer for one another and be persistent in assembling for that purpose so that we may support one another in our confession of faith. It is clear then that those who distance themselves from that practice, even though they pray privately, are not concerned about being the church of God and being strengthened in its teaching. The same can be said about the sacraments. We know that the purpose of our Lord's Supper is both to confirm our assurance that he wants to live in us and us in him, and to participate in his body and blood, just as members of the body participate in the head, which directs and controls them. So whoever wishes to withdraw from the sacrament and be content only with the word will be like a man who has a letter with a seal and wishes to break the seal and throw it into the fire, being content only with the Scriptures. Yet we know it is the seal that gives the letter its authority. Such is the Lord's Supper. It acts as the seal of God's promise so that we may be strengthened. Consequently, when we do not show the Supper its proper respect, what honour will we give the word? There is this too: when we meet in fellowship using the sacraments, we enjoy the benefits which God has showered upon us. If we reject them, it is impossible for us to be of the church of God.

Now there is still something to say about this passage, but we will reserve that for next Sunday. In the meantime, let us be careful to receive the word of God in such a way that as soon as our attention is drawn to it, we will have full assurance that it is the word which speaks, and in such a way that we will distinguish it from human inventions, and consider whether God's word is proclaimed appropriately, whether the sacraments are administered according to their proper use, and whether everyone invokes God with one heart and one mind. When we see things are proceeding along those lines, then we will be able to say the church has been restored in accordance with God's original intention.

> In keeping with this sacred teaching, let us bow before the face of our gracious God in acknowledgement of our faults, beseeching him to be pleased so to lead us that we, being members of his church, will by his intervention grow more and more in his teaching. May he give us such strength and perseverance in it that we will never fall away from it no matter what befalls us. But since by his grace he accepts us as his children, may we, for our part, seek to do nothing in this lifetime but glorify his holy name. May he be gracious not only to us, but also to all peoples and nations of the earth . . .

6

Bearing the Marks of the Church

Sunday, 2 February 1550

And fear came upon every soul: and many wonders and signs were done by the apostles. ⁴⁴ And all that believed were together, and had all things in common; ⁴⁵ And sold their possessions and goods, and parted them to all men, as every man had need (Acts 2:43–45).

Last week we dealt with what the marks of the church must be. We said that if we wish to be recognized as a Christian fellowship, we must persevere in the doctrine which we have received once and for all from God, and we must be increasingly diligent in bearing fruit in it. It is not enough that we were instructed at the outset, but we must persevere every moment of our lives. For that reason our Lord has ordained that the gospel be preached and proclaimed until the end of the world. So when we persevere in his teaching, it is a sign that we belong to him. The text here speaks of the apostles' teaching because that is the one our Lord Jesus Christ left them so that we might be instructed by them. We must be very careful not to be misled by Satan, who will incline us to abandon the pure teaching of God and adhere to the fabrications of men. He is the real scoundrel who deceives us and causes us to break this spiritual marriage which we have with Jesus Christ. We must not then be guided by any doctrine unless it is from God. We must secure our faith so that it will be founded on God's truth.

We also said there is no church in the Papacy because they do not have the word of God. When they reproach us for being separated from the church, it is a great consolation for us that we know otherwise. Who is our witness? The Holy Spirit! In addition, we must have sermons and prayers, not only in private, but we must all come together in one place to praise God as with one heart, one mouth, and one mind.

Luke adds two more things, namely, the breaking of the bread, by which we understand the Supper of our Lord Jesus Christ, and communion (*Acts* 2:42). It is true we discussed it only briefly, but we must note that just as our Lord gave us his word and wishes it to be made known, he also gave us the Supper to testify that we belong to his flock. If someone asks whether the gospel is not supposed to be sufficient to declare that Jesus Christ considers us as his own, we understand that he must demonstrate it more clearly and lead us to that assurance through the administration of the Supper. For in it we have the source of all the promises which are recounted to us daily. And just as we said above, we must seize upon the doctrine and adhere to it if we want God to keep us as his children. We must preserve this very precious pledge, which is given in the holy Supper of our Lord Jesus Christ, and not let it be taken from us. We see how the devil has worked to that end. What do the papists have in place of the Supper today? They have this foolishness, rather this damnable talisman called the mass, which is destructive of the holy institution of Jesus Christ and more different from it than fire is from water. He gave us his Supper to remind us that he offered the sacrifice once and for all to God his Father, that his death and suffering are permanent in us, and that it alone suffices to erase our sins and acquire our salvation.

The papists, on the other hand, invented the mass to initiate a new sacrifice. They teach clearly that Jesus Christ must be offered daily to God his Father. And on whom is this office bestowed? On men! It is said that this dignity will not be found in any creature in this world. Thus we see there is a contradiction between the holy Supper of our Lord Jesus Christ and what the papists do, which they call 'sacrifice'. For now, I will forgo speaking about other implications contained in the word, but I will point out, in passing, the devil's cleverness and the trouble he goes to in order to abolish the Supper by which we know that God loves us as his family. The more we are obliged to be careful to maintain this holy institution and practise it for our advantage, the more we must understand that Jesus Christ has left it to remind us that it is he by whom we live and shall live eternally. It is Jesus Christ who gives us bread and wine in his Supper to signify that our complete spiritual and bodily nourishment is in him alone and that he wishes to provide for us as his children. What will the pope do? 'Oh! It is enough that the people have the bread.' It is as if he were saying, 'Only half of your life is in Jesus Christ. Look for the other half elsewhere.' Or it is like someone giving them something to eat and telling them to get their drink wherever they can. In that, we see the irrationality in the Papacy. How could we live if we had only the nourishment of the bread and were deprived of drink? Let us then be very careful not to let anyone diminish in any way what God has been pleased to establish to remind us of him, for we understand that therein lies our life, inasmuch as by the sacraments we are taught what we must put our trust in and what we must have confidence in. If the papists reproach us for not serving God, we know very well that the opposite is true, for we have the witness of the Holy Spirit.

One of our great faults is that we do not celebrate the Lord's Supper with the zeal of the primitive church. They did not limit their practice to four times a year, but they served it every Sunday, and sometimes even every day. The faithful wanted so much to follow the evangelical teaching that when they were assembled, they served the Supper at least every Sunday. But since then, the world has become so corrupt and depraved that they came to disregard that institution. It seemed to them that since the priest had played his little game and was there on their behalf, it was enough that he had drunk and eaten by himself without the participation of the others. But we see how Jesus Christ spoke of the Supper when he instituted it: 'This cup is the new and everlasting covenant in my blood. Take it and drink, all of you' (*1 Cor.* 11:25; *Matt.* 26:27). In that, there is no suggestion that one individual should drink and indulge himself apart from others. On the contrary, in the mass everyone is excommunicated. To deprive the people of this communion is to excommunicate them. We see that happening every day in the mass. A priest eats and drinks alone and has nothing in common with the others. From that, it is easy to conclude that those who participate in such foolishness are not partaking of the Supper of the Lord Jesus Christ, for there is a very great difference between the two.

For our part, since we have the pure teaching of the gospel, we must be ardently zealous to follow what it shows us inasmuch as we see it is the rule our Lord gave the apostles, which they followed. Even though we know the teaching is pure and complete, we are still so wretched we cannot receive it as we should. For although we are to come only a few times a year to commune at the Supper, how many will come with their wicked affections? Some will come with their hatreds, their grudges; others will be full of avarice, greed, thefts, and others will cling to their blasphemies, their filthiness, or their excesses. Or else, even if they are in any way prepared when they come, they will not wait until the next day to return to their sins, to their vindictiveness, to their quarrels, and to their old hatreds. They will all return to their old ways. So we are very far from being prepared to receive the Supper of our Lord Jesus Christ every day or every Sunday. Even with great effort we cannot come prepared four times a year to free ourselves from our iniquities. We have good reason to deplore our iniquity. When we see that our Lord has favoured us with the gospel and tells us he wants to be our father and protector and nourish us with the body and blood of his Son Jesus Christ, we nevertheless distance ourselves from him by rejecting all these gracious acts. For that reason, the gospel is so far from bearing the fruit it should within us that we become worse. For there is no friendship or brotherliness among us, indeed, much less than among unbelievers.

Still, we have to pay close attention to this passage. Luke's reason for bringing the Supper and communion together is to show that there must be among us a true union based on fraternal love so that we can commune with one another and remember that God made us for one another, as members of one body, the body of Jesus Christ. In fact, an aspect of the ritual of the Supper – I am talking about when the Supper was administered more often than now – was that they kissed one another to show the fraternal love which Christians ought to have for one another. They also received alms to help those who were in need, and in that way showed that they were not hypocritically calling one another brothers and that almsgiving was as much a part of the ceremony as the rest. Since they were all members of Jesus Christ, they thought that if any among them had need, the body of Christ was suffering lack, and they would give money and alms to help. And the Papacy corrupted that too! Ignorant of the practice of doing alms, they will give their money as an offering in order to kiss an object made of silver or some other metal. Will the offerings be for the poor? No, no! Those ravening wolves will gulp them down even though they come in an endless stream. So we must not doubt that all these shenanigans have been forged in Satan's workshop to deceive people. We must be steadfast in following the true rule which we have in the apostles' teaching, namely that we are united as members of one body in true union and fraternal love, communing with one another as we have need – if we want God to approve our assemblies and the communion we have through his sacraments.

Subsequently, there is a more ample declaration of what we have said, namely that 'fear came upon every soul: and many wonders and signs were done by the apostles.' In the first place, Luke tells us that fear fell on all of them, not only on the believers. He is talking about those who might have been enemies of the gospel if God had not gathered them in. It is true that he said 'on all'. He includes them in the way that is common in Scripture. We know that the scribes and Pharisees did not believe in the gospel, but derided it. Pilate continues in his idolatry and cruelty after crucifying Jesus Christ. Consequently, not everyone was shaken by that fear, but there were many who were deeply moved, and that was so that God's church would be preserved among its many enemies, who were seeking only to destroy it. If God had not protected it, the wicked would have soon brought it to ruin, for we see today how ill disposed everyone is when coming into contact with us. Even the papists would like to devour us. Such was the case with the believers at that time. What would have happened to them if God had not done something to help? It is certain they would not likely have fled to other parts of the world. That is why Luke says God sent fear upon those who were not yet confirmed in the gospel.

We see the same thing today. For how many are unwilling to entrust themselves either to the gospel or to any other teaching? They will stand there waiting for some rumour to blow past, and they will say, 'Oh! I do not know which to believe, this gospel or another way of living. I will wait to see what happens.' That is how they willingly cover their eyes. But they see clearly that we put nothing before God's truth and that we come closer to the truth of the gospel than the papists. Then there are believers who become so enraged when confronting us that, as I have already said, they would like to devour us, and yet God restrains them to such a degree that they are powerless to exercise their malicious will, and he holds them in check so they cannot harm us. Not that we deserve it. If the gospel bore the right kind of fruit in us, the unbelievers should tremble in our presence. If, as is said, dumb animals – the most vicious in the world – will fear the faithful (cf. *Isa.* 11:6–8), what should be the reaction of those who have greater knowledge than dumb animals? Where is that power in us that lions obey us as cowering dogs unless our wickedness has effaced the image of God which should shine within us? So, then, if our lives showed we are members of Jesus Christ, there would be greater fear among unbelievers. Still our Lord bestows upon us that grace, but he obviously holds it in check, for we are not like lions, only like poor sheep among wolves. If we make a comparison between ourselves and the forces, the powers, the alliances, and the means of all those who curse God's church today, we will find that they would have swallowed us in a single gulp, as they say, if God had not restrained them. As the Psalm says, if God were not our protector when men rise against us, they would swallow us alive (*Psa.* 124:1–3, 7). It is as if we were caught in a net, but because God has been gracious to place within us a power to dumbfound our enemies, the net is broken and we are delivered. We must therefore pray that God will be pleased to give us that grace so our enemies will have such fear of us that his church will be sustained until the end.

Now we come to what Luke adds, which is still a declaration of the preceding: 'All those', he says, 'who believed were together and had all things in common and sold their possessions and goods and shared them with all according as each had need.' He gives primacy to their being together. For it is not enough for us to give alms unless we have within us a sense of true charity. We know what Paul says about it: 'If I bestow all my goods on the poor and do not have love, I do nothing, but am like a sound which dissipates in the air, which vanishes suddenly' (1 Cor. 13:3).

Now how is it that a person can impoverish himself in order to give alms to the poor and still not have love? We know that some do it out of ambition, others for vainglory or out of presumptuousness. In this way they could give until they had nothing left in order to help the poor, and yet it would profit them nothing. And why is that? Because they do not have that love without which they cannot please God. Just as we must have faith in God and knowledge of his promises, so it is that if we do good to our neighbours, we gain nothing unless our act is preceded by true charity and love toward them. So if we have charity and love for one another, we have the motive and foundation for building well. And if we do not begin there, even though we look good in people's eyes, our lives are hypocritical and vain. We must pay attention to what Luke says about that communion which existed among the faithful. For since we have but one faith in Jesus Christ, what must that one faith be like? When giving us his gospel, does he separate us from one another? Indeed not. He calls us all together and does not give one teaching for one person and another teaching for another, but this is the selfsame word which his ministers teach so that each of us may grow in charity and fraternal love into one body until we are joined to our head, who is Jesus Christ.

The unity we are talking about here must be shared among us, for the one who is not joined in true love with his neighbour is very far from God. Jesus Christ is our peace to reconcile us to God his Father and also to bring us all into harmony. It is only right that the gospel should accomplish this in us so that we can have peace with one another and demonstrate by our actions that this unity really exists among us, just as the good root of a tree is known by its fruit. There are many who will boast of their love, but how will they demonstrate it? It is not a question here of respecting their neighbours. They will be so attached to their personal welfare that they will not be concerned for others. That is why Luke, or rather the Holy Spirit speaking through him, says we must have that unity and bear its fruit if we are to do good to our neighbours and apply ourselves to the task as each of us can.

It is noteworthy that Luke says 'they had all things in common' and then adds that 'it was so they could distribute to each one according to his need'. We need to weigh these words carefully to avoid taking an extreme position. We see some who are so caught up in their self-interest that they are far from helping their neighbours and even snatch from them everything they can and inflict upon them very great cruelty. Such people well demonstrate they know no more about Christianity than dumb animals. If they were the kind of people they should be, they would not have to demonstrate what Jesus Christ, Peter, and Paul say about that charity which we must have toward our neighbours; what the prophet Isaiah says would suffice: 'We must not look down upon our own flesh' (*Isa.* 58:7). By that he means we cannot look upon another human being without having before us a living representation of our own selves, and if we deny him our help, it is as if we were refusing it to ourselves.

What is more, pagans have made the same observation as the prophet. They have said that although kinfolk are joined together by a bond of affinity and consanguinity, there is likewise a universal kinship within the human race. That is how pagans have been able to recognize what is so difficult for us to get into our heads. And because they say no one is born for himself alone but to help his neighbours, they will be our judges and pronounce judgment against us. And we still do not place a great emphasis on helping those whom we know to be in need. Will our Lord have to indict us and engage us in long inquests to show us our ingratitude? Indeed not! These poor pagans and unbelievers will convict us of our wrongdoing. Some of them are filled with such an insatiable greed that they want to consume heaven and earth, that is, everything that is under the kingdom of God, for they have little concern for the things of God. They would like to deprive others, so far as possible, of air to breathe and lock the sun in a box, so to speak, so no one can enjoy it but themselves.

Then there is the other extremity. Many crackpots wanted to say everything was held in common. That is not the intention of the Holy Spirit. We need to consider how that is to be understood. In the first place, we must not imagine things were gathered together into a pile so each person could take what he thought good. Everything was distributed in an orderly way, for the responsibility lay with the apostles. Rather, the rich sold their lands and possessions and brought the money to the apostles so no one would suffer hardship. Luke speaks of three individuals who did that, and the third was a hypocrite. Thus it is not said that there was no supervision over that sharing, but that there was such good order and such practical love that no one lacked anything.

In that, we see how that kennel of monks has corrupted this passage. They say they lead an apostolic life and have taken a vow of poverty. But what kind of poverty is that, eating the goods of others? They are lazy dogs, idle bellies, and they are still apostles, or their successors! To hear them talk, there is only love and brotherhood among them. And they say 'our cape', 'our cap', 'our this', 'our that'. It seems they have everything in common. But if a brother wishes to have a particular cap, they say, 'Oh, that is our cap', and refuse to share anything. Whatever the situation, they are always well dressed and copiously nourished. They are like pigs at a trough devouring the sweat of the poor. Did the apostles act like that? You can see the impudence of those wretches as they arrogate the apostolic life.

The text does not say that the apostles devoured the labour of the poor without doing anything or that they were lazy dawdlers, drinking and stuffing their gut until they burst, as is the case with that diabolical brood of monks. Luke is not talking about that. What he wants to point out when saying they had all things in common is that those who had abundance and could help their neighbours sold what was theirs rather than see the children of God in need. It is true he does not want to pressure those who have an abundance to cast off their wealth in order to give alms. He means that they should furnish sustenance for those who did not have enough to live on. He can then indeed say that they had everything in common, for all the wealth which God sends us has a common value as much for the poor as for the rich. Bread is a tangible creation which would not have the virtue of nourishing us if God had not given it to us for that purpose. We also see many poor people for whom a piece of bread would do more good than the best foods would do for the rich, and most often those who have an abundance will be languishing in unhappiness. That fact lets us know that it is not bread, but the word of God which nourishes us better than all the foods in this world. When our Lord permits some people to enjoy a greater abundance of goods than others, it is so they can be generous toward those who lack. Just as we wish to be recognized as children of God, so must we show by our actions not only that our lips are not uttering idle words, but that our hearts seek what our lips request. Many people are so far from helping their neighbours with what they have that they snatch greedily among themselves and cheat one another, looking like they want to consume everything. Yet they want to be known as great Christians!

We have to return to Jesus Christ's pronouncement that we must treat our neighbours justly and equitably or expect to be condemned. If a person boasts of being faithful and does not have pity on the poor, God will disavow him. People who do not harm anyone, as they understand harm, think they have done their duty. I will mention people who think they have not committed theft unless they are taken into custody, for most often those least guilty before men are the greatest thieves. And still they do nothing. As a case in point, let us take the most upright people we can imagine – I am thinking here idealistically. Here is a man who has acquired wealth by his labour without wronging anyone. He will then be able to claim that when he appears before God, he will be innocent in that respect. But that is not enough. He must be sufficiently concerned about his neighbours to help them with the wealth God has put within his hands. Compare that with what Solomon says. If a man has a fountain in his house and can draw as much as he needs from it, he will be an ungrateful man unless he lets it flow out so his neighbours can share in it (*Prov.* 5:15–17).[1] Solomon wants us to understand that that man will be inexcusable even though he harms no one and that he must disperse the goods he has received from God's hand in such a way that his fellow-man will not suffer need. That is why those men of long ago laid such a great foundation in the church. They wanted the poor to be provided for. But those bottomless pits of greed have devoured everything. Those insatiable mouths have swallowed up what was left to support and nourish the members of Jesus Christ's body.

Let us continue to ask our gracious God to be pleased to restore things to their original condition and lead us by his Holy Spirit so that our ingratitude will not cause him to abandon what he has been pleased to begin in us. But having the teaching of

---

[1] Calvin's point is well made, but the citation is taken out of context.

his gospel, let us always be joined to one another in charity and brotherly love. And when we have the true use of his sacraments and have fellowship through them, let us – if we have the kind of perfection he demands of us – at least come to him and declare that we seek in them our entire well-being, since that is to be the goal and purpose of our endeavours.

> Following this holy teaching, let us prostrate ourselves before the face of our gracious God in recognition of our failings, praying that he will be pleased to grant us the grace of being joined together in true love, having among ourselves such unity that we shall grow more and more into the likeness of our head, Jesus Christ, and after his Holy Spirit enlightens us in the knowledge of his holy word, may we never ignore it, but persevere in it all of our lives, until he takes us from this mortal body to share in the joy he has prepared for the faithful. May he grant that grace not only to us but also to all the peoples and nations of the earth . . .

7

THE PURPOSE OF MIRACLES

SUNDAY, 23 FEBRUARY 1550

Then Peter said, Silver and gold have I none; but such as I have give I thee: In the name of Jesus Christ of Nazareth rise up and walk. ⁷ And he took him by the right hand, and lifted him up: and immediately his feet and ankle bones received strength. ⁸ And he leaping up stood, and walked, and entered with them into the temple, walking, and leaping, and praising God. ⁹ And all the people saw him walking and praising God: ¹⁰ And they knew that it was he which sat for alms at the Beautiful gate of the temple: and they were filled with wonder and amazement at that which had happened unto him. ¹¹ And as the lame man which was healed held Peter and John, all the people ran together unto them in the porch that is called Solomon's, greatly wondering. ¹² And when Peter saw it, he answered unto the people, Ye men of Israel, why marvel ye at this? or why look ye so earnestly on us, as though by our own power or holiness we had made this man to walk? ¹³ The God of Abraham, and of Isaac, and of Jacob, the God of our fathers, hath glorified his Son Jesus; whom ye delivered up, and denied him in the presence of Pilate, when he was determined to let him go (Acts 3:6–13).

We have just seen how our Lord declared his goodness to the pitiable crippled man who had been healed, who was not expecting healing but received it. In that, it is clear that our Lord must anticipate our needs according to his mercy because we do not have the wit to ask him what is good and useful for us. And even before we ask him, he anticipates and provides those things which we would never have hoped for.

Besides, we need to pay particular attention to the fact that the obedience this lame man gave Peter's words bore good fruit. When our Lord wishes to deal with us bountifully out of his grace, the only way we can perceive his goodness is by not doubting his promises and by following where he leads. Otherwise, our Lord will always be true but we will not profit from that fact. If we doubt his promises, they will always be true and condemn us. When the gospel is preached, the same promises are made to one and all without exception. Yet many do not take advantage of them. That is because they have no regard for anything our Lord promises. It is as if they knew nothing about the gospel. Consequently, it is to be expected that our Lord does not fulfil for those unfortunate people the things he promised in his word because they did not believe what he had said to them. To receive the benefits he offers us, we must accept what he says as certain and true.

Now this poor lame man could well have asked, 'Why did this man tell me to get up?' That thought never entered his mind, but immediately upon hearing the command, he adds his faith, knowing that Peter had a purpose in telling him to get up. Although we are inclined to entertain many doubts, God does not want us to question whether his word will be fulfilled or not. In questioning, we blaspheme his majesty and could do nothing worse than fail to trust his word. That is an important point in this passage.

In addition, two other matters are included in Luke's words. First, we must obey God's word, consider it good and trustworthy the moment he declares it, and not doubt it. Second, we must cling to his promise in order to experience help from his kindness, as this poor lame man did.

Now, shortly afterwards the lame man gives thanks to God. In this passage we see that since our Lord exercises his kindness toward us, he also wants us to glorify his name. The only way we can repay him for all the good things he does for us is to thank him. What is more, he can very well do without all the praises we could ever offer him. He works for our salvation, for we can do nothing more important than to magnify God's name after he has shown himself to be merciful to us. That is what we must get from this passage, namely that as a consequence of our Lord's daily and infinite kindnesses toward us, we must for our part be diligent in acknowledging his benefits and thanking him for them so as not to be reproved or condemned for our ingratitude in the presence of God, in the presence of his angels, and in the presence of the whole world. For if this poor lame man was moved to thank God for a blessing to his physical body, are we not the more constrained to glorify his holy name for the many spiritual and physical benefits we receive from his goodness daily? Therefore, let us, insofar as possible, raise our voices in heartfelt gratitude to God for his many benefits.

We now come to consider the fruit which the miracle bore, for that is why it was done. Now, our Lord not only had mercy on this poor man but he also wanted the name of our Lord Jesus Christ to be magnified. He wanted to use the healing to attract to the gospel both those who had previously been estranged from it and even some who loathed it and were enraged by it. For that reason it is written, 'And they knew that it was he which sat for alms at the Beautiful Gate of the temple: and they were filled with wonder and amazement at that which had happened.' The lame man acted as a mirror so they could ponder God's power. Peter and John had been waiting for the opportunity to declare to the people why this miracle was done and what its true purpose was. The astonishment of the people served as an appropriate preparation, for it was to make them pay attention. When we are not amazed, we are not properly prepared to receive what God wishes to say to us. But when he manifests his power so that we are compelled to be amazed, he opens us to what he wishes to say so that when he speaks, we have to listen to what he tells us. The purpose of the astonishment, then, is to make the people attentive to the teaching Peter gives.

Yet, this amazement in itself, as is shown subsequently, can scarcely bear fruit because Peter begins by reproaching them when he says, 'You men of Israel, why do you marvel at this?' With that he shows, as I have already said, the people were wrong to marvel in this way, for their astonishment did not lead them in the right direction, as we ourselves have experienced. Our Lord will surely give good and salutary instructions, but they vanish immediately because we are so wretched as to pervert the things which are good and holy in themselves and which God had consecrated for our salvation. In this way we see that the people's astonishment on this occasion came from God, but it still would not have borne fruit if teaching had not accompanied it. An easy and more familiar example is that we have naturally within us the knowledge that there is a God and that if we had no preaching, no Scripture, and had never been to school, we would know there is a God who created the world and whose subjects we are. But where does such knowledge lead us? Can it lead us to a fruitful end and grow to such perfection that it can come to maturity? In no way! Instead of being good seed to produce good grain, it only produces brambles and weeds. Knowing that there is one God, each individual will create an idol to his own liking. And where do idolatries come from if not from a good source? For after our Lord gave us a natural knowledge that there is one God, we rush to invent a thousand follies in our head. Without that natural knowledge, there would be no idolatry. So we see that our Lord insists on leading us to himself. But because we are sinful, we have changed his good gifts into bad ones, and when he places us on the right road, we collapse in the middle of it.

Such is it with their astonishment, for until Peter indicated what they were to understand by it, it served them no purpose. In fact, we read nothing in this story which we ourselves have not experienced. Why did the people experience that folly and rush to make idols of God's servants, who honoured him with their lives and glorified him in their death? And what caused it if not the people's astonishment when they saw the miracles they were performing? It is true God gave them the ability to work those miracles, yet all the people immediately said these men were holy and divine. That was true, but they were to give God the glory. Yet they fixed their attention on Peter and Paul [sic] and made idols of them. That was the consequence of the people's astonishment.

Now if we are to apply this teaching to our own day, we must first notice that although our Lord makes known his power, we cannot be instructed by it until he brings us to his word and tells us the end toward which he has striven and extended his arm. It is true we will be very astonished, but our astonishment will not instruct us in the love and fear of God and in his teaching. That shows us how much we need instruction, for, as we shall see later, without instruction, miracles have been of no use to people except to lead them to idolatry and superstition. In that, we see the great good our Lord has done for us by teaching us through the gospel. He brings us to an understanding of his works so we may know their true purpose. With that instruction we become aware both of what our condition was before he called us to know him and of how much more brutish we were than dumb animals despite his having given us some wit and intelligence, and we also become aware that we were unable to grasp what he was present-ing before our eyes. In other words, that knowledge served no purpose in our instruction until he taught us its significance.

For that reason, whenever we recognize our misfortune, let us receive the remedy God gives us to endure it, namely, instruction in his word. In this way, let us always join that teaching of the gospel to the miracles unless we wish to see everything perverted, as has been done by the Papacy. As a matter of fact, Mark says our Lord caused the preaching of the gospel to bear fruit by using miracles (*Mark* 16:20). The miracles came after the teaching and were, so to speak, only accessories. Just as one validates a letter with a seal to make it more authentic, so the miracles were added to the teaching. They must not be separated, and the miracles must not be dealt with apart from the teaching. Doing so would be like a man with a sealed document who cut off the seal and put it in his strongbox to guard closely. What good would it do him? Far from serving any good purpose, it would greatly offend the one who authorized the seal and put it on his letter. We would offend God in just that way if we saw he wanted to seal the teaching of his gospel by miracles and we then set them aside. Do you think we would be excusable if we did that? Then let us learn, as I said, to join teaching to the miracles and even give it primacy. Teaching must come first. The miracles follow.

We come now to the text Luke is dealing with. He says that Peter rebuked the people because they were astonished and not, as I said, because he wanted to rebuke their astonishment in all its aspects, but he wanted to rebuke the sin that was in it. He saw the people gazing at him, and that is not what he was seeking. First, he wanted them to be amazed, but in a different way. Second, he pointed out that it was not by his power or his holiness that the miracle was done. Third, he said that 'the God of Abraham, and of Isaac, and of Jacob has glorified his son Jesus.' Finally, he showed them the offence they had committed when he said, 'whom you delivered up'. And that was to bring them to repentance, as we will see later. But that cannot be elaborated on right now.

We come now to the first point. Peter is showing here that we must not be so dazzled by the miracle that we swoon from senseless amazement, for it is as if everybody were astonished by God's power. It is true that when our Saviour does something worth remembering, we are compelled to think about it. And in doing so, we instantly take the wrong path. On the one hand, we are disposed to say that God did it. On the other, we are quick to scour through our baseless speculations for its meaning and move away from God while thinking we are growing closer to him. Let us learn to focus such wonders on their original purpose, namely, on God, from whom they come, and let us give him the honour and glory which belong to him. Otherwise, they will be of no advantage to us. On the contrary, they will be a death sentence. The experience we have had with them should incline us to that end. How did we react to them in the time of our ignorance, before it pleased God to enlighten us? It is true that if someone mentioned miracles to us, we would admit that they came from God, but did we not do that to chase after our fantasies, our vain imaginings that we created in our own minds? Then let us learn how to be appropriately amazed by raising our minds to God, being amazed by his works in order to praise him for them. For if we follow our foolish speculations, we will be more confused than we would be if someone had clubbed us on the head, so to speak. That is the way superstitions and faithlessness affect us, but when the children of God see some act worthy of amazement, they look for God in it and, having found him, they glorify him. We see how the lamentable papists react in our day. They are sufficiently amazed, but are they led to glorify God? Not at all! They make for themselves a thousand idols at the hint of a miracle. Yet, when we see such spiritual poverty in them, we are admonished to hold on to this teaching which Peter here declares to us, namely that after experiencing the wonder of God's authority and power, we remember that it is to him that we must give glory and that it is to him that we are to yield our lives.

Peter then said, 'Why do you marvel at this? or why do you look so earnestly on us, as though by our own power or holiness we had made this man to walk?' Pay close attention to this teaching. Peter does not want the people to revere him or his companion, John. When we have our eyes fixed upon created things, our eyes are clouded to such an extent that we cannot behold God. So let us take care not to allow all created things to keep us from coming to God. Our impoverished world has turned away from the straight path for just that reason. It is overly focused on created things. It is true our Lord works in many ways through his creation, but we must not stop there. Peter and Paul [sic] are to be the instruments by which we are led to God. But if we stop with them, they will hinder and not help us, as should be the case. When we fix our attention upon individuals rather than the Creator, we use them wrongly.

Peter makes an even more important declaration when he says, 'As though this man had been healed by our own power or holiness.' That is how the people wanted to perceive Peter and John, as though it were by their power that this man walked, and that is why they rebuked the people. It is true the papists confess that the Saints do nothing by their own power except as God permits. That too is the confession of the most ignorant, who still hasten not only to things created but also to their idols, to their images, to their Saints. They trot off on their pilgrimages, to all those ceremonies and that nonsense they have invented. Instead of making their way to God, they go and present themselves before a rotten piece of wood and ask it for aid and assistance in times of need. It is clear that what they say is much at variance with what they do. Even though they hold to the contention that Peter and all the others can do nothing without God's permission, their actions prove the contrary, for Peter protests that the healing was not by their power or holiness. Now let us not think that Peter is here pretending sanctity, as is the case with many who say, 'Oh, I can do nothing of myself. I am as nothing.' Their words come tripping off their tongues while their hearts are filled with ambition and pride. There are those who disregard God's gift, which is to make them humble and meek, and yet there are none more puffed up or haughty than they.

Now we must not think Peter said that pretending he did not know his true position before God. Let the papists argue to their hearts' content about the worth and holiness of the Saints, but we understand that Peter's testimony is that that accomplishes nothing. In fact, he expressly denies that it is 'by our holiness' so that the people will not attribute this healing to them. Now the papists want to say that, because the Saints received such great grace from God, they performed miracles and that there is no evil in invoking them. Then they ascribed in each Saint his particular virtue: one heals this sickness, another that sickness. John, since he received such special grace from God, heals a particular sickness. Peter cures fevers because he healed those who were sick with fever. That is how they make idols of God's servants. Thus we see that the papists' teaching is diabolical because it does not agree with the word of God anymore than fire agrees with water. Everything that is practised by them must be rejected as coming from the devil. Therefore, let us learn the consequences of giving excessive attention to miracles done by God's servants. Let us ascribe nothing to their power or to their holiness.

How then are we to handle miracles? We are to consider them as proceeding not only from God's might and power but also from the love he has for men and from his kindness, which he wants them to feel when helping them in their need. Now if we consider miracles as works of God's goodness and mercy, it is certain that the role of men's holiness will remain insignificant. That is, men's holiness will not be elevated above God's power. Yet that is not enough. We must join what follows in the text to what was said previously. After Peter rebuked the people's vice, he showed that the true way to come to God is through Jesus Christ, for no matter how much we are urged to flee from superstitions and idolatries, we will never turn from them until we learn how to from God's truth. We will not even be able to distinguish false miracles from true miracles unless we have that teaching. Whenever we want to judge what is true, God's word must come first, as Peter points out in this passage when he says, 'The God of Abraham, and of Isaac, and of Jacob, the God of our fathers, has glorified his Son Jesus.' With those words he shows us that the purpose of the miracles is to exalt Jesus Christ's reign.

So the miracles must not be viewed as empty images which have no value for us, for it is through them that we know Jesus Christ and ponder the fact that every good comes from him. That way, as I mentioned earlier, we understand even better that miracles are only seals to confirm the teaching of the gospel. For where does the gospel lead us? Does it lead us to Peter or to Paul? We will find nothing about them, but we have Jesus Christ, who says, 'Come unto me, all you that labour and are heavy laden, and I will give you rest' (*Matt.* 11:28). So he does not send us from pillar to post, as the saying goes, but he calls us to himself. So why do we not go to him when we see that he invites us so gently? Now, the miracles, which were gifts of God, as I have already said, so captivated the people's foolish admiration that they attributed all the power of the miracles to God's servants whose hands performed them.

On the other hand, the devil mimics God as a monkey mimics men, and has performed false miracles by which people, whose natural disposition is to demand such illusions, have been deceived.

Jesus Christ has warned us, as has Paul (*Matt.* 24:24; *Mark* 13:22; *2 Thess.* 2:9–10), that when there is revolt in the church and false teachings abound, there will be many false miracles to lead the reprobate astray, and they will have an appearance such that God's elect, if it were possible, would likewise be led astray. That was predicted. We have seen it and still see it fulfilled today. But let us be careful to judge between false miracles and true miracles, which we will be able to do when God's word is joined with the miracles. Jesus Christ gave one and the same teaching to all his apostles so they might glorify him. He also gave them the gift of working miracles, but not so that they would abandon the teaching and emphasize the miracles. On the contrary. As we said above, they always preferred the teaching because the miracles were done only to confirm it. Therefore, all those who would separate the miracles from the teaching are liars and traitors to Jesus Christ and his word, as is the case with the wretched papists. Not only have they perverted the miracles of God but also, by using them, they have sealed their abominations, their superstitions, and their idolatries.

Therefore, let us be guided and led by this teaching, which alone shows us the true role of God's miracles. And if we examine this statement closely, 'The God of Abraham, and of Isaac, and of Jacob, has glorified his Son Jesus', we will not attribute miracles to created beings, but we will realize that Jesus Christ has to be glorified in them. Now what will become of the others? They will be placed far below his level, for no companion can be associated with him without greatly blaspheming his majesty. Therefore, when we have learned God is to be glorified, we will no longer be so easily deceived as in the past, not even if the devil works his will as a sleight-of-hand artist or uses all the many clever and deceptive tricks he can devise. He will not be able to cloud our judgment and prevent us from distinguishing between true and false miracles, provided we have it imprinted on our hearts that instruction must come before the miracles and then that miracles come so that God's name will be glorified through them.

When the papists speak of miracles, the question of glorifying God does not come up, for they attribute everything to Peter, Paul, and others, as we have already pointed out. Yet we observe the opposite in this passage, where everything must redound to the honour of God. When Peter speaks of 'the God of Abraham, of Isaac, and of Jacob', he does so because he is speaking to the Jews, for that designation was commonly used among the people, a designation you hear spoken of sometimes, so that they would know he was talking about the God who had manifested himself to their fathers. So it was not a designation snatched out of the air, for the Lord God had so designated himself (*Exod.* 3:15–16).

The designation also made it clear that it was not enough to recognize God as Creator of heaven and earth unless one also recognized him as the God of Abraham, of Isaac, and of Jacob, the protector of his faithful, to whom he showed himself from all time as a gracious and gentle father. It was necessary that the people know that and that he was the God in whom their assurance of salvation lay. That is why their Lord was called 'the God of Abraham, and of Isaac, and of Jacob'. The Jews needed to know they had a God different from the gods of the pagans and that when they spoke of him, they were to speak of him with greater reverence than unbelievers. It is true that unbelievers had this word 'god' on their tongues, yet created for themselves idols according to their fancy. Indeed, he shows us this must not be the case for us, for we have a living God who has manifested himself to us through our Lord Jesus Christ, who is his living image and whose teaching he wants us to believe because it is the truth he wanted to manifest to the world at a time he foreordained. Therefore, we must not be ashamed to come to Jesus Christ inasmuch as our Lord gives him to us to be the means by which he draws us to himself. So when he calls us, let us do our duty and draw near to him, and it is certain we will feel his help in a way we never could without giving him the honour and worship which belong to him.

Following this holy teaching, let us bow before the face of our gracious God in acknowledgment of our faults, beseeching him to keep us from being so wretched that, after he has once called us to himself, we would turn away from him at the slightest provocation, but that being instructed by his word and profiting from it from day to day, we will be so strengthened that the devil, the world, and our carnal desires will not be able to keep us from aligning ourselves with our gracious Master and Saviour Jesus Christ, into whose care we have been entrusted. Now let us all say together, Almighty God, heavenly Father . . .

8

THE WAY TO FORGIVENESS

SUNDAY, 9 MARCH 1550

And now, brethren, I wot that through ignorance ye did it, as did also your rulers. [18] But those things, which God before had shewed by the mouth of all his prophets, that Christ should suffer, he hath so fulfilled. [19] Repent ye therefore, and be converted, that your sins may be blotted out, when the times of refreshing shall come from the presence of the Lord (Acts 3:17–19).

We have already considered the admonition which Peter directed toward the Jews concerning the sin they had committed, and we concluded that was the true way for us to be brought to God when we are made aware of our sins. Otherwise, all we do is play games, and everything we hear will be turned into fables and consequently the word of God will have no power to touch our hearts and consciences. But when someone chastises us for our sins and tells us that God is our judge, then we are downcast and begin to examine ourselves more closely.

Now he adds a word of consolation. As he mentioned earlier that people must be cast down by the knowledge of their sins, he now points out that they must be left with some hope of salvation. Otherwise, they would be overwhelmed and not brought to God. It is true that many cannot accept that consolation when they are affected by the knowledge of their sins. That is because they rise up against God and become extremely angry and act like wild people, and consequently cannot grasp that gentleness which God wants to extend to them. Yet, because they do not wish to receive him as their saviour, it is only right that they sense he is their judge. It is very difficult to convince that kind of wretched people of what I have just said.

However, when people are not completely unreformable, we must instruct them by using the procedure Peter used. He chastened them for their offences without comforting them and then showed that God is ready to forgive their sins provided they rely on his sovereign goodness. That is also the pattern we must follow when preaching the gospel to save those who hear us. We must show them how greatly they have angered God by their sins; then when they are cast down by that, we must present the grace God is ready to offer to all through our Lord Jesus Christ. Otherwise, our preaching will be in vain. It bears no fruit unless we join those two points together.

In fact, if we only proclaim how God shows himself to be our Father through our Lord Jesus Christ, a few will accept that, but to no avail unless we first lead them to a knowledge of their sins so they will be grieved by them. In this way, we also must be cast down in ourselves if we want our Lord to lift us up. Then we will know that it is not in vain that we confess that our lives are filled with nothing less than filth and contagion. Not only must we make that kind of general confession, but each of us must also confess his particular sins before God if we are to be humbled under his strong hand. May our arrogance, our rebellion, and our wicked affections not keep us from recognizing the truth expressed here, that there is no salvation except through Jesus Christ, and for that reason we must cling unreservedly to him.

That is why some people value God's grace and others reject it completely. We find two kinds of people who do not take advantage of the gospel. One kind are scoffers, mockers, and despisers of God, enemies of him and his word, and who are now destined to scoff and laugh in the privacy of their homes. The devil has so blinded them that if someone speaks to them of Jesus Christ, he provokes dispute. They would prefer to hear a bit of gossip than to hear testimony of their salvation. Whenever the word of God is proclaimed, they mock and scoff at it, or they plot together how they can vent their contempt for God and his word. There is no fear of God and his righteousness. They will make corruption so widespread that order and government will cease to exist and they will respect nothing at all. We do not need to make a special effort to recognize such wicked people, for they will show themselves readily. There is no one so limited in his knowledge of God that he cannot recognize them, for they are completely different from the true children of God and will avoid congregating in the name of Jesus Christ, just as the devil flees from his name.

The other kind are those who blind themselves with an empty conjecture they have fabricated in their heads, as the papists continue to do today. For example, when they are shown the source of their salvation and the forgiveness of sins, namely, the death and suffering of our Lord Jesus Christ alone, with no possibility of performing works, they will then say, 'Oh, what will become of our works? I have fasted frequently, given alms, distributed my goods for the honour of God, founded chapels, had many masses said, and done so many other good works with good intentions – must all that be for nothing?' That is how those wretched people want to save themselves by their own efforts and how they reject purely and simply God's grace offered to them through Jesus Christ. That is why we also need someone to show us both that all the best works which we can lay up are only dung before God and that we must seek our righteousness somewhere other than in ourselves and our salvation somewhere other than in our works. For when we have examined everything that we are, we will find nothing that is not imperfect and worthy of eternal death.

Now if we wish to arrive at that knowledge, we must confess our sins, being grieved because of them, so that God will pardon us in the name of our Lord Jesus Christ, who suffered for us, not because of any consideration of any merits within us or of which we might be worthy, but because of his pure and freely bestowed goodness. He did so to redeem us from death, in which all of us were engulfed. After being distressed by the knowledge of our sins, we must, as I have said, be left with a plausible hope. When we see a man is not totally unreformable and is open to our teaching, we must console him, for if we wish to apply too great a severity toward him and rebuke him severely when he is ready to turn to God, Satan will come and blind him with fear and he will be so overwhelmed by fear that he will fall into such despair that it will be difficult to rescue him. After we have touched the hearts of men and know they are grieved by their sins and cast down because of them, we must extend to them a hand, lift them up and say, 'Come to God. Although you have offended him, you will always find mercy in him provided you truly seek him.' That is how we must go about it, following the procedure Peter uses here. After showing the Jews they were enemies of God and worse than that pitiable pagan and unbeliever Pilate, and after bringing them to a sense of shame by thus revealing the depth of their sin so that they say, 'Alas, what shall we do?' Peter then says, 'I know that through ignorance you did it'. He added that so they would not fall into despair but return to God after recognizing their sins. However, he did not want to give them comfort, for he had rebuked them all severely in order to lead them to that grace which is offered them by our Lord Jesus Christ.

Now that passage – 'I know that through ignorance you did it' – could present a problem if those who did not sin through ignorance, but knowingly, were not able to obtain forgiveness. Many examples in holy Scripture show that they did not. Will we doubt that when Reuben committed incest (*Gen.* 35:22), he polluted his father's bed but had not been sufficiently instructed that such an abomination should not have been contemplated at all? When David committed his damnable adultery, which ended in the murder of Uriah (*2 Sam.* 11), was he not aware that that was displeasing to God and that he was grievously offending him? When the patriarchs sold their brother Joseph (*Gen.* 37:28), did they do it out of a lack of understanding that it was an evil deed? No, not at all! Before Peter denied his master (*Matt.* 26:69–75), had not Jesus Christ warned him that whoever denied him before men, he would also deny before God his Father (*Matt.* 10:33; *Luke* 12:9)? And had not Peter even been warned again and personally that before the cock crowed three times he would deny Jesus Christ (*Matt.* 26:34, 74–75)? And yet he became a base coward. When the Corinthians were indulging in all kinds of wickedness and giving themselves to all kinds of lechery, debauchery, and impurity, so that they were totally corrupt, Paul still called them to repentance and declared that God would have mercy on them provided they did not return to their vices (*1 Cor.* 5). We know that David and the patriarchs received forgiveness of their sins, that Peter was restored to his position and dignity as an apostle, and that the Corinthians, following Paul's rebukes, returned to God.

In those examples we see that the sins which men commit, well aware that they offend God, are forgivable. For that reason there was under the law the general teaching that God wanted sacrifices to be made for sins committed out of ignorance as much as for those committed willingly. In that way he wanted to show us not only that God is ready to pardon our faults if we fail through ignorance, but also when we offend him knowingly – provided, however, we go to him with the firm intention of not returning, by his grace and goodness, to our usual vices.

Why then does Peter say, 'I know that through ignorance you did it'? Now we need to pay attention to this point. Peter is not speaking here of all sins in general, but of that characteristically human rebellion of not valuing that salvation which was acquired for them by our Lord Jesus Christ. Consequently, if they refuse to accept that grace, they commit a sin more egregious than all others. For when a man rises up against God with intentional and deliberate wrongdoing and says, 'I have nothing to do with what anyone preaches to me. I would rather disavow the teaching of the gospel and extinguish the enlightenment of the Holy Spirit than to subject myself to that.' When a man is possessed by the devil like that, it is a sign that he is condemned and has no hope of salvation. That is what Peter means here. For this is not a matter of lechery, theft, usury, robbery, or other similar vice, but when they put Jesus Christ to death, they wanted to destroy, insofar as they could, the salvation that was being offered to them. Now those are sins which should make your hair stand on end – even though they might have had a desperate zeal while committing them, sure that they were doing their duty.

Nevertheless, we could still ask whether the Jews were so ignorant that they did not have some awareness they were doing wrong. We need to have a general rule that says that people never sin so much out of ignorance as they do when they are convinced of their innocence before God. If there is ignorance, it comes from an insane devotion, as we see among the papists. They think they are serving God when they hear their abominable mass and all their other spectacles, taking comfort in their good intentions, which they appeal to. It is certain all of that is done out of ignorance. But when you look closely at everything they do, you will find that they were not so naïve in their ignorance that they did not cloak it in hypocrisy, pride, and presumption. In the first place, they make for themselves idols according to their fancy and are unconcerned about inquiring after God's truth, for the natural inclination of evil men is never to want God in their hearts or to have his pure and simple teaching, as they should. They are content to have a few fictions to support them in their errors, and they will do nothing but beat about the bush, as the saying goes. They have their diabolical ceremonies, their games created to their liking, by which the more they think they owe God nothing, the more they increase their condemnation, for our Lord has declared that he wants to be served in spirit and in truth. So if we offer him the objects of our creation and all our buffooneries, in which we take pleasure, and if we abandon his true worship and fail to prize his word, and, as I have said, do nothing but beat about the bush, it is certain he will both disavow all that we do for him and punish us grievously as rebels and as those who work against his holy will. That is how those who resist the gospel sin out of ignorance without shedding a shred of their hypocrisy. Pride and ambition are near at hand, for everything they do is to be seen by men. However, they must remain under conviction before God and acknowledge guilt for their sins.

Nevertheless, let us note that even if men sin knowingly, they do not shed their ignorance. For if we were well informed, we would walk in the fear of God differently. Will a man in fact throw himself into hell deliberately? We do just that because we are blinded by Satan. Yet we have to say that when people sin, they are carried away by ignorance. That is for sure. And that kind of ignorance is condemned by God because, yielding to our own self-will, which is wicked and corrupt, we want to remain in that ignorance.

Now let us move on to the next part of this matter. We know there are sins which proceed from our ignorance and others which proceed from our wills. When man wishes to serve God according to his own imaginings and refuses to follow the will of God, there is ignorance. Nevertheless, he does not cease being led by his own will, which is condemned by God. On the other hand, when a man is so carried away by his own spirit that, knowing quite well that he offends God by blaspheming him and following his lusts and other wicked desires, when he steals from one and pillages another, in short, when he engages in so many vices that he is completely infected with them, he will nonetheless remain ignorant. For if he was aware of his duty, as I have said, he would not have given himself over so inordinately to so many sins. We can now come to a conclusion concerning Peter's remark that when we hear the word of God, we must listen in all reverence to what it says, for, no matter the level of our ignorance, we will be without excuse before God when we refuse to hear his teaching, but we will be convicted of ingratitude for having scorned the grace he has offered us.

When saying, 'I know that through ignorance you did it, as did also your rulers', Peter seems to want to excuse and lessen the scribes' and Pharisees' fault. We know they sinned in their spirit and with evil intent. The answer to that is easy. Here, Peter only wanted to speak to those he hoped would be converted to God. It is certain that notwithstanding the condition some people might have been in, although they resisted the gospel in the beginning, they were nevertheless converted shortly afterwards by the apostles' preaching. Those are the ones whom Peter addresses when saying, 'I know that through ignorance you did it, as did also your rulers.' He said to them, 'Repent therefore, and be converted, that your sins may be blotted out.' We see even more clearly, in conjunction with what we dealt with last Sunday, that Peter's intention all along was to lead the Jews to repentance so they might understand they would obtain pardon from God provided they repent of their sins and learn to walk according to God's will.

When speaking about conversion, Peter wanted to explain the significance of the word 'penitence'. That word has always been so abused that when one speaks of penitence, it seems that it is a way to acquit oneself before God, as we observe the papists practising it today. They say that this time of Lent is the time of penitence. They think they have done great and very pleasing penitence before God when they abstain from eating meat. When they hear the mass with greater devotion, when the images of the Saints are hidden, and when they are not singing the 'Hallelujah', then they are engaged in the period of penitence. Then, if they are having some service, as they term it, such as a novena or the founding of a chapel, or so many other spectacles which are but games children play, then they are truly repentant! As for the gospel, no need to talk about that! When they go through the motions of preaching, those hypocrites reverse everything. All they do is spout forth blasphemies instead of proclaiming God's truth. That is not the way we are to go about it if we wish to have true penitence, such as our Lord requires of us. We are obliged to submit ourselves completely to the word of God and follow what we know he commands us in it, beseeching him always to be pleased to lead us by his Holy Spirit so that we may be able to do those things which are pleasing to him. That is what true penitence looks like. For that reason Peter says, 'Repent therefore, and be converted', which is like saying, 'Do not think that just because you have the word "penitence" you are truly repentant. You have to be mortified. You must cease to be yourselves. You must no longer pursue those things which seem good to you. You must be completely submissive to God, hear his teaching, and allow him to be master over you. In short, you must be like new creatures.' That is the disposition of a man who truly wants to repent.

Now when speaking to them about penitence, he added, 'So that your sins may be blotted out.' With those words he points out that we cannot be led to God by some perfunctory exhortations unless we are first moved by our faults and so grieved by them that we are fully converted to God, and unless we completely abandon them and are renewed by the Holy Spirit. It is true that a man can be moved by the awareness of his sins after someone points them out to him, but if he does not come to the point of being converted, that awareness will be of no advantage to him but will only compound his condemnation. We have an example of that in both Judas and Cain. It is true that Cain confesses to murdering his brother Abel and that he grievously offended God, and thereupon he becomes as wild as an enraged animal and experiences no concern for asking God to pardon his sin, but he despairs and says that his iniquity is greater than God's mercy (*Gen.* 4:13). Judas does likewise, acknowledging that he committed an egregious sin by betraying his master and selling innocent blood, but the acknowledgment was not an attempt to return to God and ask for pardon. On the contrary, the betrayer's despair incurs his own destruction.

So let us always acknowledge our sins so that we may be grieved by them, and then let us look to God's mercy so that we may come to him in all humility and say, 'Alas, Lord, here we are on the road to hell. We are guilty and worthy of everlasting death because of the sins we have committed against your holy majesty, but you do not desire the death of sinners before they are converted and enter into life. With confidence in your great mercy, we lay claim to it, asking you not to look upon the enormity of our sins but to look upon us with pity, pardoning us by your freely bestowed kindness.' That is the way to preach the gospel. After people are overwhelmed by the knowledge of their sins, they must be brought to repentance and shown this is not a matter of putting on a happy face for God with the thought of deceiving him by pretence and hypocrisy, as people are accustomed to doing. That is not the way they are to come to him, but when they want to be truly repentant, they must be displeased with themselves and displeased for having offended God. When they are thus affected, offer them God's mercy so their sins will be forgiven, provided they return to God, as we said earlier.

Then Peter adds, 'And therefore the times of refreshing shall come from the presence of the Lord; and he shall send Jesus Christ, which before was preached unto you' (*Acts* 3:19-20). That verse is obscure insofar as the words are concerned, but Peter's intention is clear and easy to see. With those words he brings his hearers back to God's judgment and shows them that we must wait for our Lord Jesus Christ to proclaim the sentence of God's judgment. It is true that Jesus Christ will not come as judge to condemn those who have believed in his gospel, but to give renewal. For that reason, so that we may participate in that renewal, we must believe the promises made to us in the gospel. We must beseech God to forgive us our past sins and be henceforth pleased to guide us by his Holy Spirit so that we may be completely conformed to his will, obeying it according to his commands.

Moreover, we are alerted to the fact that we will never be effectively convicted of our sins, no matter the content of the preaching, unless we remember that one day we will have to give an account of our lives. We must be made aware of God's judgment, acknowledge our sins and be grieved by them. For as long as we are caught up in our vain affections and imaginings and remain in the grip of this worldly life, having someone speak to us about the things of God will be to no avail, for our hearts will be increasingly hardened until we come to that recognition of our sins. Consequently, those who are devoted to this present life cannot face their baseness or conceive of the horror their sins should produce in themselves. So what must happen? We must be awakened by a serious consideration of God's judgment, and we must always be reminded that Jesus Christ will come to judge the world in righteousness. That should resound like the blast of a trumpet in our ears.

We remember how Paul exhorted Timothy when he said, 'I charge you therefore before God and the Lord Jesus Christ, who shall judge the living and the dead at his appearing and his kingdom' (*2 Tim.* 4:1). Now Timothy was a man walking with a clear conscience. He had a great zeal for the word of God. He did his duty and followed his calling. Yet Paul gave him that charge and advised him to remember that he would have to give an accounting to that great Judge we are waiting for at the end of time. So if Timothy needed that kind of admonition, what about us? It is certain we need to be admonished even more often not to wait until that day comes to return to God. We also need to look upon Jesus Christ even now as ready to judge our case. We need to submit to his condemnation in this world and be cast down within ourselves so that we will be cleansed and lifted up when he condemns and destroys the wicked who refused to obey him and his holy word.

It must be our firm conviction that God will not tolerate such contempt for his mercies and allow us to refuse them out of hand after he has presented them so profusely. He has called us to the knowledge of his gospel so we will not follow our vain desires and our wicked inclinations, as was our custom. Yet if we do not wish to forsake them, it would have been better for us to remain papists and for God never to have manifested himself to us. That would only double our condemnation because instead of serving God we would be serving the devil – yes, and knowingly. In reality, we have no reason to expect anything but the horrible and frightful judgment of God on us unless we turn from our wicked way of living. If we continue to yield to our wicked affections, even our awareness of God's judgment upon us will do nothing but enrage us and cast us into a pit of despair. We will only become angry and gnash our teeth when someone talks to us about it. On the contrary, if we are faithful believers, we will long for the Day of the Lord to come. For it is at that time that we will achieve that perfection to which God has called all his elect. That, I say, is how faithful believers experience joy when someone speaks to them about the judgment of God.

The wicked, on the other hand, only gnash their teeth, as I said, when the subject is broached. And even while gnashing their teeth they yield more and more to their excesses, as we see today. The more God's judgment is brought to the attention of the wicked, the more they abandon themselves to their vanities and follies. We have cried out against their amusements, their dissolute behaviour, and we see how they abstain from them! These wicked man, these despisers of God, do Mardi Gras just as they always have. Then comes mid-Lent Tuesday. And they are not even content with that! They have to have their masquerades too. And what follows that? The brothel has to be open to all comers, and the trumpet must be sounded everywhere to summon everyone to the brothel in Geneva.

So where is the reformation that is supposed to be among us? What reverence do we show for God for the many good things he has done for us among the nations? His name is trampled under foot! He is everywhere blasphemed! And from now on will they not yield themselves a thousand times more villainously to their vices than they ever did when trapped in wretched slavery to the Antichrist? That is the kind of fruit we will reap from the gospel as long as such dissolute behaviour is permitted and supported. However, let those who are responsible for establishing order look more closely at the situation, and let us ask God to keep us from the hardness of heart that would prevent us from perceiving his judgment so that we may completely govern our lives according to his word, so that when Jesus Christ returns we will not be condemned but given eternal rest with him in the glory of his Father.

Following this holy teaching, let us bow before the face of our gracious God, acknowledging our sins, asking him to be pleased to touch us in such a way that, being displeased with them, we will only seek to follow him in all that it pleases him to command us, so that being enlightened by his Holy Spirit, we will never turn away from our sacred calling, but walk in it and observe his commandments until he has fully clothed us with his righteousness. May he grant that grace not only to us but to all the peoples and nations of the earth . . .

9

THE PREACHERS OF THE GOSPEL PERSECUTED

SUNDAY, 13 APRIL 1550

And as they spake unto the people, the priests, and the captain of the temple, and the Sadducees, came upon them, ² Being grieved that they taught the people, and preached through Jesus the resurrection from the dead. ³ And they laid hands on them, and put them in hold unto the next day: for it was now eventide. ⁴ Howbeit many of them which heard the word believed; and the number of the men was about five thousand (Acts 4:1–4).

Among the means by which our Lord wants our faith to be put to the test is this: Satan exerts all his power to prevent the word of God from going forth. And when his word begins to be made known, the wicked oppose it vigorously, for they are the devil's instruments for waging war against God and his Son, our Lord Jesus Christ. That is what Luke is now bringing to our attention. We have heard how the apostles taught the people and how that was a sign that the gospel was to be made public. But here the devil is, making serious inroads against that endeavour. It is an attempt to test the faith of the apostles and of all those associated with them. Seeing that everyone was resisting God's truth, they had to be armed with perseverance so they would not be daunted by that resistance. It is true the devil will make a valiant effort, but he will not be able to do anything against Jesus Christ, for since our Lord is seated at the right hand of God his Father (*Eph.* 1:20–22), all creatures are in subjection to him. Consequently, when the devil tries to prevent the spread of the gospel, he can do so only with God's permission. He can do nothing on his own authority, but God gives him leeway to do everything within his power so that when there is nothing more he can do, we will realize the power of God's truth notwithstanding the fact that his truth remains victorious whenever the world and the devil come into conflict.

Let us also note that what Luke recounts here was not for that time only. It still serves us very well now, for if the people had listened to the apostles without controversy, and had agreed with their teaching, we would not see the gospel's strength, as it is shown in this passage. But when the text says that the priests, who had all authority in Jerusalem, rise up and try to hinder the preaching of the gospel and obscure the miracle which was done, and when they do all they can to prevent the apostles from preaching in the name of our Lord Jesus Christ, they fail. Therein can we see that God has worked with his hand and that it was not by human power that the gospel has been preached throughout the world, but that God has demonstrated his power in it.

That then is a story that ought to arrest our attention because in it Luke shows us, as in a mirror, that God's adversary the devil does not sleep. As soon as the gospel appears, he immediately conspires to thwart it to the extent God permits. For, as I have said, he can do nothing unless God grants him leeway. That much is clear. Still we know that Satan is the prince of this world, that he always has enough henchmen and asks only to make war on God. Even so, God will sustain his gospel. When the wicked have made all their efforts, it will be obvious in the end that what they have contrived will fall on their own heads. Nevertheless, we must take that as coming from the hand of God. And when we see great disturbances in the church, we must not be surprised because that is the way it has always been. We must be comforted and take courage when we hear that God will be victorious over everything the devil brings to pass. Since God will conquer all things, let us take courage and persevere in the faith that comes to us through the gospel, for the world will be powerless against it. If heaven and earth should be shaken, the fact remains that God's truth overcomes every barrier, and since our foundation is built on his truth, let us not fear that the devil can rattle us and trip us up. That is the lesson we are to learn from this story.

But in order to get the most out of this, we need to note all the circumstances just as Luke mentions them. He says that as the apostles were speaking to the people, the priests come and interfere with everything. In that, we see how diligent the devil is and how vigilant he is to hinder God's work in its earliest stages. That fact shows us our responsibility. Are we not much shamed by being cowardly and inattentive when we see the devil going all out to use every means to destroy God's glory and stir the wicked to enraged zeal to eradicate the memory of our Lord Jesus Christ? Let us consider for a moment the courage the priests displayed here. It is true they seemed to be fulfilling their responsibility because they thought Jesus Christ had come to take what was theirs. It seems, as I said, that they wanted to do their duty and prevent the dissemination of false doctrine. For as soon as they heard that the apostles were teaching the people, they hastened to the place to investigate. So how diligent must Christians be when it comes to putting God's truth first? Are unbelievers to be better servants of Satan than we are of our Master, Jesus Christ? How great is our ingratitude? What reproach will we deserve when the reprobate are more diligent in their pursuit of perdition than we are in our pursuit of salvation? Therefore, each of us must be diligent to have a burning desire to uphold God's truth.

On the other hand, when Luke speaks of the priests, he is speaking of the responsibility of those who hold public office. Principally, they are ordained to bear God's word. So when some falsehood appears or Satan's wicked disseminations proliferate, it is their duty to be vigilant, confront the situation, and do everything in their power to protect the poor people from being poisoned by false teachings and to keep the souls redeemed by the precious blood of our Lord Jesus Christ from perishing, from entering into eternal death. That, I say, is how the priests – although they rose up against God – admonish us to do our duty. We, I say, who have the responsibility of teaching others, must not be cowards when we see the devil trying to propagate his lies. We must oppose them.

Next, Luke tells us about the captain of the temple. Through him, magistrates and law enforcement officials are advised of their duty. When seeing disorder, they are to use the authority given them so our Lord Jesus Christ can maintain his possession and so the wicked will not be allowed to undertake anything that might cause others to stumble. So when some false teaching arises, what are we to do? Let each of us work at driving it out. Let the voices of the ministers of God's word cry out against it, and let the magistrates, who have a sword in their hands, show that their responsibility is to restrain the wicked when they are bold to engage in their wickedness, so that each of us may fulfil our charge and our calling.

As for the Sadducees, we must first note that theirs was an abominable supposition, namely that there were factions, that the poor people who were supposed to be united in a single faith were divided. There were at that time many factions in vogue among the Jews, and yet we know that just as there is only one God, we must have one and the same Master over us, and that just as there is only one truth, we have one law to hold us together in unity and in one confession of faith. Whereas that was to apply to the Jews, it is they who are divided by factions, and each group endeavours to attract to itself followers who accept the wild concept it had worked out, and no one tries to come to God. In that, we see their situation at that time.

But if we observe those who call themselves Christians today, we will discover they create factions and divisions which are as wicked as those among the Jews – indeed more wicked. How many factions are there in the Papacy and how many groups are they separated into? It is true that they are united to make war against God. They are of a single mind to eradicate the truth about Jesus Christ and expunge his glory, if such were possible. But as for the rest, they are like cats and dogs, and the whole of their preaching will work together to rip our Lord Jesus Christ apart. Yet they have no shame when it comes to speaking ill of one another and having debates and dissensions about matters of this world. As a result there are more factions and divisions among them than among the Turks and unbelievers.

Then, we see the kind of hodgepodge there is in their way of life. Everybody boasts of his order. One will say, 'I belong to St Francis'; another will say, 'I belong to St Dominic.' But where is Jesus Christ? Where is the teaching that he left to all of us so that each of us might obey him? Just as there were many factions among the Jews, so there is a diversity of teaching under that Antichrist in Rome.

Furthermore, each group lives apart in its own way, and God's law is left high and dry. The teaching that Jesus Christ has given is too commonplace, so if one wishes to achieve a perfect state, St Francis has to replace Jesus Christ. But the opposite is true. We know all those things are not just empty, frivolous trifles, but damnable sacrilege and gross blasphemies against the majesty of the Son of God, none of which will he let go unpunished. Yet if we truly want to belong to God's church, we must each bring ourselves into line with that truth, the purpose of which is not to separate us into factions and divisions but to lead us to the true faith and unity which must be ours in God. Now if people follow their natural inclinations and withdraw into their own group, they cannot possibly learn how to come to Jesus Christ. However, let everyone renounce his own preferences and reject what seems good to him, and let him hear what Paul says in Ephesians 4: 'We must walk worthy of the vocation wherewith we are called, with all lowliness and meekness, knowing there is one Lord, one faith, one baptism, and one God and Father of all, who has called us to the knowledge of Jesus Christ his Son' (cf. *Eph.* 4:1–2, 5–6, 13).

There is one more point that we must consider. When Luke says that the Sadducees came with the others, why does he make it a point to talk about them unless they have authority, like the chief priests, who are in that group? What do they believe? They believe that God does good to those he loves, that we are not to expect a greater happiness than this world can provide, that there are no souls in paradise, and that there is no resurrection from the dead. Is it not unfortunate that the suffering and death of our Lord Jesus Christ is dismissed that way by a wicked person who denies the resurrection from the dead, who has no hope for eternal life, and is so dense he does not believe there is a happiness greater than he finds in this world?

And who are these men who foster that teaching? It was the high priest, who was like the image of Jesus Christ. Nevertheless it is clear that he is very different from what Jesus Christ teaches. Is it not unfortunate that the one whose office it is to lead men to the knowledge of God believes people do not have souls any more than dogs do? Why is it that God's church has been led by a teacher like that? It is because man's iniquity had to be punished that way. For if we consider the disarray of the Jews at that time, we will not find it strange that God allowed Satan the license to disrupt everything among them, the way that the disruption we see in the Papacy is God's just vengeance to punish human beings because they refused to obey the teaching of salvation and because they refused to receive Jesus Christ; or else after receiving the gospel, they strayed from the straight path and showed they were not worthy of receiving such a great good. And for that, God visited that kind of confusion upon them.

What then is the reason for the abominations and idolatries we find in the Papacy today? The sins of men and their ingratitude are so vile that when God presented himself to them through his word, they rejected it! Here we have a fine example of God permitting everything to fall into desolation and confusion when men cannot bring themselves under his hand. He is obliged to empower and commission Satan to govern them so that he dominates them and gives them a reprobate mind. That, as I have already said, is not only evident in the incident Luke relates but we also see it happening before our eyes in the Papacy. We have also sensed it in our persons. And now we must be all the more careful to remain fearfully, humbly, and unyieldingly obedient to the gospel because it has pleased God to snatch us from the Antichrist's wretched servitude. Otherwise, there is no doubt that if we continue in the way we began and show contempt for the word of God in this way, we will no longer be deserving even of having the pope put his hand on us and exercising his tyranny over us. The devil will certainly have taken dominion over us. If he does, we must not expect things will be as they were. What then? There will be no restraint, and everyone will want free rein to do what seems good to him without having either God or religion.

That is already largely evident. How many wretched people out there mock the teaching of God instead of receiving it with humility? It is true they are not interested in the pope's superstitions, but rather than reverencing that teaching and receiving it with great awe, as I said, they will gladly trample it underfoot – if that were possible – and hope no one would ever mention it. Why? Because they feel that someone wants to keep them bridled. They say, 'They want to make us live like monks.' That is their argument whenever someone tries to inform them that the gospel does not give us license for every evil, but instructs us in every good work (cf. *2 Cor.* 9:8; *2 Tim.* 2:21; 3:17) so that we may live holy lives in the presence of him who has called us to do just that. Those wicked people do not believe the first word of it. Consequently, they can be judged as being more brutish than brutish beasts. There is no difference between them and brute beasts unless God imprints his image on them. Moreover, they are worse than dogs if they think man and beast are the same. Let each of us take this to heart and follow the path which God has set our feet on by his word so that we may be strengthened by it and not be so attached to this world that we are wretched enough to think our felicity is found only in it. That is what we must focus on since we have so many admonitory examples. Nonetheless, we see the great folly of the pope and his ilk when they exalt their belief that they cannot err because they are the church of God and that on pain of eternal damnation they must hold steadfastly to what they have surmised once because they call themselves sovereign in the church of God.

And who was this high priest? Had God not authorized him when he established that priestly dignity in the law? Even so, the priests have not been exempted from every error. On the contrary, they have most often been enemies of God. In fact, we see those Luke speaks of engaged in incomparably severe brutishness. And the pope and all this rabble of priests and monks have followed in their footsteps. That is what papist Christianity is like since the pope says the teaching of salvation is only a falsehood so that he might have a claim for his own teaching, which is falsehood itself. And there you have the papists, who, instead of being joined to

God through the knowledge of his word, allow themselves to be led by Satan. But, as I said, men deserve that kind of confused understanding when they refuse to adhere to the teaching about salvation. We know that, according to the teaching of the gospel, we are not to follow men or be subjected to what they consider right. We are to be content with witnessing to the teaching God approves and declares to be his, even though everyone contradicts it.

Let us look closely at this passage and we will understand even better that we must not be dislodged from our faith by some hindrance contrived by the devil. So the wicked, who are instruments of Satan, can indeed rise up against God, but they only test our faith when they attack us. We must be steadfast in resisting everything they can throw up against us and not be like weathervanes gyrating in the wind. Our faith must be constant and invincible, sustained by the word of God, which is everlasting. That is the goal we must reach, as I said at the outset. We now see the disturbances and vexations and persecutions directed at the church of God by a world rabid to destroy God's word. May those things never frighten us, and let us persevere in the thing God has been pleased to begin in us, knowing that he will bring it to pass even though men will do everything within their power to destroy it. We must not get it into our heads that we will be excused from every battle today, for we know that all who have followed Jesus Christ have been hated by the world. Consequently, our Lord must deal with us in this way even today, and our faith must be exercised just as theirs was.

At this point, the apostles are imprisoned, but does that mean God's word is imprisoned? Here we have two individuals, Peter and John, who were put in prison, and because of that action five thousand are edified. And by what power was that done? By the word of our Lord Jesus Christ, who said, 'Whatsoever you shall bind on earth shall be bound in heaven' (*Matt* 16:19; 18:18). All those five thousand men were held in captivity by the devil, as we all are. Until Jesus Christ removes us from that servitude, we are excluded from God's kingdom and deprived of eternal life. Thus, the gospel is a freedom which God provides for us and which loosens the bonds of the devil. That freedom is proclaimed to us by the mouth of man. And although we hear only a voice resonating in the air, it has such power that our souls are loosed from death, and we are declared to be children of God, whereas previously we were slaves of the devil and sin. By his preaching, which converted five thousand men, Peter freed them and gave them spiritual freedom. Now it is true that his imprisonment greatly disturbed many, but that does not keep the word of God from bearing fruit, as Paul also confirms: 'It is true that I am in bondage here, but the word of God is not in bondage with me' (*2 Tim.* 2:9). He believed that what he had proclaimed had gone forth and was bearing fruit. He had sowed the gospel in such a way that God was causing his work to prosper. In that way, he exhorts the faithful to be of good courage when afflicted as he had been for God's word. Even though he was confined under strict guard, he nonetheless gloried, as I said, but the word of God was not confined with him.

So when we see persecutions arising on all sides, let us not be surprised, and let us not be like those many who, if they could have a peaceful gospel, would be glad to vote for it. We are like birds on a branch surrounded by many dangers. We do not want to share in those troubles because we are accustomed to living comfortably in this world. We, like the birds, are unwilling to subject ourselves to unpleasant times if we can avoid them. And then we think that the condition of Christians seems to be the most unfortunate in the world because everyone hates us and rejects us. It is true that we, like the birds, consider all those disadvantages and are only too careful to examine the situation, but we do not take the long view and consider that the word of God has always been the target of the grudges and calumnies of the wicked and that it still does not lose its power to overcome all of Satan's subterfuges and schemes. Our Lord wants the good news about him to flourish in the midst of persecutions. Let us not be astonished by that, and let us not think that God is asleep if he is slow to act, but let us wait for the outcome and we will see that he is using Satan's schemes and his henchmen to increase his word and strengthen his church.

However, we are advised here of the shared goal of unbelievers. Although as different from one another as cats and dogs, as I said, they persist in conspiring to destroy the kingdom of our Lord Jesus Christ. We have a good example of it here. Although the Jews differed among themselves and were divided into many factions, they were nonetheless very capable of coming together and agreeing among themselves when it was a matter of taking up arms against Jesus Christ, as I have already pointed out. We see the same situation among the papists today, for what are the differences between the priests, monks, and all that other papal vermin? They are not only like cats and dogs, as I said, but they would like to devour one another like savage animals; and if some poor Christian is engaged in warfare, they will immediately band together and conspire in his death. Why? Because the teaching of the gospel condemns them all and reveals their factions, their heresies, and their enormities. Inasmuch as they are Satan's henchmen and under his control, they cannot avoid fighting among themselves and hating one another to death, because Satan is the prince of division. But whenever there is an uprising against God and his gospel, they become closely allied first cousins. Yet we must find consolation in the fact that whatever plot they concoct, God will be able to bring them to utter destruction. And if he does not bring them to naught, he will need only to apply his little finger to confound them.

But let us not be surprised by the agreement among the wicked whenever they want to do battle against God and his word. And let us realize that when the devil does all he can to destroy the teaching preached in the name of God, we must be armed with strength from on high and not be so surprised by all the assaults he directs against us that we stop doing the work God has been pleased to begin in us. Let us, therefore, persevere steadfastly in the teaching we have heard, knowing it will be only for our good that persecutions come.

In addition, let us realize that if we are under men's tyranny as concerns the body, our souls will remain free provided we do not yield to their abominations, whatever threats and torments they may visit upon us, and do not doubt that God will sustain us until the end. And then when we see that the apostles persist in proclaiming the gospel publicly, an offence which gets them imprisoned, and when we see that the teaching bore fruit despite all human intervention, let us not doubt that it will bear fruit in us too. And because the devil is more inflamed and the wicked are more enraged against us, God has to work within us, and he will if we implore him to and are committed to bear our part of the burden and do our duty. And yet, since our Lord is putting this word before us today, by whose power we were created from nothing, may it also arm us to resist all the assaults directed against us.

Even though men reject this word, let us be confident that it possesses its proper authority. And when we see the wicked banding together against God, let us likewise be united by this same word, let us call upon God, and make a true confession of our faith so that there will be such a sense of fellowship among us that we can say that we are all members of one body, the body of Jesus Christ, and that we are in such accord that no one can say any party spirit or division exists among us. If we conduct ourselves in this way, it is certain that God will spoil the plots that the wicked hatch against us and so bless our unity that we will arrive at that blessed happiness which Paul speaks of when he says God will receive us all into his kingdom (*Col.* 1:13).

Following this holy teaching, let us bow before the face of our gracious God in recognition of our sins, praying that we will be so filled with his grace that we will walk in all uprightness and equity before him, and in this way may his name be glorified in us. Then may he grant us the grace that in the end we may be able to attain that eternal glory he has promised us, after it has been manifested in us in all righteousness and holiness. Let us now say together, Almighty God, heavenly Father . . .

10

PREACHING IN THE POWER OF
THE SPIRIT

SUNDAY, 20 APRIL 1550

And it came to pass on the morrow, that their rulers, and elders, and scribes,
⁶ And Annas the high priest, and Caiaphas, and John, and Alexander, and
as many as were of the kindred of the high priest, were gathered together
at Jerusalem. ⁷ And when they had set them in the midst, they asked, By
what power, or by what name, have ye done this? ⁸ Then Peter, filled with
the Holy Ghost, said unto them, Ye rulers of the people, and elders of Israel,
⁹ If we this day be examined of the good deed done to the impotent man,
by what means he is made whole; ¹⁰ Be it known unto you all, and to all
the people of Israel, that by the name of Jesus Christ of Nazareth, whom
ye crucified, whom God raised from the dead, even by him doth this man
stand here before you whole. ¹¹ This is the stone which was set at nought
of you builders, which is become the head of the corner. ¹² Neither is there
salvation in any other: for there is none other name under heaven given
among men, whereby we must be saved (Acts 4:5–12).

In this passage, we are to consider how Satan tries to destroy
the works of God as soon as we become aware of them. His
principal goal is to prevent people from honouring God as they
should. Now, we know our Lord speaks to us through his works. In

them he shows his power and authority, his kindness and wisdom so we may have the opportunity to magnify him. That is why Satan, the enemy of God's glory, makes every effort to obscure the works done in God's name so that people will remain in ignorance. That is shown in the present account. We have seen how Peter and John healed that poor paralytic. It was a memorable act and so outstanding that we understand God should be exalted in it and his power greatly magnified by it. Furthermore, it ought to serve as a vehicle for proclaiming the gospel. It is like a seal confirming and ratifying the teaching the apostles bring. And there the devil is again on the attack, trying to obscure this miracle so God will not be glorified and the course of the gospel will be so hindered that it will not be able to move forward. He is concerned that if the people receive this message and are brought into obedience to the gospel, they will come to salvation in the only way possible. But he, the mortal enemy of man's salvation, thwarts it in any way he can.

Now, what Luke tells us is for our instruction. So as often as God manifests himself through his works, the devil ambushes his effort and dazzles our eyes or otherwise finds some way to blind us to God's goodness, wisdom, and strength, and prevent us from extolling him as we should. As a consequence, the more the devil plots against us, the more must we apply our complete attention to analyzing what God shows us so we can profit from it. That also is why we are warned about the devil's craftiness, as much in this passage as in the entirety of holy Scripture, so that we may be armed for the encounter and resist him. Because we are carnal, we will not be remotely aware of our Lord's most obvious labours unless we are enlightened by his Holy Spirit and repulse the darkness, the craftiness, and the guile which Satan surrounds us with. Let us, then, be careful to observe closely the things God shows us. For what so easily takes our eyes off the narrow path is the fact that we do not recognize God's wondrous works and glorify him for them. We are blind because we do not recognize how God wishes to manifest himself to us. So let us learn to be more diligent in this respect than we have been until now.

Besides, we must note, as already indicated, that the devil makes a maximum effort to prevent the advancement of the gospel, for it is for his ruin and he knows it! We know the gospel is the light of God by which our paths are illuminated on the road to salvation. We know it is nourishment and eternal life. We know it is the power of God. We know it is his righteousness, by which he justifies us. We know it is his way of delivering us from sin and death. The devil, the prince of sin, seeks only to destroy us and deprive us of God's righteousness in order to lead us in paths of unrighteousness and wickedness. Let us not be surprised that he makes every effort to impede the progress of the gospel. Being aware of that, we must be armed to confront all the temptations which may arise. And when we encounter today the objections which the wicked offer against this teaching and which the wise of this world exercise mightily in their effort to thwart the gospel's progress, we understand that all earthly power resists it, and we see that most of those who once favoured the gospel have turned away from it. In short, it is the teaching which is virtually boxed in by everyone. And yet the devil cannot, despite his best efforts, impede its proclamation.

However, we also have to remember that since Satan is the prince of this world, we must not think it strange that there are so many objections raised against our Lord Jesus Christ's teaching. But we will see as this account unfolds how God keeps a mighty hand on his truth and makes it victorious against all the assaults of the wicked, by which Satan lifts up his hand against us.

Now, in order to learn more from this passage, we need to note the brutishness and ignorance of those who were supposed to be the leaders of the people and do all they could to advance and magnify our Lord Jesus Christ. They are the greatest enemies of God's truth. In addition to that, there is the condition of the people, who are so blind they do not recognize the ignorance of those who, they think, are guiding them well. And then there is the help God gives his own, such help as will be made known later. There are, therefore, three points we have to consider, not that we can deal with them now, but so we can have them in mind when we deal with them in detail later. I want to deal with them briefly now in passing.

In the first place, Luke tells us about Annas, who was the high priest at the time. Just as that worthy office was for sale back then and against God's decree – not that they bought it in every instance, but it happened regularly by political manoeuvring, just as we see priestly authority grossly abused in the Papacy today, even though the authority of the Papacy was not ordained by God, as was that of the law. For God had ordained in the old law everything that took place in the priesthood.

Now even though Luke says that 'the priests and scribes of Jerusalem were gathered together' and expressly mentions the high priest, Caiaphas, John, and Alexander, he does not do so to honour them but to increase their ignominy even more. But because God had appointed them to that status, they were supposed to do a better job than they were doing. It is true they did nothing worthy of condemnation when they came together with all the elders to deal with that matter, for it had to do with a new teaching. And we see the law said that if any difficulty arose because of religion, and even if something new occurred, such things had to be made known. Made known to whom? To the priests and elders of the people (cf. *Deut.* 17:8–13). One could then say in respect of outward appearance that they were only doing their duty and had not failed to do it. However, their purpose is clear. They cannot permit God's truth to be made manifest and allow Jesus Christ to reign, for God his Father sent him expressly for that purpose, so that he might have pre-eminence over the angels, men, and all creation. Consequently, they are indeed observing order and procedure in respect of outward form, but as for the truth, which takes precedence, they proceeded wickedly, as enemies of God.

In addition, they asked by what power and in what name this miracle was done. They admit the miracle was done, a finished act, but they asked by what power so they might know whether the apostles were being deceptive in this matter or whether the devil was up to his tricks. They know for sure that was not the case, but they wanted a reason to arrest the apostles. And that is the way the wicked resist God's truth and make inquiries about it, not to conform themselves to it, but after learning it, they are filled with rage and grind their teeth against it. That is the procedure these men are now following. In short, Luke wanted to show us, as in a mirror, how we must constantly comport ourselves because the devil is relentless in his effort to demolish God's truth. On the other hand, Luke teaches us what we must know if we are to possess the power, righteousness, goodness, and wisdom of God. He also gives us the evidence and proof we need for being confident, no matter how many distracting obstacles we might encounter. Satan will always have enough accomplices in this world to achieve his goals, for the devil must possess all those who are not joined to God and are not his children, and he must use them to fan the fires of contention and confusion everywhere.

In addition, let us consider the practice followed by the wicked and unbelievers. They will, for sure, inquire about God, not to submit to him or to glorify him or even to have a correct understanding of him, but to pervert his truth and turn it into a lie in order to do battle against him by every means possible. And since the evil intent of people is such, what are we to do?

We are to learn that there are other ways to benefit from the works of God, a thing the wicked do not do, and that as soon as we recognize a work as coming from the hand of God, we are to attribute it to his goodness, power, and infinite wisdom. In fact, we have an opportunity, generally speaking, to do just that concerning everything he does throughout the world. Even so, he does even more miraculous works in order to elevate our admiration so we will magnify his name. It is certain that when all is said and done, no work of God is so insignificant that we will not be compelled to wonder at it. But seeing that we are ungrateful and that nothing can move us to gratitude, our Lord shows us, if we are not stirred by his former works, even more wonderful works so that we will be more fully convinced. That is why God, knowing how lukewarm we are, performs more excellent works than we commonly see. That is what we need practice in recognizing if we are to know how God makes himself known to us.

Now let us move to the response given by our Lord through Peter and John as recorded by Luke. First off, he says that Peter, filled with the Holy Spirit, responded, 'Be it known unto you all, and to the people of Israel, that by the name of Jesus Christ of Nazareth, whom you crucified, whom God raised from the dead, even by him this man stands here before you whole.' It is noteworthy that Luke, in recording that, wanted to let us know that man does not have the power to exert the constancy and determination Peter had in this confrontation, and also that his mouth was guided by the Holy Spirit with such wisdom and humility that he errs in nothing. He is not so intimidated that he is speechless. His response is enough to confound them all. In it we see more clearly that man does not have the power to confess Jesus Christ unless the Holy Spirit works in him, as is evident in Peter when he was not being led by God but tried to act according to his own desire. He was so weak and inconstant that just the voice of a simple woman drove him to deny Jesus Christ his Master (*Matt.* 26:69–70). When confronted a second and third time, it is not enough for him to lie; he denies with an oath, becomes very angry, and asks God to curse him if he ever knew the man. So we see that Peter, overcome by nothing more than the voice of a maidservant, denies his master, the one from whom he received so many marks of kindness, and now finds himself in the midst of an honourable council in which the full authority of the people resides. He perceives a power and significance so great as to confound him – and a multitude of people surrounding him and railing against him, and there is no way for him to escape. In short, there he stands like a sheep among a hundred wolves. And yet there he stands, fearing nothing and answering faithfully. Shall we say that that is but the result of his natural disposition? Do we not see there a man very different from what he was before? This is how we know he was powerless to do anything without God working in him by his Holy Spirit. What weakness there was in him while he followed his natural disposition! Now that God holds him in his strong hand, Peter is no longer weak, but so greatly strengthened that no grandeur or awesome presence of any kind can frighten him.

We see then that Luke wanted to show that Peter was strong only because he was filled with the Holy Spirit. And Luke did not say that so much for Peter's sake as for ours so that we might glean a general teaching from it. Let us learn then from Peter's weakness that as soon as God slackens the bridle, we are as weak as Peter was and that there will be no strength in us until God gives it to us from on high. So let us learn that it is the Spirit of God who gives us strength of character. That is why he is called 'the Spirit of strength and power'. That is also why we are weak and infirm when deprived of him.

In addition, we need to note the significance of that response, which is that Peter shows that the only way to be strengthened is to be led by the Holy Spirit. It also shows how we can be instructed to answer whenever we are asked about the teaching of God. We even see that in this statement by Jesus Christ, when he said, 'It is not you that speak, but the Spirit of your Father which speaks in you' (*Matt.* 10:20). From this let us learn that when we are called upon to give an account of our faith, either before the wicked or before the one who will require fruit from it – and he will call us lovingly to account – we will not have to be concerned about what we ourselves are to say, but the Holy Spirit will be obliged to work in the situation. Otherwise, nothing we say will serve any purpose. For that reason, every time we are called upon to make a profession of our faith, we are advised in this passage to entrust ourselves to God so that he will be pleased to enlighten us by his Holy Spirit and strengthen us in such a way that it will be impossible for us to deviate even slightly from maintaining a true Christian stance until death. That, I say, is what we must note in what Luke records, namely that Peter did not answer according to his natural ability but according to the filling of the Holy Spirit.

Yet we have a confirmation to the teaching he adds, for we see that the teaching did not spring from the head of a man, but that the Holy Spirit inspired in Peter what Luke relates here. It is true that inasmuch as he is an apostle of God, about whom even our Lord Jesus Christ bore good witness, we should indeed believe what he tells us in the name of God. Even so, when Luke states it was the Holy Spirit who spoke by the mouth of Peter, we have a teaching which is all the more approved. And what is the upshot of Peter's response? That there is no other name given under heaven among men by which we must be saved except the name of our Lord Jesus Christ. So when we hear that, we must not reply, 'True, but who said it?' We know that the Holy Spirit was its author. We must not, then, doubt it unless we want to become enemies of God and knowingly resist the Holy Spirit. Thus we have one more very useful teaching in Luke's declaration that Peter was filled with the Holy Spirit when answering the high priest and the elders of the people.

Now this is the wording of Peter's response: 'You rulers of the people, and elders of Israel, if we this day be examined of the good deed done to the impotent man, by what means he is made whole; let it be known unto you all, and to all the people of Israel, that by the name of Jesus Christ of Nazareth, whom you crucified, whom God raised from the dead, even by him this man stands here before you whole.' When Peter says, 'Since we are being questioned about having done a good thing', it is to reproach the iniquity and impiety of the priest and the others who were with him. For why would anyone want to punish a man for doing good? We know that justice was ordained to punish the wicked and restrain them in their iniquities. It was also ordained to sustain and honour those who do good. Even nature teaches us that. So, as I said, here Peter wanted to reproach the priests for their malice and perversity because they were rising up against God. It is intolerable that people in responsible positions would use a miracle and turn the attention of the people from the pure and simple teaching of God. They are supposed to look into the matter. And it is about them that Luke is speaking. But knowing that their hearts were stirred up against God and his Son, our Lord Jesus Christ, and that this miracle was not done by the cleverness of the devil, but that it was God who displayed his power, Peter declared with good reason, 'If we are being examined concerning a good deed, since this is what I am being questioned about, it was done in the name of Jesus Christ of Nazareth.'

It is noteworthy that this word 'Nazareth' was added because it was a term of contempt. The more men disparage and reject Jesus Christ, the more Peter demonstrates the majesty which resides in him. It is as if Peter were looking down on the wicked who were trying to destroy his glory, and saying, 'That is the work of Jesus Christ, who appears to be rejected by everyone, but the fact is that he has shown his power by my hand in the healing of this sick man.' He reproaches them even more severely when adding, 'whom you crucified, whom God raised from the dead'. With those words, he makes them God's adversaries. In addition, he shows that their crucifying Jesus Christ did not lessen or destroy his power, for it was restored to him in his glorious resurrection. 'So when our Lord restored him to life, he extended his strong arm and overcame all that you devised against him.' Therein we see that Peter does not spare the priest or the entire congregation of the princes of Jerusalem.

Here Luke makes special mention of the high priest. He mentions the entire high priestly family; he mentions the elders of the people, the scribes and rulers, as if to say, 'These are all those who have the spiritual authority of the church, who are enemies and adversaries of God.' It is true Peter does well to use these honourable titles at the outset when he calls them 'rulers of the people and elders of Israel', but then he adds, 'You are enemies of God, you who crucified the author of life, you who rejected the salvation of the world, you who did all you could to hinder the advancement of the kingdom of God'. He then even tells them what is written in Psalm 118, that they who were to be the children and servants of God's household – for that is what they were called to be – had rejected the chief stone, which became the head of the corner (*Psa.* 118:22). Here we see what kind of 'respect' we are to have for those who are in authority in the church if they do not fulfil their responsibility. The priesthood was not established by men. It is true that, at the time, there were great divisions among the Jews, but the priesthood was always grounded in the ordinance which God had established in his law, from which they had their customary ceremonies and sacrifices.

Well now, the pope will say he is the high priest. But where did he get his appointing authority? Who bestowed upon him that position? Nowhere in all of holy Scripture since Jesus Christ was revealed to the world is it said that a sovereign bishop has been set above all the others. Quite the contrary. It is written that Jesus Christ was the high priest at that time and was established as such in the law of God (*Heb.* 5:5-7, 10), which is not the case for the Papacy. The priests were from the line of Levi and had to be good men of proven worth. Those who are now called priests and bishops in the Papacy, are they established in God's name? But we know how they go about it. We see only illegitimate sons and lewd and lecherous men holding their benefices. Favours are passed around. When the time comes to establish someone in a priestly office, they are passed out indiscriminately, as one would pass out something of no value. Consequently, there is not the slightest resemblance to God's institution that they can boast of in all they do. We can justifiably place them in the ranks of those Luke is talking about, not that they are worthy, but because they imitate them in their cruelty and tyranny.

However, Peter informs them that they are not contending with him and John but that in this confrontation they make themselves enemies of God and our Lord Jesus Christ because they are taking God's spiritual government and conducting it in an unjust and godless manner. In this we see how indefensible the papists' position is when they think it is enough to be ordained in their rank by God – and they are far from being so ordained. But even if they had been ordained by God, having the power to do something is very different from doing it well. A person can indeed be ordained in an office and still pervert its function. It is then a mockery of God to say, 'We have the authority to do this.' What we must give primary consideration is how they honour what has been authorized. Moreover, let us know that if the pope and all his ilk say that we are 'schismatics', that we have troubled the church and have been excluded from Christian communion, we have the consolation that the word of God teaches the opposite. Why then do they charge us with such crimes? Because we do not wish to renounce Jesus Christ and so consent to their abominations; because we do not wish to abandon the true God and submit to idols – in short, because we do not wish to be separated from God's truth. That is why the pope and his whole train of peacocks call us 'schismatics'.

Yet we see that our Lord Jesus Christ receives us and acknowledges us as his own. We see, as I have already said, that we have the witness of the holy Scripture and it approves what we do. That should be a great consolation for us. We must not be frightened by all their threats and all they can throw up against us. For it is all hot air, as we easily gather from this passage.

In addition, when Luke quotes this passage from the Psalm, saying that Jesus Christ is the stone rejected by the builders (*Psa.* 118:22), he shows that no one was more averse to Jesus Christ and his teaching than the priests, who were like the master masons of God's spiritual building. We can easily apply that to the pope and all his stupid coterie. Is there anyone in the world who tries harder than they do to lay waste and destroy the kingdom of our Lord Jesus Christ? Peter cast the priests of his day in that role. That is the way he depicted the malice and perversity that were prevalent at the time Jesus Christ was rejected by those who called themselves the great prelates of the church – and may their rejection of him not prevent God from calling all his people to himself and gathering them in. We must now be comforted by the fact that when those who wish to be known as the principal figures in the church, it will be they who wage war on God and persecute us. Still, we must be comforted, as I said, and say, 'Well, it is true that you falsely assume this honourable title of prelate and keeper of God's house. But Jesus Christ will not forgo being the foundation of our salvation. Although you have rejected him, that does not mean he does not wish to bestow his good favour on us.' That once happened to David. What happened in the Psalm happened subsequently to his church. And yet, if we persevere in the same way, we can be consoled by the fact that we are following in the steps of many notable personages. Let us therefore join with him in his afflictions if we wish to share in the glory he has promised us.

There is not enough time for the rest now. We will reserve that until next Sunday.

Following that sacred teaching, let us bow before the face of our gracious God, acknowledging our faults, praying that he will be pleased to stir us to true repentance and make us so discontented with our sins that we will, after asking his forgiveness, walk in all purity of conscience and, being led by his Holy Spirit, live in this world in such harmony and friendship with one another that unbelievers will themselves see our good works and be constrained to praise him. And as we do this, may his name be magnified and exalted in all and through all. Now let us all say, Almighty God, heavenly Father . . .

11

The Source of All Authority

Sunday, 11 May 1550

Saying, What shall we do to these men? for that indeed a notable miracle hath been done by them is manifest to all them that dwell in Jerusalem; and we cannot deny it. [18] And they called them, and commanded them not to speak at all nor teach in the name of Jesus. [19] But Peter and John answered and said unto them, Whether it be right in the sight of God to hearken unto you more than unto God, judge ye (Acts 4:16, 18–19).

We saw earlier how the enemies of truth, in their procedure, exhibit some appearance of righteousness. On that point we showed how the wicked, in their iniquity, do not show their hand at the outset but put their best foot forward so they might be exempt from every suspicion of evil before men. They only seem to be trying to fulfil their duty. But in the end our Lord confounds them all and reveals their abomination by making their iniquity quite clear even though they had concealed it for a time. And God does that to reveal their hypocrisy whenever they wish to conceal their sham under a pretence of righteousness and holiness and induce others to think they are walking in all uprightness and fairness, while their conscience is filled with fraud and deception before God. That is how our Lord sometimes wishes to close his eyes when permitting the wicked to disguise themselves with some clever mask of hypocrisy to deceive people. But what can be done? Let us wait patiently until the wicked are recognized for what they are and their iniquity is evident even though it has for some time been hidden behind the word 'righteousness' – which is abundantly clear in the current story.

For, as has already been seen, the high priest and the rest of his kind have indeed maintained some formality of righteousness in order to discuss the teaching, as was their duty. Are they confounded in that? Their rage becomes apparent. They lose their sense of judgment and moderation, and they take refuge in malice and cruelty. They condemn themselves with conscious wickedness when they say, 'What shall we do to these men? for that indeed a notable miracle has been done by them is manifest to all those that dwell in Jerusalem; and we cannot deny it' (*Acts* 4:16). And you wicked men, why then do you deliberate against them? When God extended his hand in this deed in such a way that you yourselves say you cannot deny, be aware that it is against him that you contend. So we see how the wicked condemn themselves out of their own mouths. But what difference does that make to them? They no longer have understanding or reason when they battle thus against God. The devil has so blinded them that they no longer see clearly.

Now we must not only be aware that in the end our Lord will unmask the hypocrisy of those who think they can hide from his face. He will reveal their ignorance of the truth for all to see, but we must also be aware that we have a clear indication to walk in the fear of God and in obedience to him. For once people have exceeded the bounds of propriety by abandoning what is good in pursuit of what they know is pernicious and damnable, they can only seek their own ruin and create their own destruction because although God makes himself known to them and invites them in various ways to come to him, they nevertheless withdraw from him as far as they can because they want to follow only what seems good in their eyes without bringing themselves into conformity with the will of God.

So when we see such obstinacy in these evildoers, what are we to do? Let us be careful to exercise self-control with all humility according to the law of God, before adopting a plan of action and stopping there. Let us seek what is pleasing as well as what is displeasing to God, not following our own whims, but let us be governed by his word until he grants us the grace to discern what is good or bad. That is the path we must take if we wish to walk rightly in every aspect of our lives and if we wish to be confident and resolute in doing our duty, saying, 'That is what God approves. That is the path I must follow.' When we do that, it is certain that our Lord will so lead us by his Holy Spirit that he will increase his grace in us day by day so that what was once unknown to us will become increasingly easy to understand.

Why do men go from bad to worse if not because of their addiction to their own inventions and their refusal to yield to what God declares in his word? That is a hardening that will cause us to fall into a pit because, by lingering too long over our frivolous notions, God leaves us to our devices so it will be very difficult for us ever to approach him since we withdraw from him consciously and willingly. May we never be so obstinate that we say, 'I am going to do whatever I please, no matter what I am told.' Take care to avoid such impertinence. But when we realize things are not going well even though we are well on the way, let us reverse our path as soon as we learn from the word of God that we are in error. For although we might have gone astray for a time, that will not keep us from knowing the right path to follow, provided however that we not be obstinate when admonished.

In fact, we see how Paul boasts of having followed what was pleasing to God, when he says, 'I have fought a good fight.' Why does he boast? He bore in his conscience a confident witness that he had not abandoned himself to vain and frivolous fantasies but that God had instructed him in the teaching which he had borne and received from God alone. So let us not doubt that God guides us and leads us where we must go if we permit him to govern us. Before we undertake any action at all, we must remember what God has made known to us and what pleases him. Then we must be mindful of the grace we receive from God when our conscience bears testimony that our intention is good and right. What torment must those wretches of whom Luke speaks experience when they say in protest that this sign performed by the apostles proceeds from the power of God and they nonetheless make every effort to resist it! They certainly have to be rabid and demented to fly off their hinges that way! For that would be equivalent to saying clearly, 'I shall be the enemy of God and stand against him with all my might.' So let us be aware that taking a stand against God is the worst condition that can befall a person. For we cannot possibly know how to please him unless we align ourselves with his righteousness and his word.

We still have to look at everything Luke has shown us here. On the one hand, he shows us how God's enemies try to prevent the apostles from speaking further in the name of Jesus Christ. And they do so with a malevolent awareness, thinking that in that way they will shut the mouths of God's servants and keep them from witnessing to the word, but for all their efforts they do not hinder the Lord's work. In fact, he shows us the depth of the apostles' faithfulness and how they bore up stead-fastly. Although those who were forbidding them to speak thought they were successful in their effort, the apostles remained quite resolute. 'Because God has commanded us to speak, we must not be hindered by men.' The word he has put in our mouths must run its course, no matter what roadblocks men strive to throw up before us. Such is Luke's lesson for us in the present passage.

Just as the example of these wicked men teaches us not to oppose God but to yield ourselves in obedience to everything he is pleased to show us in his word, so the apostles point us to the road we must follow. That is, we must withstand the threats and the exalted position of men and not waver in our duty. We must take a stand and faithfully fulfil what God demands of us even when it would appear that those who exercise authority over us have the right to enjoin us to forgo proclaiming and supporting our Master's cause. We must realize that they do not, for he honours us by calling us for that very purpose. Now in order to do this, we must be grounded in the knowledge that throughout our lives we are to endeavour to follow God's commands, for it is he who guides and direct us in everything we do. It is true men are able to impose laws upon us, as is the custom of princes, kings, and magistrates, who are in authority over others, but those laws are also to guide us and direct us to God. In all this, however, our Lord always reserves sovereignty for himself. When establishing princes and magistrates, he does so not to diminish his honour or relinquish his right but to be honoured by them in their position. They are to rule in his stead. They are his lieutenants, as it were, because all the world's principalities and dominions are subject to him. In the same way that a sergeant or an officer of the law is subject to the judge and under his authority and does nothing without the authority of his superior, so princes and magistrates, however great, must attempt nothing against the will of God, nor can they. The prevailing general rule is that God must govern us.

However, we must equally note that whatever office we occupy, our Lord makes our responsibility clear. There is a general rule which he sets before all the faithful. It is that law which contains the Ten Commandments. Beyond that, he declares to each officeholder his responsibility in the context of his calling. If a man has the authority to direct and govern others, the word of God shows him why he has been elevated to that position and how he must comport himself in it. The same is true for all officeholders. Our Lord will make it clear to a wicked man what he must do. Likewise, a man of low estate will be instructed concerning his duty. It is true that those who have resisted him all their lives have the notion that they are not obliged to obey in anyway whatsoever. They have such contempt for God and his word that they adamantly refuse to submit to his will. As for the faithful, on the other hand, God will not permit them to rise up against him because they present themselves to him with humility so that he may govern them. It is as I have said before. We must not presume to set up anything which contravenes God's teaching. As soon as he makes clear what his will is, we must follow where he leads. Do we understand that?

It must be clear to us that God does not exempt us from all the troubles and vexations that might arise from the malice and cruelty of men. It is true that sometimes men have an aura that will dazzle our eyes, but when we return to what God has ordained, we have a level road, a level field, where we can see in the distance our goal straight ahead of us. Try as they may to obscure our vision, God will give light to our path if our refuge is in him, even if we are surrounded by total darkness. So, the moment a person finds himself hindered in what he ought to be doing, let him lift his head high and heed God's command. It is certain God will guide him in such a way that what he feared will turn out well. For what is the most frequent cause of our greatest perplexity? It is that we do not heed God and turn to him for help, going rather in many directions, and that causes the discomfort we feel because of our unfaithfulness and ingratitude. If we were steadfast, as we should be, we would have already come to that conclusion. And since all powers and authorities are subject to God, it is better to obey him than men. That should be our mindset when we hear the answer the apostles give those who forbade them to teach in the name of Jesus Christ, when they say, 'Judge whether it is right to obey you rather than God.' It is as if they were saying, 'How presumptuous and arrogant of you to compare yourselves with God! Who are you poor wretches? Should we forgo serving and obeying God in order to please you?' That response removes every doubt we might have.

But to have a better understanding of the situation, let us take a look at the individuals the apostles are speaking to. We have the high priest and all those who had the oversight of the entire spiritual regimen. They constitute, in effect, a council of that assembly which is made up of the scribes, the Pharisees, and all the elders. We have a council in session. There can be no doubt there is among them a great display of correctness and fairness, for they seem to want to impose order upon the disorder which has arisen. And because they claim for themselves the title church of God, they say the church cannot err. It is imminently true that the true church of God will never rise up against him – for that is impossible – but because we are all capable of mistakes, we can err. When God speaks in his church, he does not rise up against himself, nor do the faithful, for he preserves them. That is why the church will never be able to resist God, but those who possess the title will resist God when they wish to corrupt and pervert everything so they can keep the title.

We have an example of that in this passage. There is no question that there was a church of God among the Jews, and it is to them that God gave the pre-eminence in his church, those who are now so rebellious they are now trying to destroy the church of God and doing what they can to prevent the proclamation of the word of life. Yet they continue to show outwardly their great zeal for God's honour. In this way, their impressive appearance and authority were able to dazzle the apostles and give them pause: 'What shall we do? For even though they are filled with all malice, they still have the title of church of God, and if we resist their injunction and command, they will consider us as rebels both against God and all civil order.' As a consequence, the apostles could have been disturbed and perplexed had they considered only that outward appearance of ecclesial authority the Jews claimed to have. But, as I have already said, they had already made up their minds to be guided by the word of God. So, knowing that God was on their side, they concluded that all those who rise up against them are minions of the devil and will finally be confounded. In all things, God must remain the master despite all opposition. Whenever confronted by people of impressive appearance, even if they seem to be angels from heaven, we must always return to this response: 'We must obey God rather than men.'

However, there is more to be said about what we have just considered, namely that the higher worldly powers must be limited and regulated by the principle that God must be in sovereign control of his empire and that we must not turn away from his word. Today we are aware of how the great of this world abuse their authority. The purpose behind their lust for power is not to rule and govern this poor world so they can maintain it in the love and fear of God and in the observance on his commandments. Honouring God and advancing his kingdom are the least of their concerns. They have in mind only their personal interests. They are filled with pride, ambition, and arrogance. It is enough for them that others talk about them. And the devil is quite aware there is no better way to mislead the poor world than when the princes and magistrates who rule it are concerned only about themselves and not about the welfare of the people. It is true that while a prince and a governor hold the power which has been ordained by God, the devil will have no power over them, but because they immediately turn away from the right path because they are ambitious and power hungry for their own advantage,

Satan will seduce them from every side. He will deceive those who have the spiritual care of the church, and he will corrupt everything to the degree that both he and they will want to continue under the noble and honourable titles they usurp, as we have observed in our experience. The pope will not admit that he wants to rise up against God and that the dominion he enjoys is diabolical and damnable, but he will say that he is the vicar of Jesus Christ, the successor of Peter, a servant of all Christians, and head and principal figure of the whole church. And that whole menagerie of priests and monks and his other mitred beasts will call themselves pillars of the church. But we understand they are the greatest enemies of God's truth who have ever lived. For they seek nothing if not the destruction of Jesus Christ and his gospel. Now what is the reason for that? It was the devil's deceit and craftiness that upset every good order and induced men to abuse the authority which God invested in his church. On the other hand, we see how the great and powerful of this world are destined to prevent God from being served as he should be. And why is that? Because they wish to continue the superstitions that have come out of the corruption of the church, which has been subverted by the traditions of men. They create statutes and ordinances which they compel men to obey, saying that every higher authority must be obeyed. That is true, but we always have to come back to what I said earlier, namely that sovereignty must always remain in God's hands, that all dominions and principalities must be subject to him, and that anything which pertains to his honour and glory must not diminish even slightly, but increase.

Let us suppose there is a judge who has a sergeant under him. If the sergeant arrogates to himself the judge's authority and attempts to work against him, which one should I obey? The sergeant or the judge? It is certain the officer will be condemned for his presumptuousness and discharged for his rebellious and disloyal behaviour. But in this case we are only dealing with mortal men.

Now if we make a comparison between God and men, what difference will we find? We have the living God, to whom belong all dominion and sovereignty, as Paul says. Are those installed in an office endowed with some natural right? Absolutely not! They possess only what God has given them. What then are all the kings, princes, and others who have dominion in this world if not God's sergeants and officers? When they undertake a project outside his authority, even taking a position against him, am I obliged to obey them? Certainly not! From this let us learn that when rendering dutiful obedience to those who have some authority over us, we must always add the condition that God does not lose his right. For example, it is true that we must listen with all reverence to those who proclaim the word of God, and we must receive their teaching in all humility so we may be increasingly strengthened by it, since it proceeds from the very mouth of God. But if they abuse their office and corrupt the pure word of God with their lies, what authority are they to have among us? We should, rather, consider them an abomination, for they are worthy of double condemnation because they wickedly abuse the name of God. The same applies to kings and princes. They are certainly to be honoured, provided they govern us according to the word of God, but when they want to rise against him and try to silence the ministers of the word of God in order to make it completely ineffective, what obedience do we owe such governors? Those who have the sword in hand must consider what God had in mind when raising them to their position. I am not speaking only about those abject wretches whose like we sometimes see. But even if they happen to be the greatest princes in the world, they must realize, I say, that they are there so that God, through their administration, may reign among them and their subjects and be served and honoured in the process.

On the other hand, what is to be done when they try hard to destroy God's teaching and obscure his all-powerful and creative word to such an extent that people no longer listen to it? They must be confronted with this teaching: 'We must obey God rather than men.' Therefore, when we are armed with that conviction and learn to walk in the fear of God and depend on him, we will never be alarmed when those things occur and the wicked rise up in such ways against God. So that we may know the arrogance and presumptuousness of those wretched men, and not be surprised by them, we must be instructed in our responsibilities. For despite all their considerable efforts to thwart God's authority, they must in the end realize that it is God who is to be obeyed and not men, and that there is no power or authority on earth, as I have said, that God does not control and govern according to his will and good pleasure. Whatever men may undertake, let it be their goal to give God the pre-eminence and not encroach on his authority, but to serve and honour him as they should.

Now just as those who are under subjection are instructed how to behave toward their superiors, so too those who have a position of authority are instructed what they are to do. Are we charged with bearing witness to God's word? To that end, we must be resolved to obey God rather than men. Let kings, princes, and magistrates bear in mind that they too must pay homage to Jesus Christ, as it is written in the second Psalm, not with pretence or hypocrisy, but in very truth, acknowledging that all they have proceeds from him and his unstinting liberality. We see from the apostles' response how true and useful the command is to 'judge whether it is lawful to obey men rather than God.' For they are using this way of speaking to show that that truth is so obvious that people ought to be ashamed even to resist it. As a matter of fact, you will not find anyone so wicked that he would dare say, 'Men ought to be obeyed rather than God.' What man, however

twisted, would not say it is better to obey God than men? Yet we
do not wish to say it out loud, but we will show it by our acts. And
we will be even more inexcusable when we show greater fear of
men by obeying them rather than God himself. And that is what
the Holy Spirit wanted to get across when he spoke through the
apostles, saying, 'Judge for yourselves whether it is lawful to obey
men rather than God'. The apostles were well aware that those
to whom they were speaking were wretched enemies of God and
his word. Yet they postponed judgment on that point, as if to say,
'Even though your wickedness extends to seeking the nullification
of God's teaching – if that were at all possible – you are reluctant
to say it is preferable to obey you rather than God. You know God
is to be honoured above all. Yet when you wish to rebel against
him, you will have less justification for your transgression, which
you will, to your great misfortune, be obliged to account for before
God.'

Therefore, when we see that God must perforce be preferred
to men, which is only reasonable, what will happen to us who have
the gospel? We have Jesus Christ as our sovereign prince. Shall we
then obey men rather than him? Shall we, because of the fear we
have of men and of displeasing them, soil and contaminate ourselves with their superstitions and share in their unfruitful works
of darkness? And in this way, do we not indeed reveal that we
obey men rather than God? When we follow their lead, there is
no doubt that God will not tolerate such betrayal. He will take
vengeance and make us feel the punishment we deserve.

Therefore, since it pleases our beneficent God to grant us the
knowledge of all these things, let us beseech him to deliver us from
everything that might keep us from following him where he leads
and from doing what he reveals in his word, so that, entrusting
ourselves to him and his goodness, we will never be kept from
reaching his everlasting kingdom, to which he is now calling us.

Following this holy teaching, let us bow before the face of our gracious God in recognition of our sins, because of which we endlessly and daily provoke his anger against us. Let us pray that he will be pleased so to touch us with true penitence and repentance that we will learn to yield ourselves to him in complete obedience. And may he be pleased to help us in our infirmities and rid us all of all our worldly burdens so there will be nothing to keep us from his everlasting care as his beloved children. Let us now say together, Almighty God, heavenly Father . . .

12

No Peace Where There Is Preaching

Sunday, 18 May 1550

So when they had further threatened them, they let them go, finding nothing how they might punish them, because of the people: for all men glorified God for that which was done. [22] *For the man was above forty years old, on whom this miracle of healing was shewed.* [23] *And being let go, they went to their own company, and reported all that the chief priests and elders had said unto them.* [24] *And when they heard that, they lifted up their voice to God with one accord, and said, Lord, thou art God, which hast made heaven, and earth, and the sea, and all that in them is:* [25] *Who by the mouth of thy servant David hast said, Why did the heathen rage, and the people imagine vain things?* [26] *The kings of the earth stood up, and the rulers were gathered together against the Lord, and against his Christ* (Acts 4:21–26).

God has many ways at his disposal to preserve us, ways that are unknown to us. And without recognizing them, we must remain fully assured and confident of their existence, so that we can rest in him and take refuge in him as often as we perceive a troubling danger, and be able to say, 'God will provide.' For guidance, let us learn to lay hold of the providence of God, and let us not yield to our human judgment and what seems good to us. For when it seems to us that we are completely lost, our Lord will find a way for us to escape which is not previously known to us, and when he shows it to us, we will be surprised. That is what Luke means here when he says that the priests, following much discussion and opposition in their encounter with Peter and John, who were like two poor sheep before devouring wolves, were nonetheless unable to do anything to them. After exhausting all the ways to find fault with them and condemn them, they had to let them go unharmed. And what is the reason for that? It is not that they fear God and, convinced of the truth, wish to align themselves with it, but they fear the people. Thus we see that our Lord granted them understanding in order to frighten them, quell their rage, and render them helpless against his servants. That is how he deals with the wicked. When it looks like they want to bring us down and destroy us completely, he knows how to save us from their hands. As to how, that is not for us to know. He will find ways that we cannot now imagine. What happened to Peter and John was not for that one time only, for our Lord wanted to use that to show us that if we put our confidence in him, he will indeed be able to prevent the wicked from exerting their rage, even though they spew their venom against us relentlessly.

Moreover, we are admonished not to marvel if the wicked refrain from doing evil at times and even do good, for it is not out of desire that they have to serve God, but their good actions stem from their human concerns. They do what they do to acquire advantage or to avoid some danger or some harm which might befall them.

The faithful, on the other hand, must behave very differently. Not only must they refrain from every appearance of evil, but they must also, while doing good, keep their eyes fixed on God and hold him in such reverence that they restrain themselves. For example, a wicked man wishes to do harm, if possible, but when it appears he cannot bring off his evil deed because of immediate resistance, he is intimidated. That fear which grips his mind prevents him from achieving his purpose. Now, where is God? For sure, God does not enter into his thinking. It is quite true that our Lord does sometimes touch the wicked with an awareness of his majesty, but mostly they are influenced by the opinions of men. The fact, however, is that God keeps them fettered, as it were, so they are unable to harm those they would have liked to devour.

That is the lesson to be learned from this passage. The fact that the scribes and Pharisees let the apostles go unharmed does not mean that they reverence God and want to honour him by obeying his truth, or even that they recognize it is unlawful for them to disparage God's majesty and impinge on his authority. What then does it mean? That they fear only the people! We see that every day in our own experience. A wicked man will do some good deed or other. If he is occasionally in a state of uprightness, he will act like a good and worthy man. And why is that? Because he thinks he is compelled to do as men do. He would say within himself, 'Unless I give some indication of human virtue, they will all spit in my face and expel me as a wicked man.' That is what impels the wicked to do something that looks good outwardly. But, as I have said, they do not act out of their zeal to serve and honour God in their conduct and in the calling which they have from him. They act only to hide their venom and their wicked hearts under their hypocrisy. Yet, what rationale will they be able to offer before God? They should not erroneously think they can hide from him and deceive him the way they do people.

Let us take the case of a judge who sets a fair punishment for a criminal. By all outward appearances, the decision is praiseworthy, but it is not if we consider that he does it for his own advantage and not out of an inward sense of justice. Now, if another comes along who is as guilty of the same crime as the former and the judge sentences him, and the judge still lets him go and himself gains the man's deliverance so far as he can as a favour to the criminal or for personal advantage – is that anyway to execute justice? Would we say such a man is just? Well, think what you like, but God says that man is a scoundrel! He might as well go cut someone's throat in the deep woods, if he is a judge and a magistrate and is not proceeding lawfully and completely impartially in everything he does.

That also follows what the prophet [blank] says. When our Lord wishes to punish the [blank] for their iniquities, he commands [blank] to take vengeance. But does he do it with genuine zeal? Not at all! He does it to get the kingdom. Yet our Lord does not praise him for that but says he will punish him as he would a base murderer. In that fact, we see the wicked could be thought of from the world's perspective as angels and still be as wicked as ever in God's sight. For if we search their hearts, we will find only hypocrisy in all they do. We will recognize their pretence in the fact that they will do both good and evil in a similar situation. When we bring God into the picture, we are always on the same footing and adhere to one and the same practice. We must not only refrain from doing evil because we can be rebuked for it before men, but because we fear God. The person who, out of hypocrisy, pretends to be an upright man changes his intent at a moment's notice. If someone comes to him for help, he will help him and in the next minute wrong him. When that happens, we know there is only evil in his heart.

Let us learn from this to abstain from all evil and do good, not to please men, not out of consideration for our advantage or disadvantage, but because we must obey God's will, which he has made known to us. It is only right that we should show we honour him by doing good because we fear offending him. That is how we will be reckoned as truly faithful. Yet, in order to fulfil our duty by obeying all his commands, we must close our eyes to all the dangers which might arise. We understand why that is necessary. For as soon as our Lord confronts us with a task and shows us our responsibility, the devil becomes vigilant and tries to turn us from it. 'If I get involved in that, what will happen? I have no idea how I will escape.' That is the way our minds work; that is how our natural reason leads us along when we do not trust God entirely. That is the devil's craftiness at work. For, as I have said, as soon as God teaches us how we are to act in all of our undertakings, the devil confronts us to thwart us and make us change our plans. In this way, he soon conquers us and turns our heads so as to lead us astray. He will entice us from the straight and narrow path if we close our eyes to the dangers which might frighten us.

We must be firmly committed to asking the Lord to continue to sustain us at all times just as he sustained those who trusted him. We must be especially strong in that knowledge when the advancement of the kingdom of our Lord Jesus Christ is at stake. In the first place, the preaching of the gospel is boxed in by the world. Most people cannot tolerate the gospel. The devil does everything he can to keep it from ever being preached. We are aware of the great difficulties and resistance which preaching encounters. Now those who are committed to serving God by preaching his word under those circumstances understand clearly that they must engage in relentless war and be dedicated unreservedly to the task, and yet, despite all the dangers that might arise, they must not shirk their responsibility. Why not? Because God is powerful to sustain us in the encounter.

Yet, let us always return to what Luke tells us here, that God has delivered his apostles from the mouths of wolves. However, even though they see very great dangers, which might have prevented them from following their calling, they persisted in serving God by preaching the gospel. The text says the priests, scribes, and Pharisees, and those who had all authority in Jerusalem forbade them with threats to continue speaking in the name of Jesus Christ. Hearing that, what might the apostles have thought to themselves? 'If we as much as open our mouths to talk about Jesus, we are done for. They will no longer accuse us of teaching falsely, but they will rebuke us for being rebels and schismatics, disturbers of the peace and contemptuous of all rule of law. That will be reason enough for them to condemn us. On the other hand, God's name will be blasphemed whenever the wicked scheme to punish us, claiming we have rebelled against the rule of law and against lawful directives.' That is how pressure from the authorities was able to frighten the apostles and influence them away from their duty. But how do the apostles react in this circumstance? They go to the entire company of believers and tell them everything that happened and about the threats to stop preaching about Jesus Christ. And after hearing what they had to say, the company of believers pray to God and entrust themselves to his promises because he said that kings and princes will rise up against his Christ but in the end will be confounded. Then they all raise their voices to God with one accord and pray that he will give them boldness to speak and bear witness to his word.

When we observe such boldness, we must take note that our Lord did not intend for this account to accrue to the praise of the apostles for what they did, but he offers it to us as a mirror to teach us to take strength from their example at times when we might be frightened, when inconveniences and troubles come to us. In such times, we must remind ourselves to say, 'Lord, the advancement of the kingdom of your Son is challenged, and you have said you will sustain us, so now may it please you to grant unto us such boldness that we will not fail to witness steadfastly in spite of all the threats and defiances of men.' That then shows we and the angels of heaven are to have our hearts strengthened in the love of God so we may serve him and honour him above all else, and strengthened in the love of our neighbour so we may love him as ourselves.

Therefore, when we recognize that Jesus Christ has done us a great good, we must be moved to thank him for it and praise his name. That, I say, is the way we ought to think. But how many of us do? That is why we ought to ponder the meaning of this passage even more, for we cannot rightly ask God to answer our prayers unless we are of one accord and obey what Jesus teaches us by his Spirit and through his gospel.

Let us now consider the content of the prayer which the apostles and other believers offer, as Luke presents it. 'Lord', he says, 'you are the God who made heaven and earth, the sea and all that is in them; who by the mouth of your servant David has said, Why did the heathen rage, and the people imagine vain things? The kings of the earth, and the rulers were gathered together against the Lord and against his Christ.' There are two main points to make here. One is that the faithful are comforted by trusting in God's promises, and that fact places them beyond all the fear and unfaithfulness which might prevent them from fulfilling what God demands of them, and then they take heart and invoke God. The second point is stated in these words: 'Lord, you have spoken through the mouth of your servant David, saying that the peoples, the kings and the rulers rise up against you and your Christ.' When the apostles quote this passage, it is as if they are saying, 'Lord, we trust in your promise that these will perish in their vanity. For try as they may to hinder us, they will not prevail because you have already declared it, and we trust what you have said.' That is how the faithful arm themselves with God's promise so as not to be frightened by all the dangers which they might encounter from men. But, not content with simply proclaiming the promises of God, they pray. And that is what we must do. And if we receive the promises of God as we should, where will they lead us if not to prayer? That is the second thing we should note.

Let us look now at the promise which elicits their prayer: 'You said by the mouth of your servant David: "Why have the great men of the earth and the people conspired against you and your Christ?"' There is no doubt that David, when speaking that way, did not wish to restrain the folly and presumption of the kings and rulers who wanted to rise up against God. We must take note, however, that he is not speaking out of his own imagination, that he is not led by flesh and blood, but that the utterance is from God himself. Therefore, he speaks with a prophet's authority and not as a private individual. It is God who is speaking through him as by his own mouth. Thus, David did not have himself in mind, but realizing that he is a figure of Jesus Christ and that what was happening within him would inevitably be accomplished in the person of our Lord Jesus Christ, he wrote this second Psalm, which extends through the whole of Jesus Christ's kingdom. It is true that when Jesus Christ appeared in the world, that prophecy was fulfilled in him and at the same time extends even farther, notably to his entire reign so we might know he will never reign in this world without turmoil, divisions, and cares. There will always be wars to the extent that Jesus Christ's kingdom will not be at peace until he has made his enemies his footstool, just as David declares in Psalm 110. Now when will this be? Not before the last day. Consequently, David is not thinking only about what will be fulfilled in the person of Jesus Christ while he is living in this world, and does not wish to restrict these words. But he does show us that while we are in this world, Jesus Christ will always have enemies who do everything they can to overthrow his gospel and keep it from being preached.

We must pay close attention to that, for it is a very necessary warning. Why so? Because we tend to think we will one day have a peaceful gospel. In that, we are mistaken, and we deserve to be, for our Lord derides our foolish hopes when we are so foolish and arrogant that we expect the opposite of what he has said. Here we have our Lord declaring to us through his word that if we wish to serve the Lord Jesus Christ and follow him, we will never have rest in this world. In this world, we want to persuade ourselves that we will have peace. And when we do that, are we not mocking him and his word? Therefore, let us not be so quick to expect this or that, but let us realize that Jesus Christ will reign in this world only with great strife and hardship, and that those who wish to be considered one of his will not be without troubles, cares, and persecutions.

But there is more. It will not be three or four who will make war against him, not the poor and not the people of low estate, but the nations and the great of the earth will rise up against him. When the great are spoken of, it is to show that the world's power will be against him; and when the nations are spoken of, it is to indicate a great, almost infinite multitude. So let us not think that a small number of people is to attack Jesus Christ's kingdom. No, no. A multitude on the one hand, and power and authority on the other, will rise up against his kingdom to beat it down and destroy it. What good will it do them? None! That, too, is what David wishes to point out when he begins this Psalm: 'Why do the heathen rage, and the people imagine a vain thing?' With those words, he derides the foolish arrogance of the kings and rulers and all who rise up against God. Why? Because it is quite obvious that they can do nothing against him, but that he will bring them down and destroy them in their presumption. That is the same point Paul makes when he says, 'If God be for us, who can be against us?' That is like saying, 'Since God is on our side and holds us in his strong hand, everybody in the world should avoid seeking our ruin. Instead of achieving their goal, they will bring themselves down.'

Now let us not think that you have to rise above the clouds to challenge God. But know that anyone who wishes to hinder the course and preaching of the gospel, and resists it with all his might, stands against God.

We do not have time now to deal with the rest of the text, but we will hold it until next Sunday. In the meantime, we must remember that our Lord wishes to advance his kingdom, knowing full well that his gospel will be persecuted and that wicked men will rise up against it, even though they profess being Christian. We, on the other hand, must take refuge in this teaching: although the kings and rulers and peoples rise up against Jesus Christ and his followers, they will gain nothing but their destruction. Among others, the in-house enemies of God and his word deserve a greater condemnation because, under the pretext of peace and goodwill, they wage war on Jesus Christ, and that is much worse than waging it openly. Let us take pains to avoid being in-house enemies of Jesus Christ. But since we profess to be Christian, let us demonstrate by our actions that we are what we confess with our mouths to be.

We must especially keep that in mind because next Sunday we are to share in the holy Supper of our Lord Jesus Christ, which will be placed before us. It is true that every day through the preaching of the gospel we share in all the good things our Lord Jesus Christ has acquired for us. But we are strengthened more when he declares to us through the Supper that we are participants in his substance, that we live in him and he in us – unless we betray him and, under the pretext of being his disciples, are his mortal enemies. Above all else, let us avoid that, for that judgment pronounced by David against all who rise up against God will fall on us also. But there are very few who bear that in mind. We see that the mortal enemies of the gospel will show no reluctance to come and present themselves as brothel whores, brazen with their hatreds, their grudges, their controversies, to participate in the holy Supper of Jesus Christ, without considering what it means for us or why it is administered to us. By that we know they come to it only to make a show and discharge a duty. The rest of the time, how often do they show up for the sermon? We only see their empty seats. Nothing more. That is not the way we are to come to this sacred table. Each person, within himself, must be prepared; he must abandon his old hatreds and grudges and come to the table with all reverence and humility. Let us all be joined together in true unity and brotherly love and, in union with our head and captain, Jesus Christ, let us truly be the people of God so that we may triumph with him in his kingdom, which he has prepared for all who steadfastly resist all the dangers that might confront those who abide in his word.

Following that sacred teaching, let us fall before the face of our gracious God, acknowledging our sins and praying that he will be pleased to grant us knowledge of his goodness, which he disposes toward us when sharing with us his well-beloved Son, our Lord Jesus Christ, in such a way that we may be able to entrust ourselves completely to him, and that we may yield to his leading so that, not being led astray by the lusts of the flesh, we may commit ourselves to his holy will until he has fully clothed us with himself by cleansing us of ourselves. In this way let us all say, Almighty God, heavenly Father . . .

13

The Prayer of Faith

Pentecost Sunday, 25 May 1550

And when they heard that, they lifted up their voice to God with one accord, and said, Lord, thou art God, which hast made heaven, and earth, and the sea, and all that in them is: [25] *Who by the mouth of thy servant David hast said, Why did the heathen rage, and the people imagine vain things?* [26] *The kings of the earth stood up, and the rulers were gathered together against the Lord, and against his Christ.* [27] *For of a truth against thy holy child Jesus, whom thou hast anointed, both Herod, and Pontius Pilate, with the Gentiles, and the people of Israel, were gathered together,* [28] *For to do whatsoever thy hand and thy counsel determined before to be done.* [29] *And now, Lord, behold their threatenings: and grant unto thy servants, that with all boldness they may speak thy word,* [30] *By stretching forth thine hand to heal; and that signs and wonders may be done by the name of thy holy child Jesus.* [31] *And when they had prayed, the place was shaken where they were assembled together; and they were all filled with the Holy Ghost, and they spake the word of God with boldness* (Acts 4:24–31).

If our works are not grounded in faith, they are not pleasing to God. We must, then, hold fast to the principle set forth here. That is, if we want our faith to be strong, we must consider God's power when praying and mention the promises which we rely on.

We have here a good example in this prayer recorded by Luke. The disciples begin by saying, 'Lord, you are God, who has made heaven, and earth, and the sea, and all that is in them.' Why do they at this point invoke the creation of the world? They do it to strengthen themselves in the power of God and in the confidence that his power is sufficient to sustain them in the presence of every danger.

We cannot have confidence in God as we ought unless we are firmly convinced that he disposes of all things in accordance with his will so that all creatures are subject to him. That stems from the fact that he created all things. We have to know that, owing to his authority and pre-eminence, everything in heaven and on earth is in his hand and is upheld by his power and might. Therefore, we need to take note of two things. The first is that if we are to pray to God certain that he will answer us, we must not doubt his power, and we must know nothing can keep him from helping us and delivering us from all the dangers which might befall us. So if we have that kind of confidence when we approach God, we will never fail to pray effectively.

The second is that we must be assured of the power of God, which we can ponder not only in the creation of the world, but also in its continuation. Our Lord did not just create the heaven and the earth and all they contain only to relinquish his rights as though he were no longer interested in taking care of it. Creation must always be sustained by his power; otherwise, it could not continue for a single minute. Therefore, since our Lord holds all created things in his hand, let us not doubt that he is sufficient to preserve us and lead us in all our undertakings provided we turn to him alone. It is not enough to have experienced the power of God. We must add to it his promises, by which he conveys his benevolent will and love toward us. Those who address the power of God and only create a fantasy in their minds without considering his promises and the goodness which he has exercised from all time and still wishes to exercise toward us – they and all their imaginings will reap only condemnation. It is true that when we think about God's exalted majesty, we are not thunderstruck. But to be truly certain, we must come to the knowledge that God is all-powerful and wishes to fulfil all his promises to us. When we are in possession of these two things, we have the right introduction to praying effectively, and our prayers will not be vain unless of course God grants us everything we could ask for concerning our salvation. That, then, is the principle manifested here and exemplified by the apostles in what they did.

We now need to pay attention to the fact that this prayer is made, in general, on behalf of the whole church and also for the advancement of our Lord Jesus Christ's kingdom. This is not a prayer for a particular moment or day. We must keep it before us until the end of the world as a perpetual reminder of a true pattern for praying to God. It is always our duty to beseech him to be pleased to sustain his church since he is her protector and takes that responsibility upon himself.

Subsequently, we need to pray that he will be pleased to magnify and exalt the name of his beloved Son, our Lord Jesus Christ, to the end that he alone will reign and that all will pay homage to him and come humble themselves before him. The fact is that when we pray for the coming of God's reign, it cannot take place until Jesus Christ reigns and everyone submits to his majesty. God does not wish to rule over us apart from the person of Jesus Christ his Son. That is the reason he sent him into the world. And yet we cannot be raised into that glory which our Lord promises his elect until Jesus Christ is exalted among us and each one of us acknowledges him as king and sovereign ruler by allowing him to lead us and make us his subjects, completely obedient to him in all things. How, then, do the disciples entrust themselves to the promises of God in this case? They know it is written, 'In vain have the kings and rulers of the world conspired to destroy the kingdom of Jesus Christ.' When God's enemies have conspired against him in every way possible, he will resist them in such a way that their futile efforts will go up in smoke. Did not David say that? Let us realize that our Lord will show us in deeds that when men have done all they can to destroy Jesus Christ's kingdom, he will sustain it in spite of them and it will increase. That is how we must arm ourselves with God's promises and use them as a shield against all possible difficulties.

The apostles' petition in this passage must not be forgotten. What do they do in face of the uprising against Jesus Christ? They take refuge in God and lean on his promises. It is true one might have thought, from the world's perspective, that there was no expectation that the gospel would continue to be made known and preached. It did indeed seem that everything would be destroyed and that Jesus Christ, along with his gospel, would be subjugated, but because the disciples have God's promises, they turn a blind eye to anything which could prevent them from witnessing faithfully to the word, for they were highly confident God would fulfil his promises and everything he had spoken by the mouth of his prophets. They cling to that truth as certain and infallible, knowing they will not be disappointed in their hope because its foundation is strong. That is a very useful and even indispensable teaching for this day and time, for the condition of God's poor church is evident. We see that the most eminent in this world are moved by a relentless intention to overthrow the gospel and keep it from being preached. We also see the great persecutions directed against the faithful. What conclusion can we draw from that when we evaluate things with our natural understanding? It seems we will not be able to last three days; but then we lift up our eyes and consider God's power. Then let us add the promises God has made to sustain us and keep us in all things and everywhere. There can be nothing then that can overwhelm us and take away our desire to serve God or to preach the gospel faithfully for the purpose of increasing and advancing the kingdom of our Lord Jesus Christ from day to day in spite of all those who connive and conspire to put an end to it. It behoves us then to remember that the kingdom of our Lord Jesus Christ will last forever.

Why do you think we will see many changes and much disorder in the kingdoms of this world? Because everything is in decay and transitory. But since Jesus Christ's kingdom is of heaven, it is of necessity permanent. On that point, the prophets testify that of his kingdom there will be no end (*Dan.* 2:44; 6:27). Then we are told it is God who sustains us by his power and might. Consequently, we have good reason for our assurance. Now is that statement about Jesus Christ's kingdom what our salvation is based on? It is certain that if he does not reign among us, we will not finally reign with him. We must always have our attention fixed on God's power and might, and then on his promises, through which he makes known to us that the kingdom of his Son Jesus Christ will be everlasting. That is all the more reason for us to engage that doctrine, for we are assailed on all sides by many enemies. Our own flesh urges us to yield to our desires and wicked affections. The devil asks for nothing but to deliver us over to despair. As soon as we encounter some minor persecution, we put on another face, as we say, not wanting to be recognized as what we wish to be. Where does that impulse come from? From Satan, who wishes to attack us on one side, while the world, our physical comforts, and our worldly conveniences assail us from the other. But if we earnestly fix our attention on God's power and on his promises, those kinds of troubles and perplexities will not befall us. When all the kings of the earth have cleverly connived and conspired and have used all their tricks to destroy the kingdom of our Lord Jesus Christ, they will have wasted their effort. Why? Because God will make a mockery of them!

In addition, there is this point to make, a point we have already touched upon. And that is that God does not wish to reign over us except in the person of Jesus Christ his Son. Whoever rises up against Jesus Christ makes war on God his Father, for the Father and the Son cannot be separated from each other. So, how does he reign over us? By our not rejecting his yoke, which is his word, by which he wishes to govern us. The gospel, then, is the Lord our God's yoke, to which we must yield, if we want him to deal with us as his people, and we must revere his gospel, which we will do when we receive it in true faith (cf. *Matt.* 11:29–30). On the other hand, if we reject it, it is certain we are resisting Jesus Christ. That is the message of the Psalm about those who conspire to break and cast off the bonds imposed on them (*Psa.* 2:2–3). In other words, they refuse to accept God's yoke because they resist him and wage open warfare against him. Since our Lord wishes to proclaim the kingdom of Jesus Christ his Son through the gospel, everyone who speaks against it wages war on God and on his Christ. Therefore, when it becomes evident that the great as well as the small are working against the teaching of the gospel, trying with all their might to destroy it, let us be confident that they will be powerless and that God will bring all their undertakings to naught. Let us be assured, then, that our Lord will apply his hand and confound them. On the other hand, let us be confident that if we wish to participate in the kingdom of Jesus Christ, we, unlike the stiff-necked and stubborn people Moses talked about (*Deut.* 10:16; 31:27), will have to honour him in his word, submit to him of our own free will and allow him to conquer us.

Now then, let us look at the great rebellion in our own nature, a rebellion so great that we must individually do violence to ourselves and do battle against our natural desires and inclinations.

Otherwise, we will not be able to commune with Jesus Christ and participate in his kingdom without submitting to his yoke and yielding to his governance. When we give ourselves over to him this way, we must not doubt that he will fulfil his promises and that we will feel their effect and power. Now, after calling to mind God's promises, we must apply ourselves even more to praying to him and making our requests known. For the fact that God promises us so many good things and will help us in and through all things is not to lull us into idleness but to sharpen us and incite us to petition him without ceasing.

It is true that if God does not draw us to himself by his promises, we are excluded from them. But as soon as he declares his goodwill toward us and we realize he is extending his hand to us, we are not to doubt that he answers us when we pray. That is why I said the more our Lord manifests himself to us through his promises, the more we must be incited to pray to him. That is what the disciples did, and in that way they instruct us what to do. They took God's promises into consideration: 'Lord', they say, 'you have said through the mouth of your servant David that the kings and great of this world rise up in vain against you and your Christ. For you will deride all their undertakings and make them null and void.' And then they add, 'Lord, consider their threats.' They are praying that they will not be disturbed or troubled by anything which might originate from men. That is what we have to do when we see God's enemies are inflamed by a mad rage. We must make that known to God so he will have pity on us, for we know God is the enemy of the proud and holds them in check when it pleases him, and they are unable to set aside the humble, so to speak. It is then his responsibility to overcome them. When they are enraged against us and seem to have swallowed us in one gulp, as we say, and to be on the verge of destroying both God and his word, let us make that known to God so he will put things right. That too is the reason the apostles said, 'Lord, consider their threats.' So let us not be astonished if the adversaries of the gospel are at fever pitch today and spew out dire threats to frighten Jesus Christ's poor little flock. But let us realize that when God chooses to show his power and extend his right arm over them, he will indeed be able to set things straight so as to bring them and their pride and haughtiness even lower and cast them into lowest depths of hell – if we, for our part, beseech him to do that. The reason God frequently does not take note of their threats is that when we see the wicked in authority over us and persecuting us, we are remiss in praying to him and keeping him in the forefront of our thoughts. In fact, we are not worthy of feeling his power because we do not make our requests with a firm faith, as we should. We ought to pay even closer attention to that teaching when we observe our laziness and lack of enthusiasm.

Afterwards, the disciples declare that the wicked have already risen up against them, as had Herod and Pilate against Jesus Christ. It is as if they were saying, 'Lord, this is not the first time the wicked have instigated war against you. We have already seen flashes of it, but it did not profit them, for you had already decreed it in your counsel. That being true, they are now able to do the same thing to us.' That is the way we are to be strengthened when we see that nothing can be done against God's providence. He has always provided for his church from the beginning of the world and has always had such concern and solicitude for his faithful followers that he has always sustained them in all times of danger.

Now God's power has not diminished. His kindness to help his own is the same as it has always been. Let us not doubt, however, that he makes us participants in that same grace and power which he bestowed upon our predecessors. Yet, at first glance, we might have said that Herod and Pilate were predominant over Jesus Christ. For when Jesus comes to that dreadful moment of hanging on the tree and dying such an ignominious death, what could one say except that God had given leeway to the wicked to do whatever they wished? But the disciples are well aware that Jesus Christ had to suffer for the redemption of the world. Yet they returned to what God ordained and said, 'Indeed, Lord, it is true that Herod and Pilate crucified your Son Jesus Christ. That is to say, after they had worked all their conspiracies and everything else they could against him, he was crucified. But that did not happen because of their power or their authority over him to put him to death, as if they had conquered him. But it was by your counsel and your divine providence which brought it to pass for the salvation of men.' That is how we must depend upon God's providence when it seems the wicked have won and possess such authority that nothing can resist their power. It is true that we will not be able to understand that or evaluate it according to our carnal senses, but we must look at it through the eyes of faith. No matter what frightening thing presents itself to us, let us know that God is powerful to keep us.

However, we must not follow the lead of many clever types. When they talk about God's providence, they engage in circumlocutions and in obscure and tedious speculations. We, on the other hand, must engage the subject with true and living faith, knowing that God, in his own strict counsel, acts only to bring about his glory and our salvation. Therefore, let God's providence serve to strengthen us in our faith, understanding that nothing will happen which is not to our advantage. In short, this is what we must pay attention to: if we see that God permits the wicked to do what we would not desire according to the flesh, we must reserve the matter for the whole counsel and providence of God. He knows why he is doing it. Besides, whenever we see the gospel being persecuted and so many great troubles occurring, it seems from outward appearance that everything must be confounded. When we see that, it is true we can be shaken. Yet we must keep in mind that God is in control of all such things and will work them out in his own good time, although we do not see it now. We also know that if we were in control, things would happen very differently. But we must honour God by attributing all wisdom and power to him when it comes to directing matters for his glory and our salvation, even if it appears they are moving in the opposite direction. That is a way we must understand that God will direct all this world's confusion toward the salvation of his faithful – especially the persecutions of his church.

In order to understand that better, let us return to what we are shown in Jesus Christ, for he is the true mirror in which we are to contemplate God's providence. When he is crucified, he seems to be utterly defeated, but that is where he shows his power and might. Although his cross was ignominious, as the world viewed it, it was like a princely chariot on which Jesus Christ triumphed over all his enemies. Therefore, since our Lord has demonstrated his providence in the death and suffering of Jesus Christ his beloved Son, let us know that it is in him we must take refuge, and let us not be surprised when it appears that the wicked have gained the day, nor let us be surprised when they are convinced they will be able to overthrow and destroy both God and his word. So, let us find our consolation in God and realize that their ruin is all the nearer and that their final condemnation will be delayed no longer and God will exterminate them completely.

Now let us look at the prayer which the apostles offered. 'Lord', they say, 'behold their threatenings: and grant unto your servants, that with all boldness they may speak your word. By stretching forth your hand to heal; and that signs and wonders may be done by the name of your holy child Jesus.' That is what the apostles asked of God. It is not that they are seeking their ease and rest in this world. It is quite true that recognizing their weakness, they ask God to strengthen and fortify them with his power. But in addition they considered a greater and more excellent thing, namely that Jesus Christ rules over everything so that he may be magnified through the teaching and by the signs and wonders done in his name. And that is what we must do. For when we understand that they did not ask God for what could be necessary for human life, but for his glory, we understand that they gave us an example to follow. It is true that we can indeed ask God for what is necessary for our souls and bodies. Jesus Christ taught us to pray in his name when we ask him to give us what we need. Yet we must look beyond that to God's glory, to the advancement and increase of Jesus Christ's kingdom, so that everyone everywhere may recognize him as the only saviour and redeemer. The apostles, then, are not seeking their own good. They are seeking to proclaim the teaching of the gospel everywhere to direct everyone to Jesus Christ as sovereign master. That was their desire, and such should be ours, following their example.

What I have just talked about is confirmed repeatedly, namely that Jesus Christ cannot exercise authority over us unless his word is known by us and preached for our edification. We also have edification from the miracles. It is true that these miracles were only for a time and are no longer the same as they were back then. However, the Lord must always have his hand extended to give value to his word and cause it to bear fruit so that his name may be glorified by it. Therefore, let us learn to pray at all times that God will give us this desire for his word to be received by everyone so that he, by our common accord, may be honoured and his kingdom increased, as it ought to be.

After recounting those things, Luke adds: 'And when they had prayed, the place was shaken where they were assembled together; and they were all filled with the Holy Ghost, and they spoke the word of God with boldness.' In that, we see first that God answered their prayer and they received what they asked for. This was not written for them, but for our instruction so that we might not doubt that God will hear us when we pray with such confidence. In the first point, we have this bit of good advice. When we pray to God, we do well to remind him of his promises and then put our confidence in them. And then let us seek above all to advance his glory through his word. When that is our desire, we must not doubt that God will extend his hand to do more than we can hope.

Moreover, we must pay attention to Luke's comment that the Holy Spirit descended upon them so that we might know by what means God makes himself known to us and helps us, namely by the Holy Spirit. Do we wish to have a strong confidence when speaking in the name of Jesus Christ? Do we wish to have wisdom and discernment and discretion and strength and steadfastness and all the other things which are necessary for our Christian walk? God must send us his Holy Spirit to lead and guide us as he leads the unlearned and is the fountain from which every good thing and every grace proceed. It is likewise by his intervention that Jesus Christ is presented to us.

Afterward, in order to connect this teaching with the practice of the holy Supper of our Lord Jesus Christ, which we are now to receive, let us acknowledge that we cannot be the body of Jesus Christ and have the kind of fellowship with him that we should unless the Holy Spirit is the means. For if we examine ourselves, how can we say we are joined in such a way with Jesus Christ that he lives in us and we in him? Will we be able to do that by our own efforts? No and no! On the contrary, if we remain our natural selves, we will never have such a union with Jesus Christ. How then does that apply to us? The Holy Spirit must renew us by his grace and make us members of the body of Jesus Christ. Then God considers us as acceptable and receives us as his children, whereas we were formerly his mortal enemies because of sin. Consequently, we are more than wretched until Jesus Christ receives us into his body, and that happens when he works within us by his Holy Spirit. That is also the case when we participate in his body and in his blood, which the Supper proclaims. When we come and take the bread and the wine, we do it as a testimony that Jesus Christ is in us and is our life. That is, his life, in all its perfection, belongs to us in common. How does that come about? By the Holy Spirit. So if we wish to belong to the body of Jesus Christ and have God acknowledge us as his children, we must ask him to send us his Holy Spirit and cause us, under his leading, to proclaim God's word with all boldness. And we must ask him to stretch forth his hand and use us to make Jesus Christ's kingdom flourish and grow increasingly until he has gathered unto himself all his elect and clothed them with his glory and his immortality.

Following this holy teaching, let us bow before the face of our gracious God in recognition of the countless sins which we do not cease to commit daily against his holy majesty, praying that he will be pleased to touch us in such a way by his Holy Spirit that we will be able so to die to the world and our own inclinations that we will ask only to follow his commands for the advancement of his glory and the rule of his beloved Son, our Lord Jesus Christ, to whom may we be joined in such a way that we will be members of his body. And may God be all in all after cleansing us of all our vices and clothing us again with his good graces. Now let us say together, Almighty God, heavenly Father . . .

14

THE FELLOWSHIP OF SAINTS

SUNDAY, 1 JUNE 1550

And the multitude of them that believed were of one heart and of one soul: neither said any of them that ought of the things which he possessed was his own; but they had all things common. ³³ And with great power gave the apostles witness of the resurrection of the Lord Jesus: and great grace was upon them all. ³⁴ Neither was there any among them that lacked: for as many as were possessors of lands or houses sold them, and brought the prices of the things that were sold, ³⁵ And laid them down at the apostles' feet: and distribution was made unto every man according as he had need. ³⁶ And Joses, who by the apostles was surnamed Barnabas, (which is, being interpreted, The son of consolation,) a Levite, and of the country of Cyprus, ³⁷ Having land, sold it, and brought the money, and laid it at the apostles' feet (Acts 4:32–37).

The word 'faith' is a very honourable term. When asked about it, we say it is an excellent virtue to have. However, none of us is willing to rely on God enough for him to consider us as faithful believers. We would like to have that reputation in the world's eyes, but God is of little importance to us. If we had the kind of disposition we should have, we would perceive what faith requires and what holy Scripture says about it to bring us into complete conformity. But we do not think about it, and therein our laziness and lack of enthusiasm are laid open. We are far from approaching the manner of living of those whom Luke refers to when he talks about the marks of the truly faithful, those who were joined together as one body and confessed their faith – although he is talking particularly about the apostles when he says they bore witness to the resurrection of our Lord Jesus Christ. Nevertheless, as the apostles bore witness to the resurrection, there is no doubt that each person, insofar as possible, followed them. In fact, we know it is common among Christians to confess Jesus Christ with the mouth just as we are to believe on him in our hearts.

Therefore, in this message we need to pay close attention to what Luke says about the way the faithful conducted themselves when they testified to their faith in the presence of God and of men. He points out what the true church is like and how we are brought into it. There must be true unity among us, and everything must be so well arranged that we look to fulfilling our individual responsibility toward our neighbours. If, in the first place, we want God to consider us in the number of his children, we must do what is said if we are to hear and be joined together with one heart and have fellowship with one another. So now, let us all take part in this teaching to which God bears witness by his Holy Spirit and makes available to us every day through the preaching of the gospel. That is how we too will be the true church. We can easily reject the pope's claim that he is the church, because what he claims resembles in no way what Luke says here. He uses that claim as a defensive weapon to frighten the simple and the ignorant. The whole of his teaching is directly contrary to what Luke says here. It is evident that the church of God does not exist in the Papacy, which we were supposed to honour and revere. It does not exist there because, as I said, nothing of Luke's teaching can be found there. God's teaching unifies men and holds them together so they will be of the same heart and soul. But are those who bear the name and title of church in the Papacy united as they should be? In no way! There is ongoing war among them. It seems to be their bounden duty to consume one another. We must not behave in such a manner if we want to show that we are children of God. It is certain that if we do not follow the principle Luke lays down for us here, we will boast in vain of being in the number of the faithful and members of the church of God.

In order to get more out of this passage, we need to take note of this: 'The multitude of them that believed were of one heart and of one soul.' Luke is speaking expressly about the multitude, and what he says is in keeping with what we said just now. It is a wondrous thing to see a large assembly of people in agreement, more wondrous than two or three or a dozen men who might enjoy mutual friendship. It is possible they can agree. But when there is a multitude, confusion will necessarily result and people will show themselves to be what they are by nature. And we know about human nature! Everyone is addicted to his affections. What, as a matter of fact, is the reason for so many disturbances and divisions except the diversity of human affections? One person wants to follow one path, another person another. And there you have the beginning of debates and dissensions, and the result is endless confusion and disorder. It is an obvious miracle when a large multitude lives in peace. The Spirit of God had to have his hand in it. Yet, if we wish to be God's truly faithful and approved by him, we must have unity among ourselves, just as Luke shows us was the case in the Christian church. For what is faith? Just as God's truth is unchangeable and cannot be divided, those who belong to the faith will be joined together. Wherever there is division, people are separated from that truth of God. Consequently, if anyone boasts of being faithful, he must do as Luke says here and live in harmony with the children of God.

It is true that Luke intended to say more. He is speaking here not only of the agreement that we all have in the church of God, but also about that oneness which must be among us as effected by love. It is possible for men to agree on doctrine. They will believe in one and the same God. They will confess Jesus Christ, who is the subject of holy Scripture. Yet, they will not forsake their divisions. Why not? Because they will not have true faith. There is a big difference between faith from God, which is to work itself out by love in good works, and some belief we get from a story. There are many extremists who will hold that the story of the gospel is true, but it will not be sealed in their hearts by the Holy Spirit. That comes as no surprise. As we have already said, if God's word has taken root in our hearts, the Holy Spirit has had to have done his work. We know that the Holy Spirit is the Spirit of peace and unity (*Eph.* 4:3), that he will be in us, and that we must be joined in true love for one another. Luke is talking here about the unity and brotherhood which must exist among the faithful as well as about the harmony which we all must have within the church if we are to make the same confession of faith and worship the same God, as we do. We must also realize that it is not enough to be joined together this way in brotherly love unless God has previously drawn us to himself and so changed us that we possess such a union with Jesus Christ that we are joined to him as members of his body.

Here Luke is speaking rightly about the fraternal union which we should have with one another. He proceeds to show how the faithful openly showed their love when helping the indigent. It is true that if someone boasts of having love for others but does not demonstrate it in action, he can be rebuked for lying. Love is not a lifeless entity. It must be made known by its outward fruits, although outward works unveil nothing if we have not love. We remember Paul's comment that a man could sell all his goods and distribute the proceeds to the poor, but that if he did not have the right kind of love, everything he does is like a sound which evaporates in the air (*1 Cor.* 13:3). Now if someone asks how it is that a man can strip himself of all his possessions and give alms to help the poor and then be told that his deed is as empty as a sound vibrating the air, the answer is that he is seeking something in return and is a hypocrite. If a man examines his heart, he will discover he does not love his neighbour as he should. Many things we do are as necessary as giving alms. We have to be benevolent if we are to forgive one another and help one another in every time of need. It is not enough that we are ready to use our goods to help one another; we must even engage our own persons. Consequently, when I learn that my neighbour needs my help, I must not only help him with my goods but I must also involve my body and my person so that it will be evident that I do what I do sincerely and enthusiastically.

Now let us note the order Luke follows. He is not just talking about love in its everyday sense. He mentions the fruits which indicate its reality. He does not mention alms first. He begins by saying the faithful have the same heart and the same soul. Now here is what we have to do if we are to show that we are children of God and that the gospel has borne fruit in us. In the first place, let us remember that God has called us to the knowledge of his truth. Let that be a link which binds us together in complete love and brotherhood so that Jesus Christ will not be divided by our dissensions since that is the way he gives himself fully to us. Second, let us realize that we have the same Father in heaven and that we are members of one body and heirs of one heritage. And let us remember that we have the same Spirit of God who guides us so that we will be joined together and have the same heart and the same soul. And, third, let us make known by our actions that our love is sincere as we help our neighbours. And inasmuch as it would be meaningless to be generous toward men in the absence of serving and honouring God, let us have such deep regard for this gospel teaching that it will be well rooted in our hearts and we will never turn from it. That is how our Lord will keep us as his church and receive us as his children.

If we now compare ourselves with what Luke has just said, we will see just how far we are from being Christian. On the one hand, we all pat ourselves on the back for being faithful. We presume no one should doubt that we are good Christians. Nevertheless, it is God's prerogative to define what true Christianity is. So let us take a look at ourselves, and we will discover that we are far from matching the standard Luke sets here. This passage can serve both as a touchtone and as a test for identifying those who are Christians.

Now let us not think that our Lord can allow his name to be blasphemed in this way. It is certain that as often as we boast of being Christian and within the hour do something that contradicts what we say we believe, we dishonour God and grandly blaspheme his name. The bolder we are in calling ourselves Christians, the more we draw God's wrath upon ourselves, for we do not possess within ourselves the truth which we claim. When acknowledging our faults, we have to ask God for forgiveness. Having done that, let this passage admonish us so that we may better receive God's word and pay attention to the teaching of the gospel more willingly than we have up till now. Why has the gospel borne so little fruit in us? Because most of us do not take a liking to it and have very little concern for it. It is true the gospel is indeed preached and people come to the sermon, but as a duty. After much has been said at those times, what do we carry away with us? We should engage in this kind of self-examination every time we hear a sermon so we can think about what we ought to get out of it and how we ought to apply it for our advantage. The sermon is not a lot of hot air! One day we will have to give an account of all that we have heard during preaching even though we have let it go in one ear and out the other. There are also many who profess the gospel and fawn over it but would like to see it degenerate completely and wish they had never heard of it.

Consequently, when the time comes to separate the sheep from the goats (*Matt.* 25:32), God will acknowledge very few as his own. When that great day comes and the evidence appears, we will no longer think about hiding ourselves, as we do now. Our hypocrisy will no longer do us any good.

In addition, seeing that the apostles have witnessed to the resurrection of our Lord Jesus Christ, let us realize that the teaching begins with us, and then as we grow in it daily, let us increase in all good works which are done out of love. Now there are two phases to that love. First, there is the love we have for one another when we realize that we are children of God through Jesus Christ, the love that teaches us to help one another and live together in peace and unity. Second, we are not to be so concerned for our individual interests that we fail to share liberally with our neighbours. That is what love is about. When I said there are two phases to love, I meant that we must understand what love is in itself and that it must bear fruit. The heart cannot have a love so narrow that it fails to show itself in the whole life of the individual and bear fruit. Otherwise, there would be no love. Let us learn to apply ourselves to what Luke shows us here. We are not to be devoted to ourselves. We are to seek the welfare and advantage of our neighbours insofar as possible, just as our Lord commands us in his law. Because each one of us is deaf to that command and by nature given to love ourselves unduly, our Lord directs us to our neighbours. 'You will love your neighbour as yourselves' (*Matt.* 22:39).

It is certain we will not be able to remain in that close relationship which he is talking about here, when there is no love in us to help us love one another. Just as we said earlier, that we will not be able to love our neighbours until we have relinquished and forgotten our love of self, so we must correct the vice of thinking too highly of ourselves. Furthermore, we must root out this inordinate desire for our personal advantage so that we will be able to endure the wrongs done to us. In short, where there is no love and devotion for our neighbours and no forgetfulness of self, there can be no godly love. The absence of love and devotion for our neighbours and the presence of self-interest are as incompatible with godly love as fire is incompatible with water. Therefore, whoever loves himself hates his neighbour. If he thinks highly of himself, he will not think highly of others, for he enhances himself and puts himself forward. If he is set on reaping his private advantage, he will necessarily be concerned only for himself as if he were the only one in the world. In short, a man who is carried away by self-love will have no compunctions about deceiving this man and robbing that one, speaking ill of one and slandering another, and doing all sorts of wicked and illicit things in order to get what he wants and accomplish his evil intentions. When that is our disposition, it is certain, no matter what fine appearance we present, there will be no more love in us than in a pack of dogs. Let us be aware then that after our Lord shows us that our hearts must be open toward our neighbours, he also wants each one of us to engage our hands fully in the task and to consider our ability to help our neighbours. When I say 'our hands', I mean everything that God has given us with which we can help our neighbours. Let us not think about retaining for ourselves, as if it belonged to us, what God has given us to distribute to others. That is what Luke means when he says that none of the faithful thought anything was his own, but everyone considered everything to be held in common. Even those who had fields and possessions sold them so that those in need might be helped by having what they required.

When Luke says that 'they had all things common', he understands that no one held proprietorship of his goods to the point that he did not distribute to others according to their need, as he will point out more fully later. Luke does not want to confuse us here by suggesting that civil order has ceased to exist, but he tells us we must not use our goods for ourselves alone and stand by and watch our neighbours die of hunger and not help them. There are many who will say, 'What is mine is mine! Let the others fend for themselves!' That is not the recommended behaviour. We must realize that God has not placed in our hands what we have without intending for us to give liberally to those in need. How does he want this world's goods to be used? Is it not so that the world's inhabitants will be nourished and sustained? Most certainly. Consequently, we must understand that this world's goods do not so exclusively belong to those who possess them that they can fail to share their goods with those whom they know to be in need, in proportion as God has given to them. That is what Luke means when he says the faithful held all things in common. That is, no one withdrew and kept his possessions so separate that he did not help anyone. They all knew that our Lord was exhorting them to help one another.

It is true, as I have said, that there was no lack of harmony among them, as Luke points out when he adds, 'And distribution was made unto every man according as he had need.' In that way, there was no amassing of goods and no disorder arising from people's taking what they wanted, but they looked to helping where there was need and distributed to each one according to his need. Now this was not written for them, but for our instruction. If we want God to accept us as his children and regard us as the body of his church, we are obliged to follow their example. We know that our Lord has not changed his purpose since that time. Consequently, we must have the same experience as those Luke is talking about. Do we want that experience to be strong and approved by God? Then we must follow in the steps of those spoken of here.

Now let us consider how far removed we are from that. Today those who have an abundance of goods are so far from helping the poor with them that even giving out of their overabundance without diminishing the principal is out of the question. It is very unlikely that a man will sell his lands and possessions to give to the poor when he does not even give anything from his excess. On the other hand, if a man has twice as much wheat as he needs, he will never be satisfied until he amasses even more. And if he amasses more, will it be to help the poor? No! But to cause them to starve. People who are not satisfied with what they possess have no compunctions about usury, robbery, violence, and extortion. They pillage this one and steal from that one. If there is scarcity, it is then that gaping mouths seek to consume everything. When they see the poor at the end of their rope, it is then that they make their best effort to devour them and pick their bones clean. Is that what our Christianity is like? If so, can we boast that we have anything in common with those Luke is talking about here? Certainly not! It is clear how far removed we are from their way of life in the 'love' which they demonstrated toward their neighbours.

In addition, extremists have tried to pervert this passage in order to introduce confusion and roil the pot. 'Look', they say. 'There are Jesus Christ's disciples. They sold everything they had. It follows then that no Christian is to possess anything in this world.' Now if that were the case, what God declared would have to be meaningless, because since man must eat, he must also work with his hands (cf. *1 Thess.* 4:11; *2 Thess.* 3:10). How could a person have food and drink if he did not have lands or possessions? We know that God has said his gospel will be preached universally and that holy Scripture will be extended to all. So who would own things? No one! The fields, the vineyards, and other inheritances would remain uncultivated, and the result would be that they would no longer produce food to sustain us. So you see we need to pay close attention to this passage, for extremists like that want to twist Luke's true meaning to their own advantage.

We also see how the monks have behaved under the Papacy. Under the cloak of brotherhood, they say that they lead an apostolic life and that the disciples had no more in common among themselves than they do. That is appropriate indeed! They are like pigs at a trough eating and consuming the substance of others. They will say 'our cowl', 'our hood', to claim there is community among them, but they continue to live separate from others. In so doing, they devour every day what the poor have struggled very hard to accumulate. That illustrates how badly they put that teaching into practice and shows they seek only to pervert everything so they can live at ease according to their pleasures. For our part, let us take under advisement that what is written here is for our instruction. Instead of being obsessed with self-interest, we need to realize that our Lord did not put us in this world for ourselves but to contribute to our neighbours' welfare insofar as we possibly can. Since we are obliged to do good to our neighbours and to help them in their poverty with our own goods, what will be the end of those who hold the substance of the poor in their hands and, instead of helping them with it, squander it on all kinds of trifles and excesses? That is the very opposite of what Jesus Christ's disciples did. They sold what belonged to them to help the poor in time of need, but these latter-day apostles ravish the goods of the poor and convert them into banquets, immoderate eating, and whatever pleases them. We ought, therefore, to fear that God will visit a great punishment upon us if we irresponsibly squander goods designed to help the members of his body.

Are we not, then, to understand that God takes this matter seriously? The answer is certainly yes. And he will not tolerate such a waste of goods given for the members of Jesus Christ. Let us remember this passage often. If we wish to be united to and joined with those who have gone before us and constituted the true church of God, we must follow in their steps, being of one heart and one mind, and extending charity toward our neighbours in such a way that each of us will give liberally to the best of our ability to the indigent. Let us not be like bad children and take advantage of one another. Let us realize that others have their share along with us in what seems to be ours by right, because we have the same Father in heaven, the same belief for making the same confession of our Christian faith, and because we are all joined to the same head, Jesus Christ, to the end that we will share in the same glory with him.

Following this holy teaching, let us bow before the face of our gracious God in acknowledgement of the countless sins we do not cease to commit daily against his holy majesty, praying that he will be pleased to touch us in such a way by his Holy Spirit that our sole endeavour will be to bring ourselves into full conformity with his will and, instructed by his holy word, live no longer unto ourselves but, completely forgetful of ourselves, look mainly to his glory and then to the well-being and interests of our neighbours. As we do that, may he so strengthen us with his virtues that we will grow in them more and more until he draws us to himself and joins us with our Head and Master Jesus Christ in that place he calls us to every day by his word. In this way, let us all say, Almighty God, heavenly Father . . .

15

THE MOTIVES FOR CHRISTIAN GENEROSITY

SUNDAY, 8 JUNE 1550

But a certain man named Ananias, with Sapphira his wife, sold a possession, ² And kept back part of the price, his wife also being privy to it, and brought a certain part, and laid it at the apostles' feet. ³ But Peter said, Ananias, why hath Satan filled thine heart to lie to the Holy Ghost, and to keep back part of the price of the land? ⁴ Whiles it remained, was it not thine own? and after it was sold, was it not in thine own power? why hast thou conceived this thing in thine heart? thou hast not lied unto men, but unto God. ⁵ And Ananias hearing these words fell down, and gave up the ghost: and great fear came on all them that heard these things. ⁶ And the young men arose, wound him up, and carried him out, and buried him (Acts 5:1–6).

We need to review what we talked about last Sunday, about the love which existed among the faithful in the period of the primitive church. That example is set before us to show us that the mark of the children of God is to be joined together with such love that no one suffers lack and indigence without being helped. In fact, we hear how our Lord says he is merciful and filled with pity for those who suffer. For the word 'alms' signifies mercy, and it is in being merciful, being moved to pity and compassion when seeing our neighbours in need, that we resemble our heavenly Father and are truly his children. In keeping with that, let us endeavour to help them in proportion to the means God provides. That is why Scripture, when speaking of alms, says that our inward parts must be open and our hearts must not be as hard as iron or bronze. But because they have the same nature that we do and bear the image of God, we must be moved and eager to help them as much as we can when we see them suffering some misfortune.

That is what Luke tells us when he says that not only the rich gave abundantly of their goods but that the distribution of them was orderly and everyone was helped as he had need. Things were not done helter-skelter. In fact, when a man gives of his goods without discerning how he is to do it, he demonstrates that he is not motivated by love but by ambition, like many who offer alms with one eye open and one eye closed, as the saying goes. Why is that? They want to deceive and make a show. Yet they have no concern for the people to whom they give, whether they need it or not. Moreover, they do not ask whether the need is pressing or greater so that they might give as liberally as God encourages them to. So whenever we are not prudent enough to consider the indigent so that we can help them according to their current need, it is an indication that love is not guiding us but that we are giving to be seen by men. In such a case, our Lord says we have already received our reward, and for that reason he will not approve our actions (*Matt.* 6:2). Let us not think that he will give us credit for it.

We need to pay even closer attention to what Luke says because if we wish to be considered children of God, we must be moved by pity and compassion when we see our brothers and sisters, who are our members, suffer need. To that end, let each of us take care to help them according to our ability. As we do so, we must, as I said, exercise prudence and discernment when considering who is hungry so that we may employ our goods appropriately. We must not, it is true, be extreme in our probing for information. If we try to turn over every stone to determine whether a person is indigent, he could die of hunger before we help him. So we must not be unduly rigorous as we examine each situation, but we must be discreet so that those who are not needy do not consume what belongs to the poor who are in dire straits. We even see that those vainglorious clods, whom I mentioned a moment ago, and who are interested only in doing those things to be seen by the world, have no insight for determining who is in need or not, and they will rationalize with God: 'It is not necessary to give so much to the poor', and that will be the end of the matter for them and, without determining to whom they should give, they will distribute their goods indiscriminately. Now do you think God will accept that gift? It is certain that he will not! He will punish that kind of presumption! What are we to do then? In the first place, we are not to wait for someone to plead starvation, but in our concern we are to ask where the need is and remedy it as soon as we know about it. Let us consider what God has put at our disposal, and let it be our disposition that the more we have received from him the greater is our obligation to provide for the needs of the indigent.

That is what is noteworthy in the incident which Luke recounts. In short, we must be touched by and moved to compassion for our brethren. Let us, then, be ready to help them according to our ability. However, we must be prudent and discerning as we faithfully dispense what we have in our hands so there will be no confusion and everything will be done according to God's will. That is why there has always been in the Christian church order and procedure in that undertaking, for we do it in keeping with Luke's account of how the apostles took the responsibility of dispensing the goods set aside for the poor. As we will see shortly, deacons were elected for that purpose. Consequently, we have to use prudence and discernment to determine how best to distribute the goods fairly. That teaching applies both to the general administration of what is to be done for the poor and to each individual in his private giving for them.

Moreover, we cannot lay down a definite rule that tells an individual whether he should give or how liberal he should be. As we mentioned last Sunday, we learn from this event that the well-to-do not only distributed liberally to the poor from the store of grain in their granaries and the wine in their cellars, but they also sold fields and possessions, diminishing their goods as necessity required. Therefore, it is, to say the least, prudent for a man who has an abundance of possessions to be prudent in his use of them to satisfy his brethren's lack, just as Paul also shows clearly in 2 Corinthians that it is for this purpose that we have the possessions which God gives us in this world (*2 Cor.* 8:14). Consequently, he who has an abundance is not to waste his excess but to consider that it has been placed in his hands to make him aware that he is not so much its owner as the one who must help his neighbours with it. That is why we cannot impose a definite rule to indicate to what extent everyone is to be generous. But the fact is that we cannot do too much.

Still, our Lord wants us to have a joyful heart, for he wants the sacrifices which we offer him to be voluntary (*2 Cor.* 9:7). He does not want us to act out of constraint but out of our free will. He does not want us to act with pretence and hypocrisy, but whenever we are disposed to help our neighbours, he wants us to do so wholeheartedly and voluntarily, as if opening our hearts to show them our goodwill toward them. Otherwise, he will surely punish us for such hypocrisy and will not put up with our dallying with him as with a small child, as we see in the example of Ananias. Because we learn so little from this incident and others, we will surely have to experience as rigorous a judgment from God, or worse, than those who have gone before and shown us the path to follow or to avoid. How many will be found who faithfully dispense the goods which God has placed in their hands? On the other hand, however, you will find more than a handful of insatiable mouths gluttonously consuming their goods and substance alone, unwilling to help their neighbours with a single scrap even if they were dying of hunger. Moreover, they are content to devour everything alone so as not to help anyone. But by usury, by robbery, and by every illegal means, they devour the poor and gnaw their bones. There are even some who are so perverse that they would, if they could, gladly deprive the poor of light, water, earth, and the brightness of the sun! They even begrudge sharing with the poor the same air and the same sun! So cruel and inhumane are they that, if they could, they would deprive them of everything they share in common with them. There is no doubt that such monsters are unworthy of being numbered among the ranks of men! They are more and more inhumane than wild animals. It is the devil who has hardened them this way so that they are no longer men but cruel and furious animals. If they had any humanity, it would be impossible for them not to have pity on and compassion for the poor, such as each of us must have because, as I have said, they are members of the same body as we.

Now the poor need to consider their position, too. One thing is for sure. The lack of gratitude among some of them disgusts the rich. And what hypocrisy we see in some of them! You cannot satisfy them no matter how much you give. Others will be presumptuous beyond belief. If you do not do for them everything they wish, they grumble and fret and fume. They would gladly demand alms like a highwayman in the deep woods. Others are incredibly ungrateful. When many see all those shortcomings among the poor, they develop an aversion to helping them. Do we still want to maintain charity among us? That is where we must begin then. We must share the same heart and the same soul. And there needs to be among the poor such a simpleness that they are content with little and work to help earn their living, walking in all uprightness and equity in their poverty so that God will open the closed hearts of the rich to help them. Now I am not saying that in order to excuse the rich, for no matter how much they cite the ingratitude and deceit of the poor, they will not be excused before God, for we must not grow weary in well doing (*Gal.* 6:9; *2 Thess.* 3:13; *Heb.* 13:16). We must focus on what God commands us to do, not on all the deceit, perversity, ingratitude, and presumptuousness of those for whom we are to do good. God's commandment is inviolable even though men's faults often give us occasion to transgress it. What I have just said, then, is to guide each of us to examine ourselves, and to lead the rich to realize that they are only the dispensers of the goods which God has placed in their hands; and since the poor are members of Jesus Christ, participating in the same grace and the same spirit, they must share with them those goods of which they are only the distributors in this world, as I have already said. And let the poor, for their part, be resigned to accept what God is pleased to send them, and let there be in them such modesty and simplicity that they will encourage the rich to be beneficent toward them. That is the essence of what we are to get out of this passage.

Luke now recites an incident which is the opposite of what we dealt with last Sunday. It is about Joses, surnamed Barnabas, who sold a possession and brought the price of it to the apostles (*Acts* 4:36–37). He now tells how Ananias also sold a possession but kept back a part of the price with the consent of his wife, Sapphira, and brought the rest to the apostles. Luke shows God's vengeance on Ananias for his hypocrisy and perjury, making it clear that God finds nothing more pleasing than innocence and uprightness. That is, we are not to be double-minded or deceitful. Our Lord loves the innocence of our hearts more than anything we can offer him. Otherwise, we could have all the virtues and still be only an abomination before God. We know that even if men hold us in high esteem, as if we were part angel, our whole life will be worthy of condemnation unless we walk in complete integrity and innocence of conscience before God. That is primarily what we are to get out of this story.

It is true that the following circumstances will arise, but let us go first to the main one. May the example of Ananias and Sapphira warn us that we are not to live our lives as double-minded and deceitful men who trifle with God. But let us be mindful that one of the things God does is reveal the secret thoughts of men (*1 Cor.* 4:5). Even so, let us entertain no thoughts except those that will be approved before him. Inasmuch as he now governs us by his word, let us realize that that word is to search our hearts thoroughly and that we must be cleansed of all wicked affections. That, I tell you, is what true Christianity is all about after we have been emptied of all pretence and hypocrisy so we can walk in all integrity and uprightness before God and with our neighbours.

We know that the natural disposition of human beings is riddled with hypocrisy and lying, which have their roots in all of us. We also know that those roots will remain until God snatches them out by his Holy Spirit. So we must pray that he will be gracious and cleanse us of such a vice so that it will no longer rule over us and our hearts will be completely dedicated to serve and honour him throughout our lives. Because hypocrisy is so embedded in us that it can be rooted out only with great difficulty, the prophets had running encounters with hypocrites and constantly denounced them. As for us, as soon as our Lord cleanses us of this vice, it will sprout again because some vestige of the root remains. Unless he continuously applies his hand, it will get worse, like weeds growing in a garden. Immediately after they have been pulled out, they will always grow back unless someone puts his hand to them. And there are in us more than five hundred times as many wicked roots and affections which have great need to be removed continually. Otherwise, they will grow in such abundance they will suffocate us and cause us to fall into everlasting hell.

The more clearly we see what our condition is today, the greater attention we should give to this story. No matter what our reputation is before men, it is obvious what judgment is pronounced upon it unless of course we walk in complete integrity of conscience. Ananias was punished, Luke tells us, by the devil's taking possession of his heart because he lied to God. So when a man is deceitful, it is a definite sign that the devil has taken possession of him and controls him completely. As we have already said, our Lord cannot tolerate being treated like an ordinary mortal. And that is what happens when we try to deceive him.

Then judgment follows. God demonstrates the execution of his judgments on those who wish to abuse his grandeur and majesty. We see that Ananias falls dead on the spot in the presence of the faithful and is a mirror of God's anger. And that ought to make our hair stand on end. It is true that men will be tested by many temptations, but the devil will not possess their hearts in such a way as to remove all uprightness and justice from them. As for Ananias, we see first that he was not only impelled toward evil; he was also overcome by the devil so that by using the lie Ananias had proposed in his heart, Satan took possession of him. That is why Peter tells him Satan influenced his heart to lie to the Holy Spirit – a point we should heed, for there is not one of us who is not enticed by many wicked temptations. The devil assails and afflicts us often. He even invades us secretly. And once he has taken possession of us, despair fills all.

Yet when we see him luring us along like little children, let us always take care to repel him and refuse him entrance into our hearts. And even if he should gain entrance, let us beseech God to cast him out. Since it is a well-known fact that 'Once he has gained entry, it is very difficult to cast him out', let us always be fortified against the temptations he presents. Let us always be disposed to line up with God so that being armed with the faith we are to have in him, and thus armed with his favour, we will be able to resist Satan and all his assaults. A man of faith must look to himself, for we are so weak that as soon as the devil raises up something before our eyes to deceive us, he straightway overcomes us. We must let the fear of God restrain us. Faith must serve as our shield (cf. *Eph.* 6:16) to ward off all the connivings and tricks which the devil can wield against us, and we are obliged to know that if we allow him in because of our negligence, our hearts will necessarily be deceitful and capricious, filled with every hypocrisy, hypocrisy which our Lord will never tolerate, but for which he will grievously punish us in life or in death.

Do not be surprised, then, if we often hear this word 'hypocrisy'. Just as the prophets always fought and decried hypocrites the moment they appeared, so must we examine ourselves in the privacy of our hearts, reproach ourselves for this vice, and beseech God to grant us the favour of removing it. We will never be so cleansed of this fault that some trace of it will not remain. Even the majority of those who wish to be known as the best Christians are so full of pretence and hypocrisy that little children will recognize their dishonesty whatever fine show they may put on. So let us not be surprised if this instruction is so frequently repeated in holy Scripture, for each one of us needs to look within and examine ourselves in depth in keeping with the admonition which I have just given.

In addition, let us look briefly at Ananias' lie. The text says he lied to the Holy Spirit. Yet he lied only to Peter. Is Peter making himself out to be God? Then Peter says, 'It is not to men you have lied, but to God. And because you tried to deceive him, you must feel the weight of his hand.' With those words, Peter shows Ananias lied to the Holy Spirit and before the majesty of God. Because of our Lord's assurance that he will be in our midst when we come together in his name (*Matt.* 18:20), we are now assembled to confess our Christian faith. We come here to declare that we have a God in heaven whom we must honour and serve. We come here to call upon his name. The sacraments are administered here in time and place. When we come here under those circumstances, Jesus Christ is present among us with his angels. We must therefore be aware that Jesus Christ is among us even though we do not see his physical presence. Nevertheless, he reveals his presence by his power. If the faithful have learned from the teaching they have heard, they feel that presence and are instructed in humility and repentance and like virtues. So when the word of God helps them this way, they know that Jesus Christ has been present and has worked among them.

Even the wicked, being cut to the heart when hearing the word of God preached, feel something of the presence of the Son of God. The power of that word pricks the depths of their hearts in such a way that they can but feel some sting from the presence of the Son of God during the proclamation of his word. Is that the way we come to this place? We must not come here to be in the presence of men, but let us be aware that we are in the presence of God. We must not come for any other reason or purpose. Many come to the sermon only to gain a good reputation. If they were not afraid of being criticized for not being good Christians, they would never set foot in this place. Some will come who are guilty of usury and theft. Some will come who are filled with envy, hatred, and ill will, others with blasphemy and perjury. And still others will bring their contagion of lust and debauchery. In short, very few will come as they should. And that is the reason the word of God has borne so little fruit among them. That notwithstanding, they still want to be considered nothing less than good Christians. Some used to come here in their hypocrisy, but that time is no longer. Those who wanted to gain status had to put on airs of being worthy people and, in their hypocrisy, come to hear the sermons, as I said. Such behaviour gained them nothing. They were trifling with God and his word. And now it is even worse, for those who wish to gain in status need only stay away from this place and completely reject both God and his word. What is that, if not lying to God? We ought to know we do not come here to parade ourselves before men, but to present ourselves before the majesty of the Son of God, who is our Master and our Sovereign King, and to profess our Christian faith. We come for the purpose of hearing the word of God. And we must do that of our own free will. Hypocrisy is out of place here. No matter how much we boast of being Christian and put on a good show, we will gain nothing from our effort unless our actions correspond to our speech. Otherwise, why does God take vengeance on Ananias this way? Because he was deceitful and completely filled with hypocrisy. It also shows that even though he lied to men, he did not escape lying to God. That is an important point to heed. Lying to God is not a difficult thing to do today. How many among us, both men and women, after committing every sin in the book, will confess them if asked? They do not worry about lying impudently before God and his angels, for they think they are scot-free unless there are witnesses to convict them.

There exists a procedure, not of man's making, however, which the faithful have observed from all time: the rebuking and reproving of transgressions within a consistory. When those who have fallen short are ordered to appear, how many do you think will tell the truth? With great difficulty will you find one in a hundred!

Is that not lying to God? There is no doubt that not a year passes that five or six hundred people are called before the consistory, but very few are found who confess their transgression. But, as I said, unless there are witnesses to convict them, all they have to do is put their hand on some paper and strike a fine pose and there they are absolved! So you can see how much perjury we have among us every year. But that really does not make any difference. For such wretched people, all that is not important. When they conceal the truth that way from men, it does not occur to them that they are lying to God. I hope they do not get it into their heads that God is a simple child. Just as he took vengeance on Ananias, he will get around to showing us that he can do the same to us. If we think we are lying to men only, we will discover that God will manifest his judgeship over us and punish us severely, just as he did Ananias for lying to him.

It is true that one could say Ananias' sin of lying to the apostles and keeping back a part of the money from the sale of his property did not deserve such severe punishment. Upon hearing that story, many people would gladly accuse God of excessive severity. But it is not our place to justify God's cause. Let us consider only what the Sovereign Judge said about the matter – that Ananias lied to the Holy Spirit. Even though he thought he was dealing with men, it was in truth God he was mocking. So let us not think that when we behave as he did and wish to make of God an idol, he will not avenge himself and show us how highly he esteems his precious truth and refuses to let men abuse it that way.

Now it is true that today our Lord will not visit that kind of punishment on those who lie to him every day, as we saw him deal with Ananias. With this example, however, he wants to show us that even though he does not act in vengeance in this world, he will nevertheless execute his judgment upon them at the end. We do not see the Holy Spirit descend upon us in visible form, as he sent it upon the apostles. And yet he does not relinquish directing his church by his Holy Spirit, as he has done from the outset. So when he sets the example of Ananias before us, it is to act as a mirror to show us that if we act like him, he will reserve condemnation until the end and then punish us. God destroyed Sodom and Gomorrah in earlier times (*Gen.* 19:24–25). He does not do the same thing now to cities which are guilty of greater abominations than those. The fire which destroyed Sodom and Gomorrah is reserved for the punishment of the wicked even though it appears that God is unwilling to take vengeance when he allows them free rein in this world. May this example serve to warn us that although God does not wreak vengeance on the wicked as soon as they offend him, the way he did on Ananias, we must not take comfort in that, but realize that our condemnation will be all the more grievous because God sustains us and gives us time and space to repent while we remain unconcerned about it. Let us know that we will eventually feel his hand more heavily and much more rigorously. So let us learn to bring ourselves into greater conformity with God's will without pretence or hypocrisy so as to give him no occasion to vent his wrath upon us, as he did upon Ananias. Rather may he grant us the grace to praise and thank him all our lives for the good things he does for us as he provides them daily in his gospel through our Lord Jesus Christ.

Following that sacred teaching, let us fall before the face of our gracious God and ask him to be pleased to open our eyes, so that we may know how dangerous it is to dabble in the vanities of this world and so that, being fully delivered, we may abandon ourselves to the Holy Spirit's guidance and governance. May it please him to forgive the sins we have committed against his holy majesty and, without holding them against us, may he blot them out through our Lord Jesus Christ his Son, to whom we are fully joined, and may he grant us to reign with him in his glory, just as he promised to all those who walk closely with him in all righteousness, integrity, and good conscience. In this way let us all say, Almighty God, heavenly Father . . .

16

JUDGED ACCORDING TO OUR MERITS AND DEMERITS

SUNDAY, 22 JUNE 1550

And it was about the space of three hours after, when his wife, not knowing what was done, came in. ⁸ And Peter answered unto her, Tell me whether ye sold the land for so much? And she said, Yea, for so much. ⁹ Then Peter said unto her, How is it that ye have agreed together to tempt the Spirit of the Lord? behold, the feet of them which have buried thy husband are at the door, and shall carry thee out. ¹⁰ Then fell she down straightway at his feet, and yielded up the ghost: and the young men came in, and found her dead, and, carrying her forth, buried her by her husband. ¹¹ And great fear came upon all the church, and upon as many as heard these things. ¹² And by the hands of the apostles were many signs and wonders wrought among the people; (and they were all with one accord in Solomon's porch. ¹³ And of the rest durst no man join himself to them: but the people magnified them. ¹⁴ And believers were the more added to the Lord, multitudes both of men and women.) ¹⁵ Insomuch that they brought forth the sick into the streets, and laid them on beds and couches, that at the least the shadow of Peter passing by might overshadow some of them (Acts 5:7–15).

Last week we talked about what lesson we should learn from what Luke tells us about Ananias' death, and we pointed

SERMONS ON ACTS 1–7

out that there is nothing God hates more than hypocrisy, being double-minded before him, and not walking in uprightness and truth. That is also the main point of service to him. However, let us not think we can take advantage of him the way we are accustomed to deluding and deceiving mortal men. But let us remember he knows the thoughts of our hearts (*Luke* 6:8; *Acts* 1:24). We cannot mislead him or lie to him, for he judges with truth and is not fooled by fine appearance, by which men are often deceived.

In addition, we also stated that gathering in the name of God is a worthy command to be obeyed because he has such concern for us that we too must be diligent in listening to and obeying him and walking in complete awe, reverence, humility, and righteousness before him, as Scripture often admonishes us to do. That is how our Lord wants us to receive his good news and say, 'Here God is present with us.' We must, therefore, be careful to present ourselves before him with a good and pure conscience.

Now, what we said about Ananias must be applied equally to his wife, for Luke tells us how God meted out to her the same punishment he had just given her husband. Let us always be aware, therefore, that if we are to serve God, our hearts must be cleansed of all deceit and malice. When someone mentions deceit, let us not think we are dealing with mortal men, who can be deceived, but with the Judge of our thoughts, who knows what is now hidden and seems to be deeply buried in shadows and darkness. Since nothing is hidden from God, everything will inevitably appear before him. This is a case in point. Let us not imagine that Ananias and Sapphira, his wife, were disreputable and inconsequential people who had no standing among the faithful. On the other hand, it is likely they were held in esteem and honoured. In fact, judging from the way Luke talks about them, they were very successful people. It is no small thing to sell a piece of property and give it to God, that is, distribute the money from it as alms.

When we see a man deprive himself of his own substance to help the poor, do we not think of him as an angel from heaven? It is an indication of great sanctity, at least in the eyes of men. There is no doubt they were very significant people, among the most spiritually advanced in the church. Yet we see the great vengeance which God drops on their heads. So let us not measure sanctity or hypocrisy by human standards, but let us take into consideration the fact that God sees much more clearly than everybody in the world. Even though we may think there is no deceit in us, we are obliged to examine ourselves closely and search our souls, and we will find that there is not one among us who does not have a well-spring of vices to draw upon. We will recognize that even better if we put into practice what John tells us, that even if our hearts do not condemn us, God sees more deeply within us than our minds can comprehend (*1 John* 3:20–21). This is John's line of thought. If a man's heart does not condemn him, even though he is the most wicked and faithless person in the world, God will examine him when his time comes to face judgment and will uncover many vices which the man himself did not know about. As for the faithful, if they condemn themselves, if they abase themselves, and in all humility acknowledge that their sins are countless, they will find forgiveness before God.

So let us acknowledge our faults, and God will not call us to account for them. But the wickedness of those who think they will escape by subterfuge and hypocrisy will eventually be unveiled before God, before his angels, and before men. What they think they have hidden and what they were ashamed to confess in this world before three or four will inevitably be revealed first to God, as is already the case, and then to all creatures, to our shame and embarrassment. That is what Luke is telling us about Sapphira. Peter is there like a lawyer presenting an indictment before God. But what occasions such punishment? She and her husband had already conspired together to gain a good reputation and an appearance of sanctity among the faithful, but in the mix were evil intentions and hypocrisy. For that reason, when Peter questions her, she does not dare confess their sin, even after Peter asks her specifically whether they sold the field for so much. She continues to maintain their lie and does her best to conceal it, but we see what price she pays for it. Therefore, using this example as a guide, let us take care not to be so in awe of men's opinions that we trifle with God and make little of his judgments. Let us not suppose that this teaching was not given to us for a purpose, but let us realize that our Lord wanted to give us a general rule, as we have already dealt with it, to show us by living example that the only way to serve him is by walking in full integrity of conscience.

In addition, let us realize how necessary humility is. When seeing these two people so grievously punished for exalting themselves and giving themselves some appearance of sanctity before men, we understand they did nothing but provoke God's wrath against themselves. Let us be aware, then, that if we desire to exalt ourselves, God will be our enemy. On that point, Scripture must be fulfilled, for he is the Adversary of the proud and it is his place to bring them to ruin. A good lesson for us to learn from this passage is that even if we do everything we can, we must be careful not to think too highly of ourselves. Let us not covet the glory of men. Let us be concerned with examining ourselves closely. We will find deep within many serious shortcomings of which we are not yet aware.

We see how Paul looks at the matter. After stating categorically that he faithfully executed his office, he adds that he was not thereby justified (*1 Cor.* 4:1–4). He was well aware that when a man has done his utmost in the service of God, he is still unable to do what he should, not even by a tenth. If Paul, with his degree of perfection, states categorically that he is not justified by having done all he could for the increase and preservation of God's church, and if he is bold enough, as I said, to declare openly that he walked in complete uprightness, we need to consider that that will be our lot too. Let us realize, then, that after making every effort to walk before God in complete uprightness, we will not be perfectly acquitted of our responsibility, and that the only thing left for us to do is to begin again. That is because, as I have already said, we have vices in us which God alone can recognize and punish, vices which we cannot see.

We come now to what Peter adds: 'How is it that you have agreed together to tempt the Spirit of the Lord?' He had said earlier 'to lie to the Holy Spirit'; now he says 'to tempt him'. That is one and the same thing. For we do indeed tempt God and abuse his patience when we want him to approve us as good while we are among the most wicked in the world. It is as if we wanted to nullify his majesty. There is nothing more characteristic of God than to judge our thoughts. It proceeds from his nature because he is spirit, as John says (*John* 4:24). So, inasmuch as God is by nature spiritual, we are to conclude that he does not look upon external appearance, as men do, and does not judge by superficial standards. He penetrates the depths of our thoughts and examines everything hidden in the hearts of men in order to offer it in evidence and make it known at a time of his choosing. So then, if we wish to put God to the test in this way, thinking we can satisfy him with a few fine outward deeds in an effort to deceive him to the extent we can, are we not making of him an idol? When we try to discharge our duty toward him by some fine outward act while full of every malice and perversity – can you imagine a more egregious blasphemy than that? It is as if we wanted to nullify God and his truth, and even his essence, and throw him out of office. On the contrary, let us learn, as I said, how not to be hypocrites, double-minded and given to deceit and falsehood, so as to avoid lying to the Holy Spirit or changing the truth of God into a lie. That is the reason for the punishment and vengeance that Luke recounts, which ought to make our hair stand on end.

As we have already said, if God does not put all hypocrites to death suddenly in our day, let us not get it into our heads that they will escape his hand. He reserves for them a much more horrible and fearful punishment. Dropping dead is a small thing in comparison with being thrown into eternal fire to endure unending pain. As for the body, enduring for a time is nothing to be compared with being in continual torment, endless and perpetual, in body and in soul. Therefore, let us not measure God's judgment against what the eye can see, but let us remember that he does not judge with respect of persons. Everything he does is done in truth. Even if hypocrites are not punished today – at least we do not see it – and if God puts it off for a while, let us not conclude that God is allowing their deceptions and falsehoods to go unpunished. Let us be aware that all their sins are recorded and that once the books are opened they will have to give account of everything, and they will receive the penalty for their sins (*Rev.* 20:12). That is why that story must always be held up before us both as instruction and as a perpetual reminder. As instruction, so we will not yield ourselves to that damnable hypocrisy which seeks men's honour and invites God's rebuke; as a reminder, so it will be a vivid picture for us to contemplate God's retribution and to encourage us to fear him, knowing that he has the power to execute his judgments upon us just as he did upon those two, and even more painfully if we are not otherwise motivated by the indications of his wrath and retribution, which he demonstrates every day.

That is why Luke adds again that great fear came upon all the church and all who heard these things. He says the believers and unbelievers alike were so shaken by that divine judgment that everyone experienced great fear. If the unbelievers were not moved by that judgment, it was at least for them an early God-given summons to appear before his judgment seat. We will do well to remember this passage whenever Luke speaks of the church. Without a doubt, he includes those whose consciences were clear and who were no longer given to their vices. They do not lose their fear or great perplexity because of what happened, for it is certain we can never arrive at such a state of perfection that we are always beyond reproach. Far from it! In this way, all the examples our Lord gives us are to serve for our instruction. May none of us fail to use them for our own good. We must not do as many when they are provided with an example and say, 'Oh! That does not apply to us in the least. Let the others take heed, if they wish.' Really? People who talk like that have never looked within themselves. When we are challenged by God's word, when our vices are rebuked and censured, and when someone declares that God's judgments are about to fall on us because of our offences, then each of us must look to himself and ask, 'Well then, how have I used my time since it has pleased God to make me aware of his truth? How have I taken advantage of it? On the other hand, I see that I am worse rather than improved. I must willingly acknowledge my guilt in this way and ask God to be pleased to receive me in his mercy.'

When we have examined ourselves this way and have individually probed the depths of our conscience, it is certain that those who think themselves exempted from the condition common to other people and think they are so perfect will find they are far from being the kind of people they think they are. Because of the saying that true love resides in the heart (cf. *1 Tim.* 1:5), God is not just satisfied that our consciences are pure, but our spirits must also be cleansed of all evil affections. Let us take the case of a man who has never been overcome by temptation and remains unpolluted by debauchery and other shameful acts, who has so effectively resisted temptation that he is free of every unwholesome lust and has no chink by which Satan might have entered his heart to plant an evil desire. Who among us, being required, as we are, to be so chaste in both body and spirit that we do not entertain a single evil thought, would dare boast of being that kind of person? The same is true of all the other vices. It is true that many have not actually stolen the property of their neighbours. They have not wronged their neighbours by their malice and cruelty. In addition, by not doing wrong to anyone, they have not wantonly coveted the goods of another, but have they not been tantalized by something they would really like to add to their own possessions without, in their estimation, wronging anyone? Being so enticed, are they not already guilty before God for not being satisfied with what he gives them? True, everybody's hands will not be bloody. They will not be murderers or highwaymen ready to cut the throat of the first person who displeases them. Their cruelty is not so evident that they would like to kill or maul anyone at the drop of a hat. Yet, how many of them would not want to get even immediately at the slightest offence? Surely we would want God to destroy our enemies completely, as if he were supposed to be the executioner for our wicked affections and unbridled appetite for vengeance. So if we examine ourselves closely, surely one of us will fully recognize his guilt before God. Let us realize that our Lord never does give us an example of punishment that is not applicable to all. That is how we must learn from all God's works and admonitions, and not project onto others our shortcomings, but accept them as our own for our own individual profit.

Let us now compare ourselves with Ananias and Sapphira. It is said that those who witnessed that event were frightened and greatly terrified upon seeing that God had visited such an execution on those two. What will be the lot of those who do not find in this example an occasion for rebuke or indications of God's wrath and retribution made manifest to the extent that they are not only condemned in the sight of God, but that their iniquity is laid bare before the world, even to little children? Or what will be the lot of those whose hypocrisy is so heavy that everyone can see it and feel it? Some will be found who pillage and steal everything they can. They think that when they give a pittance in alms, God is obligated to be pleased and that they are acquitted and absolved of all their financial abuses and thefts. And they do that as if expecting God to share in their iniquities and take a kickback.

Now, Ananias and Sapphira's offering was very different. The text does not say they acquired their property by fraud, usury, or robbery. The field belonged to them, as Peter says: 'While it remained, was it not your own? And after it was sold, was it not in your own power?' Therefore, even though they had acquired the property fairly and it rightly belonged to them, we see how they were punished because their intentions were not pure when they offered it to God. What will be the lot of those who suck the life's blood out of the poor? When we see the excessive cruelty of many, it seems they think the poor are fair game. They not only seize their neighbours' purses but cut their throats and gnaw their bones. Moreover, if they give a few pennies to God, they think they are off the hook and take the liberty of indulging in more usury, more robbery, more cruelty and financial abuse than ever before. Therefore, let those who want God to accept them as his faithful people learn to walk in the fear of God, and let them look to their own interests, for if they are not motivated by such a punishment, they will be obliged to expect a vengeance a hundred thousand times more horrible and more frightful than this one. When they are given examples, they should use them as indications of what will happen to them if their deeds are much worse than those presented in the examples. Consequently, those who profess to serve God but fail to do so in practice, and dishonour him by their works and deeds, will inevitably be swallowed up in a greater condemnation than that spoken of here, for this general rule will inevitably apply: all the acts of service and devotion of the wicked are abominable before God. We know that prayer is an offering especially approved by God. Yet it is said that prayer will become a poison for those who abuse his name. Let us not think that the double-minded will escape with a lighter penalty and not receive as great a punishment as God dealt Ananias and Sapphira.

In our day, we see the same thing Luke talks about here. The unbelievers are amazed and shaken by what happened. It is true that believers will be amazed by God's judgments, which will frighten and forewarn them, and induce them to pray for God's forgiveness and deliverance from punishment. Moreover, they are put on guard concerning the future. They are heedful that this is not a matter to be taken lightly. We must not suppose we can abuse God as we do men. We can deceive them for a time. We must not, as I said, get it into our heads that we can treat God the same way. For it is his province to judge our secret thoughts (*Rom.* 2:16). That is how believers can profit from God's judgments. But unbelievers, as I said, will only be astonished by them. They will continue to follow the herd and do as they always have. Consequently, they will inevitably feel his rigorous judgments and be overwhelmed by them. With their own eyes they now see how God deals with the wicked. They realize – or they are blind beyond belief – that he cannot bear iniquity without punishing it, and although the punishment is delayed, they still cling to all their vices, indifferent to the fact that it is God who is revealing their fate. Then they hear it preached in the sermon. And when they catch a glimpse of God's judgments, they experience a deep disturbance within themselves, but they do not know what is going on. They return straightway to their card game, as the saying goes. As Luke tells us, the unbelievers were indeed amazed and shaken, but their astonishment did not humble them or lead them to obey God and his word. They remained obstinate and hardened in their evil.

Now, Luke says a little later that 'by the hands of the apostles were many signs and wonders wrought among the people; and they were all with one accord in Solomon's porch', which was a part of the temple – not that Solomon had built it, for the temple had been destroyed, but it kept his name so that its authority would be greater among the people. That was the most appropriate place for the believers to assemble for public prayers, hearing God's word, and calling upon his holy name with one accord. That is why it is written that they would all assemble in that place. Luke adds that none of the others dared join with them and that the people were in awe of them. Now, those who are thus in awe of the large number of believers did not consider God's goodness as a reason for them to be joined to his church. Why do you think that is? Because they saw those who were terrified. Moreover, they see many other signs and wonders which are done by the hand of the apostles. God is working by the power of his Holy Spirit to strengthen the gospel more and more. The number of believers, already many, increases daily, which amazes them greatly.

That, then, is the burden of what Luke tells us here. In the first place, when he tells us that the believers assembled in Solomon's porch, he wants to make us aware that public meetings are necessary for the continuance of God's church. But there are indeed some lunatics who will say, 'What is so important about having a definite place for assembling, where all can come together in this way? Is it not enough for everyone to read Scripture at home and pray in private?' Can you imagine? We see the procedure which God has established among us and which is to be ongoing. Are we to heed those vile persons influenced by the devil rather than what God has ordained and which is to continue until the end of the world? Certainly not! In fact, we must not imagine that this procedure is established by men's wisdom or that it proceeds from human understanding. In no way! That is the way Jesus Christ wants his church to be sustained and protected, as Scripture shows (cf. *Heb.* 10:25).

Luke is here giving us the example of Christians of that time who all assembled together in that place. That should be an excellent example for us. For although there were great persecutions of the church of God at the time because the entire city was raging against them, they did not forsake assembling themselves together in the name of God. They are not driven by some pointless desire. They know what they are doing is necessary. They are guided by the knowledge that the church cannot be sustained unless those who bear the name Christian and faithful come together with one heart and one mind. All the more must we be encouraged to follow their example inasmuch as God favours us with the possibility of gathering to hear his word without being persecuted or harassed in any way whatsoever. Now, if we are remiss in assembling, especially since nothing hinders us, what excuse will we make to God? Those people were in the mouths of wolves, so to speak, at the disposal of violent governments, plagued by the persecutions and conspiracies of God's enemies. Yet they did not forsake coming together to strengthen their Christian faith more. They could see the dangers of their situation, but their fear of everything that could happen to them did not deter them. They are unperturbed and persevere in what they know to be necessary for the maintenance and sustenance of their commonly held Christianity. And by God's grace, we have his word preached to us in all freedom and we enjoy the privilege of Christian assembly without persecution. Those who want to hold themselves apart will even bear a mark of disgrace. Yet we will show how wretched we are by running the other way when the church bell calls us to worship. Most will be aware of offering some pretext or excuse for never coming. The others do not give a fig because they flee from the sermons and the gatherings of the faithful like the devil flees from God's presence. What punishment from God do we deserve and draw to ourselves? We do not have a proper concern for those things which God rebukes. In this we see our responsibility. If the Christians Luke talks about in this passage assembled amid persecutions to pray to God and hear the teaching of the gospel, we ought all the more in our day and time to come together with one accord and one heart for the same purpose.

Moreover, let us not suppose that the faithful gathered back then for only a few minutes. The opposite is true. Luke tells us there was a space of three hours between Ananias' death and Sapphira's arrival at the assembly of the faithful. Why that period of time? Their situation did not allow the convenience we enjoy today, for our civil government accommodates us. The church bell tolls to call us together at a regular hour. Most often, they had to take half a day off from work to hear God's word. By contrast, when we can devote only an hour to hearing the teaching of the gospel, do you think God is willing to tolerate such laxity? It is true that we think we have good excuses, but inevitably our indolence, rather our hardness of heart, will be punished, and those things will be our judges and condemn us before God.

Now, Luke tells us the people came together with one accord, which means that the principal aim of our Christianity is for all of us to live together in sincere peace and fraternal harmony. If we do not want our laying claim to the name Christian to be a meaningless endeavour, and if we want Jesus Christ to rule and reign over us, let us make sure that his peace dwells in our midst. It is certain that we cannot be one in heart unless our singular purpose is to draw near unto God. Why is it that each of us is so given to self-interest that we are concerned only for ourselves and are not reluctant to fight among ourselves with ill will and grudges against one another? Is it not because we do not have the knowledge we ought to have about God? There is no question that if we knew him as he wants to be known, our hearts would be different and we would be so tightly knit together that we would seek only to serve one another in all things needful.

We come now to the miracles Luke mentions. He says that many signs and wonders were done by the apostles and that all the sick, no matter their infirmity, were delivered. Indeed, even Peter's shadow was so powerful that those it fell on were healed. That was done so we might know how our Lord confirmed his word and authorized it as coming from heaven and not from men. Such confirmation was necessary at the beginning of the gospel, for the gospel could have been rejected as a new teaching. But we see that there is nothing new. Only what is contained in the law and the prophets. And the only thing we see there is that God proves himself faithful to what he promised in the Old Testament. As I have said, the gospel had to be ratified by miracles, which functioned as seals to verify its contents. Not that it was not sufficiently trustworthy without the miracles or needed greater confirmation, but the miracles were given because of the hardness and malevolence of men so that they could claim no excuse when they refused to believe.

Luke has already spoken about that and will say more about it later, but it is good for us to be admonished often by that teaching. Even if we do not see miracles today, what they teach must serve us until the end of the world. We must bear in mind what we have just touched upon, that inasmuch as our Lord healed physical diseases, he must also be our physician today and cleanse us of our spiritual diseases, which are much more to be feared than the diseases of our bodies because they lead to eternal death. We have also said about the miracles at other times that their purpose lies in the exaltation and glorification of God. As a result, we see a very evident impudence in those who completely turn the miracles to his great dishonour and, what is worse, blaspheme him because of them, as if conspiring to defy him by their wicked inventions. But we cannot develop that point right now. We will reserve it for next week and give it fuller treatment then, God willing. In the meantime, let us take care to profit from the teaching of the gospel by following the example of those Christians and faithful believers so that we may show by our deeds that we have not received the gospel in vain. Let us abandon our normal wicked life and learn to walk in the fear of God, realizing that he is by nature a spiritual being and wishes to be served with a pure and clean spirit, unsoiled by this world's pollutions. Let us in all humility and obedience draw near unto God and be fully joined with him, as we hope to be after he takes us from this mortal life.

Following this holy teaching, let us bow before the face of our gracious God, acknowledging our sins and beseeching him not to impute them to us, but to grant us the grace to be increasingly displeased with them so that he will see we are humble before him and be inclined to forgive us. And then, being removed from all the pollutions of this world by his grace, let us understand we are not to return to them and be more polluted than before. But when he delivers us, let us follow only those things he shows us in his word and recognize him as our King, our Father, and our Guide. In this way let us all say, Almighty God, heavenly Father . . .

17

REVERENCE FOR GOD'S MAJESTY

SUNDAY, 29 JUNE 1550

And of the rest durst no man join himself to them: but the people magnified them. ¹⁴ And believers were the more added to the Lord, multitudes both of men and women.) ¹⁵ Insomuch that they brought forth the sick into the streets, and laid them on beds and couches, that at the least the shadow of Peter passing by might overshadow some of them. ¹⁶ There came also a multitude out of the cities round about unto Jerusalem, bringing sick folks, and them which were vexed with unclean spirits: and they were healed every one (Acts 5:13–16).

Last Sunday, we began to talk about how useful the miracles can be for us. First, we are to use them to strengthen our faith, for our Lord extended his hand and his power to witness to his gospel and to show its sure and infallible truth. We must not, then, ever separate the one from the other. For we understand how quickly the devil inclines us to superstition and perverts the miracles so that they do not magnify and exalt God's glory and power, but blaspheme and dishonour him. Examples of that we have seen and still see throughout the Papacy.

The papists will point to their miracles, you can be sure. Why would they do that except to corrupt and twist the teaching of the gospel? Why do they extol them except to snatch from God the honour due him and transfer it to created things in order to make of them idols to their liking? That ought to keep us on the alert. As soon as we hear miracles mentioned, let us realize that God is manifesting himself to us so we may exalt and magnify him alone and attribute to him the honour and glory for all the good things and all the prosperity we enjoy. Then when we hear instruction in the teaching of his gospel, let us go straight to Jesus Christ as the one who is to lead and guide us so it will not occur to us that there are other ways to come to God, but let us be aware that Jesus Christ extends his hand to lead us to him because it is to him alone that we must turn.

Moreover, since we see that the sick were healed, let us not doubt that our Lord Jesus Christ's office is still to heal us of all our diseases. It is true miracles are not manifested openly in our day, but the fact is that the Son of God has not changed in power and goodness or resigned his office. Therefore, let us consider whether we are sick in our souls. You can be sure none of us will be found healthy. In fact, we are all in a state of death. We all need Jesus Christ as our spiritual physician. Let us consider seriously the fact that God his Father sent him into the world for that purpose – to heal us of all our diseases because we will remain dead until we come to him. That is how we are to put into practice what Luke tells us in this passage, when he says that all the sick were brought to Jerusalem to be healed of their sicknesses by the hands of the apostles, and that even Peter's shadow had the efficacy to heal the sick in the name and power of our Lord Jesus Christ. We have more than Peter's shadow. We have the power of the Son of God. It is true he was not there in his visible person, but if we lift our hearts to him on high, if we seek him through faith, it is sure he will touch us with his power and let us feel its effectiveness, not just in our bodies but also in our spirits, for it is said that he dwells in us spiritually (*1 John* 3:24). We must not even imagine that his power is diminished or that it is shut away in a secure place and experienced only there. It extends to all corners, because it is God who extended his hand to us when giving us Jesus Christ to heal us by his grace from all our diseases, and deliver us by his power from the devil, who kept us imprisoned in that wretched servitude of sin and death. That, I say, is the lesson we are to learn from the story recounted here.

In addition, Luke's comment that the sick were brought from the cities surrounding Jerusalem instructs us how we are to find Jesus Christ. Now, he does not intend for us to seek him far off. He takes the first step. He moves first. He calls us to himself before we come to him, so we have no excuse for not being saved by him. In that, we see that we lack enthusiasm, that we are far from going to the trouble to come to Jesus and humble ourselves and receive him when he is near and presents himself to us, not, as I have said, in person but through his gospel. His testimony to us is that he wants to dwell in us through his power but that we do not give him the opportunity to do so or to open our hearts to his indwelling, as he persistently calls on us to do through his Holy Spirit. There is no doubt but that that story will bring us into great condemnation because we do not use it to enhance our teaching. That is to say, we do not see in it an example of those who came to Jerusalem because our Lord was magnifying his power there. That manifestation of power dealt only with healing diseases of the body. How much more should we be moved to seek healing for the diseases of our souls!

Now, since it is true the Son of God asks only that we accept the benefit he offers, that is, the healing of all our spiritual maladies, do we not deserve eternal death if we refuse? Therefore, it is with good reason that we do not share in the grace of the Son of God and that we see everywhere so many maladies, physical and spiritual. The reason for that is that we are not charitably inclined toward one another, as were those we are talking about here, those who brought the sick to Jerusalem for healing. Diseases of body and soul are everywhere present. Of body, not just fever and similar ailments, but there is so much poverty that it tears your heart out. Some die of hunger. Others are afflicted in one way or another. But where is the charity to help both? It looks like we are wild animals out to devour the weaker and no one has compassion for those who suffer. In short, we see lack of human sensitivity in the great and the small.

Now how might that be remedied? Everyone would have to think that God does not judge us and that we will not experience his punishment unless we offend him. He invites us ever so gently to repent, but our hearts are hard. We do not want to come to him, and it has been a long time since we have individually stirred our neighbour, or rather urged him, to come to God. Consequently, we are so insensitive that we do not feel the hand of God upon us to correct us. We see in this passage the trouble the Jews go to in order to ease their neighbours' pain. There is not one who does not help those in need because of their physical health. As for us, we are not moved even when we see our neighbours perish in body or soul. We would not lift a finger. Their sense of brotherhood does not exist among us today, and that comes from the fact that there is no gratitude in either the small or the great. The small suffer many ills, but if you look at their ill will and their perversity, you will find they are filled with fraud, trickery, and deception. If they could, they would be ravening wolves. As for the great, they think the poor exist for them to prey upon. Their disposition to be merciless is so great that they will suck out their life's blood and gnaw their bones. Wild animals get along together even though there is diversity among them. But the opposite is true for us. We see one side rise up against the other. There is only war among us, dissension, and conflict, such that you would think we were created to devour one another. So let us take a look at ourselves. Just as Luke tells that story to exhort us to follow the example of those who brought the sick into Jerusalem to be healed, so it is certain that when the situation arises for us to help one another and provide some means of healing and we are unwilling to lend a hand and use our arms and legs to help the needy, we will have to give an account before God, and our lack of involvement will accrue to our greater condemnation. Luke is speaking here of the Jews who were still steeped in false teaching and did not know the gospel. Yet we see the level of humaneness which they practised among themselves. They do everything they can for the healing of the sick.

Whenever we turn to our own use those things God gives us for the alleviation of those we should help, we may be certain that God will not tolerate that kind of insensitivity. And yet we do that very thing. So let the small and those of low estate think about them. For even if they have not had the capability to do as much harm as the great but desire to, God will not excuse them on the Great Day. And whenever they endure some affliction from the great, they need to realize that it is God who is chastising them by the hand of others. The great also must bear in mind that the higher God raises them above others, the greater is their obligation to aid and sustain those who are suffering. They need also to bear in mind that if they afflict them, it is certain that in the end they will realize they have to face another judge. Let them bear that in mind early on.

The situation is the same when it comes to our spiritual infirmities. We do not think about them seriously either, for who among us considers correcting our neighbours when we see them on the road to perdition, actually perishing, and remembers to say, 'My friends, what are you doing?' How many, I ask, will be found who care enough to lead back to our Lord Jesus Christ those who have gone astray? Very few. But many depraved people will be found who want nothing more than to see everything turned inside out and to see those who want to come to the knowledge of the gospel turned away from it by the dissolute and wicked conduct of wretched people. Those who already have an appreciation of the teaching and are on the right path will be corrupted by those rabble-rousers and firebrands from hell who want only to pervert and destroy everything. Therefore, if we have failed in our duty thus far, we must make a greater effort than ever before, in our time and place and according to our ability, to fulfil our responsibility.

Since Luke tells us in this passage that the sick were brought to be healed of their physical infirmities, let us come to this great and sovereign Healer, our Lord Jesus Christ, and ask him to receive us into his way of life so that, directed and instructed by him, we may each one serve God as is fitting and our neighbours as we should.

We come now to Luke's statement that 'of the rest dared no man join himself to them: but the people magnified them.' He is including the multitude of believers which was increasing both in men and women. When he says that the multitude of believers was increasing but that no man dared join himself to them, he seems to be saying two different things. To understand that apparent contradiction, we need to note that many acknowledged God's majesty in the gospel and were terrified by it. Yet they dared not attach themselves to the company of believers but held themselves apart. That, as I said, is the reason they dared not join with the others: they saw a witness of God's presence in his church. But that should not be our reaction, for in proportion as our Lord demonstrates his power, we ought to be devoted to him and dedicate ourselves completely to his service so that we can in this way be led to the knowledge of his gospel.

Moreover, it is to our great shame that Luke says the multitude of believers was growing, whereas it is now diminishing. Even though God calls us into the knowledge of his truth and instructs us by his word over a long period, we straightway turn aside from what we know and are much worse off than we were before. That is to our great shame, as I said. Let us note carefully, however, that Luke did not relate this event just to tell us what happened, but so we might be able to profit from it by following their example. So what must we do? After we ourselves have come fully to the gospel, let us be diligent in taking it to those unfortunate souls who do not know about it. Since there is in that way a complete fulfilment, may we not withdraw from it but remain a part of it, just as we want to remain in Christ until we are wholly conformed to him and arrive at that perfection we hope. That, I say, is what we need to learn from this passage.

Moreover, when Luke says, 'And of the rest no man dared join himself to them', he intends to show, as he explains, that the people recognized a majestic presence of God and were frightened by it. There was among the believers an orderliness and procedure, as was pointed out earlier, and such great charity that no one lacked anything. Their perseverance was such that no one wearied of hearing God's word and the morning was spent in prayers and calling upon God's name. That astonished those who did not know what was happening and led them to say, 'God is in the midst of these people.' But they did not know the majesty of God as they should have. In that account, we are shown our responsibility. Once our Lord has brought us to the knowledge of salvation, we must so glorify him in our lives that people will realize we have not received the teaching in vain. That is why God's teaching must not be preached in vain among us and why we must not, by our dissolute lives, give occasion to the wicked to say, as has been their custom, 'Well, it is true those people profess the gospel, but they do not know what that means, or at least they do not act like they do.' It will be our fault, then, if the gospel is not well received and people do not give God the glory which belongs to him.

Therefore, let me repeat, since our Lord has granted us the grace to be drawn to him through knowledge of his word, let us live in such a way that his image will shine in us, for Jesus has sent us forth so that we might be like him and so that unbelievers, seeing how we live, might be drawn to him. It is true we are not to seek to be seen of men to be honoured by them. Those who do so have already received their reward (cf. *Matt.* 6:2). But we are to show that we are children of God so that we may glorify him and his image may shine in us, as I said, for that is the intention of the gospel, just as Paul speaks of it when he says that when we hear the gospel preached, we must let the image of God be seen in us with such power that when unbelievers see us, they will be constrained to say, 'That teaching does not encourage people to do wrong, but to come to God' (cf. *Eph.* 4:20–24, 29). That is why we are told our good life and behaviour are to serve as an affirmation that the teaching of the gospel is good and holy and the way to life and salvation. It is not that God needs us to confirm his teaching, but it pleases him to use our holy and upright way of life to confirm the teaching in the eyes of men. That, I say, is what Luke admonishes us to do. So, if we profess the gospel, our lives must simultaneously correspond to it and reflect such holiness that the pitiable people who do not know the gospel may have the opportunity to think and say, 'What is going on here? People say this teaching is false and a lie and considered heresy, but the fact is it has great power because those who have been instructed in it are completely changed. And we know it is a very difficult thing for man to be made new. So no matter what people say, that comes from God.' This, then, as I have said, is why we should direct all our effort toward living upright lives: so that unbelievers themselves might be constrained to glorify God.

In addition, we need to note what we must know about God's majesty in his church. We are not to be frightened by it, for Luke points out that was the reason the bystanders withdrew. It is true they saw the good order among the people, and still they did not come. They indeed show they did not learn what God wanted them to know. Luke wanted us to know that as soon as we perceive what God declares to us, we must approach him boldly despite the fact that he reveals a majesty which could terrify us. In fact, let us consider that holy Scripture tells us that man's salvation will be found only on Zion and in Jerusalem (*Isa.* 37:32; 46:13; *Joel* 2:32). When the prophets tell us that if we want God to be our Saviour, we must be counted among his people and come into his church. For the words 'Jerusalem' and 'Zion' signify the church of God. This is also the witness of our creed. What are we laying claim to when we say, 'I believe in the church universal, the communion of saints, the forgiveness of sins'? In short, concerning eternal life, our Lord wanted to instruct us that if we want to attain his kingdom, we must first of all have our sins forgiven, which we could not have without being joined to his church. So when we are separated from it, we are without forgiveness of sins and, consequently, eternal life. And yet, as I said, if we want God to be our Saviour, we have to be in his church. For anyone who remains apart, it seems as though he were consciously depriving himself of the heavenly kingdom and had completely renounced his salvation. It is clear that if God has a company of believers, his majesty is in their midst. We have to join it and fit in. Otherwise, all our knowledge will serve only to condemn us.

Now it is true that when it is a matter of coming into the church, we must not come as pigs to a trough, but with a deep sense of awe and humility. We must humble ourselves before the exalted majesty of God and not approach him as a bosom-buddy companion, as the saying goes. David gives us an example to follow when he says he will come to God's temple and worship in fear (*Psa.* 5:7; cf. *Psa.* 138:2). That is a clear indication that when believers come to the church of God, they are not to be struck with such fear that they withdraw. But, by the same token, they are not to come haughtily, as do those libertines who are so impudent they will come here and present themselves with such pride and arrogance that it seems they want to knock God off his throne. We need to pay close attention to these two things which David points out: we are to come into the church of God in all humility to present ourselves before him and call upon his name; but we are not to be so intimidated by the evidence of God's presence that we flee. Rather, let us draw near to him. It is true we will see in our day people like those Luke talks about, who are so affected by the majesty of God that they dare not approach his church.

The Lord shows his majesty for two reasons. The first is to bolster his church. Sometimes there are people who have tasted God's word, but, even should they reject it, if they ever acquire a position of authority and some case involving the teaching of truth should come before them, they will still try to gain the deliverance of a poor believer. That is because they still have some reverence for that majesty of God which they experienced before but dared not approach, and they are well aware that they are not dealing with men but with God. Thus, there is no doubt that God keeps a tight rein on such people to keep them from rigorously afflicting the faithful, as they would otherwise. That is why our Lord does not allow those people to come into his church and play on our weakness or to continue their usual practice.

The second reason is that there are others who are in awe of that assembly and dare not affiliate with the faithful. That is because they are not at all worthy. How many of us enter the church of God as we should, and with the kind of reverence I spoke of earlier? It is true the gospel is preached. So what? To what extent do our lives conform to it? It seems we have conspired to spite God in all we do. We do not hesitate to use the word 'reformation', but to what purpose? We have no difficulty, no scruples, in saying we are reformed according to the gospel. But what authority does the gospel have for us? Does it not influence us to flout God and his word? What is worse, that is the very reason God's name is blasphemed and people call the gospel a teaching for complete disintegration. But are they right? 'Those people say they are reformed, but they are more inclined to do evil than before.' That is how we will give the papists and other unbelievers an opportunity to speak badly of God's teaching and blaspheme it. It is true that one day they will give an account of their blasphemies, but we will not be excused before God, for we will have given them occasion to speak ill of it. Whereas they should be convinced by our good lives and conduct, we are the reason that God's teaching, which is the teaching of life and salvation, is called 'the teaching of devils' and labelled as false and misleading. Let us keep in mind the punishment we deserve for such sacrilege. Let us be aware that the gospel is not preached to us for that reason, but so that our lives will be completely changed by it and our sins rooted out so that God may be seen to be ruling in our midst. Otherwise, we will boast in vain of possessing the gospel and living according to the reformation it brings.

It gets even worse. We have no reverence for God's majesty when the question is one of our being brought into his church. We come with our defilements and filthiness without any reluctance whatsoever. We know that from the time of the figures of the law, it was expressly forbidden for anything unclean to enter the temple (*Lev.* 15:31; 22:3). Now, if our Lord made such a prohibition at that time, what must it be now? We no longer have a material temple, but we have our Lord Jesus Christ, in whom all the fullness of divinity abounds (cf. *Col.* 2:9). We are joined to him and from his life draw our own. That notwithstanding, we will still bring all our uncleanness and there will be in us nothing but stench and corruption. When it is a matter of coming into God's church, do we think he will tolerate such scorn for himself and his word? It is true he will tolerate it for a while, but in the end we will pay dearly. One fine day, we will have to give an account for scorning the means which God gives us to come to him. How many remember their baptism and why they were baptized? It does not cross their mind, and that should not surprise us. Instead of having to review that teaching every day, each of us should, when a child is baptized, remember our own baptism and consider why God instituted the practice and why we observe it. Instead of doing that, I say, there are these dogs, these pigs that will come here and stick their snout in the door and turn away without entering. It is true that is their custom, and they have done it for two or three days now. They will come here to honour a person but in so doing they dishonour God – and that is worse than spitting in his face, for they are not concerned about the baptism or the preaching which takes place. It seems these people are devils, as in truth they are, since they avoid the word of God and the invocation of his holy name. In that, they show they are so shameless and so unregenerate that they should be pointed out clearly. When we see that kind of scorn, let us be careful not to get on familiar terms with that kind of wretched people. For God's punishment will not long delay. But let us join the company of believers and, upon seeing God's majesty, let us not be frightened by it and flee. Let us enter boldly, but with profound humility so that we, being joined to the church of God, may participate in the benefits he provides in it, and may we learn how to magnify God in all, and through all, and in every way.

Following this holy teaching, let us bow before the face of our gracious God, acknowledging our sins and beseeching him, after he calls us to the knowledge of his word, to be pleased to grant us the grace not to continue in our usual vices, but by cleansing us of them completely, may he so remake us in his image and likeness that we will not give occasion to unbelievers to denigrate his holy teaching by blaspheming him, but by our good behaviour may they be drawn to him and walk in his holy will, and may he make us more and more like him until we all reach that perfection to which he calls us. May he not show that grace to us only but also to all the peoples and nations of the earth . . .

18

STRONG IN THE LORD

SUNDAY, 6 JULY 1550

Then the high priest rose up, and all they that were with him, (which is the sect of the Sadducees,) and were filled with indignation, [18] And laid their hands on the apostles, and put them in the common prison. [19] But the angel of the Lord by night opened the prison doors, and brought them forth, and said, [20] Go, stand and speak in the temple to the people all the words of this life. [21] And when they heard that, they entered into the temple early in the morning, and taught (Acts 5:17–21).

In this account, we have a repetition of what we encountered earlier. God's kingdom cannot be advanced without Satan's doing everything he can to hinder it. Consequently, there will always be struggle and dissension. Because that is such an important matter for us to consider, we hear much said about it. We would like for Jesus Christ to reign among us, but without persecution or any hardship whatever. He, however, wants to show us that his gospel is a treasure so precious that acquiring it is not to do us harm, being afflicted, as we are, by the world and persecuted for having it. On the other hand, our faith and our patience need to be exercised. Consequently, we must be prepared to face struggles as often as we hear the gospel proclaimed. It is inevitable. It is true that believers will not be defeated, for our Lord will hold Satan in check as well as all the wicked, whose endeavours will be thwarted. But God's children must not expect peace in this world, for the enemies of truth will always rise up against them to bring them down if at all possible. So if we are not armed against all their assaults, what will happen? Now we can defend ourselves by looking to those who have fought before us and realizing we do well to follow in their steps because they have waged unrelenting warfare to reach God's kingdom. In addition to that, let us take refuge in the one who can help us and fortify us with an invincible constancy. That is what Luke intends to convey in this story.

Now Luke had recounted earlier that the number of believers continued to increase and that God had poured out extraordinary blessings on his church (*Acts* 5:14–16). That we know. Still the church must do battle even though God is present to help her. She has to have enemies to torment her. So let us give close attention to this passage, because we need to bear in mind that God declares his presence when he distributes his Spirit to us. When he awakens us to his kindness, that ought to strengthen us against all the temptations which could possibly arise. For what do we want more than to have God show by deed and experience that he is with us to sustain us and protect us? Those are the weapons for fighting off all of the difficulties of this world. That is the way it is when our Lord lets us taste his grace as it is revealed in his gospel and sealed in our hearts by his Holy Spirit. That witnesses to his presence, and we must be assured that he helps us and watches over our salvation. Those are the weapons with which we will be able to ward off the temptations of the devil, the world, and our own flesh. It is certain that God reveals himself in his gospel, for it contains his word, which shows forth his power by the fruit it bears. Whenever we consider the preceding, if we are obliged to be vexed and tormented and if the wicked are to have power over us, let us bear it all, content to know that God will never abandon us. The acts of grace he bestows upon us confirm that that is true and that he is demonstrating his goodwill toward us. In that we must find all our peace.

We must also look closely at this situation in which the enemies of truth, of whom Luke speaks, were not pagans, people who rejected the God of Abraham, the law of Moses, or all of holy Scripture. The enemies of truth, he said, were the high priest and those who had the oversight of the children of Israel, that is, those who were revered as the pillars of the church of God. That is strange. Was it not enough for declared enemies of God to take arms and wage war against him and the gospel and level their horns against it? But here we have those who claim to be the church conspiring against it and doing the worst they can! Well, that is the way it has to be. Clearly God has his reasons. In this way he wishes to subject our faith and faithfulness to a higher test. However, he displays the majesty of his word by putting it to the test, whether attacked from within or without. It remains ever steadfast and true. That is how the apostles were put to the test. Paul, lamenting the evils he endures, says that he not only has to battle the enemy outside the church but also the enemy inside, which is worse. For one does not always know how to deal with domestic enemies, with those traitors and Judases who profess Christianity but persecute believers as much as or more than those who make open war on God's church. We see that going on every day, more than we should. Consequently, we have to pay attention to this passage because it was the high priest, the one holding the highest rank in God's church, and those of his crew who rose up against God's servants.

Luke says it was notably the Sadducees. About that we must remember what I touched on earlier concerning the great division at the time. There was no apparent church of God in the entire world except in Judea. Yet those who have full authority there are brutish people who place no value on eternal life. They are so addicted to the ways of this world that they think that man's chief happiness is to live as he pleases and that God's children have no other heritage than to exist here like pigs at a trough. That was what the Sadducees believed, and that is what constituted the faction among the Jews at that time. This can be a very useful passage provided we apply it gainfully. It warns us that if we abuse God's word, he will allow our capacity to reason and make judgments to become like that of dumb animals, and we will be no more worthy to be ranked among men than dogs and pigs. For there is no doubt that that was a just punishment from God after the wicked sect of the Sadducees had acquired complete authority in the church of God. Therefore, let us be aware that our privilege will indeed be snatched away unless we use it to honour God and truly obey him.

Now we come to Luke's account that the council came together 'and laid their hands on the apostles', 'being filled with zeal'. That is the word Luke uses. In Greek this word means 'indignation, anger'. However, we must note that Luke wanted to make it clear that that is not the whole picture, that under the cloak of religion we are like madmen. Our will must be restrained, as was pointed out in an earlier sermon. Evil men are like madmen when they want to exercise their evil will by doing what seems good to them. Consequently, God's will is set aside, as it happens among the papists. Whatever it is, they will find it good provided they have some kind of zeal. True? Do not we see that the Jews had this zeal when crucifying Jesus Christ, when persecuting his church, and working against the teaching of the gospel? You would say that 'they have a zeal for God', as Paul bears them witness (*Rom.* 10:2). But look at it! That zeal is enraged and diabolical because God is not in charge of it. Let us not, then, give free rein to our foolish minds and do what we think is good. But let us take knowledge of what God decrees for us, and let us follow only what he lays out for us in his word. Otherwise, if we want to justify our own zeal and our own good intentions, we would have to justify the people Luke is talking about.

Now, Luke tells us the apostles were put in prison. But the angel of the Lord opens the prison doors for them at night and commands them to return to the temple and proclaim the teaching for which they had been imprisoned. Now when God opens the prison door using his angel, he is acting in his usual way. It is true God can do everything by his own hand without using angels. God does not need his creatures to accomplish his will. But he ordained his angels to that office for our welfare because we are so very weak that we always doubt. Although our Lord promises to help us in all things and in all places, we are nonetheless in turmoil. That is why he uses his creatures for our welfare. Inasmuch as we can honour him by believing he alone is powerful to help us, he tells us, in order to strengthen us in our weakness, that his angels are like guards in his service to protect us and watch over our salvation. That is why it is written that 'they are established as servants for those who will be heirs of salvation' (*Heb.* 1:14).

About that we need to note two things. The first I have already touched on, namely, we know how great God's kindness toward us is, seeing that he upholds us and, when we are in doubt, gives us his angels as a testimony of his concern for our salvation. It is as if he were saying to us, 'I not only wish to tell you how much I love you by causing you to sense my power and might, but here are my angels, who will be encamped around you to protect you.' That is spoken of in Psalm 34: 'The angel of the Lord encamps round about them that fear him' (*Psa.* 34:7). And also in Psalm 91 we learn that he charges his angels to guide our steps in all our ways (*Psa.* 91:11). We have an example of that when the servant of Elijah [sic] went out and saw the great army of the wretched king of Syria, Ben-hadad, and feared to proceed further, thinking that they were all to be destroyed. But when God opened his eyes, he saw that the air was filled with chariots of fire and angels standing ready to do battle against that great army (*2 Kings* 6:15–18). That is why our Lord tells us his angels are always present to watch over us and to show he cares for us.

We need to look again at the kind of love God shows us when devoting such excellent creatures to serve us. When angels are mentioned, they are given honourable titles. They are called powers, principalities, dominions (*Eph.* 1:21; *Col.* 1:16) and by other titles given in Scripture. Not that they possess anything apart from God. They have those titles because they are his officers to execute his holy will. As already said, God's love for us is seen in the fact that he commits his angels, very worthy and honourable creatures, to protect us.

About that Luke says, 'But the angel of the Lord by night opened the prison doors, and brought them forth.' One might ask why that was done at night. If our Lord wanted to perform such a miracle, should it not be shown to everybody? Now we need to note that when God deploys his power in this way to protect his own, he does not always want the wicked to know it, for in fact they are not worthy. The wicked will not see the glory of God except to be confounded by it. Sometimes God will give the wicked a sign of his power but they will always be hardened and blind, unable to see and appreciate what is shown to them for their advantage. God does not manifest himself to the wicked unless, as I have said, it is to alarm and confounded them. That is not the way believers sense his power. That is why the apostles are delivered at night. They will eventually experience God's power and might in many other ways, as we will see shortly.

We come now to Luke's statement that the angel of God brought the apostles forth and commands them to go to the temple and preach as they had done before. The apostles could have replied, 'What do you mean? We were put in prison for preaching the gospel. Our case is to be tried. What will happen if we go to the temple to preach again? They will say that we are escapees and seditious men who wish to obey neither magistrate nor any authority, and that we are subverting all order and civil policy. Would it not be better to wait a while, just until the rage of the wicked has settled a bit?' There is no doubt that the apostles would have been tempted by such a consideration if God had allowed it. But we must consider the fact that they did not do what they would have preferred because God had chosen them to serve him. They are obliged to fulfil their charge without regard for what they might face, for should heaven and earth melt together, they must do as they are told. For always before their eyes is the conviction that it is better to obey God than men. In fact, their promptness in obeying God is made even clearer when the text says that 'they entered into the temple early in the morning.' From that you can tell they did not spend a lot of time discussing whether it was a good idea to go or whether the time was right. No, no! Following what the angel said, they come to the temple early in the morning to obey what was commanded them. They do not wish to be governed by their own wisdom. They choose only to fulfil the command to the best of their ability.

So let us learn from their example not to be wise in ourselves or to do what we think is good. But let us be wise and allow God to govern us. In fact, the whole of our wisdom is in allowing God to rule over us so that we will not pamper ourselves by doing as we please, as well as in finding God's commands good and in revering his word so that as soon as he speaks we will not balk but do our duty by obeying him in what he says. That is what the apostles did, and that is what Paul is talking about when he praises the Colossians for listening to and receiving the gospel as soon as he preached it to them (*Col.* 1:3–6). We do not need a lot of time before obeying God. When he speaks we must each be ready to receive what he tells us for our own good. And let us not even put it off from one day to the next, but as soon as he makes his will known, let us realize he also wants us to comply immediately. Let us be careful not to do as many others, who know what God's will is but say, 'Yes, he must be obeyed', but are always looking for excuses. 'Yes', they say, 'there are great difficulties in doing one's duty towards God. I know I am bad, living the way I do. I know I am on the way to hell. But look! I am taking into consideration how difficult it is to do what I know God requires of me.' That, I say, is how men take the opportunity to turn from the straight path even though God has favoured them by setting them on it. And how remiss they are in doing what they know God asks of them! That is not the way we are to respond, but 'early in the morning', 'early in the morning'. That means that as soon as God commands a thing, we are not to put off doing it until the next day!

In addition, we must also note that the text says our Lord delivers the apostles so they can place themselves again in the same danger. To be sure, he does that because he wants his gospel preached. So let us keep in mind that when God delivers his own, it is not so they will be idle afterwards, but to strengthen them even more and make them strong and steadfast by the power they experienced earlier. And especially when it is a matter of teaching the gospel, we must always take into consideration that if our Lord saves us from the hands of our enemies, it is so we can apply ourselves to serving him and sustaining his truth, not to sparing our own lives to do so.

We ought to pay particular attention to this teaching because today people are so wretched that if they are delivered from some danger, they think they are even and have already done too much. Here is an example. A man has considerable zeal after being instructed in the gospel. He is persecuted for it and God later delivers him. Previously, he was fired up, and now he has cooled off. 'Look', he says, 'I have had my turn. Let someone else take his. I have gotten close enough to the fire and I do not have to go back again.' That kind of ingratitude, I tell you, fills many people. They should instead look at it this way: 'When God delivers me, is it so I will be silent? Indeed not! But because he has given me the grace to escape the hands of his enemies, it is to make me feel his goodness all the more. Therefore, I must be grateful and thank him for such kindness and magnify him everywhere and in all places.' While they should be thinking about how better to magnify and exalt the power and might of God that they felt when he delivered them from the hands of the enemy, instead they are so cold and remiss they dare not open their mouths to say a single word about Jesus Christ.

Seeing, then, that there is such weakness in the people to whom God has given a taste of his kindness and power, let us mark this teaching and profit from it even though it is not surprising that many lose their zeal after being delivered. Most of them break free only by renouncing God. When they are in this situation, it is not a question of thinking that they are here to support God's truth and that God honours them by making them defenders of his gospel. They are pondering how, by any means, they will be able to find devious ways to escape by the skin of their teeth, as the saying goes, without concern for eternal life. They do not remember the fearful threat our Lord Jesus Christ made when he said, 'Whosoever shall deny me before men, him will I also deny before my Father which is in heaven' (*Matt.* 10:33). That is immaterial to them just as long as they break free. That is enough for them. Consequently, we must not marvel that they go from bad to worse and, after being delivered, forget God's gracious acts. For they broke free only by illicit means worthy of his reproof and condemnation.

We come now to what the angel says to the apostles: 'Go, stand and speak in the temple to the people all the words of this life.' We need to note that the gospel is here called 'word of life', for that designation bears witness that we have the knowledge of life and salvation. Who among us is so wretched that he would not like to protect his life? Not only this life, but everlasting life, in which we will share in the glory of God and be companions not only of the patriarchs, martyrs, and angels, but of Jesus Christ, joined in such a way to his body that the majesty in him will shine in us because we are members of his body, each according to his portion. Now if we desire that life the way we should, this is how we can desire it, according to Paul: 'The gospel is the power of God and salvation to everyone that believes' (*Rom.* 1:16).

In that, we can see how wretched the world is. For how does everyone receive the gospel? It is true everyone will say that he wants it; yet, where is the honour we owe to such a precious treasure? How do we often call to memory what is contained in it in order to take advantage of it? In our homes, how do we speak of it? Most people will think that when they hear a sermon on Sunday as a matter of duty, they have done enough. When they return home, instead of discussing, as they should, what was said in the sermon in order to remember better what was dealt with, they will speak only of unworthy and profane subjects. 'Not at all! Not at all', they will say. 'That is a heavy subject to think about. Let us not weary our heads with it.' Still others will be careful not to be offended by the teaching, for with great effort they will come to the sermon once every two months. Consequently, we should not be surprised if men have less understanding and judgment than dumb animals. For animals at least know how to seek the food they need, and men are so wretched they flee from spiritual food, without which they cannot live, although they think they are much at ease in this world. Consequently, we must pay even closer attention to the statement that the gospel is the teaching of life. If we wish to be quickened by God's power and might and so attain the heavenly kingdom, the gospel must be our doorway. Since God is at work in it and displaying his power through it, it has to be clear to us that there is no other way to come to him. It is certain that we will not enter his kingdom against his will. Only the gospel leads us to him. By it we embrace Jesus Christ, who reconciles us with God. By the gospel, I say, we can come to God and the salvation it promises. That is why our Lord Jesus Christ said, 'You are not of God, because you refuse to hear his word' (*John* 8:47). Therefore, those who are offended by the hearing of God's word are already marked for being thrown into the fire of hell.

Let us note also that the gospel is called 'word of life' in consideration of the law. Insofar as the law brought life to men, as Moses affirms, it was impossible to do what was contained in the law because there was a condition, namely that whoever does these things will live by them (*Lev.* 18:5; *Gal.* 3:12). So when the Lord sets the law before us, he thereby makes known the rule for right living. It is true that when giving it to the people, he said explicitly, 'Cursed be he that confirms not all the words of this law to do them' (*Deut.* 27:26; *Gal.* 3:10).

But let us now look to ourselves. Who is the man who has fulfilled the law of God and not failed in one point, but in a hundred million? Now we can think of many faults in ourselves which would condemn us. But God sees incomparably more than we do. How, then, will we be able to have life through the law when we are far from not failing in a single point, seeing that we are guilty of them all? It is true the law would indeed be life for us if we fulfilled it completely. But who would boast of such an accomplishment? That is why Paul says the law is nothing less than the teaching of death and that we are under its curse because God has established this condition: that he who does not fulfil it in its entirety will be cursed (*Gal.* 3:10–12). On the other hand, he says that the gospel is the teaching of life (*Gal.* 3:13–14) because God, after showing us our condition, has declared that we cannot be saved by our works, which we would accomplish in accordance with the commandments of the law. But inasmuch as we are completely shut out, we must seek our salvation in Jesus Christ and receive by faith the blessing which he acquired for us by his death and suffering. Let us know that he suffered for us to appease God's wrath and that his is the sacrifice which has erased all our iniquities. So when the gospel tells us that we can acquire in Jesus Christ what we will not find in ourselves, we know why it is called 'the teaching of life'. Let us, then, note this expression well, for God will not allow us to exalt ourselves by our conceit, as if we deserved something from him.

That is the principal difference between the papists and us. They think they can reckon with God and by their own works merit paradise. We, on the other hand, say that we are all accursed, and that when we have done all we can, it will serve only to make us stumble into hell unless he extends his hand. That singular teaching will humble us before God, and unless we are cast down and dead within ourselves, we will never achieve eternal life. And the way to achieve it is through the gospel, as we have already said.

Moreover, we must examine the expression 'of this life'. On the surface it appears that God is trifling with the apostles. They are in prison, they will soon return, they will be beaten, and in the end they will be led off to be executed like highwaymen and thieves. Yet they hear about life. When the angel speaks 'of this life', he seems to be speaking clearly, and yet they could only see death all around them.

Now it is certain that this life is not such that we can see it with our eyes and touch it with our hands, as God shows us our present life, but he is speaking of spiritual life, in which we are like dead men. Paul talks about it that way when he says that we are dead and our lives are hidden in Jesus Christ to be revealed only in the last day (*Col.* 3:3). That is what our lives will be with respect to the world. We will be like dead men. What is more, that is how we must be within ourselves with respect to our natural lives. The Holy Spirit bears witness to another life (cf. *Rom.* 8:16–17), which is much more precious than the life of this world. And why is that? We must now die in the death of our Lord Jesus Christ because it is in him that our lives are hidden. That is why the angel says, 'this life', as if he were pointing it out clearly for us to see and to touch so that we might be entirely and perfectly certain that the life of believers lies within the gospel. That can be stated briefly after we have simply concluded that when God reveals his gospel to us by his Holy Spirit, it is true that if we look within ourselves, we will see only poverty and wretchedness, anxieties, afflictions, and most often death. So where is 'this life'? We must rise above the heavens and seek in Jesus Christ the life which is spoken of here, for in ourselves we will find only weakness and imperfection. On the other hand, we will find in Jesus Christ all our good, our life and our salvation. And although we do not see that at present, we must still believe without any doubt that we will find it in him alone in accordance with the saying that the gospel is the teaching of life, by which, if we obey it, God will without doubt bring us to immortal and incorruptible life.

Following this holy teaching, let us bow before the face of our gracious God in acknowledgment of our failings, praying that he will be pleased to correct our faults so that, being cleansed of them, we may acknowledge him as our Master and Saviour and entrust ourselves completely to his kindness and remain obedient to his holy word. And being clearly instructed by it, let us ask for nothing but the glorification of his holy name so that he will accept us as his children and we will acknowledge him as our Father, giving him such honour and reverence as he asks of us. May he extend that grace not to us only, but also to all the peoples and nations of the earth . . .

19

ALL TO SUBMIT TO THE WORD'S AUTHORITY

SUNDAY, 13 JULY 1550

Then came one and told them, saying, Behold, the men whom ye put in prison are standing in the temple, and teaching the people. ²⁶ Then went the captain with the officers, and brought them without violence: for they feared the people, lest they should have been stoned. ²⁷ And when they had brought them, they set them before the council: and the high priest asked them, ²⁸ Saying, Did not we straitly command you that ye should not teach in this name? and, behold, ye have filled Jerusalem with your doctrine, and intend to bring this man's blood upon us. ²⁹ Then Peter and the other apostles answered and said, We ought to obey God rather than men. ³⁰ The God of our fathers raised up Jesus, whom ye slew and hanged on a tree. ³¹ Him hath God exalted with his right hand to be a Prince and a Saviour, for to give repentance to Israel, and forgiveness of sins. ³² And we are his witnesses of these things; and so is also the Holy Ghost, whom God hath given to them that obey him (Acts 5:25–32).

The first thing we have to consider in this story is the pride of the enemies of God and his truth, as well as the craftiness they devised when plotting to do evil. In addition, we have to look at how our Lord helps his own in such a way they are not disturbed by any fear and danger, and how he gives such power to his word that, notwithstanding all the obstacles the devil erects, it does not fail to have its effect and continue to advance. Those are the things shown here so that if we have to struggle against the wicked who reject God's truth, we may know they are completely blind and the devil possesses them, as this passage clearly mirrors for us. It is certain the priests assembled there were convinced the apostles had been delivered by a miracle. They had put them in prison and the guards under their authority were confident they could carry out their orders. And yet the apostles left the prison, and the guards, with doors locked, had done their duty. Is it not an inevitable conclusion that it was God who brought them out? Should not such a miracle shake those wretched men even though they had previously opposed the teaching of the gospel? Should they not say, 'It is futile to try to oppose God. For despite all our efforts, he will remain the master and we will inevitably be confounded.' But they do not take all that into consideration. They pursue their wicked undertaking. In that, we see that what I have said is true. Those who have contemplated doing evil cannot be brought back to the right path and to conformity with God's will, no matter the warnings they receive, no matter the miracles they are shown.

As for us, we need to pray that God will grant us the grace to be able to contemplate all his works so that we may honour him wherever he manifests himself. As for the others, they are intelligent enough, but because they understand everything badly, we see they are stupid and as dense as dumb animals. Where does that come from if not from God's punishment? The same will happen to us if we do not willingly listen to what he tells us and comply with complete obedience. Now if it happens that we reject his word by refusing this excellent wisdom which even the angels revere, it is certain we will be unable to avoid the brutish stupidity mentioned here. And God will always start at this point: if we see all the miracles in the world, they will not affect us. Therefore, let us be content with the teachings of the law, the prophets, and the gospel, and receive them in a spirit of meekness. If we do that, our Lord will open our eyes to behold all his works so that we can learn from them and put them to good use for our salvation.

But if we act like wild animals and our rebellion is such that we refuse to submit to the teaching proposed for us, spiritual blindness will inevitably follow. It is like this. Even if God shows us many things, we will not understand them. That is what this example shows us. We also see in it men's pride and haughtiness in that they create prohibitions, edicts, laws, statutes, and commands against God's clear ordinances. This is an example. We hear in this story how the high priest speaks: 'Did we not straitly command you that you should not teach in this name?' And where is this prohibition found? There you have God, who commanded that his teaching be preached and made known everywhere. And then these wretches come and forbid that God's ordinances be obeyed! When saying, 'We strictly forbade you to teach in this name', they band together and resolve that God's word not be heard and that what he commanded go unfulfilled. Now what is recorded here about the high priest and his accomplices ought to strike us as very strange because it is against God that they take this action. Yet we see such examples every day. People who profess the name of God rise up nonetheless in their diabolical pride, thinking they have the power to order and forbid whatever they considered right. If you say to them, 'But you are going against what God has declared', they will turn a deaf ear. They set aside what holy Scripture teaches and follow the leadings of their own mind. 'Look', they will say. 'We will finish what we have begun.' By doing that they arm themselves with the authority God gives them, as the priests are doing here. That argument in their defence, according to them, was implicit in their claim that God had established them for spiritual government and that they are his appointed angels and messengers.

Moreover, Scripture tells us that if there were some difficult point in the law, the priest should be consulted to resolve it. That is how these wicked enemies of all truth continue to clothe themselves in the name of God whenever they want to rise up in an abominable tyranny to thwart God's authority among us and prevent his word from running its course. What happened back then still happens today. What pretext does the pope proffer when it is a question of raising himself as an idol to dominate God's sanctuary, to suppress God's ordinances, and even destroy the glory of God and our Lord Jesus Christ? He will call himself 'Vicar of Jesus Christ on Earth', 'Successor of the Apostles', 'Head of the Church Universal', and 'Servant of all the Faithful'. In short, he will say nothing that does not seem to be the epitome of holiness. Yet he will abuse God's name, like the wicked liar he is. Has he laid claim to all these fine epithets? Has he masked and disguised himself with those titles? He issues edicts, statutes, and ordinances as he pleases. It is immaterial to him that he leaves Scripture behind as long as he has the title of Vicar of Jesus Christ. There he is, veiled and disguised.

Consequently, there is good reason the Holy Spirit has warned us that those who falsely claim God's name are the greatest adversaries of his truth and of his gospel. We very much need to be armed with that teaching, for we could easily be intimidated when seeing the great public manifestation of this Antichrist and all the titles he usurps, like calling himself 'Vicar of Jesus Christ', 'Successor of the Apostles', and 'Head of the Church Universal'. As a matter of fact, there are many gullible and simple-minded folk who can be influenced by them. The title 'Vicar of Jesus Christ' is enough to make them breathless with admiration, for, dazzled by such an honourable title, they are not aware of how the title deludes them. The fact that God has warned them does not give them pause.

Well, we have here an age-old image of God's enemies misappropriating his name. We see how they conducted affairs back then and we need to be all the more attentive as we consider this story. When the text says the high priest is established by God and ordained for spiritual government by the law of Moses, his counsellors are not foreigners, pagans, or unbelievers, but elders and rulers of the people of God. Yet, they consent to usurping the law's rigorous tyranny by hindering the proclamation of the gospel. Not only must each one of us apply this story to his own individual case so that we may be fortified against all temptations, but those who occupy some public office must also consider themselves as being like all those who proclaim God's word. They must carefully consider whether God has called us to this office. If he has, it was not to give us license to say what seems good to us, but to fulfil faithfully our God-given charge in such a way that we can affirm that we have added nothing of our own, but have sought only the reign of Jesus Christ, and that we have advanced nothing but what we have learned from him and his apostles.

The same is true for those who have public offices. Let them consider well that if God has placed them in positions of authority over others, theirs is not an unbridled power to say, 'We have the power to do this or that.' For as soon as a person talks like that, it would be better for that person to be a cut-throat highwayman in the deep woods than to utter the word 'power'. The devil ought to take men when they declare their power, saying, 'We have the power, we have the power.' And what are highwaymen able to do in the woods? A magistrate's duty is to follow what he knows God commands and not to do what he has the power to do or what he thinks is right. Consequently, this word 'power' is truly diabolical when taken alone without considering how a man can do what he does and for what purpose. And even if that word is not used, even though we pay close attention to what is necessary, we will understand that it is not our place to undertake what we would like, but that we have a Master above and that God must always grant his authority and we must conform to his will and not to what we have the power to do. That then is how those who hold public offices must view themselves, since those wretched men whom Luke is talking about exceeded the limits of their authority, to their dismay.

In order to understand better what is recounted here, let us consider the apostles' response: 'We ought to obey God rather than men.' We encountered that thought earlier, unless it is interpreted differently: 'Judge for yourselves whether it is right in the sight of God to hearken to you more than to God' (*Acts* 4:19). That was Peter and John's response when they were questioned.

Peter, speaking for all the apostles, now says resolutely, 'We ought to obey God rather than men.' There is no doubt the high priest and all his train had a ready reply: 'What? Are we not God's representatives?' But the fact is, the apostles demonstrate clearly that God considers them his enemies despite their boast that this responsibility has been entrusted to them. And when the apostles see that those men contradict the teaching, they have no difficulty categorizing them as God's adversaries. Consequently, the rank and all the dignity they were able to claim did not prevent the apostles from discrediting the high priest and all his crew as God's enemies because of their opposition to the gospel.

This passage requires close attention, for we see clearly today the false teaching which blinds the poor ignorant people when they hear this word from 'Holy Mother Church', from 'the Chief Bishop and Pastor', from 'the Vicar of Jesus Christ'. There they are, much frightened. Why so? They think that the Papacy could in no way be separated from God and that if there is any authority and sanctity in any position, it must be sought and found in the Holy Apostolic See, which they are usurping. Consequently, because the ignorant have no capacity for discernment, they are unfortunately led about like dumb animals, and that is why we must be the more diligent to weigh carefully what is said here. Peter is not just speaking of those who confiscate and exploit God's honour, for he shows clearly that that can be done hypocritically. Not only must we not hold such people in reverence or honour them in any way whatsoever; but we must reject them as abominable because they do not fulfil their office and faithfully discharge the responsibility God has entrusted to them.

It is true we must honour all the levels of authority which God has established in this world – as long as those who hold those offices govern us in accord with God's word. But the moment they try to subject us to their will and we, on the other hand, know that such is against God's decree, then we will be able to say it is better to obey God than men. And yet we must be careful not to be like many who, pretending to want to obey God, want only to govern themselves according to their foolish minds. Here is a case in point. There are arrogant and ignorant people who do not know whether God approves what they do. Afterwards, if they are brought to their good senses and shown they must behave according to rules and reason, they will say, 'Yes, but must we not rather obey God than men?' That is what the Anabaptists and many other sects do! Yet it does not occur to them that God does not accept them at all, even though they pretend to have a great zeal for obeying him. Consequently, we must pay attention to all the circumstances Luke implies here. He does not say the apostles made that very simple response. They explained why we must obey God rather than men, and confirmed the teaching. 'The God of our fathers', they say, 'raised up Jesus, whom you crucified. He made him Prince and Saviour over us. He has made us witnesses of these things. Therefore, we must obey him.' That is how the apostles show that our Lord sent them. They do not tell something they made up, but proclaim only what they received from their Master. And on that basis they can indeed declare that God must be obeyed rather than men.

If we want this teaching to bear fruit in us, each of us will have to consider what our calling is. In the first place, we have our general instruction, which, inasmuch as our Lord has called us to the knowledge of his truth, we must adhere to. We know that God teaches us in his gospel what our faith is and upon what it must be based. Since we have the teaching, let us know that God has spoken to us. Now that he has spoken, we must not undertake whatever seems good to us or trust in men when they try to get us to go against him, but we must be in such conformity with the gospel that when the devil devises whatever he can against us, we will remain steadfast and constant. That, then, is each Christian's calling. We must have no other faith than that shown in the law, the prophets, and the gospel. We also know that God must remain our governing authority and that we must not be subject to men in spiritual matters (I am not talking about rank and civil government), for those of lower rank must yield to being subjects, as Scripture teaches (*Rom.* 13:1–2; *Titus* 3:1; *1 Pet.* 2:13–14). But as for what God's word sets forth, men must not try to challenge it in any way. It is written, 'You shall not do what pleases you, but you shall do what I have commanded you without adding anything or taking anything away' (cf. *Deut.* 4:2; 12:32; 26:16). Since God wants us to adhere to his word and have no other articles of faith than those contained in it, we will be able to strengthen ourselves with our response if men should try to turn us from it. It is God who calls us and it is men who turn us from him. We must obey God rather than men.

Following that is the general rule that each one is to make an effort to bring poor ignorant people to the knowledge of God. When we see them going to hell and the resistance they put up, let us move on, realizing that if we fall into iniquitous hands when confessing our faith, we must, since God commands it, obey him rather than men and not be afraid of glorifying him before men and confessing our Christian faith. If they gag us, if they bind our hands, if they forbid us to instruct our neighbours and profess our faith, and if they pressure us to do something completely repugnant to our Christian faith, we must at such times remember our responsibility. Even then are we certain of God's will? There will still be opportunities to say, 'We must obey God rather than men.'

After that, there are those who have been charged with some duty. The apostles had already received this commission from Jesus Christ: 'Go, proclaim the gospel and make known to all creatures the kingdom of God' (*Mark* 16:15). Therefore, they must not resist that. They must go preach. Why? Because Jesus Christ's order once given cannot be retracted despite the devil's best efforts. The charge Jesus Christ committed to his disciples must be carried out. The same applies to us since we have been equipped with that calling. If someone wants to stop our mouths and prevent us from declaring what we have received from God, what are we to say? 'We must obey God rather than men.' But the first thing we are to learn is to proclaim nothing but what we have received from our Master. By doing that, we will be free to defy everybody in the world when they try to keep us from doing our duty. For then we will be able to declare boldly that we must obey God rather than men.

Now if that practice had been observed, Christianity would not be in the state of disarray we see it in today. Why has God's truth been perverted the way it has, and why have lies been prized above truth? It is because men rather than God have been obeyed and because they have not looked to God's commands to learn their limits. That is how God has been abandoned and men have been given precedence.

When the Lord established the high priest in the law and said that people are to go to him in times of difficultly, it was not to diminish his right and the authority which belongs to him. 'You', he says, 'will do what I command you without adding anything or taking anything away.' So our Lord did not establish the high priest in order to relinquish his responsibility and let the high priest rule in his stead, but he did so on the condition spoken of in Malachi: 'For the priest's lips shall keep knowledge, and they shall seek the law at his mouth' (*Mal.* 2:7). Consequently, God established the priests on condition that they follow his commands. But if they deviate from them ever so slightly, they are to be treated not only as private individuals but also as devils. Whereas our Lord established them as his angels and his messengers, as we have said, we must consider them as abominable and contemptuously throw mud in their face. That then is how in the time of the law God did not establish priests to teach what they thought was good, but to expound the law to the people.

Now let us consider how faithful they were to God's clear ordinance. Not only did the priests not obey God's command, but they also took a stand against the prophets and in the end even against Jesus Christ and his apostles. We see how, in like manner, those who call themselves the successors of the apostles try to subvert God's truth and change it into a lie. And yet what are we to do? The pope does not want to discuss the subject. He thinks that if holy Scripture is even cursorily examined, his abominations will be discovered and that the lamest idiot will realize everything he proposes is a lie. He thinks small children will be capable of scoffing at it all. Consequently, the only way to vindicate himself is to say that the church is infallible, but if anyone wants to know how that can be, he will never allow the question. He will invoke his Holy Apostolic See: 'How', he will say, can you question that we are the church? Since we are the church, it follows that we cannot err. Therefore, we do not need to be corrected on that point.' Indeed! As if the Holy Spirit had come down from heaven to reveal all that to them! That is the way they talk.

We can tell by what the apostles say that they are fallible: 'We must obey God rather than men.' That is said to the ones God had constituted in his name. It is clear that he is today addressing those who adamantly claim the name of God. Yet we see in this passage how the apostles set them over against God as his mortal enemies. Now when the pope wishes to demonstrate that he is indeed the head of the church and that it is he to whom all authority belongs, he cites among other passages this one from Deuteronomy 17: 'And the man who presumptuously will not obey the priest, who is there ministering before the Lord, that man shall die' (*Deut.* 17:12). In fact, that is the only passage in holy Scripture that he uses to defend his claim. But when all is said and done, we will find the passage works against him rather than for him. For the pope and those whom Luke is talking about have always appealed to the same pretext, namely that they were ordained by God. Although the pope cannot find a single reference in holy Scripture to support his ordination, he and his kind wish to do things to suit themselves without limiting themselves to the condition given at the time of their institution, namely, not to deviate from God's will. Consequently, they must not arm themselves with this passage when they claim they are ordained by God – but they must obey! They are so far from being chosen by God that they have even risen up against him, as if to spite him. And even if they had been called and ordained by God as the priests in the law were, the fact remains that they are not worthy of being obeyed, for being called to an office and fulfilling its responsibility are two very different things. How many fulfil their responsibility of serving God as they should? More serve the devil than God. Yet we know all Christians are called. How many are there, though, who renounce their baptism and eradicate the mark of God they received in it? However, as I said, we are all called. Nevertheless, we see many who do not follow their calling.

In addition, let us consider how the pope, in all his acts, works against God. We see our Lord wanted to reveal himself to us through his gospel. So that no one may make excuses for not knowing him, he wants his teaching to be made known to everyone in general. That is the ordinance which our Lord wanted to establish concerning the dissemination of his gospel. And here the pope comes, setting himself athwart everything and forbidding its dissemination, as if in spite of God he wanted to do the opposite of what he commands. We know that holy Scripture shows us the way to be saved and witnesses to our adoption as children of God by grace. Then it shows us we cannot approach God on our own, but that we must come through Jesus Christ because it is he who is charged by God his Father to reconcile us to him. It also shows that as long as we are in this world we must trust God completely. Otherwise, we are more to be pitied than wild animals. That teaching is quite certain!

On the other hand, what is the pope's teaching? In the first place, he tells us man has something within himself which will pay his debts before God. Not that that is enough, the papists will say, for they are still obliged to admit that there is much ignorance and weakness in us, but in their audacity they always attribute to themselves a part of their salvation. This is the way they talk: 'It is true God gives us a heart for doing good, but we do not relinquish some use of our free will. Then we know God will be merciful to us and forgive our faults, but we will hold on to ways to compensate him. Jesus Christ will indeed be our righteousness, but we also will have some righteousness in ourselves and in our own worth. God will cleanse us of the offences we have committed against him. Jesus Christ is indeed our Advocate, but we can have other advocates and patrons.' When we see that kind of confusion in the Papacy, what are we to say but, 'Oh! We must obey God and forsake men when they try to turn us away from obeying him.' For, as I said, we must not doubt when it comes to God's truth. A man will never be persuaded to respond that way when someone introduces him to the superstitions of unbelievers, provided he understands God must be obeyed rather than men.

In addition, we need to note that the pope disobeys God and tries to lead men into that disobedience in two ways. The one is direct, the other indirect. An example of the direct is that our Lord Jesus Christ institutes his Supper for us (*Matt.* 26:26–28). He tells us all to take the bread and the wine as a testimony that we are spiritually nourished by the body and blood of our Lord Jesus Christ. Likewise, when he speaks of the cup, he tells us all, without exception, to take it and drink from it. Now we have the pope, who issues a contrary edict and says, 'Everyone will not drink from it. Only one will partake.' Is that not great audacity, corrupting Jesus Christ's holy ordinance that way? That is like saying, 'No matter what you say, I will prevent the observation of the ordinance you established.' That is how that presumptuous man rises up against God. So, when we disobey that Antichrist, does it mean we wish to disobey God? Far from it! For see how the pope presumes to snatch from Jesus Christ his authority and his worth. He does as much with the doctrine of our faith. And that is why I say he leads men into disobedience in an indirect way. We know we are justified by faith without works. The pope comes along and inverts all that, saying our works justify us and, without them, we cannot be saved. In the face of such a great difference, we can easily see how he has inverted the whole of holy Scripture. We see it even in the Supper. Jesus says, 'Take, eat of this bread and drink of this cup.' Now how does the pope go about it? 'Oh! We have to sacrifice Jesus Christ to God his Father. It is true we do the Supper, but we do not forgo offering this sacrifice.' Yet we know God disavows all that and even abhors and rejects it. And yet this wretch expects God to accept it, like it or not.

Next, God has said rather clearly that wanting to hinder marriage is a teaching of devils, for it is an honourable estate for all, without exception (cf. *Heb.* 13:4). Nevertheless, what does the pope say? 'Oh! That is not the way it will be, for marriage will be forbidden to some – priests, for example.' After that, he wanted to establish conditions of chastity, as with monks and nuns. But what happened? He gave them the freedom to live a life of debauchery, provided they abstain from marriage. Then let them do the most damnable abominations imaginable! Thus we see clearly that there is an incomparably greater difference between God's teaching and the pope's than between fire and water, night and day. Yet, what can be done? Let us consider the fact that since it pleases God to have his gospel trumpeted abroad and that he publishes his great Jubilee, not the way that Antichrist of Rome published his this year,[1] he does so for us not only to receive from him full remission of our sins, but also to sustain us with spiritual rejoicing while we are in this world, provided we yield to him and obey him, realizing how much more profitable it will be for us to obey him rather than men. Whereas the papists place their confidence in these meaningless trifles, those children's games that God not only rejects but also abhors, we, on the other hand, look to what God ordains for us so that we can, without deviating from it in any way, adhere to it so completely that each of us, from the greatest to the smallest, will give him the praise and homage which belong to him.

> Following this holy teaching, let us bow before the face of our gracious God in acknowledgment of our failings, praying that he will be pleased to open our eyes so we may know his will and, acknowledging it, profit from it more and more to the end that we may be completely conformed unto it, obeying his holy commandments, in the observance of which may he sustain us until we abandon our fleshly bodies and are fully joined to him so that, being brought into his kingdom, we may be forever set free from law and doctrine. So let us all now say together, God Almighty, heavenly Father ...

[1] Calvin's reference is to Pope Julius III's papal bull of 24 February 1550: *'Si pastores ovium'*. [Editors' note]

20

ALL THINGS MADE NEW

SUNDAY, 13 JULY 1550 (AFTERNOON)

The God of our fathers raised up Jesus, whom ye slew and hanged on a tree.
³¹ Him hath God exalted with his right hand to be a Prince and a Saviour,
for to give repentance to Israel, and forgiveness of sins. ³² And we are his
witnesses of these things; and so is also the Holy Ghost, whom God hath
given to them that obey him (Acts 5:30–32).

There is not one of us who does not agree and say that everything ought to proceed in an orderly manner, and even the most depraved will say it is not good to see only confusion and disorder here. Yet we see there is not one of us who does not contribute to the disorder. So if we desire regular order everywhere, each of us should try to effect it where we are.

Order will be good when God rules over everyone, when everyone maintains his role in life and no one wants to advance himself, unless God urges him to, as when a man has someone entrusted to his charge. He must consider how he is to guide his family. If he has a wife and children whose care God has entrusted to him for their good instruction, may our Lord have his place of authority in all things at the same time. Does the man want his wife and children to obey him? Then his goal must be to honour God as the sovereign Father of all. Does his wife want to have her place of honour? Then she must walk in the path God sets before her. She must be humble and modest toward all, especially toward her husband (*Eph.* 5:22); and when she serves him, she should realize she is serving God at the same time. And let the children know they cannot be obedient to God except as they obey their fathers and mothers with all reverence. Let us maintain such a degree of moderation when serving others that God will always be in charge, since he is our Father, our Master and our sovereign King. Everything will be well ordered among men when God is pre-eminent and, from the greatest to the smallest, they serve in the role God calls them to, each in his own place.

But, as I have just said, there is not one of us who does not add to the confusion. Yet we complain about it anyway! But we will find the fault nowhere but in ourselves. Fathers will not value teaching their children. They will not bear in mind that they have a Father in heaven whom they must serve above all else. Children do not realize they dishonour God when they disobey their fathers. When that kind of uncivilized behaviour exists between fathers and children, God loosens the restraints, and the result is that the fathers, who ought to be obeyed by their children, are not respected by them. Why not? Because the fathers do not give God the honour which is his. We are also at fault, since we are of inferior rank, when those who have power over us loosen the restraints and trouble us, just as princes do not use restraint when governing their subjects, but impose heavy, irksome burdens upon them. And the reason is that we have not paid homage to God as our sovereign Prince. Consequently, he inevitably chastises us for our ingratitude and our failure to grant him the authority which is his. Thus, all the disorder we see in the world today proceeds from our perversity. Yet if we wish to avoid all the chaos that is hard for us to bear, each of us must, as I have said, begin with self in our own place and create order, if we want others to follow us.

Now it remains for us to learn how we are to obey God. The apostles' response tells us: 'The God of our fathers raised up Jesus, whom you slew and hanged on a tree. Him has God exalted with his right hand to be a Prince and a Saviour, for to give repentance to Israel, and forgiveness of sins.' The statement 'Him has God exalted with his right hand' is a simile taken from the roles of men in the world and indicates that Jesus Christ is like a vicegerent of God his Father to exercise all authority and government over us. Do we wish to show that God rules over us and that we honour him as we should? Then we need to yield to Jesus Christ his Son, our Saviour, whom he has given all power and authority. It is he who wants us to acknowledge our Master and Saviour. It is in him alone that he wants us to take refuge for reconciliation with himself. In short, our Lord wants to reign over us only in the person of Jesus Christ his Son. It is futile for men to try to serve God and exclude Jesus Christ at the same time. That is manifest idolatry! We make of God an idol when we want to honour and serve him other than through Jesus Christ. We must mark this passage well, for it tells us God raised Jesus his Son to his right hand to make him our Prince and Saviour. That shows, as I have just said, that it is a misguided effort to serve God without acknowledging Jesus Christ as Saviour and Mediator between him and us. That is also John's testimony: 'He that does not honour the Son does not honour the Father who has sent him' (*John* 5:23). Psalm 2 also says, 'Honour the Son whom he sends to you' (cf. *Psa.* 2:12). Do not think that God wants us to worship him while forgetting Jesus Christ. If we do that, we will be seeking God but we will not find him. For who is his image if not his Son whom he has sent? Do you think it is without reason that Scripture calls Jesus Christ 'the image of God' (*2 Cor.* 4:4)? So if we imagine some aspect of God's majesty without Jesus Christ, we take flight into the unknown, never to reach God, for we will not find him if we seek him apart from Jesus Christ.

Since we cannot know what comes from God until we possess Jesus Christ, it is certain we will not be able to serve him unless we have viewed him seriously under that image by which he has manifested himself to us. That is why holy Scripture points us to Jesus Christ, saying that we must honour him. Why? Because he has been raised to the right hand of God his Father in all glory and majesty and because every creature must be subjected to him, even the angels of heaven with all their excellence and dignity. That being the case, let us be aware that Jesus Christ cannot be our King and sovereign Prince unless he exercises his superiority and preeminence over us. Even so, it is not enough that we know only that Jesus Christ has been raised to the right hand of God to exercise complete authority over us. We must also know how he governs us. And that is what the apostles add: 'God has exalted him to give to Israel repentance and forgiveness of sins.' With those words, they return us to the teaching of the gospel, as if they were saying Jesus Christ was not exalted as King so we would not know how he is to govern us and what power he can exercise over us. But they say that 'it is so that through him we may have repentance and forgiveness of our sins.' We have that witness sealed in our hearts by the Holy Spirit, whom God has poured out upon all those who obey him.

We have just dealt with the principal point of the entire gospel, which is repentance and the forgiveness of sins. Therefore, these two matters are taught daily in the sermons and constitute what we must learn throughout our lives. They contain everything we need to know. However, we must ponder diligently what these two terms convey because of their great importance. Inasmuch as we are told the gospel is the means by which God wanted to reveal himself to us more intimately than ever before, we are shown what benefit we are to draw from it. In particular, we must have steadfast faith in Jesus Christ in order to obtain the forgiveness of our sins. On the other hand, from the beginning the devil has been relentless in obscuring these features, for he knows God's glory and man's salvation depend on them. We know that

Satan, who is God's mortal enemy and whose only endeavour is to obliterate his glory by every means at his disposal, spares no effort to demolish what he knows to be the principal source of God's honour. Following that, we know he is the mortal enemy of man's salvation and connives to destroy what he knows to be for our good. What he cannot accomplish on the first try, he will achieve by any means, if he can. We know that from experience. Throughout the Papacy, they never knew, they still do not know the meaning of the word 'faith'. If you mention the word, they will indeed say you have to have faith. But if you ask them how this word is to be understood, they will say it is enough to have some idea of the faith we owe God. And if you examine them closely, they do not know what God is, what his nature is, or even which God they worship. In fact, they say it is enough to have a 'corporate faith'– that is the way they talk – without knowing whether we are to trust in God or in faith. They will say they believe what Holy Mother Church believes, and if you ask them what she believes, they will say they do not know. That is the inane notion the papists hold concerning faith. If you ask them about the forgiveness of sins, they will tell you we need it, but they will come up with a hundred thousand ways to acquire it. But we know there is only one way to obtain it, and that is through the suffering and death of Jesus Christ. And they say that we must not be categorical, but that it is enough to have some idea about it! As a result, since they are so blind that they have no assurance of the forgiveness of their sins, we can understand that the devil has penetrated the whole world with his false teaching and corrupted the main point of the gospel, which assures us that God has redeemed us by the suffering and death of our Lord Jesus Christ. That then is the gospel's principal teaching, which the devil has perverted to deceive the poor world, as we see it today in the Papacy.

Moreover, this word 'repentance', spoken of here, has also been misrepresented, even totally corrupted by the papists. It is true they babble on in their schools something or other about repentance, but if you ask them what it is, they do not have the slightest idea. They will never arrive at giving the term the explanation it deserves, but if you go a step farther and ask what penitence is, they will say, 'It is fasting, saying paternosters, not eating meat on a certain day, trotting off on pilgrimages, and doing all sorts of other monkey tricks.' That is the kind of tomfoolery they think true penitence is. But when Scripture talks about it, we must understand a renewal of man – that he renounces himself in order to come to God. And because we cannot come to him on our own, possessing not a smidgen of good, and because we are filled with every corruption, we must be changed and moulded anew, beginning with our basic human nature and extending to all our impulses and fleshly desires. It is God who brings about that renewal by his Holy Spirit, and we cannot have it any other way. And since he has been pleased to renew us that way, not for any worth or excellence in us, but because he grants us the grace to accept him and find him good, we must not think we can please him in any other way. What are we to do? Unless God makes us new, all that remains for us is this fear of undertaking anything on our own. But let us always keep in mind the things God approves and allows. To that end, let us seek only to conform ourselves unto him so that we may be made new by his Holy Spirit and, in that way only, accepted as his own.

We see, then, that the Papacy is one of Satan's workshops where he did what he thought was good when he so blinded men that they perverted the main points of holy Scripture, which witness to our salvation. We ought to be all the more diligent in heeding this passage, which speaks of repentance and forgiveness of sins, for by so doing we can know the way God calls us to himself. That is the way we will reach salvation. If we do not have that knowledge, we are lost, for God denies us and banishes us from his kingdom. So if we really thought about these things, would we not be more ardent in thinking upon them more often in order to apply them to our advantage? But do we? We show clearly we are not greatly concerned about our salvation and are not very enthusiastic about God's honour. But in the end, he will show us we should prize such excellent things more highly.

In addition, we need to note that the text is speaking here about the office of Jesus Christ so that we may know the gospel's fullness. In fact, when we thoroughly examine the complete teaching of the gospel, we find that that is all it teaches. It is like Paul says when he tells us the purpose of his calling. 'God', he says, 'sent me to preach Jesus Christ his Son' (*1 Cor.* 1:23; *2 Cor.* 4:5). Then in another passage he says, 'I want to know nothing but Jesus Christ, even though the world scorns him and the proud are scandalized by his cross. Nevertheless, I renounce all other wisdom and desire no other wisdom than Christ' (cf. *1 Cor.* 2:2). Therefore, inasmuch as the gospel teaching consists in Jesus Christ and the knowledge of his office, let us realize that it is through him alone that we must come to God his Father. It is true we will not come by such knowledge on the first day, but we must pursue it with perseverance all the days of our lives. It is not without cause, then, that Scripture says we must glory in the knowledge of Jesus Christ (*1 Cor.* 1:31). Otherwise, we are utterly lost.

In short, those are the two main things Jesus Christ does for us: granting us repentance and forgiveness of sins. We have already touched briefly on what repentance is. It is our being made new to serve God. Now by that we are advised that as long as God allows us to go freely on our own way, we will be totally useless and we will be able to grow spiritually as much as we can – or so we think, but everything we do will only be dung and contagion, as in fact Paul says, 'All of our affections are mortal enemies of God until they are made new by the Holy Spirit' (cf. *Rom.* 8:7, 11). That is man's lot as long as he follows his natural inclination. The only thing he can do is wage open war on God, rebel against him in everything and everywhere, and confront him at every turn, as if determined to cast him from his throne. There exists great strife and dissension between God and our human nature, as between fire and water, and we must not attribute this evil and failing to God. Let us not suppose that God created us such as we are. That proceeds from the sin and corruption of our father Adam. Consequently, we are by nature full of every evil and every iniquity. Some are given to some vice; others are full of pretence and hypocrisy, even though they may appear saintly. Yet, when it is said Jesus Christ grants us repentance, we must understand that until God puts his hand on us to renew us, we will be only contagion and putrefaction. That is what proceeds from our human nature. That is what our flesh is capable of doing. Waging war against God and serving the devil and being under his power, we give ourselves to every evil and every perversity.

In addition, let us bear in mind that man has no capacity to repent unless repentance comes from God, for he alone gives it, as I have just said. The papists teach the opposite, saying that man can generate that repentance himself. It is true, they will say, that if God leaves us where we are, we perish, but when he says, 'Come', it is up to us to get up and go to him. That is how they try to garner for themselves a portion of God's power and might, saying that they can help man come to God. We, on the other hand, heed what the text says here: that Jesus Christ's office is to give repentance and forgiveness of sins. It follows then that we do not have that capacity within ourselves. We know, therefore, that theirs is a doctrine from hell when they say it is up to them to be converted and within their own power to come to God.

So much for the second point that we need to make here. The first is that until Jesus Christ draws us and calls us to himself, we are addicted to every evil. The second is that we do not have the free choice to turn to him, but it is his office to provide what we lack.

Now how does Jesus Christ bring us to repentance? It is when he strips us of everything that belongs to our human nature and regenerates us by his Holy Spirit. We are then said to be children of God. That is why Jesus Christ's Spirit is called 'the Spirit of sanctification' (*Rom.* 1:4), for he cleanses us of all our stains so that we may become children of God. As I have said, two things are required in this process, namely that everything in our human nature must be removed, and that cannot be done unless Jesus Christ sheds his grace upon us.

Now we know that men cannot change themselves and that the Holy Spirit must work within them because they are given to every evil and are even slaves and captives of sin, as Paul says: 'I am sold under sin' (*Rom.* 7:14). That is the way men are in their natural state. Just as a horse is under the control of his master and must be goaded on, we are wretchedly bound and imprisoned by servitude to sin and the devil until our Lord delivers us by his grace. It is true we will not be able to blame our sins on our being forcibly confined by sin. There is not one of us who does not knowingly and willingly sin because we are all naturally corrupt and wicked. Consequently, Jesus has to pour out his grace to cleanse us of all our evil affections and free us of sin's damnable captivity, which is our natural habitat.

That then is how our flesh is put to death when the Holy Spirit governs us and Jesus Christ, by his grace, removes the power of our affections to dominate us and conquers them to such an extent that we ask only to be conformed to him. That is what repentance is. But it is not given once and for all. Jesus Christ must continue to increase it. Let us keep in mind, therefore, that repentance is given to God's children so they may take advantage of it all the days of their lives. And let us not think it is enough for us to come to God once, but let us realize that when he puts us on the path and we take a few steps, we have to persevere until we come to that perfection to which he calls us all.

Now it follows that God is exalted for forgiving our sins. The forgiveness of our sins is the bedrock of our blessedness and salvation as men. True, unbelievers wrangle within their minds to determine whether their sins are forgiven, but they box the air. They have nothing to lean on, as is evident today among the papists. True, they talk about the forgiveness of sins, but it has no meaning for them. In that way, they think they are gaining on salvation, but they are losing ground. The reason is they do not understand what the forgiveness of sins is. We, on the other hand, know how necessary it is to hold fast to that doctrine for our salvation. In fact, the song of Zechariah makes it clear that the forgiveness of sins gives knowledge of salvation (*Luke* 1:77). Now why not seek our salvation somewhere other than in the forgiveness of sins through Jesus Christ? Shall we look in hell? God does not want us to come to him in any way except by the forgiveness of sins through Jesus Christ. In fact, that is what Paul says. We are completely justified by the forgiveness of our sins through Jesus Christ (*Gal.* 2:16). That is also found in the psalms: 'Blessed is he whose transgression is forgiven them, whose sin is covered' (*Psa.* 32:1). So if our blessedness consists in the forgiveness of sins, we conclude that that is the way God justifies us and gives us access to himself.

Therefore, let us not think that we are talking about something frivolous and insignificant when we speak of the forgiveness of sins. Let us realize that in this way we are made to share in all the good things of God and that he accepts us as his children. We even possess him fully. In fact, we also see how much forgiveness of sins costs and what high value God places upon it. Indeed, God's own Son did not spare his own life to acquire it for us. Therefore, because we were poor sinners condemned to everlasting death, the Son of God, the Lord of glory, made the forgiveness of our sins possible. He paid the price and knows how precious it is. For, as I have just said, it cost him very dearly because, for the sake of us poor wretched people, he was willing to endure being led to the ignominious death of being hung on a gallows like a common criminal, but not just on a gallows. It was like being put on a rack. For we know the torture of the cross at that time was more cruel than the gallows. Consequently, since he was willing to suffer all that to reconcile us to God his Father, we can realize how precious the forgiveness of our sins is. But that is not the chief emphasis, for he presented himself to God his Father to receive the condemnation which was due us. 'He was made a curse for all' (*Gal.* 3:13), for a person hanged on a tree was cursed in the law (*Deut.* 21:23), and Jesus Christ suffered that shame because of our curse so that God his Father might now bless us. We see how he cries out, abandoned by God (*Matt.* 27:46; *Mark* 15:34), because he had to descend into hell, that is, into those horrible pits of pain we deserved because of our sins, descending into that abyss because he bore them all on his back. Why did he endure so much? To gain for us the forgiveness of sins.

Let us pay close attention to that teaching, for it is in it that we differ from the papists. If we ask them wherein lies the forgiveness of their sins, they will indeed say God must forgive them, but they will find a thousand ways to obtain it. They have their masses, their prayers, their fasts, their merits, their reparations, their orisons. In short, there is a mountain of meaningless trifles where they search for the forgiveness of their sins. Even so, those trifles are not all there is, for if we come to the source, we will find much worse. That is, the papists are so wretched and cursed, so fiendish that they have tried to do all they could to bring down the Son of God. They have snatched away his glory by usurping what belongs to him alone. There is not a wretched creature among them, no matter how base, who does not think he receives the forgiveness of his sins. A lecher, a panderer, a pillar of a whorehouse, after whoring all year and committing the most damnable abominations you can imagine, acquires forgiveness of his sins, provided he comes and kisses the foot of an idol at Easter. A usurer who spends all his time grasping greedily and perpetrating a thousand extortions against poor people finds himself saved and washed of all his sins, provided he offers up a mea culpa, without giving the Son of God a second thought. Is it not an exceedingly abominable sacrilege when wicked scum full of contagion and stench come like that and usurp the authority which belongs to Jesus Christ? And who are you pitiable creatures who come like that and rise up against the majesty of the Son of God, whom the angels bow before and whom the devils are forced to recognize as their Judge because they cannot have him as their Saviour. So whenever the papists want to use the diabolical and infernal word 'satisfaction', being proud to the point that they think they can make satisfaction for their sins, let us realize that theirs is a diabolical doctrine invented by Satan, as are all the other means which they have fabricated for coming to Jesus Christ.

We note among other things the presumptuousness of their mass, which is their principal idol. There are so many damnable blasphemies in that abomination that the devils in hell themselves tremble. Jesus Christ will not have to open his mouth to condemn them. The devils alone will suffice to judge them for committing such damnable things that the thought of them is terrifying.

Shortly after that, the apostles conclude by saying that the Holy Spirit, whom God gives to those who obey him, testifies to all that they did. In that, we see that the apostles imagined nothing, but faithfully reported the message God entrusted to them. We must not, then, receive their teaching as coming from mortal men.

But let us take heed that God spoke to them by his Holy Spirit, whose instruments they were. That demonstrates how the gospel is not a man-inspired phenomenon. It is not a teaching open to doubt. It is God's infallible truth.

In addition, we must realize that just as the gospel cannot be preached except by the grace of the Holy Spirit, those who receive it must likewise be enlightened by the same grace. For example, I am obliged to be here to proclaim that Jesus Christ is the Saviour of the world, that by him alone we have access to the Father because of the forgiveness of sins which he has acquired for us. That, I say, cannot proceed from me or from anyone else who bears God's word unless we are confident and assured that that word is true and unless his Holy Spirit seals that certainty in our hearts; and all those who hear this word must likewise be equally assured. For that reason, let us learn to apply ourselves to that word without doubting it in any way soever so that we may know through it the source of the forgiveness of our sins, namely, Jesus Christ. May he be pleased to instruct us who have some spark of the Holy Spirit by kindling and increasing this word until we reach full perfection, whose testimony we have in his word that he will make us fellow participants when he takes us from this world.

Now let us beseech our gracious God to be pleased to grant us who have once received the gift of Jesus Christ his Son the privilege of acquiring the forgiveness of our sins so that we may also know how we shall share through him all spiritual blessings, which he has prepared for his elect. While we remain in this world, may he so bestow his blessings that we, being led by his Holy Spirit, may yield ourselves completely to his will until he changes the waywardness of our flesh to conform to himself and his righteousness. May he grant that grace not only to us but also to all the peoples and nations of the earth . . .

21

GOD PRESERVES HIS CHURCH

SUNDAY, 30 JULY 1550

When they heard that, they were cut to the heart, and took counsel to slay them. [34] *Then stood there up one in the council, a Pharisee, named Gamaliel, a doctor of the law, had in reputation among all the people, and commanded to put the apostles forth a little space;* [35] *And said unto them, Ye men of Israel, take heed to yourselves what ye intend to do as touching these men.* [38] *And now I say unto you, Refrain from these men, and let them alone: for if this counsel or this work be of men, it will come to nought:* [39] *But if it be of God, ye cannot overthrow it; lest haply ye be found even to fight against God* (Acts 5:33–35, 38–39).

The answer given last Sunday was intended to bear better fruit than it did among the priests and the council of all those who were set on attacking God's truth. For when the apostles say our Lord Jesus Christ was sent by God his Father to call all poor sinners to repentance and bestow on them the grace of the forgiveness of sins (*Acts* 5:31), was that not enough to convince and confound their harshest enemies? No one is so depraved that he still does not ask how God's grace can be obtained.

That grace offered to us is the forgiveness of sins. All we need to do is receive it by faith. The means is placed before us. To receive it, we must acknowledge that in Jesus Christ we have a definite and unquestionable pledge of God's fatherly love for us, that he has poured out his blood to wash us and suffered for all our offences. In light of that, a person has to be in the full possession of the devil if he does not accept that honour and that grace given to us only for our salvation. Nonetheless, Luke tells us that those who heard the apostles' testimony were enraged.

From that we see that God's instruction, however pleasant it may be, will never bear fruit among men unless the Holy Spirit enlightens them. That is why we said last Sunday that those to whom the Holy Spirit was given were witnesses of these things, not only those who were teaching and charged with proclaiming the gospel, but all believers. For we see clearly how rebellious and hardened a man is when led and guided by his natural senses. He not only scorns the doctrine of salvation, he also becomes angry and takes a stand against it. When we see that kind of demonstration, we must always keep our eyes fixed upon ourselves and realize how perverse our human nature is until God changes it. And in addition to that, we have to ask that the Holy Spirit be given to us and seal within our hearts this testimony of God's infinite kindness, that by faith his kindness may be confirmed in us, and that we may enjoy that blessing precisely as he promised and secured it. If the Holy Spirit works within us, our hearts will be cut to the quick. But the pain will not harden us and make us rebels determined to rise up against what he has shown us, but it will bring us to grief for offending God and make us take stock of our wretched condition. Because we are in the grip of every kind of evil, it will make us dissatisfied with ourselves and cause us to despise our flesh and its vices. When our hearts are thus deeply pierced and we are cut to the quick and become aware that we have deserved God's wrath, we will be zealous to receive God's gift. Upon learning there is nothing good in us, we will have to seek our good in God. Consequently, this doctrine is specifically cited in this passage so that as soon as we hear the gospel teaching preached, we will be hardened against it rather than advantaged by it. But as soon as God works within us by his Holy Spirit, we will be so on fire with the love of God and the knowledge of his boundless goodness as he has manifested it in his word that we will seek only to be made one with him and experience his mercy.

Luke also adds that they took counsel how they might kill the apostles. Such is the ingratitude unbelievers offer those who bring them the gospel. When God's servants proclaim that God's Son came into the world to bring all men salvation, men are so ungrateful that they gnash their teeth against the teaching and try to kill those who seek to help them in this way. But what can you do with rabid animals? And yet we must now be more sharply warned not to be ungrateful when God seeks only to call us to eternal life, and we must be aware of the blessing he provides when sending his ministers to proclaim the truth of his gospel. We must implore him to increase our knowledge of his mercy and the blessing he bestows upon us when he adopts us as his children. We must realize it is by ministers that we hear the gospel so we may know that our complete welfare and salvation lie in our acknowledgment of the mercy God has shown us in our Saviour, Jesus Christ his Son, that mercy which he wants us to enjoy in this life through his gospel.

However, Luke shows us here how the apostles were delivered by the providence of God. There they are, like sheep before the slaughter, the knife at their throats. They are surrounded by rabid wolves baring their sharp teeth. They have no hope of escaping. But they do escape this danger because God preserves them and their enemies are powerless at this time. It is true that, when all is said and done, they suffered for the witness of the gospel, but that was after accomplishing their God-appointed mission, and now the gospel is to be made known throughout the world. That is why our Lord delivers them.

The way this happens is extraordinary. Gamaliel, a member of the assembly, rises and takes a position against the entire conspiracy proposed by the elders of the people and the priests. Let us look now at what Gamaliel proposes. He says first that 'if this counsel or this work is of God, men will never be able to destroy it.' That is true. On the other hand, if it is from men and the apostles' foolish arrogance, it will eventually be abolished. That is also true, for God will bring to naught every invention and imagination of men. But Gamaliel's conclusion is foolish when he says, 'Let them alone' (*Acts* 5:38). For that was like saying the word of God should no longer prevail, that civil order and magistrates should no longer prevail, that criminals should no longer be restrained by the justice system, that the people should no longer be ruled by magistrates, and that the land should not be cultivated nor any trade practised. Why is that? If God knows whom he wishes to save, the elect cannot perish and are therefore left unimpeded. What good would it do to go to all that trouble? And why? Those whom God has ordained to salvation cannot fail, so let them go on their way. In the same way, what good would it do to go to the trouble of keeping the church from offences? For God will know how to strengthen his truth. Therefore, men need not go to so much trouble. Then we will say, 'God will keep a record of what every man is due. We do not need a justice system. God is the judge of the world. He will know how to mete out justice to armed robbers, thieves, and murderers. There will be no more need for magistrates.' Then we will say that God can sustain us because he put us in the world. All we need to do then is cultivate the land. God can take care of us and protect us from the heat and cold. We waste our time with clothing and shelter. That, I propose, would be the outcome if we followed Gamaliel's suggestion. It is clear that would be an unfortunate result of what he says here. On the other hand, our Lord wants that to be stated so that in this way the apostles will be delivered from the rage and fury of the wicked. That is an example of how our Lord will find unusual but unadvised ways which he will use especially when it is a matter of keeping the wicked from harming those faithful to him. Now if there had been among them ever so little discernment and wise counsel, they would have reacted to Gamaliel's advice, but their understanding was made dull. The only thing they thought about was accomplishing their wicked intentions. The only thing on their minds was how they could bury the gospel so no one could ever speak of it again. That was the priests' intention. However, they could not see that Gamaliel's conclusion was wrong. Nevertheless, not one of them had the presence of mind to object and say, 'True, but we still have our duty to do. If that is from God, we must follow it and exhort others to do the same, but if it is from men, we must reject it out of hand.' No, not a single one of them raised that objection. And yet our Lord uses Gamaliel's opinion to deliver his apostles, but he holds his church to a different standard. For when he delivers his own, he wants them to realize that it happens in ways he approves.

Let us note particularly that in this instance God worked to deliver the apostles from the hands and fierceness of their enemies, but that is not the means God employs in his church. That is because unbelievers are not worthy of God's showing them his power inasmuch as they refuse to receive the gospel as the message of salvation. The apostles taught those wretched men all they needed to know. They proclaimed God's grace, the role of Jesus Christ, and the kindness God showed toward us in the person of his Son – and it was useless to them. They remained hardened in their wickedness, and God could not enter them. They remained deaf to his word and rejected it altogether. That is reason enough that they are so dull of hearing, so mindless that they do not know this is from God or his word.

As for us, then, let us learn from that, that when God speaks to us, our ears must be open to listen in all humility to what he says so that we may be instructed in his will and realize that his is the true guidance we must follow and that his is the teaching we must receive. If we fail to do that, it is certain God will deal with us severely, for we will be beyond being guided by reason, and he will cause us to wander aimlessly like scattered sheep. That is why we now see the world behaving like unruly animals. Now, our Lord will make known to us what he wants the entire human race to be like, for he created us in his image and likeness. He wants us to share intelligence and rationality. I am not just talking about the teaching of the gospel but also about human government and this present life. Consequently, our Lord has a general word for everybody in the world. But because that is not enough to help them, God has to remove thick clouds and impediments from their eyes. Otherwise, people would be unutterably stupid, without the sense and understanding of dumb animals. We sometimes see people who are very wise in the eyes of the world, so much so that everybody admires them, but little children can laugh at that kind of absurdity. And why is that? Because men willingly alienate themselves from God and refuse his wisdom. God inevitably lets them wander about aimlessly. We must be all the more diligent since our Lord warns us in his word to take advantage of it and bring all our affections into line with his will.

From Gamaliel's remark we can still glean good, useful, and fruitful instruction. Two of these points are true, as I have already said. The first is that whatever is from God man will never destroy. On the other hand, whatever is from men will collapse on its own without assistance. But Gamaliel's conclusion to do nothing is wrong. According to him, men do not have to do their duty or become involved in anything or foster God's truth. Yet it is not enough for us to be instructed in what is good and right; we have to know what the power and effectiveness of the instruction are, how we are to profit from it, and why God gives it to us. When we come here to hear the gospel, we must do more than ask God to give us a good understanding of it. He must give us the wisdom and discernment we need when we consider how we are to use it.

We need to remember the conclusion Gamaliel came to here so we can avoid coming to one like it. After experiencing good, beneficial things, let us discover what God has to say to us in them. Otherwise, the experience will be of no use to us. We see examples every day of how those who hear about the gospel expose themselves to scrutinizing observations and very great afflictions. Why is that? Because they did not apply the knowledge they gained, as they should have. Let us learn from Gamaliel's example that it is not enough to have a general acquaintance with God's truth, but we must seek what God intends when speaking to us, for it is only when we learn how to apply the full teaching of the gospel to our lives that we enjoy its benefits. Otherwise, we will never learn how to benefit from it. And we can understand that better in detail when, for example, we are reminded every day that people are so wretched that, whatever they are taught, they only apply their mind and effort to rebelling against it.

Now we need to learn why God teaches us one thing or another, for we know from experience that many hear this teaching to their condemnation. They can glibly say we are thoroughly wretched and perverse without realizing they must hasten to God and ask him for mercy. But they are quick to blaspheme him, saying, 'If God knew the evil we would do, why did he not make us better?' Wicked men like that will rise up against God's sacred majesty, thinking their damnable blasphemies will deliver them from his hand. Now the intention of holy Scripture is to lead us to a different end. When it shows us what kind of people we are, it does so to teach us that until God extends his hand and delivers us from our enslavement to the devil, we are utterly lost. That is how Scripture first teaches us about humility. Then, through humility it teaches us to call upon God and find our refuge in him while we learn we can do nothing without his strength. In that way, let us entrust ourselves and our salvation to him, for we are in a state of complete ruin and destruction until he extends his hand to deliver us. As we do that, let us grieve before him, saying, 'Alas, Lord, may it please you to deliver us from this wretched condition in which we find ourselves, for we know that without your help we are the most pitiable creatures you have put on earth.' That, I say, is how we must grieve in acknowledgment of our poverty and misery. Then we are taught to give glory to God and magnify his goodness without claiming anything for ourselves, as we usually do. For we know that people are so delighted with their pride that there is nothing better, nothing more upright than they are. We must reject that attitude and acknowledge that God alone is righteous. That, I say, is the goal of Scripture. Consequently, it will not be enough for us to realize that our total human nature is perverse. We must apply that realization appropriately. That is, we must not claim to be justified before God except by faith, and we must acknowledge that all the merits we can conjure up will not provide satisfaction for our sins, but will be abominable in God's sight. And when we give an account to him in the day of judgment, we will be a hundred thousand times condemned, although we might have been the most righteous people in the world.

Upon hearing that teaching, many people fly off their hinges. 'Oh, really?' they will say. 'Since people do not deserve anything for their works, we no longer have to do good, for all our good deeds cannot get us into heaven. We will give full range to our emotions and do as we please.' The opposite is true. When Scripture shows us that we are justified by faith, it does not free us to yield ourselves to Satan. It shows us rather wherein our salvation lies and how we can achieve it, how we can be healed and delivered not only from our spiritual diseases but from death itself. And it is when we come to our Lord Jesus Christ, to him who is the fountain of all holiness, that he justifies us by faith. He gives us access to God his Father. When he does this, he dedicates each one of us to himself so that we no longer belong to ourselves. When he chooses us, elects us, let us be his abode, his dwelling place. If we belong completely to him, as the Holy Spirit witnesses to us through his word, must we not, having died to ourselves, bear fruit in all holiness to the honour and glory of his holy name? And yet that does not proceed from our works or our merits, but from God's freely bestowed election, by which he chose us without our having done anything to elicit his favour.

Therefore, we need more than to hear we are justified by faith. We need to know why Scripture declares that kind of justification. It is so that when we condemn ourselves, we will go to Jesus Christ for cleansing. Also, it is he who holds our salvation in his hand. Let us be confident then that once God has delivered us from the slavery of sin and the devil by the suffering of his Son, our Lord Jesus Christ, we will no longer be subjected to that kind of slavery, provided we are members of the body of our Lord Jesus Christ. We will also realize it was not in vain that our Lord adopted us as his children, that he imprinted his image on us, that he washed us of all our stains, and that he did it so we might remain in that state of purity in which he placed us after granting us the knowledge of his truth. That, I say, is how we must apply the teaching of holy Scripture when we are told we can be justified only by faith and that works serve no purpose. But we need to know the reason for that declaration because we see many people who, under the influence of that teaching, take extreme liberties to do what pleases them, just as we have seen many do in our day who have tried to abolish every principality, having concluded that civil government is not necessary since God knows our end from the beginning and that his plans will not change. That argument has been offered not only in our day but also in the apostles' day. They even think that because we have freedom, it does not make any difference how we live afterward, and they understand that freedom to be a license for the flesh, as if everything were allowed, as if there were no difference between whoring around and eating and drinking, as if there were no difference between eating and drinking temperately and, if the body demands it, getting drunk and engaging in excesses.

Consequently, when God speaks to us and we are aware that we have been set free by his gospel, we must remain focused on the fact that we have been delivered from the pope's tyranny, and that the yoke under which we laboured has been broken, for God declares we have been set free by the suffering and death of our Lord Jesus Christ. Now how can that be? We are no longer under the laws and ordinances of men, which forbid this or that, or tell us what we must do under penalty of mortal sin. We have seen how they forbade the eating of meat at certain times. Why? Because it had been ordered by that Antichrist, who imposed his yoke upon us. Therefore, so that the direction and governance of our souls might not be held in that wretched servitude, our Lord wanted to show us through his gospel how we are delivered from it. That does not mean, however, that from the world's perspective, order no longer prevails, that laws, edicts, statutes, magistrates, principalities, and domains cease to exist, or that we are not subjected to matters relating to civil government of human making. Let us take to heart then that when God speaks to us about that freedom, it is not so we may wander aimlessly, given to every evil, following our wicked impulses, and living like wild animals. Far from it! To the contrary! The gospel makes it possible for us to be gentle and loving toward our neighbours and kind to everyone so that we can live in all uprightness and moderation and so that the freedom we seek is the freedom to be servants of God, to the end that when we have to appear before him, we can say we have been his subjects, obedient in all things and in all places. And so, in order not to draw foolish conclusions off the top of our heads, as Gamaliel did at this time, let us always remember to keep ourselves fully in line with God's will, realizing it is not enough to distinguish between good and evil, unless we immediately pursue good and avoid evil with all our might.

Yet for our own good, we must keep before us these two points. What comes from God men will not abolish, and the inventions of men will not endure except to be destroyed. It is true we have not put that knowledge to good use, as we have seen, but the teaching is sound. And that is a passage we must heed, for our Lord often uses the wicked to make his truth known, as he did when Balaam said, 'God is not a man, that he should lie; neither is he like the sons of men, that he should repent. When he has said a thing, it will come to pass, and when he has spoken, it must take place' (cf. *Num.* 23:19). Who is speaking here? Balaam, a false prophet, a wicked man as changeable as the wind, whose tongue is for sale to change God's blessing into a curse, if that were possible! Yet an angel from heaven could not speak better than that. That is true, and yet we must glean valuable instruction from what Balaam did and even make this argument: since a false prophet, one who has no trouble blaspheming God in order to fill his purse, is nevertheless constrained to witness to God's truth, must not we who are faithful and daily instructed in God's word hold it in higher esteem and make it manifest to everyone for God's glory and honour? If the devils themselves are forced to magnify God, what must be required of those of us who are his children? When Caiaphas stated that one man should die so that all the people might not perish (*John* 11:50; 18:14), it is certain he did not say that on his own, but that the Holy Spirit wanted to instruct us by his mouth. That is why it is specifically stated that he prophesied and that our Lord wanted that prophecy to be made from that priestly office and authority. Consequently, inasmuch as Caiaphas, a mortal enemy of every true teaching, can but declare that Jesus Christ will die for the people, what are we to believe about the death of our Lord Jesus Christ? Are we to doubt that he died for us? No! Never! But we are to perceive its advantage and realize that the effectiveness and power of his death belong to us all. And even though we are poor sinners, only unfaithfulness will stand in our way unless we possess the full advantage of what he has provided for us. That is how our Lord constrains even the most wicked to make his truth known. The same can be said about Gamaliel's comment.

Therefore, we need to pay particular attention to the passage which says that men can never set aside what is of God. And even in those words, all believers find a singular consolation, which is highly necessary in our day and time. For we see how eager men are to topple the teaching God has been pleased to revive in our time. We see the machinations, the conspiracies, and concerted efforts which are made everywhere against that teaching. On the other hand, let us consider how God's graciousness is seen in his preservation of what he has begun. It is true that one might have thought previously that there should have been utter devastation. But God's hand has been clearly evident. If we think it is by human strength that God's truth persists, we are insane, but let us remember that God is able to sustain the kingdom of our Lord Jesus Christ his Son and cause it to triumph over all human machinations and enterprises. For, as it is said here, what is of men will never last and never prevail against what God wishes to establish, because man's greatest power is but weakness.

Now, that word is given to us so that we will not put our trust in ourselves. We know that nothing displeases God more than our putting our trust in created things because when we do so, we turn away from him and deprive him of the honour and reverence which belong to him. Let us focus on that better than has been our custom. Whenever we think men have to topple mountains, so to speak, and work miracles, let us remember that everything they do will have no effect except insofar as God brings it about. Let us be careful then not to place our trust in them. Rather, let us always trust in God, realizing that if he does not prosper men's undertakings, they and everything they do will remain entangled in ruin and destruction.

In keeping with that sacred teaching, let us bow before our gracious God in acknowledgment of our sins and pray that it will please him to correct us in such a way that we will seek him only. And let us come to him in accordance with the path he has laid out before us, namely, through our Lord Jesus Christ. And being led by his Holy Spirit, let us ask only to follow him in all things and in all places. Now let us all say, Almighty God, heavenly Father . . .

22

THE HONOUR OF SUFFERING FOR CHRIST'S NAME

SUNDAY, 3 AUGUST 1550

And to him they agreed: and when they had called the apostles, and beaten them, they commanded that they should not speak in the name of Jesus, and let them go. [41] And they departed from the presence of the council, rejoicing that they were counted worthy to suffer shame for his name. [42] And daily in the temple, and in every house, they ceased not to teach and preach Jesus Christ (Acts 5:40–42).

We have already seen how our Lord rendered null and void what the enemies of his truth had engineered to obliterate the memory of our Lord Jesus Christ his Son. And there we have Gamaliel giving them frivolous and childish reasons. But the fact remains, that is the way they were defeated. Earlier they thought they were in total control of preventing the gospel's progress and frightening the apostles into silence, and even discrediting them all.

And now God provides in a way no one would have imagined. As he does so, let us understand that when God executes his will, he can indeed thwart everything the wicked undertake, even though they are powerful and influential in the eyes of the world and lack nothing. And yet we see the extent of their cruelty. It is said that each agreed with Gamaliel's advice, but they flog the apostles anyway. They reproach and humiliate them severely. They also strictly forbid them to continue teaching in the name of Jesus Christ. Before that, they had to vent their rage and fury vehemently. Taking into account the restraint Luke talks about, they still go too far. What might not have happened if God had given those wicked men full rein? There is no doubt they would have perpetrated such a persecution against the church that no one would ever have dared to mention the name of Jesus Christ. We see in what happened here that they were motivated by extreme cruelty. In this we must be even more aware of God's infinite grace and goodness and the infinite wisdom by which he has provided for his church in every age. We must also be aware of his power because we see that men can do nothing but what he allows. And we must apply that to ourselves, for a horrible condemnation will be visited upon those who refuse to obey God, even though they are admonished daily about their responsibility.

Who are those Luke is talking about here? Every one of us, to the man, condemns them. They are desperate enemies of God. They are raging animals. They are men given to every barbarity. We can certainly pronounce that judgment against the scribes, that is, against that 'priesthood' in Jerusalem at that time which had complete control in spiritual matters. We now see how God overrules them through Gamaliel's advice, which was nevertheless, as I have said, frivolous and inconsequential.

Now let us take a look at ourselves. We very much want others to think of us as children of God. But how does what we hear motivate us to do his will? We can see dazzling things and yet continue more hardened than before. People will condemn us for our sins and, if we feared God even minutely, we would be moved to repentance and grieved because of our vices. In short, people will make allegations against us which would crush and move hearts of stone, and yet we will remain so hardened and rooted in our evil that their contempt will produce no improvement in us despite any chiding we might receive. Therefore, we must conclude that that example is given for our instruction. When we are so obstinate that we cannot bring ourselves back to God when he speaks to us, he makes us excellent promises which should compel us to forsake everything in order to cling to them. And when we make the unfortunate mistake of rejecting his promises and hardening ourselves to them, the members of the council will have no choice but to condemn us, for without grave warnings, they concede to a moderate approach. If those men, who were wicked to the core, were dissuaded by a rationale unapproved by God from carrying through their intention, and if he tells us what we must do to yield to his will so that he may impart to us his truth and instruct us thoroughly in our duty by his word, and if he is still unable to bring us to heel and bring us the same kind of moderate action that Gamaliel's words inspired in the council, what can we say? Therefore, let us be meek and humble. Let us display a spirit of kindness and gentleness every time God in his grace admonishes us about our salvation to secure our obedience. And when we are on the right track, may it please him to sustain us and increase his good graces within us so that we may receive everything declared to us in his name as coming from him, so that, as a result, no one will ever be able to give us good advice which does not come from God. However, if we are wilful and obstinate in our evil imaginations and fleshly desires, we are not rebelling against men, but the living God. That is the point Luke is making when telling us that those who were deliberating the destruction of the kingdom of our Lord Jesus Christ were held in check by Gamaliel, even though his argument was invalid.

Now let us consider what Luke adds. He says that the apostles were very shamefully beaten and forbidden to continue to teach in the name of Jesus Christ. He does not tell us what the apostles said in response, but he does tell us how they persevered in fulfilling their responsibility without responding to all the prohibitions and threatenings directed against them because, as we saw earlier, they had provided a general answer to all the prohibitions laid upon them, saying only that God must be obeyed rather than men. From Luke's account, we see to what extent they adhered to that conviction and did not waver despite being gravely afflicted, but honoured their God-given charge and calling more highly than pleasing or displeasing men. Even so, we must note the words Luke uses when he says that the apostles 'departed from the presence of the council'. Why is that? Because 'they were counted worthy to suffer shame for the name of Jesus.' Those two things seem contradictory at first. How can shame and honour go hand in hand? Because men do not think like God, for when Luke says the apostles suffered shame and dishonour, he is speaking from a human perspective. And when he says they rejoiced because they were counted worthy of that honour, he is speaking from the perspective of God and his angels. We see, then, the vast difference between God and the world. When Luke says that what is 'highly esteemed among men is abomination in the sight of God' (*Luke* 16:15), he is pointing out that God considers precious and supremely excellent what men call shame and dishonour.

Now let us look at these words as they are recorded by Luke. He says that the apostles were joyous as they left after being condemned and beaten. How can it be that they felt no pain? Was this sentence not difficult and painful to endure? It is certain that these men, being as mortal and subject to pain as we are, suffered physically, and we are mistaken if we think they did not feel in their bodies suffering and pain and shame from that abuse to their bodies and reputations, all inflicted by their being beaten as malefactors. Yet, knowing God approves their action and is pleased with their service, they rejoiced at enduring suffering and shame for his name's sake. Let us learn then from their example how hard and grievous and against our nature are the afflictions that we must nonetheless endure patiently for God's sake, knowing that is the way he wishes to test us, especially when we endure in his name. In spite of that, we are commanded in general to be joyous (*Phil.* 4:4) even though our Lord may punish us for our sins. However, does that mean we do not experience deep pain? To the contrary, for when a man undergoes any kind of hardship, he will necessarily feel inward pain because we are not made of iron or steel. We are not so tough that pain cannot get through to us. We know from experience that if a man's body is stricken with illness, if he is stricken with poverty or undergoes some other affliction, he cannot avoid feeling sorrow or grief. Moreover, when we are aware that God chastises us for our faults, we experience an additional sorrow, which we need not only to overcome the wicked inclinations of our flesh, but which is also advantageous for our salvation. For where is our repentance if there is no grief for offending God? Repentance is also that sorrow Paul speaks of as coming from God and approved by him (*2 Cor.* 7:9–10). But when we, under these circumstances, uphold God's honour, knowing that whatever persecutions the wicked may put upon us, our Lord has not forsaken our salvation or abandoned us as his children. For that we are to rejoice, knowing that by his power he will sustain us and that everything we endure in this world will be turned into our joy and consolation because of our salvation, as Paul also says in the eighth chapter of Romans: 'If we suffer with Christ, we will also be glorified with him' (*Rom.* 8:17). Still, we must have within us that spiritual rejoicing we spoke of earlier. It is true we will not escape being grieved, but that sorrow will not turn us from God but will provide us with the way and reason to take refuge in him.

The wicked, feeling the afflictions which oppress them, are deeply tormented and, moved to despair, grind their teeth and rage against God. They have nothing to console them or lessen their pains. We, on the other hand, when we are greatly grieved and tormented, when we suffer great pain and grievous anguish in our hearts, we do not fail to look to God. Feeling the goodness and love God has for us, we have reason to rejoice. Even though we are sorely tormented, we still receive some comfort which makes us patient in our afflictions. That, I say, is the joy that God's children are to experience in the midst of their sorrow. But, as I have said, that has to happen, especially when God grants us the honour of suffering for his name's sake. In that way, he testifies and acknowledges that we are his own because we champion his warfare.

Moreover, in order to get a better understanding of this point, we need to return to what Luke says about the apostles, that they were joyous because our Lord had counted them worthy of the honour of suffering for his name. With those words he shows that the apostles had a definite witness from God that he approved them as his servants. Indeed, he had set them apart for an honourable service. As a matter of fact, do we want something more excellent than sustaining the cause of God's truth and being appointed his advocates? Whenever a man wishes to appoint an attorney to set his affairs in order, he proves his affection and trust by placing his property in his hands. Now our Lord does not use us in a frivolous and insignificant undertaking. There is nothing more important to him than the truth of his gospel, for it is through the gospel that he wishes to rule over us, as Scripture says when speaking of the gospel: 'Behold God's sceptre.' [1] 'Behold his throne, from which he wants to preside among us.' Now that truth is entrusted to us inasmuch as we are God's advocates and patrons suffering in support of that truth. Paul speaks of it that way (cf. *2 Tim.* 1:8; 2:9). God does not want his cause to be supported with weapons. But when we suffer in our bodies, in our reputations, in our possessions,

[1] For this expression, the editors refer the reader to *Inst.* 3.20.42, *OS* 4,352.19; *Inst.* 4.2.4, *OS* 5,36.5.

and in like things, and when we bear it patiently for his honour, we are defenders of his truth. Not that God needs us! For who are we that we can sustain God's truth? We know it is written that from men come only lies and vanity (*Isa.* 59:4). Yet if we suffer in that role, we must magnify God's loving-kindness even more for calling us to that purpose although he does not find it in our nature. For, as I have already said, there are only lies and vanity in us, and we are by nature God's mortal enemies. It is not for anything that we have done that he has chosen us among all the others to sustain his truth, but the fact remains that when God wants us to suffer in witness of his gospel, we are granted the privilege of a service surpassing excellence. Consequently, Luke says that when the wicked beat the apostles in this way, God does them great honour. God wants us to know that when we become aware that he puts his mark upon us and lets us know we are not only of his household but have also been entrusted with the very excellent and worthy position of being chosen to sustain his gospel, we have occasion to rejoice! That is why Paul, in prison, boasts so often of his bonds and chains. And he offers it as evidence, as a prince or a king gives evidence of his greatness and power, when he says, 'I have this many provinces and this many towns, lands and castles.' In the same way, Paul says, 'Here I am in prison.' And where is he? Among thieves, lowlifes, and murderers. And there he receives reproaches, taunts, and curses from everybody, but that is his glory. He is not concerned for what men think. He is content that our Lord considers it an honour and privilege that he is tormented in this way for his gospel. He knows that the angels in paradise respect and praise that and that one day he will be honoured by all believers everywhere. In other passages (*1 Cor.* 9:25; *2 Tim.* 4:8), he speaks of his crown in the same way, that crown he is to receive pursuant to the work he will do on behalf of God's church. And not only for his preaching and teaching, but because of what he had endured and was still enduring in his body. And that is what the text means when it says that 'the apostles rejoiced because they had the honour of suffering for the name of God.'

However, it is very difficult to persuade us that that would be an honour. We think so highly of this world's honour that we do not consider what is of value in God's sight, as we read in the twelfth chapter of John: 'They loved the glory of the world more than what God approves' (*John* 12:43). After relating that many were converted to God but did not dare confess him before men, he gives the reason: 'Because they were so blinded by man's honour that they refused to give honour and obeisance to God by confessing Jesus Christ' (*John* 12:42). We see every day, more than we should, that we are unable to believe or trust Scripture when it says that the reproach and shame we endure in the name of our Lord Jesus Christ is honourable and that it is an excellent thing to suffer persecution in witnessing to his gospel. We ought to pray all the harder that God will open our eyes and keep us from being so blinded by this world and its enticements and vanities that we pay less attention to God than to the things of this world. We are far from being willing to suffer for the sake of the name of our Lord Jesus Christ. Rather, many who call themselves believers do not quit pursuing what they know to be opposed to God and his truth. We find many, I say, who want to be thought of as the great defenders and pillars of the gospel. Even so, they, tantalized by some juicy morsel from the Antichrist's kitchen and cloaked with benefices, as they call them, are wretchedly bound to those abominations and idolatries of the Papacy. Why is that so? Because they prefer the honours and goods of this world and the good opinion of men to being held in esteem in God's house. Indeed, they boast relentlessly, brazenly, of a lofty Christianity, but what kind of Christianity is that? There is not a shred of it! For when men limit themselves to what cannot be reconciled with Jesus

Christ, they clearly demonstrate they have nothing in common with him, especially when they hold the reproach and ignominy of the cross up to shame.

And then we have among us those who are such devils and she-devils who blaspheme God so openly that we should be horrified. They find fault with those poor believers who have endured some kind of persecution in the name of God and exclude them. That, for those scoundrels, is the gospel. But what kind of gospel is that? For them it is the gospel of hell, for they are so wicked that they turn into reproach and shame the things God's children have endured in order to witness to his name. If they speak of the believers' persecutions, burnings, and banishments, they do so for their amusement and to make them objects of reproach and abhorrence. But let them expect God to exact vengeance for such cruelty and severity. For they are not directing their remarks to men, but to God himself. When they taunt believers that way, it is as if they came and spat in the face of the majesty of the Son of God. Yet they are like shameless brothel whores, and they will say, 'The gospel, the gospel!' But if there is such a thing as the devil's gospel, you will find it among such liars.

We see, therefore, what a rare thing it is to consider it an honour to suffer for Jesus' sake. And yet, unless we do, we cannot be accepted as God's children. Our Lord Jesus said, 'Whosoever shall deny me before men, him will I also deny before my Father who is in heaven' (*Matt.* 10:33). That pronouncement by our Lord will always be in effect and will take place. I tell you, our Lord Jesus Christ, when he makes that statement with his own mouth, is not joking. We know he is speaking seriously. So let us be aware that we are truly renouncing Jesus Christ before men when we think too highly of this world's honour and vanities and refuse to suffer for the name of Jesus Christ in our bodies, in our possessions, or in other ways, no matter how. We must not be influenced by our ease, our conveniences, and the grandeur and appearance which can characterize this world. In fact, let us consider what characterizes our worth and excellence. Let us set before ourselves the most worthy and excellent of men. Who will he be? He will be a piece of pure filth. He will be a rotting corpse who will nevertheless possess some virtue God has given him. But what does that man have to exalt himself with? Nothing at all, for he is tangled in many vices. And yet the least of these will so love their honour and men's esteem that by comparison God's truth means nothing. Even so, let us not be surprised that very few are able to suffer for Jesus Christ's name, for men are so depraved that they prefer themselves to the glory of God. I tell you, we, being only filth and defilement, will want to be held in honour while God's honour is trampled under foot. And that happens when we turn our backs on God's truth or fail to confess it so that we may preserve this world's honour and repute.

Now although it is difficult and irksome for our flesh to bear up under reproach from men, each of us must nevertheless try very hard to fight against our evil affections. Therefore, since God calls us to serve him and wants us to uphold his honour, let each of us, the moment we receive an indication he wants to use us in his service, make preparations to that end in defiance of men and everything else, without regard for public opinion, without regard for anything our human nature desires. That is what Paul did, as we see in another passage: 'Let no man trouble me, for I bear engraved in my body the marks of the Lord Jesus' (*Gal.* 6:17). There he compares the marks of Jesus Christ's wounds to the horror of being marked on the forehead or some other part of his body as a sign of reproach and ignominy, as is commonly done to thieves and cheats so that the marks of the wounds will remain engraved there forever. So Paul, speaking of those marks, glories in them more than in all the coats of arms of this world's princes. As for all of this world's high pomp and acts of gallantry, are they not but dung in comparison with the signs that Jesus Christ gives in testimony of our being defenders of his truth?

Let us learn to put God's honour first, along with everything that glorifies God and that men find seemly and exceedingly worthy. Everything they value among themselves, that must we treat as filth and dung, being content with what God approves in the presence of his angels and all creation. It is true we can say, 'That is easier said than done', for we are far removed from the beatings. Yet the fact remains. Such must be our practice at all times. We do not know what God is reserving for us. In order to support the gospel, we must not, if we want to be Christians, be so in word alone, although we are in the shade and at ease in the absence of persecution. But if God has spared us for a while, let us remember that he is able to put his hand upon us when it pleases him, as we well deserve. Even if we do not see bare swords and burning stakes now, let us be reminded of our poor brothers who are bearing up under the torments and persecutions of the wicked, and as often as we hear them mentioned, let us say to ourselves, 'There go those whom Jesus Christ has chosen to suffer in defence of his truth.' We, therefore, must be prepared to receive whatever God wills to call us to. And so must we do our duty, as we have in fact seen others do who lived among us and were burned elsewhere. I tell you that is how we must be prepared to follow the road wherever it pleases God to lead us, either to life or to death. For anyone who thinks he is always going to have it easy in this world, without hardship or affliction or any kind of persecution, does not know what Christianity is all about. Consequently, we must anticipate what the wicked might do to us if God gives them free rein, so that if he should let us fall into their hands, we will be able to resist steadfastly whatever they may throw at us.

That, then, is what we must learn from the teaching Luke presents here. Since he tells us here that there is a vast difference between God and men, let us make every effort to avoid pursuing this world's honours so that we will not be led astray by a desire for men's approval and thereby offend God. But let God's approval, and his keeping us as his own, be enough for us. Although the service we render him is rejected by men, it is very pleasing to him. Besides, as far as we are concerned, let us know that because our Lord has graciously granted us the knowledge of his truth, he has in this way brought us into his house, and that is the greatest good that he can do for us. Moreover, we must be much more content with that than if we had all of this world's goods and conveniences, as David had, who, though a king, sought only to be in the courts of the Lord (*Psa.* 84:10), that is, to be one of the least in God's church.

Now how does that apply to those who wish to play at having great zeal for the gospel? At the drop of a hat, they are willing to give up everything and would refuse to listen to anything about it because they think they are not respected as they should be and because they prefer to be in men's good graces and not in God's. It ought not to be that way. At the least, we should prefer honour from God to anything that might come from men, for we know it is only lie upon lie. Therefore, what they think is honourable and excellent, let it be to us as dung. To the contrary, if we suffer in the name of God and if that is considered the greatest disgrace in the world, let us take consolation in the fact that God approves it, as I have already said, and that it will be found good, holy, and worthy in the sight of God and his angels. And in order to suffer more courageously when it pleases God to call us to himself in this way, let us keep before us the examples of the apostles. Let us remember that they were mortal like us. Let us also remember that if the Lord provided grace for their time, his power and will remain unchanged, and he will be able to strengthen us so that we can resist all the assaults against us. And when men hold us up to shame and reproach, let us not fail to boast, as Paul did, for in so doing we will be following in the steps of our Lord Jesus Christ, being conformed to his image so that one day we will be participants in that glory and glorious immortality which he has prepared for us in heaven.

Following this holy teaching, let us bow before the face of our gracious God in acknowledgement of our sins, praying that he will be pleased to receive us in pity and in mercy and so correct us by his Holy Spirit that it will be our purpose and aim to please and obey him in all things and in all places. May he join us to the body of our Lord Jesus Christ his Son, whose members we are, in such a way that we will not fear suffering shame, reproach, ignominy, and even death for his name and the advancement and growth of his kingdom and glory. In this way, let us all say, Almighty God, heavenly Father . . .

23

The Qualifications of Deacons

Sunday, 10 August 1550

And in those days, when the number of the disciples was multiplied, there arose a murmuring of the Grecians against the Hebrews, because their widows were neglected in the daily ministration. ² Then the twelve called the multitude of the disciples unto them, and said, It is not reason that we should leave the word of God, and serve tables. ³ Wherefore, brethren, look ye out among you seven men of honest report, full of the Holy Ghost and wisdom, whom we may appoint over this business (Acts 6:1–3).

So far, we have seen the care with which the Christian church supported the poor, how everyone gave of his own substance so that there was no lack or want of anything. It was as though those who enjoyed abundance had taken the food from their own mouths to help their poor brothers with it.

In this account we have the same teaching, which shows us our duty, namely that we must not allow those who are fellow members of Jesus Christ to go without this world's goods while we have more than we need. For if God gives a man wealth, it is to put his charity to the test. We are to give an account of what God has placed in our hands. However, if our neighbours endure hardship because of our lack of mercy, it is certain that will not go unpunished. If we cannot learn from that example, it will serve as so much condemnation when we appear before the great Judge. We know what he has already declared and that his position will not change: 'I was hungry and thirsty and you gave me something to eat and drink. I was naked and you clothed me. For that, come possess the kingdom which has been prepared for you from the beginning of the world' (*Matt.* 25:35–36, 34). On the contrary, they will hear, 'Depart from me, you reprobates and cursed of God my Father, into everlasting fire. For you have no part with me, because you did not help those who were in need and want' (cf. *Matt.* 25:41–43). With that, we see how our Lord banishes from his kingdom all those who do not share their goods liberally when seeing their neighbours' need and offer no aid or assistance. And he says that he recognizes what we do to the least of those whom he entrusts to our keeping, he recognizes it and accepts it as done unto himself (*Matt.* 25:40, 45). In other words, he says that if we do not show our gratitude for his benefits when faced with those who are destitute of this world's goods, our action is not against a mortal being, but against the Son of God.

Luke now tells us the procedure they established so that that charity might continue and the alms given by the believers might be distributed fairly. First, he points out that it had to be done this way because grumbling had arisen. With the number of disciples increasing, the Greeks and those from foreign countries began to grumble because it appeared to them that their widows were not being treated like the others. In that, we see that it is very difficult, when you have a large group, to agree on something that pleases everyone. The proverb is as true as it is old: 'Large numbers beget confusion.' If we but set about remedying a situation, we will discover that is the way it is. It is true that when goodwill exists, God will always provide a remedy. But human nature is so sinful that there is always something to complain about unless care is taken to do everything right. We even see here the extent of our evil. There is nothing more delightful than seeing the number of believers increase and grow. Since we ask God everyday for his kingdom to come, it is understood that he is pleased to draw unto himself and into obedience to himself poor scattered creatures and bring them into his church, which, being well ordered, can grow daily. That is how God's kingdom will prosper and bear fruit, as if Jesus Christ were most highly revered. I tell you, nothing is more pleasing than that. And yet, sheer numbers initiated the grumbling. That is like I have already said. That very fact shows us the extent of human perversity, namely, no blessing of God is so great that our capacity for sin cannot pervert it. We need to humble ourselves even more and pray not only that he will extend his hand to us and cause us to sense his goodness and his grace, but also that he will guide us by his Holy Spirit in such a way that we will know how to use well the good things he has provided for us. And may we use them in such a way that everything will redound to his honour and our edification.

Inasmuch as the devil is constantly at war with God's church, disseminating discord, disputes, quarrels, and dissensions, we ought the more be on guard to resist him. I tell you, that is how clever Satan is. He knows God cannot rule among us unless there is peace and harmony. In order to separate us from God, he comes and sows dissensions. Has he separated us from one another in this way? That is how we become his victims and are thereafter easy prey. Aware that the devil is always working to achieve that, should we not ask God to keep us strong in peace and unity and to incline our hearts in that direction so that we may apply ourselves diligently to that end? For if we do battle under Jesus Christ's banner, we must know our enemy's tricks and subtleties. But there is no doubt that Satan is always after us to distract us from the love and peace which should exist among us. Let us, therefore, uphold his banner the more diligently.

However, let us not be surprised if human depravity sometimes finds many things to grumble about, for people always have many concerns which cannot be satisfied. No matter what we do, they always find something to fault and to lash out at, as was the case in the apostles' time. Do you think there was something to rebuke and criticize the apostles for when they distributed the alms entrusted to them? Yet they were accused of wrongdoing and maligned. That shows us that after we have in good conscience done what is required of us, we will still be accused of wrongdoing every now and then. Let us not be surprised when people reproach us, insult us, and make false accusations against us, for the apostles lived very faithful lives and conducted themselves devotedly in their charge and office and yet were not exempt from that kind of malice. However, if we ever see any lack of orderliness in God's church, we must immediately seek to remedy it as quickly as possible. For even though the apostles might have said, 'The duty we have been performing, we still want to perform', they knew it was not expedient to do so. They are still in strong agreement about that, for they consider that that command prevents them from preaching God's word as they should. Not that they had not preached, but they had not preached as they would have preferred because the responsibility they had been given was taking some of their time. Consequently, the apostles, hearing the grumbling begin, are not slow to react.

What they did was to call upon the congregation, as was the custom in the church. Would to God that it were still the practice today that every time public decrees and mandates are proclaimed, there would be a vote by all the people so that nothing would be allowed except what had been approved. That is how we handle the public offices of the world and spiritual charges. Those matters are handled easily, but it seems that we ask only not to be bothered when it comes to choosing a minister of the word of God. Each of us should have a burning desire to be able to choose a man who is very well suited for that position. But is that the way it is? That shows us we are only mediocre Christians and how little we care about the way God's church is governed.

But that was not the way it was according to Luke's account here. As soon as the apostles realized that grumbling was beginning in the church, they called all of the believers together to elect deacons, as they call them. That word simply means 'minister', that is, 'servant'. Those who have the responsibility of serving in the church, whether for distributing alms or for preaching, are aptly called 'ministers', and all of the apostles held that title in common. All those who are charged with administration by the churches are aptly called 'ministers of the word of God'. But the church, without further definition of the word, designates as 'deacons' all those who are appointed in behalf of the poor.

There were two kinds of ministers, or servants, in the Christian church. One had the responsibility of distributing the alms and goods which had been given to help the poor. The other was charged with doing domestic and normal chores, caring for the sick, and doing everything pertaining to the household, as it were. Paul notably deals with those two functions in Romans chapter 12, saying that those who are responsible for distributing alms must not be miserly and lament the good they do, but they are to try to help the needy as long as they can. And, he says, those who have the care of people are to be cheerful and pleasant, without dissension and ungrudgingly (*Rom.* 12:8). It will only make the poor person sad if someone helps him in his need and grumbles at the same time. It is as if the person hit him with one hand and gave him a piece of bread with the other. For that reason, Paul says that those who are entrusted with domestic matters must have a glad heart when helping the poor who are sick and refrain from berating them, and that whatever they do they must do with gladness of heart and cheerfulness of spirit so that the poor will be cheered when seeing they are being helped caringly and affectionately. Those commendable qualities must characterize the deacons and those who are stewards for the administration of the goods. Therefore, let those who are stewards delegated to carry out that responsibility not play at being thrifty managers and withhold from the poor their share. We see people who want to please men and play at being good servants, but who will hold back the goods dedicated to the poor and let them languish. The devil take such 'good managers' if they are not careful to do what they should! The devil take them!

And then, as for those who are to have oversight of individuals, let them show a cheerful face and a pleasant demeanour so that the poor will say, 'Well, what they are giving us they are giving with goodwill'. If the hand gives freely, the heart does as well. That, I say, must be the disposition of those who are entrusted with such responsibilities, according to what Luke tells us here when he says that seven people were chosen to oversee the distribution of alms and aid for the poor and to supervise it all. Now, as I have already mentioned, that was done so that it might be the continuing order for God's church. From the beginning, the apostles have wanted that responsibility, although it was for them a great inconvenience and an imposition on their time, as I have already pointed out. Nevertheless, they did it because it was evident that gifts were made much more willingly when they were responsible for receiving the alms for the poor. So when we see that the apostles endured such hardship and inconveniences to distribute goods to the poor, we must take it as instruction to do the same, for there is no doubt that their contemporaries have been encouraged to do good to the poor, since they themselves had undertaken that responsibility. And that is why they were led to undertake it. But they are well aware that that cannot last forever. That is the way we are to go about it. We must not be obstinate when it is a matter of bringing order into God's church. Although things continued to be distributed for some time in a way different from the one revealed in God's word, the fact is, they must be improved, provided they continue in good order, not only during our lifetime, but also after our death. That is to be done even in matters concerning human life.

Now if in this present life we are to make every effort to make good things better and prevent the world's decline into evil, we must be even more diligent in ensuring that the continuity of the church is well regulated and that what is well begun today is perpetuated, not for twenty, thirty, or forty years, but from generation to generation. That is what the apostles intended when they chose deacons. In fact, examining how Paul speaks of it, we find that he makes it into a general rule. He does not just recount an event, as Luke does here, to give us an example of what is to be done, but he says to Timothy, 'This is how you will select deacons.' After speaking about pastors and those whose office it is to proclaim God's word, he adds that deacons must be serious people, well behaved, temperate, not double-tongued, not liars or lovers of money or lewd, but men of good conscience, prudent, instructed well enough in the faith that they can teach others. After talking about them, he adds requirements for their wives just as he does for ministers' wives, saying that they must be chaste, modest, good managers of their households and families, and examples for all the others. He says the same thing about deacons' wives. Then he adds that those who serve well gain a good standing for themselves and great assurance in the faith which is in Jesus Christ (cf. *1 Tim.* 3:1–13). That is not a low-ranking position. It is true that people sometimes think that serving God by serving the poor is an office of little importance. But Paul says it is a position of honour, indeed, an unrestricted freedom in the faith for those who walk uprightly in the execution of this responsibility.

Consequently, we can relate that passage from Paul to Luke's comment, which does not simply recount an event that happened once and for all. It shows us that this must be a perpetual order in God's church, that those who are established to govern it must care for the poor, and that things must be as well organized and implemented as possible by men. In fact, we see how the church was regulated long ago and that there was a very well-established order. But, as I have said, men are so wicked that even if there are incomparably well-established regulations here below, they still pervert everything with their evil. It is true that the early church established good ordinances so that what was dedicated to the poor would remain theirs. Now we have the priests and all that kennel that devour everything and gather everything they can to themselves. Each one of them asks for a part of it, so that there is no longer order. And have they not succeeded so well that in the end everything has come to this horrible confusion which we find in the Papacy today?

As for the early church, the deacons have the responsibility for everything belonging to that office, and everything given to the church was entrusted to them. We see how strictly they were commanded to walk before God and to remember that theirs was not a profane or mundane office, but a spiritual charge. It is for that reason they were given the cup when it came time to celebrate the Supper of our Lord Jesus Christ, and that those who were charged with the care of the poor joined with the ministers of God's word at that moment so that they might be recognized as having a charge in the church and so that they themselves might realize they had to walk uprightly in order to say, 'We are no longer our own, but we must dedicate ourselves completely to serving God.' And that too is why Luke recounts in this passage that after the election of the deacons, the apostles laid their hands upon them to show they were set apart for God, just as for all sacrifices made under the law the laying on of hands was required, as it is put forth in Moses. The apostles observed that order. And even today we would do well to follow that ceremony. For if we reject human superstitions and inventions, we are not saying that we scorn what comes from God and his apostles. When it is a question of becoming a minister of God's word – according to Luke's comment that hands were laid on the deacons – there should be a solemn declaration that these are no longer private individuals who do their own will, but that they must be completely dedicated to God's service. And we see how in the ancient church this order lasted until God, because of men's ingratitude, allowed everything to be confused, as is now evident in the Papacy. We see how they thoroughly mock God. What do the papists create and ordain their deacons for? To play-act and do juggling tricks, as if God were a totally blind idol.

It is good that we understand and recognize such games so that we can detest these wicked men, these devils, who are so beside themselves with disdain for God that after defiling his church, they are so brazen that they boast of it. When the pope and his ilk want to condemn us as heretics, the only thing they can charge us with is not being counted among their fine 'sacred hierarchy', as they call it. And who is it made up of? The pope will say, 'I am the head, and then we have the bishops who represent the apostles, the priests who represent the disciples, and the deacons who are in the subsequent order.' That is how, I say, the pope and his ilk attribute to themselves all the orders of God's church. And it is under the cover of the noble title 'sacred hierarchy' that they usurp them.

Let us look now at the role of the deacons ordained into the Papacy. They are to receive not the alms given for the poor – that in itself is a mockery – but to receive what is placed in the offering, and that disappears into those insatiable abysses for the upkeep of their whores, their pimps, and all their kind. That is their office!

Then they have to play-act in the mass disguised as clowns. And yet the people take that to be complete holiness and perfection, so much so that they say it is an image of paradise. They must be more than insane when they say, 'That is the image of paradise', about something we know is not only so stupid and frivolous that even little children should spit at it, but also detested and abominated by God. It is good, then, as I have already said, that we recognize such abominations and hold them in contempt and thank God that he has been pleased to remove us from the kind of pollution and odious abomination that Satan formerly held us trapped in.

Moreover, let us be careful that we, after condemning the papists, are not included in the same vengeance from God. We must, then, walk in such purity, simplicity, and uprightness that we share nothing in common with them and are in no way like them. And then, although they make deacons the way they want them to be and have this rule in their orders that they have to pass this way before entering the priesthood, as they put it, let us realize, however, that it is all just mockery. The deacons who were made in the early church were ordained to minister to the poor. And what is their role in the Papacy today? Is that their purpose? What is more, they are told nothing about it. They are told, 'We grant you the right to bear the cup and to chant the gospel.' That is what deacons are ordained for in the Papacy. That is their principal function. That indeed is all that means. There is no question about it. And then in short order they are made priests to chant their great mass. That is how those wretches mock God so impudently that little children can condemn them.

Now let us take a good look at ourselves and understand why we have this text and why God declares what kind of government, what kind of order and regulations he wants to prescribe for our use. If we wish to be respected and esteemed as his church, we must practise what he declares to us here. Consequently, what the apostles did must be a perpetual example for us. Thus we have a general rule laid down for us by Paul, who not only shows us what the apostles did but also what all Christians must do if they want Jesus Christ to rule and have order in the church. The poor must be cared for. And for that, we need deacons. And yet it is not enough that we elect as deacons just any kind of men; but quality is required in the mix, as this passage specifies: 'Choose men from among you, especially men of good repute.' That conforms to what Paul says: 'Let them be tested first', he says, 'and then let them give a good witness of their conscience' (*1 Tim.* 3:8–9). It is as if he were saying, 'We must not put a man in there with expectation, as if to say, "Well, we will see how he turns out", for that is mocking God.' But he must be tested. His good life and conduct testify that he qualifies to exercise that office. And then let us find out how he deals with others. Let us pay close attention to how he conducts his family, how he rules his wife and children. And then, if he is wise and prudent, let us acknowledge that he is suitable and capable of serving God in that position. That is the kind of men of good repute Luke has in mind here.

But he is not satisfied with that quality, so he adds: 'Let them be full of the Holy Spirit and wisdom.' That is because a man can be of good and scrupulous conscience, of upright life an behaviour, and still be incapable of administering such a responsibility because he lacks common sense and judgment. Now we are aware that the task requires judgment and discrimination. So if a man lacks judgment, no matter how capable he may otherwise be, he would do better to decline that office and remain as he is than to accept the advancement. For it would be to his condemnation if things went badly in the absence of good management. First, God would be mocked, and then the poor would be deprived of good directors. So Luke notes particularly that prudence must play a role. Paul speaks of gravity and says a man must be sincere and upright and speak with integrity. So let a man be prudent, wise, and discriminating. All that adds up to the good repute, to the prudence, Luke speaks of here. What Luke does here is sum up in a single statement the prudence, the wisdom, the worthy life, the good conscience, the good judgment, and the common sense required of those who are charged with caring for the poor and are responsible for that ministry. Consequently, they must not be hard and wooden. They must be chiefly men of good repute and good and pure conscience, as we have just said.

Now the text not only says that there have to be individuals who are responsible for electing people suitable for that service, but also that the entire church is commanded to be involved with the care of the needy. When elections are held for any position, it is as if we were heaping the wrath of God upon ourselves. We must realize that electing ministers and deacons is no small matter. For the man of God, as Paul calls him (*2 Tim.* 3:17), is first in order. And then the poor, whom the Lord Jesus Christ has highly recommended to our care, must be helped because he accepts what is done for them as if it were done to him (cf. *Matt.* 25:40, 45). For that reason, we must always call upon God, as the apostles did. But is prayer offered? Even so, let them realize that they are subject to being deceived and misled by human nature. For one of the seven elected was evil.[1] By that fact, God shows us that after we dutifully call upon him, he must, to keep us humble, show us that there is nothing more difficult to achieve than human perfection and that there is always something to reproach. We ought to beseech God all the more diligently to be pleased to correct the evil in our nature. When we see that even in the holiest of matters we fail so miserably and when we see that we are more inclined to fall from

---

[1] The editors cite sources that show the church from early times believed that Nicholas, one of the seven, was believed to be the founder of the sect of the Nicolaitans mentioned in the book of Revelation (*Rev.* 2:6, 15).

good into evil than to withdraw from evil to do good, we must make an even greater effort to see that good things continue when we see they are well ordered. But the opposite prevails. We pervert everything by our evil. We even see there is still something praiseworthy in the Papacy, which they call poorhouses,[1] houses of God.[2] That is something that has been erased from our list of things to do. Consequently, we ought to be deeply ashamed that while we were in ignorance and still in that horrible darkness of the Papacy, we used to call poorhouses 'houses of God' to indicate that that was where God wanted us to serve him in the person of the poor, and we ought to be equally ashamed that we still hold in high regard the name 'house of God', but, what is worse, we abandon the poor there without being concerned for or solicitous for their welfare. In fact, there is no reason to elect stewards to supervise the care of the poor or deacons to administer the alms given for the poor because nothing is given for them, or very little. Consequently, what good would it do to have ten or twelve stewards elected to oversee such a responsibility when there is no money in the purse? Therefore, let us know that after we have condemned the papists, we will be doubly condemned. Why so? Because we clearly demonstrate that our love for our poor brothers has grown cold, even in this time when God has granted us the grace to recognize fully what is pleasing to him and what he requires of us.

Now we must first, as I have said, give liberally of our substance to those whom God has given the charge of caring for the poor. And let us not be satisfied with giving liberally and with the alms that would be distributed by the hands of the deacons. We should also give alms privately, for we should not suppose that in the early church each individual was unconcerned for the needy

[1] French: *hospiteaulx*.

[2] French: *maisons de Dieu*.

and did not help them beyond what they received from the hands of the deacons. So let us do the same if we want God to choose us and sustain us as his church and if we want to progress from good to better, as the apostles show us here. That, I say, is what we must do. And since we cannot of ourselves possess those virtues and since we are incapable of doing the smallest of things without God's instructing us, let us pray that he will be pleased to correct the things which are still poorly organized and to further what is established according to his holy institution so that people cannot say that we created something from our imagination, but so that they may know we have followed the pure, simple, and complete teaching of our Lord Jesus Christ.

> Following this holy teaching, let us bow before the face of our gracious God in acknowledgement of our sins, praying that he will be pleased to draw us to himself and to obedience unto himself in such a way that we will seek only to be in conformity with his holy will, just as he has declared it through his word, and in such a way that all of us, in common accord, will desire that he be honoured and served as he should be, not only by us, but also by all those who will be instructed upon seeing our worthy lifestyle. And in the meantime may he be pleased to forgive us our past sins and lead us to better things so that as long as we are in this world we may strive for the goal he has set before us, until we have all reached it. May he grant this grace not only to us, but also to all peoples and nations of the earth . . .

24

TRUE DISCIPLESHIP

SUNDAY, 17 AUGUST 1550

And in those days, when the number of the disciples was multiplied, there arose a murmuring of the Grecians against the Hebrews, because their widows were neglected in the daily ministration. [2] Then the twelve called the multitude of the disciples unto them, and said, It is not reason that we should leave the word of God, and serve tables. [3] Wherefore, brethren, look ye out among you seven men of honest report, full of the Holy Ghost and wisdom, whom we may appoint over this business. [4] But we will give ourselves continually to prayer, and to the ministry of the word. [5] And the saying pleased the whole multitude: and they chose Stephen, a man full of faith and of the Holy Ghost, and Philip, and Prochorus, and Nicanor, and Timon, and Parmenas, and Nicolas a proselyte of Antioch: [6] Whom they set before the apostles: and when they had prayed, they laid their hands on them (Acts 6:1–6).

Last Sunday we began the exposition of the present text and explained what the office of deacon was in the early church. According to what we have already seen, there can be no good order among the faithful unless the poor are helped. However, much commotion and grumbling among the faithful cannot be avoided without involvement and supervision and the kind of administration that avoids confusion, so far as men can avoid it.

And now we must mention again what Luke relates here. In the first place, he says a grumbling arose because the number of followers had increased. By that, we understand we are so sinful that the more liberally God bestows upon us his graces the more we take it as an opportunity for evil. Now there is nothing in this world to be desired more than to see the church grow and have an infinite number of believers. In that particular, we are in common agreement with the angels. We know that that heavenly host is innumerable. So when our Lord's church in this world gets so big and great that the invocation of his name is heard everywhere and everyone has one confession of faith and one and the same doctrine so that all follow God with one accord, there you have, as I have said, one song which is shared in heaven and on earth. Yet we are so wretched we cannot maintain that union which God has established between himself and us, for we cannot be united with him unless we preserve that brotherly love.

In this passage we see that in the church, where there were still apostles, dissatisfaction had arisen because the numbers had grown. That does not mean we must not do everything we possibly can to draw people to God. If Satan thought that by encouraging tumult and turmoil he could keep the kingdom of our Lord Jesus Christ from growing, he would immediately have gained an advantage over us with his craftiness if growth in numbers discouraged us and we said, 'Oh! Because of the grumblings, dissensions, and quarrels, fewer Christians would be better. We would do better not to be concerned with bringing a lot of people to the knowledge of Christ.' Should that have happened, the devil would have the upper hand. So even though we have tumult and turmoil, let us do as we are commanded and work to win the whole world to God and bring it to obedience unto him. Also we must find ways to resist dissension and then, after it occurs, root it out. But the way is not to let Satan rule over us and have his way or for us to yield ground to him as if he had won. That is not the way, and we must pay attention to everything that Luke tells us here. He says it is because the number of believers was growing that this murmuring arose. He does not add that the apostles repented of growing the church and of drawing a large number of people to the faith. But, to the contrary, we see how they did not cease, but always preached to reach out to the unfortunate people who do not know their doctrine, so that everyone might be resolute in it and so that each person might receive it. Consequently, the apostles did not veer from their calling because of the grumbling which had arisen, but instituted instead a suitable solution. Therefore, we must do as much and desire especially that the gospel be extended and increased throughout the whole world.

In the meantime we understand that the devil will insinuate himself into the mix. He will come and sow weeds in order to stir up trouble among us. What are we to do? Are we to draw apart and separate ourselves from the fellowship of the church? That would be lying to God and totally approving evil. But let us take care to look for approaches that God approves, such that Satan will in the end be thwarted in all his contrivances and wiles. That, I say, is how we must make our effort if we are to follow the apostles' example given here.

Besides, sometimes good people come along who do not forgo grumbling while indeed possessing some shelter and some vestige of possessions. The kind of grumbling that Luke is talking about here did not come into play. Some might complain that they were being rebuked for their vices or that they were being chastised, as we see happening today, when most of those who vent against the gospel are lowlifes who are angry because someone wants to rein them in. They want to be permitted the full range of dissolute living. They want to live like wild animals, without rules or correction. Consequently, they become very angry and blaspheme

God. But those Luke talks about here are not like that. They are grumbling because they think the alms are not being properly distributed because consideration is not being given to the widows who were Greek, that is, foreigners. It was as if a kind of jealousy had arisen among the Christians because some were from Jerusalem and the rest had been gathered from many regions included in the word 'Greek', for it was common in Scripture, when a distinction was needed, to say 'the Jew and the Greek' (cf. *Acts* 14:1; 19:10). Consequently, it seemed to the foreigners not only that the alms were not being well distributed, but also that their widows were not being shown due respect. In that regard, those who are grumbling give some appearance of worthy zeal, for they are not talking in their own behalf or for their individual advantage, but so that there might be good order and good administration among the believers. That must encourage us to be loving and sincere as we prepare to establish a polity and government among ourselves. In those matters where we cannot be one with God, Jesus Christ cannot rule over us and we cannot hold on to him as our master and guide. That is the kingdom of which I spoke. Even if we try to do good and show goodwill, the devil will be able to lead us astray and we will give rise to offence and disturbance in God's church. Therefore, each of us must be careful to comport ourselves steadfastly and not to be overly confident in our worthy zeal. But let us learn to restrain ourselves and exercise moderation so that we will not put too much store in our opinion. But let us fellowship together. Let us love one another, and let no one be excessively wise, for we become divided when everyone wants his own counsel to be followed. If the devil finds access and catches us off guard, he will, you may be sure, no matter how genuine our love is, take occasional advantage of our worthy zeal. Consequently, let us not be completely given over to our own predilections, wanting what we think is right to be done forthwith. But let us look farther ahead to that unity which is to be ours, that unity which is to be a bond of perfection, in Paul's words (*Col.* 3:14). That is what we are to learn from the statement that 'there arose a grumbling among the disciples.'

Afterwards, let us be careful to avoid all conflicts, disturbances, and turmoil so as to avoid division and alienation among ourselves. 'In Jesus Christ', Paul says, 'there is neither Jew nor Greek nor barbarian' (*Col.* 3:11). All that must be brought under subjection because we are members of one body, whose head is our Lord Jesus Christ. Therefore, inasmuch as we have been brought into God's church, we must no longer consider anything that will create divisions among believers, but we must let Jesus Christ so rule over us that we no longer seek him according to the flesh. This is how Paul says it: 'Though we have known Jesus Christ in this world, we are not to know him according to his human nature, but in the spirit' (*2 Cor.* 5:16). Indeed, we must know him in such a way that the earth and the world cease to attract us. Consequently, since God has adopted us as his children, let us keep in mind this immortal heritage which he offers us on high. And may nothing deceive the nations, regions, and countries any longer, but let us keep before us the main point, namely that God has united us so that we may all participate in a common heritage, the kingdom of heaven, where we have the same Father and the same Redeemer. That, I say, is the closeness which we must experience together. Do not let the flesh keep us from sharing an enduring peace and from extending our hand to each of our neighbours so that we may draw those who are unfortunately uninformed to God and to obedience to his will.

Now if the devil caused grumbling during the apostles' time, what about today, when we have so many troubles and quarrels and offences among us? We are still far from achieving the kind of perfection they had, for they had such order and such regulations among them that they are like angels. And yet when we hear that there arose grumbling among the apostles, let us not be surprised if we encounter many stumbling blocks within God's church today. There is a lot of wickedness and there are many who are inclined to rebellion and who want everything to be governed according to their insights. The very ones who have less understanding, less judgment and experience, and who are the most presumptuous are the ones who want to rule and direct everybody as they see fit. And yet they go around creating conflicts! They will certainly say, 'Why is such and such not done this way? Why can we not do it thus and so?' To make a long story short, God would have to make them a world of their own! If you put a dozen such clever people together, they will claw one another's eyes out and still presume to govern everybody. Now I would really like for such 'governors' to know what true Christianity is, namely that we interact with our neighbours in such a way that we show we honour other people, as Paul instructs us (*Phil.* 2:3). That means we think more highly of others than of ourselves. But some of them, indeed the majority, think they have the skill to manage something, such that, to hear them tell it, they seem to be angels whom God has sent to restore everything that is badly built. And when it turns out for the worst, they stand there all confused. That is what we need to glean from the first point that Luke deals with in this account.

Now let us come to what he says about the apostles: They call together the company of the disciples and tell them that it is not good or fitting to serve tables and to abandon the teaching which had been entrusted to them. Afterwards, they counsel disciples to choose from among themselves men of honest report, full of the Holy Spirit and wisdom. And as for themselves, they would continue in their office, which is to be busy with the ministry of the word and prayer. We need to take note of the word 'disciple', which Luke uses twice in this passage. That means if we wish to

322

be good Christians, we must be learners, for that is what the word 'disciple' means, a learner.

Now let us take into consideration how many there are in the world, indeed even here, who erroneously call themselves Christians. There is not a single person who does not admit right off, without hesitation, that he is a Christian. Yet if we ask for evidence of that Christianity, where will we find it? Most are pitiable animals, with no learning, no instruction. Let us not think the Spirit of God, the Spirit who spoke by Luke's mouth, is received without instruction. He declares that we will not be considered as Christians unless we are learners. And if we call a useless person a donkey or an animal, it is certain that was not Luke's intention when he used the word 'disciple'. Let us be advised then that those who do not grow in the teaching about God and who do not continue or who even withdraw from the number of the faithful are rejected by God because they have no knowledge of him.

In short, two things are required of us if we wish to be known as true disciples. First, we must demonstrate that we have been to Jesus Christ's school, that we can give a good account of our faith, and that people realize we are not ignorant of the gospel. It is true that not all of us can be teachers, but the prophet Isaiah's statement that 'all will be taught of God' (*Isa.* 54:13) is ever true. That, I say, is a general statement wherein is no exception. If we wish to be pupils and disciples of God in the Christian church, we must allow him to teach us, and we must show that his word has guided us. Subsequently, we must continue in that school all the days of our lives. For it is not a school that we must attend for a while simply to prepare ourselves, but we must apply ourselves until we die. Even if we should live in this world a thousand or two thousand years, let us always be willing, indeed let us always be resolved, to have Jesus Christ as our teacher. Therefore, all those who are annoyed by and surfeited with the teaching of the gospel and think they are already wise and have nothing more to do with doctrine or any kind of instruction are as much Christian as dogs. For we must not resist what the sovereign Judge has declared, namely that Christianity does not exist unless we are always under the tutelage of our Lord Jesus Christ and unless we grow increasingly in the word of his gospel.

Moreover, this admonition by the apostles tells us, first, that 'It is not good that we leave the word of God and serve tables.' At first, that might seem strange since the apostles had fulfilled the office of deacon until then. And now they are excusing themselves from the responsibility, saying they cannot fulfil it because they must give preference to teaching and preaching God's word. Might one think they wrongly used the word insofar as they did not follow their calling? But what Luke has already recounted helps us resolve this question. He shows that the apostles were always faithful in their calling. To be sure, he shows with what continuing diligence they remained there teaching and preaching God's word for four or five hours. Likewise, as we saw in the account of Sapphira that between her husband's death and hers, there was a period of three or four hours during which the believers remained perseverant and diligent in teaching the gospel proclaimed by the apostles (*Acts* 5:7). Therefore, when the apostles say in this passage that they do not think it good to abandon their charge in order to serve tables, they do not mean that when serving tables they stopped preaching, nor do they intend to belittle serving the poor and put everything else aside, but they for their part want to leave off serving tables because, as they might have said, 'My friends, the word of God is so precious that it must be preferred above all else. Moreover, it is so difficult to do that well, but if a man does nothing else, he does enough. The burden bears so heavily on his shoulders that if he is involved in anything else, he is necessarily distracted from his charge and unable to accomplish it. Are we not right to do this? Then we must be allowed this freedom so that we may preach in public and particularly admonish those who need it. That is what our Lord called us to when ordaining us to this office and entrusting this charge to us. Therefore, it is not good for us to have any other office which might prevent us from fulfilling this one faithfully.' And that, I say, is the apostles' meaning here, as is clearly evident, and they never forsook their charge. But because serving the poor might present some hindrance, they are content to lay it aside.

Now we need to emphasize what I have already touched upon, namely that God places no higher value on anything than the preaching of the gospel, for he wants his kingdom to be dominant in this world, and preaching is the way to lead men to salvation. That is how he displays his power, as Paul says in the first chapter of Romans (*Rom.* 1:16). Now we know that God prizes nothing above his honour, which lies mainly in men's knowing him and poor souls' being brought to salvation. So let us not be surprised if our Lord wants his gospel to be proclaimed with such diligence that nothing can hinder its course. For the only way men can come to salvation is through instruction in what the gospel teaches. Now since that is God's will, let us follow it. For even if we do all within our power to bring men to the knowledge of God so that Jesus Christ may be exalted and magnified by everyone, his kingdom will not be perfect among us from the outset. Far from it. In fact, why do we pray for God's kingdom to come? We do so to point out that we are very far from having it among us in its perfection. It is very important for us to be aware that the more we understand how difficult it is to get everybody to acknowledge God as they should and how difficult it is to bring about the preaching of the gospel, the more we must be encouraged to pray that God will be pleased to give his word such power that the ignorant will be built up and that those who are far from him will come to him through the preaching of his gospel, so that the kingdom of our Lord Jesus Christ his Son will be increased and extended.

Moreover, we can gather from Luke's words that that charge is not as easy as it seems. Many think one only needs to get behind the pulpit and discourse and hold forth for an hour, and that that is all there is to it. It is true that eloquence will always be eloquence, but we have to consider whether that eloquence is used appropriately and whether there is skill in applying it to life's needs and to what people need to be reproached and criticized for, depending on the dominant sins and the offences which occur every day. Now that is not easy to do. If the apostles, who were endowed with God's most excellent gifts, found it difficult, where does that leave us? It is as Paul exclaims, 'And who is sufficient for these things?' (*2 Cor.* 2:16). By that, Paul means that when it comes to proclaiming the doctrine of Jesus Christ, our speech must be alive and penetrating so that the teaching will be impressed on the hearts of men and so that the Holy Spirit will issue forth from our mouths and be like a burning fire warming consciences to God's love and like a sword excising all evil affections and mortifying men, to the end that he may make them new creatures. We cannot even have a good thought. God must provide it! We must be aware that we cannot proclaim the word easily unless we go about it right. And this is how Paul, speaking to Timothy, puts it: 'Consider well why you have been established in this office. The government of God's house has been placed in your hands. And his gospel, which is the pillar of righteousness, has been entrusted to you so that his truth may be maintained through preaching. In short, he has established you to direct his church by his word. Consider then in what fear you must walk' (cf. *1 Tim.* 3:15).

Now, that instruction is addressed to those who bear the word of God. If the apostles did not possess the required sufficiency for completely fulfilling their office, there is all the more reason for us to consider our weakness and apply ourselves with greater effort to the commission entrusted to us, knowing that we will not achieve our goal without much criticism. Let that then stir us and prod us to be even more diligent. For this is no small matter. First, we must proclaim God's word faithfully without adding anything of our own to it. We must have zeal and burning desire that everyone be brought to the knowledge of God for his forgiveness and for salvation. Let us respect this application of the teaching and use it correctly so that this word may have its full and complete effect and so that we may present it seriously, mindful of how we do so. Many people would like for me to preach with my eyes closed, not considering where I live, or in what locale, or in what time. As if those whose responsibility it is to proclaim God's message did not proceed the way it was done in the time of the apostles – as if the prophets did not apply the law of Moses to their day and time, and as if the apostles did not follow the same practice! And as if we were not to honour God's command through Paul to apply that teaching as we observe the offences, the dissolution, the vice, and disruption among us! Now as I have already said, these matters are of such magnitude that a mere mortal must not presume that he can achieve them, since he is distracted by many other concerns. Therefore, we must fully give ourselves to the task, as Paul tells us in yet another passage, where he makes a comparison with soldiers: 'A man will leave his home and all his affairs in order to follow his commander and will think of nothing but fulfilling the duty placed before him until he has finished his course' (cf. *1 Cor.* 9:25–27; *2 Tim.* 4:7). So what will we do when God calls us into his spiritual army and bids us follow him in guiding his church? Must we not be so preoccupied with that that nothing in the world can divert us from our calling? It is true that men will never be so perfect that they can reach that goal. Even if we were angels from heaven, such a charge would be of so great importance that we would not be able to discharge it in every respect and everywhere. And what does it mean to be clothed in this mortal body? How can we possibly serve God with the required undivided loyalty? Still we must consider our goal, fix our eyes upon it, and not justify ourselves for being distracted in any way. Our slightest deviation will be too much.

In that, we see how God has been mocked, indeed greatly blasphemed by this wretched Papacy. There you have the bishops, those mitred beasts, those monsters, who call themselves successors of the apostles. And just what is that succession, which is their great protector. Let us consider now how and in what they succeed them. The apostles say it is not good that they serve tables, which hinders the word of God. And what do the successors do? They have on their shoulders a thousand and a thousand more charges, which they bear well and with pleasure. Suppose a bishop has three or four hundred parishes under him. He will say that these are ecclesiastical charges. Let us overlook that, provided he fulfils his responsibilities. Following that, he has temporal jurisdictions, having usurped the sword and the authority of the magistrate, which is a responsibility that is to be governed apart, but he is not to interfere with God's church. Then he had to have cities and castles, lands and regions, and finally principalities. All this demonstrates that bishops have nothing in common with the apostles and bear no resemblance to them, no more than devils resemble angels. But they have found a more subtle means than the apostles, for the apostles said, 'We cannot serve tables and leave aside the preaching of God', but the bishops look only to serving themselves individually at the so-called 'episcopal table'. They are not concerned with the others except insofar as they, like insatiable gulfs, are able to swallow up what was appointed for the poor. When the distribution was made thirteen hundred years ago to provide for the bishops, it is expressly stated that the distribution was not only for them, but also for the support of those who were to follow. There were alms for those who lived in the city and were for the maintenance of the poor widows and orphans. The third part was dedicated to them. And then the fourth part was given to the bishops. But their canons specified that they were obligated to receive all poor strangers and support them with those funds which had been given to them. Now serving tables is very difficult, but they devised that release from responsibility. Now they will serve only one table – their own. What will become of the pulpit and the office of preaching? Oh! They do not condescend to engaging in such a foolish undertaking. Their office will be to anoint with holy oil, to dedicate and bless churches, baptize bells, consecrate the churches' vestments and trappings, bless organs, and engage in other such fanfare. But preaching, oh, that is for mendicants! So we see how God has been and continues to be mocked and blasphemed by bordello whores: the pope, his bishops, and all his vermin, who have no shame in assuming the mantle of succession of God's holy apostles, and yet in this way they spit on the majesty of God's Son.

Therefore, we ought all the more to praise God for snatching us from such an abyss. Let us take care to hold to the charge that we have received from him. He wants the charge kept inviolate until the end of the world so that preachers of the gospel will be able to accommodate the teaching according as they see a need and proclaim the word both in public and in private. And even if we sometimes see wicked men, men who are rebellious and thoroughly incorrigible, participating in this proclamation, and even if we see many scandals and much reprehensible behaviour, let us not fail to follow our calling always. But may that encourage us more to proclaim the judgments of God on the wicked in order to rebuke and reprove them for their vices and declare to them their judgment: that if they remain obstinate in their evil, God is condemning them through our mouths and that we are but the instruments of the Holy Spirit.

Following this holy teaching, let us bow before the face of our gracious God in acknowledgment of our failings, praying that he will be pleased so to humble us that we may approach him in all reverence and ask forgiveness for our faults, seeking only to entrust ourselves completely to him and, so doing, persevere until the end. And may we realize that our Lord Jesus Christ, having given himself over to death on our behalf, has not conquered our bodies and souls to no purpose. So let us now say together, Almighty God, heavenly Father ...

25

LEARNING, TEACHING, AND LIVING THE GOSPEL MESSAGE

SUNDAY, 24 AUGUST 1550

And the word of God increased; and the number of the disciples multiplied in Jerusalem greatly; and a great company of the priests were obedient to the faith. ⁸ And Stephen, full of faith and power, did great wonders and miracles among the people. ⁹ Then there arose certain of the synagogue, which is called the synagogue of the Libertines, and Cyrenians, and Alexandrians, and of them of Cilicia and of Asia, disputing with Stephen (Acts 6:7–9).

We have often pointed out that if we want to profit from the book of Acts, we must always keep in mind that Satan is relentlessly conspiring against everything within his power in order to stop the gospel in its tracks, for he is the mortal enemy of truth, resists God with all his might, and is the adversary of men's salvation. We also see how our Lord sustains his own so that they are never overcome by the trials which may befall them. He gives his word such power that it remains victorious over all the assaults Satan and his minions direct against it. This, we are told, happened in the time of the apostles so that we might be disposed to withstand the same battles. For God's word will necessarily be assailed in our day just as it was in theirs. And since this is the way God grants us the grace and honour of declaring it in our day, so must each of us declare it in our station in life in accordance with the means and ability God gives us. Therefore, aware of what we are told here, let us know that although Satan is trying mightily to abolish God's truth and obscure the teaching of the gospel, he will never on any occasion succeed or even divert us, provided we walk in the confidence that God will help us. With this certainty, let us be assured that we will be victorious. And although there are many difficulties in resisting Satan's repeated assaults, the fact is that in the end Satan will always be under subjection to us. May God strengthen us so that we can walk steadfastly in obedience to him.

That is why Luke says, 'The word of God increased; and the number of the disciples multiplied.' There we have the real triumph of God's church! It is when his word is received in obedience that he increases the number of his people. In that way the gospel bears fruit and flourishes, not with worldly pomp or in the ways of this world. But since God's kingdom is spiritual, the true blessedness of the gospel resides in the fact that God is served and honoured, that his word will not be proclaimed in vain, but that it will be received in all humility, with everyone being instructed in such a way that we will all be joined together in true concord and fraternity to serve God with one accord.

However, even if we are persecuted, even if unbelievers mock us and even defame and despise us, we will still have, in the eyes of God and his angels, the kind of esteem we should covet. And that is one thing we should note well. The impression is that God's church is nothing if not a beautiful external appearance, with its pomp, ostentation, and great wealth. That is how we, with our carnal eye, perceive the state of the church. All the more then must we take note of this teaching, which instructs us in the true dignity of the church. In it God has his throne, where each takes his place and obeys him, where the gospel is preached in its purity and entirety, and where each is disposed to yield in obedience to our Lord Jesus Christ, without being fixed on the things of this world. And although Satan has many avenues by which to assail us and come against us and although we, because of our nature, cannot prevail in the face of the many battles he and the wicked wage against us, let us be confident that God will give us an invincible constancy to repulse them all, provided we take refuge in him the way the apostles did in their day. Despite being rejected and shunned as filth and excrement, they did not abandon their calling, for they were sure God approved it, even though men despised it.

But very few pay any attention to that teaching today. If a triumphant church appeared here below today, oh! many would make profession of the gospel and be happy to have it preached. But when they see that we are fearful and that, from the world's perspective, our adversaries are so numerous that they appear irresistible, they will say, 'Why come here and be destroyed willingly? Why put ourselves in this danger of losing all that we have, even our very lives, for this thing?' Such is the rationale of many who withdraw from Christ and his church. They do not perceive the ostentatiousness and vain dignity of the world. And why is that? Because we fail to receive the teaching Luke shows us here. The fact is, the faithful do not spend their time with pomp and circumstance or with the things of this world. They are satisfied that God is glorified, and they are satisfied when they see God exalted and magnified. They know that is the great blessedness of the church of God and his great triumph, and after that they have no trouble being members of such a body. So that is how we must take advantage of that teaching, such as Luke presents it to us with that in mind.

However, we have to note that God's word increases in two ways, both when it is proclaimed abroad and again when it produces better fruit in us than it did before, and when we are strengthened in faith and in all holiness of life. That is what Luke adds when he says that 'the number of the disciples multiplied.' Now, God's word increases in proportion as men receive it. It is true that God's word, in and of itself, always remains unchanged, just as we know that truth is unchangeable. But just as it is said that God's name is sanctified when we give him the honour due him, so God's word grows in us when those who were formerly ignorant and unbelieving yield in obedience to God and to our Lord Jesus Christ in order to be guided and governed by his Holy Spirit. It is as if a new land has come into existence, a land where the gospel had never been spoken before and we now hear that it reaches into new regions. That is like the growth of God's word in a city where there are two or three believers and each one wins a half dozen others. When the number of disciples grows, the word increases at the same time. Not, as I said, that the word can increase or decrease, but Luke has people in mind when he speaks this way.

Now just as God's word grows when people are won to Jesus Christ and join his church, so it grows in each of us when we become more firmly established in God's will. It is indeed right that we should always be growing. We must not always remain unchanged. When we are instructed today, we must grow in proportion to the amount of knowledge we received at the time. Tomorrow we will have another message and a different Scripture passage. Must that serve no purpose? No! We must prize that knowledge of God according as he is pleased to teach us to be increasingly inspired to follow his holy will and give ourselves to the teaching of his word. For the more men are enlightened, the greater must be their zeal and passion for serving God so that they will be stronger as they face the temptations of the world and Satan when he attacks them.

That is how God's word increases in them. It is in accordance with that example which our Lord Jesus Christ compares the kingdom of heaven to leaven that has been put in dough. In its initial stages, you cannot tell that the dough has risen, but after a short time, you realize the power of the leaven. Therefore, after receiving the gospel, we must grow in it to such a degree that the power and efficacy of God's word is recognized and that his word has not been sown in us in vain. Likewise, it is not without reason that the gospel is compared to a seed, even a mustard seed. For only a small seed is needed to produce a large branch on which even the birds of the air can make their nest. That is the way the word of God is to bear fruit in us. The seed must not remain in the ground; it must grow and produce ears and finally be harvested.

Therefore, in keeping with the teaching Luke gives here, let us learn that we constitute a true church of God when we try our best to increase the number of believers. And then each one of us, where we are, will apply all our effort to instructing our neighbours and leading them to the knowledge of God, as much by our words as by our showing them good examples and good behaviour. That is also why holy Scripture exhorts us so often to win to God those who remain alienated from his church, for we see unbelievers as poor lost sheep. Our Lord has not given us insight into his truth for our advantage alone, but for sharing it with others. Because we see them as madmen casting themselves into hell, we must, to the extent we can, prevent them from doing so and procure their salvation. That, I tell you, is the zeal all Christians must have if they are not to limit themselves just to the public worship of God. They are to seek to encourage everyone to come willingly and affiliate with our Lord Jesus Christ so that there will be only one God, one doctrine, and one gospel. Let us be so closely conjoined that we will all be able to speak with one voice as we call upon God our Father. Unless we do that, we give a clear indication that we have scarcely learned anything in the school of our Saviour Jesus Christ. Each of us must extend our hand to our neighbour and encourage one another to grow more and more in the knowledge of God's truth, which he has been pleased to reveal to us. And when we see someone fall short, let us correct him with gentle admonitions and point out how we must serve God and forsake our iniquity.

That is not said only to preachers and those who expound the word of God. It is the charge of all Christians in general, as Paul says. He does not tell Titus and Timothy to preach, exhort, rebuke, censure, and admonish. But he does say to them, 'Be diligent in fulfilling your office and carrying out the charge which is entrusted to you. Rebuke, exhort, and censure each person when you know their manner of life so as to turn them from their wicked ways and lead them to salvation' (cf. *1 Tim.* 4:13; 5:1-2; *2 Tim.* 2:15; 4:2; *Titus* 2:1-10). That is Paul's instruction to all whose charge is to bear the word of God. He exhorts everybody in general to admonish one another.

Now, as I have already said, we must make every possible effort to lead those who have not been instructed in the knowledge of God so that they and we may serve and honour Jesus Christ, and in so doing increase the number of believers. But is that all? We are far from doing all we should. Surprisingly, we have, it seems, conspired against God by obscuring the truth of his gospel by no longer talking about it. What, then, should be our approach?

There are two ways to draw the poor uninformed to salvation. The first is that our disposition be considerate and consistent as we teach those who lack instruction, exhort the fainthearted, and reprove and denounce those who refuse to obey the teaching. The first way, then, deals only with verbal instruction. Now the second is that we give good examples by our lives so that those who see our good behaviour will be constrained to say, 'That teaching is surely holy, since those who profess it lead such holy and upright lives.

We have to acknowledge that teaching as being from God.' That then is how our lives are to serve as instruments for instructing the uninformed.

But when most people see that God provides an opening for them and a way to instruct the uninformed, they will remain silent, keep their mouths shut, and not say a word. But they will say, 'Oh! That is not important. Let everyone do as he feels led.' Alas, wretched people, our Lord has not given that knowledge for us alone. If a man thinks he has fulfilled his office and discharged his responsibility by walking as uprightly as he possibly can, yet without the slightest concern for others when he sees them go astray and has had the opportunity to reprove them, but did nothing – that man is not justified in thinking he has thereby discharged his responsibility. He will be guilty of other peoples' sin because he had the means to admonish them and did not. Consequently, we are very far from manifesting a true mark of Christianity when God provides an occasion to draw to himself the poor uninformed and we do nothing and perversely refuse to say a single word to instruct and enlighten them so that they can share with us in the knowledge of the gospel of our Lord. But when it comes to talking about what the gospel teaches, they do so mockingly so as to give unbelievers a distaste for it. They will say, 'After all, what good are all these sermons? The preachers are always working to proclaim publicly, and we know only too well what we are supposed to do.' That is how the mockers manage to set divisions so as to make God's word objectionable. And we find such devils among us. They are so wretched that they seek only to subvert and pervert everything. The result is that Jesus Christ is not lifted up and we are not instructed in his name so that we may pay him the honour and homage due him.

Now as for the Christian life, we well understand that we can take no credit if people are drinking enthusiastically from the gospel. For what opportunity do we provide the uninstructed for receiving that sacred teaching so that they can abandon their foolish superstitions when they become aware of the iniquities predominant among us? Some among us are given to every cruelty and inhumane act, to every injustice, to usury, robbery, and extortion. Still others will be filled with every impurity and contagion, given to lechery, debauchery, and drunken revelry. And still others will be blasphemers of God, drunkards, gluttons, rabble-rousers, rebels, and quarrellers. In short, we see that we have almost reached the height of every iniquity. Do we think this is the way to draw the poor unbelievers to the knowledge of God? Oh! Far from it! Even though our Lord is to be honoured by our worthy lives and behaviour, we try only to dishonour him. Consequently, we are far from resembling the Christianity Luke depicts for us here. In fact, we do not endure hardship and apply ourselves diligently to attract the poor uninformed to God so that the number of believers will increase and everyone will serve God with one accord.

Luke is speaking particularly about the priests when he says they were also obedient to the faith, for inasmuch as the priests were mortal enemies of the truth, it must be said that God worked in that situation with a particular power. We also see how the council comes together to condemn Stephen. We saw earlier how many inconveniences, hindrances, and obstacles the priests were throwing up before the apostles as soon as they began to advance the gospel. Therefore, it must be said that God worked miraculously in those who yielded to the teaching of the gospel. Since they belonged to that accursed group that rose up against Jesus Christ and since wretched people like that do come into line and obey him, we have a sign that God's hand is at work. In fact, it is as if our Lord wants his grace to be magnified when he extends his salvation to the gates of hell and pulls those who are thought to be totally lost from the pit of the abyss and places them in his kingdom. It is a great sign of his goodness that he gives us, and we have good reason for glorifying him for it.

In fact, when the priests are mentioned, we must each think of ourselves. Although we have not continued in that diabolical papal priesthood, each of us was far too involved in it. God had to extend his mighty hand to pull us out. Let each of us in our own situation think about our involvement in it. Those among us who used to be involved in the curse of the monastic life, which they call 'religious orders' – let them know that they have been delivered from the depths of hell. And may they also realize the danger they were in. And since our Lord has granted them the grace to escape that abyss, they must all the more magnify that grace and praise him as long as they live. Even so, let us think about ourselves, more than has been our custom. We were like poor brutish beasts that the devil possessed and held ensnared in his grip. As a result, he made us rise up in contempt of God and his word. Many of us were even like madmen whom God had to tame like wild animals. Otherwise, we would never have come to him. When we grasp that fact, let us not imagine that it was our doing, but that God extended his hand to lift us out of those pits of hell. We do indeed have good reason to hold to the faith and teaching which he has given us, for it is from him that we have received such a blessing. The might of the entire world could not have helped us!

As for the way Luke speaks here, when he says, 'A great company of the priests were obedient to the faith', he uses the word 'faith' to mean the teaching of the gospel, as does Paul in Romans 10, when comparing the gospel with the law and explaining to what end the gospel is preached (*Rom.* 10:8). 'It is', he says, 'so that everybody may obey God through faith.' Now here, Luke uses the word 'faith' for the teaching which God sends us to draw us by faith to himself. Luke notes particularly that 'they are obedient to it' and so points out that it is not enough that we attribute to

God the truth of his word. We must be held under its authority. We must come to the point that we no longer belong to ourselves, following our fleshly desires and living as we please. But let us be so dedicated to the service of God that we seek only to follow him in all things and everywhere and to serve and honour him, as is his due.

Then the text says, 'Stephen, full of grace and power, did great wonders and miracles among the people. Then there arose some in the synagogue, which is called the synagogue of the Libertines, and of the Cyrenians, and of the Alexandrians, and of those who were from Cilicia and Asia, to dispute with Stephen.' Here Luke is talking about Stephen because his death occasioned a great persecution directed against God's church and because he wants to recount the sermon which Stephen gave in the assembly of priests and teachers of Jerusalem. Now, before coming to that point, he says, 'Stephen was full of grace and power.' That fullness was not absolute, for it will never be found in a mortal. But the text says that God fills us with his grace when he confers it upon us in such sufficiency that it appears in us and people see that he has worked powerfully in us.

That is also what Luke meant when he said Stephen was full of grace. Not that he did not have some imperfections, for our Lord distributes his blessings freely upon all men in moderation. Only Jesus Christ has received them in their fullness so that he may be our fountain and we may draw from him, as John says in the first chapter: 'And of the fullness of Jesus Christ we have all received grace for grace' (*John* 1:16). If we wish to share in those blessings, we must come to him, for he has received them in their fullness from God his Father. And in the third chapter he says, 'God has given his Spirit to Jesus Christ without measure' (*John* 3:34). That is how our Lord Jesus Christ alone was filled with the Holy Spirit in all perfection. Conversely, no mortal has ever received more than a measure of the Holy Spirit in proportion as God gave him according to his will. Stephen was necessarily one such mortal. Yet the text says he was filled with the Spirit because God's glory was very especially manifested in him and necessarily worked through him. And he brought that grace and that power together in the miracles, for the time was such that the gospel had to be confirmed by miracles, as we saw earlier and will see again later.

After recounting that, Luke tells us that there were nevertheless some men so perverse that they rose up against Stephen. He wants to teach us that we must always be aware that even though God reveals himself to men, there will always be some who are so wretched that they will fight relentlessly against the obvious truth. So our Lord reveals his gospel so clearly that we have to be astonished that men are not dismayed and that they do not individually stick their heads in the ground out of shame! Is it not outlandishly diabolical malice and unbridled arrogance on the part of men to rise up against God and willingly wage war against him? That is what Luke tells us about now. Concerning Stephen, he says that God had granted him such grace that everyone could clearly see that what was coming from him was from heaven. And yet all those who spoke against him could realize that when we resist his teaching, we are not resisting a mortal man, but the living God. I tell you, that is what should have been going through their minds. But, conversely, Luke says that they rise up enraged and, completely defeated, continue to persevere in their evil. What conclusion can you come to, except that the devil possessed them? It is certain that it is a true judgment of God when such wretched men are reduced to error, as Paul says, and the god of this world, who is the devil, has so blinded them that they realize neither the danger they are in nor the ruin that is about to befall them (*2 Cor.* 4:4). God has, as I said, allowed Satan to blind them so that they had no more understanding, judgment, or intelligence than brute beasts, as exemplified by those whom Luke mentions. He does not tell us that just so we will condemn them, but so we will be warned by their example to humble ourselves before God and pray that he will be pleased to open our eyes, and, with eyes open, we will be able to recognize the grace he has granted us to the end that we will thank him for it.

In addition, when the text speaks of the synagogue of the Libertines, and of the Cyrenians, and of the Alexandrians, and of those from Cilicia and Asia, we must consider the customs of that time. Back then, synagogues were like schools in the city of Jerusalem. It is true that having schools was a very useful and holy thing. In fact, where will the seed of the gospel abide if the little children and even the young people are not instructed and if that instruction does not continue? We see what importance it had in the past. There were well-funded schools and much money was spent for the instruction of children. Everyone wanted the children to commit themselves to learning. But today we are not enthusiastic about all that. It seems to us that having students study is a trifling matter. How many will be found today who will put themselves out to have students instructed? It is true that they will be taught to read and write, for that seems to be sufficient for cheating someone in a shop. But they do not have to go beyond that. Even in papal times, fathers shared that viewpoint and said, 'Oh! My son is going to be a Canon. He will be a Curate. He will have to study to do that.' And today they will say, 'What will I gain by sending my children to school? And why become preachers? That is to say, a scoundrel. Oh! I will not have any part of it.' When you see such contempt for letters and the sciences, you really need to fear that we are becoming more brutish than we have ever been. For if we are careful to preserve wheat for seed so as to be able to sow and harvest the next year, how much more should we be diligent in preserving some good seed for God's church.

Now we ought not be astonished if things are as bad as we see them today. What about all these colleges that make up the universities which people praise so highly? A child could not learn as much evil or become accustomed to as much filth and degradation in a brothel as they would there. Why is that? Because everything there is given over to dissolution and the headmaster fails because things are not regulated according to God's word. Therefore, as children are guided, so will they conduct themselves. However, if our Lord grants us the favour of well-regulated matters in our day, let us take pains to insure that they continue, praying that he will not allow them to grow worse, but rather to improve steadily, so that it will be known that we have been to his school and profited from it. Let us always be subject to and obedient to what he is pleased to command us in his word, and let us consent to be governed by it until we attain to our Lord Jesus Christ and are fully joined to him.

> Following this holy teaching, let us bow before the face of our gracious God in acknowledgment of our sins, praying that he will be pleased so to open our eyes that we will recognize that he alone is our teacher and that it is from him that we must learn our straight path so that we may always aim at the goal which he has proposed for us. And as long as he permits us to remain in this life, let us never stop glorifying his holy name so that the uninformed may be stirred to do likewise, to the end that everyone with one accord may be able to serve and honour him by obeying his holy word. So let us all say, Almighty God, heavenly Father . . .

26

DEFENDING THE TRUE OBSERVANCE OF THE SACRAMENTS

SUNDAY, 30 AUGUST 1550

Then they suborned men, which said, We have heard him speak blasphemous words against Moses, and against God. [12] And they stirred up the people, and the elders, and the scribes, and came upon him, and caught him, and brought him to the council, [13] And set up false witnesses, which said, This man ceaseth not to speak blasphemous words against this holy place, and the law: [14] For we have heard him say, that this Jesus of Nazareth shall destroy this place, and shall change the customs which Moses delivered us. [15] And all that sat in the council, looking stedfastly on him, saw his face as it had been the face of an angel (Acts 6:11–15).

According to what we have previously dealt with, we are admonished by the Holy Spirit to strengthen ourselves if we are intent on maintaining the teaching of the gospel because there will always be rebellion in the world and because men are so malicious we must always be struggling against them. And without the struggle we cannot serve God by proclaiming his word. That is demonstrated by the example of Stephen, who by the grace given to him, tried to advance the gospel. But we see how he was attacked; we see the rage that was directed against him to hinder him.

345

Yet Luke will show us how steadfastly Stephen has maintained that teaching which he had previously proclaimed. All that, I say, is recounted so that this may be a mirror for us and we may learn not only to be ready to proclaim the gospel to the extent we can, but also that we may be armed because there will always be enemies who resist that truth and because Satan will be relentless in his war against Jesus Christ.

Now Luke tells us that just as these wretched men who resist Stephen have maintained an evil cause, so have they used similar tactics. 'For', he says, 'they suborned false witnesses against him and charged him with blasphemy against God and Moses.' True, there seemed to be evidence for charging Stephen falsely with that accusation. There is no doubt that he had spoken about the ceremonial law and had said that it was to be abolished, and that all the ceremonies of the law were to last only until the coming of our Lord Jesus Christ and that there would no longer be a material temple where God would be served, as was his established purpose for the Jerusalem temple. So that was the source of their apparent evidence, but surely we see their malice and understand that they, testifying against what they knew to be true, perverted what Stephen had said, so that he might be accused of blasphemy.

Now, by that we ought to be alerted to the fact that there will be many enemies and many devious ways to dissuade us from our calling. Nevertheless, we must be unyieldingly steadfast in the face of all the harsh words which will be hurled against us. For what implication does that have for us if we yield too readily? So we will do well to be aware of all of Satan's crafty and subtle wiles lest we be surprised when he confronts us with them. That is what Paul says in 2 Corinthians: 'We are not ignorant of his devices' (*2 Cor.* 2:11). That is how Paul exhorts the faithful to resist Satan so that they will not be taken by surprise as those who do not know his ways. But because we do understand the tricks he uses as he rises unobserved out of nowhere to do his utmost against us, we must also be careful not to be taken unawares. We must always be armed against him, as Paul says. That is also why Luke tells us how Stephen was falsely accused.

In addition, we must not be surprised when we preach God's word in its purity and fully, if there are always some so wicked and impudent that they find fault with the things which have been explained clearly and interpret them wrongly. But that must incite us to be even more circumspect. We understand, I say, how God's truth is open to being reviled and corrupted by the world. That being true, what are we to do? We are not to give the wicked an opportunity to disseminate false statements which will encumber God's word. Rather let us silence them insofar as we can, for if we, by our behaviour, are the reason the teaching of the gospel is scorned and defamed, it is certain we will be punished doubly – and rightly so (cf. *Luke* 12:47). Let us pray that God will give us the grace to grow so much through the proclamation of his word that the wicked, who seek only to invent means by which to fault the teaching of the gospel, can only acknowledge their impudence as a result.

Have we done all we can? Have we tried to teach the gospel in its purity so that no one will take offence at our teaching? If, however, we understand that the devil is always raising up wicked people to take what we say and distort it and find fault with it, we must not let that stop us from doing what God commands. We know what our charge is and we must persist. Whatever happens as the world does its worst to prevent the teaching of the gospel, we must, as the wicked rage, remain steadfast and persevere in doing what God has once and for all entrusted to our charge. In this way we understand that this story will serve us very well, provided we apply it for our instruction and profit. Now as for the first, as I have just said, just as the devil, the father of lies, is always plotting treachery, always seeking perverse and illicit means to achieve his goal, let us remember that he will raise up wicked men to pervert and corrupt every good doctrine in order to find an opportunity to revile and malign it. In short, since Satan's cause is evil, he also conducts its evil intent. What are we to do? Well, since our Lord has given us knowledge of his truth, let us, if we wish to follow his command, consider whether our cause is good and approved by him, and then let us engage in it with a pure conscience. In other words, let us proceed with simplicity, for he wants us to approach it wisely. Let us not think that God's glory can or has to be advanced by our foolish inventions, but let us realize that he does not want to be served with them. That, I say, is a part of what Luke shows us here, namely that because our Lord has favoured us with his pure truth and because, as a consequence, our enemies rise up against us, we must – if our cause is good – endeavour to engage in it forthrightly.

Now I say that because many think they can get people to accept the gospel by any means at all, on the spur of the moment. 'Look', they say, 'we have to proceed in such and such a way. If we want to advance the gospel on our first outing, the world will never accept it.' Some will want to have God glorified by using their hypocritical means; others will look for who-knows-what kinds of other ways. Now God rejects all of that. And for good reason. But let us follow the course the Holy Spirit lays out for us. In other words, since we have to fight against the devil, let us not use his weapons to defend ourselves from him, but being armed by God, let us engage in our cause with a pure conscience, uprightly and simply. And not only must we adhere to that rule in the matter of doctrine, but in our entire life. As for doctrine, I have already mentioned briefly that we must not follow those who say, 'Oh! This is how we can further the gospel. We must use this dissimulation or another; we must do thus and so to attract the ignorant to the knowledge of the gospel.' It is like those Nicodemites who say, 'It is good to assume some pretence. If I go to mass every day, they will think I am very devout, and eventually they will find some small fault and initiate a discussion and respond in such a way that the mass will be abolished.' Such is the pretext those poor wretches want to hide behind as they counterfeit being Christians today. And yet they wallow in their filth and support others of like mind. It is true that those who employ those kinds of tactics say, 'It seems to us that the gospel will be better served in this and that way', but when all is said and done, there is no doubt that we will discover they want to flee from the cross and persecution, but will find in so doing that they are going about it in the wrong way. As I said, our Lord commands us to proceed with all simplicity. But also when we have to deal with people for whatever reason, let us, if our cause is good, lay it out fully and well. And we do indeed need that admonition. For when a man has tried to do well and act uprightly and faithfully in all his dealings with his neighbours and people still return evil for good, then, since we are of the flesh, we will want to get vengeance and give as good as we got. Now our cause was good and we handle it badly when we handle it that way. For however good our intention may be, God rejects everything we do if we want to defend ourselves in ways that he does not approve. Let us not run about aimlessly following tortuous paths. Rather, let us stick to the straight path by considering what God approves. If we see a way that seems good to us but that God condemns, let us reject it every time.

Now I have said we very much need that bit of wisdom, for we see how people live today. We always put our trust in the ways and means of getting things done, thinking we will achieve our goals while well aware that God condemns them. I have said that even if we had an angelic goodwill, our effective and efficient means would still need God's approval. For example, whenever I make an effort to do something good and try my best to do what God commands, I must consider how to proceed. And what is this procedure to be? According to God's rule and commandment! Whenever we see that our Saviour wants us to proceed in a certain way, let us proceed confidently, for we cannot fail. But if we have devised something repugnant to God's will, knowing that he rejects it, let us also detest it and refuse to follow through. In this way, we will be acting in complete conformity with his will, as I have just said.

In addition, we need to realize that there is no case so good or just that we do not make it bad and condemnable in God's eyes when we have handled it badly. For the whole of it will be considered wrong. And even when we are persecuted and afflicted unjustly, we must not rise up against those who have injured us and take vengeance. But we must return good for evil, just as our Lord commands. And when we see our enemies employ every manner of cruelty and violence against us, let us put it all in God's hands without wanting to return evil for evil. For, as the saying goes, that would make two devils out of one. That proverb did not arise without reason. As often as we see someone wrong us and act maliciously against us, we think we are authorized to retaliate. Now that person was already the devil's captive, and if we side with him in doing even worse than he did, there was but one devil at first and we make two of him. To avoid doing that, there is but one remedy, the one I have just provided: if someone wrongs us, we must put our cause in God's hands and, to the extent it is good, we must deal with it in such a way that he will not be offended and we will do only what he permits.

Let us now look at this accusation against Stephen. They charge him with saying Jesus Christ intended to destroy the temple, the ceremonies, and the law of Moses. Luke tells us that those accusations were made against Stephen. It appeared that he had done so, as I said at the outset, but their accusations sprang from an evil source, and his accusers misrepresented what he actually said. That is why they are called 'false witnesses' by Luke, or rather by the Holy Spirit, who pronounced the judgment. We will not be guilty before God just when we openly say something against the truth, but also when we alter the content so that its meaning is different. We are then liars and deserve punishment. Where are the true witnesses now? We will find that the whole world is filled with false witnesses, and only with great difficulty will we find one out of a hundred. If we ask them what they know, they will have no trouble perjuring themselves or at least they will try every means at their disposal to disguise the truth and will never get to the point unless they are pressured by force, and even then they will not tell the whole truth. Are people like that rare? No! They are commonplace. Normal. So let us consider what we might do should we have to appear before this great Judge who holds his truth in very high regard, a fact which shows that he despises a lie, for we cannot lie without severely defacing God's glory. Nothing characterizes God better than truth, so much so that he attributes this virtue to himself. Consequently, if we lie and disguise the truth so that it does not remain whole, are we not doing all we can to rise up against God and obscure, indeed destroy, his glory? And yet everybody is doing it so regularly that before long it will shortly be made a law! Now we ought to pay special attention to this passage where Luke declares that those who had a fine external appearance before men of good conscience are nonetheless condemned by the mouth of God and by the Holy Spirit as false witnesses who have been corrupted as liars and perjurers because they did not proceed with humility, forthrightness, and integrity, as they should have done.

Let us now look at their accusations. There is no doubt, as I pointed out above, that Luke could have said, 'This temple has served you during the time of figures and types of the law. And even though it was designed and built as God commanded, the fact is that he no longer wishes to be honoured and served in a specific place, but throughout the whole world.'

We see that in our Lord Jesus Christ's remark in the fourth chapter of John, when he explains to the Samaritan woman what the worship of God entails. 'The time has come', he says, 'that those who worship will no longer come to this mountain or to the temple in Jerusalem, but God will be called upon throughout the whole world' (*John* 4:21). It is true that during the time of the law, there had to be a specific temple in which God was worshipped, because it was not at that time as fully disclosed as it now is in the person of our Lord Jesus Christ his Son. Even so, although God had instituted nothing else like it, the temple had to be established and last until Jesus Christ was revealed to the world. That, then, is how the material temple in Jerusalem represented the Son of God and was built to hold men in the fear of God and in obedience to him until Jesus Christ's coming. But has Jesus Christ come? We must no longer linger over types, because we have the truth about the things which all the ceremonies of the law signified. Since we have the truth, we no longer need to go chasing after the figures, or shadows, as Paul says, for they no longer serve any purpose (*Col.* 2:17).

Consequently, Stephen was able to speak this way, and his teaching is necessary. But as long as those who would like to have the temple and all the ceremonies of the law without having the truth, they blaspheme against God and against Moses. And why is that? If the Jerusalem temple signified nothing, if all the ceremonies practised there had no meaning and contained no doctrine, it would have only been farcical and child's play to kill calves and sheep, to take blood and pour it on the altar, and to sprinkle it on the people. What good would all that have done, if there had been no understanding behind it? It would have only been useful as busywork for those who had nothing else to do. So anyone who separates the truth from the types blasphemes against God and the law. So Stephen was able to say, 'Do not think that God gave you children's games when he instituted the sacrifices and commanded so many ceremonies to be performed in the temple, but know that these ceremonies contain great mysteries, as was declared to Moses: "You will do all these things following the pattern that you saw on the mountain." That is to say, there is nothing earthly or profane, but everything was made to conform to that heavenly image' (*Exod.* 25:40; *Acts* 7:44; *Heb.* 8:5). That is how Stephen speaks, teaching the abolishment of the ceremonies of the law, because we possess their truth and perfection. Yet they accuse him falsely. And who are they? They are the ones who think they possess goodness, integrity, piety, and the perfection of the full teaching within themselves and who imitate the great believers and resist so strongly God's teaching.

Therefore, let us return to what I touched on at the outset, namely that we will never be able to proclaim God's truth without our teaching's being subject to unjust reproach and without our adversaries' finding some way to level accusations of betrayal and falsehood against us. We must be fortified beforehand if we are to repel the affronts and false accusations. Let us, I say, be relentlessly steadfast.

Moreover, let us not be caught unawares, if possible, but able to answer, always standing ready when they taunt us, courageous and speaking graciously in order to expose the malice of those who revile us. Not only was that kind of talk attributed to Stephen, but also to Jesus Christ. Yet it is quite certain that the Son of God neither forgot nor omitted anything that might prevent his teaching from being accepted. He gave no occasion for anyone to stumble on his account. And yet by accusing him of coming to abolish the law and of destroying and laying waste everything, they put him under pressure to respond. And because his intention was never to abolish the law, but to fulfil it and restore it, the Son of God has to make that response. And there is no doubt that he did so to answer the false accusations they laid on him.

We very much need these examples and an understanding of all the incidents associated with them. Today it is clear that many have been turned away from the gospel by the brazenness of our adversaries, who do everything within their power to make people doubt God's teaching. In fact, their false charges against the pure teaching of God are in our day just like those Luke has recounted here. When you read what the supporters of the Papacy allege against us, or rather against God, you will find an enormous and lamentable brazenness. They think they are permitted to do everything. And why is that? Their zeal reflects precisely what Luke is talking about here. They are filled with an enraged zeal which knows no reason or restraint. And during that time, the devil roused in them such fury that they stop at nothing as long as they can sustain their cause, no matter what! Now to what lengths will they go? In the first place, they will balk at subverting and perverting the whole of sacred Scripture. They will not always act out of ignorance – dumb animals though they are – but out of very profound impudence. They will gladly pervert Scripture and twist the meaning of passages. They will erupt with fierce hostility, no longer restrained by fear of or reverence for Scripture. They will mangle it. 'Oh! That is all right', they will say. 'We are dealing with heretics. There is no harm in abusing Scripture to abolish their teachings.' Then they go and misrepresent everything we say in their effort to convince the ignorant that we permit every evil and have blurred every distinction between virtue and vice, and that when we say we are justified by faith and saved by God's grace, we do so to allow everyone to live as he pleases. That is the way they fault the gospel of our Lord Jesus Christ.

Now if we did not have these examples, we could be alarmed and even turned away from our calling and say, 'It is true that we must all try to put God's truth first. But what good will that do? God's name will still be blasphemed. We see that the wicked use the occasion to blaspheme and spite God rather than praise him.' So it seems that it would be better for us to renounce the gospel and abandon it. But when we see that the same thing happened to our Lord Jesus Christ, who is the example and pattern that we are obliged to follow, we must not lose courage. Rather, we must be armed with relentless steadfastness so that we can advance God's cause and God's claim and persevere with all our might. For Stephen's steadfastness shows that we must be fearless. When we see the wicked spewing out blasphemies and devising every kind of evil against us so that others will despise our teaching as wicked and perverse, let us respond with such diligence in advancing the teaching we proclaim in its purity that people will know by our good and holy behaviour that those who misrepresent our words do so wrongly and without cause. For not only has our Lord entrusted to us the charge to proclaim his word, but he also wants us to defend it, not that we are sufficient for the task, but he will provide the means. Nor does he need us, but he honours us by making us its defenders. The more we see the strenuous efforts of the wicked to overthrow Scripture and interpret it against us, let us be all the more ready with answers to defend ourselves. That is why we are constrained today not only to demonstrate by word and in writing the teaching which we advocate but also to answer the false accusations laid on us by these hypocrites who, only wanting to satisfy their stomachs and their fleshly pleasures, seek to maintain their claim zealously and with raging passion, but without explanation or discussion. Consequently, we are obliged to take our case to them.

Why must we? We would be betraying God's truth by remaining silent when seeing them making every effort to abolish the truth and the teaching of the gospel. What would happen if we refused to do our part? Would we not be traitors and disloyal to God? We must not be surprised then if we are engaged in many combats against the gospel's adversaries, for our Lord has appointed us for that purpose, and it is our duty to fulfil it. Stephen shows us how to do it, as we will see later. In fact, our Lord gives us sufficient resources to resist our enemies. He provides what he promised his apostles by providing his people with the wisdom no one will be able to resist (*Luke* 21:15). Similarly, the papists are now accusing us of a crime like Stephen's, namely that we are destroying the full worship of God. Yes, but let us look briefly at what the papists practise.

Now the worship of God everywhere in the Papacy consists only of the idiotic antics they engage in. One person will torment himself with making a pilgrimage, another with attending many masses, another with making many religious gestures, fasting on a certain day and, on another, saying such and such a prayer to a Saint, and then another such prayer to a different Saint. In short, those things in the Papacy today that they believe constitute devotion and the worship of God would fill a bottomless gulf. And who invented all that? Men imagined it in their heads, or they acquired it in Satan's workshop. For it is certain that the source of all superstition resides there, where the devil blinds men so profoundly that they confidently do the things that seem good to them. And everything called 'the worship of God' in the Papacy is only some kind of antic by which they dally with God as if he were a small child.

Now what do we say? We say we must worship God with obedience. He has given us an unmistakable guideline, namely that whenever we do what he tells us without adding or taking anything away, we are worshiping him the way he wants us to. That is what we proclaim. God has not provided us with a short version of what he has given as doctrine. He has given us the full version. So we conclude that if we wish to worship God appropriately and as he requires, we must reject everything invented by men.

Now when we say that, our adversaries immediately accuse us of what they accused Jesus Christ of, namely, of wanting to destroy the law. Inasmuch as we say that the forgiveness of our sins is a free gift (it must be this way; otherwise we are all condemned), we say that if God wishes to judge us rigorously, he will not find anyone who is not guilty in a multiplicity of ways. When we think we have lived a good life and come before this great Judge, we will discover that our lives are filled only with pollution and filth. Consequently, we say we must think about doing good, but when we have worked hard at it and done the very best we can, we must take refuge nowhere but in God's mercy. We are his, not because of our merits, but because he has adopted us once and for all without considering our worth or without looking at who we are. He has chosen us by his free grace and loving kindness. That is what we teach.

Afterwards, when we offend him, he must receive us in mercy; otherwise we are condemned. On that point, the papists charge us with destroying the law of God and extending license to everyone. Yet, it is clear that we insist much more on keeping the people in the fear of God and in obedience to him to encourage them to all holiness of life, a status the papists do not persist in. They have only their traditions to recommend, but we focus on the main thing, namely, on what God has commanded, which we endeavour to conform ourselves to. And we encourage others with all our might to do the same without adding or subtracting anything.

They also charge us with destroying and abolishing the sacraments of God. Now why do they do that? It is true that we do not retain many of baptism's insignificant trappings, which for the Papacy represent the full sanctity and fullness of baptism. If anyone says it is necessary to baptize with water only as our Lord Jesus instituted it and as the apostles practised it, they will say, 'Oh! There is more to it than that. You have to speak incantations over the water and breathe upon it before it is suitable. Jesus Christ used river water for baptizing, and that was quite appropriate. It must be prepared differently. There must be salt; the water must be 'waxed';[1] and all must be accompanied by other vacuous blessings and crossings. Then there must be oil, salt, spittle, candles, and other lighting effects. Oh! That is what is most holy and devout.' Inasmuch as we do not have all that fanfare because it is all a diabolical invention to draw the poor world into idolatry and nullify the value of baptism, they charge us with abolishing baptism.

But what is the teaching about baptism? Must we stop with the elements and the earthly signs, even though they are ordained by God? Certainly not, but we must seek our salvation in Jesus Christ, who is the truth and substance of baptism, and to whom we must come. Then, as for the water, we say we must be content to do what our Lord Jesus Christ has shown us and what the apostles practiced after him. Consequently, when we give that response, do we not prove that we refuse to deprive baptism of its due place?

Thus, we have a situation very much like Stephen's. Their charge is that he wanted to destroy and abolish the law of God and Moses. The opposite was true. When Stephen says, 'My friends, do not put your confidence in the temple or in ceremonies or in

---

[1] French: cyrée. Hughes Oliphant Old helps explain this expression. 'The pre-Reformation tradition had put considerable emphasis on the relation between the water of baptism and the waters of creation as well as the relation to the prenatal waters of the womb. The baptismal font was commonly called the womb of the Church … The ceremonial which accompanied the rite went so far as to plunge the paschal candle into the font in order that the font might be impregnated.' Hughes Oliphant Old, *The Shaping of the Reformed Baptismal Rite in the Sixteenth Century* (Grand Rapids, Mich.: Eerdmans, 1992), p. 262.

sacrifices or in all the rest, for God ordained all these things only for the purpose of keeping us in the fear of him until his Son's coming, and now that Jesus Christ has come into the world and we have the fulfilment of all things in him and now that we have the substance, we need no longer deal with figures.' We now say the same thing about baptism, namely that we must keep our eyes fixed on God's truth, particularly the grace which our Lord Jesus Christ has acquired for us by his suffering and death, that grace which baptism represents, and we must reject all of men's inventions, for they are but abominations.

The same is true for the Lord's Supper. With this, we will conclude the message, because we are to celebrate the holy Supper of our Lord Jesus Christ next Sunday, and this will serve as preparation. About this the papists will say, in order to make us odious to everyone, that we are wicked because we destroy the holy sacrament of the altar. But how do we destroy it? What we do is to observe the procedure our Lord Jesus Christ instituted and just as the Evangelists and Paul taught. 'Our Lord', they say, 'takes bread, breaks it, and gives it to his disciples, saying, "Take and eat. This is my body which is delivered up for you. So that you may be participants in my body, I want to give you this sign." Then, when he takes the cup, he says to them, "Take and drink, all of you, of this cup, for this is the cup of my blood, by which the covenant with your God is ratified and confirmed"' (*Matt.* 26:26–29; *1 Cor.* 11:23–25).

Now what do the papists do? Oh! Everyone does not have to commune using this sacrament. All that is required is for the priest to be there by himself and eat everything in his trough while saying that he eats for everyone as the people stand idly by. Then, instead of giving it to the people according to the ordinance of our Lord, who said, 'Take and eat', they will have the people adore it, and in addition they will present it to God and say, 'Here is a sacrifice which we offer unto you.' Did Jesus Christ command that? Absolutely not! Then, instead of proclaiming this teaching so that it might be heard by everyone, they have to breathe on the bread the way sorcerers blow on their amulets, and say softly, 'This is my body', as if the bread had some intelligence. 'Oh! Those are sacramental words', they will say. 'It is no longer bread. It is the body of Christ, and we must adore it.' And doing that, they manage to make a god out of a piece of bread and kneel before it, as if to say, 'This is my God.'

Is that not a damnable blasphemy against the majesty of God? We now reject all those abominations and adhere to God's pure institution. Can it be said that we are abolishing the sacrament? Far from it! Rather, we advocate as insistently as we can that the sacrament be re-established in its pure and unadulterated state, just as our Lord Jesus Christ ordained it and celebrated it with his disciples. That is how we must answer our adversaries whenever they want to accuse us of abolishing the sacraments.

And we must note that it is not enough to answer to the papists. We must also answer to God. Since we practise the unadulterated institution of the Supper, a very high and exalted thing, everyone must look at himself and examine his conscience. And when we have effectively resisted the papists and rejected their abominations – if God grants us the grace in our day to participate in the Supper of our Lord Jesus Christ his Son, according to its true usage and pure ordinance – we will be much more inexcusable if we come to it hypocritically and fail to approach it with true sincerity of heart as it is properly administered to us.

Well what do you think about that? Many will have no difficulty in presenting themselves at the Supper without considering their condition. Some will bring along their hatreds, their grudges, their jealousies; others will bring their usury, their thefts; others, their pride, their ambition; others will bring their debaucheries, their filthiness, their wickedness; others, their gluttony, their excesses;

others will bring their blasphemies, their perjury, and yet others will bring their backbiting and shameful speech. And that is how we will profane this holy sacrament which Jesus Christ instituted on our behalf, not that the teaching is not pure, not that it will not be observed as Jesus Christ ordained, but the profaning of it results from our perversity. So let us look within ourselves, and, as I said, let us take care that we not have to answer for this before men alone. But when we appear before the great Judge, may we be able to answer that we have not destroyed this sacrament, as our adversaries charge, but that we have communed in purity and in truth.

Moreover, when we hear in this passage dealing with Stephen that those who had assembled to judge him saw his face as the face of an angel, we know that it is to show us that we too must present such a face when we appear before God so that the angels will recognize us as their companions, as people who have taken pains to praise God in every aspect of our lives and to conform ourselves to his holy will so that after he has taken us from this world, we will also participate with the angels in his immortal glory, fully obedient to his will, asking only to fulfil it as they do.

> Following this holy teaching, let us bow before the face of our gracious God in acknowledgment of our innumerable sins, which we persistently commit against his holy majesty, praying that he will be pleased so to touch us to the quick that we, being displeased with them, will obtain his forgiveness. May he remedy all of our evils in such a way that after remitting our sins, not only those which are evident to men but also those which remain hidden, he may be able to keep us in purity and simplicity of conscience, so that once being called to communion with the body of our Lord Jesus Christ his Son, we may never be separated from him until we are joined with him in full perfection and integrity. So let us all say, Almighty God, heavenly Father . . .

27

FAITH'S TOTAL COMMITMENT

SUNDAY, 7 SEPTEMBER 1550

Then said the high priest, Are these things so? ² And he said, Men, brethren, and fathers, hearken; The God of glory appeared unto our father Abraham, when he was in Mesopotamia, before he dwelt in Charran, ³ And said unto him, Get thee out of thy country, and from thy kindred, and come into the land which I shall shew thee. ⁴ Then came he out of the land of the Chaldaeans, and dwelt in Charran: and from thence, when his father was dead, he removed him into this land, wherein ye now dwell (Acts 7:1-4).

We have already looked at the accusation against Stephen, which charged him with wanting to destroy the law of Moses and the temple of God. Now we have talked about the occasion he had given the wicked to speak that way, and we have pointed out that it all stemmed from their malice, the way the devil always finds some pretext for obscuring and nullifying God's word or making people hate and distrust it, if he cannot do worse. Stephen was right to say that these ceremonies were not intended to sanctify men, that the material temple was not a place where God was enclosed, and that the purpose of the entire service conducted there was to lead people to our Lord Jesus Christ. In brief, Stephen's teaching is the same one we preach every day, namely that God wants to be served in spirit and in truth (*John* 4:24) and that all the ceremonies performed there had no other goal or purpose than to lead us to Jesus Christ, and we are not to look for any other teaching. Consequently, Stephen was falsely accused.

The long description he now gives makes it clear it is very difficult to turn men from their superstitions and fantasies and lead them directly to God. Stephen could have answered very briefly: 'I did not say what I am charged with, for I am trying only to show what the truth of God's law is, what the temple is, and why the services ordered in the law are performed. It is so we may realize that, inasmuch as God has been pleased to call us to himself and has chosen us to be his children, we must be separate from the pagans and unbelievers of this world. In addition, we need ceremonies to teach us about our weaknesses, but by looking more deeply into the matter, we must always consider that their true purpose is to lead us to Jesus Christ, who is their perfection and fulfilment, a fact we have to consider if we wish to please God.' Stephen, therefore, could have stated that teaching in a few words. But he gives a long recitation. And why does he do that? Does he say more than he needs to say? Indeed not! But as I have said, we are so influenced by the flesh that it is very difficult for us to discard our foolish imaginings and demonstrate the true worship of God, which is spiritual and will lead straight to Jesus Christ. So we have to work very hard, and even then we cannot reach our goal. And in our day we see an even too common example. What is the reason for all the battles we have with the papists? Is it not because we want everybody to look to Jesus Christ and no farther? May everybody acknowledge him as the fountain of all righteousness, of all power, and of all wisdom. May men be thoroughly humbled and not spend their time seeking salvation in things created. That is what we ask for.

Now it is true that if the world were not as ungrateful and inclined to evil as it is, we would soon have arrived. But there is such wickedness and rebellion that we cannot reach our goal, even though people cry out every day against the wicked imaginings, superstitions, and idolatries. Yet the fact remains that most people refuse to be corrected and remain rooted in that accursed thought which came into their heads one fine day. We should be more attentive to the response Luke offers because we understand it is a very useful and much-needed teaching that we will not learn in a day. For we are shamefully remiss in this matter and, what is more, we back away from the lesson because it is contrary to our nature. For if we follow our inclination, we will always remain trapped in the flesh. In that condition, we will not approach God because of his nature. He is spiritual, as the whole of Scripture shows, and we must serve him in a spiritual way, not with ceremonies of human devising.

Continuing, let us follow the order of events as Stephen presents them. He begins with Abraham. He does so because we will never be disposed to receive God's word unless we renounce all things and leave them behind to follow God. That is how, I tell you, men abandon all their superstitions. When they are no longer attached to their natural reason and stop busying themselves with men's opinions, and when they are satisfied that God has spoken to them and are content with the declaration of his will, then they will follow him peacefully and without objection. That is Stephen's purpose here. Now the Jews were blinded by a foolish presumption of wisdom as well as by a vain reputation for holiness, both of which they made into idols, just as today the papists are hardened against God and his word. Why? Because they think that they are wise enough to govern themselves well and that for that reason no one can discipline them. They also think God has to accept their empty devotions, as if that were the true and approved worship he requires of us. Now that is not what we have to do to come to God. There is no other way or means than this: men must stop thinking that they are wise and they must go beyond their natural reason for resolving and concluding matters. In short, let them turn away from the world and be content with being instructed in God's will.

That is Stephen's – or rather the Holy Spirit's – response. Now we must realize that he did not give that response just for that particular occasion, but as a perpetual teaching. For that reason it has been written down for our daily use and advantage. Do we want to be sure we please God? Do we want to be free of all superstitions? Then let us follow this rule which has been revealed to us, namely that we give attention to how our Lord Jesus Christ made himself known to the early fathers, and with that certain knowledge, let us follow this instruction as we would a straight and narrow road. For the moment we get off course, we will be like pitiable wanderers. It is on that knowledge that we must rely. So we must carefully weigh Stephen's words: 'The Lord of glory appeared to our father Abraham.' When saying, 'The Lord of glory', he indicates that everything men can imagine about God is but vain speculation, an idol fabricated in their heads. There is only one God, to whom all glory belongs and to whom glory must be attributed. Consequently, the title 'Lord of glory' is not an insignificant attribute of God. So let us learn not to devise conjectures and say, 'God will be thus and so', or 'We must serve him in this or that way.' The moment we want God to conform to our worldly understanding, we have created an idol and disparage the majesty and authority of the one to whom all glory belongs.

Now Stephen says, 'He appeared to Abraham.' So if Abraham, after that experience, had attempted something contrary to God's will, he would have intruded himself by saying, 'I want to devise a way of worship I think is good.' If Abraham had doubted the promise made to him, how would he have been different from the pagans and unbelievers? Whom would he have served? The devil, the way all the pagans did, who became very animated after their foolish devotions! To what avail? They only provoked God's anger, just as Abraham would have done, had God not had pity on him. That is why Stephen said, 'God appeared to Abraham', as if saying, 'My friends, the rules Moses gave us in his law are not from men. Our father Abraham did not make something up. He did not waver, as did those who wanted to follow their own mind. But as soon as God spoke to him, he obeyed. Inasmuch as God appeared to him, we are assured that we cannot go wrong by continuing on that path.' In short, at this point we must formulate a general teaching, namely that we not intrude ourselves, for it is utter folly and arrogance to proceed, thinking, 'That is what God is like. This is how we must worship him.' But let us just open our eyes and look at him, not with our physical but with our spiritual eyes, when he shows himself to us. For he reveals himself to us only in spirit and in the living image of our Lord Jesus Christ. Our ears must be attuned to hear his teaching, to linger over it and hold to it completely. Therefore, anyone who goes beyond that falls into the most horrible abyss imaginable, because that teaching provides the only way to acquire the knowledge of God's truth. In fact, how did Abraham live until God appeared to him? Like a poor animal. And that is the same reproach Joshua addressed to all the people: 'Consider what your father Abraham was delivered from! Were not he and his kindred pitiable idolaters? It was after God extended his hand and showed himself that Abraham obeyed his word. So realize that your primary worth did not come from the house of Abraham or his kin. You have no grounds for glorying in the flesh. But know that God in his mercy has chosen you and adopted you as his children, not because of your worth, but because our Lord has desired to manifest his kindness toward you and your fathers' (cf. *Josh.* 24:2-4)!

Therefore, in the person of Abraham we have a double mirror. Because God called him, let us acknowledge that he was one of God's elect. Even so, he was a poor wretch and if God had left him that way, he would have been on the road to hell. Why so? Because he was willing to serve God in his ignorance, in accordance with his own will. Now such a practice had to be condemned as perverse, accursed, and completely forsaken. That is the first mirror that we see in this story about Abraham. The second is when Abraham is called and walks the path which our Lord shows him. He leaves the country of his birth behind in order to go to a strange and unknown country. Therefore, when we are told Abraham pleased God by faith, it is because he completely accepted the promise which had been made to him. That second mirror shows us the road to salvation. So let us follow his example. We see how difficult it is to please God as long as we follow our own imaginings. Before God appeared to Abraham, Abraham honestly thought he was worshiping God, even going to great trouble, but he was really serving the devil, to his condemnation.

Now we understand what Stephen means when he says, 'The God of glory appeared to our father Abraham.' Everyone must come to that understanding because that is the only way to find salvation: men must abandon all their superstitions and foolish imaginings in order to be wiser and abide fully by what God shows them through his word, without deviating from it in any way. By doing this, we will realize it is not in vain that the Lord of glory has appeared to us. If we do not, everything we do will end in confusion. For just as the idols which men invented are nothing in themselves but foolish imaginings, so also all those who worship them can only do so to their ruin and condemnation, as Psalm 115 makes clear (*Psa.* 115:8). And we have also observed the curses given in Isaiah and Jeremiah against all those who wish to worship God according to their fantasy.

Now let us consider what is demanded of our father Abraham: 'Leave your country and your kindred and come into the land which I shall show you.' Two things here deserve to be considered closely. One is that God demands of Abraham something which is very difficult and painful. He commands him to leave his country, his home, and his kindred. The other is that God does not name the country he is to inhabit, but calls him to an unknown land. 'I will show it to you', he says. That is how Abraham's faith is tested in two ways. Since he can miss his kindred and the land of his birth, he shows his faith is firm by refusing to let all those considerations keep him from following his calling or obeying God's commands. The second witness and test of his faith is that he disregards everything he might confront and abandons himself to God's guidance. Although he is ignorant of what the undertaking involves, he nonetheless pursues it and is not apprehensive about where he is going, as long as God is his guide. That is why the apostle says in the Epistle to the Hebrews that when Abraham was called, he obeyed out of faith. He wants to point out that everything Abraham does is founded on that faith. Otherwise, it would have been impossible to please God, which in fact he would never have been able to do if he had not accepted God's promise by faith. That is why he set out and made the journey, persevering to the end without ever deviating from the path once it was taken. Moses expands on this point. He says that God spoke to Abraham, saying, 'Leave your country and the kinsmen of your father's house' (*Gen.* 12:1). It is as if God wanted to test him with a lancet to the heart to tell him, 'I know that it will be difficult and painful for you to leave your country, your father's house, and those whom you know; I know it will seem strange to you, but you must leave everything behind.' It is true that at first sight we could conclude that what Stephen says here would not be in keeping with the story of Moses, for in Genesis 11 Moses says that Abraham had already left his country and had come to live in Haran in the land of Canaan, and then adds in Genesis 12 that God revealed himself to Abraham, saying, 'Leave your land and your country.' This presents no difficulty when we know the order Moses was accustomed to following. He adds a longer statement about the story after mentioning it briefly, giving a summary of what he wants to say later about what happened. Consequently, we must not think that Abraham was not still in the country of his birth, but in Haran, when God said to him, 'Leave your land with your kinsmen and friends; leave your father's house.' There is no doubt, as I said, that God would not have spoken this way, had Abraham already been in the land of Canaan. Abraham was still among his kinsmen and had not budged from his nest when God commanded him to leave.

We must now note that what was recounted about our father Abraham's obedience to God was not told so that we might know his merit and constancy, but so that we might be instructed by his example. For if we wish to be known as God's children, we must be the children of Abraham, as Scripture says (cf. *Gal.* 3:6–7). That is why he was given the name Abraham (*Gen.* 17:5), for in the beginning that was not his name, and God named him that because his spiritual lineage was to be spread throughout the world. That is why our Lord Jesus Christ tells us that if we wish to be children of Abraham, we must resemble him and be conformed to his life and example (*John* 8:39). So let us observe that his calling serves as a general pattern for all believers. When God says to him, 'You will leave your country', it is not because God wants every-one to leave his country without some need to do so, but because he wants to show us that all of us are to be strangers in this world. In fact, the Epistle to the Hebrews says as much. When our Lord gave that honour to the patriarchs to keep them as his heirs, it was because they walked in the world, not as those who considered it a permanent dwelling, but as those who were only passing through (*Heb.* 11:13–16). Moreover, whenever it pleases God for us to leave father and mother, kinsmen and friends, lands and possessions for his name's sake, we must be prepared to do just that, as our Lord Jesus Christ himself says, not to one or two but to all, that anyone who does not leave father, mother, sister, brother, wife, and children for the sake of his gospel, is not worthy of belonging to him (*Matt.* 10:37; *Luke* 14:26, 33). Now that does not mean we should change countries just for the sake of changing dwelling places. It means that we must stand ready to depart this world when God calls us. We must indeed do even more. Each of us must get out of ourselves. And that is harder to do than anything else, for we must learn to put our affections to death and no longer yield to our nature, but, as I said, we must get out of ourselves.

It remains for us now to consider the fact that Abraham's calling is our own and that God wanted to give us a clear picture of what we must be ready to do to follow him so that we may be his church and continue in the number of his children. It is true, as I have just said, that everyone is not constrained to leave the country of his birth, but all of us are obliged not to be attached to this world. Our hearts must not be so rooted in it that they cannot leave it, but they must be like birds on a branch, as the saying goes. Let us realize that this life is only a passageway to lead us farther along. We must not be attached to it and say, 'Life is good here.' Let us avoid that kind of security, but let us place ourselves completely within the will of God. And no matter what our advantages are in this world, let us be aware that they do not compare with the inheritance prepared for us in heaven. May none of these things, not even life itself, keep us from reaching our goal.

In addition, let us be aware that when we are unable to worship God in one place, we remain free to follow what he has commanded. There is nothing to keep us from leaving that place. For where does our good lie if not in being joined with our God? Where is our blessedness if not in having a true and perfect spiritual union in which we dwell forever in him and he in us? Therefore, if we are separated from our God even as we live in the land of our birth, we are wretched people. The question then is whether to prefer our salvation and the honour of God over everything we can possess, even our own life, which is only a vapour. We find many today, however, who hold back because their benefits are in the land of their birth. Yet, they cannot live there without offending God and fouling themselves with many abominations because of their frailties.

It is very possible for a Christian to live anywhere, provided he is not saving his own life. But those whom I am talking about want to be exempted from every persecution and, in order to please unbelievers, they foul themselves in the midst of idolatries and superstitions. In that way they distance themselves from God and quietly renounce him because they are unable to leave the country of their birth, or the country where they are accustomed to their pleasure and their carnal benefits. Consequently, they cannot follow God and hold on to him by worshipping him as he requires. On the other hand, we ought to tremble when we hear we are not worthy of Jesus Christ unless we are able to leave father, mother, wife, children, kinsmen and friends, lands, possessions, and inheritances, indeed our very lives, for his name's sake (*Matt.* 10:37; 16:24–26). Therefore, having our father Abraham's example imprinted on our hearts, let us realize that in order to worship God, we must close our eyes to all the things the world offers, things which could confront us and turn us from the path God sets before us.

We must now remember that our lives here below will not remain forever and that our hearts must not be rooted here as if we were never to leave. We must realize that our lives are worth nothing, and that we must always stay focused on Jesus Christ's dying and being raised again to rule over the living and the dead so that we might live and die unto him because our lives are not our own, for we completely forsake them (*Rom.* 14:8–9). Therefore, Paul shows us that our lives are now hidden, that we esteem as nothing this life which we live before men, knowing that it is nothing, but that our lives are in heaven, because Jesus Christ is there (*Col.* 3:1–3). We must, therefore, forget everything else in order to achieve that goal, and everyone must renounce himself, according to the lesson given by Jesus Christ. He says, 'Whoever wishes to be my disciple must begin by forsaking himself' (*Luke* 14:26, 33). That is also why it is written, 'Listen, daughter. Forget your people and your father's house' (*Psa.* 45:10). That was said to Solomon's wife, but she was the figure of the entire church of God. As for the first statement, God declares we must forget our father's house, and that includes everything men deem precious in this world. So let us cease to be attached to our 'country' and to our 'paternal home', so that we will no longer be dominated by all fleshly and earthly desires. Let us no longer be concerned for our lives. Let us subjugate everything, and then the King will take pleasure in us. If we wish to please Jesus Christ, the bridegroom of our souls, we must overcome our fleshly affections so that they will no longer reign within us (cf. *2 Cor.* 11:2; *Eph.* 5:2).

Now because we find self-denial difficult, we must make a greater effort to ponder what is said here in order to learn from it. The statement to Abraham is noteworthy: 'Leave your country, your father's house and all your kinsmen and friends.' That will put an end to all the excuses we are accustomed to making. When

God declares his will to us and lets us know how he wants us to serve him, we offer so many excuses that we never get around to it. We always struggle against him and think that in the end we make a good case for ourselves. 'Yes, but what shall I do if I undertake such a task? Is that not a great temptation to expose my life and my possessions? If I lose everything, I will be vulnerable. What will become of me? It is difficult to live up to those requirements. Now there are better ways to go about this.' Those are arguments which we make against God daily. He wants us to hear him immediately when he speaks. He wants us to stand still with our mouths shut, making no reply, and follow him without resistance.

So that we will offer no resistance or arguments, the text says, 'Leave your father's house', as if our Lord were saying, 'I know that men will find my commands painful, so much so that they will object to something or other because they will think it difficult. And they will make excuses, saying that the thing cannot be done or that if they do not do it, their fault is quite insignificant and easily pardoned. That will never happen', God says, 'for all their excuses will be groundless, no matter how many they come up with. Despite their efforts, they will remain guilty of not obeying my law.' That passage is indeed noteworthy because it shows us we are given to the vices I mentioned earlier. We will never be able to obey God without bargaining with him with everything we can muster and then some. We do not come to him promptly when he speaks. We do not realize that the thing must be done the moment he commands it. True, in the end we yield a little bit, but the fact is that we do not come to him immediately, as did Abraham, who realized that the moment God spoke to him he had to gather his possessions and depart.

Seeing then that we also are inclined to resist, we must be even more attentive to what is said here. It will be of no advantage to us if we make a good case for ourselves and argue it well and present all our reasons and make all our excuses. In the end we will not escape hearing the sentence that condemns us.

Now we come to the second point. Scripture says that God commands our father Abraham to go into a country which is unknown to him. We have already said that this is an extreme test of faith. However, there is nothing more associated with faith than God's withholding from our sight the things he promises us. 'For', as Paul says, 'where would hope be if we had full possession of what God declares to us? What we see', he says, 'we no longer hope for' (*Rom.* 8:24–25). On the other hand, hope is for things hidden. Consequently, there would be no hope in the world if men did not believe in what they cannot see and what is completely invisible to them. But again our Lord wanted to give a very definite example of it in Abraham, who is a mirror for all believers. True, Abraham had to have many more excellent qualities than the common people or even we ourselves, who are his children, have. Yet we must at least follow him from a distance. That is why our Lord did not want to show him the land of Canaan. He could have said to him, 'I have assigned to you a country where you will dwell; it is located in such and such a place; there is the road; you have only to follow it.' Our Lord, I say, could have given all these instructions to Abraham to give him more courage to say, 'At least God was gracious to show me the place where I am to serve him. There is where I must go.' But that was not the case. God closes Abraham's eyes and says to him, 'You will not know where I intend to lead you. I will show you the way, but only from day to day. Your dependence on yourself must come to an end. Think about the next day as much as you wish, but you will not know where you are to walk, except as I show you.' That is how our Lord closes his servant Abraham's eyes so that he will have no guidance except that enlightenment of faith which leads him where God is pleased to call him. If

375

someone had asked Abraham, 'Where are you going?' he could have answered, 'I know only that it is where God is leading me.' 'How far is it?' 'God will instruct me.' 'In what country will you live?' 'Wherever God settles me.' That is how Abraham's eyes were closed to everything so that he might yield to God's will.

In fact, not only is God's command spoken of here, but it is also said that Abraham followed him in order to show us we have no excuse, unless we do likewise (cf. *Luke* 9:57–62). All the excuses we are accustomed to making will serve only for our greater condemnation because we are often tempted to say, 'Yes, but why does God not allow us to have a better grasp on things than we have?' The answer is that God is not pleased to do so. He could have established his church in Mesopotamia or in Haran, where Abraham was living. The land of Canaan was not better at that time, for we see that the people were as wicked as any in the world, and yet our Lord leads Abraham to that place in the midst of devils. For these people are given to every wickedness, but God wants him to live there instead of in his country, where he could have lived at ease and enjoyed all its conveniences. Yet he is content and not concerned about where he is going, provided that God is his Guide. So let us not find it strange in our day if God leads us against our preferences to places where we would not want to go. For if our country holds us back in such a way that we dishonour God, it would be much better for us to be aliens in another place for the sake of his honour and his glory.

Now to conclude. Since we do not have time to consider these matters further, let us apply that teaching to the holy Supper of our Lord Jesus Christ, in which we commune together today, as it is now set before us. We see how our father Abraham followed God without seeing the things he had been promised, but since he had to seek out what was hidden from him, let us know we have to do the same thing. We must live in this world as those who are not in

376

it, whereas the unbelievers are given over to it and place their trust in it. Our way of living must be quite otherwise. And how is that to be? Let us search for what we do not see and is beyond every human sense, beyond anything man can imagine within himself. For who will reveal the love God has for us? Who has shown us the things which we are to receive in glory one day? Therefore, we must have our eyes fixed on all that God says if we are to apply our faith to what he makes known in his word, so that nothing can make us doubt it. We must accept it by faith, as if now seeing him face to face. We must look at it that way if we are to follow Abraham's example.

Now we see it in the Supper. We have bread and wine. Now all foods are for the stomach (*1 Cor.* 6:13). Are we coming then to this table looking for a meal for our bodies? Indeed not! As Paul says, each of us has a house for eating and drinking (*1 Cor.* 11:22, 34). So we come to the table seeking nourishment for our souls. Will we find it in the bread and wine? No! But we must come to Jesus Christ, who is the substance and fullness our souls need. These elements well instruct us that our Lord teaches us how we are spiritually nourished and sustained through the sacrament of the Supper. But we must not stop there, as if the fullness of the sacrament were incorporated within it. We must look beyond it, to the one who is its infallible truth. Do we wish to profit from the Supper of our Lord Jesus Christ? Then we must not, as I said, seek him in what we have seen with our eyes. When we see the bread and wine, we must lift up our hearts on high and say, 'It is God who is speaking.' The Supper declares that we have our spiritual nourishment in the body and blood of our Lord Jesus Christ his Son and that we are so united with him that we live in him and he in us. Therefore, inasmuch as we cannot truly commune using the holy Supper of our Lord Jesus Christ unless we cleave to him, let us be careful not to bring with us our hatreds, our rancour,

our usury, our thefts, our filthiness, our lechery and villainy, our blasphemies, our backbiting, our perjury. But let us be careful to renounce the world and all the wicked affections of our flesh so that there will be a true unity which joins us together in such a way that we possess him and he possesses us as his heritage, and in such a way that we no longer live unto ourselves, but that he lives in us by his Holy Spirit.

Following this holy teaching, let us bow before the face of our gracious God in acknowledgment of the innumerable sins we do not fail to commit daily against his holy majesty, praying that he will be pleased so to touch us to the quick that, being aggrieved in ourselves for having committed them, we will no longer yield to the many vices which have turned us from him in the past. But may we be so unified by true charity and mutual fraternity that we will be able to cleave to him and acknowledge our Father and Saviour so that God will accept us as his children. And since we are not worthy of presenting ourselves before his face because of the many infirmities which envelop us, may he be pleased to receive us in the name of and through our Lord Jesus Christ. Now let us all say, Almighty God, heavenly Father . . .

28

FAITH MUST BE TESTED

SUNDAY, 14 SEPTEMBER 1550 (AFTERNOON)

And from thence, when his father was dead, he [God] removed him into
this land, wherein ye now dwell. ⁵ And he gave him none inheritance in
it, no, not so much as to set his foot on: yet he promised that he would give
it to him for a possession, and to his seed after him, when as yet he had
no child. ⁶ And God spake on this wise, That his seed should sojourn in a
strange land; and that they should bring them into bondage, and entreat
them evil four hundred years (Acts 7:4–6).

Last Sunday we dealt with what Stephen said about the proof
Abraham gave of his faith, namely that Abraham had no
difficulty concerning leaving his country, his kinsmen, and all the
services he was accustomed to receiving from others. Following
God's call, his primary focus is on obeying God and regulating
his life according to God's commandment. And he has no human
attachment which prevents him from achieving that goal.

Now we are shown that Abraham did not give such proof
of his faith on a single occasion but that God wanted to test
him thoroughly and that Abraham continued until the end
so that we might not only have a pattern for following his
example but also know that we have to fight against our fleshly
affections until we overcome them. That is the Holy Spirit's

intention as he speaks through Stephen, such as Luke recounts it here.

In the first place, he says that Abraham, following the death of his father, came from Haran into the country that God subsequently gave to his successors. His father's death is mentioned particularly to show that Abraham, after bringing him on the journey and seeing him die, was probably experiencing deep sorrow, for his father's death could be attributed to him. He could be accused of causing it and being the executioner. But that is not such a stumbling block for him that he loses his resolve or sight of the promise made to him so that he might say, 'Nevertheless, we will move forward until we reach that country where the Lord wants me to live.' Yet it is said that God consoled him by promising to give him the land into which he would come, the land of Canaan. But how does God make his promise? In a way that would seem strange to us. He says to him, 'You are the heir of this land; this day I make you Lord and master over it' (cf. *Gen.* 12:7; 13:14–17), and yet he does not possess one foot of it. He is there like a poor foreigner. He is even obliged to buy a burial place for his wife (cf. *Gen.* 23). That is all he owns. We would find the promise ridiculous and think that God wanted to mock Abraham. That, I say, is something we would not be able to judge according to the flesh.

Now that is not all God says to him: 'This will be for your seed. It is true that you will not enjoy it during your lifetime, but those who will descend from your lineage will possess it.' And where are they? Abraham is already an old and frail man. In the flower of his age he never had a child. His wife is sterile. There is no hope that he can ever have children, yet our Lord says to him, 'This land is for your successors.' And Abraham is consoled by the promise God gave him, even if according to the flesh he sees no evidence that it can happen. There is the possibility he might think the promise is empty. But his faith has to be put to the test.

And yet there is another test. It is said that when Abraham yields completely to God, he hears even worse news. For when God said to him, 'Those who come after you will enjoy this land, but do not think that it will be soon after your death. When you have passed on, your children will continue to wander in a foreign land and be treated cruelly. They will endure a captivity so harsh that worse cannot be imagined. And this will not be for the length of one man's lifetime. Do not suppose that for four hundred years either you or yours will possess this land.' When Abraham hears that, will he not be dumbfounded? That is a strange way to do things. God wants to console Abraham. About what? About nothing, as he says at the beginning. And then he mixes so much vinegar with the oil that Abraham can only think, 'God would have done better to leave me there than to make me journey so far and endure so many hardships. It is true I am a poor wretch, but at least I could spend this mortal life as I might if there were no way to escape it. But when God comes to me and says, "I will give you such and such", and I have no prospects except that my heirs will have to endure cruel bondage, what is the purpose of it anyway?' That is the conclusion that Abraham could draw following human logic. It would have been better if God had not revealed himself to him than for him to be in such pain and to put his posterity in such great danger. But he prizes God's grace more than possessing the whole world. Consequently, he prizes a single word from God's mouth more highly than everything he might desire in heaven or on earth.

That is why this story was recounted for us. For, as we said at the outset, we must not think of Abraham here as a private individual. But because he is called 'father of the church of God', we must all be conformed to his image. Otherwise, it will be futile for us to argue that God will keep us as his household. Do we then want to be reckoned as faithful before God and before his angels? Then we must be children of Abraham, not in the flesh but in spirit.

In that way, we will belong to his spiritual lineage, as Paul says (*Gal.* 3:6–7).

Let us now develop each point in the order it is presented. First, the testing of Abraham's faith recounted here occurs after our Lord showed him the land in which he was to dwell, but he does not give him a foot of his inheritance. We must remember that Moses says we need to keep in mind the kind of people Abraham lives among. After entering the land of Canaan, he had, as we have already mentioned, to deal with the most cruel and most treacherous people you can imagine. They persecute him. They afflict him severely. Even though he tries to placate each group so that no one will be able to complain about him, he is nonetheless tormented and everyone wages war against him. Consequently, he has to endure a very difficult trial. Still he perseveres. He is not unhappy about having left the country of his birth to follow God. He is not saddened by leaving behind his acquaintances and kinsmen in order to ally himself with unknown and barbarous people who greatly harass him. He is content that God has spoken to him and provides the grace to obey his voice. Let us learn then that it is not enough for us to experience some good intention or some worthy desire; we must persevere in these conditions until the end. And we must not do as many, who begin quite well and lift their defensive shields to defend the faith, but thereafter fall away from their calling and hate everything they pretended to love and follow the most. I tell you, we must not be like them! We must be fortified against all the temptations of the world, the devil, and our own flesh, so that by resisting them, we will be able to persevere to the end in those things which God wants us to undertake without wavering in the slightest. We must not think that we can live in this world without being tested. It is a thing common to all believers, as we see in the example of Abraham. True, we will not all be tested with the same rigour. We will not be equally tested because we do not all possess the same measure of faith. Many of us will have only a tiny spark of faith, and if God wanted to test us as he tested Abraham, it is certain we would not be able to stand fast. So it is that our Lord knows what he has placed within us and deals with us according to our ability. However, we need to understand that no one will be excused from undergoing many trials, especially those who are set on serving God by renouncing the world and all its vanities. Everyone will be obliged to engage in great and difficult combats. And yet we are told that Abraham, after entering into the land promised him, did not possess a foot of ground, a matter that could have angered him according to the flesh, but he did not forsake following God. Let us also realize that his example is set before us to inform and instruct us that after having a good experience, we are not to turn our backs overnight on a worthy undertaking and become angry when seeing that things are not going as we would like. But when God, from a human perspective, seems to put a curse on everything we do, causing things to go wrong so that he seems to be against us – when all that happens, what must we do? We must fortify ourselves against all those trials by asking God to be pleased to give us the kind of steadfastness we find in our father Abraham.

The second point we see here is that Abraham is not attached to the present life. He wanted to live at ease in the land of his birth and enjoy all its worldly comforts. We know it was a fertile country abounding in all the wealth and good things one could want from the world's standpoint. He is there in the midst of friends and acquaintances. But his eyes are shielded from all that. It is true he could have become discouraged at the outset and could have lost interest upon hearing he did not possess a foot of land in this country to which God had led him. But because none of that concerns him, we understand even better what I have just said, namely that he was not attached to this world and realized it was only one of life's passageways through which he must go. And Abraham had to keep that in mind.

We come now to our situation, for we have a better vantage point on the spiritual life than Abraham had. True, God worked harder in him than he ordinarily does in men. But if we consider the promises of the gospel, it is certain we have to have a much greater teaching and a more excellent witness concerning this eternal salvation than Abraham could have had. Things were much more obscure then. Jesus Christ had not yet been revealed. Abraham desired to see the Saviour of the world, but he did not see him (cf. *Heb.* 11:13). But to us he has been made manifest. We have come to the fullness of time, as Paul says in 1 Corinthians 10 (*1 Cor.* 10:11). Since our Lord has made such a declaration about the spiritual life, it is certain we must be even more fervent to achieve it. And if we are not, we will be less excusable than Abraham. His was only an obscure and hidden teaching in comparison with ours. A very important point for us to notice is that Abraham and all the patriarchs did not become attached to the life of this world, knowing that the inheritance God has prepared for his children is in heaven and not here below in this world. Let us also learn to slough off its carnal attractions so that our spirit and our minds, yielding to our strong tendencies, will not be fixed on the fragile things of this world, but let us look beyond to that eternal life for which we must work hard, and not limit our vision to this present life, which is only fleeting and quickly perishing. It is true we will all confess that our hope is elsewhere than here below and that our lives will be much more excellent than we now realize. Yet, after acknowledging that, what do we expect? What are we most attached to? Still in the world, we seek our convenience and ease. We would like for God to pander to our worldly desire. And what is that, except that we would like to have our reward here, as if that were the fullness of our bliss and our sovereign good? Even more, then, must we note that Abraham did not refuse to follow his calling no matter what awaited him, however difficult and unpleasant.

We must come now to the primary way by which we can grow stronger, without the things we desire in this earthly life. We grow stronger by listening to God when he speaks to us, by leaning on his promises, and by putting all our trust in him so that we may seek in him our delight and our peace. That is what Stephen wanted to convey when saying God spoke to our father Abraham. It is as if Stephen were saying Abraham could have found it difficult to refrain from grumbling against God and being angry for being removed from the land of his birth, where he had been reared, only to be brought into a strange land with fine promises and nothing to show. The way he managed, according to Stephen, was to stake everything on the promise God made to him, even though it was not apparent how it would be fulfilled. Are we then willing to cast off our fleshly pleasures? Are we willing to conquer the wicked affections of our nature and all the temptations we might encounter? God's promises must be imprinted on our hearts if we are to trust them to the extent that we will never doubt them or his word. Let us stay fixed on that alone and not on the things we see and perceive with our human understanding.

However, we must consider how God speaks to us. He does not speak to us in a way that we can understand, for we always ask for currently accessible things. But he directs us far ahead. 'Wait! Truly I have made you a promise', he says to Abraham. 'When will you receive it? Not today, not tomorrow, not in this world, not even after you are dead. You must be patient for a long time. Your children will be greatly afflicted after your passing. They will undergo greater conflicts than before.' That is how our Lord speaks to us. Thus we must note that he does not speak to us to give us what might please us, but to say, 'All of your affections must line up with me; I need a bridle to restrain you and to direct you in the right path. For men want to see immediately what they seek, but I want you to long for it expectantly.' That then is the rationale the Lord uses when he wishes to test the faithful. In other words, he does not immediately give them what they ask for. He makes them wait for it and long for it so that it appears that he wants to disappoint their hopes. But he does that only to test our obedience. Let us not think that God takes pleasure in deferring his promises from day to day and from year to year, except that he knows it is good for us. It is true we do not understand his ways right now, but in time we will know it has been for our advantage. But if we now want to examine his ways closely, this is how we can do it.

Let us consider our own situation. There are, for example, believers who mingle with the idolaters in this world. If God were to give believers everything they want as soon as they want it, what would happen? How would they show their steadfastness in maintaining his honour in defence of his truth? How could outsiders know whether believers would obey God or not? If a father indulges his children by giving them everything they desire and obeys them by giving it to them as soon as they ask or wiggle their little finger, how will people know whether the children of that kind of father obey him or not? He does everything they want. That is the way things happen with us. Our obedience must be demonstrated when God calls us against our will. But if we obey him then, we show we are his children and claim him as our Father. That is what we need to learn from this text, which says that God promises to give our father Abraham the land on which he was living as his inheritance, while not possessing a foot of it and having the promise postponed a long time, even four hundred years.

Now let us look at what Stephen adds. Abraham's descendants will dwell in this foreign land and be badly treated for four hundred years. It is for good reason that these matters have been recounted, as I pointed out. We have been forewarned that our faith must be tested. Since it is more precious than corruptible gold and silver tested by fire, to use Peter's analogy (*1 Pet.* 1:7), we must expect that our faith, which is much more noble and precious, will likewise be put to the test by the tribulations which God sends us. We will admit all that is true, while acknowledging we are incapable of practising that kind of faith, for when God sends some trouble or other our way, we are so surprised that we forget what we have heard or even said to others about the testing of our faith. When it comes to teaching the requirements of faith, there is no one, not even someone with a master's or doctor's degree, who has the slightest idea of what to do when called upon to practise faith in the midst of hardship. Consequently, we ought to ponder the demands of faith frequently and in depth.

Following what Stephen tells us in this passage, let us be strengthened when it pleases God to test our faith. Let us not look upon the things of this world; rather, let us look to God for strengthening by the power of his Holy Spirit so we will be able to withstand such testing. In short, we must consider the long haul if we want God to acknowledge us. For even though he is near to us, even though his power lives within us, he will appear outwardly to be far off, and he will seem to have rejected us and stopped caring for us. That is why we must keep our eyes fixed in the distance, for if we wish to receive God's promises according to the world's perspective, we will be disheartened at every turn. I tell you, our hope must be beyond death whenever God wants to test our limits. And what if someone asks how God tests us beyond death? That seems like the ultimate test. It is certain that a man of faith is not to be concerned only for his own person, but for those who come after him. Moreover, knowing God, we must not only instruct the people of our day in the same knowledge we have of God's truth, we must also provide for those who come after us. That must be the extent of our love for our neighbours and our zeal for God's glory.

If God declares to us at this moment that there will be great disturbances after our death, so great that the entire world will seem to be on the verge of collapse, that the unfortunate believers who remain will be violently persecuted and cast out everywhere, will we be astonished upon hearing it? We will indeed! To avoid that situation, we must do everything within our power to teach God's promises to those who follow us so they will know how to withstand such assaults on their faith when they come. That, I say, is how we must struggle against the trials that God sends us not only during our lifetime, but also beyond our death. Our Lord Jesus Christ tells us that the end times will be like the most horrible cataclysm one can imagine. There will be injustice throughout the world. There will be rumours of persecutions, and murders, and massacres. The predominant impulse will be to kill and overthrow those who want to proclaim God and his truth. And how will God's church survive when it is already obvious that there are very few who will take courage and defend it. And then there are those who pretend to be exemplary Christians, those who, people think, are the world's most zealous. Not one tenth of them, I tell you, will persevere. So there you see the kingdom of our Lord Jesus Christ falling into decay. It seems obvious that it will soon to be in ruin, especially if we look only upon the outward appearance. But let us remember the promises we have concerning how this kingdom will be maintained in spite of the machinations of the wicked, and we will discover that, if heaven and earth should be thrown into confusion and everything destroyed, the word of God will always continue and subdue all the attacks and difficulties which now disturb us and make us think that the church is going to be totally subverted. That, I say, is how we must fight against the things which are to occur after we die.

In addition, we must give attention to what is said here about Abraham's seed, namely that it will inhabit a foreign land for four hundred years and even be badly treated there. The text is not talking about the people God rejects, but about those he has chosen. There was only one family at that time which God had raised up and on which he had manifested his grace. If there was to be right of succession anywhere on earth, it had to be in Abraham's family. They are God's beloved, whom he adopted to be his church, but who, as the text says, are very cruelly treated, as we will see shortly in Stephen's account. So if unbelievers deal badly with God's church today and persecute and molest it, are we to find that strange? Let us consider what happened to Abraham's race, for we always need to keep this mirror before our eyes because his race is a living image of God's church. Such is the meaning Stephen draws from this story. Abraham's successors were in grievous bondage so that we might understand what we will have to endure whenever it pleases God. True, sometimes God grants respite to his own and does not permit them to be relentlessly tormented and held in such cruel tyranny. But the fact is that we must not expect the kind of deliverance that would let us place our foot on the necks of unbelievers and give us the kind of control over them that they most often have over us. On the other hand, let us always be assured the wicked will torment us whenever God loosens the bridle. We must therefore endure much anguish, many hardships and many troubles at the cruel hands of the iniquitous. Since that is what Stephen's example proposes for us, let us apply it to our instruction.

But we still need to weigh the import of Stephen's comment: 'For four hundred years'. If God sends a violent tempest upon his people and it passes through like a mere storm, it can be borne more easily. But it is very hard for men to languish for such a long time in bondage and even die in it. They see no hope for their children; they see that those who suppress them are strong and powerful and even very cruel and barbaric. God must then work in us miraculously or our seed will never escape without being completely exterminated. That, I say, is very difficult and loathsome for them. We ought to pay all the more attention to the story so that we will not always expect to live at ease in this world and expect that if we have enjoyed the good life for a time, God is obligated to continue it. That would be like counting our chickens before they hatch, so to speak.

But let us consider those four hundred years which passed before our Lord helped his church. Was he neglecting it, or was he not vigilant in the salvation of his people? Certainly not! For the days were numbered. God fulfils his promise at the end of the term and makes it very clear that he forgets nothing. He does not wait for the people to come to him. He comes and draws Moses to be the leader and captain of that deliverance which he wishes to provide for his people, who are living under Pharaoh's authority. He draws them from the abyss of hell, so to speak, to show he has forgotten none of what he had promised.

Now everything that our Lord did in ancient times for this people was for our instruction and must be applied for our benefit. It is true he performed great miracles when removing his people from Egyptian bondage. But let us be aware that when our Lord freed us from bondage to the devil and brought us out of the depths of hell, he again demonstrated his power and might more fully than when he extended his hand to grant us this freedom we now enjoy. Yet it is not enough that we know we have been thus delivered, but we must realize why he has freed us. He did it so that we might serve, honour, and follow him wherever he calls us and dedicate ourselves to that calling throughout our lives by applying all our wit and all our effort.

Following this holy teaching, let us bow before the face of our gracious God in acknowledgment of the countless sins we commit daily against his holy majesty, praying that he will be pleased to grant us the grace to obey him so that we will prefer his commands above all the things we customarily take pleasure in in the world and so that we will so honour and revere his holy word that as soon as he speaks, we will not hesitate for a moment to do what he says, so that he, accepting that kind of obedience, will acknowledge us as his children and show he is our Father through our Lord Jesus Christ his Son. And as the gifts of his grace continue in us, may his kingdom be increasingly advanced for the sake of his honour and glory and the salvation of those whom he has chosen and elected. May he grant that grace not only to us, but to all the nations of the earth . . .

29

THE MEANING AND USE OF THE SACRAMENTS

SUNDAY, 21 SEPTEMBER 1550

And he gave him the covenant of circumcision: and so Abraham begat Isaac, and circumcised him the eighth day; and Isaac begat Jacob; and Jacob begat the twelve patriarchs. ⁹ And the patriarchs, moved with envy, sold Joseph into Egypt: but God was with him (Acts 7:8–9).

Continuing along the lines of our earlier conclusions, Stephen points out to the Jews that after our Lord chose and called their fathers, he gave them the sign of circumcision to confirm his covenant. Despite that, it appears that the Jews had nothing to boast about, as if circumcision were the cause of their salvation or they possessed some personal dignity for which God was obligated to them. So we understand Stephen's intention is to crush that foolish arrogance so characteristic of the Jews. Moreover, he wants not only to show that all the ceremonies they trust in are nothing unless they are illuminated by God's promise, but also to point to their object and express their true meaning. He shows here that God chose Abraham before Abraham was circumcised, but that fact does not detract from the sacrament of circumcision unless we fail to value its real purpose and truth. We must follow this procedure when dealing with those hypocrites who, with their superstitions,

393

obscure and invalidate the sacraments ordained by God. We need to have a precise understanding of what has been instituted if we are going to demonstrate current abuses clearly and how men have abused the sacraments. Therefore, Stephen acknowledges that circumcision was a sign and mark of the covenant which God made with his church. That shows us Stephen does not wish to invalidate the sacrament, as he was charged with doing. But at the same time he points out that circumcision is not the basis for salvation, because Abraham was already serving God before being circumcised.

That is also how Paul deals with the matter in the fourth chapter of Romans (*Rom.* 4:1–12). Inasmuch as he is dealing with the same subject, he shows that Abraham was reconciled to God before receiving the sign of circumcision. He was already justified. To show this is true, he uses Moses' argument that Abraham accepted God's promise at the time God declared to him his gracious will. Thus, our Lord already had him in his grace and considered him as righteous. And at that time, Paul remarks, there was no circumcision. If Abraham was already a child of God, we must not attribute that fact to an external sign, but to the free gift of God's goodness. That is why Paul explains to the Jews that the true purpose of all their ceremonies was to point to our Lord Jesus Christ, who fulfils them and gives them their meaning.

But in order to understand the whole matter better and to be well assured of our salvation, let us begin with Stephen's comment about the covenant: 'God', he says, 'gave Abraham the covenant of circumcision.' His main reason for saying that is to indicate the purpose for which the sacraments were established. It was to make known God's gracious will, how he wants to be joined to us, and how he wants to receive us into his grace and love. That is the purpose the sacraments have served from all time and the purpose they must serve even now. They are to confirm us in the love he has for us and to lead us to acknowledge him as our Father, in the assurance that he views us as his people and his children. Now, do we want a more excellent confirmation that God declares his gracious will toward us and ratifies it so that we will experience no doubt that he makes his graciousness known to us, such as he declares himself through his promises? Do we want, I ask, to hold these God-ordained sacraments in greater honour and reverence than to receive them with that condition? It is true that the papists do not exhibit that restraint, but make idols of the sacraments. Do they honour them in that way? No! By no means! The papists think that their salvation is enclosed in baptism. Since we say that baptism must bring us to the blood of Christ, that we are washed and cleansed by it, and that the power of this blood is communicated to us to strengthen us by God's Spirit, who then, if not God's Spirit, is the one who mortifies our flesh and corrects all our vices and the unwholesome lusts which are in us, and who leads us and directs us to God so that we may be obedient to his righteousness? The papists acknowledge none of that. They restrict themselves to the external sign. They dwell on the corruptible element of water.

They do the same thing with the Lord's Supper, although they do not practise it as such. When they come to their mass, we know that it is the most damnable idol that exists. Not only do they say that when performing it, they are celebrating the Supper of Jesus Christ, but they also say they are presenting a sacrifice to God his Father for the remission of sins. That is how they make the mass a sacrilegious act which annuls the death and suffering of our Lord Jesus Christ. In addition, that is how the papists try to exalt the sacraments more than we do. But how do they do that? By making idols of them! Now the greatest honour we can render to the sacraments is to consider why the Lord instituted them. As I said, the word covenant is added because God is making himself known to us, and after speaking to us and giving us his promises, he ratifies and confirms them by the signs he adds so that we will have greater confidence in him.

We now have to point out that it is impossible for the sacraments to benefit us as God intended if we do not have his declaration of love for us and if that love is not made manifest in them. A contract for five pennies cannot be made between men unless the two parties understand what is being contracted, unless one party knows what the other is promising, and unless what is promised is agreed upon. If such is required in contracts of little consequence, what will be required when it is a matter of our salvation? When it is a question of God's revealing himself to us, must there not be words to explain the signs? If there are only external signs, will they be more than a farce and nonsense?

Therein we see how the Papacy has corrupted the use of the sacraments and falsified everything. It is true that man's infidelity has not been able to destroy God's truth. What is of God in baptism remains in spite of Satan and the papists. The baptism ordained by our Lord Jesus Christ remains forever, incapable of being destroyed by men, but the papists have indeed falsified it because they have removed what it teaches. All they do is mumble words as if it were a magic rite. They mutter an unknown language. And I am not even mentioning all that insignificant twaddle they have added, and the spitting and the candles, the salt and the oil, and whatever else. But not a single word about the meaning of baptism will be heard. For, as I said, they have to use an unknown language. Opposed to that is the general statement that all the sacraments must witness to God's love for us. But how can they unless someone first declares what God wants us to understand? Or unless we know what is represented by the external signs which he establishes for us? In baptism we realize how the power of our Lord Jesus Christ's death and suffering is communicated to us in such a way that we are assured that we are cleansed of all our stains by it. And if we do not understand all of that, what good is it? Thus we see how the Papacy has profaned and corrupted the sacraments.

As for the Lord's Supper, there is an even more horrible profanation. Everything in it is upside down because the mass has as much in common with the Supper of our Lord as day with night, as Satan with Jesus Christ. But even if the mass were not such a detestable sacrilege and remained as it stands, we can still say that it is a very ridiculous rite. Why? Because no teaching accompanies it. We must take note of this word 'covenant' so we can know that if we want to honour the sacraments the way our Lord instituted them for us, we must always put his word first, not as mysterious sounds, as is the custom of the papists, but as preached doctrine, its contents proclaimed aloud, so that the people will know what the sacraments represent and so that we can be like two people making a contract. On the one hand, God must speak, making promises such as please him and obligating us by his free grace, and we, on the other hand, are there to accept what is promised. Now how can we accept it without knowing about it? That is the first point we need to understand here. That way, we know the sacraments must serve our faith. They are more than witnesses and signs to which we bear witness as a result of making our profession of Christianity before men. It is by them that our Lord wants to reinforce our knowledge and awareness of the grace he wants to bestow upon us.

And what if someone asks whether the word is sufficient? True, it should indeed suffice, and we must blame our vices and our unbelief for the fact that we do not attribute enough weight and authority to God's word. The fact is that we are so weak that even after God speaks to us, we need him to add some confirmation to bring us to the understanding of what he wants to show us. For example, we will be told daily that our Lord Jesus Christ yielded himself to death for us in testimony of the love which God bears us and by which he adopts us as his children. That information will be repeated often, and it is worthy of our trust and of our receiving it as teaching from heaven. But our natures are so weak that even if we are instructed in it every day, we cannot accept what God says to us, but are always doubtful. There is no steadfastness in us. Our Lord supplies our deficiency and adds baptism, by which he gives us a visible sign that we are washed by the blood of Jesus Christ. And in it he provides an example that just as truly as your bodies are washed by water, so also the blood of his Son serves to cleanse us spiritually. So there we have a confirmation given by God, like a letter sealed with a public seal for greater authenticity. That is precisely how God works with us. Why? To help the weakness of our faith. True, if we did not have complete faith in God's word, the sacraments would be useless. They can profit us nothing unless teaching comes first. But, as I have already said, we are so weak that unless we have the right kind of faith, we cannot, without God's further strengthening, receive what God tells us. In that way, we understand that the sacraments are to reinforce our knowledge so that we can have a greater assurance of God's grace.

And yet, whenever we are put to the test when Satan entices us to sin, let us repulse him by remembering God's promises. And if that is not enough and we perceive there is still some doubt, let us add the sacraments as God's validating signs. Consequently, we will not only be able to say that our Lord has made us that promise because he has redeemed us from everlasting death by Jesus Christ his Son and has made us alive by his resurrection, but beyond that we will also be able to say we have the signs imprinted on our bodies. God has marked us with his seal, which he placed upon us by baptism. When we take the Supper, we have a testimony of that same grace which Jesus has likewise given as a testimony that we are incorporated into him so that we may enjoy all his benefits.

That is how we must make use of the sacraments if we are to be strengthened when Satan comes and arouses distrust within us. That is how the sacraments are to serve our faith.

Now it is true, as I have said, that the sacraments are nothing in themselves. The Holy Spirit must give them value. When we receive baptism, does the sign of water have such power that we are refashioned in the image of God and begotten into new life? In no way! We observe the opposite. Everyone is baptized equally. And how many baptized individuals continue to be cursed and rejected by God, even though they have received baptism? So we see that receiving the external sign is not everything. But we must make an effort to be conformed to what it represents. It is true that when it bears no fruit, men's evil nature must be blamed. But even so, the sign in itself has no power unless we receive power through the Holy Spirit. Therefore, when our Lord represents our spiritual washing by baptism, the Holy Spirit works in us to cleanse us of our wicked affections and to put off our old nature and the old man, as Scripture says (cf. *Eph.* 4:22; *Col.* 3:8–9). That then is how the Holy Spirit makes up for our deficiency. Otherwise, everything we get from doctrine will be of very little use to us.

Then there is a very small step we must take to come to the truth of the sacraments, which is Jesus Christ. As under the law, before Jesus Christ was made manifest in the world, all the sacraments God had decreed for his church were to lead the people to Jesus Christ. Now, by that same decree, we have to come to that same point. Otherwise, we will have nothing but an empty figure. In short, the substance of the sacraments is embodied in Jesus Christ. And that is the end to which baptism directs us. Otherwise, where will we be washed clean if not in the blood he shed for our redemption? As for the Supper, we do not seek eternal life in a piece of bread and a little wine, but the signs lead us to Jesus Christ, who has been offered for us once; he has now been communicated to us so we may possess him and all his gracious gifts. That is how we must consider the signs. In themselves they have no power but the power that is in Jesus Christ. Their effectiveness is in his Holy Spirit, because he gives it to us out of his free grace.

Now inasmuch as that understanding pertains generally to all the sacraments God has ever established, Stephen applies it here to circumcision. For circumcision was to serve the Jews the same way baptism serves us today. Paul confirms as much in Colossians 3, when he says, 'We have been renewed in Jesus Christ, in whom there is no difference between Greek and Jew, circumcision or uncircumcision, but Christ is in all things' (*Col.* 3:10–11). But because it could be doubted that we need any sign at all, he adds that that is the reason we are baptized. Consequently, when this passage makes clear that circumcision was like a covenant of God with his faithful, let us realize that God has declared his promises of salvation and that he has confirmed and demonstrated the power of his covenant with those who were called.

It is true that the sign is no longer used today, since Jesus Christ has come in the flesh. Its significance, however, is perpetual, for there is a similarity between that sacrament and our baptism. What God wanted to make known by circumcision is that everything pertaining to man and his nature must be pruned within us. It is true that the sign, as it stands, will be insignificant in the minds of men. But we must not measure the decrees of God by our understanding and our reasoning. Although men may think it ridiculous that a spiritual sacrament is performed that way, God nevertheless had a reason for instituting it. He wanted, as I said, to make a visible declaration to that people, within the limits of their understanding, that he wanted everything in their human nature to be pruned so they would no longer live unto themselves but unto him who had called them. What, in fact, is the burden we bear because of our father Adam and all the parents who begot us? What have we received from them if not every curse? There is nothing in us which is not worthy of God's rejection and which does not deserve condemnation to everlasting death. That is what we have inherited from our predecessors. We are so completely inclined to their disposition that we can but sin. And God's wrath is upon us. Therefore, was it not right for God to declare to his people that there is nothing in man which is not to be totally destroyed so that we will come to him and receive his grace and his blessing?

Now it was still not enough that God declared to the Jews that they had to be punished because of their nature, so he adds that his grace was to proceed from human seed. There, then, are the two aspects of circumcision, namely that man is condemned in himself and that God must bring him to newness of life. Man is also shown how such grace will be provided for him: Jesus Christ must take on human flesh and, in him, we will possess all righteousness and holiness. So when in our day and time circumcision is mentioned, let us remember that this is the way our Lord chose to point out the same things under the law which baptism shows us, namely that we, as far as we and our natures are concerned, are dead and need to be made new with a better life. But because that cannot be done by our power, we seek in Jesus Christ what is lacking in ourselves.

Let us now consider what God said to Abraham before giving him circumcision. He declares to him, 'I am your God and the God of your seed, and in it all the nations of the earth will be blessed' (cf. *Gen.* 12:2–3). That then is our Lord making a contract with Abraham. Inasmuch as a declaration is made in good faith, they deal as any two parties would: Abraham accepts all the promises made to him, and thereupon God adds circumcision to seal what was contracted. Then we see how Moses and the prophets always continued to declare the purpose of circumcision so that it would not be a worldly sign which served no purpose, but so the people would always be accustomed to anticipating our Lord Jesus Christ. That is what all the other ceremonies of the law pointed toward. The same is true today concerning baptism. Our Lord, for his part, wants that anticipation to continue and he wants us to hear as he tells us about his purpose in instituting baptism. We see how we are reminded of that every day. We, for our part, must be increasingly assured as we receive the promises given to us so that baptism will be meaningful for us.

In the second place, as a matter of fact, Stephen tried to explain what the real use of circumcision was as he reasoned with the Jews concerning their groundless confidence in it. They claimed to be very zealous for the sacrament which God had ordained, and hearing what he said, they charge him with wanting to abolish the rite. The first thing he touches upon here is how they use the sacrament wrongly, inasmuch as they were putting their confidence in it for their salvation. Now was that the thrust of his comments? He adds that it was not his intention to reject the sign, since God instituted it. Rather, he explains its true meaning, as if to say, 'Through it, we have the confirmation of that covenant which God made with Abraham and with us also because we are descendants of his lineage.' There we have a seal which redeems and ratifies what God had made clear in his word. Paul speaks of it this way when he says, 'That is how Abraham was justified before he received the sign of circumcision' (cf. *Rom.* 4:9–11). In that, we see that we have the free gift of righteousness before God, that our righteousness does not proceed from us, and that we must receive it from God's pure promise. However, we need to be strengthened because our weakness is such that if we do not have some signs to help us, we have a very hard time trusting what we are told.

After discussing those matters, Stephen points out to the Jews their deceit and perversity. Even though they had apparently intended to maintain circumcision, they had greatly misunderstood God's sacraments. 'For', he says, 'consider now how your fathers observed circumcision.' He adds that the patriarchs themselves, moved with envy, sold their brother Joseph. 'Such', he says, 'is your glory that you think you have such excellent worthiness that you have to despise all others. And this pride is not only directed against men but also against God. And yet there is not one of you who is not the offspring of murderers. Did not all the patriarchs conspire against Joseph? Except little Benjamin, who was at home. But the ten others were there. After talking about killing their brother and even after burying him alive, the greatest kindness they can do him is to sell him like an ass or an ox. If you then are descended from them, what do you have to boast about? Moreover, realize that when God gave Abraham the sacrament of circumcision, he had already pulled him from the great abyss in which he found himself, as we have just seen.' So we can see what Stephen was aiming at. It is as if we were to say today, 'It is true that the gospel is so precious that a price cannot be put on it. Inasmuch as our Lord favours us with its preaching, and inasmuch as we have the benefit of the sacraments in their entirety and they are administered to us rightly, that is no small good!' But so what? That is not all there is to it. We must accept what God makes known to us and practise it with full awareness.

Let us now consider how we receive baptism and the Lord's Supper and how the teaching is imprinted on our hearts. We will find that we only tarnish the things God has set apart for our salvation. Consequently, we are doubly guilty because God gives us the purity of his word and yet, for our part, we do not do our duty by receiving it as we should. It is true there will be excellent directions, but they will be written on paper. Great store is not placed on following them. So if we want to take pride in saying in

Geneva today, 'What? Have we not become reformed according to the gospel? Do we not use the sacraments in their purity and integrity?' Indeed we do! But let us look at what good all that does us. After establishing prohibitions, are we more concerned about them than anything else? There is a prohibition against blaspheming God's name, but not a day passes without thousands of blasphemies flying everywhere. All the other prohibitions we have equally ignored. And that is the way Stephen proceeds. Even so, let us realize that everything he said to the Jews is what the Holy Spirit is saying to us today through him. So if we boast that there is such a reformation, as we say, where is it? We have the gospel. But that is not the only thing that needs to be reformed while God is being dishonoured. On the one hand, we see drunkenness and lust; we hear of usury and plunder, on the other; we hear of scandals and debauchery; we see hatred and rancour, and we hear of blasphemies and perjury. In short, those vices are rampant among us. Can we boast? Not on your life! Let us rather bow our heads in shame and keep in mind that the evangelical reformation to which God has been pleased to call us will be a double condemnation on our heads as long as we manifest such obvious rebellion against God. Consequently, we must pay close attention to Stephen's line of thought when he says, 'The patriarchs, moved with envy, sold their brother Joseph.'

Also, why has God granted us the grace to call us to the knowledge of his gospel? Do you suppose he found some worthiness in us? If we compare the Jews with our ancestors, we will find that they were only born out of due season and that we have been like wild trees grafted into the good tree to bear fruit. Thus, this passage advises us that God has not told us everything, but that we must have his word and receive it in true faith; it must enter into our hearts and touch us to the quick so that our lives may then bear witness to the fact that this instruction has not been bestowed upon us in vain.

Therefore, let us be aware of how we must join the word, the sacraments, and their effect together if we want to profit from them. God has not given us empty and useless figures in order to play games with us, but he wants to rule in us by his Holy Spirit. So, as I said, it is not enough to say that baptism is administered in Geneva according to God's command. What good will the true use of baptism do if we each yield ourselves to every kind of evil and the world rules in us more than ever and we do not realize we are to die with Jesus Christ and be cut off from our carnal affections? Let us rather bear in mind that the sacraments, as we use them today, will condemn us doubly before God. Therefore, let us ponder the gifts of grace which God provides, and let us remember well that we are not of the same company and number as those Stephen is talking about. After our Lord has marked us with his blood in baptism and sealed us with the testimony of how he died for us, let us not then be so wretched as to defile ourselves with our wicked affections, but let us continue in the purity to which Jesus Christ calls us and which he offers us. That is what Stephen means when he says that 'the patriarchs, moved with envy, sold their brother Joseph.'

And still we must note that men have always been accustomed to using the gifts of God's grace wrongly, even against him who is the author of all good. It is too bad we can never give God the glory he is due. If he deprives us of everything good, we grumble and grind our teeth against him. We only display our despair. On the other hand, if he sends us good and liberally bestows upon us the gifts of his grace, we immediately forget who we are. We begin to think it is not God who provides us with everything. And yet we are still willing to profess that we are Christians. We want baptism to cover all our iniquities, and when we say we are baptized, we think we ought to be absolved of every evil. Then we want the

Supper of our Lord Jesus Christ to be a cloak to hide our filthiness and wickedness, and we say, 'Oh! We have the holy sacrament of our Lord Jesus Christ.' It is true the sacrament is holy, but where is the holiness that we bring to it? Consequently, we rightly deserve God's withdrawing his hand from us and depriving us of all his gracious gifts, for we so grievously misuse them.

That, I repeat, is what Stephen points out here, so that by following that teaching we will not be quite so likely to react negatively when we are rebuked and keenly reproached for our sins. Let us not think that Stephen took pleasure in criticizing the patriarchs so long after their death. Nevertheless, he gives evidence of an offence so egregious that each of them should despise it. Yes, to be sure, but his purpose is especially to get the people to humble themselves and say, 'We have to magnify God's goodness toward us and our fathers. He was good to our fathers despite their wretchedness and this enormous crime, as this passage shows, and yet he forgave them their great transgression and all the others, and he is good to us because he promises to have pity on us and receive us mercifully.'

That then is how the Jews were to humble themselves before God and acknowledge that they had nothing to boast of, not of their ancestors or anything else. And the main reason is that, to the extent we seek to have honour, God's glory is diminished by that much. What must be done then? God must confound us so that we will learn to humble ourselves – since we cannot do that of our own free will – and so that we will give glory to God for everything. And that is what Stephen intended when he added: 'God was with Joseph.' And then he adds that God poured out his mercy on the patriarchs. Those are the two factors we must note, namely that, first, we have to be reproved and brought to ignominy and shame, and, second, God's mercy toward us has to be declared. For if we heard only God's threats and judgments, we would be reduced to despair. But when God's goodness is declared after we have been made to feel our sins, we are then even more inclined to go to him and beseech him to receive us in mercy. For after demonstrating that we have been rebuked and condemned for our vices, he adds his reasons for doing so: to let us taste his goodness, as he did our fathers, and to let us benefit from what he blesses us with as long as we are in the world.

Following this holy teaching, let us bow before the face of our gracious God in acknowledgment of our sins, praying that he will be pleased so to touch us to the quick that henceforth we will examine ourselves better than we have in the past so that, being cleansed, we may be joined to the body of our Lord Jesus Christ in such a way that our superstitions and carnal lusts will never be able to separate us from him. Now let us all say, Almighty God, heavenly Father . . .

30

OUR SHIELD AND DEFENDER

SUNDAY, 28 SEPTEMBER 1550

But God was with him, [10] And delivered him out of all his afflictions, and gave him favour and wisdom in the sight of Pharaoh king of Egypt; and he made him governor over Egypt and all his house. [11] Now there came a dearth over all the land of Egypt and Chanaan, and great affliction: and our fathers found no sustenance. [12] But when Jacob heard that there was corn in Egypt, he sent out our fathers first. [13] And at the second time Joseph was made known to his brethren; and Joseph's kindred was made known unto Pharaoh. [14] Then sent Joseph, and called his father Jacob to him, and all his kindred, threescore and fifteen souls. [15] So Jacob went down into Egypt, and died, he, and our fathers, [16] And were carried over into Sychem, and laid in the sepulchre that Abraham bought for a sum of money of the sons of Emmor the father of Sychem (Acts 7:9–16).

Last Sunday we dealt with what Stephen said about the patriarchs, how they conspired against their brother Joseph. Now he adds that God had pity on Joseph and preserved him, and he tells how in the end God delivered Joseph from his afflictions to signify he approved his cause. For in fact what can Joseph do? But if God revealed to him he was to be dominant over his brothers, he undertakes nothing with foolish pride. Whatever haughtiness or ambition he might have had did not come into play, but since our

SERMONS ON ACTS 1-7

Lord decreed that he hold that pre-eminent position, it did not emanate from him, it does not have to be conferred on him. That is evident from the fact that the patriarchs addressed themselves to God rather than to their brother, but without success, as is the case with all who resist God and his decree. God's plan must be fulfilled in the end and have its effect, whereas men's rebellion must precipitate their ruin.

In addition, when the text says that 'God was with Joseph', it is to give us hope that the same will be our lot if we are unjustly afflicted. That example is to serve us as a general pattern, just as there is a pattern in holy Scripture teaching that we bear patiently afflictions and adversities. And while suffering patiently, we must not doubt that whatever misfortune may befall us, God's hand is upon us for our defence and salvation because in the end we will need to know we have not trusted in him in vain. But when seeing that God worked this way in Joseph's behalf, we have a confirmation of his promise and recognize its truth. With that, then, we must realize that our expectation will not be disappointed any more than his was. That is the first point we are to get from this passage.

And that point needs to be all the more impressed upon our memory since we see the opposite happening in our world today. How many people today have such foresight and good sense to put themselves in God's hands and trust he will guide them that, should some affliction befall them, they will not grow angry and grumble against him? How many will be found to endure with such patience that they will patiently bear everything God is pleased to send their way? Their number will be very small. True, we think we preserve ourselves by our endeavours, by our diligence, by our friends and all the rest of it, but it does not occur to us to trust in God. On the one hand, if we are enjoying times of prosperity and ease and have everything we could want, we think it comes to us by chance and we stop looking to God. On the other, if we lack some trifle, we think God is remote unless he shows himself, that is, unless he puts into our hands everything we desire. That is why adversities disturb us to the point that we think God has abandoned us or that he no longer thinks about us, and sometimes we even think that he is against us and that it is he who is waging war against us. However, let us arm ourselves with the teaching we have here that God will be beside us to help us when we are unjustly persecuted, just as he helped Joseph.

Now that ought to serve us both as a comfort in our faith and as a teaching that causes us to walk in all uprightness. For just as we are assured that God will keep us if we walk in all gentleness and kindness, so also we are assured that if we trouble our brothers, we must avoid doing them harm or violence, or we will be warring against God and he will be our enemy. That, then, is what we have to learn from this present teaching, namely that we live with our neighbours in sincere love so that we will give no one occasion to be aggrieved by us. And when we have done what we should and have led a peaceable life, and if the wicked still persecute us, let us take refuge in him who is the just Judge and has said he will not permit his people to be afflicted and will avenge them (cf. *Psa.* 9:13; *Rev.* 19:2). Let us then have the wisdom to entrust ourselves completely to God. Nonetheless, let us each one take care not to be disdainful of our neighbours and use extortion or violence. Let us remember, since our Lord is with the innocent to help them, he will have to show himself as inimical to and contrary to all those who wrong and harm their neighbours.

Now we need to keep this teaching in mind, as I have already said, because it is so poorly practised. For just as there are very few who hope in God and wait for his help when they are afflicted, neither do we have great difficulty inciting him against us when one of us uses violence against his brothers and another engages in some wicked activity God condemns. It does not occur to us that in this way we provoke God against us. But in the long run we will of necessity feel it in spite of ourselves. It is a great pity we are admonished and advised concerning that every day but profit so little from the teaching. That shows us clearly that we concede less trustworthiness and authority to God's word than to a mortal man's. We fear the threats of men, who are full of lies and inconstancy, but when God speaks, we do not get excited. That is pretty good evidence of our unfaithfulness. So do not be astonished if it is often said there is no faith in the world, no Christianity. For if we were Christian, as we would like for people to think, would we not have a different reverence for God's word? Would we not hear what is said to the prophet Isaiah, that if God speaks we must listen to him (*Isa.* 65:12; 66:4)? But when we see in men such hardness of heart that they assail God without considering with whom they have to deal, we realize that for them God's word is no more than a figment. But since they are unwilling to listen to him today as their master, they will one day learn that he is their judge.

As for us, let us learn to correct our innate wicked affections, which cause us to offend one another, and let us not fight like cats and dogs. If we want God to live in our midst, let us be united in strict love, and let us each endeavour to abstain from every evil and every hurtful act so that we will not be stumbling blocks for the upright and innocent. And when we do offend, we need not doubt that God is our protector and sustains us and is our defender against all those who want to wrong us.

I tell you we must examine ourselves along those lines if we are to grow more than we customarily do. A trifle spurs us on against one another. The smallest trifle imaginable, once initiated, will set a mortal quarrel in action. The moment you loosen the bridle, caution and restraint disappear. Everyone would like to destroy his perceived enemy. In short, there is so little harmony and love among those who call themselves Christians that you would think they had never heard a single word of the gospel. Now once that evil has taken possession of us, it will continue to grow, and finally even greater evils will follow in its train. Experience makes that clear. For when offences have been sown, as Paul remarks, quarrels and disputes will follow (*Gal.* 6:8). And the ultimate consequence is that each side works at cross-purposes with the other. We ought to focus on finding some way to correct this lest the devil come and take possession of us and dominate us. If we do not, we will come to hand-to-hand combat. You can depend on it! Men, once they have loosened the bridle of evil, will be like mad dogs and more cruel than wild animals. Is this the way we intend to live in obedience to God and be at peace with him? Let us look for ways to do good for one another while abstaining from all evil. That kind of evil behaviour portrays the 'quality of Christianity' that exists in people who are dead set on harming their neighbours, striking one and goading the other, without any more compassion or sense of humanity than you would find in ferocious animals. But we wrong wild animals by comparing them to such scoundrels, for we know that wolves do not eat their own kind. Their very nature prevents them from doing such an outrageous thing. Now when men attack their brothers that way, it is an indication, is it not, that the devil is ruling them, since they are more cruel and inhumane than wild beasts, which have no powers of reason?

Let me summarize what I have just said. Evil gets into us and grows until it does its utmost. We see rather ordinary examples of it. What happened here three days ago? The only question now is no longer one of a beating. Murder necessarily follows. How can that happen if somebody gets involved, as he should, and if the witnesses are concerned about it? And how does that come about except that someone does not get involved, as he should, and those who see it are unconcerned. It is true, since I am talking about it right now, that the parties will think I wish them ill, but I am seeking the salvation of both their souls and their bodies. For if those who had authority over them had punished them, they would have made them good men, but because there was no punishment, the gallows will have to play a role in the situation. And even those who permit that deserve to have their throats cut! Why? Because we all value the infinite treasure of God's grace, which allows us to live in peace and move about day and night without danger and difficulty. And when we knowingly forfeit that privilege, are we not, I ask you, scorning God? And even striking and wounding, indeed without cause! That is the behaviour of drunkards, not just drunk with wine, but totally enraged, who come to blows, with or without a quarrel. It is all the same to them. Now when we think like that, is it not time to do something about it? We can close our eyes, but God will watch for acts of extortion and violence and will also demonstrate that he judges a city and a country, wherever such things are done. In addition, we see that vile lechers and low-down drunks and whoremongers will take advantage of the situation. And, yes, we can complain about it. And if I had been there, I would have done even more.

Now there is no need to talk a lot about it. We know well enough our wickedness without any preaching. Consequently, we see they are worse than rabid animals and that whatever warning you give them, gentle or harsh, does them no good. And yet we must grieve when seeing these poor wretches, God's creatures, going to hell this way. Still we must not be surprised, for when they have once resisted God and his word, they have been totally blinded and are without reason or understanding. Now, as a matter of fact, this teaching was not idle instruction. If, as I have already said, we want God to rule in our midst and acknowledge us and keep us as his own, we must abstain from all violence and wrong and extortion in regard to our neighbours. And still we must be patient during times of adversity so that when persecutions arise we will turn the matter over to God and not make two devils where only one exists, as the saying goes. But let us wait for God to work and accomplish what he did in Joseph, for in him God made a comprehensive promise to all his own.

Besides, although our Lord was with Joseph, the fact is he did not deliver him the first day. Joseph endured hardship earlier, as we see in Moses' account (*Gen.* 39:2, 21; *Acts* 7:9), and even by what is said in Psalm 105, where it is stated that the iron pierced his soul, his feet were fettered, and he was in a prison so narrow it was harder and more painful for him to bear than if he had been mortally wounded in the heart (*Psa.* 105:18). And that did not last for just a short time. He had to languish there as in a grave. And yet we might find it strange at first that God was with Joseph to help him but kept him in a prison so cruelly that he is looked upon as a poor slave. And with everything he endures, whether accused as wicked, as a traitor and disloyal to his master, as an adulterer, as one who tried to violate his master's wife – all imaginable crimes are laid on him. So when he finds himself oppressed this way, he could have been moved to despair, as if God had no concern for him. And in fact, as we read this story, it might seem to us at the outset that God was not concerned about sustaining him at the time. But the fact is we must hold off on such an extreme temptation because what Stephen tells us here is that God was with him. Yes indeed. For he does not always reveal his presence when he is near. So God hides himself sometimes, although he loves us, watches over us, is more solicitous for our welfare than a father, and wants to help and sustain us. Yet we do not understand that. We can look in every direction, but it will seem that we have no help. That is the way our Lord works with his children without their knowing it.

And that is one thing we need to note well. For there is no more dangerous temptation than to doubt God's providence and think he is not mindful of us. When we come to the point of thinking he is unmindful of us, that, I tell you, is enough to cause us to give ourselves to every evil. So let us be armed against that kind of temptation. The armour God provides is our ability to evaluate his providence from a non-worldly perspective. For if we evaluate it from a human perspective, his providence will never be ours. We must hold firmly to what he says to us without seeing with our eyes that he is near. Let us hold to his promise, then, until he reveals himself at an opportune time. Even if he remains hidden until then, let us know he has not forgotten us and will indeed show he has kept us from harm. Let us cling to him and be confident that whatever trials come our way, he will not allow us to fail. For at those times when we are in direst need, it is then that he will show his power.

In fact, if we look closely at this story, we will discover that our Lord exhibited his might and power more effectively when Joseph was confined in that narrow prison than if he had never been placed there or if he had undergone a different affliction. Nevertheless, Joseph does not despair, nor does he repent of having walked in the fear of the Lord, even though he paid for it very dearly at the hands of men. If he had been willing to be disloyal to his master, he could have had everything he wanted. But for fearing God and comporting himself uprightly he was condemned as if he had perpetrated the very wickedness he had tried to flee. Even though unjustly accused, he remains firm in his purpose and does not fail to call upon God for help. Consequently, God looks upon him with favour. What might have happened to him if the Spirit of God had not guided him? That then is how our Lord helped Joseph without his being aware of it. For could he not have been led straightway to the gallows as one accused of trying to violate his master's wife, who was, to be sure, the wife of a man of great authority in the house of the king? There he is, a poor foreigner, a poor slave who was sold like a donkey or some other animal and who was of little value anyway. Why does he not suffer death, except that God preserves him? Consequently, Joseph's afflictions, however great, do not keep God from helping him and letting him feel his presence.

And sometimes God even has to allow us to be afflicted so that when he helps us we can realize he is watching over our salvation. Now we do not see that and we do not understand it with our natural perception. Rather, we think that if we are delivered from some misfortune, it is because of our good fortune. So we do not feel the hand of God except in times of great affliction. For that reason, he will let us languish and we will not be delivered on the first day. He wants to test our faith and lead us into deep abysses to make us humbler and allow men to magnify his grace when they find themselves delivered from their greatest agonies and compelled to confess that God has placed his hand on them.

Moreover, let this not be our instruction for a day or a year, for God's time must not be limited, but let us always remember that fact and say, 'God has promised to be the shield and strong defence of his people, not just in respect of our possessions or our bodies, but he will defend our souls against Satan and all the assaults he can level against us' (cf. *Psa.* 18:31–36). And yet whatever hardships and whatever afflictions we endure, let us always look to that promise and not lose heart. And if we have been obedient today, bearing patiently what it pleases him to send our way, let us beseech him to continue his kindness toward us and give us such grace that our hearts will never be weak and lose courage.

Now Stephen adds, 'And God delivered Joseph and gave him favour and wisdom in the sight of Pharaoh king of Egypt, and he made him governor over Egypt and all his house.' Here we see that even though Joseph experienced many afflictions, it was not for a particular occasion he felt God's hand helping and undergirding him, for God was always favourable toward him. And Joseph's only expectation is in God and his only hope is in God's goodness. And even though Joseph was honoured in Egypt and enjoyed great respect and authority as the king's lieutenant, he does not rest on those laurels. He is anticipating a different inheritance and wishes to be buried in the land of Canaan. And although that cannot happen soon after his death, he nonetheless wants his ashes carried there long afterwards to show that he has no regard for the delights, pleasures, riches, and honours of Egypt at the cost of the spiritual inheritance which God promised him, his children, and all the house of his father, Jacob. That is what Joseph focuses on.

So when Stephen says God delivered Joseph from all his afflictions, he does not mean he was delivered from everything in this world. For even if God delivers us from some evil or other, he is not indicating he wants us to have everything we want, as if it were bad for us to be trained by many afflictions in this life or to expect our ultimate happiness here. Consequently, when God delivers us from an affliction, we must always be ready to receive others whenever it pleases God to send them. That is the way we must look upon affliction, for we will not enter our true rest until our Lord Jesus Christ comes to judge the world. We must continue to acknowledge God's blessings if we are to be moved to thank him and then realize we have not hoped in him in vain. Let us be strengthened in his love. Moreover, after we have received all the blessings God grants us in this world and considered carefully his purposes, may our ultimate conclusion lead us to say, 'Every good thing God does for us now is to lead us higher, to that eternal salvation he has promised us.'

We come now to what Stephen says about the favour Joseph had in Pharaoh's eyes. He says 'favour and wisdom'. With the word 'wisdom' he wants to express the way our Lord delivered Joseph from prison. True, God could have delivered him in a different way, but he wanted to favour him so that Pharaoh would know him to be a wise and prudent man so that, after knowing him as such, he would put him in a very honourable position and give him such authority in the entire kingdom of Egypt that all his lineage would be preserved from the famine to come. And in that way God shows us that if we are wise or have any aptitude for serving men, we must freely share it with others, realizing that this special gift from God strongly binds and obligates us to him.

We must pay even more attention to this teaching inasmuch as we see the world's ingratitude and lack of thankfulness. For how many pay homage to God for what he has given them? What we see is men abandoning themselves to every evil and perversity after receiving some good or other. When they receive some gift from the Spirit, instead of turning it to God's honour and the general good of their neighbours, they try to turn it to Satan's service. Now how many in the Papacy today, under the cover of proclaiming Christian teaching with the view to perverting the entire kingdom of our Lord Jesus Christ and exalting their idolatries and superstitions, will end up more malicious and crafty because they have more grace and gifts of the Spirit? That is an example of the horrendous ingratitude seen everywhere. When God gives a man good intelligence and grants him the favour of knowing more than others, that man ought to use his advantages to the praise of God and the honour of his name, but he will do everything within his power to accomplish things completely contrary to God and his command.

Since that is clear, we need to take note of what is said here, namely that God gave favour and wisdom to Joseph, who used them to serve others greatly. And we also see how God used one individual to provide for the entire country of Egypt. It is true he is principally concerned about Joseph. It is to him that that favour is addressed, but the entire kingdom of Egypt benefits from it. Therefore, let us acknowledge that it is a singular favour that

God does for men when he sends them people of intelligence and wisdom. It is a sign he has pity on a country and on a people, especially when those who are favoured share one heart and one passion to exalt what God has given them and dedicate themselves to the charge entrusted to them. When that situation exists among us, let us realize that God is at work in our midst.

In addition, just as we are admonished to pay homage to God – if he gives us understanding and good judgment to thank him as we should for being more dependent on him – so let us apply all our efforts to serving and honouring him, the more so as we receive his gracious gifts, praying that he will be pleased to increase them in us daily until we come to him in all perfection. The mischief in it is that we are rather diligent in the pursuit of things relating to this present life. We are so well acquainted with daily life that we do not walk in it as if doing so were a burden, and we do not hide the fact that our minds yield easily to it. But as for the knowledge of God, wherein lie the salvation of our souls and our spiritual welfare, we are so unbelievably stupid that when we hear preaching daily and our ears are bombarded by what we must do, we will still be like blocks of wood. No preaching, no exhortation, no admonishment will do us any good at all. It will only be sounds in the wind, as they say. So, seeing that kind of hard-heartedness in ourselves, let us pray that God will be pleased to illuminate us by his Holy Spirit so that the teaching which is preached in his name will bear fruit in us, and may the same be true of all the other gifts he has conferred upon us out of his goodness. For we must appreciate the fact that all the means at our disposal for conducting and governing our present lives are as many particular gifts God gives us, by which we must seek him. And after receiving them, we are obliged to acknowledge where they come from and thank the one who gives us the grace to use them for our advantage.

Moreover, we must note the fact that even if our Lord has

put these gifts at our disposal, we must make them effective. Otherwise, they are of no value. We see a lot of restless people. They expend so much effort running here and there in useless activity and seem so busy with so many things that we can only conclude that those things are very important to them. They are nevertheless wasting their time and effort, for instead of moving forward they are moving backward. Why is that? Because God wants to point out that all the things men have to do will profit them nothing unless he bestows his blessing upon them. So let us not be so foolish or presumptuous as to think we can go forward without our God's help and blessing, but let us try as hard as we can to render unto him what belongs to him alone. May his glory not be obscured by men's foolish presumption, as happens every day when they inappropriately try to exalt themselves above God. Even more ought we to be stirred to serve God when we realize the things that his hand provides for us to do are given so we may honour him. He will make them so fertile that they can but bear fruit.

Then the text says that famine came to the lands of Egypt and of Canaan, that the fathers, unable to find food, were sent to Egypt to bring some back, that in the end Joseph is known by his brothers, and that he sent for his father, Jacob, who is also brought to the land of Egypt, and they remain there for a time, until, following their deaths, they are buried in the land of Canaan. Stephen summarizes these stories to show that God guided that people in all things, as Psalm 105 recounts, as has already been pointed out. Now God even forbids them to be touched or harmed when he says, 'Do not touch my anointed and do no harm to my prophets' (*Psa.* 105:15). We also see how our Lord always preserved them, what wonders he worked by the hand of Moses to deliver them from the servitude which confined them. The text says God, after choosing them as his inheritance, always watched over them, even sustaining them against the kings and the powers of this world. By that we understand that if God is on our side and is for us, we must not fear, although from the world's perspective it is very obvious we are completely lost. Therefore, let us entrust ourselves to him so that if we want him to lead us as he led that people and even as he guided Joseph in all his undertakings, we may be obedient to him and receive in all meekness and humility the things he is pleased to send upon us to conform to his image and share the glorious majesty which is in Jesus Christ, our Head.

In which direction must we walk if we are to acquire the enjoyment of such good? Our Lord shows us the path in Joseph's example. That is, it is through much adversity, poverty, and affliction that we approach Jesus Christ's cross, which we must share if we want to share in his glory. Let us not be aggrieved if we are persecuted in this world, for this is the path by which God wants to guide and lead us into possession of that heavenly glory which he has promised us and to which he will bring us through the agency of our Lord Jesus Christ.

Following this holy teaching, let us bow before the face of our gracious God in acknowledgment of our sins, by which we do not fail to provoke his wrath against us daily, praying that he will be pleased to open our eyes to the knowledge of the providence by which he governs this world, so that we may be the more moved to entrust ourselves completely to him as we lean on his goodness and his grace. However, may all our affections lead to his being glorified in all our lives so that the afflictions and tribulations which befall us may not turn us aside and so that we may always persevere in serving and revering him and rendering him the honour and homage due him. So let us all say, Almighty God, heavenly Father. . .

31

PRIDE AND PRESUMPTION IMPEDE GOD'S GRACE

SUNDAY, 5 OCTOBER 1550

So Jacob went down into Egypt, and died, he, and our fathers, [16] *And were carried over into Sychem, and laid in the sepulchre that Abraham bought for a sum of money of the sons of Emmor the father of Sychem.* [17] *But when the time of the promise drew nigh, which God had sworn to Abraham, the people grew and multiplied in Egypt,* [18] *Till another king arose, which knew not Joseph.* [19] *The same dealt subtilly with our kindred, and evil entreated our fathers, so that they cast out their young children, to the end they might not live* (Acts 7:15–19).

James says that our Lord bestows his blessings upon us in abundance and without reproach (*James* 1:5). So why does the Lord remind us so often of the benefits we have received from his hand? It seems that he keeps them ever before us as if to chide us. And if we consider our ingratitude, we will realize that there is good reason for his reminding us so often of the good things he has done for us and for calling them repeatedly to our attention.

On the other hand, although we have mightily experienced his grace, we are unable to have confidence in him. And even if we are delivered from some misfortune or enjoy some good fortune, we think it is a bit of good luck and cannot realize that it is the result of God's goodness. That is why he gives evidence of his many kindnesses. His point is to rebuke our ingratitude and point out that by hoping in him we will lack nothing at all. And especially does our pride need to be brought low because we always use the blessings we receive from him as an occasion to think more highly of ourselves before God than we should. Those blessings should only stir us to humility, but our nature is so perverse and accursed that we always take an adverse path, as is seen in the example Stephen deals with here. He is talking with the Jews, whom God had exalted above others and to whom he had accorded outstanding privileges. They are therefore bound to God and ought to be humility itself, but they are so filled with pride and arrogance that they do not understand who they are. They think they surely deserve everything they have. And what is more, instead of obeying God, they rebel against him in every way. If they are shown their sins, they think they are unjustly accused and refuse to be subjected to yoke or discipline. Consequently, Stephen is obliged to deal with them the way he does by showing them that without God's absolute goodness they are nothing, that their fathers, in whom they glory, were afflicted in many ways, and that, by comparison, their fathers would be more worthy of enjoying the blessings God bestowed upon them, even though they did not deserve them. We must conclude then that it is Stephen's intention to show them that they have no reason to exalt themselves as they are doing, and that they are egregiously abusing God's blessings.

That is why he now adds that 'Jacob went down into Egypt and there he died with the patriarchs', as if to say, 'We think we have been exalted to high heaven because God has assigned us an inheritance apart. We forget who we were and where we came from, but we must remember that God chose our fathers at a time they were a people rejected by the whole world as worthless. Therefore, we must attribute all that to God's unvarnished mercy. And we

424

also see that when God wanted to call our fathers and manifested himself to them even though, in so doing, he would have exercised special grace on their behalf, they had nonetheless been trained by many hardships. There you have the patriarchs, and especially Jacob, who were carried into Egypt and were there a people disappointed by the promise which had been made concerning the land we now possess. Those events, then, are to instruct us that we have nothing to be puffed up about, that our presumptuousness and arrogance derive from our careless regard for God's goodness, and that we do not appreciate how much we are bound to and obligated to him.'

Therefore, from this we must formulate a teaching which will be to our advantage, namely that we always remember what we were until God had pity on us, and that we reflect upon what we would be if left to our human nature and deprived of the grace we have received from him. But the moment we seek to know what kind of people we might be without God's grace, we discover the reason for our foolish arrogance, which is the reason we grow haughty. And for that reason, God has to deprive us of a blessing he bestowed upon us. And because this vice is deeply engrained in us, let us take care to correct it in the way shown here.

Now there is nothing so common among us as something we all condemn. For example, when we see a man who is ungrateful toward his benefactor, there is not one of us who does not condemn him, and even though we did not acquire that attitude from some sort of instruction, the fact is that God imprinted on our consciences the conviction that ingratitude is a vice which is not to be tolerated. So if it is so despicable among men, what will be the result if we are ungrateful toward our God? Therefore, let us take care to turn to good advantage the exhortation that Stephen urges here. If the Jews, with all their worthiness, are now criticized for not being submissive under the hand of God, who knows their poverty and indigence, what will happen to us, who are like stillborn children in comparison with them? We are, as Paul says, wild plants, so to speak, grafted into a good tree to bear good fruit (*Rom.* 11:17–22).

In addition, when Stephen says that Jacob and the patriarchs died in Egypt and that their bodies were buried in a sepulchre which their father Abraham had bought, we must note that the patriarchs, not having obtained in this world what God had promised, nevertheless did not cease to persevere in the faith, not just in the present life, but also after their death. It is true that we do not read in Moses that all the bodies of the patriarchs were buried in Abraham's sepulchre. Nor does Stephen intend as much. He understands here a part for the whole, because when Jacob has himself buried there, it is to represent his whole lineage and show them that they were all to aspire to that inheritance for which he had waited, although he had not enjoyed it during his lifetime. Joseph also commands that he be carried from Egypt, even though his body is already in ashes. His ashes are taken to the sepulchre of his fathers so that his lineage will not want to remain in Egypt and be separated from God's people. The incentive to remain was great because Joseph had been the king's vicegerent. Great authority had been conferred upon him there, and it was a perilous temptation for his children to remain in Egypt and be deprived of the inheritance which God had assigned them, which was a figure of the eternal kingdom that he had prepared for all his chosen.

In that, then, we see the intention of these holy personages. Even though our Lord long delays fulfilling the promise he made to them, they still persevere until the end, for even in death, they testify that their confidence is not crushed. Now that did not come about without great patience. In keeping with what is pointed out here, let us learn that if we do not receive on the first day what we seek, we must not grow weary, but that when we have confidence in God, we will be strengthened by his word and, leaning heavily on his promise, we will overcome all the trials that befall us in life and in death.

Now, because we are impatient and fickle, we need to hear this lesson repeatedly. Whenever God does not favour us in a way that pleases us, we are not reluctant to grumble against him, and we are unable to wait from one day till the next for our blessing. Seeing that we are in such a hurry and so impatient, we must learn from these examples from Scripture that the patriarchs, though carried far from the inheritance that God had promised, still did not lose their confidence. And they were considering not only that temporal inheritance of the land of Canaan, but also that heavenly kingdom, of which this earth, which constituted their promise, was the figure and representation. In fact, we have a much greater opportunity to take heart and always aspire after what God calls us to, for he does not offer us a land solely as a sign and figure. He is leading us to heaven, and the door is always open to us in the person of our Lord Jesus Christ. There you have the holy fathers who seek after the land of Canaan. And why do they? Because it is a pledge of the inheritance that we too await and have in common with them. But the fact remains that God does not open the heavens to them immediately and say, 'Come to me', but he gives them a rather strange sign for the very excellent inheritance he promises them, namely, the land of Canaan. Yet nothing keeps them from having the confidence to return to that land which is assigned to them and always remains the steadfast object of their aspirations, namely that they prefer to dwell in the land God assigned to Abraham than to have the rest of the world at their beck and call. Therefore, since God grants us the favour not only of giving us some figure of this world, but of also calling us directly to the open door of his kingdom, Jesus Christ our Lord, we must strive for it as much in life as in death, following the path he sets before us.

The passage which says that 'Abraham had bought the sepulchre in which he was buried with all his lineage' illustrates even better Abraham's zeal and abiding expectation. Two things

are to be noted here. One is that he prefers to live in the land of
Canaan as a lowly foreigner. He has no possession or inheritance,
as noted above, where he can plant his feet. Nevertheless, he waits
for God to fulfil that promise and asks no other inheritance, nor
does he miss the land of his birth, but is content that God has
spoken to him, and he rests completely in his word. The second,
which is recounted for us here, is that Abraham was not devoted to
the goods of this world as they related to his life. He is content to
possess nothing. As for his body, he wants to have a sepulchre that
is his own, not that he needs one, but for the assurance of those
who come after him. Abraham, therefore, having fulfilled his duty
to teach and instruct his family while he was alive, still wishes to
speak through signs after his death. He wants his sepulchre to be
a message to his children, as if he were saying to them, 'Be assured
that God will give you what he has promised me, for he is faithful.
Here is my sepulchre. It will be for you a memorial to strengthen
you in the faith that I received from God and to encourage you
to remember always what I have told you. Since my mouth will
be closed by death, know that I am still teaching you through my
sepulchre.' That was Abraham's intention.

That too is why Jacob admonishes his son Joseph to have him
taken there, which Joseph promises to do with a solemn oath. And
he is indeed taken to the sepulchre of his fathers, for Joseph faithfully
fulfils his oath. And that is not the result of superficial devotion, as
among the papists, who, filled with superstition and idolatry, seek
only to corrupt and pervert the whole of sacred Scripture. They
have in fact stuffed their canons with them and have decreed that
everyone will be free to choose to be buried where he wishes. 'And
how', they ask, 'do we view our revered fathers who have done so?'
It is very appropriate. As we have already shown, it is not a matter
of Jacob's body resting more at ease in one place than in another,
any more than Abraham's. But all that takes place so that their

descendants can say, 'Here are our fathers. Although they do not possess land here, the fact remains that since God had made them a promise, they always kept it before their eyes.' Consequently, we must realize that the blessing we await from God does not belong to this life, but our inheritance is in heaven. Our desire then must be for that, and this world must not hold us back, whether we suffer hardship or enjoy its good things. Let us always follow the path that God shows us, remembering so well this goal and target which he has set before us that no matter what happens to us, we will remain firm and steadfast. Therefore, whenever we hear about the burial of the patriarchs, let us keep in mind that they were not influenced by foolish ambition, as the unbelievers were, but they wanted to instruct their descendants that way.

Then we read, 'But when the time of the promise drew nigh, which God had sworn to Abraham, the people grew and multiplied in Egypt until another king arose in Egypt, which did not know Joseph. He abused our kindred and dealt badly with our fathers and caused them to abandon their children to death so that they might lose the generation.' That is why Stephen tells these stories. He wants those to whom he is speaking to be more aware of what mercies God showed their fathers so that their foolish and vain pride might be struck down, for it was impossible for the Jews to be brought to the gospel without first being subdued so that they might not think too highly of their own superiority, as they were accustomed to doing.

We see what repelled the Jews who did not come to Jesus Christ. It was their arrogance, which puffed them up even to the point of wanting to establish their righteousness against God's, just as Paul says: They think they do not belong to the human race, which makes them think too highly of themselves, for they always have this before their eyes: 'We are a holy lineage; God has raised us above others; we are descended from holy fathers;

we have the law and the Scriptures' (cf. *Rom.* 10:3). That, I tell you, is the reason the Jews found occasion to exalt themselves and be proud. But knowing all that, they should have said, 'We are therefore deeply obligated to God. For what were we before? Are we not all descendants of Noah? Furthermore, where was our father Abraham when God called him to himself? He was mired in all abominations; he was a pitiable idolater, like everyone else. And yet God deigned to choose him. So we see in that act an example of his kindness toward us. On the other hand, who were our fathers? Were they more excellent than others? What did God see in them? Why did he elect them? For no reason! But what he did for them he did out of sheer goodwill. And then our fathers were put to the test in several ways, ways that lead us to recognize that God had his hand on them, that they were in so many dangerous situations and endured such poverty and miseries that if God had not had pity on them, they would have been lost, and more than lost. Let us therefore realize that God wanted to show his mercy toward us.'

Such is the acknowledgment that the Jews should have made of God's benefits. But, as I have already said, under the claim that God chose them from among others, they rise up enthusiastically and try to act like untamed horses. They think they are worth vastly more than others. And in fact such presumption is the reason, as I said, that they neglect and reject the grace which is presented to them by our Lord Jesus Christ.

Now God sent us his Son so that we might seek our complete welfare and happiness in him, and inasmuch as we are empty and destitute of every virtue, we must find our strength in him. Because we are of a perverse and corrupt nature, we must be sanctified by him. The Jews, on the other hand, think they lack nothing, and that is why they are far from coming to Jesus Christ. Consequently, Stephen must root out of their hearts their pride and presumption. Otherwise, if they persist in such ingratitude and remain negligent of God's blessing, what is said to them here will serve to condemn them, and they will be doubly guilty of making themselves unworthy of the blessing which had been set before them. So let us be aware that if we want to enjoy the Son of God and participate in all his blessings, we must always begin by acknowledging what we are in our nature so that we can learn how to attribute everything to God. For as long as men acknowledge the gracious gifts already bestowed by God, they will attribute them all to his goodness alone, without ascribing anything to themselves or to their worth. But because we are inclined to foolish presumptuousness, as soon as we prize anything about ourselves or our own merit, we are immediately stripped of whatever good there was in us. And instead of magnifying God, which is the right thing to do, we end up exalting ourselves. That is what we need to note in what is said here.

God increased their numbers the way he did because he wanted to declare that it was he who directed all their affairs and that no one should think it had happened by the hand of men. And even on the basis that the circumstances given here, we have two main points to look at. One is that our Lord will always give good issue to his every action and that he will so direct things that when the time comes, the matter will be finished without the intrusion of the hand of man. He needs only to execute his word to make it effective. The second point is that God humbles us in many ways and wants us to step back, or so it often seems, rather than move forward. He wants us to be less self-assertive so that his power will be better known and manifested, and yet we cannot receive a declaration of it that is not obscured by our indifference. Those then are the two points that Stephen makes here.

It is true that Stephen was speaking to the Jews, but this teaching is also for our instruction. And when he says that the time drew near for the promise to be fulfilled, he indicates more clearly how our Lord is faithful in accomplishing what he had said to Abraham and had confirmed and ratified to Isaac and Jacob. Now it is noteworthy that Stephen said, 'When the time of the promise drew nigh'. It is true that the promise had already been made, but its fulfilment had to be deferred and they had to wait for a period of four hundred years – not that they remained that long in Egypt, but the Lord has in mind the time he spoke to Abraham. For four hundred and thirty years later the people left Egypt and the law was given, as Paul says in Galatians (*Gal.* 3:17).

From that we are to infer a general rule, namely that God knows the appropriate time to bring to pass what he has said. And because of our impatience, we must especially note that comment, for there are two phases of the promise. We must receive God's promise when he speaks, without inquiring further, just as we must now receive the promise of the forgiveness of our sins, by virtue of which he accepts us as if we were righteous and innocent. Following the assurance of forgiveness, we hope that after shedding this mortal body, we will one day rise in glory and be heirs of the entire world. Now let us understand that we will not likely discover any sign that we are to be participants in the glory of God. For who are we? We are pitiable sinners who daily and ceaselessly provoke God's anger against us. In addition, we are surrounded by countless miseries. The world is like an abyss in total chaos. And where then is this glory of God which we have been promised? As for the glory of this world, it is clear that we must not cling to it. Moreover, God deprives us of it, and rightly, to show us that we must not busy ourselves with it. When is our time for his promises to us? Now is the time we are to lean on his promise, satisfied that he has made his will known to us and that his word alone is sufficient. Today is our time for the promise. But there is another time when the promise will be fulfilled. This will be when God tests our faith and patience by making us wait, for he wants us to wait hungering and thirsting. He will be well able to effect what he has declared. But the time has not yet come. So we must remain in suspense until God shows us that the time is appropriate for accomplishing what he has promised us. And that is what Stephen intended his hearers to know, that the people had to long for God to accomplish the things he had determined in his own counsel.

We come now to talking more at length about a topic already mentioned, namely that God, after promising what is necessary for our salvation, knows when he will bring it to pass, and that men must not intrude themselves with their counsel or wisdom. So God knows very well how to manage things by his eternal counsel and by his hand alone, as is admirably shown here. He causes Abraham's lineage to grow and increase until the right time comes to deliver them from Egyptian servitude. We might have thought earlier that God had abrogated the promise that 'Your descendents will possess this land in which you live as a foreigner' (cf. *Gen.* 12:7; 13:15). Now there we have all of Abraham's descendants very severely bound in Egypt. How then are they going to be returned? But God provides. Now it is true that that was not done at one fell swoop or according to human preference. Things were hidden for a time so that it seemed they were never to be fulfilled, but that is the way our faith must be exercised, for, as Paul says in Romans 8, there would be no faith or hope in us if we could immediately see all that God promises us (*Rom.* 8:24). Therefore, after taking everything into account, we will find that it is to our advantage not to see those things we are to wait for, so that our faith may be tested by patience and so that we may learn in this way to reject all the trials Satan might confront us with and to resist all the battles he might direct against us.

In addition, it is to be noted that Abraham's lineage did not multiply naturally, but miraculously, just as our Lord manages things for the salvation of his people. And especially when it is a matter of the whole body of the church, it must be handled in such a way that we are constrained to admit that God has overcome every order of nature. And in that, we see the ill will and perversity of those who think it impossible, indeed completely incredible, that God could increase this people in so little time. 'How indeed', they will ask, 'could that be done?' Now what is the cause of such arrogance? It is because they want to judge the works of God by their understanding. So let us guard against such folly and presumption and realize that all things are subjected to God and that he will one day dispose of them as seems good to him. And especially will he surmount every natural order, as we have already said, and no one will be able to attribute to any but him what he does for the salvation of his people. In that brief statement we are to understand that our salvation is not by means visible to us here below, but that we must rise above the heavens in order to say, 'That is our God who can do all things in a way that his works, effected according to his will, are incomprehensible to us.' And yet we must make no judgment concerning them except as he reveals them in his word. If we trust in his promises, he will not need to fulfil what he has promised us. And even though the promise is not fulfilled as soon as we might like, he will so grant us the grace to persevere in the faith he has given that Satan will have no power to make us waver. And that is because our Lord Jesus Christ says that the gates of hell will not prevail against our faith when it is firmly grounded (*Matt.* 16:18).

We come now to the second point which I touched upon, namely that although our Lord is diligent for man's salvation, he holds it back, or seems to, instead of advancing it. He does that so we will walk in humility and realize even better that all our benefits depend on his grace and that, when misfortune befalls us, we must receive it as correction from his hand. That is what Stephen points out when Pharaoh oppressed Abraham's descendants by going as far as he could to remove all his male seed. That was not done without God's permission. And yet it could be said, 'Since this is the way God prepares to deliver his people, why does he permit such tyranny and cruelty? It seems he wants to destroy and not to deliver.' That is indeed the way things look. But let us consider why he works that way. Now, as I have already said, if our Lord followed human procedures to advance our salvation, we are so wretched that we would think the implementation of our salvation was no big deal. And in that way his goodness would appear to be nullified, and we would not be able to experience it. Moreover, we are so indifferent that we cannot observe his works and use them to magnify his power and his might. Consequently, it is not only useful, but more than necessary, for God to draw us to himself by things we do not comprehend so that we may learn to place ourselves completely in his hands and commend to him both ourselves and all we are to do in this world, knowing that he will bring everything to an excellent conclusion and direct everything toward our salvation. That is the second point we have to note in this passage: that even though our Lord has resolved to remove his people from Egyptian servitude, he still permits Pharaoh to mistreat them severely and even do everything he can to destroy all their male seed, not that he does so, but even so the small children are murdered and their own fathers are their executioners.

Now today we must apply this story to our situation, for we see how Satan works deceptively today to bring down God's church. We see the kind of slavery it was subjected to, not a slavery of bodies for carrying mortar and straw for making bricks, as was the case of God's pitiable children, but a slavery of the poor souls which are tormented and even thoroughly oppressed by the spiritual tyranny of the Antichrist in Rome. He holds them together with false doctrines in order to bind them very tightly and to fetter them and to keep them in subjection to Satan, whereas they should be taught by the word of God, which is the true teaching of freedom. But we know that the submission which God demands of us is worth more than all the kingdoms of this world. It is not a severe and irksome yoke to be borne, but, as our Lord says, easy and light (*Matt.* 11:30), and even more beneficial for the salvation of the soul.

Let us then submit ourselves to him. And although Satan tries hard with every means at his disposal to destroy God's poor church, let us not lose heart. And even though the wicked, Satan's instruments, use craftiness and deceit to remove all the male seed, that is to say, God's power and might that are found in the teaching of his word, let us remember that the wicked will fail in their effort and that the more agitation and rage their failure provokes in them the nearer will be their ruin and the collapse of their power. But if we wait patiently for him to accomplish what he is pleased to do, we will finally not only sense that he will deliver us from their hands so that we will no longer be subjected to their cruelty and tyranny, but also that, by delivering us from this mortal body and all the afflictions we are accustomed to enduring in this world, he will bring us into the possession and enjoyment of his eternal kingdom.

Following this holy teaching, let us bow before the face of our gracious God in acknowledgment of our faults, praying that he will be pleased so to quicken us that, sensing the depth of our sins and comparing everything in our nature with his good graces, we will be prompted to return to his mercy and pray that he will be pleased to make us sense his mercy and realize how dependent we are on him, so that we will honour him in the name of our Lord Jesus Christ, which is our only adequate response. Now let us all say, Almighty God, heavenly Father . . .

32

Faith's Struggle against Unbelief

Sunday, 12 October 1550

In which time Moses was born, and was exceeding fair, and nourished up in his father's house three months: [21] *And when he was cast out, Pharaoh's daughter took him up, and nourished him for her own son.* [22] *And Moses was learned in all the wisdom of the Egyptians, and was mighty in words and in deeds* (Acts 7:20–22).

In all the teaching we hear daily, we have two principal goals. One is to acknowledge God's goodness in order to know how he gains and furthers our salvation. The other is to consider and acknowledge our duty and how we must order our lives to serve and honour him.

Now we have both kinds of instructions in the present reading. On the one hand, we are told how our Lord saved his people, how he delivered them from Egyptian bondage, and how he fulfilled the promises made to Abraham. Moses is presented here as another example to show each of us our duty and how we must employ ourselves in the service of God and our neighbours. As for the first, Stephen shows how our Lord saved his church in a miraculous and unexpected way, a way that could not even have been hoped for. The approach is so unusual from a human perspective that no one would ever have thought that a deliverance like that of the people of Israel might be accomplished in such a way. In the first place, he says that Moses was born at the time Pharaoh had commanded that all the male children be killed. Consequently, it does not appear that Moses will live. Hope of deliverance by his hand is very remote. Yet he is brought up for three months in his father's house. Not without great fear, however. For that reason, it is recorded in Hebrews 11 that Moses was saved by his parents' faith (*Heb.* 11:23) and that if they had not leaned on God's promise, they never would have been bold enough to provide for their child. Faith, therefore, played a necessary role. Nevertheless, that faith was still so weak that at the end of three months they proceed to cast the child out. They fasten him in a basket and place it in the water on the bank of the Nile, as if he were already in the tomb. And the only thing the parents could say was: 'We have brought him up as well as we could with our life in danger. Since we can now no longer protect him, we must commend him to God.' And in fact they leave him there as one buried. So we see that Moses, who is to give life to others, is there as one dead. It is as if he, while still an infant, were in the grave. That much for the first point.

Let us also note that he was taken up by Pharaoh's daughter. Although he is placed in high society, it nevertheless seems that he is cut off from his people and no longer has anything in common with them. Even though he was brought up quietly in his father's house, it no longer appeared that he was to serve the people of Israel, especially since he enters the king's palace and is brought up there as an Egyptian. So he is like one completely alienated and apparently cut off from the people. That is the second point Stephen makes here. And finally we are told that when he tries to engage in God's calling to help his people, he is driven away by threats. Even one of the people of Israel reproaches him for killing an Egyptian. Consequently, he is obliged to flee into a foreign country, where he is even further removed from the possibility of discharging the responsibility God ordained for him, namely that of delivering the people from bondage.

Now the fact is that God, beyond the realm of human imagination, used Moses to accomplish what he had decreed. As a result, we understand how our Lord works to effect the salvation of his church. It is he who initiates and perfects it, and because he cares for us, we do not perish. That is the main thing Stephen shows us here, for he wanted to chide the Jews for their ingratitude because, as we have already seen, there was in them an excessive pride stemming from God's many blessings. There is surely great perversity in men when they exalt themselves this way instead of acknowledging in all humility the blessings and gracious gifts they receive from God's hand. What do you say to that? The Jews were not the only ones to receive good things from God. We have the same streak of ingratitude in ourselves, and we need to be similarly condemned. We deserve Stephen's admonitions more than those Jews to whom he was speaking. So let us realize that in the deliverance of the people of Israel we have a living image of how God initiates and sustains and perfects our salvation. Let us also realize that the source of all our blessings is due only to his absolute goodness.

Let us also realize that God perfects our salvation not in the way or manner of men, but that he has at his disposal incredible means unknown to us, and he perfects it in such a way that his power will be better known and magnified. If he used ordinary means, we would be able to fancy that our own industry resulted in our salvation. Otherwise, we, ingrates that we are, would little appreciate God. Consequently, he must compel us to magnify his works.

We now have to recall what was mentioned above, namely, when our Lord wishes to lead us to life, we must pass through death, as we see here in the example of the person of Moses, who is to be the people's deliverer, but he was not yet born and was already dedicated to death. After his parents protect him for a while, they must cast him not just to the mercy of men, but also to the mercy of wild animals and the water. Was his life not then already in death? But our Lord can indeed find a way to give us life when we are as dead and thrown into a pit. And so that we do not think that that was done only for the Jews, let us consider how our Lord Jesus Christ has redeemed us. Who would have ever expected that Jesus Christ, born in a stable, would be rejected by men so that by his grace and power we would live in the heavenly kingdom? When we see him sojourning in this world, scorned and in complete poverty, who would have associated him with the kind of glory and great majesty given to him by God his Father? In the end, how does he deliver us from our bondage to the devil? How does he acquire eternal life for us except by dying, and dying on the cross, about which it is said, 'Cursed is the one who hangs on a tree' (*Deut.* 21:23; *Gal.* 3:13)? Therefore, as men see it, it is curse and only curse, but that is the way he provides the entrance to eternal life. So let us not think that Stephen intends to give us a singular example in Moses. But let us know that he intends to offer us a mirror in which we are to contemplate how God leads us to salvation. We must, as I have already said, pass through death to arrive at life. Now that seems very strange to men, but it allows us to magnify God's grace even more as we realize that it is he who is at work with his mighty hand. It is he who does everything, and he does it in such a way that his power cannot go unrecognized and we are compelled to magnify it.

Now although that is set forth in few words, it needs to be pondered at length, thought about often, meditated upon, and studied diligently, for it is not a subject that is understood on first encounter. Even if we do nothing else all life long, we will have profited from it only by half. We see that men are so inclined to ingratitude that they forget the good things they have received from someone else, and above all when it comes to God, we never ascribe to him his due honour by thanking him. It is true that we are remarkably ungrateful with respect of people, but if someone does us a good turn, we will be more grateful to that person than to God. Must we not say we are beyond wicked when we are more diligent to acknowledge the good turn received from a mortal man and more grateful to him than we are to God our Creator, the one who gives us all things? Now we cannot be helped or supported by men in any way except insofar as God has made them his deputies and placed in their hands the ability to do us good – then sometimes, with respect of men, we return the kindness. But when it comes to God, we do not give him the opportunity to let us sense his goodness in providing some worth or excellence that might be in us. Moreover, he does not take or borrow from somewhere else the good he bestows upon us. He is himself its source. We do not motivate him to do us good, as I have already said. His goodness alone must shine forth. That and that alone motivates him to shower us with the benefits and blessings we receive from his hand every day. Must we not then say that we are despicably ungrateful when we do not give him greater recognition, honour, and reverence than we give a mere mortal?

Seeing that there is such a tendency to wickedness in us, we ought to pay even closer attention to the teaching he provides: that it is he who initiates our salvation, that it is he who continues it and perfects it. Yes, in such a way that we cannot say we have anything to do with it. That, I say, is what we must apply our minds to all our lives, for by doing so we will understand the reason for our lack of trust in him. If God does not place before us the things we need, we fall into doubt and perplexity. 'What', we ask, 'is going to happen to us?' 'What will become of us? How will this turn out?' Sometimes we are only too apprehensive and worry about all sorts of things. But when it comes to trusting God, we are so dull minded that the devil gets the best of us and we no longer rely on God, and at that moment we look for any means to turn from him and distrust his promises. In that way we keep trying to measure God's grace according to our understanding. When God calls us and declares that he wants to be our protector and that after sustaining us in this present life, he is preparing for us another life which is incomparably more excellent than this one – when we hear those promises, we straightway fix our eyes on what we can see and touch. And if things are not the way we want them to be, we find nothing to credit God with. Now is that the way we deal with everything that is contrary to what we wish for? And there we are, very far from praising God for all his works. Consequently, we need to pay all the more attention to this passage in which our Lord shows us he does not work the way men do. And why does he not? So that we may learn to close our eyes and not debate within ourselves whether he has the means to save us. But let us come to this conclusion and say, 'Since our salvation is in God's hands, we must not doubt, for he is powerful enough to perfect it. It is true that we will not be able to grasp any of this. It seems that we are already dead and the grave offers itself to us as the only thing remaining for us – our burial. But our Lord will indeed accomplish what he has promised, although it seems impossible.' That, I say, is how we must struggle against our lack of confidence, just as we must struggle against our ingratitude.

In addition, after hearing what we have been told in this passage about Moses, we have to talk about our Lord Jesus Christ. In him we will see not only an image of the redemption and salvation of all the faithful; we will also see in him the fulfilment of the full truth and perfection of our salvation. And after realizing what has been accomplished in the person of the Son of God, let us be apprised that because we are members of his body, we must also be conformed to the image of the one who is our Head.

As for Moses, we need to consider here how God saved his church. Here we have the people Israel, whom God chose to be his heritage. As we have already seen, he allows them to be oppressed by tyranny and forced labour. And that lasts a long time. In the end, when he wants to help them, he raises up Moses. And what is the sign that Moses is appointed to undertake such an outstanding act? He is viewed with great fear. Even so, in the end, his life must be put in danger. There he is, like a child cast too soon from his mother's womb. He moves from one stage of death to another, and yet God has his hand upon him and shows by observable evidence that he has preserved him.

Moreover, when it seems that Moses is to be prepared to lead the people out of bondage, we find him being brought up in Pharaoh's house as if he were Egyptian. And then when he has the courage and desire to serve his people, he is obliged to flee. All that is so contrary to what might be expected in connection with God's promises that there is no sign that men could see. And yet God has worked in such a way that what he had previously promised is performed and fulfilled. Seeing that in the ancient church, let us not be surprised if the situation is similar today.

But, as I have already said, we must not only consider that story, but when we come to our Lord Jesus Christ, we will also see in him how God perfects our salvation in a very unusual way. That is to say, he does not use means men are accustomed to so that we will attribute everything to him and nothing to ourselves. God's Son came down to call us to heaven. And where does he begin? We find him at his first advent in a stable and rejected by men. As a result, there is no nook or cranny to be found where his mother can give birth to him (cf. *Luke* 2:7). How can he then make us heirs of the whole world, when he has no place to dwell on earth?

However, after living here below, he is so poor and wretched that he is rejected by everyone and is not deemed worthy to be in the company of men. At the end, when he is supposed to have mastery over the devil and sin, death and the world, there he is, hanging on a cross, under a curse. It seems that no one can approach him without being cast down. So when we see the Son of God in such an ignominious situation, let us take into consideration how God perfects our salvation and perfects it in such a way that we can honour him alone for it.

And what we find in our Lord, we must each apply to ourselves because we are members of his body. Do we then want to share in the salvation God has ordained for all his people? We must pass through death to arrive at life. Not just that we die as it is established in the course of nature, but I mean that throughout our whole life we must appear to be dead. That being so, let us be conformed to that image of God which he has given for us to meditate upon in his word. If a man should find himself more overwhelmed by misfortunes and afflictions than he can bear, he should lean upon God's promises and hold on to them firmly, for that is the way he will resist all the trials that can befall him. And it is very necessary that we take refuge in those promises in order to strengthen our hope of salvation. On the one hand, we see that we are immeasurably weak; we are senseless to the point of being incapable of serving God as we should. On the other hand, the desires of our flesh are still so strong that they urge us to evil, and we see the devil's temptations from a different perspective. I tell you, when we see ourselves confronted with these dangers, there is no doubt that we can fall into great confusion and great doubt, but we must never abandon the certainty that our salvation is sure. Why not? Because we are in God's hand. So let us hold fast the certainty that he has given us once and for all so that whatever may come our way, we will not be thrown into confusion. Why?

Because we must have it firmly fixed in our minds that if we wish to enjoy that felicity he has prepared for us in heaven, we will not be able to reach the heavenly kingdom unless we have previously died and are cleansed of all our carnal affections. That, I say, is how the faithful must be conformed to Jesus Christ, their head.

And we must practice this teaching all the more because we see that it cannot enter into our hearts without great difficulty. It is true that each of us will indeed confess what I have already declared about Jesus, as concerns his person, that he redeemed us in a marvellous way. But we are unable to draw near unto him as we should and be made like him. Therefore, let us understand that this teaching has not been made known to us so that we might know how Jesus Christ redeemed us. We must also add this aspect, namely that he is accomplishing our salvation daily and reinforcing the blessings he has poured out upon us so that we may feel their power and effect within us. That is what we are to learn from this point: that God procures and advances the salvation of his church in such a way that nothing can be attributed to men and everything must be acknowledged as coming from him. In that way, he wants to crush our pride and presumption first. And then he wants to prune all our wicked affections and our distrust so that we may learn not to measure our salvation by the notions we conceive in our minds, but so that we may know that our salvation surpasses anything we can discern or understand from the things of this world. For, as I have already said, we must each examine what is within ourselves and hope from God what we do not see. Thus, when we examine the general condition of the entire church, we must have that same hope.

We see how God's poor church is beaten up today. We see how the poor children of God are exposed as prey to the wicked, like sheep among wolves. They are in fear and anxiety, and it seems like their lives are hanging by a thread. We see tyrants who are like rabid animals seeking only to murder and devour. If God's word is preached today, it seems that everything ought to be destroyed right off. I say that because the powers of tyrants are much greater than the powers of those whom our Lord has granted the grace to serve him. In short, it seems that no male seed is to remain in the church today and that everything is to be obliterated. In short, if we look at the situation from a worldly standpoint, we are justified in evaluating things that way. But let us get back to what the text says, namely that our Lord has redeemed his people by means deemed impossible by the world. Nevertheless, he did not fail to accomplish the redemption he had promised. And it was accomplished even better in our Lord Jesus Christ, and he accomplishes it daily in each of us. Let us realize then that God works so well for the preservation of his church that he sustains it by his power and not by human means, and that he delivers it from bondage and death itself. But the church must first die. In other words, she must be oppressed on all sides so that she will learn that she cannot grow unless God alone is her refuge.

We must now note that all the obstacles at Satan's disposal will be powerless against God and in the end, in spite of Satan's devices to thwart God's ordinance, will be effective against those for whom our Lord will accomplish what he has determined to do in his own counsel. That is what happens when Moses is exposed to death. If Moses had died, would it not have been like abolishing the promise and never delivering the people from Egyptian bondage? That, I say, is how the devil plotted as he tried to prevent the deliverance of God's children. And yet our Lord overcomes that obstacle easily. What is more, he uses it for his work and accomplishes the task. Since Moses is brought up in Pharaoh's house, it looks like he is to be the enemy of the people of Israel rather than their help, for he is there as one having royal parentage. Pharaoh's daughter adopts him as her son. So, being brought up in the house of this cruel

446

tyrant who proposed to eradicate the memory of the children of Israel, does it not appear that Moses is to be one who consents to such tyranny? But what happens? Our Lord uses that means to move his work forward, although the devil's intention was the complete opposite. Later, when he is forced to flee, does it not appear that Satan has won and that Moses will play no further role? And yet our Lord makes better use of him than if he were still there, for we see that after he remained in the land of Midian for forty years, God does not fail to call him back to accomplish his work. Consequently, we see how Satan does his best to destroy what God does for the salvation of his people, since we know that he is the mortal enemy of our well-being. He will not stop devising whatever he can to deter God as he procures our welfare and our salvation. Why is that? When the devil has done his work well, he will be disappointed in the result. When I speak of the devil, I include all his minions and the stratagems he uses, for we see that the wicked try hard to keep God from sustaining us. We see how they labour every day to find ways to bring us down, but let us know that our Lord will provide and that they will always be thwarted and their efforts vain.

Yet we must be exercised by these struggles, just as the people of Israel had to languish for eighty years following Moses' birth (*Acts* 7:23). There you have our Lord giving sufficient evidence that he wants to have pity on his church. He establishes Moses as his lieutenant to bring that redemption about. After Moses is thus exposed, he lives about forty years in Pharaoh's house. In the meantime, the people increase. For after fleeing from the kingdom of Egypt, he remains forty more years in a foreign land (*Acts* 7:30). So the faith of the believers is well tested and proved in many ways. So let us realize that God will indeed allow us to languish and endure much and that we will be downcast sometimes. The devil will contrive to destroy us; the wicked will torment us; God will loosen their restraints against us so it will appear that we will never escape their hands. But when we are so overwhelmed that we no longer know what to do, it is then that God will show his power by helping us. That is what we have to bear in mind.

Meanwhile, let us look beyond our present situation. Let us consider the outcome of so many obstacles, of so many cruel tyrannies, and the torments and forced labours inflicted upon God's people. This prophecy had to be fulfilled: 'I will judge the people whom they have served' (*Gen.* 15:14). Yet that was said more than four hundred years before being fulfilled. And that was to show it was not a prophecy which vanishes like fine man-made ordinances that will last for a while and in short order be abandoned and forgotten. That is not the case with God. Everything he says must be fulfilled in its entirety. And although he spoke of it long ago, it must still be accomplished as if he had declared it that very day.

So what we are to note is that our Lord will permit us to be like downtrodden people for a while, that the devil will have the advantage over us, and that, as the stronger, he will overwhelm us while devising our downfall; but if God graciously gives us the power to wait patiently, we will see the kind of outcome depicted here, namely that God will cause us to overcome all of Satan's efforts and cause us to be steadfast and invincible against all his assaults. And what is more, he will use Satan's attacks while delivering us, despite the efforts of Satan and all the wicked. In fact, that is even more evident in the person of our Lord Jesus Christ. Does it not appear that the devil is victorious and has won the day when Jesus is hung on the tree, indeed so profoundly exiled that he bears the very curse which was written in the law: 'Cursed is he who hangs on the tree' (*Deut.* 21:23; *Gal.* 3:13)? There then is Jesus Christ, rejected as one deserving to be cursed, both by men's judgment and by the judgment already pronounced by the mouth of God. It does appear, I say, that the devil has won everything, but God determines that, because his Son submitted to such a curse, we now receive its blessing and that, because he has borne the burden which was on our shoulders, we are completely delivered from it. Because we were guilty before God, Jesus Christ had to bear all our sins, and we are now looked upon as innocent. As a result, God no longer finds any sins in us because they have been erased by the blood of his Son and by this sacrifice which he has offered once.

We see then how the ways the devil had concocted to prevent the salvation of the world were changed into our welfare and our advantage. And that will be the case for everything the devil is able to do today to bring down the building which is God's temple and to subvert our salvation. Therefore, God will change everything Satan devises and use it for good. Provided we have the patience to trust his promises, we will realize, no matter the afflictions we endure, that there is nothing better than having our refuge in God and being able to say, 'Well, it is a fact that God did not intend to deceive us. Therefore, let us cling to his word. Even if heaven and earth are thrown into confusion, let us trust that God will bring everything to a good end.' That, I say, is how we must fight against all the temptations Satan puts before us to dissuade us from the calling which God sets before us and to prevent us from hearing his voice, which indicates the road we must travel to reach his kingdom and enjoy the good things he has prepared for us there.

We come now to the second principal point that we mentioned, namely that in the person of Moses we are to learn what our duty is and how we must apply it to God's service. In order to do this, we must individually consider what each of us is called to. When we realize that God has established a rule for us, let us follow it without resisting. And whatever worldly difficulties we may encounter, the fact is that if we trust in God, we sense that he will hold us by the hand because it is he who has laid out the road which we are to travel, and it is he who teaches us as if he were saying, 'Go this way', while pointing us to it. That is what we can learn from the example of Moses.

Now it is said that Moses, while in Pharaoh's house, is instructed in all the wisdom of the Egyptians. We could question whether Stephen alone recounted that or whether Moses was instructed in such knowledge in order to serve God better. Now as for the wisdom of the Egyptians, it is certain that they had good and useful sciences, such as recognizing the order of nature, having an understanding of natural things, both in the heavens and on earth. Astrology was common among them inasmuch as they practised it extensively. Therefore, Moses was thus instructed in these sciences, but the Egyptians still had many wicked superstitions. They even used astrology for divination, just as the Chaldeans did. And we still see today people who are so lunatic and irrational that they want to affirm that the world is governed by the influence of the stars, for that is the way they talk, presuming to recognize in each person's birth how he must govern his life. Moreover, there are so many other superstitions that their number is infinite, as we see in the Papacy. They have their rationale for their divine service. There they explore their mysteries of the mass; there they discourse together to find some appearance of reason so that they will not appear to be simple-minded and witless, as they are. That is the way it was in Egypt. The Egyptians, after devising so many superstitions, in which they were immersed, also thought they had the finest pretext and the most serious motive in the world for worshipping an onion, an ox, a cat, and other animals. What is the reason for all that? They wanted to find clever ways in which they might differ from other peoples in some way and to be seen as ingenious in knowledge and discovery, as the mass is employed in the Papacy today. You do not have to inquire deeply into all the foolishness done there before learning that they cannot move a single finger without conveying some mystery. Why? As I said, so they will have some appearance of reason in what they do, although they cannot praise it or define it in such a way that you cannot recognize it for the abomination it is.

Now Moses, as Stephen says, was brought up on the Egyptians' wisdom, not that he was corrupted by their wicked superstitions, but he so profited from it that God used it for the redemption of his people. Let us learn from his example and follow God's calling so that nothing will keep us from pursuing it till the end. Moses had no trouble joining his people and forsaking all the delights and pleasures he could enjoy in the king's house, and he preferred the shame and torments of his brothers to everything one could want. Let that, I say, encourage us to do likewise and to prefer remaining in the company of believers and being God's church to everything that we could cling to as precious in this world.

Following this holy teaching, let us bow before the face of our gracious God in acknowledgment of our sins, praying that he will be pleased so to touch us to the quick by his Spirit that we will be able to renounce our vices and all the wicked affections which distract us from his service. And because we cannot be constant and steadfast in resisting the temptations which the world, the devil, and our own flesh urge upon us daily unless we depend on his promises, may it please him to turn our minds from the vain things of this world so that we may lean on him and completely rely upon his infinite goodness, which he will let us taste while he sustains us here below and until the day he draws us to himself to know it in all its perfection. Now let us all say, Almighty God, heavenly Father . . .

33

PERSEVERING AFTER A GOOD BEGINNING

SUNDAY, 19 OCTOBER 1550

And when he was full forty years old, it came into his heart to visit his brethren the children of Israel. ²⁴ And seeing one of them suffer wrong, he defended him, and avenged him that was oppressed, and smote the Egyptian: ²⁵ For he supposed his brethren would have understood how that God by his hand would deliver them: but they understood not. ²⁶ And the next day he shewed himself unto them as they strove, and would have set them at one again, saying, Sirs, ye are brethren; why do ye wrong one to another? ²⁷ But he that did his neighbour wrong thrust him away, saying, Who made thee a ruler and a judge over us? ²⁸ Wilt thou kill me, as thou diddest the Egyptian yesterday? ²⁹ Then fled Moses at this saying, and was a stranger in the land of Midian, where he begat two sons. ³⁰ And when forty years were expired, there appeared to him in the wilderness of mount Sina an angel of the Lord in a flame of fire in a bush. ³¹ When Moses saw it, he wondered at the sight: and as he drew near to behold it, the voice of the Lord came unto him (Acts 7:23–31).

As was pointed out last Sunday, we must not scorn this blessing from God when he is pleased to admonish us not to allow anything in this life to prevent us from obeying his voice. Therefore, let us always follow this rule: as soon as God speaks, let us obey what he commands. It is true we can always invent multifarious excuses or hindrances for ignoring him, but we must close our eyes

453

to everything. The world must not win out over us and keep us from following our God's calling. Now, that has been made clear enough and, with the example of Moses, we know what our condemnation will be if we are ill disposed to obey. For Moses had many obvious excuses, if excuses were ever acceptable before God, but he does not proffer them, for he well knows that nothing in the world should keep us from listening to God and that we must not allow our endless excuses to confuse our priorities.

We must add now to what has been said, namely that it is not enough to have begun well; we must persevere to the end in what God calls us to. We see in Moses his great virtue in turning his back on the kingdom of Egypt and all the delights and pleasures he enjoyed there. But we must examine his perseverance. It was no flash in the pan, for many people will give evidence of admirable zeal for a while, but straightway become slack and so cold that they abandon their well-begun endeavours. Such was not the case with Moses, for just as he is prompt in obeying God, so he remains steadfast in pursuing his calling.

In the first place, when a countryman said to him, 'Who made you a judge over us?' he saw his people's ingratitude, and it was enough to make him lose courage. He is even threatened. Such is Moses' situation. Moses, who chooses his people's afflictions over all the riches and pleasures he could enjoy in the court of the king of Egypt, wants to join the company of his unfortunate, afflicted brothers and identify with them. He bears with them and puts himself in danger for their sake, and in the end, in return, he is threatened with death. Would he not have been justified in saying, 'Alas, who is this I am dealing with? I took upon myself the responsibility of helping these oppressed people. I ask only to be their companion in misery. I had much rather help them at the risk of my life than see them in their afflictions while I am at ease. And now, instead of recognizing the good I am accomplishing for them and my genuine longing to deliver them from this wretched bondage, they repay my good intentions with evil, threatening me with death. With everything that is within me, I want to end their forced labour and their affliction, and they will not let me. Not one of them would dare lift a finger to avenge his mistreatment. And since God has given me the authority to do so, I can avenge them, and rightly. In addition, they do not recognize the love I bear them.' That, I say, is the kind of ingratitude which could have discouraged Moses, and could have every day. People who are most dedicated to serving others leave them alone when they understand their attitude. How is that? They say, 'It is not to my advantage to spend my time doing everything I can for them. They refuse my every effort and could not care less. Oh! You must not do people a favour when they do not want it.' Since they do not want your help and reject every good turn you do for them, they deserve to be left alone, do they not?

We should, therefore, admire Moses' persistence. He was not deterred from obeying God because of the people's ingratitude and servile disposition. He was also sure that God would not abandon his work because of that. Moreover, he has to be firm in God's word inasmuch as he idles away forty years pasturing animals instead of being invested and established in a position of authority. He has to pasture animals in the mountains and deserts. That is indeed a change of status in life, and not for a day, not even two. He has to wait forty years before God tells him he wants to use him to deliver the people. True, he had had that revelation before, but he could have thought that God was mocking him or that the deliverance was not to happen. How is that? 'If God intended to deliver his people, would he leave me here? I have been waiting here for a very long time and I see nothing. He had told me that I would be their redeemer, but he does not show me how. I am already growing old and grey.' Moses was already forty years old before God appeared to him. He was already forty years old when he went to visit his kinsmen, and then he was a fugitive for forty years. A lot of time has passed. Yet he sees no indication that God wishes to raise his hand to bring about the deliverance he had promised. Consequently, Moses has many occasions to doubt and throw up his hands in the end and say it was foolish of him to hope God would deliver his people from bondage and to say that his promise is steadfast, if he does in fact always remain firm in what he says.

So we must take note of Moses' perseverance so that when God grants us the grace to set us on the way after calling us to himself, we will demonstrate that quickness to obey him, and so that, come what may, we will not grow weary. Let us be armed with such strength against all the trials the devil can throw at us that we will not be turned from our way or the path which God first set us on. That, I say, is how we must be victorious over all the dangers that can come our way. For God's calling is not for one day. God does not bargain with us to serve him for a short time. He wants us to be his all our lives. That goes without saying. So let us not think we have done our duty by serving him for a time. We must always go further. When Paul asserts that he forgets those things which are behind and always looks to what lies ahead (*Phil.* 3:13–14), it is as if he were saying, 'My friends, whenever we think about what we have done, we think God ought to be satisfied with us and we say, "Well, look at what we have accomplished. Is it not time for others to get involved in this?"' Now we must not think that way, but count as nothing what we do, not that God forgets it or that we have wasted our time, but so that we will not think that, because of our work, we are freed from our obligation, by which we are bound to and indebted to our God. Let us leave behind what is past and look to what God is calling us to so that we may always pursue our course and apply all our understanding and all our strength to that end. That, I say, is how we must do everything after Moses' example and Paul's. And that is also what Paul is praising the Corinthians for when he says that as soon as the teaching of the gospel was proclaimed to them, they received it without hesitation (cf. *1 Cor.* 1:4–7). That promptness is the first point. We must not wait until the next day to obey God. But as soon as he favours us with the word of his mouth, let us say, with foot raised, 'Lord, where do you want me to go?' Let us be alert and diligent to obey.

And then he adds, 'After you once have that grace, remain in it, and follow your calling.' With those words we are admonished not to become discouraged straightway or to lose everything as the result of our angry disappointment. But let us have a complete faith which continues and even increases.

And let us be assured that Satan will not sleep and that he will try to discourage us. But if we wish to resist all his temptations and remain steadfast and invincible, we must beseech God to enlighten us by his word. Consequently, God must remain within us and we must be guided by the invincible power of his Holy Spirit so that we will not grow weary for any reason.

Now that kind of resistance comes from the certainty that God will give us his help and protection. Even though we encounter great obstacles and think it foolish to struggle past them, yet if God makes it known that he wants us to travel that path, we must not make of it a hardship. Why not? He will provide everything we need. God cannot be mistaken, as can men. When a man undertakes a task, he will not consider all the details so well that nothing is overlooked, because his mind cannot grasp everything. That also is why we are disappointed and nonplussed when we want to accomplish something we have conceived in our heads and are dumbfounded when we have to change our plan and purpose because we were badly counselled. But that cannot happen to God.

Therefore, let us note that whenever God commands us to follow one path, he knows all the bad experiences we can undergo.

And yet he will provide so that nothing will happen to us except for our good and our salvation. The certainty that God wants to lead and guide us undergirds us. Otherwise, we will always be perplexed, fearful, and easily terrified. But when we have it firmly fixed in our minds that God is for us, we will persist in pursuing what he has put within us to undertake even though the devil directs all his efforts to diverting us from our calling.

Now Moses is praised for killing the Egyptian who was doing wrong to his kinsmen. Why so? Did he support a good cause? Yes indeed. But that is not all. It is noteworthy that the text says God had established him as the defender of the people and had placed them under his leadership. Consequently, he conducts himself in accordance with the revelation he had. If Moses had been a private individual and had taken the sword in his hand to kill the Egyptian, he would have acted foolishly and presumptuously. But we need to consider what God commanded him to do and that Moses did not exceed his authority.

Now there exists a general rule which applies to all of us, but there follows a special rule for each individual according to his calling. Since it will be said to those who are appointed to proclaim God's word that they must be ready to instruct, to teach, to reprove, to exhort, to censure both in public and in private, let them be vigilant concerning those entrusted to their charge, and let them take care that there be no disorder or occasion for offence in God's church. In short, let them be like a shepherd over the sheep. That commission God does not give to everyone, but only to those who are charged with preaching his word. But he does say to everyone, 'Admonish one another that each be diligent in giving good counsel to his neighbour.' But the particular function of the office is to proclaim God's word in the church.

Therefore, everyone is to heed the role ordained for him. Our Lord gives magistrates the administration of justice to ensure that each person receives his right. He does not permit the innocent poor to be oppressed, nor does he allow the weak and infirm to be wronged or injured while the great are supported and favoured at their expense. For if they pervert a poor person's just right, they will be worthy of great condemnation, just as if they had cut his throat. Therefore, our Lord is giving here a lesson for those whom he has placed in public office.

And yet the magistrate must not heed what the world commands or how he will please this or that person, but let him confine himself to what God has commanded him. Now we will sometimes find excellent excuses for not fulfilling our duty. But in God's sight that will win us no credit. Therefore, as for that particular calling, all people who have a jurisdiction are to maintain God's honour because it is he who has set them in his own place. They must strive with all their might to see to it that God is dominant and that his principality is sovereign.

Then let them see to it that everyone enjoys his just right and is neither wronged nor harmed. Every merchant must consider his calling and conduct his business in such a way that he does not try to cheat others in order to enrich himself. Let him not provide adulterated and misrepresented merchandise or engage in usury, robbery, violence, or extortion, or any such thing.

Likewise, let a labourer work with his hands and earn his living honestly and serve his neighbours. Let a craftsman understand his calling and follow it for God's honour and glory.

As for those who are married, let the husband consider his duty to his wife, and the wife to her husband. Let the man who has children and others under his authority keep this thought in mind: 'It is God who gives me this family with the stipulation that I am obliged to take care of it and, principally, to instruct it in the love and fear of God.' And let the children keep these words in mind: 'We must be submissive and obedient to father and mother.'

Those, I say, are the special callings which complement the general rule God gives us. Now it is impossible for a husband to do his duty toward his wife, a father toward his children, and a magistrate toward his people, if he does not keep these ordinances.

Therefore, let us learn to govern our lives according to God's word and yield completely to his will, and whether we do so in a group or in private, realizing that it is God who is guiding us, we will no longer have trouble or difficulty in following our calling. But if we wish to follow a whim and do whatever we please, we could be among the world's most virtuous and most highly esteemed, and still God will reject us and even condemn us. Why? That is the reward men can receive when they refuse to yield to God and when they reject the restraints and guidance provided by his word. Moses took his lead from that word and yielded completely to what he knew pleased God. And that is why he is praised and approved by God. So do we want God to approve us? Then each of us must take our lead from his word, and having done so, let us not deviate from it in the slightest.

We now come to what Stephen adds. He says that after forty years God appeared to Moses in the desert on Mt Sinai. He says specifically that it was an angel of the Lord. But then he adds that our Lord says, 'I am the God of your fathers, the God of Abraham, Isaac, and Jacob' (*Acts* 7:32). He does that to show God is declaring his presence there and manifesting himself. Then he says that that occurs in a flame of fire in a bush, and when Moses sees this, he is frightened and dares not draw near to watch. He is astonished to see the bush is not consumed even though the fire is all around it.

Then God says to him, 'Put off your shoes from your feet: for the place where you are standing is holy ground. I am the Lord of your fathers. You must now carry out the charge I committed to you forty years ago' (*Acts* 7:33; *Exod.* 3:5). Now, in the first place, we must note that God uses visible signs to show us what he wants to tell us.

460

And we must follow the general rule which is occasionally brought to your attention touching the sacraments, for the sacraments are likened to spiritual things which are represented in them, like the water we see in baptism. Why is that? Because the blood of Jesus Christ washes us. And then water is put on our heads to show that we must die unto ourselves and bury all our carnal desires so they will no longer reign in us and so we will enjoy the spiritual blessings which God wants to confirm in us.

In the Lord's Supper, we have bread and wine to teach us that we are spiritually nourished by the substance of our Lord Jesus Christ, that we are dead unless he is our nourishment. Such is the case with all the sacraments the church has ever had. Now I am passing over this hurriedly because it is enough to recall those comparisons so that we can understand this figure given to Moses.

Here is a burning bush that is not consumed. What did our Lord want to signify by that? Although the people of Israel were in Egypt like flaming fire, they always retain their status: the fire does not consume them. Now it can be said that it was such a wondrous miracle that it can but astonish us when we hear of it. The people, burdened beyond endurance in that place, are so oppressed that they no longer know which way to turn. They are commanded to kill their male children as soon as they are born. These poor people are everywhere so afflicted that they are considered as less than animals; yet they continue to grow and increase abundantly. When we see the multitude that results in so little time, what can we say? The people have grown in number beyond anything imaginable. Who would have said that the seventy or seventy-five people who went into Egypt would have come out as one hundred sixty thousand in such a short time? We must admit that God was at work in a miraculous way. So we see the sign given to Moses is not trivial. But what is signified to Moses and what he sees with his physical eyes he sees also with his inner eyes and realizes it represents the people of Israel's situation. True, it was a great miracle. It was a wood fire and nothing was consumed. It was an even more wondrous miracle in that God preserved his people during such a cruel bondage, such as it was in Egypt, when the poor people were worked like beasts of burden and considered as less than dumb animals. For, as I have already said, they were forced to kill their male children as soon as they had come into the world, and that was done so the lineage of the house of Israel would wither away.

So we see now why and for what purpose that vision was given to Moses. It was to strengthen him so that when he returns to Egypt and sees the peoples' wretched condition, he will realize, 'Well now, the people are like wood.' That is to say, 'I see nothing here but a people who are like wood and subject to being burned with fire. But what God has preserved until now, must he not preserve it according to his promise? Therefore, there is no doubt. God will work in such a way that our undertaking will succeed.'

And how would Moses have even had the courage to leave the land of Midian if God had not strengthened him by that vision. He could have said to himself, 'Pharaoh has treated the children of Israel harshly for a long time now. If God had wanted to remove them from that tyranny, he could have done so sooner. He has waited too long. In fact, there is no indication that he is about to fulfil what he promised.' Consequently, God has to anticipate such doubts, which he does when he says to Moses, 'Look, it is true that your poor kinsmen are like wood thrown into the fire; yet the wood is not consumed, for it is preserved by my grace.'

Now it is true that the people's affliction was not always as extreme as it was at that time. But the fact is that God always wants to test his people. Therefore, the church will never be at rest or at ease, for there will always be some kind of affliction and a fire lighted within, as the Psalm says, 'The wicked have fought against me from my youth; they have ploughed upon my back as one ploughs arable land, and torn me asunder' (cf. *Psa.* 129:2–3). That has been the lament of God's church, not for a limited time, but from her youth. Let us realize, therefore, that we are subject to enduring many hardships and many afflictions, that the devil is urgently busy afflicting us, that the world is against us, and that the wicked will bring to bear on us the harshest and severest attacks they can conjure up. This, then, is what we have to learn from that vision as it is presented to us, that we are, in our nature, only wood. So we are subject here to being consumed, for our natures are weak and fragile.

Moreover, we need to note that there will always be a fire burning within us and that, in addition, the devil will always find enough wood to keep it going, and it will not be his fault that we are not completely consumed, but our Lord is not willing that we should perish and go to hell. True, as I have said, there will always be a fire and we will see its flame, but God will show his might, as he displayed it in Egypt, and we will be preserved in the midst of the fire. In that way he gives even better evidence of his power.

For if our Lord maintains us here in a state of ease without struggles, what good would that do? We would think that there is no blessedness apart from this world, and few would look to God for help. But when we realize that our nature is very fragile and that we are pitiable creatures destitute of all help, it is then that we understand there is no strength in us. The more the devil lights the fire and strives with all his might to burn us up and consume us, the more will we have to cry out, 'Alas, if God had not helped us, what would have become of us?' We can indeed say what is written in another Psalm: 'If God had not looked upon us with pity, we would have been undone. If he had not been our Protector and watched over us, we would have been swallowed up' (cf. *Psa.* 124:2–3). For what, I ask, are the persecutions and torments of believers at the hands of the wicked if not bottomless pits? If God leaves us in the midst of the fire and the flame of this world's persecutions, we are then like people who have been devoured. But he delivers us from them when he knows the time is right and does not allow us to be consumed.

So that is how that vision given to Moses is not only for him, but also for us, for we must extrapolate from it a general teaching so that we will know how our Lord intends to maintain his faithful in this world while promising that his church will be preserved until the end. However, that is not to say that she will be welcome here below in this world and that everyone will leave her in peace. In no way! No! To the contrary. It is as though she were in the midst of a fire, and yet it is not as though the faithful were like iron or steel and incapable of being quickly consumed. They are like wood, straw, or stubble. That we are like wood in a fire, yet stand fast and are not consumed, is nothing short of miraculous. How can that possibly happen? God unquestionably extends his hand over us, and we have to realize that, as he does, he does not use human means or other means available to the world, but his own divine and miraculous power. We have to pause here because we need to realize that it is God who leads and governs us in the midst of all our afflictions. If he did not, what would become of us? Would we think we could stand firm by our own power? We could not. Our attention is always fixed on the things here in this world. If we think we are far from danger, then we take courage. But if we see that we are about to be overwhelmed and that the fire is to destroy and consume us, we are so dumbfounded that we think we are lost. And when that happens, what honour do we show God? We measure his grace by human standards. That is a very treacherous infidelity, and yet it influences all of us in some way. Therefore, we should fear this punishment even more if we do not understand that we are wood soon to be consumed unless we are preserved by our God's might and power, and we will be preserved provided our hope is in him and our eyes are fixed upon him alone.

We now come to what is said to Moses. 'Put off your shoes from your feet: for the place where you are standing is holy ground' (*Acts* 7:33). That is said to Moses so he will be better disposed to listen to what will be said later. For God does not immediately tell him what he intends to make known. He uses this as a preface, as he commonly does. When we wish to make a statement, we use a preface or exordium to introduce the subject we are to deal with. This is what our Lord does so Moses will know it is God who is speaking to him.

Now, the ancient fathers have to be confirmed in all their revelations, for what would all that teaching mean if we did not have a true knowledge of them and if that knowledge were not firmly imprinted on our hearts so that we would be assured of what God tells us? Consequently, we must have no doubt about where the teaching comes from. Let us realize that it proceeds from the mouth of the living God. We must, I say, be convinced of that truth and remain confident of it until the end. So we need to note that when God revealed himself to the ancient fathers, he not only gave them signs and testimonies of his presence, but he also declared to them his will and the reason he was revealing himself to them in this way so they could know that it is not the devil who comes to deceive us, or an apparition, or some deceptive vision, but that it is God who is presenting himself to us.

We see how the Papacy built itself on these visions. Satan worked in them in such a way that he infected everything with superstitions and idolatries because of their false perceptions, by which the poor unlearned are beguiled, as they continue to be at present. Now it is quite possible that doddering monks had dreams. How about that? Some hollow and deranged brain dreamed that souls are weeping and wailing in the fires of purgatory. We need to look at this, they say, because it is a revelation. And they end up inaugurating All Souls' Day. They did that based on a dream of a Cluny monk who had that revelation on the way to Rome. Oh! That must be celebrated with a solemn feast day. And immediately they decide to do it in their cloister. Still there is no certainty, for it was not God who manifested himself to this monk, but it was the devil – who changes himself into an angel of light, as Paul says – who deceived the monk and all his ilk.

Now that was not the way God revealed himself to Moses, but Moses was fully and completely certain it was God who spoke to him. And we must be even more convinced about his teaching so that we will know he did not insinuate himself into the situation but was sent by God and so confident of his calling that he persevered in it until the end and was like an angel from heaven so that we might know that the teaching he brought to the people of Israel came from God and not from him. That point must be understood.

Therefore, let us know that each time the word of God is preached to us, we must first and foremost receive it not as a human teaching, but with all reverence and humility as proceeding from God's mouth, just as we are told we must obey that word above all others. In that way, when God opens his mouth to teach us, we will be better prepared and more inclined to listen to him than to yield ourselves to the most covetable things in the world.

Moses is then told that the place where he is standing is holy ground. That is because God is there, declaring his presence and manifesting himself. That is the way Jacob speaks when he returns to the country from which his grandfather Abraham had come, saying that God reveals himself to him. He says, 'Truly, this place is none other than the house of God' (*Gen.* 28:27). The same is said to Moses in this passage. Now, was the land of Midian holier than the others? Not at all! To the contrary. The people who lived there were unbelievers. And since that time, it has not been said that it was made holy, but it is holy because God declares he is present there, just as every place he manifests himself possesses holiness, for there can be no majesty but the majesty that is in him, and it must shine forth all around him. That is why that place is called holy.

However, we must fend off superstition. Let us not think that one place is holier than another, as has happened both among the papists and among the Jews. The Jews worshipped on the mountain where God had appeared to Jacob and called that place 'the house of God' (*Gen.* 28:19). But we see that our Lord, in horror at what they were doing there, calls it by the mouth of his prophet 'a house of iniquity' ('Beth-aven': *Hos.* 4:15; 10:5). From that, let us know we must not attribute importance to what has happened on a single occasion, unless we have the support of God's word. For there is nothing more dangerous than men when they fabricate in their heads what they think is good, claiming that God has done the thing to which they attach themselves. When men are not led by God in everything they do, no matter how excellent it appears, it is only an abomination. Consequently, the Jews misunderstood holiness, thinking it resided in one place rather than in another.

The same thing has happened in the Papacy. They give great importance to worshipping in holy places, as they view them. It is true that they do not even have as many plausible reasons as the Jews, or as much evidence. For what witness do they have that God appeared in all the places, that they were so holy, and that they make such a fuss over? What holiness is there in Loreto and Santiago [de Compostela] that people would go to the trouble of trotting off to those places? It is true that the devil was able to create a few illusions there, but that is all there is to it, complete delusion and deception by which the devil misleads poor ignorant people.

When they go to Rome, it is because many martyrs were killed there. At an earlier time, the city gorged itself on the blood of the poor believers who were murdered there. That is a fine holy place where they go see what Satan's instruments were when he used many devices endeavouring to destroy God's poor church and abolish the memory of our Lord Jesus Christ at a time when members of his body were murdered by tyrants and enemies of his truth!

Thus we see that the papists do much worse than the Jews. Yet, as I have already said, let us not use it as an occasion to do anything contrary to God's will and unleash superstition's bridle, claiming that it was done at some past time. We must hold to the word of God and rest upon it firmly without wavering in any way. So let us note that if the land of Midian was called holy at one time, it does not mean that men should give that fact great weight for worshipping God in one place rather than another simply because God once declared he was present there.

Therefore, let us remember this passage since time does not allow us to say more about the presence of God and since we must not think that his majesty is confined to one place rather than another, but that it extends everywhere, and we must think upon his majesty in all his works – especially when he manifests himself to us in his word and we receive it in all fear and humility, yielding ourselves to it. And that is how we will make places holy with his holiness; and that will also happen when we receive in true faith the promises he makes concerning our salvation. In this way, we will be joined to him and he to us, so that he may draw us to himself and cause us to reign with him forever.

> Following this holy teaching, let us bow before the face of our gracious God in acknowledgment of our countless sins, by which we fail not to provoke his wrath against us daily, praying that he will be pleased so to touch us that we will be displeased with them to the end that we will seek only to serve and honour him and to dedicate our whole life to his honour and glory. Let us be so joined to him by his word that we will remain in him until the end and until he is all in all (*1 Cor.* 15:28). Now let us all say, Almighty God, heavenly Father . . .

34

RELEASED FROM FEAR THROUGH GOD'S MERCY

SUNDAY, 26 OCTOBER 1550

And as he drew near to behold it, the voice of the Lord came unto him,
³² Saying, I am the God of thy fathers, the God of Abraham, and the
God of Isaac, and the God of Jacob. Then Moses trembled, and durst not
behold. ³³ Then said the Lord to him, Put off thy shoes from thy feet:
for the place where thou standest is holy ground. ³⁴ I have seen, I have
seen the affliction of my people which is in Egypt, and I have heard their
groaning, and am come down to deliver them. And now come, I will send
thee into Egypt. ³⁵ This Moses whom they refused, saying, Who made
thee a ruler and a judge? the same did God send to be a ruler and a
deliverer by the hand of the angel which appeared to him in the bush
(Acts 7:31–35).

On the basis of what is recounted here, that our Lord commands
Moses to take off his shoes as an indication of his reverence,
we have already pointed out that when approaching God, we must
cast off all our affections, all our natural dispositions, and our vices,
for we will never be able to hear clearly what God says to us unless
we relinquish everything that is natural to us.

We have also pointed out in general terms how this passage
advises us concerning the kind of reverence we must have as we

present ourselves before our God's majesty when he gives us a sign that he wants to come to us. We must be disposed to receive him in all fear and humility and submission.

Yet it seems that some controversy arises when Stephen says that Moses, drawing near to consider what that vision was, hears God's voice. Then he adds, 'After hearing that voice say, "I am the God of your fathers Abraham, Isaac, and Jacob", he does not dare look at it.' With that he shows us that the more God manifests himself to us the more deeply we are to be moved by such fear that we can only be confounded unless he gives us courage and extends his hand to lift us up.

In fact, those who are in no way touched in their hearts by him give evidence that they have no knowledge of God, and they remain thus hardened, for we see many who are so dull of hearing that if they are admonished day and night and exhorted endlessly, the effort bears no fruit. In addition, they do not consider how far they distance themselves from God when they harden their hearts in that way, or else we do not see that they have any inclination to say, 'We have to deal with God, who is our Judge.' This matter must not be treated lightly, for those people have no idea about God as Judge.

But a man who knows the true fear of God is so frightened when he realizes God is speaking to him and giving him some sign of his majesty that he will stand motionless and distraught. Whenever God revealed himself to his servants, they experienced such apprehension and fear that they thought they were like dead men. In ancient times, it was common to hear people say, 'Who will see God and live?' (*Exod.* 33:20) The fathers are well aware that we are like fuel in a burning fire which consumes everything. It is said that God is a consuming fire (*Deut.* 4:24). Now what about us and our nature? How shall we come to such a fire and not be consumed?

Consequently, we must not find it strange that Stephen says that Moses, although God drew near to reveal something to him, did not dare give the vision the consideration he might have, but stops, filled with fear. In that, we see Moses knew how fragile our nature is. For if Moses, a man already practiced in the knowledge of God and having received other visions in Egypt, a man of such worth that God bestowed upon him such wondrous favours, was thus distraught, what will be our lot? When God gives us the grace to reveal his will to us, must we not, therefore, experience fear until we know him? Now we must not remain in such a state of fear that we withdraw from God, but we must follow Moses' example and renew our courage as we read that he did when God declared why he appeared to him.

We have therefore two items to note briefly here, namely that we consider both God and ourselves and that we are lost, and that we do not know what to do or what will become of us. When I say we are to consider both God and ourselves, I mean that we must acknowledge, on the one hand, what the nature of our weakness is, that we are nothing, indeed less than wisps of smoke. On the other hand, when we come to God, we will, as I have already said, find him to be a burning fire to consume us. That then must be a clear warning that we are as people lost.

However, we must also take into consideration that it is by our God's grace and kindness that we are not consumed, and that fact should give us courage to come to him without creating obstacles that would keep us from presenting ourselves before his majesty. Therefore, when our Lord inclines us to draw near to him, we will realize then that he is acting to instruct us in humility and fear. And after frightening us, he tempers our fear by showing us his love and mercy toward us. In that way we are strengthened after he has shown us wherein we are weak. That is how he lifts us up after bringing us low. When our Lord Jesus Christ himself gives a sign of his divinity, the texts says that his disciples were afraid, but when he says, 'Do not fear; it is I' (cf. *Matt.* 14:27ff.), all their fear goes away. So it is when God reveals himself to us. And it is good and necessary that we be brought low because of the excessive foolish pride in men who always want to rise too high. God must then conquer them and teach them humility, which he does by means of the kind of fear just mentioned. But when we are shown that it is he who is revealing himself to us for our salvation, all fear is then removed because we realize he is not coming to throw us into the pit. But to the contrary, he comes for our welfare and our salvation. So when we have this word of consolation from him, we must no longer fear to approach him boldly even though we were formerly far away from him.

So let us pay close attention to this passage which says that 'Moses wondered at the sight.' By doing that, he shows the love he had for God because he well knew that God wanted to tell him something. He is attentive. He applies his full mind, raising his eyes to look at what God wants to show him. Following his example then, as soon as God speaks to us, we must open our ears and be ready to listen. As soon as he shows us some sign for our instruction, we must concentrate our whole mind and all our wits on it. For if we are indifferent to God's voice, what excuse can we offer, seeing that he wants to teach us in such a personal way? Let us not react as do many who use their ignorance as a defence. They do not think God is worth listening to when he speaks. Following Moses' example, let us be careful to listen when God favours us with instruction. As we do that, let us offer the kind of honour and reverence we know God's dignity is due and worthy of. And recognizing it, let us humble ourselves and free ourselves from all presumption and arrogance, for we will never be of a mind to come to God unless we are lowly, as holy Scripture mentions frequently. In other words, when God speaks to us, let us be ready to yield to his will. For when God wants to bring us to himself, he does not use a heavy hand to drive us away. Rather he shows himself to be gentle and kind so that we will take heart and come when he calls.

We must now consider the content and substance of these things God said to Moses. First, he said, 'I am the God of your fathers, the God of Abraham, of Isaac, and of Jacob.' Then he adds, 'I have seen, I have seen the affliction of my people; I have heard their groaning. I have come to deliver them and I want you to undertake that charge.'

As for the first point, it is noteworthy that God, when calling himself the God of Abraham, of Isaac, and of Jacob, wishes to remind Moses of his promise to be always mindful of the children of Israel and to protect them with his hand. For that people was separated from all the other nations of the earth, not that they were more worthy than other peoples, but his setting them apart stemmed from his pure kindness and his freely bestowed love, as Moses makes clear to them when he says, 'It is not that your fathers were more numerous and possessed some excellence the others did not have, but he chose you out of his kindness and love' (*Deut.* 7:7–8). And why? You will not find the reason in the people, but only in the fact that God loved them. That way, he shows that only mercy is at play and that human merit has no role.

That then is our Lord's intention when he says to Moses, 'I am the God of your fathers.' It is as if he were saying that '[Moses] is reminding you of the promise I made to your father Abraham, often repeated and confirmed since the days of Isaac and Jacob, that you may be founded upon it. For therein does your salvation consist. Therefore, know now that I am faithful and truthful when I speak. True, your fathers died long ago, but I have not forgotten what I promised them, for my truth is not for the lifetime of just one man. So, even though Abraham, Isaac, and Jacob have passed on, my truth will remain forever, and I will now show its power and effectiveness. I will fulfil what they expected and hoped for from me.'

It is true that our Lord has always attributed those titles to himself in order to bring the people back to his word. From that fact we can formulate a very useful teaching. We see how we are inclined to wander and exalt ourselves in pride and presumption. An amazing audacity resides in men. They boast of penetrating both heaven and earth with their minds. At the same time, we understand the extent of our weakness. Our understanding is dull and grossly inadequate. And yet we think that nothing can be beyond our comprehension. We even want to confine God's majesty to the limits of our imagination. As a consequence, men are so unsure of themselves that they argue about all the things that they conceive of and tangle them so badly they cannot make heads or tails of them.

Now, that presumption is not confined to human matters. It also extends to the question of knowing God, of worshipping him, and of putting our trust in him. On that subject, we are bolder, more attentive, and more diligent than if we were measuring out a piece of ground. And that has been the status quo in all times. Men have always come up with wild speculations. When they wanted to know what God was like, they formed endless fabrications in their minds. And where does all that come from? It comes from that foolish curiosity, so prevalent among men, that leads them to seek to know more than they should. True, men do indeed confess that God is Creator of heaven and earth, but in short order they create him as they want him to be, and everyone makes for himself an idol that he fancies. That is because people conceive wicked images of God when they think of him in terms of their own understanding.

It has been like that from time immemorial. We still see it today. The Turks, the Jews, and the papists will confess that there is one God, Creator of heaven and earth, but they nonetheless overflow with thousands of superstitions, and instead of worshipping the living God, they have idols upon idols. And what is the reason? It is because they have alienated themselves from God's word and because, when they tried to seek him out, they forged thousands of speculations in their head and subsequently found themselves deceived. So when the Turks confess that they worship God as Creator of heaven and earth, they make for themselves a god to their liking. And there you have an idol, a devil. What then is to be done? This is the only remedy: we must not be wrapped up in our foolish imaginations if we want to understand God as he wants us to know him. We must adhere completely to the way he sets before us, and it is through his word that he wishes to reveal himself to us. Therefore, because God is incomprehensible to us in his majesty, he shows himself to us in his word. That, I say, is how God will be known to us when we think upon him as he is taught in his gospel, in which he manifests himself to us because it is necessary for our salvation.

Therefore, when it is said that he is the God of Abraham, the point is that we are not to limit our thinking to a mortal man. Here we must consider Abraham as a public individual representing one who has received God's covenant. God made him promises of salvation so that those who would come after him might understand that Abraham did not know God through vain human imagination, but through the revealed path. God's intention was and is that we might follow his will as set forth in his word and draw from it all our wisdom, to the end that we might be decisive, content and satisfied that God declares himself to us for our good and advantage. Therefore, we must say that we are subject to his word, for those who do not wish to submit to it will find themselves so distanced from it that they will think they can approach God in other ways.

And this is why our Lord has always attributed to himself the title 'I am the God of Abraham, of Isaac, and of Jacob' – because those men always followed him according to his word. Now if the ancient fathers under the law had to be restricted to that title because of the promises God had given their fathers, what does that mean to us in our day? Today God makes himself known much more fully than he did under the law. In times past, he spoke to our fathers in many ways, as the apostle to the Hebrews says, but in his final act he has spoken to us definitively in his Son (*Heb.* 1:1–2). So, Jesus Christ reveals the heart of God his Father, not in part, but in its fullness, in such a way that we cannot fail to be aware of what constitutes our salvation. How firmly, then, ought we to trust what he tells us, since he makes himself known to us in the person of his Son! We must not wander about aimlessly seeking his will. We need only to hold to the pure teaching of his gospel, and in so doing we will have sufficient confidence in that truth.

That is also why Jesus Christ is called the living image of God his Father. We now see the advantage that accrues to us in this teaching in which our Lord does not simply name himself, but adds another title so we can learn to seek him out in his word. Now that title served Moses because it confirmed him in the promise that had been given to the ancient fathers. For the poor people of Israel were so cruelly afflicted that they seemed to be a people without hope whom God himself permitted to be beaten down by evil practices because he is rebuking them and rejecting them and because he wants them exterminated from the earth. If they had been compared with the rest of humanity, others would have said, 'That is one miserable group of people!' What hope are they ever to have of escaping those misfortunes? From a human perspective, there was none. And yet we must return to this promise which God declares once again when he says, 'I am the God of your fathers.'

Why must we return to this promise? Because it is now and will forever be unchanging. So let us note that when our minds, from a human perspective, are confused and we are as people lost, without hope, and when it seems God will never have pity on us, it is then that we must come to his promise and affirm the guarantee of our salvation in the word he has given us.

That then is how a man of faith will be completely victorious when the world is against him, when all creation has conspired to dissuade him from the trust he must have in God. He will always conclude, 'The fact is that God has promised to be my Father and my Saviour; I will put my confidence in that fact and find strength in his word even though I seem to have no access to him and no way ever to approach him. Since I have his word, I am assuredly joined to him, for he cannot abandon his truth. In this way, I have no doubt that he is my Protector and Saviour and that he helps me both in body and in spirit.' That then is how we are to be taught to hold to our confidence in God's promises as we wait for his help in the midst of our adversities, and since we confess that God saves us as much in body as in soul, we must be decisive and adhere strictly to his word. As I have said, even if we are drowning in all sorts of miseries, as long as we have God's word, we have a key to escaping all the afflictions and anguish that might befall us.

And then we still need to note all those occasions when our Lord calls himself the God of Abraham after Abraham's death in order to signify that his truth does not die with men. In fact, God is not subject to variation or change but remains an everlasting constant. So we can live and die, but the word of God will always be a living reality, for his word must share the nature of the one from whom it proceeds. Thus, inasmuch as our Lord promised Abraham he would protect all his lineage, that truth is steadfast and inviolable even though Abraham is dead. If that was the situation with the ancient fathers, the greater is the reason that we ought to be strengthened today in the promise of our salvation, such as it is given to us. Our Lord presents it to us and bestows it upon us liberally, not from the hands of Abraham, but from the hands of our Lord Jesus Christ his Son, who received the promise from God his Father for our sake and for our profit. He covenanted in our behalf. Moreover, we are not dealing with an empty promise or with one which fades with time, but one for which the blood of our Lord Jesus Christ is our surety. His blood is the seal which confirms what God promised by his own mouth. Jesus Christ died but rose again straightway.

Therefore, when we enjoy this blessing of being able to rely on Jesus Christ, we know that he shed his blood for the sake of the promise of our salvation, that it is he whom God received into his hands and that he offered himself to God his Father on behalf of that promise in order to validate his suffering and death and give the promise integrity and power. Can we not honour God by trusting him at least as much as the ancient fathers did? And Moses is greatly strengthened by this statement alone: 'I am the God of Abraham.' Moses, I say, who was contrarily tempted often, remembers that he was estranged from the land of Egypt for forty years, like a poor vagabond in a wilderness. Yet, when God uttered this simple statement: 'I am the God of Abraham', he took courage and was completely certain that God wanted to redeem his people.

God now speaks to us in another way. He says to us, 'I have sufficiently manifested myself in the person of my Son. Know that his suffering and death testify to the love that I have for you. He was raised again so that you might know he has such power that he can never fail you.' Since we have all these things, are we not worse than unbelievers if we cannot comprehend the love God has for us? Is it not a sign of great unbelief that we cannot know him as he reveals himself in his word? So let us learn to compare ourselves with the ancient fathers. In no way did they doubt God's promises, even though, when given, they were very obscure and practically impossible to understand. Consequently, we have a very strong reason to receive them without difficulty and to rely upon them completely.

We also know that this passage shows the immortality of the soul, as Jesus Christ himself explains it. He says that God is not the God of the dead but of the living (*Matt.* 22:32). It is as if he were saying, 'God calls himself the God of Abraham after Abraham died.' Consequently, Abraham has to be alive. It would be meaningless for God to say, 'I am the God of mankind', were it not so. It would be like a man saying he was the prince of a country that existed nowhere in the world. Would that not be a mockery? That shows us that those who have died in this world do not cease to be alive in God's presence. That point we must note well, for the ancient fathers had to have that resurrection imprinted on their hearts just as it is made known to us in the gospel.

And, as I have said, by calling himself the God of those who have died, our Lord shows that he does not give us life in this world only, but that we are alive in him after he removes us from here below. In fact, what would our situation be without that knowledge? We would be the most miserable men on earth, as Paul says, if we set our hearts on the things of this world (*1 Cor.* 15:19). So let us learn that God does not want us to hope in him in this life only. Our faith must extend beyond death so we will know that even though our lives are now hidden (*Col.* 3:3–4), they will one day be revealed at the coming of our Lord Jesus Christ.

We come now to what Stephen adds: 'I have seen, I have seen the affliction of my people.' That is the account he gives of Moses' story: 'I have heard their cry and have come to deliver them' (*Exod.* 3:7–8). Our Lord says that he saw the affliction of his people and heard their cry, which signifies that he sees our adversities and provides for them beforehand, even though we do not now see his care for us and his desire for us to know that it is in him that we must trust and that we possess nothing that does not come from his grace to make our faith sure. Sometimes, God has to hide himself from us. Yet he does not fail to undergird and help us, even though we do not have the good sense to come to him as we know we should, and while we do not have the good sense to come to him, he pities us as his little children. In fact, he could not be the Judge of the world if he did not know our need of his help better than we do. But the fact remains, as I have said, that we must seek him out if we wish to share in his grace. We must come to him and seek our complete well-being in him.

Also, we need to note the order of events as stated here. God heard the cries of his people before coming to their aid. That then is how the aid and support God wishes to give his people depend upon his freely given promise. He does not act because we support and advocate him, but because his goodness is boundless. He commits himself to us by his word. The children of Israel could have groaned and lamented without first being prompted by God, but it would have profited them nothing, and they could not have groaned while calling upon God if they had not relied on him.

Therefore, the first thing we are to learn from this passage is that there is no way to take refuge in God unless he leads us to himself and he himself provides the way, leading and guiding us with his hand so that we will arrive not by our efforts, but by knowing that his promises to be our Saviour are not futile. That then is how God is obliged to speak to us before we can implore him. That is what Paul says: 'How can men call upon God except that they first know him and have heard by the preaching of the gospel how he wants them to pray?' (Cf. *Rom.* 10:14) It is true that it is natural that men are moved to inquire after God. But how can this be? I am speaking of pagans and poor ignorant people. They indeed believe in God; yet they are in such confusion that they do not know what to ask of him, and they know even less what to expect from him in the way he answers. Why? Because they have imagined so many ways to approach God that that acts as a barrier between God and themselves and prevents their cries from reaching him. Whatever the situation, as I have said, even if we had never had a single word of instruction, nature urges us to acknowledge that there is a God to whom all things are subject. God has imprinted that in our minds so we will be even more inexcusable. Even when the most wicked and reprobate desire to spite God, we see that that natural instruction is still within them and that they must acknowledge that there is some power and some divinity to which they are subject. Consequently, the most ignorant will acknowledge God and invoke him, but theirs will not be a pure and holy invocation.

Moreover, as we have said, when men have created in their heads services for worshipping God as it seems good to them, they have created idols that they worship instead of the living God, and they will even call upon idols unless they are taught by God and have a testimony of his goodness and know that he wants to answer their prayers. Now unbelievers, principally the papists, pray to God by chance. They have no certainty about their prayers, whether God is obliged to answer them or not. And that should not surprise us because, most often, they do not address God in their prayers, but their idols, their patrons, and their saints, which they themselves have forged. That shows us how few there are today who know how to pray to God. Now one of the principal features of our Christianity is just that: being able to pray.

It is when we come to the sermon that we should make good use of our intelligence in order to ask God that the things we hear will bear fruit in us in such a way that we will be strengthened in our faith and in our hope. But how many think about that? Very few. All the more then ought we to heed and put into practice the teaching that we must be assured of the love God has for us, of the fatherly concern he bears us, and that it is he who exhorts us to take refuge in his grace, being assured that we will not seek for him in vain. That is one point that needs to be made.

As for the second, we must note that when God hears us, it is not that our prayers deserve to be heard because they have such worth that when we open our mouths, he is bound to grant what we request. Everything originates in his promise because he has obligated himself to us voluntarily out of his pure beneficence. Therefore, although God has promised to hear our requests and does in fact hear them, let us not attribute that to some merit, but, as I have said, we must come to that beneficent promise which he has made out of his pure goodness.

And that is why it is written that he said, 'I am the God of Abraham, of Isaac, and of Jacob. I have heard the cry of my people', before saying, 'And I have come to deliver them.' Now in the end, after God gives Moses the promise to deliver his people from their bondage, he says to him, 'Now come, I will send you into Egypt.' That is the command that is added to the promise. So Moses must, upon hearing God's promise, make immediate preparations to accept the charge entrusted to him. From that we must learn this very useful lesson: that when God presents himself to us and calls us, he does not do so intending that we remain on the road and use the occasion to settle down after setting out to come to him, but he wants us to combine a strong constancy with our faith so that, receiving the promises he makes to us, we will be ready to follow him wherever he leads and dedicate ourselves completely to him and say, 'Lord, what can I do to please you? Here I am, ready to obey your holy will.' That is what we must note in this passage.

That is why he says, 'I have come to help them. Now come, I will send you into Egypt.' And how is that? Could not God deliver his people some other way? What need does he have of

Moses? He could certainly have done without any human help, but he wants Moses to guide the work he wants done, not, as I have said, that he could not have done without him whenever it pleased him. But if he wants to honour us by using us in his work, we are even more bound and obligated to him.

Now finally Stephen concludes 'that Moses was made a ruler and a deliverer of the people', even though they had already rejected him, saying, 'Who made you a ruler over us?' With that statement, Stephen wanted to give the Jews evidence that God had had mercy on their fathers despite their lack of gratitude. In that way, he wanted to crush the pride and presumptuousness of this proud and arrogant people, just as holy Scripture accuses them of and condemns them for that vice. But let us note that this day we need God to humble us. Let us briefly examine just what foolish human presumptuousness is. It is not a vice peculiar to a single people. It is a vice common to and operative in the entire human race. It is true we have many wicked affections. But this is the main one: the pride and presumptuousness within us that keep us from bowing our heads in submission to God and humbling ourselves before him. We need to pay close attention to this passage in which Stephen points out to the Jews that the grace God granted them was not that they might welcome it, but that they might make themselves unworthy of it by their ingratitude while he continues to work out his plan in such way that he accomplishes the redemption he promised their fathers. Therein we see that even though we provide God with many opportunities to withhold his good graces from us, he nonetheless never fails to do good things for us so that his goodness and mercy overcome our evil, although it is exceedingly grievous and heinous. As a consequence, we have good reason to trust him and have confidence in his promises because we know that everything he does and makes known is for our good and our salvation. We will take up here next Sunday.

Following this holy teaching, let us bow before the majesty of our God in acknowledgment of our sins, praying that he will be pleased to touch us with such sharp repentance that we will approach him with sincere reverence and humility and ask his forgiveness. Even though we know they are grievous and heinous, let us not fear presenting ourselves before him in the name of our Lord Jesus Christ, knowing that it is not in vain that he calls us to himself and that he will not reject our prayers, but will hear them as he promised, provided we offer them in faith and truth. Now let us all say, Almighty God, heavenly Father . . .

35

REDEMPTION IS OF GOD ALONE

SUNDAY, 2 NOVEMBER 1550

This Moses whom they refused, saying, Who made thee a ruler and a judge? the same did God send to be a ruler and a deliverer by the hand of the angel which appeared to him in the bush. [36] *He brought them out, after that he had shewed wonders and signs in the land of Egypt, and in the Red sea, and in the wilderness forty years.* [37] *This is that Moses, which said unto the children of Israel, A prophet shall the Lord your God raise up unto you of your brethren, like unto me; him shall ye hear* (Acts 7:35–37).

Our redemption is God's undertaking, and his alone. Still we are told that Moses was the people's redeemer. Yet we must realize that God bountifully bestows his blessings upon us by using men. By doing that, he lays upon them the dignity that belongs only to him. He does it so that we will receive the good things he does for us while including the human means which he has established. True, in spite of any pride that may be in us, we will not reject God as our Saviour. Yet we thwart his effort to teach us by using men, and we do not acknowledge that he employs them as his ministers and instruments. So it is noteworthy that the text says Moses was the people's redeemer. The power to be the people's redeemer did not proceed from him, and the credit for redeeming them must not be given to him. To give him the credit would be to obscure God's glory and nullify his majesty. But everything must be attributed to our God's goodness, power, wisdom, and might, for it is because he used Moses that the people were saved. Let us then use men in such a way that God's worthiness and authority will in no way be diminished and that God will always have his proper due, which is wholly reserved for him, and at the same time let us discern how he wants to make himself known to us.

Now it is noteworthy that the text says Moses was appointed to be the redeemer of the people in spite of the fact that they had already rejected him. That makes it appear that the people did not deserve to be redeemed. With that, Stephen reminds the Jews that God did not elevate their fathers to such honour and esteem because they had earned it. The only thing they can do now is to confess that they are fully and completely obligated to God and that neither their virtue nor their worth had anything to do with their having this privilege more than others. On the other hand, he points out that everything Moses did was under a greater and higher guidance than his own. He was under the hand of the angel who had appeared to him in the bush.

Then Stephen adds that Moses refers the people to another master and teacher, saying that Moses did not want them to cling to his teaching as if it were the perfect goal. When he speaks of the angel, there is no question that it is Jesus Christ. True, the law was given by the administration of angels (*Gal.* 3:19), as we will see later, and it is also true that Moses was accompanied not by a single angel, but by a celestial army. But here Stephen mentions a single angel in order to point to the one who is sovereign and ruler of all the others, namely, our Lord Jesus Christ, as has been said. And Paul says that is the way the passage is to be understood: that Jesus Christ was the people's guide when they were taken from Egypt and dwelt in the desert, as he spoke of it more fully in 1

Corinthians 10 (*1 Cor.* 10:9). For when declaring how the Jews put God to the test and rose up against him frequently, he said they were rebelling against Jesus Christ. Now why would he say that? Because Jesus Christ had them under his care and was the Shepherd of God's church.

It is true that that fact is now more expressly stated. Since he has been manifested in the flesh and has come down to earth, yet, under the law, believers had to accept the Son of God as their Saviour and Guide. That is precisely what Stephen meant in this passage when he said that Moses delivered the people, and he did that by the hand of the angel which had appeared to him and was his superior master and guide. His was a lesser role.

The instruction that we are to conclude from this, briefly stated, is that it is from God's hand alone that we receive every blessing and every grace and that he alone is our Saviour and Head. We must also note that when God governs us, he cares for us and his care is in the person of our Lord Jesus Christ. Therefore, we must always consider the means God has provided for our access to his majesty. That means is Jesus Christ, who comes to unite us with God his Father. That office was given to him to bestow upon us lavishly the blessings of God, for he holds them in his hand and distributes them.

Consequently, when we want to receive some blessing from God, we must address our petitions to Jesus Christ and to none other. If we fail to do so, we seek God in vain. Never will he make himself known to us in any other way. The more we think about drawing near to him in some other way, the farther away he will be. So let us learn to follow the way shown here.

Even though his is the only way, our Lord Jesus Christ continues to share his blessings with us by the hand of men. But as he does so, he always maintains control and power over the entire process so that the praise will be given to him. As we confess now that Jesus Christ is the Head of the church and is our Master, whom we must hear, even so will we shortly declare it more fully. It is he who has the authority to teach us, for all fullness and wisdom and divinity lie in him. And yet we are daily taught by men. How can this be? It is not because Jesus Christ has signed his right over to us. For since we possess the teaching of the gospel, it is not so that we may forge a new law, but so that we may leave its honour and authority in his hands alone to the end that he who teaches must be a learner the same as others and that Jesus Christ will be the Teacher of us all. . That then is how our Lord Jesus Christ will utilize men in such a way that he will always remain faithful to his word. In short, that is the lesson we are to learn from this passage where Stephen says that Moses was established to be the people's redeemer by the hand of the angel who appeared to him in the bush.

Now Stephen adds that Moses 'showed signs and wonders both in Egypt and in the Red Sea for forty years in the desert.' He then gives a brief summary of what deserves greater elaboration, but he relates in few words what the Jews could understand, for they had a good knowledge of all those things.

In the first place, our Lord had provided Moses with adequate approval by performing so many mighty acts and miracles by his hand. With that, Stephen shows that the accusation against him of detracting from Moses' honour and authority was false. Therefore, he both concludes and confesses that Moses was an outstanding prophet of God and had done great things for the people's redemption. We can judge from that that his intention was not to encourage disobedience to the law of Moses. But he does want to show that all of the outward ceremonies had come to an end because Jesus Christ, who is their truth, fulfilled them all with his coming. And that is the main thing we must consider here. The account of this story would be of little value if we did not always have before us what Stephen asserts. For just as he spoke to the Jews of that period, so also is that teaching recorded for us so that we might know that Jesus Christ did not come to destroy the law but to confirm it (*Matt.* 5:17). The gospel then is not a teaching contrary to the law of Moses. It is rather a more adequate revelation and confirmation of the things shown earlier. And in that, we see how the whole of holy Scripture is in agreement. We see how all those whom God instructed from the beginning of the world are in agreement, as if they had spoken with a single voice.

We also see the gospel's superiority in the fact that Moses and all the prophets were agents for what was to be fulfilled with the coming of our Lord Jesus Christ. We also see God's grace in those whom he used for such a long time as our servants and as the servants of our salvation, as Peter says (*1 Pet.* 1:10–12). Nevertheless, we must always bear in mind that whatever miracles Moses performed, the people persisted in rejecting him. They always grumbled against him. Their ingratitude is evident in the fact that Moses' miracles did not move them to collaborate with him and acknowledge that he was sent by God and that they could not ignore him and his office without at the same time manifesting obvious rebellion against the living God. Now that shows that the Jews were indeed worthy of condemnation. But after fully examining ourselves, it is certain we will not find ourselves to be better than they were. We will find, I tell you, that there is today a greater rebellion against God than there was back then.

True, we will not see the heaven darkened, the water changed to blood, and the other wonders done by Moses in Egypt. We will not see the sea become dry and make a passageway. We will not see manna fall from heaven and streams flow from rocks. Yet God still labours on our behalf in such a way that we indeed have reason to obey him in all humility. Moreover, all those miracles done in Egypt pertain to us. God, as we have already mentioned, not only wants us to learn a valuable and useful lesson from them, but he also wants us to entrust ourselves completely to him. Then, let us realize that all the miracles done at that time are to help us today. Those done by Jesus Christ and his apostles serve the same purpose. That then is how our Lord approves and confirms the teaching of his gospel by all the miracles performed from the beginning of the world. Nevertheless, we still cannot put our trust in them. We cannot acknowledge that it is God who must receive all the credit. In that, we see our ingratitude is not less today than theirs was among the people Stephen is talking about here.

Let us therefore learn how better to profit from the works God shows us, which are witnesses of his majesty, his power, his goodness, and his infinite wisdom. Let us be more careful than we have been to take advantage of that lesson so that it will incite us to love him and to accord him the fear, the honour, and the lordship which are his.

The reason our Lord performed so many miracles in Egypt was to declare his concern for the salvation of his people. We see then the love God has for all his own and that he has shown in heaven and on earth that there is nothing in creation which does not declare how highly our Lord prizes and values us. Now what he has done for the people of Israel also shows the affection and solicitude he has for all those whom he has chosen as his inheritance. And he makes that known more fully through the teaching of his gospel. So whenever we seek the confirmation of our God's paternal love, let us go to his miracles and we will find nothing but a clear declaration of the singular concern he has for us. That then is primarily what Stephen wanted to show so that we can know we are valued by God, and he also wanted to show that we are deeply indebted to God because he has declared himself to our fathers from early times and shown how he has exercised his grace toward us so that all he has done might convince us to acknowledge all his benefits and thank him for all his blessings.

Now it is true Stephen does not censure the people for their rebellion at this point, but he wanted the Jews to keep it in mind, and he will speak of it again later. Everything cannot be said in a single statement, but when he uses the word 'prince', he wishes to point out that God persisted in confirming Moses' call so that the people would understand he had ordained him to deliver them.

We see then how our Lord never wearies of doing good for us and that he persists even though we are unworthy and reject him often. For we see how his people had given themselves over to every wickedness. We see how they had polluted themselves with idolatry, how they grumbled later, and how they were filled to overflowing with evil desires. In short, there was no end and no limit to their wickedness, and God was provoked anew every day. Yet he still continues to do good for them. Moses fulfils his office as redeemer; manna falls from heaven to feed them; God leads them night and day. We see the extent of his mercy and patience in the fact that he continues his blessings and makes such an ungrateful and rebellious people sense his goodness. And if we examine ourselves, we will find that there is no less evil in us than in them, for we do everything we can to provide God with an opportunity to stop doing good for us. Why then does he continue except to overcome our evil with his mercy?

Thus, when the stories of holy Scripture are recounted for us, let us always keep these two things in mind: with one eye let us consider men's evil, their unfaithfulness, and their rebellion against God; with the other, let us contemplate how God has worked on our behalf so effectively that he has overcome every iniquity in our nature by his goodness and infinite mercy and always makes us sense his goodness although we deserve to be treated harshly.

Now after Stephen spoke of the miracles Moses did in Egypt, at the Red Sea, and in the wilderness, he adds at the end that it was Moses who said that God would raise up a prophet like him from among the children of Israel and command that he be heard. Here Stephen shows that Moses did not want the people to limit themselves to his teaching alone, and he gave them hope that God would reveal himself more completely.

The passage cited here is elaborated more fully in Deuteronomy 18. There it is written that the people must not be discontented with God as if they did not have a definite declaration of his will. 'I am now speaking to you', Moses says. 'But after my death, God will always raise up from among you prophets like me' (*Deut.* 18:15). It is worth noting that he says that so the people might not turn to sorcerers and soothsayers, for men are by nature exceedingly desirous of knowing everything. As soon as something comes to our attention, we want to have it resolved immediately, and we wonder what it means. And that is the reason we have so much foolishness in the world and so many perverse ideas. And men are so inclined in that direction that they prefer to believe Satan's lies and deceptions over God's truth. And Moses wanted very much to protect us from that. For he says, 'Be careful that you do not consult sorcerers or witches or soothsayers or anyone who seeks the counsel of a familiar spirit or of the dead, for you know how the devil changes himself in a thousand ways to delude men and deceive them by his cunning and stratagems' (cf. *Deut.* 18:10–11). That is how the fathers were taught.

Now Moses says, 'Be content with the way God will choose to instruct you. After my death, you will have prophets who will come among you and serve as instruments of God, and he will speak by their mouths. Therefore, if you desire to be taught by him and know his will, you will have to follow what he shows you by his prophets. For he has ordained the ministry of his word and wishes men to serve him in that ministry. You must not, therefore, run helter-skelter in search of revelation, as the pagans do. You must not go to sorcerers or soothsayers or think you will get a new revelation from the dead. But listen to the prophets, who, as I have said, will be God's instruments' (cf. *Deut.* 18:15–22).

Now Stephen concludes from that that Moses wanted to lead us to Jesus Christ. And not without reason, as has already been pointed out in chapter 3 in Peter's sermon.[1] In that sermon, Peter expressly applies that passage to the person of our Lord Jesus Christ. It seems on the surface that that is not apropos, for Moses is speaking in general terms about all prophets, and in this passage Peter is speaking only about Jesus Christ. So it seems that there is some discrepancy here. But when we examine the point closely, we will find it is not without reason that this passage is applied appropriately and that we must acknowledge that Jesus Christ is the end of the law. For since God promised his people to continue to send them prophets, that promise must be maintained and inviolable.

Let us now consider whether God has stopped speaking to the children of Israel. If we reply, 'They did not deserve it', that promise nonetheless remains in full effect, so much so that what God promised in those words from Moses had to be fulfilled. Such we see fulfilled in God's sending Jesus Christ, even though the people were not deserving. From that we see that his gracious act did not result from men's faith, but only from God's freely bestowed goodness. Therefore, we must acknowledge that Jesus Christ fulfilled all prophecies, as he in fact clearly demonstrated by the prophets themselves, and especially by Malachi, who said, 'I am sending my messenger who will go before me' (*Mal.* 3:1). In that passage, our Lord shows that although he sent his prophets to instruct the people in the law, he will bring it to a conclusion by the one who is its completion. Now, that messenger of whom Malachi speaks was John the Baptist, through whom God brings

---

[1] The sermon referred to here has not survived. [Editors' note]

to a final conclusion all the prophecies until the coming of our Lord Jesus Christ.

So we understand that this passage about Moses must be applied to God's fulfilling his promise, because he always continued to lead the people by the ministry of prophets until the time drew near and Jesus Christ came and was manifested to the world, at which time all prophecies ended. Such is their perfect fullness. Thus we see that just as Stephen cites this passage, so also Peter quoted it appropriately to show Moses did not want his teaching to be received as if it represented the be-all and end-all of God's purpose, but he tried to bring the people to that fullness which we now see as being entirely in our Lord Jesus Christ.

We must now conclude from this passage that the law and the prophets have served to lead us to Jesus Christ. Furthermore, they all constitute for us today witnesses to what the gospel teaches, as Paul speaks of them in the first chapter of Romans (*Rom.* 1:1–3). For when he says that we are justified by faith and are saved by God's grace as it is offered to us in Jesus Christ, he says that that does not come to us through the law, that is, because of our works or through the services we have done for God, but by his pure mercy. The law, therefore, is not at work here, but this is the way God wants to save us: even though the law cannot justify us, it nonetheless tells us that our salvation resides in and consists in the grace of our Lord Jesus Christ, in that pure goodness that God has shown us in his person. That is what Stephen meant. And we need that teaching very much, for we know how inclined we are to be distrustful and slow to believe. It is true that we are only too quick to accept lies. We are unbelievably steadfast in believing them after hearing them only one time, and as a result we lose the kind of confidence we should have in God's truth. Consequently, we ought to pay even more attention to what supports this teaching, as when it is said that Moses served the way he did the rest of his life because he wanted to give the people hope that God would send them greater guidance, namely that they would be under the governance of our Lord Jesus Christ and hear from him everything we should desire as instruction from the mouth of God. For it is said in the first chapter of Hebrews, 'God spoke to our fathers in many ways through his prophets, but he has now spoken for the last time in the person of his Son' (*Heb.* 1:1–2), through whom he has more fully declared his will to us than he had to all his prophets.

And we should be ashamed for not attributing to Jesus the honour due him, which the poor Samaritan woman does. The Samaritans were only half Jews, so to speak, and they were foolishly arrogant in that they were descended from Abraham's race but still did not worship the God of Abraham, as they should have. In fact, Jesus Christ says as much: 'You do not know what you worship, even though you think you serve the God of Abraham' (*John* 4:22). And she says that Jesus Christ is the Teacher and sovereign Master who, after being revealed to the world, will instruct his people so thoroughly that they will have no doubts about anything.

We who are now Christians, who have been baptized in the name of our Lord Jesus Christ, who make open declarations of having the gospel, let us at least honour Jesus Christ by attributing to him the same authority that a woman does, indeed a pitiable, loose woman who had never been instructed or taught. Let us therefore realize that the certainty of the gospel is such that, from the beginning of the world, never has God spoken except for man's instruction. But since God has blessed us with the coming of the fullness of all things, we must be more confident of our salvation than the ancient fathers were.

Now this teaching must not only serve to test our faith and our Christian belief, but it must also serve as a bridle to restrain us from wicked speculations, toward which our nature urges and encourages us. In order to understand that better, let us always look to this passage about Moses which we have already dealt with, namely that when he says God will send prophets, it is so the people will not be carried away by a mad desire to run to sorcerers and soothsayers or to have a revelation from the dead; it is because they are to be content with the teaching God will send them by his prophets. Now when Moses labours to get the people to turn from such practices, it is because he knows that that kind of vice is highly common among men and that we do not always have within us the power and constancy to deliver ourselves from it. As I have said, we are more inclined to believe lies than God's truth. And then we are so arrogant we want to know more than God shows us, and we are so curious that we seek only to inquire about things that are completely beyond our province.

In short, that is how men will be led astray by their foolish curiosity to inquire into irrelevant matters. But that is not a new vice. It has been around for all time. So let us consider how Moses wanted to remedy such a vice when saying, 'God will send us prophets.' Now, if it was necessary for the ancient fathers to listen to the prophets and hear what they said to them and if they had to obey them, what is required of us in comparison? Those who were under the law will be more excusable than we, although they are inexcusable. And what is the reason for that? The teaching was not as clear for them as it is for us today through the gospel. At that time, our Lord led his people using very obscure images. Now we have Jesus Christ, who is the truth of the law and the prophets, and he speaks to us more intimately than God spoke in the law. For Jesus declares, 'I will no longer call you servants, for a master does not speak familiarly with his servant, as I do with you; I am revealing to you the secrets of God my Father and I am speaking with you as with my companions' (*John* 15:15). Therefore, Jesus Christ condescended to that point so as not to conceal from us anything useful for our salvation.

Therefore, since our God so gently invites us, what will happen to us if we do not listen to him? Nevertheless, we see that the world has not been incorrigible and must be brought under subjection without surrounding itself with these foolish imaginings by which it has always been deceived. How did it happen that God has been forsaken for so many foolish inventions? Today, for example, all the things practised throughout the Papacy are but rampant follies and inanity, and if we examine all they hold as articles of faith, we will find them to be just so many fabrications and fantasies devised by the minds of men. They have layered doctrine upon doctrine. There has been no limit to or restraint in what they have done.

Then there is the public worship of God, so-called, but what does it consist in? Everyone has put in his twopenny worth, and the result is a terrible jumble, and once Satan gets into the mix, he can but add disaster upon disaster, confusion upon confusion. And then as the crowning iniquity, which results from men's audacity in assaulting God's teaching, madness alone survives. After forbidding eating, they will forbid tasting. Then, after forbidding tasting, they will also forbid touching. And, as I have said, that proceeds from the fact that men have been so presumptuous as to want to add to the teaching which has been revealed to us by the Son of God, as it is contained in the gospel, and not everybody is acquainted with it. And if we consider what we can observe, we will have the impression that the gospel has been buried as a result of its being so badly understood by everybody.

It is true the papists will say they devise nothing of their own, for the pope does not say that something needs to be added to the word or that he has done anything wrong. But he uses such eloquent words that only the Holy Spirit abides in everything they do inasmuch as the church cannot err because the Holy Spirit guides her. The poor people do not understand that that is having faith in the pope. All the fabrications they have created are so well embellished by that elegant language that the poor ignorant people think everything comes from heaven, but we understand that all that is nonsense. Jesus Christ declared that when the Holy Spirit comes, he will not diminish his majesty and his authority. The Holy Spirit was not promised so that he might introduce new things, but so that he might strengthen us in the teaching that the Son of God proclaimed once and for all. After all, Jesus Christ did not intend to send his Holy Spirit to renounce the teaching which he had received from God his Father. Therefore, he must always occupy the highest rank, and his gospel must be received with all fear and reverence without the addition or deletion of anything under any pretext. For if we add anything to or take anything away from it, we renounce what the Son of God has done.

In fact, that is why the pope and Muhammad are companions and have spoken with one voice, so to speak. As for Muhammad, after dispensing his devil-inspired teachings, which bewitched the poor world, he declared that everything he had taught was revealed by the Holy Spirit. He did not wish to abolish the teaching of the gospel completely. He did not say that Jesus Christ did not have the gift of prophecy. Yet he does affirm that Jesus Christ did not possess such great perfection that we must not wait for another. That is how the glory and majesty of the Son of God are covered over by Muhammad's false teaching.

And the pope. What does he say? The same thing. Both speak, as I said, with one voice. In that, we see that the pope and Muhammad are like the two horns of the devil for the establishment of Antichrist's kingdom. So when someone mentions the Holy Spirit, we must determine whether the teaching is in keeping with the teaching of the gospel. For, as we have already stated, Jesus Christ did not want to teach us partially. In fact if he had not taught us perfectly, he would not have fulfilled the charge which he had received from God his Father.

Now we must nevertheless note that if we are to be taught by God, we must not come in search of more knowledge than we need, and we must renounce all means which originate with men, unless those means are approved by God. Those who yield time and again to their foolish imaginings are like those who renounce Jesus Christ and everything he has taught us by his word.

So if we wish to be counted as and esteemed as true servants of God, let us be careful not to incline either to the right or to the left of what he has shown us by his word, and let us not inquire after more than it teaches, but let us be content that God has spoken once by the mouth of Moses, by his prophets, and for the final time by our Lord Jesus Christ his Son, beyond whom we must not go if we want to participate in that wisdom which he promised all those who belong to him. Now the rest will keep till next Sunday.

Following this holy teaching, let us bow before the face of our gracious God in acknowledgment of our sins, praying that he will be pleased to bring us to such repentance that we will be able to recognize the source of all evils, namely, the unfaithfulness which is in us. Knowing how strongly we are inclined by nature to be unfaithful, let us profit so much from his word that we will be increasingly encouraged to fear him and to love him and to believe what he declared once and for all by Moses, by his prophets, and finally by our Lord Jesus Christ, his beloved Son. Now let us all say, Almighty God, heavenly Father . . .

36

God Speaks through His Servants

Sunday, 9 November 1550

This is that Moses, which said unto the children of Israel, A prophet shall the Lord your God raise up unto you of your brethren, like unto me; him shall ye hear. ³⁸ This is he, that was in the church in the wilderness with the angel which spake to him in the mount Sina, and with our fathers: who received the lively oracles to give unto us (Acts 7:37–38).

We have already explained why the promise that God would send prophets was given to the children of Israel. Inasmuch as men are inclined to vain things and their nature urges them in that direction, God has to restrain them in some way. For that reason, he established a definite procedure for instructing his people. He does not want us to wander aimlessly like unbelievers, but he wants us to have his truth to guide us. The way to acquire it has been shown to us, namely that from the beginning he sent his prophets to testify to what he wanted men to know. After speaking many times and in various ways to the ancient fathers, he brought things to a final conclusion in his Son Jesus Christ. And the gospel is for us a conclusion of all the revelations we are to expect from God's will. Therefore, that promise was completely fulfilled when God raised up prophets under the law. But the fact remains that we have the promise in its perfection today in that our Lord Jesus

Christ is the sovereign Prophet through whom God wanted men to know what was necessary for their salvation.

That being so, as has been pointed out, we must learn that God wanted to correct men's inquisitiveness and arrogance, which drive their relentless desire for new revelations. In fact, we see their unflagging zeal. For even though we have a full and perfect teaching, even though our Lord has declared his will fully in his gospel, we see how men have been diligent in that pursuit, like Muhammad and the pope, who are the two horns of the devil set on killing the poor world and imprisoning it. And on what pretext? On the pretext that the gospel does not provide all we need to know and that there are other and higher revelations which are necessary for our salvation. Such is the homage they pay Jesus and his teaching, which he received from God his Father for our instruction. But the pope dares to attribute to himself the distinction that it is in him and all his decrees and statutes that perfection and all knowledge lie.

Therefore, in order to fend off such satanic lies and deceptions, we need to be armed with this passage, which says that Jesus Christ is the sovereign Prophet by whom God wanted to manifest himself to men. We must cling fast to his teaching without wavering. All our wisdom consists in that. If we depart from that teaching, we will no longer be in God's school, but in the devil's, which is a school of hell.

In addition, when it is said that we must listen to those through whom God speaks to us, although they are mortal men, we see the kind of reverence our Lord wants his teaching to receive and how precious it is. Since it is said that we cannot reject those whom our Lord Jesus Christ sends as his messengers, let us not reject him himself as if he had come to us in his person. That then is what God wanted to communicate through Moses. We must not see the men who proclaim his word with their mouth, but we see beyond them and consider where the word comes from and whether God has entrusted to them that rank and office. In fact, our Lord wants to put our humility and our hope to the test by sending us his word through men. Could he not manifest himself to us from heaven or send angels to instruct us? Now he does not have to. There is a definite rationale behind it. For if angels descended from heaven to proclaim God's will, there would be no testing of our reverence for him inasmuch as the testing of our reverence is recognizable when he speaks to us through men. And when we receive what is said to us in his name, we declare at that time that we truly wish to be in subjection to him.

And that is what Paul is talking about when he says, 'When we proclaim the gospel, which is a precious treasure, it is at that time like gold in earthen vessels' (cf. *2 Cor.* 4:7). People will indeed put a great treasure in a vessel having no value. That is what our Lord does concerning his gospel. If we know the value, the price, the power, and efficacy of the gospel, we will see, first, that it is a very precious treasure, for it is called the kingdom of God, and, second, that it is his power for saving all believers, as Paul says in the first chapter of Romans (*Rom.* 1:16). That is how our Lord Jesus Christ makes himself known to us face-to-face, so to speak, and we see his glory shine.

Consequently, it is impossible to value the gospel too highly. And yet our Lord communicates it to us using men. And he especially does not choose the greatest, but he chooses men who are not of high estate or wealth, as the world values things. He does that to show us we must not become attached to those who speak to us and honour the gospel in accordance with the quality of their persons, but to show us that we must always honour and revere God by yielding ourselves completely to his word. That then is what we must note concerning Moses' express teaching that we listen to those whom God sends, even though they are mortal men.

However, we also realize the singular grace of God in his being pleased to communicate his gospel to us by men, for he shows us greater honour than if he sent angels from heaven. 'Who are we?' as Paul asks (cf. *2 Cor.* 2:16). Where is the man who thinks he is fit and sufficient for the great responsibility and commission of being God's ambassador to bear the spiritual message of the remission of sins and the salvation of souls? The task surpasses all human capacity. But the fact is that God uses men to accomplish that work. In that, we see how he honours our nature and how greatly obligated we are to him for doing so.

We are, then, doubly ungrateful if we do not deign to receive God's word when it is preached for us by men. In the first place, we reject God, who is speaking to us, and then we do not acknowledge the honour he is doing us. In other words, God does not consider whether we are worthy of such a blessing, for we can do nothing, but he chooses us as his ambassadors to bear the message of salvation. Consequently, we very badly miscalculate if we do not humbly and reverently accept the good thing he is doing for us. To sum up, this passage shows us how our Lord wanted to restrain us so that we would not act like wild horses running loose, following our foolish fantasies with each of us wanting to be taught what we wanted to be taught.

Now there exists a common rule for all believers. Namely, we must adhere to what God has declared to us by his prophets and finally by his Son Jesus Christ, in whom he has summed up all knowledge and wisdom. If we desire to be instructed appropriately, let us hold fast to what is contained in the law, in the prophets, and in the gospel as the source of everything we need. And then let us, as we hold to that knowledge, honour it as it deserves to be honoured, and let us be assured that this is the way God ordained to speak to us and that we must not turn a deaf ear to men when they faithfully proclaim the message entrusted to them. Let us hear them as if they were angels descended from heaven.

And then we must note that this is an inviolable procedure: God has always spoken to us by means of his servants. And when he sends us men to proclaim his will, we must not receive it as coming from them. Otherwise, it would not be the will of God. But when we acknowledge that what they proclaim is drawn from the true source, which is the teaching of the prophets and the gospel, we must receive it without any resistance, for if we reject it, the devil will surely be our teacher. There is no way that our Lord Jesus Christ will reject us and the devil take possession of us unless we refuse to submit ourselves to the teaching about him. As experience shows us, it turns out that all those who despise him and his word are forthwith alienated from him, are no longer members of his school, and necessarily accept the devil as their teacher. But what happens to them in the end? They do not follow the papists' teaching, for they are unworthy of it, but they are like dogs, without God and without religion. Seeing such punishment from God, let us learn to submit ourselves to the yoke which he imposes on us here, for our Lord has from the beginning wanted his people to be governed by the ministry of his word. And he wants that procedure to be observed until the end of the world, as Paul says in the fourth chapter of Ephesians (*Eph.* 4:11–13).

Now Stephen adds that 'Moses was in the wilderness with the fathers', but while the angel who spoke to him on Mt Sinai was in charge, Moses was always inferior. It was not he who had the principal position. We have already pointed out that the angel was Jesus Christ, according to Paul's exposition given in the tenth chapter of 1 Corinthians (*1 Cor.* 10:4). So it is as if Stephen were saying, 'Moses did not lead the people for one day only. He kept them together in the wilderness for the space of forty years.' Yet, as I said, Moses was not the chief authority, but Jesus Christ presided over it all, as if he were saying, 'Moses did not advance his own ideas, but was faithful to God and proclaimed his will as he had received it.' In fact, he gives a fuller explanation later. He received the living word, he says, in order to proclaim it to us. In so doing, he shows that Moses fabricated nothing in his head but faithfully preached the teaching he had received without making any changes in it. In fact, it would not be a living word if it did not proceed from God. For what can we find in men when they speak to us from their own resources? There is in them only vanity and lies. That much we know. Can they then proclaim the word of life? Far from it. Therefore, since Moses' teaching was living, we are obliged to conclude that it had God as its source. Now we see here that our Lord does not want to teach his people for one day only but wants us to sit at his feet all the days of our lives, the very thing we need to do.

This is a passage that needs to be underscored, for there are many foolish and arrogant people who consider themselves inordinately wise. As soon as they have some small sip of the gospel, they are inebriated. 'What more do we need?' they will ask. 'We know more about it than we want to!' – a byword common among them. They are telling the truth, but they do not know what 'knowing' is, for those who have already profited from the word of God want only to seek more. That is one of the good things we do when God instructs us. We always hunger to grow stronger in what we have heard once concerning his teaching, and we want to hear again and often the things we have already learned. Thus those who have had their fill of the word of God show clearly they never knew its worth. Let us note then that when God proclaims himself to us, we must not think that when he speaks to us once, he immediately hides, but he wishes to continue so that we, for our part, will persevere until the end in our pursuit of a better knowledge of his word. That is what Stephen wanted to make clear when saying, 'Moses was in the wilderness for forty years with the people.'

And he still wants to point out the ingratitude that filled those who rejected Moses. Despite the fact that God had given him many signs and testimonies of approval with regard to his commission, they still rebelled against him. In short, he means that we need God to seek us this way, as he says through his prophet, 'He watches over us morning and evening, as a father watches over his children and even as a mother suckles them' (cf. *Isa.* 49:14; 63:16; 66:13). Therefore, because God is so solicitous to draw us to himself, we are guilty of an even greater and more grievous vice when we manage to push him aside. And that is what Stephen wanted to show here.

Now it is true that he was speaking to Jews. But that teaching is addressed to us today. So let us note particularly that when God favours us by instructing us in his teaching, we must not grow weary even though we are often reproved. We have not reached the end yet, and we must continue to proceed earnestly while under-going instruction. That is one point. So let us guard against doing as the Jews did. Since God continues to teach us over a long period of time, let us not be worse than they or even like them. Let us know that that teaching must be a guide to lead us on the path of salvation. As a consequence, we will understand that when God blesses us by giving us instruction, it is not without purpose that we have been instructed in his truth.

In addition, this passage also indicates what we must learn. It is true that God teaches us using men, and it is in this way that he wants to have authority over us. In fact, we know that Jesus Christ was given to be our Master and that we are particularly commanded to hear him. That then is the main thing said about Jesus Christ. It is true that we must hear those whose office it is to bear his word, but not when they are speaking on their own. We listen because we see Jesus Christ speaking in them and through them. The fact remains, as I have already said, that God reserves for himself alone the right to speak with full authority and refuses to be usurped by anyone. But that authority is given to Jesus Christ his Son. Therefore, no one is to presume to teach anything that does not come from him. That is what Stephen declares: 'The angel spoke to Moses and Moses received from him the teaching that he communicated to men.' It is as if he were saying, 'Moses invented nothing; he did not advance his own ideas but faithfully administered the things God had entrusted to his charge.' In that way he followed his calling and did not exceed his authority. Now let us consider who Moses was. He was the greatest prophet who ever lived, but he did not have Jesus Christ's lofty position, for he has surpassed all the others. He is not like Moses. Consequently, he must hold sovereignty over all. True, as I have already said, Moses was an outstanding prophet and endowed by God with many gifts. Yet, he is not to be listened to except insofar as he speaks for God.

How then will we listen to others who do not have those credentials? Now we have the pope and Muhammad, who say that they must be heard too. And who are those two? If we examine briefly what confirmation they have indicating whether God sends them, we will discover that they are wretches, dung, and vermin. They are not at all like Moses. Far from it! And yet Moses' confirmation lay in the fact that God had put the word in his mouth; otherwise this teaching would have had no power. And to show that this is true, let us look briefly at the source of the pope's teaching. He forged all his teachings in the devil's workshop. This then is a passage that we must note closely. Moses' teaching can be accepted only insofar as God gave it to be communicated to men. About that we can have no doubt. It is God who speaks to us when our faith is based on his teaching and not on men's fantasy.

Therefore, let us ask God to bless us by teaching us through his Holy Spirit so thoroughly that our faith in his teaching will be strong. Let us not be doubtful and say, 'I do not know whether that is good or bad or whether I am to abide by or avoid it.' But let us acknowledge that this teaching which we have learned from God is his unassailable truth sent to us from heaven. Let us be resolute about that. Then we will be fortified against all the temptations to the contrary which could possibly come our way.

At this point, we could ask how it is that Stephen calls Moses' teaching 'living oracles', since Paul says in the third chapter of 2 Corinthians that it is a teaching of death and that it has the power to kill and utterly destroy (*2 Cor.* 3:6–7). Now we need to note that Paul, when speaking of the law, has in mind only the things which were added about the promises and threats. Why is that? Here we have God telling men how he wants them to live. 'You will love me', he says, 'with all your heart, with all your strength, and with all your soul, and your neighbours as yourselves' (*Luke* 10:27). When God shows us how he wants us to live, he adds that 'he will do these things and provide their recompense. But take care that you not offend in a single point, for whoever offends in a single point will be guilty of all and should then expect only death on his head' (cf. *Deut.* 28). That, then, is how the law works, when we consider it in its pure state.

Now Moses is pointing toward another goal. He has given the promises about our Lord Jesus Christ. In fact, when he established the sacrifices and the cleansings and similar practices, it was to teach men that they needed to be reconciled to God and that if they were to find favour before him, they needed to find it in Jesus Christ, who was the figure of all the ceremonies which had been established. That then is why Moses was commissioned by God to make known his mercy and the way they are saved by the free gift of his goodness. But as for the teaching of the law, he makes known to men how they are to hearken unto God. And with that he promises them salvation, provided they accomplish before God all that the law contains. On the other hand, if they do not, he threatens them with eternal death.

Now Paul expounds Jesus Christ for us. Why? Because the Jews wanted to be saved by the law but were unaware of the grace brought by Jesus Christ. And Paul, knowing they were unwilling to be moved from that position, says to them, 'The law is a teaching about death' (2 Cor. 3:6–7). The reason? When we have only the law, by which God instructs us how we are to live, it is certain that we will always be condemned, and hope vanishes. There is no other way to be saved since God gives us only one option: 'I command you to do everything contained in the law' (cf. Deut. 5:32; 11:32). If God stops there, we are lost. At that point, we are bereft of any salvation. Why so? No man will ever be able to acquit himself before God in any way whatsoever.

True, when the promises are first presented to us and God says, 'Those who keep the law will receive a very ample reward, for they will be saved', it seems that paradise is wide open and that we need only to enter. And when men in their foolish arrogance seize upon that statement, they can come up with wondrous notions, for we see how in the Papacy the word 'merit' pops up everywhere, and they think they will have paradise because of their merits.

Now the opposite is true. When Paul announces the promise that 'he who does these things will live by them' (Rom. 10:5), it does indeed seem like that will be quite easy, but when we take into consideration that the law does not promise men salvation apart from the condition that they accomplish everything God commands in it, we will discover that no man has ever been saved by it. For it is written, 'Whoever does not fulfil all these things will be cursed' (Deut. 27:26; Gal. 3:10). And so it is that no man has ever fulfilled them. Therefore a general curse rests upon the whole of the human race. And there is yet an even stronger statement, for it is clearly written, 'Cursed be the one who raises up idols but will not acknowledge God's bounteous favours. Cursed be the one who will not worship him with his whole heart, the one who will not keep the Sabbath or honour father and mother' (cf. *Deut.* 27:15–26). The same applies to all the rest. Now everyone must accept his condemnation on that point and answer individually, 'So be it!' And if it is true that everyone who does not keep all these things will be cursed, even so will no one be found who keeps them.

In addition, let us consider briefly how human beings will be able to fulfil the law of God when they are incapable of a single good thought as they prepare to do so. Thinking about it is a very simple matter. Yet our thoughts are so wicked that we cannot entertain a single good thought that will predispose us to doing good. Therefore, since we cannot entertain a single good thought, as Paul says (cf. Rom. 8:7), how will we be able to acquire the will to do so? God will have to give it to us. Since we are devoid of the will to do, how shall we accomplish the deed? Again, God will have to apply his hand. And when he does that today, he will have to begin again tomorrow, and he will have to undergird and help us daily. Otherwise, we will utterly fail. That, then, is how our Lord initiates and brings everything to perfection in us in order to bring us to salvation. That is so true that if we take the most perfect people who have ever lived, we will find that they needed God's help. Take Abraham, for example, who stood above all others and was a mirror for all righteousness. It is nonetheless written that he obtained mercy through faith because there was weakness in him. True, there was not so much weakness in him as was in many, but the fact remains that he is as indebted to God as all others are. Then there is Moses, whom we mentioned earlier. There were significant indications of perfection in him, but he was obliged to take refuge in the truth of the signs that God had him put forth, namely, the grace of our Lord Jesus Christ. Otherwise, he would not be able to stand before God's judgment without being confounded.

Therefore, since that was true of the most outstanding individuals who ever lived, how will we fare? Let us be aware that if we have nothing but God's commandments, we are all condemned. For if he does nothing but say, 'That is what you must do', what will happen? It is true that we will see clearly how we are supposed to live, but we will be incapable because we will have no inclination to live that way because our nature is so wretched that it will turn us in the opposite direction. Unless our Lord shows us in his word the path to salvation, we will all go to hell.

After giving the law, Moses strongly affirms that the sun and the moon testify to the fact that he has shown them the way of salvation. True, he has shown them the way, but that does not mean they can follow it. What then must we do now? Here is the remedy. After God shows us we cannot do what he commands, he imprints and engraves upon our hearts what is totally contrary to our nature. That is how our Lord will remedy our deficiency when he mortifies our hearts and changes them so radically that we will seek only to obey him and to subject ourselves completely to him and his holy word.

That is one remedy, but it alone does not suffice. We must add to it a second, which is that God receives us in mercy, that even if we are not worthy of presenting ourselves before him to ask for forgiveness, he still does not reject us. Inasmuch as our Lord Jesus Christ shed his blood to wash and cleanse us, he gave himself over to death to deliver us from that obligatory death in which we once found ourselves. That is the second remedy God promises us in accordance with what Moses has made known to us.

Thus we see that Moses bore the living word. It is true that if the law did not find men so thoroughly disposed to evil, it would be a word of life, but its failure originates with us. If we examine human beings, we will discover the reality that they cannot fulfil the law because their nature is accursed and perverse. Yet, when God speaks to us in his law, we must couple it with the grace provided in our Lord Jesus Christ as it was promised and imaged by Moses. If we lived accordingly, the law would then be for us a living word. That is why Paul says Jesus Christ is its heart and soul (cf. *2 Cor.* 3:17).

Let us now summarize this teaching so that we may apply it to our edification. So let us note first that when we come to be taught, we do not do so just to learn how we must live. That would be a minor consideration. Nevertheless, some people are so brutish minded that when they come to the sermon, they think the only thing they have to learn is how to live. If all we learn is that God commands this or that, we will learn very little at his school, for we see, for example, that in the Papacy they talk about nothing but the necessity of doing one thing or another, but they do not advance God's commandments. On the other hand, they will recommend highly the inventions and superstitions of men. One must fast on a certain day, refrain from eating meat on another, or do this thing or that. That is how the papists are engulfed in the superstitions they themselves created, heaping commandment upon commandment, without end and without number. Now those who still hold to the Papacy's old leaven think that all they have to learn about the gospel is to hear God's commandments. But, as I have said, that is a minor consideration if we go no further.

What then is required? When we come to the sermon and God teaches us his commandments, we must consider how we are to fulfil our duty toward God. We know to what extent we are bound and obligated to him. Nevertheless, instead of doing what pleases him, we do not cease to provoke his anger against us every day. As Paul says, all our affections are just so many enemies of God, and we do not cease to wage war against him (*Rom.* 8:7).

Realizing that Paul's assessment is true, we have to acknowledge how deeply we are indebted to God. Now have we learned that? We must humble ourselves before God and ask him to pity us and be pleased to heal us of all our faults. In other words, we must ask that he be pleased to correct the evil within us and that, because we have hearts of stone, he will change them and bring them into conformity with his will so that we will strive only to bring ourselves into subjection to him. That then is what we must do when we realize what the law of God is.

And then we must come to that other refuge, which is the forgiveness of our sins. Although we are imperfect, may it please our gracious God to accept us in the name of our Lord Jesus Christ, and may we, by his goodness, be deemed righteous and innocent before him, in spite of the fact that we are not. But that is precisely the reason Jesus Christ has washed us of all our uncleanness and redeemed us by his suffering and death. That is also what is proclaimed to us every day, for when we preach, we do not just say, 'That is what God commands.' We then add that Jesus Christ is given by God his Father and that we share in his Holy Spirit so that we may be justified by his grace. That then is how the Holy Spirit is given to us through the Lord Jesus Christ and how that promise of grace, which we must also accept by faith, is made to us every day in the name of God.

Moreover, we hear the proclamation of the forgiveness of sins. We are told God is always ready to have pity on us provided we come to him in faith and repentance and ask him to receive us in mercy through the suffering and death of our Lord Jesus Christ, and ask him to accept us now as his children despite the fact we previously waged war against him. Those things, I tell you, we must do. In that way, we see how the law of God was alive for the children of Israel. That is to say, not only did they hear the commandments God gave them through Moses, but they also leaned on God's promises and came straight to Jesus as if they had been led there by the figures and ceremonies of the law. That, I say, is how the law will give life to men. That is also why Paul says, 'Jesus Christ is its soul' (*2 Cor.* 3:17). If he is separated from the law, only eternal death will remain because the law by itself is like a body without the soul. That is how the law is living instruction when it is rightly received.

Now how does that apply to the gospel today? Do we not have a life that is more certain than those people could ever find in the law? True, those who were under the law were living in that hope of salvation which was promised through the Lord Jesus Christ. But today we have a much fuller proclamation. That is why Paul says in the passage we cited, 'Jesus Christ sends his power to save all believers, when the gospel is preached' (*Rom.* 1:16). That, then, is a witness which should indeed incite us to receive the gospel with all fear and reverence and submit ourselves completely to its teaching, for that is the only path God sets before us to come to him. That is, when the gospel is proclaimed to us and we receive it, he will, although we were previously dead, quicken us and regenerate us so that we will live unto him forever. Since it is written that 'Moses brought the living word', how are we to apply what has been brought to us in the name of our Lord Jesus Christ?

We have the Son of God, who is life eternal. He speaks to us even though he is not here with us in person and does not show himself to the world as long as he ordains men as his ministers and agents to proclaim his word. And since we are assured that he himself wishes to teach us in this manner, accept us as his children, and have us in his care, what can we say? And yet we see many who use their ignorance as a defence. But ignorance is deceitful, especially when we do not wish to listen to God. It is true that those who have no knowledge, instruction, or doctrine do not escape condemnation, for God knows why he withholds those things from them. But when God favours us with the preaching of the word, by which he makes his will known, we are guilty of a much greater sin if we refuse to hear it. In addition, the penalty for our refusal will necessarily be doubled. Let us be very careful then not to reject this God-given blessing for fear of being totally deprived of it in the end.

And especially must we note what Stephen tells us in this passage about the importance of not observing human behaviour to find a reason to turn from God. For although we understand that men are very remiss in following God, we must always follow our calling and try not to find fault, as many do. Indeed, when they resist and begin to say, 'I will come later', let us be careful to avoid falling into that trap. That is the way we lead one another to hell. Therefore, when God calls us, let us set out without delay and without making excuses for one another. And let us not look to our fathers, as many do, saying, 'We want to live as our ancestors did.' Let us not be hindered by these meaningless trifles. For if our fathers were unbelieving, they deserved to be condemned. But let us acknowledge that God is our sovereign Father and that it is to him that we must give all obedience. That, I say, is how we must avoid finding an occasion to turn from God because of the influence of men, but we must always keep our eyes fixed on God and his truth so that we can receive the teaching of his gospel which he communicates to us through the grace of our Lord Jesus Christ.

And then let us not doubt that he will give us the strength to overcome all the temptations Satan puts before us, and in this way we will realize that it is not in vain that we follow the path he shows us.

Following this holy teaching, let us bow before the face of our gracious God in acknowledgment of our sins, praying that he will be pleased to instruct us in his will so that, knowing how we must live, we will be so completely cleansed of the evil affections of our flesh that we will be completely dedicated to his service, and may he receive our service as acceptable in the name of and through our Lord Jesus Christ, and may he accept us as his children so that we will be bold to call upon him as our Father. Now let us all say, Almighty God, heavenly Father . . .

37

GOD'S WORD FREES FROM IDOLATRY

SUNDAY, 16 NOVEMBER 1550

[Moses] received the lively oracles to give unto us: ³⁹ To whom our fathers would not obey, but thrust him from them, and in their hearts turned back again into Egypt, ⁴⁰ Saying unto Aaron, Make us gods to go before us: for as for this Moses, which brought us out of the land of Egypt, we wot not what is become of him. ⁴¹ And they made a calf in those days, and offered sacrifice unto the idol, and rejoiced in the works of their own hands. ⁴² Then God turned, and gave them up to worship the host of heaven; as it is written in the book of the prophets, O ye house of Israel, have ye offered to me slain beasts and sacrifices by the space of forty years in the wilderness? (Acts 7:38–42)

The story Stephen recounts here is worthy of our frequent attention. He points out to the Jews the evil and rebellion their fathers exhibited against God. But we too see it as a mirror of our nature. The fact is that after our Lord draws us to himself and favours us with the proclamation of his will, he can sustain us only if we are not unduly inclined to evil and given over to it. But, even if we are not, we are immediately corrupted by idolatries and superstitions. Even though we know how to serve God well, our minds turn straightway from truth to falsehood. That is why I said we must pay close attention to this story. In it we contemplate a vice common to us all. And it is not limited to us and our time. From the time man separated himself from God by his sin, this accursed seed has always been in the human race and will be until the end of the world.

Let us look now at what Stephen says in summary: 'Our fathers', he says, 'would not receive the living word but in their hearts returned to Egypt.' Here Stephen condemns two evils. One is that the Jews, after God's law was given to them, did not adhere to it. It is not that they did not yet have an adequate declaration of it, for our Lord had already manifested himself sufficiently to them through Moses in anticipation of its solemn appearance when Moses would bring it written on two stones. Now the Jews demonstrate their very wicked ingratitude, because after God redeemed them and showed them the concern he had for their salvation, they still refuse to hear.

Their second evil is that after being oppressed by such cruel servitude in Egypt, they prefer to be like those tyrants who treated them cruelly more than to being like the one who was appointed their redeemer. And there is this additional circumstance. Moses had not been gone from them for a long time. What is more, they knew his being on the mountain was for their advantage and welfare. It is not as if he is unconcerned for their salvation, but he is there to be instructed by God so that he will not bring them human teaching or something he has invented, but only so he can make known to them in all purity what God revealed to him.

There is yet another evil pertaining to the Jews in connection with Moses' absence from them. They kept saying they did not know what had happened to him. Now even if we have reason to find fault with the Jews in what is recounted here, the Holy Spirit, as I have pointed out, wanted to show us what kind of people we are, as our experience does in fact show us only too well. In point of fact, although God calls us to himself, we can draw near to him only after coming to him. There is such inconstancy within us that a trifle distracts us from him. It is true that even if we never hear a single word preached and even if God does not grant us the grace of having his word, we will be inexcusable in our idolatries. The pagans did not have prophets to teach them, yet God condemns them in their ignorance. When all is said and done, men's ignorance is never without pride, and they are so presumptuous that they prefer to turn from the living God to idols rather than to have a pure and holy religion. But when God draws near to teach us and says, 'You do not have to be like pitiable blind people, not knowing the way you must go. But I am showing you the path you have to follow. Once you are set upon it, do not stray from it in any way.' So when our Lord shows us that kind of grace, do we not deserve a more grievous condemnation if we reject that blessing from him? There is no doubt a deep-seated evil within us if we behave that way. Let us then compare ourselves with the Jews. According to what is recounted here, they received the living word but refused to believe it. Let us, on the other hand, in all humility receive that word which is proclaimed to us today, knowing that it is God's trustworthy and infallible truth and that through it we have salvation and life and that the moment his truth is taken from us we can only be in a state of death.

We hear the disciples' response to Jesus when he says, 'Do you want to go away also?' because many had abandoned him. But they say, 'Where would we go, Lord? For we know that you have the words of life' (*John* 6:67–68). So do we want to be confident in what we are taught? Then, let us lay hold to the pure teaching of the gospel. If we are tempted to deviate from the truth in any way, we will end up only in perdition and destruction if we pursue our foolish notions. Why is that? As soon as we are separated from Jesus Christ, our salvation is snatched from us. We are then lost and condemned. So, let us be sure to yield in obedience to our God after he once reveals his word to us. And even as we know that all people on earth, content with their personal insights and fantasies, can only come to ruin, we also know the devil will provide us with many plausible reasons not to obey that we like. But our hearts must incline to him and not be focused elsewhere.

Now the third point we touched upon is that the Jews alleged they did not know what had happened to Moses, which shows us that the people soon forgot God's grace. As I have said, Moses had been appointed for their redemption and deliverance. They experienced God's wondrous power in the many signs performed in Egypt. Later, when they passed through the Red Sea and were nourished in the desert, they experienced several mighty works. They had innumerable miracles. And no sooner do they turn around than they say they do not know what happened to Moses, while knowing quite well that God withdrew him to the mountain for their good. That is the way we are. The purpose of the good things God does for us is to make our eyes pop out, as the saying goes. Yet, either we do not think about them any more or we immediately forget them. That is a lesson we are to learn from this story, in which we see that the Jews are condemned so that we will not fall into the same temptation and share their fate. Rather let us beseech God to be pleased to lead and guide us by his hand so we will take advantage of his blessings, and may he imprint them so firmly in our memory that we will never say we do not know what it is happening.

But the principal point of this story is what Stephen adds, citing from the thirty-second chapter of Exodus, where the people say to Aaron, 'Make for us gods who will go before us' (*Exod.* 32:1). Thereupon they forged a calf and worshipped the idol, Stephen says. This comment that the people demand gods to guide them is very important inasmuch as it is the source of all the superstitions which have ever existed and will exist until the end of the world.

If you want to know the original source of all idolatry, here it is. People want to have around them the presence of a god who suits the fancies of their flesh. God knows our weaknesses and descends to our level. He knows that we cannot reach his majestic height, and for that reason he makes himself small, so to speak, so that we can contemplate him in our need. But even though God descends so low to our level in his desire to draw us to heaven, he does not transform himself and say that he is flesh, as we are. But he is like one who reaches down very low to raise us above the heavens.

Those then are the means God has ordained from all time to draw men to himself. He sees our inability clearly. For that reason, he does not speak from his glorious majesty. He comes to us. Why? It is not to entertain us down here; it is not to say that he no longer resembles himself; but it is so that when he comes down, he may cause us to rise up. For example, when we hear sacrifices and the other ceremonies spoken of, what are they but ways God has provided for men's weakness, seeing that their senses are base and that their nature is not angelic enough to lift them above the clouds? That then is why he helps their weakness. That also is why the tabernacle was built, as I shall explain more fully later. And without recourse to the examples in the law, let us look just at the way our Lord instructs us today. We have the preaching of the gospel. We have the ceremonies of coming together, of lifting our hands to heaven when calling upon him, and other signs that indicate our reverence for him.

Moreover, when he wants to assure us of the forgiveness of our sins, we have the water of baptism, with which he shows us visibly how we are washed by the blood of our Saviour Jesus Christ, how he causes us to die to ourselves and to the world in order to be raised again, so to speak, by the grace of the Holy Spirit. Do we not see, then, in baptism how our Lord descends to us because of our lack of knowledge? For we cannot understand these spiritual matters because they are too high for us and surpass our capacity. So that is how far our Lord is willing to go to accommodate our ignorance.

The same can be said of the holy Supper. In and of itself, this would be a very difficult matter to understand: how we are fed on the body and blood of our Lord Jesus Christ. In the Supper, we see the bread and the wine. From personal experience we understand how bread sustains us, and also wine. Jesus, then, takes this figure and shows us he has the power to nourish our souls. We see in that, as I said, how our Lord lowers himself because of our frailty. But does that mean we are obliged to remain here below and focus on what we see with our eyes? Not at all! For it is on this very subject that the world began to pervert the signs God had established for us. In fact, we see what happened to them in the Papacy, how they worship a piece of bread as God and think he is enclosed within it. God's intention is the very opposite. His intention in everything he does is to draw us to heaven.

Let us learn then that God, after coming down to us, wants to draw us to himself but does not want us to call upon him according to our fantasies. But what happens? It turns out that when men want to lay hold of some presence of God, they always forge a presence convenient to their nature. And that is what we see here in the Jews' comment to Aaron: 'Make gods for us who will go before us, that is, gods we can see and touch with our hands and have present with us.' Has it been only the Jews who have made that kind of demand? As I have said, idolatry is a damnable vice which has reigned for all time in the world. In fact, its root grows so deep within us that there is no one who does not have an idolatry forge within himself, because it is inside ourselves that we are nourished and so engulfed by it that we will remain locked there forever unless God removes us forcibly.

In addition, we must be aware that on this point men's failure is twofold. First, they want to have a crude way of worshipping

God, a way that pleases them. And then, in addition to that, they are bold to give themselves leeway to manufacture anything they like. But in fact it belongs to God alone to make himself known to us. Men must not presume to produce whatever they fancy. As soon as men give themselves the license to say, 'We must have such and such an image to represent God', the devil straightway takes possession of them and everything they do and fills their heads with so much nonsense that there is no end or restraint to their inventions, as is evident in the many trifling playthings in the Papacy. Yet there is no foolish trifle that does not convey some great mystery. A candle represents the Holy Spirit, salt represents God's wisdom, and spittle, oil, and other items in endless array all add their spice to the sauce, so to speak. Into the mix they add play-acting and mimes, and yet God is everywhere. Indeed, men grossly abuse God's name whenever they invent what pleases them and then try to compare God, his power, and his majesty to their foolish inventions.

So let us remember that there are two vices which signal the perversity of the entire human race. It is that men, being of the flesh, want to make God like themselves. We look at things from an earthly perspective. Our natural disposition is worldly. We want to have some conformity with God now, not so that we are transformed into his image as we should be, but we prefer to fashion him in our image. Now because we have that vice rooted in our nature, we ought to pay even closer attention to this passage, which says, 'Make for us gods who will go before us.' We must shield ourselves from those foolish inventions. That is why it is written, 'Guard against making for yourselves any image of things in heaven above or on earth below' (*Exod.* 20:4). That is not only stated in Exodus, but also even more strongly in the fourth chapter of Deuteronomy: 'Remember that when God appeared to you on Mount Horeb, he did not appear to you in human form or in another image, but you heard only his voice. Be content then with that and be careful not to give full rein to your foolish imaginations. For Satan will turn you from the straight path the moment you forge some new image and say, "Look upon that which is good for representing God for us'" (*Deut.* 4:15–19). Likewise, let us not be brash, thinking we appease God with what we deem to be good, for as soon as we do that, we rebel against him.

We have all experienced sickness, have we not? Let us think about the remedies we receive. One remedy for our spiritual sickness is that we remain steadfast in the teaching we receive once he has made himself known to us. Do we wish to remain steadfast in the truth? Let us not turn from it when we please and wander here and there. The lesson we are to learn here is that we must not attempt or invent anything we dream up, but to listen to what God says and tells us about himself, because everything men conceive or imagine will be just so many idols that they themselves manufacture. The moment we release the reins of the foolish fantasies we project here and there about God, we have an idol. Therefore, we must maintain the simplicity of God's word so that we will seek to know nothing but what God has revealed to us, for it is his initiative alone to manifest himself to us, as I have said. If we fail to follow his word in its simplicity, we will fall from one abyss into another. Whenever we choose to pursue our vain speculations about God – for human nature will always be a pit of hell – we will be cast out and lost the moment we enter our own understanding and remain bogged down in it. So we must guard against remaining ensnared in our evil affections. So let us renounce them completely and apply all our effort to bringing ourselves into conformity with God's will, which he declares to us in his word. That is our first remedy.

The second is this. After hearing it is God we must follow, we must simply adhere to what he makes known to us lest we be so wretched as to reject the means he offers us to come to him. Men have always had the kind of pride and arrogance that keeps them from being satisfied with just the voice and word of God. Yet his word gives a true picture of him, and it is there that we have to contemplate him. And that accords with what we have already cited from the fourth chapter of Deuteronomy: 'You heard a voice but did not see a form' (*Deut.* 4:15). Do we really want to see God? Then let us receive his word! 'Yes', someone will say. 'We have surely heard the voice, but God gives us nothing whereby we can contemplate him.' We cannot in our fleshly nature see him, but we see him easily with the eyes of our faith. That must suffice us for being conformed to his glory. It is as Paul says in the third chapter of 2 Corinthians when speaking of the gospel, 'It is the light which must enlighten our entire life and in it, seeing God face to face, we are transformed into that light and continue to grow in it until we come to maturity' (cf. *2 Cor.* 3:18).

But for all that, as I have already mentioned, our Lord is not content with giving us his word, knowing as he does the extent of our weakness. He adds other aids, as the sacraments, for example. But let us guard against abusing these means. So what are we to do? As for baptism, we have water, which is sprinkled on the head or face of a child. Let us be aware, as I have already said, that it is our Lord Jesus Christ who calls us to himself so we can place the full confidence of our salvation in his suffering and death, knowing that until he washes us, we are like poor lepers covered with stench and contagion before our God. Then let us realize that from our mother's womb we bear every curse so that we must be reforged, so to speak, and our nature and affections changed. We must become new creations. And where does all that come from? From Jesus Christ himself, for we must be transferred into his death in order to receive life in this world. That then is how baptism is to lead us on high to heaven and not lull us to sleep here below.

Coming to the Lord's Supper, we have only bread and wine. But do we linger over these corruptible elements? Indeed not. They must lead us to Jesus Christ. We do not make an idol of them here below and worship him in the bread and wine, but we seek him on high in the eternal glory of God his Father, where he lives. We must give the greater attention to the teaching we are examining, for we are inclined to do the opposite, as I have said. Man must conquer his natural inclinations if he wishes to be steadfast in God's pure truth. Why so? There is a reason that we are called 'liars'. It is as difficult for a man to remain steadfast in God's pure truth as it is to make a river flow upstream. There is no hope that we could make that happen, but for God it is possible, as we observe him working by his power in all his faithful. But if we had to remain steadfast in his truth by our own power, we absolutely could not because we are so weak. Such do we see clearly if we but observe how the world has trundled along since its creation and if we observe how superstitions dominate everywhere even today. How few are they who follow the path that I have pointed out!

But the fact remains that if we practise the two things that I have mentioned here briefly, we will be delivered from all of Satan's attacks in spite of the nets he stretches out against us to lead us in the wrong direction. There you find the papists. They relentlessly forge gods in endless number. What about that? If we look closely at what influences them to do that, it is because they have abandoned that word from God and do not realize it is the living image by which our Lord reveals and declares himself to us. Therefore, the papists, being diverted from God's word, are soon off in search of statues of Saints, as if God had not adequately instructed us in his word. And then they create their idols in order to have some image to represent God for them. Then they go looking for Jesus Christ in a piece of bread, which is idolatry so damnable we cannot think about it without horror. And why does that happen? Because, as I said, they have abandoned God's word to follow their lies.

But this will be better understood by what follows in the text: 'They worshipped their idols after having a calf made for themselves.' And how did the Jews intend to worship that idol? As a calf in the manner of the Egyptians, for the great god of Egypt was a bull. One might ask whether the Jews expected to worship that image which they had made. It is certain they did not. We understand from the account of the story of Moses that they affirm that they worship the God of Israel, the God who delivered them from Egyptian bondage. Aaron proclaims the solemn feast. He says, 'Come to the sacrifice' (*Exod.* 32:5). Then he says to all the people, 'These are the gods who brought you out of the land of Egypt' (*Exod.* 32:4). And the people consent to that. So when we have taken everything into consideration, we will find that the Jews intended to worship the God of Israel who had formed them. Nevertheless, Stephen says, 'They worshipped their idols.' So it seems that in saying that he wrongs them. Now we must note it is not enough for men to want to worship God. If they want to worship God in an unusual way, in a way not in keeping with his will, they go against what they have promised. It is as if I promise to obey a prince while in complicity with his enemy. What do you say to that? Such is the case when men say to God they desire to worship him but come to him and make idols, create new services like the ones they create every day according to their fantasy. Now our Lord decries all that. That is a point we need to take seriously. There have been pagans from all time and they have never thought that God was wood, stone, gold, or silver, and it is clear from their books that if you asked them, 'Come now, do you think that your idols are God?' 'No', they would say. 'But that is what he looks like.' Yet the prophets cry out against them, saying that they have whored around with wood and stone, gold and silver. Why so? Because they placed in their idols the full confidence of their salvation, and when they wanted to offer prayers to God, they had to go to them.

We see that more clearly among the papists. They think they have the most absolute defence in the world. So it seems to them! They will say they are not so foolish as to believe a piece of wood is God. They will say he is in heaven, but that still does not excuse them. Let us consider now what they do. When they want to worship God, where do they turn their attention? To that idol! That is how they transfer God's majesty to an inanimate object. Afterwards, when they want to pray to God, where do they go? To that very idol, just as if God had attached his ears to it, just as if his hand and his might were there. In short, we understand that those earlier people who wanted to make images of God never thought there was any power or divinity unless they saw some image of wood or stone, gold or silver. And we see that even more clearly among the papists. I am not talking about the even more lame-brained practices among them, for they will just as soon say their 'Our Father' before an image of St Barbara as before the image they make to represent God. From our perspective, supposing they used idols only to give form to God, how can they be so presumptuous as to think they can represent him with a corruptible object? What do God and a piece of wood have in common? Scripture says, 'What honour do you show me by trying to represent me by a tangible object which has no reason or intelligence?' (Cf. *Isa.* 40:18; 42:8) God is stripped of his majesty when we deal with him that way and do all we can to snatch his honour from him. If we make some image to represent him and whenever men take the license to fashion him according to their pleasure, that is how, I say, he is stripped of his majesty because his honour is transferred to an idol and a lifeless object. And then, since God is depicted by it in men's minds, they imagine at the same time that they will feel his strength in it. Thus God is destitute of everything. That is what has happened to him from all time, and that is how we see him even better today in the Papacy than he has ever been seen among the pagans.

So let us pay close attention to the passage which says that 'the Jews worshipped their idol', notwithstanding the fact that they declared they wanted to worship the God of Israel and not pay homage to a calf, but to sacrifice to God. It is said that God replies that it is not to him that they are making sacrifice, but the devil. As soon as we move away from the truth, it is meaningless for us to say, 'We want to serve God. Our intention is good.' God condemns us, and all that will serve no purpose for justifying us. Why not? Because he wants to be served according as he commands and not according as we think good.

We now know that idolatry occurs when men have been bold and diabolically presumptuous enough to create an image to their liking and have a tangible God suitable to their senses, because they are given over to base and corruptible things. They want God to resemble themselves. That is the kind of subtle, crafty trick used by Satan to poison the poor world. We have looked at the remedies that will work against that evil. In the first place, men do not presume to imagine anything about God except what he shows us in his word and is pleased to reveal to us. So let us be content with his pure teaching and add nothing to it.

In the second place, if God descends to us, it is not to confine us to this world, as I have said, or to give us some image to our liking, but to lift us up so that we can contemplate him by faith at a higher level. Consequently, all these revelations which God gives us are intended to be, of necessity, spiritual in nature. So then, let us follow as he leads us in the knowledge of his truth through the preaching of his gospel.

In addition, let us note that the moment we fall ever so short of the light that God shows us when he enlightens us by his word, we will be so blind that we will see nothing, not even the most evident things

– which is what happened among the papists. They will indeed say, 'I want to worship God.' They will stick the name of God on idols, but idols they will be, no matter what they call them. And God decries all that. Let us look to our own house when God speaks and calls us to give ourselves to him as his subjects. That is where we see his living image. And then, since we have his sacraments, we also have true images of God, which we must not flout inasmuch as God has established them for our salvation and to strengthen us in our weakness.

Now Stephen adds that 'the Jews rejoiced in the work of their hands.' For that reason, God turned aside from them and gave them over to the worship of the host of heaven. He says that to show how the Jews rejoiced in their idolatries, just as we see that men are pleased with their follies and inanities. Why is it that we do not take pleasure in what God has established for us? Because there is no conformity with our nature and our inventions always seem more beautiful than anything else, like a monkey which finds no face as beautiful as its own. That is the way it is with men when they have created something or other. They are so pleased with it that they think they are already in paradise. That much you see in the Papacy when you enter a church and see more ostentation and fanfare than anything else. You hear organs on one side, singing on the other, and censers, torches, lamps, and many other trappings. In short, there is enough there to occupy every eye, ear, nose, and who knows what else. So when you are in a papist church, you will think you are in a terrestrial paradise. Why so? Because all those things please men. And still we encounter the pride of those papists who are enraged and inflamed against God and his word, so to speak, and if you talk to them about God's teaching, they resort only to crying murder and mayhem.

That is also why the prophets, when speaking of idolaters, say they are like whorehouse prostitutes who are more brazen than harlots when it comes to maintaining their idols and grotesque images. That is how the devil, once he has won men's minds, stirs them into such a frenzy that they are worse than rabid and do their worst to spew their venom and their poison against God and his faithful.

We must all the more take great care to avoid engaging in that kind of abuse, for the things that please our eyes must be suspect, and rightly so. We must cling only to what God shows us in his word without adding anything of our own to it. The moment something in it pleases us, we are to reject it as suspect. Why? Because our judgment is corrupt and can of itself invent nothing which is not damnable and abominable before God. Therefore, everything we see which seems to us to be fine and good must be looked upon with grave doubt. That is how man protects himself from himself, for never will we find such accomplished deceivers or creatures more pernicious than ourselves.

It is noteworthy that the text says 'the work of their hands', because men are so filled with pride that they want God to approve what they do. We understand that the contrary is true. God admonishes us in many passages that he wants us to be in such conformity with his will that we will not violate his commands in any way. Moreover, we are not to think of him as being of the flesh, as we are, but we must contemplate him by faith and in spirit. So there are two things we must note. First, we must not take pleasure in what we consider beautiful, for there is a vast difference between God and us as natural beings. Second, the work of our hands is a wicked thing, and everything we can produce and offer is but stench and abomination before God. Why? Because God has left us his teaching in such a state of completeness that he does not want men to add anything to it.

So that we can have greater certainty about these things, Stephen adds, 'God turned aside from them and gave them over to the worship of the host of heaven', which, however, we cannot now discuss at length, but it will be reserved for another time. But it is as if Stephen were saying, 'Since the Jews rejected the grace God had bestowed upon them and proven themselves unworthy of it by turning away from him in favour of their foolish inventions, he also turned aside from them and gave them over to the worship of their idols. For that reason, they will fall into such confusion that one idolatry will follow another until they reach the bottom of the abyss.'

> Following this holy teaching, let us bow before the face of our gracious God in acknowledgment of our sins, praying that he will be pleased so to move us by them that we will be driven to align ourselves with his word, follow it as a rule for our entire lives, and remain steadfast in it because he has revealed it by the hand of Moses and has confirmed it by his prophets and finally by our Lord Jesus Christ his Son. And may it please him to sustain us in our infirmities until he fully delivers us from them. Now let us all say, Almighty God, heavenly Father . . .

38

The Penalty for Idolatry

Sunday, 23 November 1550

Then God turned, and gave them up to worship the host of heaven; as it is written in the book of the prophets, O ye house of Israel, have ye offered to me slain beasts and sacrifices by the space of forty years in the wilderness? [43] *Yea, ye took up the tabernacle of Moloch, and the star of your god Remphan, figures which ye made to worship them: and I will carry you away beyond Babylon* (Acts 7:42–43).

We pointed out previously the extent to which men are naturally inclined to idolatry, and we summed up by saying that we carry within ourselves its root. The reason is that, because we are carnal, we think God has to be like us and we would like to change him to suit our fancy. That is why men have from all time made idols and worshipped them, holding creatures in greater reverence than the Creator. We also mentioned men's foolish impudence in being pleased with what they have created. And even though God despises everything they make, they do not cease to present it to him in the hope that he will accept it as good.

Now all that is clear in this text which Luke recounts concerning Moses. In the first place, the children of Israel want to have a God who reveals himself to them. We see in that the point, already made, that we cannot lift our minds on high to contemplate

God in accordance with his commands. But following our human instinct, we want to have some visible image of him. That is how we forge a god according to the flesh.

On the other hand, the text says that those who forged golden calves rejoiced in the work of their hands. That also confirms what I have said, namely that we do not pay much attention to God's condemnation of the superstitions which we invent, but we value them so highly that we think what God has ordained is less good and less well made. Since that wicked inclination and vice are deeply rooted within us, we ought to be even more on guard. So let us not think that all the excuses and plausible pretexts we can conjure up have any value, for whatever we offer up is only abomination before God. Let us be satisfied then with our God-given simplicity and not go astray in pursuit of our wild fancies and all human inventions, for they will all come to naught.

It follows that since men have begun to go astray, they will go from bad to worse, and they will continue to increase their idolatries and abominations once they fall away from God's truth. And that is what Stephen says: 'God gave the children of Israel up to be a reprobate people and gave them over to worshipping the stars of heaven.' It is as if he were saying, 'God, seeing that he could not keep the people obedient to himself, loosed their bridle and let them give themselves over to every evil.'

So we have two matters to consider in this passage. The first, which I have just dealt with, has to do with the fact that men have not adhered to the pure teaching of God and have consequently had to enter a labyrinth of every confusion and have had to compound evil with evil until they reach the depths of every iniquity. In addition, we must note that that proceeds from God's righteous judgment. That is because, after calling us to himself, he sees our rebellion. He has to throw us into a state of confusion and reprobation so that the devil will be completely free to drag us from one predicament to another and so that we will have no greater sense of reason and judgment than dumb animals.

Now as for the first point, we need to be warned to remain obedient to our God because of the evil which can ensue if we do otherwise. Once we begin to yield to our foolish imaginations, there will be no end and no limit to them. That is why our Lord so expressly forbade deviating from the purity of his Scripture, either to the left or to the right (*Deut.* 5:32). We have also shown that God tells us to hold fast to what he has established. And then he adds that 'we are not to turn from it in any way soever.' For it follows, as I said, that we always go from bad to worse, and until we reach the pit of total confusion and of everything described here, we have the rather common experience observed in what happened in the Papacy. How did these diabolical abominations increase to the extent we see them there? Let us not imagine that with one stroke the world abandoned the teaching of the gospel. It happened over a period of time, and at the outset people entertained a few superstitions which did not appear to contradict God's word. That did not seem bad, and they thought God would find that very acceptable. Then one thing and another had to be added. Our God cannot, as I have said, tolerate the scorn and contempt men heap upon him by not being satisfied with what he has established. But they come and add from their own fantasy what they think is appropriate for serving and honouring him. And that is how the devil has from all time exploited men's inventions and superstitions when they are bold to create something or other in their heads.

Now we must return to what I have mentioned. God is angry with men when they are unwilling to be satisfied with what he tells them. He leaves them alone and turns the reins over to Satan to blind them. That is how men by God's just vengeance fall into the horrible pit of confusion we see in the world today. We see it not only in the Papacy. If we read the history of all times past, we will find that vice to be commonplace. From the beginning, instances of idolatry have not been as prevalent as today. Yet, men did not have that tendency to forge idols without God's making himself known to them in some way. All the trouble started when they were unable to adhere to his pure teaching and insisted on inventing one thing and another in their heads. So they have always had their own creations. And God allowed it. And in the end they would be in such disarray that only confusion would reign. In just that way God punished the pagans of those days because of their rashness, which resulted from their failure to adhere to his word. Consequently, those who rejected the gospel had to fall into such a pit and become blind, as is the case now. And it was especially right that that kind of punishment took place. Men, because of their ingratitude, deserved to fall into greater confusion than they are in today.

We have Jesus Christ, the path of salvation, indeed salvation itself. The teaching of the gospel is a burning lamp by which the Holy Spirit shines his light on us throughout the world. But since men have been so unfortunate as to close their eyes to that light and turn consciously from the true path of salvation, was God not obliged to reach out his hand and punish them with all rigour? So if today we see grossly excessive practices in the Papacy, let us realize that the world's lack of gratitude had to be punished that way. And then the papists will use this as a shield to defend themselves against God when they are warned that they will be punished for the idolatries and abominations they are guilty of. 'Look', they will ask. 'Did our Lord not promise to help his church?' (*Matt.* 28:20) Now let them be careful when they say that. They are so far from being God's church that they even provoke it to wrath with everything they do.

Consequently, we must examine ourselves and remember that the vice criticized here is commonplace among men. And these things are written for our teaching and instruction so that if we want God to grant us the grace of walking uprightly, we will not be like animals gone astray. We must not veer from his pure truth. In proportion as he reveals himself to us, we must also acknowledge his will according as he declares it and adhere to it firmly without deviating from it ever so slightly. For if we happen to become separated from him, we will of necessity fall into a pit much more horrible than the one he has already graciously pulled us from. Therefore, let us be diligent to hold to the simplicity of the gospel if we do not want God to blind us to the extent that, like dead men, we will no longer be able to stay on course. That is the blindness we see in the papists, and that should serve to goad us on toward humility so that we will each one come into line with God and his teaching.

Let us also learn to glorify God when he punishes men in this way. Although he ought to do us ill, we must, when we see poor souls going to hell that way, try to draw them back to the path of salvation. Yet, let us not attribute that judgment to God's cruelty and blame him as if his punishments were excessive. Let us acknowledge, rather, that men are rightly blinded in that way, rebuked and thoroughly confounded.

In addition, as for Luke's speaking the way he does here, we must note that he does not do so to say that God turns his back on us. He rightly treats us that way if we do not think he is favouring us when he grants us everything we desire. Now our Lord shows us his favour and his kindness when he sustains us in our present life and provides us with everything we need. If we have enough food, if we have clothing, if he keeps us in health, if we have peace, our Lord is showing his favour toward us. That is how God shows us his face.

On the other hand, when we experience poverty or famine, when plagues and other diseases come upon us, when we endure strife and controversy, it looks like God has turned his back on us. Now, as I have said, we are deeply pained if some adversity befalls us, but we do not realize that the main thing is that God leads us and makes us aware of his help and his presence in our hearts. In the meantime, he guides us in such a way that we are certain he is with us. So the main thing we are to desire is that God lead us in such a way that we will walk in obedience to him. That is how God makes his face shine upon us, and that is why it is written in Psalm 4, 'Lord, make your face to shine upon us' (*Psa.* 4:6). That will mean more to us than an abundance of grain and wine. Now David wanted to express in that passage the fact that men seek God only for their stomachs' sake and for the conveniences of the present life and clearly demonstrate that 'they have no affection for you, Lord. But it means much more to me that I know you have given me some indication of your fatherly love. That brings me much greater contentment than possessing all that men can desire, for they always seek what is natural to man.'

Moreover, let us take note that God presents his face to us in the gospel, as Paul says in 2 Corinthians 3: the gospel is a mirror in which God makes himself known to us so that our eyes may be fixed on him and remain fixed on him so that we will think upon him to such an extent that we will never turn away from him (*2 Cor.* 3:18). If we do that, it is certain he will never hide himself from us. He does not reveal himself with the intention of hiding himself later. He intends to give us that complete vision Paul speaks of in 1 Corinthians 13, where, after contemplating God by means of the gospel mirror, we will contemplate him in his glorious majesty (*1 Cor.* 13:12). Likewise today, we are changed into his image so that we will be perfectly like him. In that way, our Lord will never withdraw from us, but it is our duty to behold him with the eyes of faith and remain unyieldingly steadfast in him, as he has commanded. And how can we? After being instructed in the gospel and realizing it is God's truth, we will not stray aimlessly. Although the devil uses many clever tricks to induce us to stray, let us remain firm and steadfast in the faith we have received. So let us abandon our superstitions and take increasing advantage of God's teaching. Let us beseech him to grant us the grace of never being separated from him so that in the end we will be so steadfast that when the devil works all his wiles on us, we will remain firm and invincible against all his attacks as we hold fast to what God revealed once and for all when he showed himself to us in his word. So let us never be sidetracked. That is the teaching we are to gather from Stephen's comment that 'God turned away and showed his back to the children of Israel.'

And that is especially said about all those to whom our Lord made himself known once. If the unfortunate blind who have never had doctrine or preaching are without excuse for turning their backs on God's truth, what will happen to us once we have known the teaching of the gospel and God has graciously adopted us as his own? If afterward we happen to fall into our foolish imaginings and each of us pursues his vain thoughts, what will be our excuse? It is certain we will be convicted by our own deeds. Let us examine ourselves closely, and inasmuch as he has come near to us out of his infinite goodness and given us the teaching about our Lord Jesus Christ his Son, who is our true light, let us make our effort to walk in the way while it is still day (*Rom.* 13:12–14) for fear that the night will take us by surprise and plunge us into a darkness more terrible than the Papacy's.

When Stephen says a moment later that 'God gave them up to serve the host of heaven', he follows the general teaching of holy Scripture, namely that God releases men into the devil's power when they turn from him. Now it is certain that that should frighten us and that we should experience a great fear upon hearing that God delivers us into Satan's tyranny and we are in servitude to him.

But we ought to prize even more highly this incomparable blessing when we learn that he wants us in his service and that we are not even compared to servants, for we are like his own children. Let us then determine to remain in his service and persevere in yielding to him in all humility. It is a great pity that men consider this so lightly. Everyone's hair should stand on end when hearing that the devil might become our master, and yet everyone yields to him willingly. The Lord wants us for his own and we refuse to hear him. That is how the devil takes possession of us. It is true that the devil will have no power over us unless God allows it, but he is indeed permitted to dominate us when we refuse to hear what God says to us and receive what he offers us. That is what Paul understands when God reveals to him 'the punishment that will befall those to whom the gospel has been preached but refuse to believe the truth and walk in the light that God gives them' (cf. *2 Thess.* 1:8–9; 2:11–12). God will be obliged to make them serve the creature and fall into an abyss of error and confusion following their rejection of such a blessing.

And we see what happened in the Papacy. Even though God had blessed the world by making his gospel known everywhere, because men refused to honour him as he deserves, the devil gained possession of his kingdom as we see his domination in the person of the Antichrist, who sits in God's sanctuary (cf. *Matt.* 24:25; *Dan.* 11:31). Consequently, knowing that, men must become aware of the fact that of themselves they cannot remain steadfast in God's service. Still we must pray that since he has by grace extended his hand to us once to guide us till the end, we cannot take a single step without his guidance. And we must also pray that he will keep us steadfast. We are so incapable of long resisting the assaults made upon us in this present life that we cannot even wiggle a single finger unless he gives us the ability and strength. We must not, consequently, take anything for granted, and we must realize that it is God who initiates and brings everything to fulfilment.

When Stephen says, 'God gave them up to serve the host of heaven', we understand the evil nature and perversity of men when they turn into evil everything God himself has established. It is true that here on earth we have an adequate witness of God's glory, for he shows us his infinite goodness and power and wondrous wisdom so that we have plenty with which to magnify his name. But when we lift our eyes to the heavens, we have even more than we have on earth. In this way our Lord reveals himself and witnesses to his divinity so that we may learn from him and honour him as is his due. The truth is that this world is filled with enough wonders to lead us to God.

But we see that is not what men do. They abuse him with flagrant malice when they see the light of the sun and worship it. God's majesty is scorned and replaced by a thing ordained for our use. That, I tell you, is precisely how perverse we are. It is not that God did not instruct us in his will. We see how he spoke to the children of Israel. After forbidding them, in general terms, to adopt the superstitions of the pagans, he particularly admonished them to be on their guard against being deceived by the host of heaven. 'You see', he said, 'that all created things, however noble, are established to serve you' (*Deut.* 4:19; 17:3). As the sun was created to serve you by day, so were the moon and stars to give you light by night. Those then are the creatures God has lifted up above us in the heavens. Nonetheless, they are subjected to us and are for us to use. When we go and worship them, what dishonour we do to the majesty of God, who created them to serve us! In that, I say, we see the capacity our corrupt nature has to change into something evil all that God has established for our well-being.

Now what the children of Israel did there can certainly be found in us. It is a shortcoming much too common among men. The Jews were not the first to invent that. We see that Eastern populations worshipped the sun. And many others also made idols to their liking to worship. Therefore, what we need to learn from this passage is that we are of such a perverse and corrupted nature that we turn everything God ordained for our salvation into evil, as I have said, perverting God's well-established and perfect order. Such is the human condition. And that is evident not just in idolatry. Everywhere we look we see that bread and wine, which God has ordained for our nourishment, are instruments of gluttony and drunkenness. And we defile them by our evil when we thus misuse those good creations which God designated for our use. On the other hand, we see the place for justice, which is a holy and sacred thing we cannot do without. And yet in the name of justice people perpetrate the greatest acts of violence and extortion imaginable. In short, there is nothing so good, so holy and praiseworthy that human evil does not pervert it. And the very things they should use for their advantage they apply to their hurt. That is how we do things. As a result, we have good reason to hate ourselves and from now on to be well advised not to be foolish enough to give free rein to our lusts and wicked affections, but to pray that this bounteous God, after sharing his blessings with us, will grant us the grace to use well everything he has created. For it would be much better for us to die from hunger here with only bread and water received from the hand of God with thanksgiving, than to have all the goods and all the wealth of this world, indeed all of creation at our disposal, and to misuse them. For there is nothing which will not require vengeance against us. In fact, it is certain that those who abuse the things God has created will be like drunk and gluttonous men, whether in ostentation and things dissolute, or in idolatries and superstitions. God's creations will necessarily be like so many negative entities that require vengeance against the men who defile them.

Therefore, as I have already mentioned, whenever God bestows his blessings upon us, knowing that with each blessing, we need him to grant us the grace of his Holy Spirit so that we can utilize his benefits the way he commands. And as we do so, may the things he has provided, which are good in themselves, not be changed to evil by our disposition to evil. That is what this passage warns us against.

In addition, it is not without reason that Scripture designates that wondrous company of the stars as 'the host of heaven' (*Deut.* 4:19). We see an infinite number of them. (That is, they seem to us to be infinite, but astronomers could calculate their number.) And God wanted men to know that so we will have the opportunity to be moved and delighted with wonder, as David was when he considered the company of the heavens and marvelled (cf. *Psa.* 8). What company do we see there? We see how constant it was when once created. Yet there is no doubt that therein God showed us a living image so that we might contemplate him in it as we should and serve him. But we do not do that. We see that men are so wretched that they obscure every testimony of him no matter how clear or evident it is. In fact, they give everything a contrary meaning. Consequently, after God declares himself in the whole world, above and below, he must add his word to guide us to the knowledge of him. Otherwise, we would not be able to arrive at it with our own natural mind. God's word must be our eyeglasses so that we will not mistake one thing for another. But let us learn how to evaluate everything God shows us in the heavens and on earth so that we may apply it to our good. That is the way we are advised to look upon and contemplate God's glory, his might and his power in all his works on high and here below, and to think upon them in such way that we do not misuse the things he has created by giving them the honour and authority which are his alone. In fact, just as the Jews worshipped the sun and the moon, are not those today who worship a piece of wood and a stone and all other images – are they not, I ask you, guilty of a greater enormity than that of the Jews?

In other words, if we make a comparison with the Papacy's idolatries, we will find that theirs are more flagrant and more despicable than those of the Jews. But the fact is that, despite the papists' offering excuse after excuse after excuse, we will still find that their superstitions are more abominable before God than those of all the pagans who have ever lived. So let us learn to adhere to the pure simplicity of God's word so that we do not abuse and misuse the things he has created for our use and subjected to us.

And it is worth noting that Stephen said, 'You made these figures to worship them.' We need to pay close attention to that. If you do not use the word 'idol' in the presence of the papists, they think they have escaped detection. They too abominate the word 'idol'. Whenever they are called idolaters, they think they have been gravely wronged, for they call their statues 'images'. Now we see that the word 'idol' is not expressed here, but they have an honourable word, one by which they can offer a more plausible pretext for excusing their superstitions. And that word is 'figure'! Now that is the same word they apply to the sacraments because God has imprinted his mark upon us, which is given as a figure of what we see in the sacraments. But when men create figures in their head, God disavows and rejects them because they have nothing in common with the things he has instituted for us, which are like living images. That, I say, is the difference between the sacraments of God and the figures invented by men. And even if we concede to the papists that their statues are not idols, that is, even if we do not call them by that name and say they are images, as they do, the Holy Spirit still declares that 'when men make some figure to worship, it is only an abomination, as it was then' (cf. *Deut.* 27:15). It is the devil possessing them, and God rejects them as rebels and disobedient to his majesty. Now the papists cannot deny they worship figures. It is even one of the cardinal points of their brand of Christianity that they have to have figures to represent both God and the Saints. If that is the case, what becomes of the pronouncement God made by Stephen's mouth? So let us pay close attention to this message, for it is not a question of the word 'idol' because he condemns all figures in general. Last Sunday, we said concerning the sacraments that men can abuse them too, as they have done from the beginning. It was not God's intention to give us figures for the sacraments in order to keep us focused on the here and now or to worship those kinds of figures. Why then? To advise us by things visible that we must remember his power and that the sacraments are like wings to bear us on high.

If men use the sacraments as an occasion to remain focused on this world, they profane what God has ordained, which is what we see the papists doing. In the first place, as for baptism, they do not acknowledge that the truth and substance of baptism reside in our Lord Jesus Christ. They do not acknowledge that we are regenerated by the power of the Holy Spirit, but they think their salvation resides in the water, which is only the figure. That is how baptism has become an idol for them. In this way, they have corrupted baptism and perverted God's ordinance.

As for the holy Supper, they completely destroyed it when they elevated that idol, that devil in their mass. It is as if they eradicated God's pure ordinance in order to make way for their inventions. That, then, is how men have perverted the sacraments. For our part, because it has pleased God to grant us the grace of hearing the declaration of his will, we know the purpose for which he calls us. Therefore, let us so use the sacraments which he has ordained that we may always keep our eyes fixed on high and see what our Lord wants to show us by means of these figures. For as soon as we become attached to this world, we create idols, which God detests. So we must hark back to last Sunday's Scripture, not to consider the signs and the figures of this world, but to have our eyes lifted on high so we may know that the sacraments serve us only as a means by which we are to seek God. But let us not, out of our presumption and arrogance, place some figure before ourselves and say, 'God will find this good', for there is nothing that he despises more than our adding to his word that which pleases us. Yet Stephen quotes what Amos says in chapter 5 concerning the reproach God directs at his people, saying, 'You have not offered me sacrifices in the wilderness for forty years, but you have worshipped your gods, your figures, which you yourselves created' (*Amos* 5:25–27). The main reason Stephen quoted that was to show that the people were always inclined to idolatry.

Stephen's intention, as we stated at the outset, was to subdue the Jews' pride because they thought they were a holy people and possessed a special worth above others and should not to be afflicted in any way. He shows them that both they and their fathers never did anything but provoke God's anger against them. In general, he cites the book of the prophets because they all speak with one mind. Yet he draws from the prophet Amos, for it is there that our Lord utters a grievance against his people, but not against those who were alive at that time, when he says, 'You have rebelled against me from the beginning; I fed you in the wilderness so that your fathers might obey me, but they gave themselves over to idolatry. It is obvious, therefore, that you are a perverse and incorrigible generation, and that from the beginning your fathers rebelled against me and rose up against me. You have continued to increase their vices, so you are worse than they ever were' (cf. *Amos* 5:25–27). And that is how Stephen applies that passage even to those of his time, not that they had idols then, for we do not read that the Jews ever had idols after returning from Babylon unless Antiochus forced them to (cf. *Dan.* 11:31; *1 Macc.* 1:58). And yet Stephen reproaches them for that because they always had some superstition or other which they fabricated according to their liking in order to obscure the true worship of God. And that, as we have already said, proceeds from men's natural disposition not to be satisfied with God's pure decree, but, being rashly presumptuous, they always create something they fancy. And in proportion as they abandon themselves to that practice, they only heap evil upon evil until they reach the height of confusion. So, understanding that we are inclined to such vice, let us be on guard lest we fall again into that pit from which we have been delivered. And because there is no constancy within us and we cannot continue on our own, let us learn to walk in fear and humility in obedience to our God, and let us pray that he will always guide us and strengthen us by his Holy Spirit so that we will not fail.

Moreover, when we grasp the fact that there is within us the seed of pride and presumptuousness and when we think that every notion we have conceived will necessarily be considered good, let us not cling to what we have created ourselves. But let us realize that it is God's place to discern between good and evil. On the other hand, whenever our Lord is pleased to bestow upon us his blessings, let us pray that he will be pleased to let us enjoy them only as he commands. And especially since we have his word, may he never allow us to be drawn away from him, but yielding to his word, let us always fear him until we arrive at the perfection to which he calls us.

Following this holy teaching, let us bow before the face of our gracious God in acknowledgment of our sins, praying that he will be pleased to impress upon our hearts fear of him and obedience to him so that, as we walked in accordance with the rule he has given us in his law, we will seek only to follow it and bring ourselves into conformity with his holy will. And as long as we are in this world, may he guide us by his Holy Spirit in such a way that, after shedding this mortal body, we will be able to enjoy the blessing he has promised us in our Lord Jesus Christ. Now let us all say, Almighty God, heavenly Father . . .

39

DIVINELY DIRECTED WORSHIP

SUNDAY, 30 NOVEMBER 1550

Then God turned, and gave them up to worship the host of heaven; as it is written in the book of the prophets, O ye house of Israel, have ye offered to me slain beasts and sacrifices by the space of forty years in the wilderness? *43 Yea, ye took up the tabernacle of Moloch, and the star of your god Remphan, figures which ye made to worship them: and I will carry you away beyond Babylon. 44 Our fathers had the tabernacle of witness in the wilderness, as he had appointed, speaking unto Moses, that he should make it according to the fashion that he had seen* (Acts 7:42–44).

We saw earlier that since men once turn away from God's pure truth, their inventions become a bottomless cesspool and they proceed relentlessly from bad to worse. We have to be even more on guard once God has instructed us to remain in the pure simplicity of his word.

There remains one more point to be discussed concerning the passage cited here from the prophet Amos. Our Lord reproaches the Jews for not offering sacrifice to him for a period of forty years. And yet we know that they did. So how is that to be understood? It is because the Lord does not accept every act of worship men offer unless they offer it in purity, with no hint of superstition. For as soon as we mix our superstitions with what God has ordained for us, everything is corrupted. God gives his approval to none of it. In his view, we have done nothing in his honour. He says as much through his prophet Ezekiel: 'Go', he says, 'and serve the devil; you are no longer going to serve me. I wash my hands of you' (*Ezek.* 20:39). There the children of Israel were, quite content to worship God and do what the law commanded concerning the sacrifices and other matters, but they wanted to enjoy their inventions at the same time, the way we see it today among the papists. They do not say they want to reject God completely. What is more, they will cover all their abominations with this fine phrase: 'worship of God'. Now the papists still want to have their patrons and advocates. They will build a temple in the name of St Peter, another in the name of our Lady. They will raise an altar in honour of some Saint. They will have to make an image of some patron. Then they will have to make a pilgrimage and have some devotion or other. That is the way it was back then. Now our Lord, seeing the people place their companions ahead of him in that way, declares he much prefers the Jews to serve the devil fully. 'Do not', he says, 'come and add me to the mixture of your filthy practices, for that blasphemes my name even more. I no longer want you to speak of me. Let the devil be your prince, and do him all the honours you imagine you are doing me. Whatever you are doing in my name, no matter what it is, does not please me and I will not praise you for it.' That is what the prophet Amos says to our day, because the people are polluting themselves with idolatrous acts and God rejects everything they could do and declares those acts as just so many abominations in his sight (*Amos* 5:25–27).

Therefore, let us learn to lean completely on God, and in order to render the worship he requires, let us mingle nothing with it and let us add nothing to it. We can certainly argue later, saying, 'My intention was good', but God will condemn it all. That is how the prophet presented the admonition he directed at the people for not offering sacrifices to God. He does not accept all those rites because the people had many idols. God's purpose is to push them farther, namely, to Babylon (*Amos* 5:27). It is true the prophet speaks of the city of Damascus because it was like their bastion; it was their refuge and they put all their confidence in it. And that was even the place all the worship of God was corrupted. As is seen in holy history, the altar in the temple of God was modelled on the one in Damascus (*2 Kings* 16:10–11). So our Lord said to them, 'You know about that wicked city from which idolatry came, but I will remove you farther from it, and you will no longer have it as your fortress.' Now instead of saying that, Stephen says that 'they will be carried away into Babylon', which is a declaration of what the prophet Amos said, although phrased differently.

Now to aggravate the sin of the Jews even more, Stephen adds, 'God had given them a tabernacle.' That means he had ordained and established a form for honouring and serving him. If we had not been instructed, we would not have the rules God gave so that we might know how to worship him, and we would have an excuse for saying, 'Look, we want to worship God, but we do not know what his will is.' Men could say that, not that such a defence would be worth anything or acceptable. Even though the pagans claim God did not instruct them in his will, they will not escape being condemned for their superstitions. For it is certain that men have never given themselves over to idolatry except out of their evil inclination. And yet the fault is not so blameworthy when those who fall short have not been instructed, because there is no open rebellion, only an evil inclination and ignorance.

Stephen now says that such was not the case with the Jews, who had been adequately instructed. 'Your fathers', he says, 'had the tabernacle of witness.' When he uses the word 'tabernacle', he includes all the ceremonies God had ordained. It is as if he were saying, 'Our fathers did not fall into the corruption of superstitions for lack of being instructed or because God failed to give them some definite form for worshipping him. They had all that and still they proceeded to pursue the inventions of pagans. The obvious conclusion, then, is that their disposition to evil was so great that they refused to obey God's word and adhere to the guidelines he had given them, rules which were so complete and perfect that they could not be excelled.' That, I say, is the argument Stephen makes to show that the people's sin was the greater and more inexcusable. For he says that this tabernacle was laid out and built in accordance with the layout and pattern which God had shown Moses on the mountain, as it is recorded in Exodus 25 (*Exod.* 25:9) and as the apostle likewise mentions in the eighth chapter of Hebrews (*Heb.* 8:5). Now that is a point we need to note well, for we can conclude from it that it is not for men to create ways to worship God as they wish, but that God reserves for himself the authority to declare what pleases him and is agreeable to him. And more than that, he shows us that what God establishes for men is not meaningless or without a worthy purpose. God always has a reason for the commands he gives so that nothing will be done in vain.

Next, we must note that the purpose of all these ceremonies which we employ must relate to our Lord Jesus Christ, who is their truth and substance. So in the first place, when the text says, 'See to it that you perform the rites according to the pattern you saw on the mountain' (*Exod.* 25:40), our Lord is declaring to Moses that he does not want him to presume to make up something in his head. Now if Moses is not permitted to do as he pleases, what does that mean for others? Does it mean that men today are permitted to formulate ways to worship God as seems good to them? Who is allowed to usurp greater authority than Moses had? It is written that he is above all the prophets, that God makes him sovereign over all the others, and yet he is told to be careful not to do what

God has not commanded (cf. *Exod.* 3:14–4:17). From that we learn it is an act of pride and diabolical arrogance to invent ways to worship God, as has been done in the Papacy. The pope arrogates to himself the license to establish statutes and edicts, to create laws and ordinances. Why does he do that? To worship God the way he dictates!

Let us now consider whether the pope is to be preferred to Moses. Where do we find in holy Scripture that God gives him greater authority than Moses had? We will not find it. Moses is strictly forbidden to do anything that is not commanded. That being true, will the pope usurp greater authority? And when he wants to usurp what does not belong to creatures or even the angels in paradise, are we not permitted to declare that he is a devil who rises up against God's majesty? Here is a word that condemns everything ever invented by men for the worship of God: we must exercise that single-mindedness which is so often commanded, and we must not deviate from it in any way.

That goes for all the ceremonies by which people think they worship God, like the pope, who has established a hundred thousand empty formalities. By establishing them, he says God will be worshipped this way, provided God accepts them. We see things differently. Therefore, if we had no other testimony in all of holy Scripture for rejecting all the Papacy's superstitions, it would be enough for us that God forbade Moses to do anything that was not in conformity with the example he had seen on the mountain. So much for that.

Now, as I have already said, God gives no command that is without purpose, but he has in mind what will be useful for men so that there might be some good instruction for our salvation in what he establishes. As we see in the law, there were many ceremonies, but let us not think that God was engaged in child's play when he commanded that one altar be built in one way and another in another way and that atonement be made in a particular place and that those ceremonies be set up that way. Let us not think, I say, that God was being frivolous or wanted to amuse his people with meaningless actions. Those things have a spiritual purpose and truth. Moses did not see a physical tabernacle on the mountain. He was lifted up above all things. So the pattern is spiritual, heavenly. That is the way God instructed his people to their great advantage when he established the ceremonies which existed in the time of the law.

It is true that looking for some mystery in the details of each ceremony is not our province, for our intelligence is not keen enough to know what Moses knew. So let us wait until what is now hidden is revealed, and then we will understand why those ceremonies were established. But the fact remains that we have been adequately instructed, as I said. In fact, we see how careful Moses is to detail everything from the loops (*Exod.* 26:4–5), to the nails, and to the bolts. There is nothing, not even a hair, whose measurement and material he does not specify, just as it was revealed to him. The truth is that by proceeding thus he demonstrated his obedience. He adds to each statement 'as God ordered Moses' to show that human effort was not involved, but that he simply followed everything God had ordered. What Moses primarily wants to communicate is that he was obedient to God's word without insinuating himself or doing anything out of his own rashness. He always bears in mind the vision he had, and he wants to let the people know that when they have that tabernacle, they must not think of it as being terrestrial or as emanating from man, and that they must always be lifted up to that spiritual truth in heaven. That is what Moses wants to get across.

However, let us note next that none of the ceremonies we use is intended to bind us to this world. They contain a spiritual truth that lifts our spirits and minds to God. For we know that God is by nature spiritual. He does not want to be worshipped according to men's notions, but in spirit and in truth, as we are told in John 4 (*John* 4:24). In the matter of baptism, we see the water, but we must not encapsulate our salvation in this visible sign. We must not think that with baptism God wants to keep us focused on the world. It is to signify a spiritual thing. The same is true for the holy Supper. It is not a question of having the lives of our souls contained in bread and wine, but by those elements God wants to teach us how weak we are. In that way, the things we see contain, as I have already said, a spiritual significance to lift us up to heaven. Now we would never understand that if we did not know Jesus Christ is the substance of all God wishes us to value in his church, as I have already said. That then is the truth we have concerning the worship of God and all the elements we use. In short, when we have our eyes fixed on Jesus Christ, we yield to him and remain completely in his hands, once we have come to him.

That, in fact, is evident both in baptism and in the Supper. For what is baptism the figure of if not that we are washed in the blood of our Lord Jesus Christ and renewed because he is raised from the dead so that by his power he puts our wicked nature to death and brings us into conformity with the image of God his Father (*Col.* 3:10) in order to present us before him. That is, in a manner of speaking, the substance of baptism in Jesus Christ.

As for the holy Supper, it too leads us to him. Because he offered himself for us once in sacrifice, our trust must remain entirely in that fact alone. As a result, we see how the entire worship of God does not reside in the external form. But the truth lies in Jesus Christ and must conform to him. Such was the case of that ancient tabernacle with its appurtenances and accessories. True, there were many ceremonies, but everything was done to sustain and nourish the people in the hope of the Redeemer who had not yet been revealed. And because Jesus Christ was hidden, there had to be more ways to assure the people, as Paul says (*Col.* 2:17). Those ceremonies were like shadows and figures of Jesus Christ because he had not yet been revealed. Now that we have the substance, we must dispel the shadows. And even they would be useless if we insisted on holding on to them and obscuring the light we have in the gospel. On that point, we see how the apostle points out to the Hebrews, and teaches us in so doing, that Moses refused to teach the people anything that would confine them to sacrifices, but he wanted to lead them farther, namely, to Jesus Christ (*Heb.* 9:19–26). And with that, he points out the conformity and likeness between the ancient figures and what is now revealed in the person of the Son of God.

Now for the tabernacle which was raised up. There was the enclosed court in the front, which was for the people. When the people came to worship God, they did not approach the Holy Place. There was a veil between the two. Then there was 'the simple Holy Place', as it was called. The people stood farther off. That was to show we are not worthy to approach God's majesty. Because we are nothing but filth and contamination, we must not presume to present ourselves before God as if we had private access to him. That is what was symbolized to the people. But does that mean God rejected the Jews, saying, 'You have no association with me'? Not at all! For they were his well-beloved people whom he had chosen to be his children. How, then, can we reconcile these differences? Now there was the priest, who wore engraved on his two shoulders the names of the children of Israel (*Exod.* 28:9–12); there were two precious stones where the names of the twelve tribes were inscribed. There were two other precious stones before his breast, where there were additional images of the names of the tribes of Israel. So even though the people dared not enter the Holy Place, still the priest, when entering, drew all the people to himself. For that priest was not acting as a private individual.

He was not there in his own name, but as a representative of the figure of Jesus Christ. And that is also the reason he was dressed in strange garments. He was not there as a man, for he had a different appearance, which signified that although we are not worthy to go to God, yet Jesus Christ is the one who leads us to him. He bears us on his shoulders. We are his breastplate, and he keeps us there as in his heart because of the love he has shown for us. That is how in the person of our Lord Jesus Christ we have access to heaven, although outcasts because of our unworthiness.

Now that priest, we know, could not come to God, for he was a sinner like the rest. Yet it was only a yearly sacrifice, as holy Scripture calls it (*1 Sam.* 1:3, 21; 2:19; 20:6; *Heb.* 10:1, 3). But what was symbolized in it as a shadow was accomplished in Jesus Christ. We now have the fulfilment because Jesus Christ has ascended into heaven. There he presents himself before God his Father so we will be able to enter in his name. That also is why the veil of the temple was split when Jesus Christ died (*Matt.* 27:51 ff.), signifying that now things are no longer what they were under the law. It also means that Jesus Christ dedicated and consecrated the way by which we can come to God and that he has so poured out upon us and clothed us with such blessings that we are able to come and present ourselves before God's majesty. And how is that? Jesus Christ broke through the veil that separated us from our inheritance and our salvation. And how was that done? It was by the blood of Jesus Christ which was shed, as under the law the priest was forbidden to make a solemn entry into the Holy of Holies without blood. Some sacrifices were made daily, a solemn sacrifice was made only once a year (*Lev.* 16:34). And at that time the priest would enter the Holy of Holies with his fingers stained with blood to sprinkle the mercy seat and the ark. Why did he do that? To signify that Jesus Christ gave us access to God his Father when he shed his blood and that we are so sufficiently washed that God's anger is appeased and our sins are no longer imputed to us. Because of the sacrifice made for us, we are cleansed of all our filthiness and pollutions. Except for the sacrifice, we would not have access to God because we are very wretched, like poor lepers who have to have the blood of Christ to cleanse us. Otherwise, God would never have received us into his grace and love. So we now see how Jesus Christ was the end of everything God had established in the law and how Moses incorporated nothing from his own understanding, but considered the purpose which required the figures of that period to be related to Jesus Christ, who was their truth and substance.

And then there was especially the covering of the ark, which was called the 'propitiatory' [mercy seat] (cf. *Rom.* 3:25; *1 John* 2:2). Paul and John point out clearly that it was a figure of Jesus Christ, and the word itself also conveys that. For what does this word 'propitiatory' mean? It is a way of appeasing God so that he will be propitious, merciful, toward men. Whereas we deserve to be thrown into the bottomless pit by God and destroyed because of his anger against us, he has provided the means for us to find grace before him and in this way be our Father and Saviour. Can the covering of an ark do that? We know very well that it cannot. Therefore, let us be aware that when we fix our attention on God, Jesus Christ must precede us. For if we come to God without putting ourselves in Jesus Christ's hands, that majesty which is in God will so frighten us that, instead of drawing near to him, we will be the more distanced from him. It is certain that those who presume much when coming to God have the idea that he has to receive them, and do not abide in the grace of Jesus Christ – it is certain, I say, that they are possessed of the devil. But in order to use this comparison appropriately, we must acknowledge such a majesty in God and realize that its purpose is to confound us unless Jesus Christ precedes us.

That then is how we will be able to approach God, how we will find favour in his eyes. That is how it will be whenever we contemplate him in the living image which he has provided for us, his only Son, who has reconciled us to himself by his death and suffering. We are now assured of his love, despite the fact that we are poor sinners. Now because the people needed to be sustained in many ways in the knowledge of God, they also had to be strengthened in the faith of our Lord Jesus Christ because he had not yet been revealed to the world.

That is why there were so many ceremonies, according to what I have already said about Exodus. There was always a burning light in the sanctuary (*Exod.* 27:20–21; *Lev.* 24:2–4) to signify that we must not approach the worship of God casually, as if unsure of what we were doing, but in need of enlightenment. And where will the light come from? There was the sacred candlestick which also signified that God must guide us by his Holy Spirit. Without that, we are poor blind people who will only stumble about and wander from the path. That was what was pointed out to the people. Then there was never any leaven in any of the sacrifices (cf. *Lev.* 2:11), and that was to show that men must bring nothing of their own, for when men come and add I-know-not-what from their understanding, they infect and vitiate God's ordinances. Sacrifices were not to be made without salt (cf. *Lev.* 2:13). Why not? He adds the reason, namely, the salt of his understanding must permeate everywhere. Afterwards, men who were about to enter the sanctuary, even as they stood in the outer court, had to be washed,[1] signifying that we are laden with blemishes. Every time we think about invoking God, we must begin at that point: 'Be pleased, O Lord, to cleanse me, for I am covered with filth.' We

---

[1] The editors suggest considering *Exod.* 29:4 and 30:17-21, adding that only the priests are mentioned in those verses, not all the people.

will never be inclined to ask God to pardon us and forgive our sins unless we take refuge in this cleansing by our Lord Jesus Christ.

Then, there always had to be blood, both morning and evening, in the sacrifices being made to God. That was to show that no matter what we are involved with, we will never be able to please God, unless the blood of Jesus Christ intervenes. That then is what has always been required to sustain the people, and even though we do not have those shadows and figures in our day, yet knowing their truth and substance, we understand the purpose they served, and we in particular are strengthened by them. The ceremonies of the law were not just for those people, but for us also. And how is that so? Not that we must employ sacrifices. We no longer have dead animals to reconcile us to God. And that is especially why the papists have occupied themselves with the shadows, and upon seeing there was a light in the temple, they say, 'Oh! We have to have some in ours.' They are monkeys quite simply, for they want to imitate the ancient fathers while not considering that all those things are perfected for us in the gospel and that God abolished the former at the coming of our Lord Jesus Christ his Son. Consequently, the papists are nothing but stupid since they want to imitate the ceremonies of the law when we no longer need them.

Still, that is not to say we do not receive some advantage from them, for if Jesus Christ had appeared to the world without being prefigured, would the correctness of our faith be such as it is? If the promise of Jesus Christ and the gospel had never been made, it would have been more difficult to believe. For inasmuch as we know that every new thing is suspect, the Jews could have said, 'What are you saying? That is a new teaching. You are talking to us about the remission of sins which is acquired for us through our Lord Jesus Christ. What has become of our ancestors? Was there no remission of their sins? Now that Jesus Christ has come into the world, what was the situation before him? Was there no salvation for them?' That, I tell you, is how we could doubt, but since we see that, from the beginning, God wanted Jesus Christ to be figured, we also understand that all those who have walked uprightly had that very goal of knowing that all of their confidence had to be founded on Jesus Christ. Now that we understand that, are we not greatly strengthened? Moreover, when we see that what existed at that time conforms to what we have declared in the gospel, are we not all the more assured that our faith is not to be doubted? Will we be able to say today that what we believe the gospel teaches is baseless? So when we come to contemplate that comparison in the way the apostle deals with it in the Epistle to the Hebrews, we see how God's wondrous wisdom gave order to everything. We see how our Lord led by the hand, as little children, the fathers who were under the law until all things should come to greater completion. As I have also said in connection with the veil, the veil was torn to announce the end of all those shadows because Jesus Christ, who was their truth, fulfilled everything. Yet, even though the veil was torn, we still have Jesus Christ who leads us and in whose name we come boldly to offer ourselves to God his Father. That then is as desirable a figure as we could wish for.

In addition, since we see that all those figures and shadows have been fulfilled in the Son of God, we have to consider how everything was prefigured before it was fulfilled. Therefore, we are even more aware that Jesus Christ did nothing in vain, but that everything was directed and arranged for the welfare and salvation of us all. That instructs us in the fear of God and in charity for our neighbours so we will always be increasingly trained in obedience to God. We are then strengthened in our belief that we can invoke God's name and be assured he will answer us. That is how all those things can instruct us. How so? Since we see that a prayer was never offered without the shedding of blood, we realize we will never open our mouths in prayer to God without first taking refuge in the suffering and death of our Lord Jesus Christ. If we did not have access to him by the grace acquired for us by the suffering and death of his Son, who would so embolden us to call God 'our Father', seeing that we address him every day as 'Our Father which art in heaven'?

Then when it is said that 'the people must wash' (cf. *Heb.* 10:22), we are thereby instructed to acknowledge our uncleanness. We now need no other washing than the one provided when Jesus Christ shed his blood, which is figured in baptism,which acts as a sign and seal of all that Jesus Christ has acquired for us. In that way we are also instructed that we must acknowledge our vices and experience true sorrow for them, realizing our nature is so perverse that we pray God will change us and effect correction in us. That is the kind of instruction we must receive from those ancient sacrifices without making playthings out of them, as the papists have done. They have to have water that has been blessed. Why so? Because in the law washings were once required. In that, I say, they pretend to follow the ancient fathers in having water over which blessings and incantations had been uttered. But they do not consider its intention, namely that Jesus Christ has obtained for us newness of life and that he wants to resurrect us so we will no longer live to the world, but be conformed to God his Father. And then we are strengthened with a true confidence that we will lack nothing because we will be able to present ourselves to God and obtain everything we need, such as we have it in Jesus Christ. Therefore, let us no longer doubt. Let us no longer be uncertain, realizing that if our confidence in him is not firmly and securely fixed, our uncertainty would blaspheme the Son of God and offend his suffering and death.

That is how the ancient sacrifices and all the ceremonies still serve us today even though they are no longer in use. And even when we are told Moses sprinkled the blood of the sacrifice on all the people and the book of the covenant (*Exod.* 24:8), we understand how we must receive simultaneously the blood of our Lord Jesus Christ and the promises of God contained in holy Scripture. That is how God promises to be our Father. And how will we be certain of the promise? When it is sealed by the blood of Jesus Christ! The book of the law, having proceeded from God, was so sufficiently sanctified that it was not unclean. Why then does he sprinkle it with the blood of the sacrifice? He sprinkles it so we will realize that the blessings of God would be of no use to us unless they were given life by Jesus Christ, who is the Yes and Amen of all things and through whom we share in the grace of God. We must not think that those are empty promises, but that they have to be sprinkled with the blood of Jesus Christ. That is how we must apply to our instruction all the figures given to the ancient fathers in the law. It is true that we will not utilize all that, but that does not mean their truth has been abolished.

In addition, Stephen shows how very little the people profited from having a tabernacle established by God, for they were still unable to keep it free of idols. That is a vice common among men. What are we to learn then from this passage? We are to learn that God, for his part, did not fade away after revealing himself initially to the children of Israel, and that he gave them all the instruction they needed. But what did they do? They were ingrates and wicked. They perverted the things that were instituted for their salvation. But as I have already said, that is a characteristic almost universal among men. It is in fact, generally speaking, common to their nature. Consequently, God must instruct us and grant us the grace to enjoy the good he does for us so that the good things which come from him will not be corrupted by us and our evil disposition. We see an example of that in what happened in the Papacy. Was there anything that had to be changed in our Lord's ordinance concerning the Lord's Supper? Yet they have changed it into a damnable idol, which is obviously a more egregious blasphemy against God than pagans ever came up with. It is evident that the devil rules there more dominantly than he ever did among all idolaters. The long and short of it is that they will say the mass is a sacrifice for the remission of sins. There you have a priest, when he arrives to perform his tricks, who presumes to reconcile sinners with God and redeem souls from damnation. Are not those blasphemies so abominable that your hair stands on end? True, they would indeed say that their mass is founded on the suffering and death of our Lord Jesus Christ. But the fact remains, they openly renounce all the graces and benefits which Jesus Christ acquired for us. And experience demonstrates as much, for when they say that their mass is a sacrifice offered to make peace between God and men, they could not more impudently renounce the benefit and merit of our Saviour Jesus Christ's suffering and death. And then we see that idol worshipped as God. The sign given to us in the Lord's Supper is to lead us on high and not to bind us here below. And we see that those poor wretches go prostrate themselves and worship a piece of bread instead of lifting their minds, as they should, to heaven to think upon what the sign means for us. In that example we see how men pervert the things God has established for their salvation.

And we see especially that they have also corrupted baptism with their inventions. And I am not just talking about all the foolishness, incantations and charms, such as salt, spit, oil, and many other inanities. But the teaching of the papists regarding baptism is diabolical because they do not lead the poor people to the blood of Jesus Christ, but they lead them to believe that the salvation of their souls is dependent on the water. Therefore, if we had no other example than the one found in the Papacy, we would understand men are much inclined to corrupt what God has ordained for their welfare. The same thing was obvious among the Jews under the law of Moses, for they corrupted with their superstitions what God had established for them.

As for us, although we are not swallowed up in the papists' superstitions, let us consider how we take advantage of the things God has given us. We have the simplicity of his gospel and the preaching of it. We have public prayers, baptism, and the Lord's Supper. Do we take advantage of that as we should and as God intended? Alas, we fall far short! For even if we have no idols, we cannot bring ourselves to serve God as we should. Many people will think they have done their duty and have even done too much when they have sacrificed half an hour to listening. And it is never a matter of changing their way of living. They simply will not learn they must be refashioned in the image of God if they are to be joined to Jesus Christ. When they profess to be Christian, much is lacking. So let us learn that if we are going to serve God, we must not do it half-heartedly, as many do, and we must not take refuge in something we have contrived, but we must, in all obedience and humility, accept what God has ordained without adding anything to it, for we know that God does not wish to be served in a worldly manner.

And, in addition, may all possible ceremonies lead us to Jesus Christ, since he is our goal, and if ever we are separated from him, everything we do will not be accepted by God, but he will reject it and we will not be able to approach him by that means. Now in order to come to him, what must we do? We must not go beyond the pure teaching of the law, the prophets, and the gospel. If we do not stop there and if we do not remain steadfast, without vacillating, we will be like pitiable, blind people. In fact we see that that is what has happened in most of the world, just as it is still evident in the Papacy today. Consequently, we must make an even greater effort to remain steadfast in our obedience to God. And because Jesus Christ has extended his hand to us, let us allow ourselves to be led to him in everything we do until we achieve that glorious immortality to which God is calling us.

Following this holy teaching, let us bow before the face of our gracious God in acknowledgment of our sins, praying that he will be pleased to draw us to himself in such a way that we, dead to our fleshly affections, may ask only to obey him and cause his holy name to be glorified and magnified in every aspect of our lives. And bowing before his exalted majesty, let us say humbly and sincerely, Almighty God, heavenly Father . . .

40

WORSHIP IS SPIRITUAL AND PERSONAL

SUNDAY, 7 DECEMBER 1550

Which [tabernacle] also our fathers that came after brought in with Jesus into the possession of the Gentiles, whom God drave out before the face of our fathers, unto the days of David; [46] Who found favour before God, and desired to find a tabernacle for the God of Jacob. [47] But Solomon built him an house. [48] Howbeit the most High dwelleth not in temples made with hands; as saith the prophet, [49] Heaven is my throne, and earth is my footstool: what house will ye build me? saith the Lord: or what is the place of my rest? [50] Hath not my hand made all these things? (Acts 7:45–50)

We need to remember what we discussed previously, namely, the reason that, according to Stephen, the Jews had a tabernacle. It was to show that God was not to be faulted because the Jews did not serve and honour him as they should have, but that they were so perverse that they tarred with superstition everything God had established for his worship. So Stephen told the Jews that their fathers were so corrupt that even though God had drawn them to himself and had instructed them faithfully, they were still unable to turn anything to their advantage. Everything they touched went bad. That is why he recounts what Moses said: 'The tabernacle was made and constructed according to the pattern and figure which was revealed on the mountain' (*Exod.* 25:9; *Acts* 7:44). In saying that, he pointed out that God did not intend to direct those ancient people toward earthly things to induce them to superstition, but that in all the ceremonies of the law there was a hidden content which would lead us to that spiritual truth which is our true goal. That, then, is why our Lord did not want to be worshipped in a commonplace manner. But look! The Jews misunderstood all that. And therein we understand men's disposition toward evil. No matter what God does to draw them to himself, they back away and distance themselves from him as far as they can and always end up in their vain follies.

In addition, since God presents himself to men the way he does, we see that there is no excuse for ignorance. He shows them how and by what means they will be able to come to him, and still they distance themselves from him. Since God favours us by showing us the way of salvation, let us take care to follow where he calls us. Let us always be aware of the purpose of all his ordinances so they will focus us on his intention and counsel.

We come now to what Stephen adds. He says that 'the tabernacle was carried into the land of Canaan, as God had promised his people' (cf. *Acts* 7:45). It remained there until the time of David, who found such favour before God that at his request a definite place was designated for building the temple. That was like saying that God did not visit the Jews for a time, but that he increased his favour toward them. After the tabernacle had remained until the time of David, the temple was built. So with that event we see that God continued to reveal himself to the ancient people to assure them of their salvation and give them a more ample confirmation of his desire to live in their midst. But that did not help them in any way, for they remained hardened in their evil. And no matter what God did to draw them to himself, they always refused to obey him. That, I say, was Stephen's intention.

We now need to note these words: 'David found favour before God.' As a result of his request, a place was designated for building the temple. It did not seem that a specific place for building a material temple was a matter of great importance, but we see the opposite is true. We even see the zeal with which David requests it. He pledges and vows that he will never sleep and be at ease until God reveals to him where he wants the people to worship him as he commanded. That is the way David shows it is not an insignificant matter and that the people must not consider lightly having that place which was promised beforehand in the law.

One could argue here that David was overly excessive in his rash desire to have a place designated. The opposite is true, for God approves that zeal, and David's zeal is especially welcomed because it shows the great desire he had to elevate and establish the worship of God so that it might be perfect, indeed at the very time when religious practice could implement the worship. That is, at the time of the ceremonies. In fact, when our Lord commands the temple to be built, he designates a definite place where he wants his name to be invoked and does so to show the people that he would reside perpetually in the land of Judea and that it would be there that the people would know his power and his grace. Until the temple was built, it seems that God did not have a fixed residence in the midst of the Jews while the tabernacle was being transported from place to place. When the place was indicated by the angel (cf. *2 Sam.* 24:16) as David requested, then our Lord declares that his promises are certain and that he will never withdraw from the midst of the people.

It is true that those ceremonies lasted only until the coming of our Lord Jesus Christ. When he was made manifest in the flesh, all those figures ceased, but it was very important for the people to know that God wanted to inhabit that place until Jesus Christ should fulfil the things necessary for their salvation. It is because of David's great desire, then, that God designates a definite place to be worshipped so that the ark would no longer be transported from place to place.

Now when we see David motivated by such great zeal, we must take him as an example. Otherwise, what he earnestly affirms will be a witness of condemnation against us. For that shows us we must long for nothing in this world more than the presence of God and saying we are joined to him and want him to guide us and always make his help available to us. What more do we want? Unfortunately we see how men are devoted to their empty pursuits, everyone striving to satisfy his appetites and affections despite the fact that nothing is more despicable before God. Still we want to subject God to ourselves and hear him say he is our Father while we scorn him. And yet we ask him to let us sense his grace. That is not the way we are supposed to respond to him. But, as I have said, let us pray as David did, asking him to grant us the strong confidence that we can find our refuge in him.

Moreover, may our worship of him be so well established among us that we will seek only to honour and glorify his holy name as we should. Where can we find the kind of concern needed to do that? We will find it in very few people. Even those who want God to be served and honoured are quite indifferent when compared with David. In him was a king sanctified by God. God established him in an immeasurably high position. He was able to live comfortably and enjoy all the pleasures and delights of this world. Nothing prevented him from being fully obeyed in everything and everywhere. Still he says he will not sleep even though he is in his house, in his palace, and will never rest until God shows him where he wants his temple built. Thus we see that David scorned all the things of this world when it was a matter of honouring God and sensing his grace and power. Now who among us is not so intoxicated with the things of this world that we are not indifferent to God and his grace? If we have a zeal for worshipping and honouring him, it is not driven by the kind of ardour shown here. Rather, we will find it very difficult to sense some subtle impulse to do so, and soon even that will die out. David's urgent desire for God to designate where he wanted his temple to be built grievously condemns us because we lack his zeal.

We must now be more greatly concerned than David was, for we are now no longer talking about a material temple, but about the worship of God as it is revealed in its purity and perfection. We have the true temple in which he lives, our Lord Jesus Christ. The fact remains, however, that what was done in ancient times is for our instruction. We no longer need the shadows and figures since we possess the truth. So let us learn not to become attached to the things of this world, as we formerly were, but let us lift our minds and our thoughts on high, to what is above us, to God, who resides among us and is near us whenever we take refuge in him.

Furthermore, when men come to him in all humility and render him his due obedience, it is then that we find grace in his sight, which is the greatest blessing we can receive from him. He is the one we must desire above all others. That is what Scripture tells us so often: that men do indeed have an opportunity to be content and rejoice when they are aware that God is living in their midst. We are content and rejoice despite the fact that all our worldly desires are not met, things are in a state of confusion, and poverty afflicts some, sickness others, and others have their cross to bear, according as God knows how to bridle us in, knowing what is good for us. Although we are variously afflicted, let us be content because God favours us with living in our midst and showing us that he wants to make his eternal residence there. Because we have the freedom to worship and honour him and to confess our Christian faith, having imprinted on our hearts the certainty that God is near, that, I say, is an invaluable treasure which we must prize more highly than all the pleasures and comforts of this world.

We come now to what Stephen adds: 'The sovereign God does not live in temples made with hands, as it is written in the prophet: "The heaven is my throne and the earth is my footstool. Where then will you build for me?"'This passage is taken from the sixty-sixth chapter of the prophet Isaiah (*Isa.* 66:1). Now we have already stated Stephen's intention. Inasmuch as the Jews could not walk in the simplicity they were taught by God, but had perverted everything with their superstitions, Stephen cites that passage as if to say, 'God granted David the singular grace of indicating Mt Zion for the building of the temple in which he wanted his name to be invoked. But you have wrongly understood that. Why so? Because you have set up a worldly and human worship, thinking that God had to be enclosed in this temple as a man would be in his house. That is how you have wrongly abused the grace which had been bestowed upon you.' That was always Stephen's purpose, for which he was accused of wanting to destroy the law of Moses. He shows that that was far from his intention and that he wanted rather to reform it and restore it to its status, as if he were saying, 'The ceremonies, which distracted our fathers, were not ordained by God to bind them here below, but to instruct them in his spiritual worship. If our fathers, whom Satan blinded, did not understand that, does that mean we are not to learn now what is necessary for our salvation? So let us learn that God did not ordain the building of his temple so that he might be confined within a material place.'

Now that we have taken a good look at why Isaiah spoke that way, it will be easy for us to apply his witness to the matter which Stephen deals with and expounds. The prophet Isaiah does not debate about the habitation and presence of God. But he does return to an imbecilic notion men entertained in his time. They thought that after presenting their offerings, after worshipping God with pomp and outward show, they had done enough and that God should ask nothing more of them. Their vain confidence comes out in these words: 'We come to the temple, we offer sacrifices, and since we worship God with so many beautiful ceremonies, what more can he ask of us?' That is how the Jews became insensitive to their iniquities: they thought that by using these fine pretexts they had done enough to honour God.

That has been a common vice in all times. As men are carnal, they also think God is influenced by what they fancy. That is exactly what we see in the Papacy today. There is great pomp, organs resound on one side, singers on the other, and there are many candles, everything is decked out, there are incense and fine fragrances. When all of that is present, you have a worship of God that sweeps them away with admiration. When you enter a temple belonging to the Papacy, it seems you have entered an earthly paradise. Such is the reaction of the foolish people who do not realize that this is about God or how he wishes to be worshipped. That vice did not appear yesterday or last year but has been perpetual in men. For it is our nature to be always creating something new and imagining that God is obliged to fall in line with our meaningless gestures and accept and approve as good those things we have invented. That is what the prophet Isaiah's words mean. He looks at the Jews as hardened in their evil disposition. He sees that they are filled with every kind of vice and that usury, robbery, violence, and extortion reign on every side. On every side we see nothing but blasphemy, perjury, excess, lechery, gluttony, drunkenness. In short, he sees that everything has gone wild. Yet, to cover their wickedness and filth, they use more of the superstitions they invented and still think they have done everything they need to do toward God. 'How is it that we are not performing the sacrifices the way God commands? Do we not worship him the way he established? Why are we railed against? Are we to be rebuked in every way possible?' Those are the excuses offered to the prophet whenever he rebuked the vices common in his time. That is why he said to them, 'Yes, and do you think you are going to manufacture in this a God to your liking? When you come to the temple to make some impressive outward show and present some kind of offering, do you think God is appeased and content with that? Do you think God is compensated by all those things? Realize that his nature is different from yours, and do not imagine he is confined to one place rather than another.' That, I say, is the point the prophet Isaiah was speaking to.

Now it seems that that line of thinking is useless here, for the Jews were not so stupid that they were not well aware that God resides in heaven. And yet they could reply, 'What is your reason for telling us God does not live in the temple made by men? Do you think we have not known that until now? We are not so stupid that we have not been quite aware of that.' Now, as I have already said, the prophet is not discussing here the essence of God, whether or not it is infinite, but he only wants to show that he is not like men have made him out to be and that they think they do everything they need to when engaged in some act of worship or other.

Now he says God takes no pleasure in all that. And why not? It is because he is not like us. That is why he adds, 'Where is the place of my rest? Have I not made all these things?' (*Isa.* 66:1–2). It is as if he were saying, 'I can do without all the worship you give me. It does not do anything for me, as the saying goes. In fact, the sacrifices I ordained are for you. I do not need them except insofar as they are useful for your instruction.' We understand, I say, what the prophet meant. But as concerns the words 'seat' and 'rest', we are not to imagine God as seated in human fashion. We know for a fact that he has neither a body nor legs. So why does the prophet speak in those terms? He does so to point out that God comprises all things and that he, being spirit, must have spiritual worship. Moreover, his nature is not the same as men's, and human appetites and affections do not influence him. That is what Stephen understands. Thus, when Scripture tells us that 'God is in heaven', it is to lift our thoughts on high when it comes to worshipping God and invoking him. Indeed, when we think about him, we must not think about anything connected with this world. If we consider the heavens, we are, every one of us, caught up out of ourselves. If we consider this world, well, we see things the way they are. If we look on high, we see that things surpass our capacity. If we did not say God is above all things, we might think he was about our equal and make him our companion.

That is how men customarily exalt themselves. We know that from experience. Consequently, Scripture lifts us up to heaven, saying that God resides there, so that when we worship him, we may do so in all humility and not as unto an idol. But let us realize that his majesty is so exalted that it exceeds all things created and that we must be extremely humbled when we think upon him. So let us note that the reason for that manner of speaking is to get men to strip themselves of all superstitions and insane fantasies. It is also to show us that we must not measure our earthly disposition against God's power, but that we must acknowledge he is above all things, inasmuch as we now understand what the prophet Isaiah means.

It will be quite easy to apply this testimony to what Stephen is discussing, for he demonstrates to the Jews that their fathers abused not only God's temple but also the Scriptures because they believed God lived in a material place. Not that the Jews would think God had a body, but, as I said, because they thought that they could satisfy God with their ceremonies and that God ought to ask for nothing more. After making sacrifices, they felt they had made sufficient recompense for all their shortcomings and iniquities. That is what the prophet Isaiah said. He was cited by

Stephen. But we must now acknowledge that that teaching was addressed to us. I have already said that that vice was not restricted to a particular time, but that since the creation of the world, men have been inclined to that evil. They want to understand God from a material standpoint.

And we see what has happened throughout the Papacy. There, when a temple has been filled with incense, they think God is obliged to rejoice in that fragrance. Yet those who make the incense are filled with filth and stench. All who come there to worship God bring with them nothing but their contagion and impurity. Some are filled with lechery, others with murder, still others with usury and robbery. There is only hatred, rancour, dissension, and strife among those who come there and play the hypocrite. In that way they incense our Lord with every contagion and stench. But they still think that they have acquitted themselves well and that all their sins have been erased because there is incense and many burning candles. God surely must be satisfied, they think, but their eyes are blinded by Satan. They walk in darkness and are so embedded in their wicked affections that they can never view God correctly.

Then there are beautifully adorned altar pieces. So what? How are their hearts adorned? They are filled with every cruelty and barbarity. That, I say, is how we perceive the papists' image of a world-oriented God similar to themselves. Why? Because all the worship they offer him is only fine, external appearance. And on the inside, what kind of simplicity and uprightness is there? It is pointless to look for anything like that. It is enough for them to be well adorned with outward show. But we know that the worship of God is spiritual. And why? Because we have to know God's will according to his nature and not ours, for we are flesh. Consequently, we should not be surprised if God's will is not like that of men. It is true he will always be present with us. He will even dwell within us provided we are humble enough to yield to him and conform ourselves to him in order to bear his image. Therefore, whenever men seek to be like God, then he will live in them. But when they wish to hold on to their own nature, he is obliged to turn away from them. That, then, is how the papists must show us by their example that human beings are always inclined toward superstition and desire to worship God in a manner that conforms to the world.

Now let us look at ourselves. True, we do not have the papists' idols and statues of Saints. We do not have a piece of bread enclosed in a bottle or I-know-not-what so we can say, 'There is our God.' Yet we do not forgo worshipping God as we please, as men have always done. True, as I have said, we no longer practise the papists' foolishness and infantile games. God has favoured us by delivering us from all that nonsense. When we come to this place, we come to hear the teaching, and then to offer communal prayers and administer the sacraments appropriately. Do we do all those things? If we do, we fail to take advantage of them. Be that as it may, let us consider briefly how most go about their business. It is true we prize the gospel and say we are reformed Christians. As for the papists, we condemn them roundly. How can they not be utterly contemptible for having a piece of bread as their God? They think God is beholden to them because they have trotted off here and there on pilgrimages and have invented every kind of worship imaginable. They think God has to be satisfied with that, as if it were true perfection. And are they not rankly stupid?' That much we can say!

About ourselves we say, 'We worship God as he ordained and have added nothing of an earthly character.' After we say that, people look at how we live. The person who boasts of being the greatest Christian will not stop talking about once selling a harvest of wheat, rye, oats, and beans for eighteen gold coins. That is the gain for waiting a year. And the poor, who are starving to death erroneously believing they are being treated kindly by Christians, would be just as well off in the hands of highway robbers. That is how Geneva will become a food paradise! But if someone takes a good look at the way things are, he will discover it is a hell. To hear us tell it, we are angels, but if someone looks closely, he will find we are worse than devils. So if the prophet Isaiah proclaimed to his generation that 'God is on his throne in heaven and earth is his footstool' (*Isa.* 66:1), he is saying the same thing and more to us today. Why? Well, how do we worship God? We want to deal with him as with a little child. If he complains, give him an apple and he will be happy even if he has been threatened and beaten. The same is true for us if we think we can disregard God and then think that he has to be satisfied because we put on some fancy display and say sweetly, 'Oh, the gospel teaching is good!' We think he does us great wrong when he chides us. So let us not think that the prophet Isaiah spoke as he did just for his generation. But let us realize that he wanted to restrain a vice which is rooted in human nature and is always active, just as it is today. Do not think that only the Jews are condemned in this passage. We are the ones God is addressing. He is arguing his case and making a case against us to show us that we too believe that he is still bound to us and that we are worshipping him with outward show and that he must surely be satisfied with our saying clearly that we have the gospel. Now, let us understand that if we think this way, we will find ourselves seriously disappointed and deceived. Why? Because God does not approve of anything we do unless we adhere fully to what he has ordained. That is what we must learn from what Stephen gathers from the prophet Isaiah.

When he adds, 'Where is the place of my rest?' (*Isa.* 66:1), he means that God wants to dwell among us, provided, to be sure, that we live strictly for him. The prophet Isaiah even calls the church 'the dwelling place of God' in the eleventh chapter (*Isa.* 11:10). He says that dwelling place is glorious. The same is said in the Psalm: 'This is my rest: here will I dwell forever' (*Psa.* 132:14). That is God speaking. How then does the prophet Isaiah now say, 'I have no place to rest'? It seems he is contradicting himself. Not so. But the problem here stems from men's foolish notion that God will be joined to them while they are hardened in their evil. They follow the devil but want God to be close behind. That is how men get carried away by foolish, overweening pride and wisdom when they have some external sign.

In short, the prophet Isaiah is here rebuking the same vice as Jeremiah. 'It is only lying words', he says, 'when you say, "The temple of the Lord, the temple of the Lord"' (*Jer.* 7:4). And was not the temple of God the one in Jerusalem? Yes, provided it was being used as God had commanded. But when the Jews did not consider the purpose God had in mind, it was only a pollution of God's temple, a pretext and a cloak for every iniquity. When men are at their most wicked but have ceremonies in the temple, they think they are acquitted in God's sight and have served him well. As we see, some in the Papacy, the most 'devout', are the most wicked. When there is a man who is filled with every cruelty and inhumanity, who has eaten and devoured his neighbours and done nothing in his life but kill, beat, murder, whore around, and get drunk, oh, all he has to do is to listen devoutly to the mass, mumble a lot, make a lot of meaningless gestures, and not forget to take a little holy water when he enters and leaves, and drop in the poor box a few coins gained from his highway robbery and usury, as if God should share in the booty. There you have an upright man, after he has done his duty by all those trappings! The same can be said of everything else done in the Papacy. Their ceremonies and diabolical inventions serve only as a cloak to cover their pollution and villainy. Provided they have heard the mass, even though they are so wicked that the air is infected by them, people will say, 'They are good people.' That, I say, is how the devil blinds them.

But we still have to look to ourselves also. If we want God to have his rest in us, as in his church, we must live to him, as I have already said. But then does God call us? Let us consider that. How does he call us? We must get out of ourselves. Otherwise, the church we claim to be will only be a den of thieves because we will be more audacious in doing evil when we do it under the cover of God's name. Like a thief in plain sight, he will be afraid to cut someone's throat. Why? He is afraid someone somewhere is watching him. But when he is in a den, he is bold. Why? He is under cover of darkness. That is the way hypocrites are. When they have engaged in fine ceremonies, they think they have shielded themselves and God can no longer recognize their iniquities. Now that is not the way we are to act, for it will serve no purpose. Let us not use lying words, saying, 'The Lord's temple, the Lord's temple'. Rather let us consider what God commands in his word and stay focused on it without vacillating in any way. If we want to possess the promise that God will find his rest among us, let us be careful not to drive him away with our evil. But as long as he favours us by living in our midst, let us also pray that he will grant us the grace to be able to deny ourselves so we may come to him. And when we come to him, let us pray that he will sustain us to the end so that we will never be separated from him or from the grace of his Holy Spirit.

Following this holy teaching, let us bow before the face of our gracious God in acknowledgment of our sins, praying that he will be pleased to privilege us with knowing him better than we ever have before, so that by knowing him we will also learn how to know ourselves and be displeased with ourselves and so that our desire will be so fixed upon him that we will seek only to yield ourselves in obedience to him. And inasmuch as he has given us the rule for living the right kind of lives, let us bring our lives into conformity with it, and at the same time may he be pleased to exercise his infinite mercy toward us by sustaining us in the name of our Lord Jesus Christ. Now let us all say, Almighty God, heavenly Father . . .

41

GOD'S AUTHORITY REJECTED

SUNDAY, 14 DECEMBER 1550

Ye stiffnecked and uncircumcised in heart and ears, ye do always resist the Holy Ghost: as your fathers did, so do ye (Acts 7:51).

God's servants will definitely be subjected to attacks because the world hates the teaching God has placed in their mouths. And that is because they do not relent in demonstrating the authority this teaching has for condemning the whole world. Therefore, the wicked and unbelievers gain nothing by raising their horns against God and using force and violence to suppress this word. That fact must certainly contribute to their very great confusion. I will go so far as to say they would use force and violence if they ever acquired the power to do whatever they wish. We have here an excellent example of that, one worth remembering, for it is written that Stephen was accused just as if he had wanted to destroy God's law, just as if he had been against Moses. As a result, we see that he was led before the council. And who are his judges? The mortal enemies of God and his truth, who would have liked to destroy the gospel and banish it from the face of the earth. Even so, Stephen does not abandon his cause because he knows that it is God's cause and because it shows that that false charge was brought against him wrongly.

He now adds a condemnation for all the judges and does so because he understands that despite all the admonitions he has given them, he has convinced none of them. He sees then that they are hardened and obstinate in their evil. For that reason, he rises up against them with thundering vehemence, as we see. It is true that in the end he is dragged outside the city and cruelly killed (*Acts* 7:58). But, as I have said, he still adheres to the authority of God's word. In that fact, we see what I said at the outset, that the wicked, after strong resistance, after venting all their rage, gain nothing but condemnation from God's word, against which they are waging war.

But to understand all this better and to apply it better for our use, the first thing we need to notice is that Stephen changes his style at this point and he calls the Jews 'stiff-necked and uncircumcised in heart and ears'. At the outset, he called them 'brothers and fathers', speaking with gentleness and goodwill. He even showed great deference when it was not enough to call them 'brothers' as a sign he was seeking fellowship with them, but he gives them a more honourable title when he calls them 'his fathers', indicating that he is only seeking to be obedient and in subjection to them if, to be sure, he should find that they were being subject to God. But after realizing they are completely rebellious, refuse to come under subjection, and have contemplated battling against God, he no longer acknowledges them as fathers and brothers and wishes to have no association with them, but condemns and considers them accursed. So we see how we are to proceed when announcing God's word to men. If possible, we are to try to lead men to God and his truth. To that end, we proceed with gentleness and goodwill. But if we make a great effort to teach and give good information only to discover that we have wasted our time, we must then employ the bluntness Stephen uses. We must tell them what kind of people they are, calling them what we hear them

586

called: 'people without judgment and discernment'. When he calls
them 'a stiff-necked people', he compares them with animals that
refuse to come under the yoke. It is an unruly animal that cannot be
tamed. Thus Stephen applies that expression to the Jews, pointing
out that they are more bestial and dumber than dumb animals.

He adds that they are uncircumcised in heart and ears, which
is stronger than saying to them, 'You have a heart of stone; you are
enemies of God.' It is as if a Jew had become uncircumcised and
allied himself with the uncircumcised in order to follow another
religion. Now the Jews found all their glory in circumcision because
it was the sign of God's covenant and they could say, 'God has
chosen us for his own.' But Stephen could contradict them and say,
'Your circumcision is only a sign of falsehood and deceit insofar as
it concerns you. You have destroyed its meaning because you wear
it only in your body. And as for your hearts, it is clear that they are
uncircumcised.' That is the way he speaks to those who refuse to
come under the obedience of the gospel. Now, as I have already
said, that is the way we are to proceed if we are to be bearers of the
teaching.

And that speaks not only to those who are charged with the
responsibility of teaching God's word, but to everyone in general.
For on this point the Holy Spirit, who must be our guide, is not
disparaging the right way to teach. If we wish to serve our Master,
that is the way we must go about it. We must make every effort to
draw everybody to the knowledge of the gospel. For when we see
people going to hell who have been created in the image of God
and redeemed by the blood of our Lord Jesus Christ, that must
indeed stir us to do our duty and instruct them and treat them
with all gentleness and kindness as we try to bear fruit this way.

But still Stephen had a special reason. He was speaking to
the Jews, who professed to be God's people. That then has to do
with the 'brothers' Stephen was talking about at the outset. That

is the relationship we now have with the papists, although they differ from us. They confess that Jesus Christ is the Redeemer of the world and then destroy his power while still retaining some sign of the gospel. They confess that Jesus Christ is the Son of God and that what the Evangelists wrote about him must be adhered to as God's truth, even though they do not believe it. So if we have that in common with the papists, there is some appearance of brotherhood. That was the relationship Stephen had with the Jews. Moreover, there was the priesthood, which men did not invent rashly, for our Lord had commanded that it have a place in his church. And that is why Stephen called those assembled 'his fathers'. True, he realizes that they are in fact wicked, but because the office is from God, he continues to attribute some honour to them. If those who are called 'prelates' in the Papacy had been set up and commanded by God, even if they were his mortal enemies, we would still have to acknowledge them. But because they make open war against the gospel and exercise every cruelty against God's children, we must denounce them utterly.

But there is yet another special reason. For God never instituted and commanded anything they claim they created out of their own heads, like the kind of fatherhood the pope and his ilk have set up, a tyranny against the will of God. It can never have the kind of approval the Jews had because the priesthood was approved by the law of Moses. But the pope has usurped everything he has today with his mitred beasts at his side, all those bishops and prelates who have intruded themselves. Consequently, they are unable to claim the kind of prelacy possessed by those to whom Stephen is speaking here, those who were in charge of the entire spiritual government in the church of Judea.

Still, let us look at the case of the pope and all his ilk who, because of their offices, might be worthy of being called 'fathers'. However, that does not mean that the authority of God is to be diminished by that kind of fatherhood. Even if they had a fully God-approved pre-eminence among men, God must always be granted his full authority. So let us note that even if there were holier and more honourable offices than we can conceive of, God must always be placed above them and his authority must continue in his hands and remain undiminished in any way. Let us suppose for a moment that God established the pope for this purpose, that this seat in Rome is truly what it is called, the principal seat in all of Christendom, and that the bishops had been founded on Scripture and that God had approved their office (although that is not the case), the fact is that they cease to be fathers the instant they declare they are God's enemies and refuse to be his servants. So where does that fatherhood come from? It does not come from those of high estate on whom titles are bestowed, but from God. Let those who find fault with that go make a case against God. Those who grasp after the titles in the Papacy not only use them wrongly to God's great dishonour, but, under the authority of those titles, lead everybody away from obedience to him. That is why we must establish every authority and every high office given to men by God according to his will without detracting from the right that is duly his. No matter what high office men may possess and no matter what fatherhood they attribute to themselves, God must always remain pre-eminently the Father. If men exalt themselves above him, there is no fatherhood in them. That point is worth noting, for many people depend on dignities and titles and say, 'We still need prelates and superiors!' Yes indeed, but does that have to obscure God's glory? Must his honour be diminished in order to exalt men? Where will it all end? Therefore, when men in authority learn to act with such modesty and humility regarding God's honour that they exalt him rather than themselves, they should not take offence when they are rebuked, threatened, and even reviled. That, then, is how we must always render to God what is his without elevating creatures at the expense of his majesty.

It is true that God has established social ranks in the world in such a way as to express his desire that those who discharge their responsibility badly will nonetheless be honoured in the very ranks which are so necessary among men that, should a man not do his duty, he will still remain at the rank he holds. For example, concerning the ancient priesthood, God had given it to Aaron's house. In addition, he wants that order to prevail in his church; he wants Aaron's lineage to exercise that priesthood always. And although they do not fulfil their duty, they always remain in their rank. Why? Because that office was from God. However, that does not mean the priests had not diminished God's word, as we see the prophets crying out against them and showing them their baseness because they perverted the teaching God had given them. They tell them that the high office they claim is but filth and dung. Nevertheless, the priesthood still retains its integrity despite the fact that the prophets had to cry out against the wicked who abused God's ordinance in the way they did.

Let us now look at the other ranks of this world. As for the ranks related to the civil order, we have kings and princes who have been established by God. No superiority exists apart from him, says Paul (*Rom.* 13:1). Now if it sometimes happens that princes practise tyranny, abuse their power, and wrongly seize others' property and exercise violence, what is to be done? Their subjects must be patient even though they endure a great deal, knowing that God will punish them for their sins. For if we have good princes, it is a testimony of God's love. By the same token, they are God's scourges when we have offended him. On the other hand, that does not mean that if princes want to constrain us to offend God and are obviously the mortal enemies of the gospel and want to turn us from honouring God, we must attribute to them no more authority than we would to dogs. Inasmuch as they want to diminish God's majesty in this way, they are not worthy of being called animals. Therefore, every high rank and all authority must yield to God's honour, for he must not be deprived of his authority in any way whatsoever.

The same is true for the fathers. If the fathers want to constrain their children to do evil, the children must bear in mind that they have one Father in heaven, whom they are to obey because, as Paul says, he is Father of bodies and souls (*1 Thess.* 5:23). Therefore, children must obey their fathers, but according to God's will. For from the moment the fathers encroach upon God's honour, the children must not in this instance obey them any more than they would the devil.

As concerns the spiritual care of the church, the pope cannot undertake what the emperors and the kings of this world can or what falls to the responsibility of governors and magistrates. Why not? Because our role was instituted to bear God's word, to rebuke vices, to administer the sacraments, and to keep order and support civil government so that God's honour will not be diminished, and to utilize excommunication so that unbelievers whose lives are wicked and dissolute will be excommunicated and expelled from the company of the faithful. That then is what God has appointed us to do. Therefore, anyone who arrogates more to himself, no matter who he may be, must be cast out without compunction. We now understand what restraints must be placed upon the honours and ranks of superiority in this world. In other words, God is always to remain pre-eminent, the greatest are to be subjected to him, and there must be no pretentiousness among men. If we maintain that perspective, all will go well.

So we will render to the princes over us what is due them. Even if they are wicked, even if they are not doing their duty, even if we know that they are abusing their power, even if they are burdening us, let us not fail to obey them since this is the way God wants to chastise us by their hand. But if it happens, as I said, that they try to turn us from God's honour and push us toward idolatry and superstition, they must then have no more authority over us than frogs have, or fleas, or lesser creatures. Why not? Because they want to constrain us to do something contrary to the will of the sovereign prince, whom we are to obey to the exclusion of all other men in the world, regardless of their authority and pre-eminence over us. As Paul says, since all power is ordained of God, he must be sovereign over all things (*Rom.* 13:1).

As for spiritual government, those who are to be constituted as the church and charged to proclaim God's word in the simplicity and purity in which we received it, there is no longer any superiority, I tell you, if they should deviate from it in the slightest, for we are not living in the time of the law when God appointed a definite lineage. That has not been the case since the coming of our Lord Jesus Christ. It has been necessary to elect those who exercise this office. Are they fit? They must discharge their duty and be answerable to God for the task he has put in their hands each and every time he calls on them. That, I say, is what Stephen sets before us here. Now we understand why the pope calls us 'schismatics'. He tries to make us odious by accusing us of holding a false and heretical opinion. Why? Because we do not want him to be over us! What does he expect? His intent is to debase the full majesty of our Lord Jesus Christ and remove all authority from the gospel while expecting us to accept all his abominations and his false and diabolical teachings without objecting. If we have to be schismatics to obey God, so be it. But, as I have already said, we know that that accusation is wrongly applied to us. In addition, if his position rested on the best foundation in the world, he and his doctrine would still have to be rejected. Why? Because he rises up against God and wages deadly war against the gospel.

And now there is another reason we must extend this teaching
a bit further. It is, as I have already said, that, seeing that men
are created in the image of God and that their souls have been
redeemed by the blood of Jesus Christ, we must try in every
way available to us to draw them to the knowledge of the
gospel. First, we try to reach them through gentleness and kindness. But have we determined whether men can be brought
into obedience unto God in this way? Since we see that there is
such hardness and rebellion in them that they cannot be won in
this way, it is no longer a matter of using gentle tactics. Rather, we must storm out against them, as the Holy Spirit shows
us here. And because of that, we understand why many people
think they would like for us to refrain from all harshness when
we speak of the pope and his ilk, calling him an antichrist, a
murderer, a robber who kills poor souls, a thief who pillages God's
honour. Those people, I tell you, will come to us and say, 'Now
tell me what good that does? Would it not be better to refrain
from those criticisms than to be so severe?' In that way, they show
clearly that they have no more zeal for God than a pack of dogs.
Is it right, when God's honour is being trampled underfoot, that
Jesus Christ should be held up to mockery by this Romish robber
who sets himself up as an idol to the extent that there remains
nothing of God's majesty, power, and might that this evil man
does not wish to claim as his own? There is no ordinance of God
that he has not corrupted and perverted. He has profaned the
sacraments. And yet we do not open our mouths and say that he
is an evil man. While witnessing all these abominations, we say
nothing. We keep our mouths shut when we see God blasphemed
and his kingdom brought to ruin and all things holy profaned.
What other outcome can there be? Therefore, let us follow the
Holy Spirit's procedure, such as it is demonstrated for us here. Let
us no longer be gentle when we see such a wicked and egregious

obstinacy against God and his word and when we see that men are totally incorrigible.

Then there is another matter to lament, which is similar to the first. Many times we are compelled to speak out and cry out against these mockers of God who do nothing but flout the whole teaching of salvation. Today we see these condemnable evil people who fear dogs more than they do God. They have no reverence for the gospel and are as brazen as brothel whores. What are we to do about that? Are we going to say simply, 'My friends, that is what God has made known to us; we must make an effort to abide by it'? Oh, we will be their friends if we talk that way! But we understand that God will be mocked, that his honour will be trampled under-foot, and we will not object. Is that the way to proceed? We would have to condemn Stephen, or the Holy Spirit, who spoke by his mouth, because, as we said earlier, Luke declared that Stephen did not speak for himself, but that the Holy Spirit urged him to such vehemence that God sustained him. So let us now go make a case against God and say that he did not proceed well at this point! But, as I have already said, those people show their colours as soon as they say, 'Is that any way to object?' That is a clear sign that they have no love for God or for his word. Now, for our part, we must remain steadfast. Since we are appointed to preach God's word, we must confront the rage of the wicked and adhere to the procedure God has shown us. We must thunder out against them because gentle admonitions cannot reach them. We must confront them with the judgment of God if we are to bring them down. And this is precisely the way we can acknowledge the certainty that God's word must not yield before the malice of men. It is at those times that we must show the power and authority of the word.

On the other hand, when God extends his hand to us, we need to be advised to come to him because he is inviting us in a kind and fatherly way. But when we stubbornly rebel, God's word must be like a hammer to knock some sense into our heads. That is why holy Scripture says he is kind and like a father and is called the bread of life (*John* 6:35, 48). Those attributes are found in many other passages that we could cite. Among others, the prophet Micah, as we have seen recently, said that God's word does good to those who walk uprightly (*Mic.* 2:7). But whenever we want to be hard-headed and butt heads with God and refuse to submit to him or his word, then we must feel the force of what the prophet Jeremiah says when he speaks of God's word as a hammer to break our heads and as a fire to burn and consume men, and because they are but straw, they must be cast into the depths of hell whenever they want to rise up against that word (*Jer.* 23:29). So let us each examine ourselves. And while God favours us by inviting us with fatherly gentleness, he asks only that we come to him, and he helps us so we can sense the gracious comforting of our Lord Jesus Christ. Then if we back away, is he not justified in letting us go our own way? Therefore, when our Lord Jesus Christ calls us, let us not be so wayward that we completely oppose him, but let us acknowledge that we must find all our consolation in his word.

Now it is quite true that many wicked people are little concerned when others treat them austerely and tell them things that should put them to shame. They could not care less. They do nothing but hatch their own thoughts, but in the end they will learn that God will not allow a jot or a tittle to fall from his word (*Josh.* 21:45; *1 Kings* 8:56). I tell you, they will learn that the sentence pronounced against them today will be inscribed before God and will one day be carried out. Yes, they will escape the hands of men. They will even have power over men and inflict them with all kinds of afflictions and suffering at their disposal. They will even despise God and mock him and his word, but after engaging in such wicked acts, they will, when all is said and done, acknowledge that it is with their master that they have trifled. All of it will come back to haunt them. The only thing that remains for us to do is to ask to come to God while he is extending his hand and then follow him where he leads.

In addition, we must likewise note what Stephen says here: 'stiff-necked and uncircumcised in heart and ears'. By speaking that way to the Jews, he points to the kind of people the faithful ought to be. There is no doubt that he wishes to state that it is in vain that they profess to be the church of God. It is as if he were saying, 'It is true you bear the title 'prelates of the church' and occupy the priesthood, yet in no respect do you belong to the church of God. Why not? You are stiff-necked. So what is lacking? If you want God to give you his approval and consider you as his children, then learn to submit your neck to his yoke' (cf. *Matt.* 11:28-30). That submission is the true mark of your Christian faith. When the Lord's yoke is not difficult or burdensome for us, it is then that we are not rebellious when he wants to bring us into subjection to himself. We will voluntarily yield to his lordship. That is a point we must pay close attention to in this passage.

We now ask what God's yoke is. It is his desire that each one of us bring himself into conformity with his word. That is the rule he has established for us. We must now adhere to that teaching, submit to it as to a yoke, and come to it gladly, knowing that God will deal with us with such gentleness that we will have no occasion to withdraw from his service. If we say, 'Alas, we are weak, indeed completely powerless, but God requires of us too great a perfection', then how in the world can we please him in anything? Now to compensate for our shortcomings, God goes so far as to be always ready to forgive them in the name of our Lord Jesus Christ. Consequently, men have no excuse for not yielding to God's yoke. For if we yield willingly, there is no doubt that we will find him sweeter and more gratifying than all the freedoms this world affords.

As touching what is said here about circumcision, we must consider what sign and what mark God has given us today so that we may know we belong to him. We have baptism, which has taken the place of circumcision. Now the truth of baptism and its efficacy do not consist in an external power. It is not enough to have water applied to our head. What then is required? That we take refuge in the blood of Jesus Christ, which purges us and cleanses us of our impurities, so that when they are washed away, we are truly cleansed and are assured and certain that God has forgiven our sins and will no longer charge them against us. That is the first truth about baptism. The second is that we are, in a manner of speaking, thrust into the water in order to die to the world and that we are already in the process of dying to ourselves, to all our lusts and evil affections so that we might live unto God. In other words, God lives in us by guiding us by the Holy Spirit. If that is not the case, we will be able to boast of our baptism, but that will be a lie. That is why Moses said to the people, 'Therefore, circumcise your hearts unto God this day' (*Deut.* 10:16). He shows them that it was not sufficient to use an outward sign, but that they had to come to the truth, because our Lord never limited himself to figures, but required the faithful to consider what they signified. So our hearts must be circumcised unto God. And how is that done? We remove from our hearts everything that is superfluous, like evil thoughts, wicked affections, carnal lusts, and such like. It is as our Lord tells us. We must die to the world and to ourselves. Otherwise, we stifle our baptism and will be accused before God of having invalidated this sacred sign (cf. *Mark* 8:35; *Rom.* 6:8). Now it is true, as I have just said, that the truth of our baptism does not consist in these externals. Jesus Christ must validate everything by his Holy Spirit. For Scripture says it belongs to him alone to baptize with spirit and with fire (*Matt.* 3:11; *Luke* 3:16). It says that men will be able to baptize with water, as John the Baptist did and others after him, as we still do today, but that does not mean we can bestow the Holy Spirit. Who then can? Jesus Christ, who reserves for himself the power and authority to give the Holy Spirit. We must then pray that the Son of God will not allow our baptism to be a dead figure, but cause it to prevail by the grace of his Holy Spirit so that we may be renewed to live for him, as he calls us to do. And as Moses said when speaking to the people, 'Circumcise your hearts', so must we do today as we remember the promises we made at the time of our baptism. We must renounce the world if we are to dedicate ourselves totally to God and his service because the reason God has chosen us and marked us as his own is so that we will not doubt that he wants to receive us into his heavenly kingdom. So let us be careful not to deprive the sign and mark he has given us of its meaning. Otherwise, we will be deprived of his grace if we are so wretched as to take a stand against him. That is how we nullify the grace that God has granted us. And, as Paul says, we grieve his Holy Spirit (*Eph.* 4:30). Let us take counsel then and take greater advantage of it than we have before, and coming back to him in true repentance, let us receive this blessing from his hand as it is presented to us.

Following this holy teaching, let us bow before the face of our gracious God in acknowledgment of our sins, praying that he will be pleased so to touch us that we will abandon all of them so that nothing will prevent our coming to him in the name of our Lord Jesus Christ his Son. And as long as he permits us to remain in this present life, may he lead us by his Holy Spirit in such a way that we will ask only to yield ourselves to his will, such as he has made it known in his law, until we are so clothed in his righteousness that he will live fully in us. Now let us all say, Almighty God, heavenly Father . . .

42

SUSTAINED WHEN PERSECUTED AND AFFLICTED

SUNDAY, 21 DECEMBER 1550

Which of the prophets have not your fathers persecuted? and they have slain them which shewed before of the coming of the Just One; of whom ye have been now the betrayers and murderers: [53] *Who have received the law by the disposition of angels, and have not kept it.* [54] *When they heard these things, they were cut to the heart, and they gnashed on him with their teeth.* [55] *But he, being full of the Holy Ghost, looked up stedfastly into heaven, and saw the glory of God, and Jesus standing on the right hand of God,* [56] *And said, Behold, I see the heavens opened, and the Son of man standing on the right hand of God* (Acts 7:52–56).

We pointed out last week that even though it is mortal men who proclaim the teaching sent from on high, it is God we resist if we refuse it. Now our Lord wants to be heard with all reverence, which explains why the messengers he sends are only human beings like ourselves. So let us take to heart that God's teaching, when faithfully proclaimed, is so thoroughly his that whoever refuses to receive it in all humility wages war against God and resists the Holy Spirit. That is a state of affairs we should recoil at in horror. Indeed, everyone who hears that says that situation is abhorrent. Yet to our detriment we do not hesitate to collide with God. Seeing then such resistance and obstinacy in men, we are particularly obliged to take note of this teaching. That is to say, if we wish to be at peace with God, if we do not want to grieve his Holy Spirit, we must in all humility and reverence receive the teaching that is preached to us in his name and with his authority.

Now Stephen confirms that point even more strongly when he adds, 'Which of the prophets have not your fathers persecuted? Did they not kill those who were proclaiming the coming of the Just One?' He was saying in effect, 'Your fathers murdered the prophets.' It follows then that they waged war against God and the Holy Spirit. We now see that that judgment is a confirmation of what was said long ago. So let us not think that we have a dignity that places us over others when we are so wretched that we resist God's teaching. But let us realize that if we are to obey him, we must accept what is proclaimed in his name. That is the way he wants us to honour him. He wants his word to be received. Consequently, whoever rejects God's prophets, as I have said, is already God's enemy and will feel God's hand upon him to wreak vengeance. When someone speaks to us in God's name, let us learn to accept the great blessing of being prudent enough to take into consideration what we are told. And since it is God's will that we have preaching, let us be aware that we will not be able to reject men for fear that God will be offended and consider the outrage as being directed against his person. As it is written, 'Whoever rejects you rejects me, and not only me, but the Father who sent me' (*Luke* 10:16). Those are the words of our Lord Jesus Christ.

Moreover, Stephen points out to the Jews that their killing the prophets who were proclaiming their salvation was the result of their unbelief and ungodliness. If that were the only thing we could not stand to hear from God, would that not in itself be diabolical madness? What excuse could we have for being so proud and arrogant that we cannot listen to the one who formed and created us? Also, our guilt is compounded because God has favoured us by speaking to us about our salvation and seeking only our good and our obedience to his teaching. That is what Stephen intended when saying, 'The prophets spoke to you about the coming of the Redeemer. They wanted to lead you to eternal life, and you rejected them, and killed them.' Now it is true that he is reproaching the Jews here when he says their fathers were like that, and he said that to come to his next point: 'You are murderers of the Just One; you have therefore surpassed your fathers in iniquity.' This passage tells us that the more our Lord shows himself to be gentle and gracious toward us for our own welfare, the fewer excuses we have for rejecting the grace he offers us, and we deserve, I say, greater condemnation before him if we do not accept the good he wants to do for us.

Now the Jews are reproached for killing the prophets who spoke to them of the coming of Jesus Christ. What will now happen to us, then, if we do not listen to God now that he is speaking to us and has already sent his only Son and has brought us the message of salvation, though not as it was delivered to our forefathers in the law? Now that it is apparent and obvious to us that the kingdom of heaven has been opened for us by the resurrection of our Lord Jesus Christ, we have a reliable testimony that we are victorious over death and that he has won life for us. Since all that is ours, what wrath do we not deserve if we should be so wretched as to reject such grace?

And we must pay even closer attention to this passage, which says, 'Behold those who killed the prophets; they are completely without excuse before God' (*Matt.* 23:37; *1 Thess.* 2:15). And how is that? They sinned doubly. In the first place, they did not render to God the honour he was due. And then they were ungrateful because they heard about the Redeemer of the world but refused to share in that great blessing. And if they were punished for such wickedness, what will our lot be? True, our Lord spoke about those days, but he is now speaking in a different way. He declares that his Son has already been sent to us and we are no longer under the figures of the law. We have clearly revealed truth! Therefore, let us know that a much more horrible punishment hangs over our heads if we do not in all humility receive that good thing God wishes to do for us. In conclusion, Stephen says, 'You have received the law by the disposition of angels', which is the same as saying, 'God has sent you his law. It is true that Moses was the messenger, but its authority was greater because angels administered it. God sent it from on high in order to establish it among you and to give it to you by their hand. That, I tell you, is an admonition God gave by the agency of angels, but you did not heed it. What excuse then will you have for being traitors like that and for being false witnesses of God?' Now when Stephen reproaches the Jews that way, he does so to point out he was not guilty of the crime they accused him of. He also wanted to point out that they were not motivated by the kind of zeal they were displaying, for they were pretending that they could not tolerate a violation of the law of Moses. That is why Stephen declares to them unambiguously, 'That is not what incites you against me. It is an accursed madness, because you cannot tolerate the truth of God. The truth is that you do not walk according to his law and his commandments. It is evident that you have not done so. The necessary conclusion then is that you have no zeal in you, but only malice, and that it is the devil in you, urging you to persecute me.'

Now on this point one could allege, 'If the Jews are wicked, that does not mean to say that Stephen's case is good and just.' We have to note that he is speaking to men who were totally hardened and that he understood they completely rejected God's teaching. On that point he says to them, 'You have not kept the law.' It would be a waste of effort to pursue this further and continue to speak with people who are as rebellious as you.' That is what Stephen means.

Now there is a good lesson to be gleaned from this passage. First, we learn that the law of God has been given to us so authoritatively that we must not consider it as a teaching fabricated here below. For it says notably that the angels were God's commissioned officers to establish the law so that it might be received without any difficulty, as Paul says in Galatians 3: 'It was', he says, 'ordained by angels in the hand of a mediator, who was Jesus Christ' (*Gal.* 3:19). He is not speaking of Moses, but the fact is that the angels are appointed so we might know that it is God who is speaking and that Moses was only a deputy and presented nothing that he had created in his imagination. That is the first point we need to note here, namely that when someone speaks to us about the law of Moses, we must not look upon the man's outward appearance, but we must understand that it is God who sent him. The proof that this is so lies in the fact that the angels testified that this teaching had come from on high and that God wants to be received with total obedience. Consequently, when we refuse to obey God's law, the angels witness against us and pronounce sentence on our rebellion. It is true that God could have bypassed the use of angels when setting forth his law, but he wanted them to be there as witnesses so that if we now become disobedient, they can testify against men's refusal of the blessing offered to them at the time. It is true that the law without Jesus Christ is of no advantage but works for the condemnation of men. However, if we receive it with the promises it contains, we will at that time find everlasting life because Jesus Christ is encompassed within it, for he is its soul.

Now we also need to note that when our Lord deigns to address us, our sin is compounded if we do not obey him. As for the knowledge we have to have concerning him, it is true that his desire is for everyone to preach the gospel, and none will be excused. It is true that in our day and time the Turks have no more preaching than we had when we lived in ignorance and were without the knowledge of the truth about God, just as that knowledge still does not exist in the Papacy, where the devil is in such control that they seek only the absolute burial of God's teaching, although they want to pretend some appearance of ignorance. Nevertheless, all of them are inexcusable. But a much more grievous punishment awaits us. That is because it is God who especially appeals to us as one opening his mouth to address his word to us. He grants us this blessing, but we do not yield and receive it. It is certain that if we do not profit from his teaching, he will raise up others and make himself known to them. Even so, we must give serious attention to this word: 'You have received the law, but you have not kept it.' It is true that all the pagans did not know God during that time. But it is also true that unbelievers are definitely inexcusable, for it is said that those who sin without the law will likewise perish without the law (*Rom.* 2:12) and will not be excused because of their ignorance. Those who have been instructed and have heard the teaching and yet sin, their condemnation, I tell you, is sealed.

Just as Paul spoke that way to the Jews at that time, these letters are now addressed to us. Since God has now favoured us with the blessing of instruction, let us realize that it is as if he were extending his hand to us and saying, 'I want you to come to me and not consider those pitiable, ignorant people.' True, we must have pity on them and make an effort to draw them to the knowledge of the truth in which our Lord has instructed us. But let us not be like them, following in their idolatrous and superstitious ways. Rather, let us follow the path God shows us. That is the meaning of this passage which says, 'You have received the law but you have not kept it.' Because our Lord had made himself known to the Jews, they were considered perjurers and covenant breakers because they did not receive the teaching when it was presented to them. The same will be said of us, but we will be more inexcusable if the teaching we hear today does not enter into us. And why is that?

Let us now compare the law and the gospel. It is written that the law was given by the hand of angels. And the gospel, by whose hand was it sent to us? It was Jesus Christ, who came down from his heavenly glory, was manifest in the flesh, and opened his sacred mouth to instruct us. But being dissatisfied with that, he ratified his teaching with his own blood and even bore the penalty which was our due because of our sins. Therefore, since our Saviour Jesus Christ has graciously condescended to be our Master and Teacher, will not our punishment be much more rigorous than that of the Jews if we do not receive the word coming from his mouth? Is God not right to grow increasingly angry with us for such wickedness and ingratitude? And that is why Paul says in chapter 3 of 2 Corinthians, 'If that which does not merit being glorified has been glorified, how glorious will be that which God sheds his glory on and causes to shine with such splendour?' (Cf. *2 Cor.* 3:7–11.) Now Paul, in this passage, dealt with the distinction which I have just touched upon. So he says, 'When the law was manifested, wonders accompanied it. Thunder and lightning were heard and seen. After the cloud appeared on the mountain, the burning fire and the sound of the trumpet were such that the earth trembled' (cf. *Exod.* 19:16; *Heb.* 12:18–19). So when we see that God made his law known that way and that there was great fear, and when we see, on the other hand, that the gospel was proclaimed in all gentleness and meekness, and because our Lord Jesus Christ, the fountain of all kindness and mercy, brought it to us himself, we are the only ones standing in the way of the gospel's being received with greater authority than the law. It is true that he is indeed speaking today just as he spoke in those days, but he is speaking differently. Therefore, if those who rejected the law of Moses remain inexcusable, what will be our lot today if we do not think it worthwhile to hear that teaching, which must cause not only the earth to tremble, but heaven itself? And when the law was revealed, our Lord did indeed shake the earth. But there is now an even more wondrous shaking: heaven and earth must be shaken by the preaching of the gospel. So if our Lord reveals the truth of that teaching so fully that all creatures above and below are shaken by it, and if he knows that we cannot be shaken and that we are more insensitive to it than dumb animals, what punishment do we deserve? Consequently, we cannot reject it without trampling under foot the blood of our Lord Jesus Christ. It is our Lord Jesus Christ who poured out his blood. Why? To wash us with it, for it is our cleansing. And yet by our ingratitude we nullify it today. The Jews were reproached because they violated the law, which had been given to them by angels. That was a witness against their wickedness as covenant breakers, disloyal to God. Such ingratitude must not remain unpunished. Let us be aware then that we will be even more worthy of condemnation because the teaching of the gospel was not only given to us by angels, but by the Son of God, their Master, and ratified and approved by his own blood. God wanted his majesty to be known here below, for it is a teaching which is to shake heaven and earth. We must not be so hard-hearted and obstinate that we reject it.

Moreover, if we wish to show that we are zealous for God and his word, we must demonstrate it in our lives. Many will put on airs of being very zealous, and they will refuse to hear God's word spoken against. They will play the role very well, but they want to have the leeway and freedom to live as they please. That is not the way things are done. If we want to demonstrate that our zeal is real, let us walk with a pure conscience and make sure that everyone keeps God's word.

Consequently, the text says that those who heard Stephen speak gnashed their teeth against him and were cut to the heart.

That points out that he was so far from influencing them and mollifying them and purging the venom and bitterness in them that they became even more venomous and more outraged against him because of his charges against them. From that it is quite clear God's teaching will not help everyone. Why not? Because the teaching must enter our hearts. Otherwise, we will not be moved to come to God. Consequently, there is such a great difference between God and men that when he calls them, they go in the opposite direction until he changes their wicked hearts and gives them a new affection to bring them to his will. So this passage teaches us the extent of the evil and perversity of human nature. It is true that Luke is talking about the Jews who were enemies of the gospel. But we are so far from being better than they that our zeal and our affection are not different from theirs unless God works in our hearts by his Holy Spirit. In short, we have here a mirror image of human nature which shows that when God speaks to them, they only kick back like horses and rear up against him in rejection of his word until he corrects them himself. Now it is true that men do not see this at first, for at the outset some semblance of religion exists and men do not react like madmen in their resistance to God. We are not able to hear what he says and receive him as we should until he opens our hearts, conforms us to his will, and brings us in line with his word. Otherwise, in the end we will be obliged to endure the kind of hardness within ourselves that he is talking about here. That is to say, the more God pursues us for our welfare, the more we experience rage and gnash our teeth against him and his ministers and resist them with a diabolical anger and rebellion. That, I tell you, is the way all human beings are. Understanding that, we have much to guard against. And we must seek the remedy so that after recognizing the evil within us, we will come to God and beseech him to be pleased to remove that hardness and rebellion from our hearts and give us that gentleness and kindness which are so necessary if we are to hear him, and we must beseech him to give us a spirit of meekness to yield completely to his will and obey it. So much for that point.

Still, we must note that God's word is not the source of men's unbridled behaviour, bickering, and madness. Such cannot be attributed to God's word, for it does not proceed from his nature. The fact is that we are ill-disposed to pay attention when God speaks to us. For his part, he asks only to instruct us in all gentleness and kindness. But because we find God's word is unpalatable, all that behaviour proceeds from us. Men are so different from God that they never want to conform to his teaching. The greater their estrangement from him, the greater their desire to withdraw farther and farther from him.

Moreover, this alerts us to the fact that he must not be surprised if the world rejects God's word or even if many are scandalized that it is not received as it ought to be. This is the way they react: 'What? If that word is from God, why does he permit men to receive it as something else?' That is how many ignorant people are scandalized when they see that the world scorns and rejects the gospel that way. Now we must guard against such a temptation, for there is nothing new in that, as we learn from this passage. Here we have Stephen, filled with the Spirit of God and yet unable to change the minds of his hearers. So let us not be surprised if we find the same thing among ourselves. Did a change occur throughout the world when the Son of God spoke? Did everybody amend his ways upon hearing his voice? Indeed not! So what will happen when we speak? Do you think we will be more privileged than our Master? Now we have in this passage a general remedy for the temptation that could confront us when we see holy Scripture being rejected. So, those of us who have the responsibility of proclaiming God's word are counselled to be patient if we do not see the teaching bearing fruit in everybody. We must persist in the pursuit of our commission and do what God commands. We must, it is true, expend much effort and do everything we can to make our teaching bear fruit among all, weeping and groaning when we see the word is not received as it should be. And when it is not, we must not grow weary, for if God does not want everybody to be converted to him, that is, if he does not wish to favour them in that way, it is not our place to go against him. But our only obligation is to follow the calling he has laid upon us, for nothing will hinder us, because it is God who says to us, 'Preach!' Nevertheless, we see that people often grow increasingly worse because of our preaching. We see some who are like devils running loose. It would seem that we would do better to keep our mouths shut. But how can we? It is God who says to us, 'Preach!' So let us pursue the charge laid upon us, no matter what happens. That is another point.

It is true that when he says, 'Preach', he promises to make that teaching bear fruit. But fruit is not evident in everybody, but definitely in some. So let us realize he manifests himself to those to whom it pleases him. It is a special gift. However, that turns out to have even graver consequences for people when they refuse to take advantage of the teaching, for we realize they have been completely forsaken. When the right medicine is prescribed but fails to help a patient, what can we say except it is all we can do? And if the patient himself refuses everything good for him, what can we expect except that he continue to die? The same is true for those who resist the gospel, gnash their teeth against it, and act like madmen, for it is the medicine that will heal us not only of our spiritual ills, but of death itself. The gospel has the power to redeem us from eternal death and lead us to the kingdom of God. Now that medicine, because of us and our evil, becomes a deadly poison. That is evident in the fact that our nature is so perverse we corrupt all of God's gifts. That then is what we need to note in this passage where Luke says the Jews gnashed their teeth against Stephen and their hearts were rent.

Now Luke also adds that Stephen lifted his eyes on high and fixed them there because he was being afflicted by men. He sees himself as a sheep in the midst of wolves. He sees only diabolical rage all around him. He must then commend himself to God and take refuge in him, which he does, as is shown here, and God does not fail him, for the heavens are opened to him. He sees Jesus Christ standing at the right hand of God his Father. Now that is not for his consolation only, but so that the wicked and adversaries of the truth may be even more convinced, as we will see, for he declares that he sees the heavens opened and Jesus Christ standing at the right hand of God, that is, in his majesty, where he is Ruler and Sovereign Prince over all creation.

Now it is worth noting that Luke says, 'Stephen, being filled with the Holy Spirit, saw the glory of God and of Jesus Christ', which he says to point out our need to be led by the Spirit of God. Even though his glory is quite apparent, we will not see it any better than blind men unless the Holy Spirit fills us and opens our eyes. That is what Stephen wanted to point out. But in order to glean the substance of the teaching contained in this passage, we must first notice that Stephen points out that we must take refuge in God when we are in extreme affliction and see only men's fury and rage against us. That is the only remedy that can give us assurance, namely that we totally entrust ourselves and our undertaking to God. Our Lord has a reason for declaring that he will help his people in time of need. It is true that we always need his help and that he is also ready to provide it. And he particularly declares that he will sustain us whenever we are oppressed by evil and afflicted on all sides, and that it is at those times that he will show he is even nearer. So let us learn from Stephen's example that when we are in confusion in this life and surrounded on all sides and so heavily oppressed that we can take no more, God will manifest his help at that time, declaring to us that that is the way he wants to draw us to himself, provided he is our sole refuge. That then is a primary teaching of this passage that we must take to heart. The teaching deserves greater elaboration, but let us look to applying it to our instruction, and although we are dealing with it in few words, let us not fail to imbibe it and profit from it.

In the first place, when some evil presses upon us, when men persecute us, and when we are tormented in some way or another, let us follow Stephen's example and turn to God as he did in this passage, and we will find that God will help us even better than we hoped. However, as I have said, we must be filled with the Holy Spirit. Not that we might have him as fully as Stephen did, but the fact is that if the Holy Spirit does not appear to us and give us the ability to see, we will never glimpse God's glory – provided we do not think God grants us the grace to contemplate him without first enlightening us by his Holy Spirit. There is a difference between God and us; we cannot reach him; we cannot have the minutest knowledge of him unless he cleanses us of all our wicked affections. And how will he do that? By his Holy Spirit.

Now we might ask at this point, 'How is it that Stephen was able to see the glory of God inasmuch as God is invisible?' That would call into question what has been declared heretofore, namely that we cannot comprehend God in his majesty and in his being. We must understand that God has manifested himself at all times to his servants whenever it is expedient for him to do so, whether in large or small measure. There is no doubt that Stephen had a much more perfect manifestation than was ever provided before, for our Lord Jesus Christ had not yet been seen in his glory the way Stephen now sees him. But he still did not see God's infinite majesty. So God had to manifest himself to him only to the extent that he could endure it.

We could also ask how Stephen was able to see Jesus Christ, for Scripture says, 'He is higher than the heavens' (*Heb.* 7:26), and our eyes cannot see that far. And the papists misuse that passage, as if Jesus Christ were everywhere visible in this way. That is an outlandish notion, if we compare Stephen's sight with our natural faculty. Why so? Well, Stephen sees Jesus Christ, but those who are in the room with him do not! Why not? Because they are blind and also because Stephen did not see him with natural vision, but miraculously, because God gave him eyes to see. Consequently, heaven was not only open to Stephen, but our Lord also gave him new eyes so that he might contemplate the things which are, in the natural order, incomprehensible. That ought to be sufficient for us against all the claims that might be made about this passage.

When the text says that Stephen saw Jesus Christ seated at the right hand of God his Father, it does not mean that we should imagine anything fleshly about our Lord Jesus Christ. When Scripture speaks in those terms, it does so to signify that he has all authority and all power to govern everything by his might. He is God his Father's lieutenant for judging the world and all creatures under him. That was the glory that Stephen saw. And as for us, if we are obedient to our God, long-suffering in our afflictions and totally reliant upon him, it is certain he will not hide from us, but will, under those conditions, show himself for our good, just as he did for Stephen. Now it is true we will not have the kind of miracle he had. We will not see the heavens opened, but God will show himself in such way that we will have enough to satisfy us and to be guided by his Holy Spirit, and we will be able to remain steadfast in our resistance to all the temptations the devil puts before us and never be overcome by the temptations of this world.

We also need to pay attention to this passage so that we will be better prepared to receive the holy Supper, which we are going to celebrate next Sunday, God willing. So when we come to the Supper of our Lord Jesus Christ, we see before us bread and wine. We do not come seeking sustenance for our bodies. 'For', as Paul asks, 'does not everyone have his own house to eat and drink in?'

(*1 Cor.* 11:22) So what are we looking for in the Supper of our Lord Jesus Christ? We are seeking to be fed by him so that he will be our meat and drink, nourish us, and live in us by faith. We are joined to his body so that we may share in all his blessings. Now that is not what we actually see. We see only a piece of bread and we take a sip of wine. That will not be found among the elements that make up this world. What we must do is lift our eyes on high. It is true, as I said, that God will not work the same kind of miracle that he did in Stephen. But just as the Holy Spirit was visibly bestowed on the apostles so they might know that our Lord will guide us until the end of the world by his Holy Spirit, so did our Lord Jesus Christ reveal himself that one time to Stephen so we might understand he will also reveal himself to us. So what are we to do? We must lift up our eyes on high in faith since the promises given to us also wait for us there. Jesus Christ does not say, 'Look for me in the bread and wine', but he says, 'Come unto me' (*Matt.* 11:28). And where will we find him? He tells us that he is in the glory of God his Father. Since Jesus Christ calls us to himself, we must, if we want to go to him, get beyond this world by raising our thoughts on high and not doing as the papists, who look for God in a piece of bread and even make a damnable idol of it. Rather let us, like Stephen, look to heaven without doubting that God will give us the vision that we will obtain by faith the things necessary for our salvation. That way, Jesus Christ will live in us and we will be so joined to him that we will share his power and all the good things he has received from God his Father. Not that he needs them for himself, but so he can communicate them to us, as we see him do by his Holy Spirit every day.

Following this holy teaching, let us bow before the face of our gracious God in acknowledgment of our sins, praying that he will be pleased so to quicken us that our attachments to the vanities of this world and our evil affections will not hinder our pursuit of the calling to which he has called us. And may he not allow us to waver from his holy teaching, so that by submitting ourselves completely to his holy word, we may be brought into conformity with his holy commandments. As we do this, may he alone be worshipped and exercise such authority and pre-eminence over us as he deserves to. Now let us all say, Almighty God, heavenly Father . . .

43

REWARDS AND REPRISALS

SUNDAY, 4 JANUARY 1551

But he, being full of the Holy Ghost, looked up stedfastly into heaven, and saw the glory of God, and Jesus standing on the right hand of God, [56] And said, Behold, I see the heavens opened, and the Son of man standing on the right hand of God. [57] Then they cried out with a loud voice, and stopped their ears, and ran upon him with one accord, [58] And cast him out of the city, and stoned him: and the witnesses laid down their clothes at a young man's feet, whose name was Saul (Acts 7:55–58).

When we are hard-pressed by our enemies, our only consolation is in the knowledge that God helps us. That is also the point to which Scripture leads us when it wishes to give us a firm assurance. 'The Lord is on my side. I will fear no living man', David says, 'when I am assailed by a countless multitude; so long as God defends me, that is enough for me' (*Psa.* 118:6). And Paul says, 'If God is for us, who can be against us?' (*Rom.* 8:31) He is our only refuge when we realize we can do no more. We know that God is watching over us and is concerned for our salvation. It is true that we must always be confident of that. And we must not be so blind that we fail to look to God except in time of need. But when I say 'except in time of need', it is to point out that there is no evil so great that this good and dependable remedy cannot overcome it when we seek after it. And especially when we fight for the truth, God, in order to maintain his cause and his purpose, will grant us the privilege of being persecuted by the world. The wicked will rise up against us with unrestrained rage, and there will be no way to resist them. We must not reach that point. God has not forsaken us. He wants to help us in our need.

That is exactly what Luke is recounting. By proposing Stephen as an example, he indicates what we all have to do. If we had a brief account of Stephen, it would not have such power as when he shows us that Stephen, being persecuted by the enemies of the gospel, commended himself to our Lord Jesus Christ and how he endured death and remained strong and invincible. When that is recounted for us, we have a much greater confirmation than we have from the teaching, and we can no longer say, 'Yes, but we are infirm and weak by nature. We know we cannot maintain God's cause as we ought.' And we have before us Stephen, who has the same nature we do. But because he is strengthened by power from on high, is armed with prayers and petitions, and sustained by God's grace through his Holy Spirit, we see there is no weakness or infirmity of the flesh that prevents him from doing what God commands of us all. So let us imitate what he shows us here. In other words, let us call upon the name of God and be assured that he will help us in such a way that we will never be overcome, for, as we have already said, persecution is sure to come upon us. We must look to our Lord Jesus Christ when men afflict us and seem to have all power over us.

We also need to note in this passage that Stephen says, 'I see heaven opened, and the Son of man standing on the right hand of God his Father.' We have said it was by a miracle that Stephen had that vision and that believers will not see Jesus Christ as Stephen saw him, even when facing a similar death. As a general rule, we must rise to heaven by faith if we are to learn how Jesus Christ is all-powerful to help us. And let us not doubt that we will be enlightened by the Holy Spirit so we can see things hidden and invisible, provided we ask God to be pleased to lift us to himself.

Now Luke has already mentioned that Stephen was filled with the Holy Spirit. That is why he was able to see the heavens opened. Therefore, inasmuch as our sight is so limited that we can see things only on this earth, let us pray that God will give us better sight. In other words, let us pray that he will so enlighten us by his Holy Spirit that we can see what is now invisible to human reason and maintain our assurance that Jesus Christ is at the right hand of God his Father, even though he has not yet appeared in his majesty. In fact, we will only be hypocrites if we do not look to heaven, for every day we say, 'I believe that Jesus Christ ascended to heaven, is seated at the right hand of God the Father Almighty.' If we confess that with our mouths and yet do not have that belief imprinted on our hearts, is that not a mockery? So let us do a better job of looking to heaven than we do so that the delights and pleasures of this world will not be like a blindfold that prevents us from being able to contemplate Jesus Christ in his power. Now the text says, 'Stephen saw him at the right hand of the Father.' That means that Jesus Christ has been established as sovereign Prince so that he might be Lord over all creation and have everything in his hand and under his authority.

Now let us consider the reason Jesus Christ rules and governs. It is for our good. Consequently, all the power given to Jesus Christ is for our salvation, and it is his desire to bring it to pass. In short, we must not limit our concentration simply to Jesus Christ; we must realize that he was exalted by God his Father so that every knee must now bow before him and every creature give him honour (*Phil.* 2:10–11).

So, in the first place, let us now learn to bring ourselves into subjection to Jesus Christ, since he is the sovereign King of the entire world, with the angels themselves, God's glorious principalities, in subjection to him. What then can we do but humble ourselves and bring ourselves to obey him? That is what we are to learn from the words 'the right hand of God', where Jesus Christ is. However, let us not doubt that he holds in his hand all the good things necessary for our salvation and is dispensing them liberally for us. On the other hand, let us not doubt that he can overcome the devil and all his minions and hold them in check to keep them from doing us harm. In short, that right hand of God constitutes the unshakable assurance that we must have. Being under the protection of our Lord Jesus Christ, we need not be surprised or astonished in any way – provided he has received us into his care and we have that confidence in him – that we are assured that whatever the devil contrives when the world assails us, our salvation, being in his hand, is in an invincible fortress. So let us not imagine that the expression 'the right hand of God' refers to some remote corner of heaven. But let us realize that the right hand of God reaches both high and low, and that the power of our Lord Jesus Christ is here in this world and is able to resist all the efforts of the devil and his minions. No matter what they do, they can do nothing to harm us.

However, it is true we will continue to be persecuted, as we see in Stephen's case. Even though he saw our Lord Jesus Christ's power and majesty and experienced it, he was nonetheless stoned, and that because it pleased God that he should witness to the gospel and that innocent blood should be shed as a stronger confirmation of his teaching. So it could well be our lot that we, knowing the power of our Lord Jesus Christ, will not escape being afflicted by men and that God will loosen their reins for a while. Yet the fact remains that we will sense his help and aid in such way that men, after venting their full fury, will have accomplished nothing against us without advancing our salvation comparably. For, as Paul says, death cannot prevent our lives from being blessed if we accept it in honour of our God (cf. *Rom.* 14:7–8). In another passage he says that if we have Jesus Christ, death will be to our advantage, just as life is, for all is gain for us, provided we possess Jesus Christ, because he sanctifies everything for us (cf. *Phil.* 1:20–21).

In addition, we must note how cowardly we are in the face of persecution, how fearful we are, how minimal our steadfastness and courage are, when it is a question of bearing witness to the truth. All of that is the result of closing our eyes so that we do not know how to look to Jesus. What keeps our vision from glimpsing that heavenly glory? Is it not our weakness? As the apostle says, if we had real faith, we would have an anchor in heaven (cf. *Heb.* 6:19). Our faith would then enter into the incomprehensible secret places of the kingdom of God. If, however, we do not reach that height, it is because we are lacking in faith. Now, seeing the fault within us, let us also seek the remedy, which is praying to God that he will be pleased to reveal the glory of his Son to us and make us profit more from the gospel than we have, so that we may know his power and be fortified against every temptation. Let us likewise apply our study to that end inasmuch as we have not yet sufficiently learned what the power of our Lord Jesus Christ is. And when it comes to preaching, we do not have the kind of liking for it that we should. That being true, let us acknowledge that we have not been appropriately diligent in listening to God's promises so that we may receive them as certainties and meditate upon them continually. So, let us learn to be more fervent than we have been. Even the times we live in invite us to do as much. We see how God's poor church is going through uncertain times today. If we are now in the time of rest, well, it is a moment of respite God is providing. But we see our brothers being persecuted for witnessing to the gospel. Every day we see the plots against us. We see the threats of our enemies and we even see their power, and we do not know what God will allow them to do, either to chastise us for our sins or to test our patience, so that those who are true believers may come under scrutiny. We do not know what God has in mind, but our responsibility is to get ready beforehand so that we will not be caught unawares.

Now this is how. As long as we are still in this world, despite not seeing Jesus Christ with our fleshly eyes while he is in his majesty and in that celestial glory mentioned here, we will be able to contemplate him through faith in the same way we rise above the heavens. Being assured that sovereign control has been conferred on Jesus Christ, let us come directly to him, and, praying that he will gather us into his flock, let us not doubt that his power is sufficient to sustain us against all of Satan's efforts and all of the tricks and schemes of the wicked. To that end, let us entrust ourselves completely to him after the example given us here in Stephen.

It is also worth noting that Stephen says he sees the Son of man. With that statement he rebukes the Jews' pride and arrogance. It is as if he were saying, 'It is true that you reject the Son of God because he appeared to you in human flesh, because you crucified him and despised him, and even because he was subjected to shame and abuse. You think you completely destroyed him and reduced him to nothing. But I see him', he says, 'in his sovereign majesty and the glorious immortality of heaven, and I see him seated at the right hand of God his Father.' True, the word used here does not signify a literal seat, but it means he is there until he appears and comes to judge the world. Now Stephen's comment counsels us that even if Jesus Christ is not glorified by men as he should be, with some rejecting him and others slighting and scorning him, we must not, for that reason, cease giving him the honour which he is due. In other words, let us remember that, in his humanity, in which he was once destroyed, he did not relinquish being the God of glory, to whom all honour belongs. It is true, as I have already said, he humbled himself, indeed abased himself completely, as Paul says, when he was crucified and hanged on the tree (*Phil.* 2:7–8), which signified a curse. But let us realize that even that could not diminish his authority or his divine power. That was said so we might acknowledge his mighty power after he was hung on the tree, and be stirred to humble ourselves before him and pay him the homage all his subjects owe him. It is true that the devils of hell are forced to bow before him, but we must give him voluntary obedience, as do the angels of paradise.

Now as Luke had previously recounted that the Jews had interrupted Stephen's message with their outbursts, he adds, 'They cried out with a loud voice, and stopped their ears' so they might not hear his testimony that Jesus Christ is at the right hand of God. That should not surprise us, for an unbeliever can experience only deep fear when someone speaks to him of Jesus Christ. Why is that? Because he recognizes in him his judge. True, we will indeed acknowledge that Jesus Christ is the Judge of the whole world, but we also know that he will not judge us, but will rather be our advocate to argue our case, already won in his sight, because he will be our defender and demonstrate the power of his blood for the forgiveness of our sins. Therefore, acknowledging Jesus Christ as our Saviour, we do not look upon him as our Judge. On the other hand, his rigour does not so frighten us that we flee from his presence. Rather, when we are told he will come to judge the world, we will rejoice. 'For then', he says, 'your redemption will be drawing nigh' (*Luke* 21:28). That then is how believers experience incredible rejoicing when they are told about Jesus Christ's coming.

But the opposite is true for unbelievers. They can only be stricken with fear. They know very well that Jesus Christ will bring them to shame and destruction. Yet when they hear him spoken of, they enter a furious rage, as Scripture mentions here. True, we will see the wicked mock the last day, when the Son of God comes and all flesh appears before his throne of judgment. All that is foolishness to them. But when we speak of Jesus Christ in earnest, we are obliged to be convinced, as we see later, that King Agrippa and the governor of Judea are stricken with fear when they hear Paul speak of this day of judgment.[1] They came there with a sense of curiosity to hear Paul speak of something amusing in which they might find some recreation to help pass the time. But when he brings them to the last day, they are greatly disturbed. 'Come, let us lock him back up. We no longer want to hear about it.' The same is true for these Jews unless the devil takes greater possession of them and instils a greater rage in them and they refuse to listen. Now we must not be surprised if the enemies of truth are stricken with fear when someone talks to them about their judge. As I have said, they fear appearing before him because they know it will be their final undoing.

When Stephen says that he sees the Son of man, he does so for two reasons. One is that he strengthens himself against the trials which are assailing him. The other is that he holds in contempt those who are thus rebellious and smitten by a guilty conscience before God. 'Here I am now accused by you', he says. 'I am in your hands and my body will die, but I have Jesus Christ, who maintains my cause, and my salvation is assured in him because God his Father has given him all power, by which he keeps me. But as for you, I assure you that he is your Judge and you will render account to him, as much for the cruelty you are now inflicting upon me as for your resistance to his truth. You will in the end become aware that he is your Judge. This is why he is seated at the right hand of God. One day, you will have to appear before his judgment throne and give an accounting.' As a result, those wretched men are painfully tormented

---

[1] Intended is probably Felix; cf. Acts 24:25. In Acts 26 there is no explicit mention of the fact that Paul also discussed the future judgment with Agrippa and Festus, the successor of Felix. See for their reaction Acts 26:24, 28. [Editors' note]

by a furious rage. Why? Because they are faced with an endless reproach and condemned, and all that remains is for the sentence to be carried out, for they are thoroughly rebuked by God.

Now when these things are recounted for us, we are to be so open to receiving Jesus Christ and the promises we have in the gospel that when we are told about him, we will know that he is our Saviour. When we are told that he is going to come to judge the world, let us rejoice at that message because we know he is coming to deliver us from all evils and receive us into his kingdom and into the glory he has acquired for us. And let us be careful in all things to conform ourselves to the gospel inasmuch as we see great vengeance visited upon all those who have rebelled against him. Because of that rebellion, most of the world is still in confusion and error today. For what is the source of our joy, if not Jesus Christ? Now we see the Jews become enraged when they hear about him, and they stop their ears so as not to hear. We also see the perdition that is their lot. So let us be very careful not to be like them unless we wish to be condemned like them for resisting God and his word. For if we act like them, we will not experience a better fate than theirs.

Even so, although they have exerted great effort and tried their best to destroy and abolish the gospel completely, they have made no progress in that endeavour. In fact, we see the evidence today, if indeed we have eyes with which to see it. Even though the enemies of truth make every possible effort to bring contempt upon the teaching of the gospel, they cannot escape being compelled to concede to it some authority.

We see the papists raging anyway. It is true, if they had their say in the matter, no one would pay any attention to what we preach. Still, in spite of their criticisms, they acknowledge a power in God's word which cuts them to the quick and torments their consciences. We see the reactions of those who are wholly given over to Satan, who in no way wish to conform to God's teaching. They will pretend to be joyous and they will laugh, but their laughter will not escape their mouths. In fact, we see they are always gnashing their teeth and fretting and fuming, whatever they do. It is true that is not the case for all those with a wicked heart, but there will be some who are so brazen that they have to show their colours and reveal their fury against God and his word. And what is the reason for that? They are unworthy of sharing that joy which God gives his children. In the midst of all our ills, we find consolation because Jesus Christ is our Saviour and the redemption he has gained for us will not be fruitless. Therefore, knowing that, there is reason for us to rejoice in all our hardships. On the other hand, the wicked are necessarily confounded when Jesus Christ is mentioned, for they know he is their Judge and their polar opposite, and they will of necessity learn of God's wrath, whereas we have the assurance of his love. That, then, is the consolation we must receive from this passage, in which Stephen's persecutors stopped their ears and cried out so as not to hear what he declared about the glory of our Lord Jesus Christ.

Now let us not be surprised that the wicked continue from bad to worse and are hardened so that they can in no way be brought to the knowledge of salvation or show any sign of mending their ways. What Stephen recounts here should certainly disturb these wretched men, even if they had been as hard as rocks and even if he could have softened them, as the text suggests. But since the devil possesses them and they are consigned to the obstinacy of their errors, they continue in their obstinacy, as they rightly deserve. Therefore, when we see that kind of unfortunate obstinacy in those whom God has deprived of his Holy Spirit, we have every reason to be in fear. So let us humble ourselves and pray that this gracious God will not allow us to have ears that are stopped when he speaks to us or allow us to be so evil that we cry out against him. Rather, let us yield ourselves completely to him in all humility and meekness, and let us be of a kind and gentle spirit and listen when he speaks so that we may receive the comfort he is ready to give us.

Now the text continues: 'And they ran upon Stephen with one accord and, casting him out of the city, they stoned him. The witnesses laid their robes and clothes near a young man named Saul', who, as we will learn later, was consenting to his death and was a murderer along with the others. Now it is noteworthy that the text says Stephen was stoned by the Jews so as to make it clear that the testing was severe and hard for him to bear. Why so? Because he was executed as an evildoer. And it was not pagans who put him to death, but those who call themselves the church of God. In those days there was only one people whom God had elected and chosen. And those who boasted of having full authority in the church are his persecutors, adversaries, and judges all at the same time. So we can say Stephen was in deep trouble according to man's judgment. And he understands that he is: 'Here I am, rejected by all those who boast of being God's people. They have excommunicated me and have now stoned me as a false prophet, as an enemy of God's truth.' Since Stephen is enduring such hardships, he has a great need to be armed with an invincible power, for he would have otherwise been immensely tempted to lose all courage. That, I say, is primarily brought to our attention so that when we are attacked as Stephen was, we will always have his example when we take refuge in God.

But to receive the maximum advantage from this passage, we need to note that Luke does not want to say that the Jews are wrong in stoning Stephen. Why not? They are following the form of justice and procedure such as God commanded, in part at least, concerning carrying out the sentence. Their wrong consists of two things. The first is that Stephen asks only to bring the law to its true and full conclusion, but the Jews exhibit pure hypocrisy while pretending to be zealous for the law. They are not concerned whether the worship of God is corrupt or not, provided they have authority over others. That is one point we must not miss. The other is that they achieve it by force, ungodliness, and violence. They did not listen to Stephen when he tried to explain his position, witness to it, and make a good confession. Their insolence is evident. They all begin to cry out so he cannot be heard. And what is the reason for that if not their preoccupation with wicked affections and their deliberations to resist God, whatever the situation. Those are the two things wherein they fail.

However, it was God's command that if a false prophet arose, he was to be stoned, as we see in the command recorded in Deuteronomy 13, where it is said that a false prophet is a person who turns the people from God, who puts forth dreams to establish idolatries and abolish the true worship of God and that unity of faith which comes through his word. God wants people like that to be exterminated from the world (*Deut.* 13:1-5). And in so doing there is no cruelty.

Now let us consider how God's honour must be precious to us. When a highwayman is killed, that is, when he is executed with legal authority, everyone says it is done justly. Why? Because we abhor murder. And the law is clear: 'Whoever sheds man's blood, his blood must be shed, because man is formed in the image of the living God' (*Gen.* 9:6). Consequently, we do not find it strange that highwaymen are punished. Let us now consider which has the greater priority, human life or God's honour. Moreover, a murderer must die because he has violated God's image. Now we know that God's image is greatly obscured in men, indeed almost totally erased. Since that is true, when it comes to dealing with God himself, whose honour some have tried to destroy and abolish completely, the person who has rebelled that way against his Creator, is it not right that he be punished more stringently than a murderer?

In the same vein, we hang embezzlers, and when an embezzler makes a career of stealing and ends up on the gallows, everybody says he deserved to be punished that way. Yet, when someone tries to steal God's honour and bury it completely, even trying to do away with the salvation of souls, is it not a cardinal matter when such thieves are not punished and they go about looking for ways to destroy us both in body and soul? We do indeed punish embezzlers, who go about snatching away our possessions. The salvation of our souls and God's honour mean nothing to us. Therefore, a false prophet, who turns us away from God, steals chiefly the honour and glory which belong to God, and then becomes a murderer when he does his best to do away with the salvation of souls. All those elements are there and we still do not take them into account. On the other hand, if someone offends our honour, oh! immediately we throw ourselves wholeheartedly into vindicating ourselves. And who are we? Pitiable worms! What is our honour? Yet God's honour is violated and we do not think that is important.

So let us not think it is cruel or unjust to punish those who stand against God. For there is neither murder, nor larceny, nor robbery that we should hold in greater contempt than those who murder poor souls by poisoning them with false teachings. Let us then be more zealous in correcting and chastising that than all the other vices in the world. Why? We should consider God's honour to be pre-eminent over all things. It is our great shame when we talk about who we are. We say we are Christians when people talk about the city of Geneva. 'Oh, it is the best reformed city in the world!' And if someone slanders a man or woman, a compensatory fine must be paid. It goes without saying, some completely worthless people are often slandered, and their honour must be restored. And if God is blasphemed and his name is torn to pieces, what is the punishment? Oh, all you have to do is kiss the ground. That is the ordinance! What sort of reformation is that? Are we so wretched that we suffer men to be preferred above God? Or say that a man is more privileged than God and that his honour will be better protected? How about that for blasphemy! Now the fact is that we will still be accountable. Let us not get it into our heads that God does not uphold his honour when we profane him that way. That was the point of the law directing that false prophets should be stoned.

It was the custom for witnesses to throw the first stones. And with good reason. A witness is the one who condemns the individual, properly speaking. It is true that the judge has the authority to pronounce the sentence, but he is restrained by the fact that he cannot condemn a man without being convinced by good witnesses. Consequently, it is the witnesses who give the sentence. Now we know that words are often cheap when it comes to oppressing the innocent. That is why our Lord ordered witnesses to carry out the sentence. And it was not a shameful thing to do, as it is today when it is a disgrace to be an executioner. Consequently, what is recounted here about Stephen was in keeping with the common practice and the order which God had established. Back then, there was greater respect for witnesses than there is now. In this day and time, we see that people have no difficulty lending their witness to one another. In fact, it is a common proverb among the wicked that when it comes to witnessing to truth, they will never say anything to condemn the guilty or clear the innocent. In so doing, they show clearly their rebellion against God. For he says that he abhors the one who wrongly condemns the innocent just as much as the one who clears the wicked (*Prov.* 17:15). That is how we must examine ourselves more closely when it comes to witnessing in God's name. We must not have greater regard for one than for another, but we must proceed justly without making distinctions between persons. It is to be noted that it is said that the son must not spare his father or the father his son or the husband his wife, even though she sleeps in his arms. 'Nevertheless', says the Lord, 'you will reverence my majesty more highly than anything else' (*Deut.* 13:6–8). That, I tell you, is how we must act. As for the rest, let us pray that God will not allow our emotions to govern us in such a way that we will be tempted to bear false witness against our neighbours. Rather, in everything we do, may he lead us and guide us in such a way that we will do nothing against his glory and the advancement of his kingdom.

Following this holy teaching, let us bow before the face of our gracious God in acknowledgment of our faults, praying that he will be pleased to cut us to the quick so that we will confess our sins, experience true repentance and, with our repentance, hasten to our Lord Jesus Christ and ask him to be pleased to present us to God his Father so that we, receiving pardon through him, may be led and guided by his Holy Spirit, walk according to his commandments and learn increasingly to renounce our wicked affections and all the desires of this world and our flesh. Now let us all say, Almighty God, heavenly Father . . .

44

FAITH IN PRACTICE

SUNDAY, 11 JANUARY 1551

And cast him out of the city, and stoned him: and the witnesses laid down their clothes at a young man's feet, whose name was Saul. [59] *And they stoned Stephen, calling upon God, and saying, Lord Jesus, receive my spirit.* [60] *And he kneeled down, and cried with a loud voice, Lord, lay not this sin to their charge. And when he had said this, he fell asleep* (Acts 7:58–60).

We have already dealt with the vision given to Stephen to strengthen him so he would have a steadfast confidence when dying in witness to the gospel. So Jesus Christ showed himself to him in his own kingdom and power so that Stephen might know he was not vainly championing the cause of the Son of God, to whom authority had been given to keep and save his own.

Now we have pointed out that that vision was not given just for Stephen's sake alone. It is also useful for us today. Our Lord Jesus Christ, having risen to heaven, will reign until the end of the world, which assures us that we, by his power and might, will be victorious against all our enemies. That assurance will be our sole refuge when we undergo affliction. As a result, we know Jesus Christ was not exalted in his kingdom for no purpose, but that it was for the salvation of all who believe in him, and he will make us aware of that provided we put all our hope in him. It is true we will not see him with our eyes, but we will be able to contemplate him with such confident faith that it will be sufficient to lift us above all the temptations of this world.

We have here two points to note which Luke recounts concerning the death of Stephen. The first is that Stephen called upon Jesus Christ to receive his soul. The second is that he besought God to pardon his enemies for the sin they were committing. That is the way Stephen witnessed to the faith he had in Jesus Christ. Then he demonstrated the kind of love he bore not only toward his friends but also toward those who were cruelly persecuting him. So in the first instance, he made this request: 'Lord Jesus, receive my spirit.' We understand that Stephen, with these words, was resolved to die. He is no longer thinking about the present life. He knows God is determined to take him from the world. Certain of that, he is seeking that eternal life for which we must all strive, keeping our eyes fixed on it even though we still have to live in this world without knowing when we will have to leave it. But Stephen, knowing he must die, presents himself to the Son of God so that his soul will be received into his safekeeping. So consider how Stephen scorned the world. That way, he shows this is not our abiding place and our affections must not be attached to the world as if we were never to leave it.

In addition, we must note that it is with no small strength that Stephen overcomes that trial. When he perceives that he is considered a wicked enemy of God and his teaching and that he is judged to be a heretic, he sees death before him. He sees the world enraged against him, those very men who call themselves prelates of God's church. Nevertheless, he does not fail to beseech Jesus Christ to receive his soul. We see, I repeat, how he was strengthened by the Spirit of God and that it would have been otherwise impossible for him to overcome that trial. Because we do not know what God has determined for us, we must, following his example, commend our spirit to him so he will keep us in this world only as long as he wishes. And then, when he is ready to take us, may he receive us unto himself until the day of resurrection. That is also what David says in Psalm 31, where it reads, 'Into your hand I commit my spirit, O Lord' (*Psa.* 31:5). It is not just because he is facing death that he offers that prayer, but also because he sees himself surrounded by adversaries and in imminent peril that he finds his refuge in God and says, 'Lord, you placed me in this world. It is your responsibility to keep and sustain me. Therefore, my soul has to be in your hands and you must protect it.' That is how David entrusts himself to God's providence and, certain that God takes care of him, goes on his way. Even though he sees the present evil, he knows he will escape it by God's grace. And yet as he looks beyond to the time God wishes to take him from this world, he sees that a better life is ready for him in heaven and that our expectation and hope must not be fastened on the things of earth, as if our lives had something in common with brute beasts. Consequently, David, being assured of the immortal heritage God has promised all his children, not only has confidence that God will preserve his life for a while longer on earth but also that instead of dying he will live because he knows there is an eternal glory which has been prepared for him and for which all of us must also wait.

Now, as I said, we must pray the way David did, for we do not know what God has appointed for us. Let us commend our lives to his providence and, because he has placed us in this world, may he watch over us and sustain us as long as it pleases him. But if we see there is no longer any hope of living in this world, we must speak like Stephen, as even our Lord Jesus Christ did and say, 'Receive my spirit' (*Luke* 23:46). Let us put our spirit in God's hand. True, Stephen is addressing Jesus Christ here. And we must pay close attention to this, for we have our Lord Jesus Christ commending his soul to God his Father. Why? We see the fruit of that action. He commended his soul to God his Father not only so that he might keep it, but also so that he might exercise guardianship over our souls. Just as we see that God kept his Son's soul, let us not doubt that Jesus Christ has the power to keep our souls and that we must take refuge in him in accordance with the example given to us here.

But so that we may better understand that teaching, we have here, in the first place, a testimony of how man's soul is not some temporal force which disappears like the wind, but a spirit or spiritual substance which has its own permanent life. Otherwise, it would be futile to say, 'Lord, receive my soul.' The body turns to dust and we have the words 'Receive my soul.' So let us conclude that when the spirit is taken from this world, not everything within us perishes, as it seems, but God receives our spirit, as it is said, until the body returns to the earth from which it came and the spirit returns to God, who gave it (cf. *Gen.* 3:19; *Job* 4:19; *Eccles.* 12:7). It is true that, given our fleshly existence, we will not understand that, for there is no difference between the death of a man and the death of a horse. It seems that everything rots away. But when all is said and done, we will find that we are taken from this world by a different death, so to speak, because God has imprinted his image on us, and our souls will live forever. So the point we have to note in this passage is that when we leave this world, there is a different life, a permanent life, for our souls.

In addition, we are shown here how we are to call upon the name of the Son of God. It is true that when we pray in public, our prayer is not addressed to Jesus Christ but to God his Father. In fact, that is the regular way to pray. We beseech God the Father because he is the author of every good thing. It is to that fact that Jesus Christ leads us. When he commands us to pray that way, he affirms that he will be our advocate and offer our requests in our behalf, and that we will be answered in his name and through him. That, I say, is the instruction he has given us for prayer. Yet it is still permissible for us to call upon our Lord Jesus Christ, as we see later when Ananias says, 'Lord, Lord, this Saul persecutes everyone who calls upon your name' (*Acts* 9:13–14). That statement makes it clear that in all times believers have called upon Jesus Christ. In fact, all power is given to him by God his Father so we will seek it in him. Therefore, we have to pray to God the Father and invoke Jesus Christ our Advocate and Intercessor so he will guide us and cause our prayers to be heard. We are equally obliged to pray to Jesus Christ. Why so? Because he is our eternal God, because, being sent as our Mediator, he is our Advocate as well as our Redeemer, and because all things must be in his hand and under his direction. Since God the Father has magnified his Son in that way, it is only right that we seek our good in him. That must be our intention when we call upon him, as we are taught here.

Still we must note that if we are to offer that prayer, we must be fully certain that Jesus Christ receives our souls in his hand to keep them until the day of resurrection. It is true the souls of the wicked do not perish, but the life which has been given them is a death more severe and harsher than they can endure. This is the certainty which belongs to the faithful, that Jesus Christ will be the keeper of their souls. Since he now calls us to himself as his flock, let us not doubt that when it pleases God to call us from this world, he will keep us even more securely. We must remember Jesus Christ's declaration that he will keep everything given to him by his Father and that nothing will be lost (*John* 6:39). It is a great consolation that Jesus Christ declares that his charge is to be our protector and that indeed that power comes from God his Father.

Then he adds that when we come to him, we must not be

afraid. Now in this world we encounter many things that can cause us to fear. We live in the midst of a million dangers, and it seems our salvation is exposed as prey. We see the devil's cunning and the ways he ransacks and destroys us. But the fact is that in the midst of so many difficulties we must be confident our salvation will be protected by our Lord Jesus. Why so? No one who comes to him will perish. Now what would happen if he removed all these dangers that hold sway over us in this world? Do we think he would protect our lives less well then? Well then, let us learn we must be certain that we are in the Son of God's safekeeping in life and in death. In life, he cares for our bodies and our souls. In death, even though our bodies turn to dust, they will not fail to rise someday by his power, and he will sustain and safeguard our souls until then.

Now we must acknowledge that we need this assurance because of the power which indwells us all. For if our bodies are a pit of abomination and iniquity, our souls are even more so. Let us look briefly at the wicked affections within us. Let us look at how filled with evil and cruelty we are. In short, because there is only evil and perversity in our souls, must they not be rejected and condemned by God as abominable? Consequently, we must come to Jesus Christ, or we are more than hopeless. But when the Son of God receives our souls, we know there is something to wash and cleanse them, even though they are filled with spots and blemishes, leprous before God. Only the blood of Jesus Christ can cleanse them. Consequently, when we come to him, we are certain all our sins are not imputed to us when the Son of God applies the blood he shed once for our cleansing. Yet, if we are indebted to God because of sins we have committed, Jesus Christ holds the debtor in his hand to crush and destroy him. For that reason, he endured such a harsh and cruel death that he spared nothing to deliver us from the bonds of the devil and to erase and destroy the debt as if it had been nailed to the cross, as Paul says in Colossians

(*Col.* 2:14). Therefore, we understand how necessary it is for Jesus Christ to offer himself for us and tell us that he is the guardian of our souls and that he must guide us all with his hand. Having that, we must no longer doubt, as I have just said, that God receives them. That is the first item Luke includes in this passage, namely that Stephen demonstrated his confidence in our Lord Jesus Christ when he commended his soul to him. With that lesson, we are strongly advised what we have to do. That is, as long as we are in this world, let us remember that our lives are in God's hand. In addition, as we approach death, let us not be gripped with fear and dread as unbelievers are, but let us be aware that there is a better life prepared for us in heaven.

Let us come now to Stephen's second request, which shows the love he has for people. And that is how we must react both in life and in death. Two things are required of us in which the perfection of our Christianity lies. First, we must put our confidence in God and acknowledge the means by which he calls us to salvation. That is, we must put our trust in the grace he has conferred upon us in our Lord Jesus Christ. Therefore, let us find our complete refuge in him, knowing we must not seek our welfare elsewhere. Our faith, then, is the sum of our Christianity. By it we are encouraged to call upon our God, to dwell completely in him and to walk in fear of him, in obedience to him, and in all purity and cleanliness of heart. Then comes the love we are obliged to have toward men. That is why holy Scripture, when speaking of living right, leads us to these two points. We have no excuse then when we are tempted to say, 'Oh, I do not know what I am supposed to do; I do not pay much attention to what God demands of me.' Do we want something easier than God's command to trust him when we know that the grace of our Lord Jesus Christ is the only means acceptable to him and that our complete welfare is in him and in calling upon God in his name? And second to that, we must live

637

with our neighbours in true love and charity, do no man wrong, and be kind and gracious to everyone. In short, let us do to men as we would have them do to us (*Matt.* 7:12). That is a rather easy lesson to learn, but it is very difficult to practise. We must make an even greater effort when we recognize the great resistance our nature puts up and we go against what God commands. We must make a greater effort to fortify ourselves with these two teachings in order to regulate our lives along these two lines: the trust that God demands we have in him and in our Lord Jesus Christ; then the love he commands toward our neighbours. As for the first, we will not repeat what has already been said. What remains, then, is that each of us must realize that we have to lean on God's mercy in the assurance that Jesus Christ did not die and rise again in vain, but that it was through him that we have our salvation and the boldness to call upon God and find our complete refuge in him. If we are cruel to our neighbours and seek only their ruin and destruction, how can we think that God is granting us grace? Jesus Christ shed his blood for the redemption of the world. Now if we ask for the destruction of what he has redeemed at a high price, do we think we are sharers in the blessing he has acquired for us? Do we think he is obligated to acknowledge us as his own? To the contrary! We must consider it a certain fact that he will avenge such cruelty and visit upon us a punishment much more severe and horrible than the pain we have inflicted upon our neighbours because of our inhumanity.

So, do we want to possess Stephen's kind of faith? Do we want to enjoy the privilege of calling upon our Lord Jesus Christ to receive our souls into his safekeeping? Then we must be in accord with and united with people in sincere love, for we know God has indeed given us that nature so we will live in love and brotherly affection. But we must surpass that, for Stephen not only prayed for all men but especially for his enemies, even those who were stoning him and engaging in such horrible cruelty against him. Even so, he says, 'Lord, lay not this sin to their charge.' Although they are putting him to death, he is asking God not to punish them for this sin, but to receive them compassionately and show them mercy. It is true this is the opposite of our human understanding and all the dispositions of our flesh. But the fact is that the Holy Spirit has recounted this story for us so we will know our responsibility and imitate Stephen, who at his death prayed for his enemies. What he did becomes a command for us all. Our Lord Jesus Christ did not speak to just one man when he said, 'Pray for those who speak evil of you, do good to those who wrong you, and love those who hate you' (*Matt.* 5:44). That is a general teaching which we must follow if we wish to be disciples of the Son of God.

But since we claim the weakness, or rather the evil disposition, of the flesh, we think that will serve as an excuse before God. But this is a testimony against us, for Stephen was a man subject to the same passions that we are, and yet he overcame his nature and said, 'Lord, forgive them this sin.' That is what Jesus Christ had done earlier. But we can say we are far removed from the perfection of the Son of God. That is why Stephen is given as an example for us. We are left defenceless, for we no longer have a clever turn of phrase by which to excuse ourselves. But we should say, 'Alas, it is true God commands us to love our enemies, but how can we? It is not possible, for everything within us resists.' So that we will not think such frivolous excuses serve some purpose, Stephen is given to us as an example to follow. The Holy Spirit admonishes us to renounce all the wicked affections of the flesh so we can pray for our enemies. In short, this passage is not to serve us only as doctrine, but it is to goad us and urge us to realize both that God did not idly command us to love our enemies and that we must make every effort to do so. A true confirmation of our Christianity is found in the necessity of our being in conformity with the Son of God. If we cannot do that on our own – for it is certain that doing so surpasses all human strength – let us ask God so to strengthen us by his Holy Spirit that we will be able to follow the example given for us here, after we have been freed from all our lusts and carnal affections.

What do you think about that? There are very few who will think about putting a great deal of effort into that, for it should be our responsibility to exercise control over all our carnal affections, just like holding back wild animals on leashes and keeping them captive. We will never be able to yield ourselves to God's service until we have forcibly restrained our human nature because all the affections of our flesh and all our thoughts, as Paul says, are just so many enemies working against God (*Rom.* 8:7; *Eph.* 2:3). All the desires, all the wicked thoughts which can assail man, are like soldiers at war with God and his truth. As a result, we will never be disposed to dedicate ourselves completely to God and his service until we learn to put our human nature to death, so wretched and accursed is it. But, as I have said, very few will go to such trouble. To the contrary. Everyone delights in his own vices. We think it is enough to say, 'We are not angels and we are not that perfect.' Well, if we are not angels, God will destroy us along with the devils if we are unwilling to come into line with his will. It is true that no man is so perfect that he can love his enemies the way Jesus Christ does. But the fact is we must strive to do so by putting to death all our wicked affections, because we know they are God's enemies. To that end we have to pray not only for all people in general but also for our enemies. And yet few are they who do it. But what is worse, there are many who, when done some wrong, are not content to seek vengeance and return evil for evil. If anyone tries to rebuke them for their sins, they think they have been gravely injured. That is a great pity. I do not know how most people can avoid feeling shame when they call themselves Christian, since that impudence is the rule everywhere. It is a common practice when our vices are reproved that those who realize their guilt most keenly think they have been deeply offended and want to inflict an ignominious punishment upon the offender. In fact, some discontented people are so incensed they complain because they are unable to spew their venom. Against whom? Against those whom they have accused of rebuking them. In short, if someone tries to rebuke sins in our day and time, he needs to make an appointment with death at the same time – as if he had committed some grievous offence. But, as I have said, if someone has rebuked a person in order to show him his faults, the rebuked person needs to make peace and say, 'I forgive him for offending me.' And what did that person who was appointed by God do to you? He rebuked you for your sin, as he was obliged to do, and he must be forgiven. But because he has tried to rebuke sins, everybody comes and takes sides against him. And what does that say about our progress? It is still a common problem among us today in Geneva.

So let us not give ourselves too much credit. Rather, let us take a close look at what this passage says. It shows us that, as children of God, we must pray for our enemies. But this is what everybody says: 'True, but I have done him no wrong. Why did he have to hurt me? So how can I forgive him?' Please! Let us consider Stephen. Who among us can lay claim to such innocence and declare as sincerely as Stephen does here, 'I committed no such offence; I have tried to gain the salvation of those who are persecuting me'? We see the spiritual disposition which drives him. He is not praying insincerely and hypocritically for God to pardon the sin of those who are stoning him the same way many do, protesting glibly, 'Oh! I wish him no harm. I forgive him everything he has done to me', while harbouring a heart filled with rancour and hatred. That is not what was driving Stephen when he offered this prayer: 'Lord, lay not this sin to their charge.' He always pursued their salvation as if he wanted them to understand his meaning: 'Unfortunate people, you are persecuting me as if you were doing God a great service, but you have wrongly understood what I am doing. So understand now that I am only seeking your salvation, whereas you are only pursuing your destruction. I am not motivated by a passion like yours.' So when Stephen makes that point, he is trying to find out whether there is some way to instruct them and lead them to repentance.

Now Stephen's prayer did not bear fruit immediately. In other words, the fruit did not appear forthwith. For there we see that Paul was consenting to his death. The witnesses do not stop their cruelty against him. They condemned him and remain intent on their purpose, intoxicated by their malice. We do not see Stephen's prayer answered the moment it is uttered. That is true, but like the seed sown in the ground (*John* 12:24), it does not appear straightway and produce its fruit. It remains hidden there, just as sometimes the petitions and prayers of the faithful do not come to pass and into evidence. But in time God makes known that he has answered them. We see Paul remains without hope for the time being. Who would have said at the time that he would teach others? He was a young man enraged against Christians. He harasses them. He torments them. He takes pleasure in destroying them, as will be seen in the course of events. And yet in the end we witness the miraculous conversion brought about in him, how our Lord Jesus Christ extended his hand to him and delivered him from the bottomless pit and destruction. That is how the prayers of the faithful are not in vain, even though on the surface they seem unheard and unanswered. Whereas Paul persecuted the gospel, we see him made its minister. We see the grace which he was given later.

Seeing then that Stephen's prayer was answered, let us return to God emboldened. Since our nature is inclined to evil and to refusal to forgive those who have wronged us, let us ask God to cleanse us by the power of his Holy Spirit so that there will be nothing to keep us from coming to our Lord Jesus Christ and conforming ourselves to him. As he presented his soul once to God his Father, may he now receive ours.

> Following this holy teaching, let us bow before the face of our gracious God in acknowledgment of our sins, praying that he will be pleased to cut us to the quick because of them so that, being displeased with them, we will seek to bring ourselves into complete conformity with him as we use the examples he presents to us daily in holy Scripture. And may he daily make us aware of the grace he has granted us through our Lord Jesus Christ his Son. So let us now say together, Almighty God, heavenly Father . . .

INDEX OF SCRIPTURE REFERENCES

ROMANS

1:4	269
1:16	242, 325, 503, 515
2:12	604
2:16	212
3:25	560
4:9–11	394, 402
6:6	7
6:8	597
7:14	269
8:7, 11	267
8:7	511, 513, 640
8:16–17	245
8:17	293
8:24	433
8:24–25	375
8:31	615
10:2	236
10:3	430
10:4	63
10:5	510
10:8	339

ROMANS

10:14	480
11:17–22	426
12:8	307
13:1–2	254, 590, 592
13:12–14	541
14:7–8	619
14:8–9	373
15:16	21

1 CORINTHIANS

1:4–7	57, 457
1:23	267
1:31	267
2:2	267
4:1–4	206
4:5	195
4:13	2
4:14	17
5	99
6:13	377
9:25	295

COLOSSIANS

2:2–3	63
2:9	229
2:14	637
2:17	352, 558
3:1–3	373
3:3	245
3:3–4	479
3:8–9	399
3:10	557
3:10–11	400
3:11	321
3:14	321

1 THESSALONIANS

2:15	601
4:11	186
5:23	591

2 THESSALONIANS

1:8–9	542
2:9–10	91

2 THESSALONIANS

2:11–12	542
3:10	186
3:13	194

1 TIMOTHY

1:5	209
2:5	61, 64
3:1–13	309
3:2, 6–7	49
3:8–9	313
3:15	326
4:13	336
5:1–2	336

2 TIMOTHY

1:8	294
2:9	118, 294
2:15	336
2:21	116
3:17	116, 314
4:1	106